Russia: From Proletarian Revolution to State-Capitalist Counter-Revolution

Studies in Critical Social Sciences Book Series

Haymarket Books is proud to be working with Brill Academic Publishers (www.brill.nl) to republish the *Studies in Critical Social Sciences* book series in paperback editions. This peer-reviewed book series offers insights into our current reality by exploring the content and consequences of power relationships under capitalism, and by considering the spaces of opposition and resistance to these changes that have been defining our new age. Our full catalog of *SCSS* volumes can be viewed at https://www.haymarketbooks.org/series_collections/4-studies-in-critical-social-sciences.

Russia: From Proletarian Revolution to State-Capitalist Counter-Revolution

Selected writings

Raya Dunayevskaya

Edited by
Eugene Gogol
Franklin Dmitryev

Haymarket Books
Chicago, IL

First published in 2017 by Brill Academic Publishers, The Netherlands.

Published in paperback in 2018 by
Haymarket Books
P.O. Box 180165
Chicago, IL 60618
773-583-7884
www.haymarketbooks.org

ISBN: 978-1-60846-933-8

Trade distribution:
In the U.S. through Consortium Book Sales, www.cbsd.com
In the UK, Turnaround Publisher Services, www.turnaround-uk.com
In Canada, Publishers Group Canada, www.pgcbooks.ca
All other countries, Ingram Publisher Services International, ips_intlsales@ingramcontent.com

Cover design by Jamie Kerry and Ragina Johnson.

This book was published with the generous support of Lannan Foundation and the Wallace Action Fund.

Printed in Canada.

10 9 8 7 6 5 4 3 2 1

Library of Congress Cataloging-in-Publication Data is available.

GCC/IBT

MIX
Paper from responsible sources
FSC® C103567
FSC
www.fsc.org

Contents

PART 4
Russia's Transformation into Opposite: The Theory of State-Capitalism

PART 5
From State-Capitalist Theory to Marxist-Humanism, 1950s–1980s

Editorial Note and Acknowledgements

Within the text of some documents the following abbreviations are used: Hegel's *Science of Logic*, Volumes I & II—SLI or SLII; Lenin's *Collected Works*, Volume 38—LCW 38; Dunayevskaya's *Marxism and Freedom*—M&F. Fuller annotation given in the Bibliography.

The Marxists Internet Archive (MIA) has posted the English translation of Lenin's "Abstract of Hegel's *Science of Logic*" from Volume 38 of *Lenin's Collected Works* (https://www.marxists.org/archive/lenin/works/1914/cons-logic/index.htm) with formatting to represent the way Lenin wrote in his notebooks. It also includes links to works by Marx and Hegel as posted by the MIA where Lenin cites them. Within the MIA's Hegel Archive, the online *Science of Logic* contains links to Lenin's Abstract wherever he has commented on a specific paragraph.

We wish to thank the Raya Dunayevskaya Memorial Fund for giving permission to publish documents from the *Raya Dunayevskaya Collection—Marxist-Humanism: A Half Century of Its World Development* (www.rayadunayevskaya.org). We thank the following members and friends of News and Letters Committees (www.newsandletters.org) for their editorial assistance in preparing Dunayevskaya's documents for publication: Daniel Bremer, Bob French, Roger Hollander, Ron Kelch, Georgina Loa, Fred Mecklenburg, Héctor Sánchez, Susan Stellar.

Introduction

Eugene Gogol, Terry Moon and Franklin Dmitryev
For the *Raya Dunayevskaya Memorial Fund* and the Marxist-Humanist Organization, *News and Letters Committees*

Raya Dunayevskaya, the founder of the philosophy of Marxist-Humanism and of the organization News and Letters Committees, had a unique relationship to the Russian Revolution. She was seven years old in 1917. Escaping her parents, she ran through the streets of Yarishev and saw its destruction and the rapes and beheading of townspeople by counter-revolutionary troops retreating from the Bolsheviks. That the Bolsheviks were welcomed as liberators shaped her actions when the family settled in Chicago in 1922 after fleeing the famine in Russia the year before. In Chicago's Near West Side, Dunayevskaya and her sister Bessie traveled Maxwell Street, looking for the sign of the hammer and sickle. In 1978, she articulated the power of that moment of revolution:

> ...I come from Russia 1917, and the ghettos of Chicago, where I first saw a Black person.... You know, you're born in a border town—there's a revolution, there's a counter-revolution, there's anti-Semitism—you *know* nothing, but experience a lot.... It isn't personal whatsoever! If you live when an idea is born, and a great revolution in the world is born—it doesn't make any difference *where* you are: *that becomes the next stage of development of humanity.*[1]

1 The Present Moment and the Russian Revolution

On its hundredth anniversary, the Russian Revolution continues to elicit contradictory interpretations from historians, Marxists and other revolutionaries. We live in the shadow of that momentous event of the early 20th century. Dunayevskaya's experience is key as we begin with the Revolution's meaning for those who lived it, and who acted, thought and wrote about it.

In the immediate aftermath of the revolutionary explosion of February, and most especially of October, masses within what became the Soviet Union participated in new emancipatory moments. Revolutionaries in Russia and without

1 *The Raya Dunayevskaya Collection—Marxist-Humanism: A Half-Century of Its World Development*, Wayne State University Archives of Labor and Urban Affairs, Detroit, Mich., #5818. The Collection is viewable online at www.rayadunayevskaya.org

sought to develop and extend the revolution to the world, while seeking to come to grips with its significance.[2] It transformed them for the rest of their lives.

The complex vicissitudes of counter-revolution in the two decades that followed V.I. Lenin's death did not obliterate the profound changes to those influenced by 1917. The consolidation of power by Joseph Stalin, the implementation of the first Five Year Plans, the exiling of Leon Trotsky followed by his assassination at the hand of Stalin's agent, the Hitler-Stalin "Non-Aggression" Pact and the Soviet Union's participation in World War II—all became moments of fierce contention within the radical left movement.

These moments played out in Dunayevskaya's life. In 1928 she began to question the Communist Party's policies and actions after the expulsion of Trotsky. When she suggested that her comrades hear Trotsky's response to his expulsion, she was literally thrown down a flight of stairs and kicked out of the Young Workers League. Then eighteen years old, she began a revolutionary sojourn that took her from New York City to Los Angeles. Moving to Boston in 1929, she met Antoinette Bucholz Konikow, a birth control advocate who spoke out for legal abortion and had formed a group of independent Trotskyists—almost all women—who had also been thrown out of the Communist Party.

Back in New York, she became secretary to Trotskyist leader James Patrick Cannon, but did not stay with him long. She hitchhiked across the country to workers' strikes at various sites, arriving in San Francisco in 1934 just as the general strike of July 16–19 had begun. More than one hundred thousand workers in San Francisco and Alameda Counties stopped work in support of longshoremen and seamen who had gone on strike along the entire West Coast. The next year she was in Los Angeles, where she taught Karl Marx's *Capital* and worked as an organizer for the Spartacus Youth League. By 1936, she had moved to Washington, D.C., where she worked with Ralph Bunche on the Washington Committee to Aid Agricultural Workers.

In this period she also corresponded with Trotsky, who was in exile in Mexico. In 1937 Dunayevskaya, thwarted from joining the International Brigades to fight fascism in the Spanish Civil War because she was a woman, heard Trotsky was in need of a Russian language secretary. She wrote him directly and left for Mexico without obtaining permission from the branch of the Trotskyist party. She worked with Trotsky in Coyoacan, Mexico, during the years when Stalin waged the infamous Moscow trials. She helped Trotsky respond to the fantastic slanders against him, many times with only two hours' notice.

---

2 See John Randall's monumental documentary studies on the history of the International Congresses.

Dunayevskaya was with Trotsky and his wife Natalia when Stalin had Trotsky's only surviving child, Leon Sedov, murdered. She took the phone call that told of his death and she then had to tell Trotsky. She wrote of how Trotsky and Natalia stayed locked in their rooms for eight days until Trotsky emerged with a hand-written memorial to Sedov. "His face was deeply lined. His eyes were swollen from too much crying.... The very next morning, the morning papers carried the announcement of the Third Moscow Trials (March 1938)."[3]

In 1938, the deaths of her father and brother forced Dunayevskaya to return to Chicago, where in 1939 she broke with Trotsky over his insistence that Russia was still a "workers' state" even after Stalin made a pact with Adolf Hitler. Twenty-nine-year-old Dunayevskaya disagreed with Trotsky, the man she considered the greatest living revolutionary. She lost her power of speech for two days. Then began what she later asserted was "my real development."

In our age, investigating the process leading to the Russian Revolution, understanding the contradictory years 1917–1923, as well as grasping what transpired in the USSR after Lenin's death and within the capitalist world under the impact of the Great Depression are all crucial to unearthing the significance of the Revolution 100 years later.

Today, however, we are making that investigation in a world whose dominant ideologies deny the Russian Revolution's singular importance, dismiss it as a deviant historical footnote and obscure its contradictory meaning. Two dimensions of the present moment stand in our way.

First is a world in economic, political and social disarray that includes: a permanent drive by the U.S. for world hegemony in conflict with nuclear-armed Russia, China and the nuclear ambitions of North Korea; a multitude of reactionary regimes and non-state powers determined to crush any authentic opposition from below under the cover of religious dogmas and narrow nationalisms; and an unprecedented refugee crisis involving millions of people in the Middle East, Asia, the Americas and Africa, with tens of thousands already massacred in ongoing wars. *We are in a cauldron of seemingly permanent war and suffering.*

Second is the ideological pollution. A host of ideologues seek to smother the idea of liberation and dismiss as unreasoning the human beings needed to achieve emancipatory social transformation. They wish to consign authentic revolution to the distant past and imprison us within a no-exit future. While this is to be expected from neoliberal and other modes of reactionary thought, more distressing—and a somber indication of the depth of the ideological

3 See Chapter 4, p. 144.

pollution—is the lack of an emancipatory vision from many who see themselves as radical critics of today's oppressive reality but for whom revolution is hopelessly utopian and doomed to be dictatorial rather than liberating.

A *critical return* through the revolutionary mind of Raya Dunayevskaya to the world-shaking events of 1917 that forged a giant leap in humanity's emancipation, as well as a devastating transformation into opposite in the decades that followed, can provide us with a needed vantage point to confront our own contradictory, unfree world.

II 1914–1917: War and Revolution as Testing/Turning Points

1917 was a world historic turning point—the first successful social revolution against capitalism. But, before that, there arose a crucial test for revolutionaries—the outbreak of the First World War in August 1914. It was a test that the established Marxism of the Second International failed, betraying the world's masses. Despite a decade and more of anti-war proclamations, speeches and demonstrations, once war broke out the vast majority of the socialist and trade union groups backed the governments of their respective countries. The largest socialist organization, the German Social Democracy, supported the war, and its members in parliament, save for Karl Liebknecht, voted to fund it. He and the great Polish revolutionary and theoretician Rosa Luxemburg would break from this betrayal of socialist principles.

From Russia, a crucial exception came from Lenin and the Bolshevik Party, who sharply opposed the war. To Lenin the betrayal was such a shock that he sought to work out its root and to establish theoretical ground for his revolutionary viewpoint through a return to the philosophic origins of Marxism within the Hegelian dialectic. His *Conspectus of Hegel's "Science of Logic"* (*Philosophic Notebooks*) provided "philosophic preparation" for the events from February to October 1917, and for the first conflictive years of Soviet power, 1917–1923.

Lenin, the Bolsheviks, and other revolutionaries, most notably Trotsky, were open to the Russian Revolution's turning point. In the darkest hours of war, a new beginning became possible. It was based on the activities of masses of workers—including women workers—and peasants, together with radicals who opposed the war. What Russia meant to those who lived it in the aftermath of the betrayal of the official Marxism of the Second international was revealed: a new revolutionary moment that became the first workers' revolution against capitalism.

Dunayevskaya never lost that experience of living at a time when an "idea was born" and expressed the excitement of that new beginning 65 years later, writing of the "greatest of all events," March and November 1917:

> [T]he March Revolution...was initiated by women. It was initiated on International Women's Day, against the advice of all tendencies—Mensheviks, Bolsheviks, Anarchists and Social-Revolutionaries. Those five days that toppled the mighty empire demonstrate that it is never just a question of leaders, no matter how great. Rather, it is masses in motion.
>
> In the continuing imperialist war, which had wrought such havoc and brought such misery to the Russian masses, the various left organizations thought it right to celebrate International Women's Day at a regular meeting. As it happened, the Bolsheviks' printing press broke down and they could not even issue a leaflet, but the *mezhrayontsy* group did address a flysheet to the working women who opposed the war. However, the women of the Vyborg textile factory categorically refused to limit themselves to a closed meeting.
>
> Despite the advice of all political tendencies, they went out on strike, fifty thousand of them. The next day they appealed to the metal workers, led by the Bolsheviks, who then joined the strike: now there were ninety thousand out. Someone cried, "To the Nevsky!" and the demonstration was joined by a mass of other women, not all of them workers, but all demanding "Bread!" Whereupon that slogan was drowned out with, "Down with the war!" By this time, the third day of the strike, there were two hundred and forty thousand strikers; the Bolsheviks issued a call for a general strike. The police opened fire and some fell dead, but the Cossacks had not yet unleashed their fury against the strikers. The women went up to the Cossacks to ask whether they would join them. They did not answer but, wrote Trotsky, "the Cossacks did not hinder the workers from 'diving' under the horses. The revolution does not choose its paths: it made its first steps towards victory under the belly of a Cossack's horse. A remarkable incident!"
>
> On the decisive fifth day, the prisons were opened and all political prisoners were freed. At the same time, the mutinous troops descended on the Tauride Place. "Thus dawned upon the earth the day of destruction of the Romanov monarchy." By November the Kerensky government was also overthrown and the Bolsheviks took power on 9 November.[4]

The focus of this book is to help catalyze much needed discussions by presenting documents from the Marxist-Humanist revolutionary philosopher, Raya Dunayevskaya, who, in the mid-20th Century, sought to give meaning to the

4 Raya Dunayevskaya, *Rosa Luxemburg, Women's Liberation, and Marx's Philosophy of Revolution* (University of Illinois Press, 1991), pp. 84–85.

magnificent Russian Revolution and to its devastating transformation into opposite, and thereby construct a new beginning for Marx's Marxism.

III An American Revolutionary Born Out of the Russian Revolution

The Russian Revolution was central to Dunayevskaya's life and thought. She experienced it as a child, then grew up active in the Communist and then Trotskyist Left in the U.S. After serving as Trotsky's Russian language secretary in Mexico, her realization of Trotsky's error in insisting that Russia was a still a workers' state "though degenerate"—a mistake that limited the total revolutionary change that she envisioned—forced her to immerse herself in economics, revolutionary theory, and philosophy.

By early 1941, Dunayevskaya had written her first essay on the theory of state-capitalism. She showed that the USSR operated according to the laws of capitalist production. That same year she met Cyril Lionel Robert (C.L.R.) James, who, under the pen name J.R. Johnson, had also written a position paper on state-capitalism. Dunayevskaya, writing under the name Freddie Forest, and James formed the State-Capitalist Tendency—also known as the Johnson-Forest Tendency—within the Workers Party, which had been formed in a split from the Socialist Workers Party over the latter's continued defense of the USSR. From 1941 to 1947 she was a member of the party's Harlem, New York, branch.

In the 1940s, Dunayevskaya thought that "the relationship between philosophy and economics had intensified." She was seeing "philosophy as inherent in new revolutionary forces—labor, Black, women, youth."[5] Seeking out the dialectical opposite of state-capitalism in such revolutionary forces, she singled out workers' strikes and national resistance movements against fascism during the war, as well as anti-colonial revolts.

She had felt an affinity with the Black struggle for freedom shortly after her arrival in Chicago. As a young woman she worked with the *Negro Champion*, the newspaper of the American Negro Labor Congress. She wrote book reviews that were published widely in African-American newspapers and journals. When she graduated from Medill High School in 1928, her date with an African-American classmate created a protest that threatened to cancel the scheduled prom. The NAACP took up the case.

While the Second World War was raging, there were Black uprisings in Detroit and Harlem, as well as a miners' strike that included large numbers of Black miners. Dunayevskaya and James wrote a series of pioneering studies on

5 *Guide to the Raya Dunayevskaya Collection*, p. 59.

African–American struggles and their relation to socialist revolution and the Marxist movement. She took up Lenin's writings on the national question and on the condition of Black sharecroppers in the U.S. after the Civil War. Racism and struggles against it were the subject of much of her revolutionary journalism in the 1940s. The Tendency chose Dunayevskaya to put forward its position on the validity of independent Black struggles in debate with David Coolidge (Ernest Rice McKinney) at the 1946 Workers Party Convention. McKinney was the leading Black spokesman for the Shachtmanite position, which hewed to a long tradition of white U.S. socialists subordinating race to labor.

In July 1947 the Johnson-Forest Tendency left the Workers Party to rejoin the Socialist Workers Party in September, where they remained until 1951. That same year Dunayevskaya presented the Johnson-Forest Tendency's theory of state-capitalism to the Fourth International at their conference in France, where she debated Ernest Mandel. In 1948 she moved to Pittsburgh to work with steelworkers there and miners in West Virginia.[6]

In 1949–50 Dunayevskaya was working on three things simultaneously: she was an activist supporting the coal miners' general strike in West Virginia; at night she was translating Lenin's Abstract of Hegel's *Science of Logic*; and she was working on a book, "Marxism and State-Capitalism," which over the next several years became transformed into *Marxism and Freedom: From 1776 until Today*. This activity led to a three-way correspondence with C.L.R. James and Grace Lee Boggs, who was also a leader of the Johnson-Forest Tendency.

In 1953 Dunayevskaya made what she called a "philosophic breakthrough." In two letters of May 12 and 20, 1953, she discusses how she discerned in Hegel's Absolutes a dual movement—a movement from practice that was itself a form of theory, and a movement from theory reaching to philosophy. Six weeks later, the June 17, 1953, East German mass revolt broke out.

By 1954 differences between Dunayevskaya and James reached the breaking point and, just when Correspondence Committees was listed as subversive by McCarthyism and war threatened to break out over the islands in the Formosa Strait claimed by both China and Taiwan, James fled to England, leaving Dunayevskaya and the organization to face McCarthyism alone. The break with James finally came in 1955. Immediately afterwards, Dunayevskaya, along with most of the worker members of Correspondence Committees—including the Black autoworker Charles Denby, who became the founding editor of *News & Letters*[7]—formed a new organization, News and Letters Committees.

6 Andy Phillips and Raya Dunayevskaya, *A 1980s View: The Coal Miners' General Strike of 1949–50 and the Birth of Marxist-Humanism in the U.S.* (Chicago: News & Letters, 1984), p. 33.

7 See his autobiographical *Indignant Heart: A Black Worker's Journal* (Detroit: Wayne State University Press, 1989).

Its first Convention charged Dunayevskaya with completing her book, *Marxism and Freedom*, began regularly publishing the newspaper *News & Letters*,[8] and published their first pamphlet: Dunayevskaya's translation of Lenin's *Philosophic Notebooks* together with her May 1953 letters.

The new organization's Constitution singled out workers, Blacks, women and youth as revolutionary subjects in the U.S. Its center was in Detroit, Michigan, because of its African–American and proletarian nature and because Dunayevskaya refused to start a paper without a worker as editor and Denby lived in Detroit, where he worked at the Chrysler Mack auto plant.

Dunayevskaya was involved in every aspect of News and Letters Committees: she wrote a column for each issue of the newspaper; participated in local meetings; went on annual speaking tours; met with members and worked out ideas to help their self-development; and chaired the biweekly meetings of the Resident Editorial Board, which took responsibility for the day to day running of the organization. She took on an increasing amount of correspondence with intellectuals and activists alike, such as Erich Fromm, Adrienne Rich, Maria Barreno, Leopold Senghor, and Herbert Marcuse, who wrote the Preface to *Marxism and Freedom*, calling it "an oasis in the desert of Marxism."

Marxism and Freedom (1958) aimed "to re-establish Marxism in its original form, which Marx called 'a thoroughgoing Naturalism, or Humanism.'"[9] The first edition included her translations of Lenin's *Philosophic Notebooks* and "Private Property and Communism" and "Critique of the Hegelian Dialectic" from Marx's 1844 *Economic-Philosophic Manuscripts*—the first time those essays were published in English. It also includes much of her study on Russia as a state-capitalist society. Her methodology of writing was unique. Dunayevskaya presented draft chapters of the book in speeches to auto and steelworkers, miners, student youth and intellectuals who, she felt, "In their own words and out of their own lives...contributed a new understanding."[10]

After the publication of *Marxism and Freedom*, Dunayevskaya spoke at an international conference in Milan, Italy, of revolutionary tendencies opposed to both the U.S. and Russia. In 1962 she traveled to Africa, visiting the Gambia and Ghana, and her articles on the trip included ones on the role of women in the African Revolutions. In this period she instituted a series of "Weekly Political Letters" that took up crucial topics of the day, including the Bay of

8 All issues of *News & Letters*, which is still in print today, are viewable online at www.newsandletters.org.

9 Raya Dunayevskaya, *Marxism and Freedom: From 1776 until Today* (Amherst, New York: Humanity Books, 2000), p. 21.

10 Ibid., p. 24.

Pigs Invasion in April 1961 and the Cuban Missile Crisis in October 1962. None of this was separate from supporting concrete activities: from workers battling automation to the civil rights movement's Mississippi Freedom Summer and the Montgomery Bus Boycott—including singling out the self-organization of women hospital workers in Baltimore's "Maryland Freedom Union" and Woman Power Unlimited, a support group for imprisoned freedom riders in Mississippi.

In 1963 she wrote the pamphlet *American Civilization on Trial*,[11] which provided a Marxist-Humanist perspective on U.S. history, past and in the making, and demonstrated the two-way road between African and American freedom movements. Its central category, "Black Masses as Vanguard," became the pamphlet's subtitle in later editions. She continued to develop that idea for the rest of her life, measuring it against the activities and thoughts of Black masses.

As the anti-Vietnam War movement arose and the Sino-Soviet conflict deepened, Dunayevskaya was invited by radical social psychologist and philosopher Erich Fromm to write an essay for *Socialist Humanism* (1965), a book he was editing. In 1966—after correspondence with Japanese theorist of state-capitalism Tadayuki Tsushima and help from the Zengakuren, a revolutionary student group that had broken with the Japanese Communist Party—Dunayevskaya traveled on a speaking tour in Japan. Back in Detroit she wrote and lectured on world events including the Arab-Israeli conflict, China's "cultural revolution," Czechoslovakia's Prague Spring, the 1968 uprising by French students and workers, and "Lenin on Hegel's *Science of Logic*."

By 1969 the objective crises compelled Dunayevskaya to intensify her work on a new book that she felt was needed to theoretically clarify revolution. *Philosophy and Revolution: From Hegel to Sartre and from Marx to Mao* (1973) developed Marxist-Humanism's "original contribution": "Absolute Negativity as New Beginning." She made presentations on *Philosophy and Revolution* or read or sent draft chapters to groups of African Americans, youth, women's liberationists and East European revolutionaries.

When the Women's Liberation Movement burst forth in the mid-1960s, Dunayevskaya's reaction was unique among the Left. Rather than castigating it as a "diversion from revolution" as so many did, she welcomed it and sought to make its revolutionary character explicit. "The Women's Liberation Movement as Reason and as Revolutionary Force" was the concept she created to make her philosophic breakthrough of 1953 specific to women's liberation: that the movement from practice—in this case the women's liberation

11 Raya Dunayevskaya, *American Civilization on Trial: Black Masses as Vanguard* (Chicago: News & Letters, 2003).

movement—was itself a form of theory and that the movement from theory had to meet and help develop the new movements from practice.

The 1970s began with the revolutionary uprising of Polish workers beginning in the Gdansk shipyards in Poland, whose breadth and depth included Polish housewives. The decade ended with revolutionary Iranian women chanting against Khomeini on International Women's Day, 1979: "We made the revolution for freedom and got unfreedom." In between, Dunayevskaya wrote of every revolution and counter-revolution—from U.S. President Richard Nixon's invasion of Cambodia, to the gunning down of students at Kent State, Jackson State, and the six African American youth killed in Augusta, Ga., for protesting the murder of a 16-year-old killed by his jailers.

In 1974–75 the Portuguese Revolution burst forth and Dunayevskaya wrote passionately of its beginnings in the African Revolutions. She singled out Portuguese women, including the practice of the MLM (Portuguese Women's Liberation Movement) who fought not only the capitalists but "our own comrades who are refusing us equal pay," as well as the concept of *apartidarismo* (non-partyism) raised from within the revolutionary Left by Isabel do Carmo. Dunayevskaya's critical analysis of the economic crisis in the U.S. in those same years saw a new economic phase of state-capitalism.

In 1977 the Women's Liberation Committee of News and Letters Committees published *Sexism, Politics and Revolution in Mao's China*,[12] Dunayevskaya's analysis of the vilification of China's "gang of four" that included a critique of Roxanne Witke's book *Comrade Chiang Ch'ing*, along with an interview Dunayevskaya had with a Chinese woman revolutionary, "Jade," who spoke passionately about the difficulties of living under Mao's state-capitalism.

Dunayevskaya completed her third book, *Rosa Luxemburg, Women's Liberation, and Marx's Philosophy of Revolution*, in 1982. Her aim was that the book's three parts be seen as a unity that "will illuminate the totality of the crises of today, and the whole new continent of thought Marx discovered which remains *the* ground for perspectives for the 1980s."[13] The book brought out the relationship of Marx's "revolution in permanence" to Dunayevskaya's original contribution, "Absolute Negativity as New Beginning," and created what she considered a new category, "post-Marx Marxism as a pejorative, beginning with Engels." This work separated Marx's Marxism from that of his followers, including Lenin, Trotsky, and Luxemburg. She further argued that the transformation

12 Raya Dunayevskaya, *Sexism, Politics and Revolution in Mao's China* (Detroit: Women's Liberation-News & Letters, 1977).

13 Raya Dunayevskaya, *25 Years of Marxist-Humanism: A History of Worldwide Revolutionary Developments* (Chicago: News and Letters, 1980), p. 24.

of the relationship between women and men was fundamental to a Marxist concept of a new society.

In 1985 Dunayevskaya published her fourth book, *Women's Liberation and the Dialectics of Revolution: Reaching for the Future*, a collection of essays written over a thirty-five-year period, which sought to articulate Marxist-Humanist views over the entire post-World War II period so as to confront unfinished revolutions.

In November 1984, Dunayevskaya suffered a stroke, but by March 1985, she gave a lecture at the Wayne State University Archives of Labor and Urban Affairs, the first given by a living person whose collection the library housed. Her last years were dominated by studies for a book with the working title, "Dialectics of Organization and Philosophy: The 'Party' and Forms of Organization Born out of Spontaneity." In the midst of this activity, Raya Dunayevskaya died of an abdominal hemorrhage after surgery for a broken leg.

IV The Form and Content of the Present Volume

This collection of selected writings of Dunayevskaya on the Russian Revolution, on the development of state-capitalist theory, and on its relationship to the birth and development of Marxist-Humanism was created almost three decades after her death. The documents are drawn from the vast depository of her writings in *The Raya Dunayevskaya Collection*.

The selection from among hundreds of documents that discuss the subject matter at hand, written over more than four decades, has been guided by theoretical and philosophic categories that Dunayevskaya forged in her study of the Russian Revolution. That study did not end with analyzing the revolution and the contradictory practice of the period afterwards, but continued with its transformation into its opposite, the establishment of state-capitalism, and its global impact in the 20th century. Crucial—after this first attempt to build a workers' state was transformed into the monstrosity of a state-capitalist tyranny—was Dunayevskaya's determination to find *new beginnings for revolutionary Marxism for her age.*

Three of the categories she created were directly related to this: 1. *Lenin's philosophic preparation for revolution*, as well as *Lenin's philosophic ambivalence*; 2. *What happens after the revolution?* which referred to the first years after November 1917, and would come to have meaning beyond the particular outcome of the Russian Revolution; 3. *State-capitalism*, the theory born in her analysis of the Russian economy using Marx's economics from *Capital*, and the conditions and human relations of Russian workers at the point of production.

Two additional categories are also crucial: 4. *State-capitalism as a global phenomenon.* 5. *Marxist-Humanism* as a *philosophic-practical-organizational* body of ideas that reaches back to *Marx's* humanism, his philosophy of revolution in permanence, and forward to what she saw as the ongoing challenge for revolutionaries to develop further.

For Dunayevskaya, these concepts did not exist in isolation from each other. She wrote, "Without Marx's Humanism, the Theory of State-Capitalism Is No Great Divide [in Marxism]"; while pointing out, "[W]e must say that without the theory of state-capitalism it would have been impossible to reach Marxist-Humanism." The intertwining of Marx's original Humanism, the theory of state-capitalism, and Dunayevskaya's philosophy of Marxist-Humanism provides the framework for the present volume.

The book begins with writings analyzing three moments in Russian history: Lenin in 1914–1917, the immediate post-1917 period, and Stalin's implementation of the first Five-Year state economic plans and consolidation of power. It was the Hitler-Stalin "non-aggression Pact" in August 1939 and the subsequent beginning of the Second World War that triggered the first writings in which Dunayevskaya concluded that Russia was not a workers' state, but a state-capitalist one. She then delved into Lenin's philosophic preparation for revolution and examined the first years after the 1917 Revolution, when Lenin was still alive.

In the process of studying what Russia was economically, Dunayevskaya discovered Marx's 1844 *Economic-Philosophic Manuscripts* and Lenin's *Philosophic Notebooks*, neither of which was available in English. Even in the early and mid-1940s, when her focus was on developing the theory of state-capitalism, the seeds for re-conceptualizing Marxism were present. She was also making sight translations of Lenin's *Philosophic Notebooks* in the early 1940s. By 1948, she had decided to translate them into English.

What began as the urgent need to grasp the *economic* transformation of the Russian Revolution into its opposite with Stalin's consolidation of power, as well as the subsequent Great Depression changing the nature of private capitalism globally, developed into an exploration of the *theoretical-philosophic* roots of Marxism for Marx and Lenin. This was compelled by the reality that *Russia's transformation into state-capitalist was being carried out in the name of Marxism,* and that the anti-Stalinism of Trotsky and Trotskyism was insufficient to meet the challenge. Dunayevskaya sought to fill that gap.

The first four parts of this volume trace Dunayevskaya's labors on the Russian Revolution—what led up to it, its reality, and its aftermath. Part 1, "Philosophic Preparation for Revolution: The Significance of Lenin's Hegel Notebooks," contains Dunayevskaya's translation of the *Philosophic Notebooks* and the letters she wrote during that process. Two documents—"Lenin on Hegel's

Science of Logic: Notes on a Series of Lectures" (1967) and "Hegelian-Leninism," a presentation to the 1970 Telos International Philosophic Conference—speak to her interpretation of those Notebooks.

In each of her "trilogy of revolution"—*Marxism and Freedom: From 1776 until Today, Philosophy and Revolution: From Hegel to Sartre and from Marx to Mao,* and *Rosa Luxemburg, Women's Liberation, and Marx's Philosophy of Revolution*—she returned to Lenin as revolutionary and theoretician. In the process of working on a new book in 1986–87 on "Dialectics of Organization and Philosophy" she returned again to Lenin and was developing a "Changed Perception of Lenin's Philosophic Ambivalence." Notes and presentations on this changed perception, including his failure to relate philosophy and organization, are included in Chapter 2.

In Part 2, "On the Significance of Lenin's 'Great Divide in Marxism'; Contrast with Trotsky, Bukharin, Luxemburg," presentations and essays reveal Dunayevskaya's interpretation of Lenin's political practice and writings of 1915–1917 on imperialism and self-determination of nations. They are rooted in his new view of the Hegelian dialectic, in contrast with how Dunayevskaya viewed Trotsky, Luxemburg, and Bukharin, leading revolutionaries who lacked a fully dialectical viewpoint in their political-revolutionary practice and theoretical labors. Among the topics are Trotsky's theory of permanent revolution, including an exchange between Dunayevskaya and the Trotskyist theoretician Ernest Mandel (Chapter 4), Lenin's differences with Bukharin on self-determination (Chapter 5), and Luxemburg's important writings on the Russian Revolution, as well as Lenin's critique of her *Junius* pamphlet (Chapter 6).

A more personal but equally theoretical view is in Chapter 7, "On Women Revolutionaries in Russia." Dunayevskaya's "In Memoriam" to Natalia Sedova Trotsky, with whom she maintained a warm correspondence, discusses the role of women in revolution, especially those "who had not gained theoretical leadership and therefore were very nearly disregarded except as faithful wives and mothers." She shows us a Natalia Trotsky who dared "in speaking out even against those who had led the movement her husband had founded, because nothing at all could stay in the way of principles."

In Part 3, "What Happens After?—Lenin 1917–1923," Dunayevskaya develops this crucial category in the case of the Russian Revolution. In *Marxism and Freedom,* she had formulated the problematic thus:

> the two biggest tasks [the new workers' state, the "dictatorship of the proletariat"] faced theoretically were: (1) *how* would labor assert its mastery over the economy and the state? And (2) since the dictatorship is supposed to be a transitional state—transitional to socialism—*how* would it achieve its own "withering away"?

Chapter 8 begins with the Trade Union Debate between Trotsky, Alexander Shlyapnikov and Lenin, of which Dunayevskaya wrote:

> Before [the Trade Union debate] ended, subjects in dispute ranged far and wide: (1) What is a workers' state? (2) What is the role of trade unions in such a state? (3) What is the relationship between workers at the point of production and the political party in power? (4) What is the relationship between leaders and ranks, party and mass?
>
> *Marxism and Freedom*, p. 197

The second document in Chapter 8 takes up Lenin's sharp critique of the growing bureaucracy in the newly born workers' state, and the evaluation in his "Will" of Stalin, Trotsky and Bukharin.

Part 4, "Russia's Transformation into Opposite: The Theory of State-Capitalism," contains documents that detail the development of state-capitalist theory with a focus on Stalin's Russia. These essays, written while Dunayevskaya was a member of the Workers Party, were the first comprehensive economic-political analysis of Russia as a state-capitalist society. The debate was not alone against Stalin's Russia and its ideological defenders, but also against the anti-Stalinist Trotskyist Left, the majority of whom either continued to analyze Russia as a "workers' state" that was almost tantamount to "socialism," or argued for "new" social forms such as bureaucratic collectivism.

Dunayevskaya's first essay on the theory of state-capitalism was her 1941 "The Union of Soviet Socialist Republics Is a Capitalist Society." She followed it with "An Analysis of the Russian Economy" in 1942–43 and "The Nature of the Russian Economy" in 1946–47, both published in *The New International*. "Labor and Society" (1943) cited passages in Marx's 1844 Manuscripts in charting a return to his concept of labor, its alienation, and labor's total emancipation as central to the abolition of capitalism and the construction of a new society.

In 1944 she challenged the Russian theoreticians who had suddenly reversed the official line to declare that the law of value—what Karl Marx had singled out as the hallmark of capitalism—also operated under "socialism." She obtained a copy of the Russian economic journal, *Pod Znamenem Marxizma* (*Under the Banner of Marxism*), through a diplomatic pouch after it failed to reach libraries in the U.S. Her translation of the journal's article on "Teaching of Economics in the Soviet Union" was published together with "A New Revision of Marxian Economics," her critique of this drastic revision, in *The American Economic Review*, 1944. It created a hot international debate that was reported on the front page of *The New York Times*, lasted for a year, and elicited responses in *The American Economic Review* from Paul Baran, Oskar Lange and Leo Rogin, with a rejoinder by her, in 1944–45. As the U.S. and the USSR were allies, the U.S. State Department also tried to keep her article from being published.[14]

After World War II, intense economic developments in Russia unseparated from deepening exploitation of labor eerily echoed Marx's description of capitalism as "production for production's sake." The nuclear arms race escalated as the USSR sought to match the U.S. A-bomb, and then H-bomb.

Though her focus was on Russia—where the transformation had taken the extreme form of a workers' state turned into its opposite, into full-blown state-capitalist tyranny—Dunayevskaya saw state-capitalism as a world stage, born of the Great Depression and encompassing various state formations. They included the New Deal in the U.S., Nazism in Germany, and the "Co-Prosperity Sphere" in Japan, among others. She would develop the concept of world state-capitalism throughout the post-World War II decades.

Part 5, "From State-Capitalist Theory to Marxist-Humanism, 1950s–1980s" takes up the development of the philosophy of Marxist-Humanism, singling out key moments.

Following the March 5, 1953, death of Stalin, Dunayevskaya immediately wrote on its significance and the ramifications that she was sure would follow.[15] Working out the meaning of Stalin's death, amid rising tensions among the leaders of the Johnson-Forest Tendency (James, Dunayevskaya, and Boggs) over her analysis, Dunayevskaya was compelled to return to the philosophic origins of Marxism within the Hegelian dialectic.

The Philosophic Moment of Marxist-Humanism

Where both Marx and Lenin had found rich new beginnings in the dialectic—Marx particularly in Hegel's *Phenomenology* and the early parts of *Philosophy of Mind*, and Lenin in the *Science of Logic*—Dunayevskaya probed Hegel's Absolutes: Absolute Idea in the *Science of Logic*, Absolute Knowing in the *Phenomenology of Mind* (Spirit), and Absolute Mind in the *Philosophy of Mind*. She wrote two letters on May 12 and 20, 1953,[16] on what she would later call her breakthrough on Hegel's Absolutes. Within them she found a dual movement—from practice to theory, and from theory to practice. So crucial did she feel this breakthrough was that she returned to it again and again over the following

---

14 *The Raya Dunayevskaya Collection*, # 9971.

15 See her articles in the March 19, April 16, and April 30, 1953 issues of *Correspondence* newspaper, #2180 in the Raya Dunayevskaya Collection.

16 They are included in Chapter 2 of *The Power of Negativity*.

decades. This concept of a movement from below, from practice, that she discerned as a form of theory, and a movement from theory to practice reaching for the fullness of philosophy, would determine Marxist-Humanism throughout Dunayevskaya's life. She called this breakthrough "the philosophic moment of Marxist-Humanism."

To follow the development of Marxist-Humanism comprehensively, her trilogy of revolution, as well as *The Power of Negativity: Selected Writings on the Dialectic in Hegel and Marx,* are essential. In 2018, the 200th anniversary of Marx's birth, The Raya Dunayevskaya Memorial Fund and News and Letters Committees will be issuing another collection of her writings tentatively titled *Marx at Two Hundred: The Meaning of His Philosophy of Revolution in Permanence for Our Day.* That volume will also take up the philosophic moment of Marxist-Humanism in that context.

Part 5 begins with a document that discusses the development from the State-Capitalist Tendency to the birth of a Marxist-Humanist organization—News and Letters Committees. When she became fully a Marxist-Humanist, her analysis of Russia not only included a chapter on Stalin from *Marxism and Freedom* but crucial writings on "The beginning of the end of Russian totalitarianism." The "beginning of the end" was manifested in revolt and outright revolution within the Soviet Union and its satellite states. The documents included in Chapter 11 chronicle the East German Revolt of June 17, 1953, only six weeks after the death of Stalin, the Vorkuta prison uprising of July 1953, and the Hungarian Revolution of 1956. She continued writing on movements from below, including the movement toward "socialism with a human face" in Czechoslovakia 1968, and the Polish workers' strikes that led to *Solidarnosc*. These writings can be found in the Raya Dunayevskaya Collection. She documented the ongoing development of state-capitalist Russia, including Khrushchev's rise to power, so-called deStalinization, Andropov's regime, and the Gorbachev-Reagan maneuvers. A number of these documents are in Chapter 12.

The concept of state-capitalism as a world phenomenon took on a new concrete form with Mao Zedong's rise to power in China. He openly called his regime state-capitalist. Two of the major articles Dunayevskaya wrote on the first decade of Mao's rule are included in Chapter 13: "Only Freedom Can Solve The Crisis" and "Let 100 Flowers Bloom ... But Only One Party Rule." Her most comprehensive analysis of Mao's rule and ideology are chapters in *Marxism and Freedom* and *Philosophy and Revolution*: "The Challenge of Mao Tse-Tung," "Cultural Revolution or Maoist Reaction?" and "The Thought of Mao Tse-tung." Two other writings, "Sino-Indian War Reveals Relationship of Ideology to State-Capitalist Imperialism" and "Indonesian Communism: A Case of

World Communism's Decomposition," take up her analysis of China and state-capitalism in the Asian sphere.

From the 1960s to Mao's death, Russian and Chinese "Communism" were preoccupied by the Sino-Soviet Conflict. Dunayevskaya wrote extensively on this for *News & Letters* newspaper. Chapter 14 contains her commentary on it from *Marxism and Freedom.*

At the same time as Dunayevskaya hailed the Cuban Revolution's daring challenge to U.S. imperialism, she analyzed Fidel Castro's tying Cuba to the Soviet orbit and being pulled toward state-capitalism. She sharply critiqued Regis Debray's advocacy of the strategy of *focoism* as elucidated in his *Revolution in the Revolution.* This material is in Chapter 15.

In Chapter 16, "State-Capitalism as a 'New Stage of World Capitalism' vs. the Humanism of Marx," are a number of writings that sharply differentiate state-capitalism in its many manifestations from the humanism of Marx.

Lastly, Chapter 17 on the "Battle of Ideas" contains a number of Dunayevskaya's discussions and critiques of Left intellectuals and revolutionaries in relation to Russian state-capitalism and Lenin's *Philosophic Notebooks*—among them Herbert Marcuse, Cornelius Castoriadis, Georg Lukacs, and Tony Cliff.

***

Raya Dunayevskaya lived freely when women were not free and was fierce in her determination to fulfill and deepen the promise of the Russian Revolution at its best, to transform a world she viewed as brutally inhuman into one where everyone could experience self-development and freedom. Readers will find in her a thinker-activist who lived and wrote profoundly on the meaning of the Revolution and its transformation into opposite. Her questioning and passion for a world that transcends capitalism compelled her to become a Marxist philosopher who was determined to create Marxism anew in the last half of the 20th century. That task is no less urgent in the 21st century.

PART 1

Philosophic Preparation for Revolution: The Significance of Lenin's Hegel Notebooks

CHAPTER 1

Translation of and Commentary on Lenin's "Abstract of Hegel's *Science of Logic*"

Dunayevskaya's four-decades-long engagement with the dialectical thought of Lenin stands alongside her exploration and breakthrough on Hegel's Absolutes, and her thought-dive into Marx—rooted in how she saw his confrontation with the Hegelian dialectic and her view of Marx as "philosopher of revolution in permanence," 1843–1883—as crucial philosophical vantage points for her development of Marxist-Humanism.

Her engagement began in the early 1940s with sight-translations of portions of Lenin's Philosophic Notebooks on Hegel's Science of Logic, *continued with a full translation of his 1914–15 Hegel Notebooks (1949). In the 1950s she began writings on what she termed Lenin's "philosophic preparation for revolution," and its political concretizations after 1914, as well as 1917–1923. In the 1960s and 1970s, she continued these studies and wrote as well on what she saw as Lenin's "philosophic ambivalence" with regard to his not publishing the Notebooks, and not sharing their content and methodology with his Bolshevik colleagues.*

A brief selection of Dunayevskaya's writings on Lenin and the dialectic is presented below. This chapter's appendix is her translation of Lenin's commentary on the Science of Logic *as published in the first edition of* Marxism and Freedom *(1957). Her first commentaries on the Notebooks can be seen in the three letters she wrote to her colleague C.L.R. James accompanying her translation. Two documents from the 1960s and 1970s, "Lenin on Hegel's* Science of Logic: *Notes on a Series of Lectures" (1967) and "Hegelian Leninism," a presentation to the Telos International Philosophical Conference (1970), show her determination to share her labors of reading Lenin on Hegel with her Marxist-Humanist colleagues in News and Letters Committees, and are part of her preparatory work for "The Shock of Recognition and the Philosophic Ambivalence of Lenin," Chapter 3 of her* Philosophy and Revolution *(1973).*

Three Letters to C.L.R. James in the Process of Translating Lenin's "Abstract of Hegel's *Science of Logic*"

Letter to James of February 18, 1949

Dear J:

I decided to translate the *Philosophic Notebooks* on the *Science of Logic* in toto as excerpts cannot avoid the appearance and actuality of being forced. Here is the first section, dealing with the Prefaces, Introduction and Doctrine of Being. Note that the Leap (translated by Hegel's translators as Jump) you made so famous in your *Notes* [*on Dialectics*] is not in Quality but in Measure. It is the climax, that is, to entire first volume [of the *Science of Logic*]. He begins by objecting to the pedantry which listed the title of the Observation to the Nodal Line of Measure-Relations: (Examples of Such Nodal Lines; *natura non facit saltum* [nature makes no leaps]) in the contents pages but not in the text itself. He then proceeds to introduce his conclusions with "gradualness explains nothing without leaps," then he repeats the title of the Observation "as if Nature did not make jumps" which he emphasizes further by repeating the word "Leaps!" at a side, then softly emphasizes "Interruptions to gradualness" [M&F, p. 330; LCW 38, p. 123] and ends with quoting pages 389–390, "It is said, *natura non facit saltum*" and two more Leaps! follow that. You would think at this point that he feels gaily and can transit to Essence easily. No, he complains here that the end of Vol. I, "Transition of Being to Essence is analyzed doubly obscurely" [M&F, p. 330; LCW 38, p. 125]. How much that man knew and how much more he was searching for!

You will enjoy the notes on Being which you practically skipped over in your hurry to get to Essence. It seemed to me one of the reasons was the necessity to begin with simplest categories, because both in philosophy, economics, politics and what have you those simple categories "contain in germ the whole." An excellent example of this firm grasp of the dialectic at its simplest is his remark, after complaining that Hegel is unclear, or rather he is unclear about Hegel's full meaning in "*Die Objectivität des Scheins, die Notwendigkeit des Widerspruchs* [The Objectivity of Appearance, the Necessity of Contradiction]" (inherent negativity):

> Is not this the thought, that appearance is also objective, since it is *one of the sides* of the objective world? Not only *Wesen* [Essence], but also *Schein* [Appearance] are objective. Even the distinction between subjective and objective has its limits.
>
> M&F, p. 328; LCW 38, p. 98

No wonder that man could write of *appearance* so profoundly! *Imperialism: A Popular Outline*. Need I harp on my favorite peeve: compare this analysis of appearance to Rosa [Luxemburg]'s analysis of essence in her *Accumulation* [*of Capital*].

Another thing that struck me anew was emphasis on Method, Method, Method, "the dialectic which it has in itself" [SLI, p. 65]: The first reference to *Capital* occurs here when he quotes Hegel, "not a mere abstract Universal, but as a Universal which comprises in itself the full wealth of Particulars" [M&F, p. 328; LCW 38, p. 99]. When you add to his emphasis on the development of thinking through "its own necessary laws," his attack against "using" forms of thought "as a means," the attacks both on Kantianism and his "thing-in-itself" and Transcendental Idealism and its "subjectivism," you can see that the concretes which Lenin had in mind when he was reading *Logic* were both the economic conditions—*Capital* plus the *Imperialism* he was going to work out—and Ideology of the Bernsteins, Kautskys and, yes, Rosa Luxemburg since in that very period he also made notes on her book. What rich years were 1914–16 for Lenin in his "study room"!

Evidently for the first time he was struck also by the fact that in the back of Hegel's mind when he worked out the "self-development of concepts" was the whole history of philosophy. (He had made these notes before those on Hegel's *History of Philosophy.*) Along with this was the emphasis on how "materialistic" rang the sound of Hegel's statement, "What is first in science has had to show itself first historically" [SLI, p. 101; LCW 38, p. 106]. Lenin gave a very, rather truly materialistic interpretation of history as it meant to him also the *economic* foundations of society. At the same time he contrasts "Sophistry and Dialectic" in general when he quotes Hegel:

> For sophistry is an argument proceeding from a baseless supposition which is allowed without criticism or reflection; while we term dialectic that higher movement of Reason where terms appearing absolutely distinct pass into one another because they are what they are, where the assumption of their separateness cancels itself.
>
> SLI, p. 117; LCW 38, p. 107

Both Hegel and Lenin hit at "baseless assumptions"; this is very important for our work, of course.

Among the "baseless assumptions" are those that divide finite from infinite by an impassable barrier, or, as Hegel would put it, by making one "a this-sidedness" and then establishing an "other-sidedness," a beyond. It is at this point that he deals with "Ought and Barrier as moments of the finite" [SLI, pp. 144–145], but very briefly; I went back to Hegel very carefully on that, and the correspondence with G [Grace Lee Boggs] on the relation of this to the general contradiction of capitalism you are acquainted with. I will return to that again at another time.

No one reading Lenin can resist temptation to quote him on the dialectic, although they know the reader is all too anxious to stop reading this to get to Hegel himself, so here goes: This comes after Hegel's "The things are, but the truth of this being is their end" [SLI, p. 142].

> Thoughts of dialectic *en lisant* [in reading] Hegel. NB. Sharp and wise! Hegel analyzes concepts which usually appear dead and he shows that there *is* movement in them. The finite? That means *movement* has come to an end! Something. That means *not what Other is.* Being in general? That means such indeterminateness that being = Not-Being.
>
> All-sided universal flexibility of concepts—flexibility reaching to the identity of opposites. This flexibility, subjectively applied = eclecticism and sophistry. When this flexibility is *objectively* applied, i.e., reflecting the all-sidedness of the material process and its unity, then it is dialectic, it is the correct reflection of the eternal development of the world.
>
> M&F, p. 329; LCW 38, p. 110

Have fun with Lenin and be patient about his Notes on Essence since this is a very large section and I do this between many other activities.

Yours,

R

∵

Letter to James of February 25, 1949

Dear J:

Herewith Lenin's Notes on Essence; I am moving faster with the translation than I had counted upon mainly because I had thought it would take time "to find" the quotations but now find that as I myself internalize Hegel I nearly always flip open the right page.

The deep richness of Lenin's Notes would overwhelm me if it were not for their utter simplicity. As if you did not believe me, let me cite but one instance. He is talking about a "purely logical" working out of the dialectic and continues "*Das fällt zusammen* [It coincides]. It *must* coincide as does induction and deduction in *Capital*" [M&F, p. 332; LCW 38, p. 146]. Not for one instant does he permit you to think that to compare the dialectic "merely" to the deductive and inductive method of *Capital* is "narrow," for the comment occurred as an addition to: "The continuation of the work of Hegel and Marx must consist in the *dialectic* working out of the history of human thought, science and technique" [M&F, p. 332; LCW 38, pp. 146–147]. Moreover, "technique," or the technology which sets the ground for our mode of production, production relation[s], and generally the whole intellectual development, is nowhere here so overpowering that you think of the mind's development as a *mere* reflection of the economic relations; that too not only has its own laws but "works upon," so to speak, the economic material and the result is not any one of these things *alone* but *all* of them together. This can be seen, for example, in the three dates that he sets down for universal development: (1) 1813—*Science of Logic*, or the theory of development, (2) 1847—the *Communist Manifesto*, or the application of dialectic to society, (3) 1859—[Darwin's] *Origin of Species*, or "application" of dialectics to man [M&F, p. 331; LCW 38, p. 141]. Whoever is still so foolhardy as to look for a "primary cause" may do so if he has enough time to waste; Lenin will have none of that—he will have only totality and movement and break-up and movement.

If the three sections of the Doctrine of Essence had to be summarized in three words, I'd say *Manifoldness* for Show (Reflection), *Law* for Appearance, and *Totality* for Actuality. Manifoldness is particularly important if you consider that Lenin wrote his Notes when the world was being rent asunder. Lenin, in quoting Hegel on the fact that both Skepticism and Idealism admitted manifoldness and yet the one dared not "affirm 'it is'" and the other dared not "regard cognition as knowledge of the thing-in-itself" [SLII, p. 22], comments: "You include all the manifold riches of the world in *Schein* and you reject the objectivity of *Schein*!!" [LCW 38, p. 131]

Lenin notes, further, not only that Essence must appear (rather he comments on this statement of Hegel's, thus: "The little philosophers dispute whether one should take as basis the essence *or* the immediately given.... Hegel substitutes 'and' for 'or' and explains the concrete content of this 'and'" [M&F, p. 330; LCW 38, p. 134]) but he emphasizes that even more, [it] is "*one* of the determinations of essence" [LCW 38, p. 133]. Naturally, he does not fail to underline that one-sided determinateness of Essence has no truth, but he emphasizes also (permit me to skip here): "Causality is ordinarily understood by us as only a small part of the universal connection, but (a materialistic addition) the small part is not subjective but the objectively real connection" [M&F, p. 335; LCW 38, p. 160]. I could not help but feel that these "small parts" which had "objectively real connection" were the elements of the phenomena about him which became the book *Imperialism*.

May I be permitted to linger a moment on Law of Contradiction, seeing that both Lenin and you considered [it] so much the essence of the book as to quote it in toto? I however wish to limit myself only to its relationship to the general contradiction of capitalism. I began to harp on the applicability of parts of the dialectic to that general contradiction even when I was in the Doctrine of Being (Section on Ought and Barrier in relation to infinite production—production for production's sake, that is) and now I find that Hegel notes (p. 67): "Infinity, which is contradiction as it appears in the sphere of Being," and then moves rapidly on to demonstrate that "the principle of self-movement ... consists of nothing else but the exhibition of contradiction." Having moved that rapidly, he concludes, "Motion is *existent* contradiction." The emphasis is Lenin's and suit[s] me perfectly for grappling with the law of motion of capitalist society in philosophic rather than in value terms. If [I] am wrong, I can always return home—to the law of value—but something bids me continue with it.

Some time back I wrote to Grace about the fact that "kingdom of laws" in *Phenomenology* had me baffled since there seemed to be a contradiction between that analysis which fitted the primitive conception of the Stalinists and the economic laws to which Marx refers as dominating over society regardless of the consciousness of men. I was on the point of considering myself still as a mere "Woman of understanding" when I met with Lenin's notes on the Law of Appearance, where he not only sends himself back to the very same section in the *Phenomenology,* but after listing no less than ten definitions of law in Hegel, he concludes that all these definitely differ from the final conclusion, p. 135. Allow me to take these summations step by step as they will help me transit to totality. Law is, says Lenin, paraphrasing Hegel:

(1) unity of show and existence; (2) *one* of the steps of the cognition of unity and connection of reciprocal dependence and totality of the world process; (3) the enduring and persistent in appearance; (4) the identity of appearance in its reflection; (5) the *quiescent* reflection in appearance; (6) narrow, incomplete, approximate; (7) essential appearance; (8) law and essence of concept are homogeneous... expressing the deepening of man's knowledge of appearance; (9) reflection of essential; (10) a part; appearance, totality, wholeness is richer than law. [M&F, p. 333; LCW 38, pp. 150–153]

But here Lenin stops himself to note: "But further, although it is not clear, it is acknowledged, it seems (p. 135 especially), that law can overcome this inadequacy and grasp also the negative side, and *Totalität der Erscheinung* [totality of Appearance]. Must return here!" [LCW 38, p. 152]. Now pp. 135ff has what appears to me the key sentence: "The determination of Law has thus changed [in] Law itself." At which Hegel proceeds to show what it was "at first," what it became as "negative intro-Reflection" developed it [SLII, p. 135], and concludes "Thus Law is *Essential Relation*" [SLII, p. 141]. The emphasis is Lenin's and brings us precisely to the comprehension of law in the sense in which Marx uses "absolute general law,"[1] which can only be abrogated by the mediation of the proletariat establishing different social relations.

What a dialectician that Hegel was; nothing else can explain the sheer genius of that man's language which defines identity as "unseparated difference," and now as he enters Actuality and *Totalität* [totality], asserts that totality is found as "*sundered completeness*" [SLII, p. 170]. The emphasis is Lenin's [LCW 38, p. 156], which shows he was not going to be outdone by a man who lived and died long before World War I. You will like the way Lenin weaves in the Smaller Logic to clarify the essence of the dialectic. He underlines Hegel's *"The sum total of the elements* which, as it opens itself out, discloses itself to be necessity" [*Encyclopedia of the Philosophical Sciences,* ¶143]. And then translates: "The unfoldment of the whole totality of moments of actuality NB = essence of dialectic knowledge" [M&F, p. 334; LCW 38, p. 158]. He also asks himself whether by "moments of concept" Hegel does not mean "moments of transition." He is full of "all-sidedness and all-embracing character of world connection" [M&F, p. 335; LCW 38, p. 159]. Always it is: Connection, relation, mediation, necessity, motion, unity of opposites, break-up of identity, transition and motion, motion and transition, and that is totality. I believe I am ready to follow him into Notion.

Yours,

R

∵

Letter to James of March 12, 1949

Dear J:

I am extremely happy in being able to send you the conclusion of Lenin's Notes on the *Logic.* If you wrote your *Notes on the Dialectic* for me, then I translated Lenin for you. Surely you who have gone into a regular "conspiracy" with Lenin on the analysis of Hegel deserved seeing Lenin's notes in their entirety, and not merely in extracts. Being the only Russian, it was my duty to have done this long ago. The only reason (and it is the real ground, not a mere excuse) I have for not doing so is that I could not have without first having digested your Notes; so now we are "quits." Perhaps I'll even be conceited enough to say that when you come to rewriting your Notes I can be of service.

---

1 See Dunayevskaya's *Philosophy and Revolution, from Hegel to Sartre and from Marx to Mao,* pp. 92–94. —Editors.

Let me say at the start that, although you have entered into this "conspiracy" with Lenin, the outstanding difference between the two "versions" is striking. You will note that Lenin's notes on the Notion are as lengthy as those on the Introduction and Doctrines of Being and Essence combined. Yours were too—but in your notes on the Notion you included the actual application of it, both insofar as a balance sheet of Trotskyism is concerned as well as in outlining our own leap, but Lenin's Notes on the Notion are that bulky *in and for themselves*, with bare indications as to how to apply. The difference is not accidental. Lenin was looking for a new Universal. He found Hegel's Idea, and said, if I may steal an expression from Marx, who stole it from someone else: *hic Rhodus, hic salta.* And even then Lenin couldn't fashion his new universal—revolutions to a man—until there appeared the Soviets, 1917 version. The Idea had him pose the question correctly; the Russian masses supplied the practice; and then Lenin arrived and unified the two and called it: *State and Revolution.* We, on the other hand, although we are looking for our (this age's, that is) universal, have something to go by as Lenin had not. Hence, although you spent that much time on Notion, and included its practice, the thing you chose most to stop at and say: *hic Rhodus, hic salta* to was the Law of Contradiction in Essence. That too is not accidental since what we are confronted with is not a "betrayal" (like that of the Second International) but the *contradictions* of Trotskyism which still passes for Leninism and in which we too have our roots and being, so much so that even when you come to the Notion (in your Synthetic Cognition) you return back to Essence, contradiction of form and content, cause and effect, etc., in order once and for all not only [to] do away with, but overcome, transcend Trotskyism.

Just as the LEAP characterized Lenin's comprehension of the Doctrine of Being, LAW as Essential Relation his grasp of the Doctrine of Essence, so PRACTICE characterizes his very profound analysis of the Doctrine of the Notion, and why he chooses to single out the section on the Idea as you had Observation.

Lenin begins with the fact that "The dialectic road to cognition of truth is from living observation to abstract thinking and from this to practice" [M&F, p. 337; LCW 38, p. 171] and never lets go of this for a single second. He insists that the laws of logical cognition reflect objectivity in the subjective consciousness of man, but he does not stop at reflection. No, he states categorically, "Man's cognition not only reflects the objective world, but *creates* it" [M&F, p. 347; LCW 38, p. 212]. (My emphasis.) But if you think for a moment that that means you can get off into the high clouds of the land beyond, he brings you right back to earth and practice, practice, practice:

> "Conclusion of action".... For Hegel *action*, practice is the *logical "conclusion"* of the figure of logic. And this is true! Of course, not in the sense that the figure of logic has by its otherness the practice of man (=absolute idealism) but vice versa: the practice of man repeating itself billions of times, fastens itself in consciousness of man by the figures of logic. These figures have the solidity of a prejudice, an axiomatic character precisely (and only) because of this billion-timed repetition.
>
> M&F, p. 348; LCW 38, p. 217

And again:

> The activity of man, composing for itself an objective picture of the world, *changes* the external activity, transcends its determinateness (=changes these or other of its aspects, qualities) and thus takes away from it the traits of appearance, externality and nullity and gives it being in-itself and for-itself (=objective truth).
>
> M&F, p. 348; LCW 38, p. 218

And before that:

> undoubtedly practice in Hegel stands as a link in the analysis of the process of cognition and precisely as a transition to objective ("absolute" according to Hegel) truth. Marx, consequently, clings to Hegel, introducing the criteria of practice into the theory of knowledge: cf. [Marx's] Theses on Feuerbach.
>
> M&F, p. 347; LCW 38, p. 212

And before that: he had traced the embryo of historical materialism in Hegel, quoting and emphasizing (in caps) the following from Hegel: "In his tools man possesses power over external nature even though, according to his ends, he frequently is subjected to it" [SLII, p. 388; M&F, p. 342; LCW 38, p. 189].

His *whole* emphasis on the *End* and *Subjective* notion is that the aims of man are generated by the objective world but that he changes, subjectively desires change and acts; there he goes so far as to call the objective world non-actual and the desires of man *actual*, and the reason he hangs on so to the Idea is that "it not only has the dignity of a universal, but also the simply actual" [LCW 38, p. 213]. Let me see whether I can do with the Idea, what I tried to do with the Law, listing it in detail, for Lenin has no less than 17 definitions—more correctly, manifoldednesses: (What a word I just made up!)

(1) Notion *and* objectivity; (2) *relations* of subjectivity to objectivity; (3) *impulse* to transcend; (4) *process* and subordination of thought and object; (5) contains strongest *contradiction in itself* since notion reaches freedom and *eternally* creates, *eternally* overcomes; (6) is *Truth* (only as *totality* and relation does it realize itself); (7) is *Reason* (Subjective and Objective); (8) is objective *activity*; (9) *develops* through (a) Life, (b) process of knowledge, *including practice*, (c) reaches the Absolute Idea or complete truth; (10) *logical* notion, which = nature AND concreteness AND abstractness AND phenomena AND essence AND motion AND relation; (11) not only dignity of universal but also simple *actual*; the richest *is* the *most concrete*; (12) *unity* of cognition and practice; (13) three postulates summarize it: (a) *good End* (subjective End) vs. *actuality* ("external actuality"); (b) external *means* (weapon) (objective), (c) correspondence of subject and object, the verification of subjective ideas, which are (14) criteria of objective truth; (15) Absolute Idea as unity of theoretical and practical idea; (16) *method* of absolute cognition, after which is (17) the summation of the *dialectic.*

For that Lenin gives 17 other aspects which constantly develop through relations, objectivity, contradiction, struggle, transition, unfolding of new sides which seem to be a return to old (negation of the negation), motion, practice. He sums up science which he considers, after Hegel, "*a circle of circles*" [LCW 38, p. 233] as the movement from "subjective Idea to objective truth *through* practice" [M&F, p. 343; LCW 38, p. 191], with no end of emphasis on technique *and* the objective world *and* subjective aims: "*Technique, mechanical and chemical, thus serves the aims of man, in that its character (essence) consists in its determination by external conditions (by the laws of nature)*" [M&F, p. 341; LCW 38, p. 188]. Finally concluding that the only verification of all these dialectical laws is the application to *individual* sciences and hence the emphasis on our restudying Marx's *Capital*, which *none* of the Marxists of the 20th century understood [M&F, p. 340; LCW 38, p. 180], and a remark against himself: "Marxist*s* criticized the Kantians and Humists at the beginning of the 20th century more in the Feuerbachian (and Buchnerian) than in a Hegelian manner" [M&F, p. 340; LCW 38, p. 179]. The emphasis on the plural (Marxist*s*) is Lenin's; it follows the remark against Plekhanov; and has an additional remark: "The question of the criticism of contemporary Kantianism, Machism, etc." [M&F, p. 340; LCW 38, p. 179]. In other words, the emphasis on the plural includes himself as he is the only one in addition to Plekhanov who had bothered much with Machism.

It is a masterly understatement to say that I am immensely impressed. A better way to express it is that I am dying to get down to apply all this to two things: (1) the American economy to which I hope to get to seriously this summer; (2) to Marx's *Capital* on which I hope Grace will collaborate; I have written on some of the aspects already and will tomorrow send off another letter on other aspects.

Because I have been very anxious to finish this ([George] Novack's visit took a week out) I have not read either the notes on the Puritan Revolution or the one on the Negro question; I hope I can keep both till next week and will let you have my reactions then.

My love to Connie [Webb].

For: "The Materialist Friends of the Hegelian Dialectic"

Notes on a Series of Lectures: Lenin on Hegel's *Science of Logic* (December 14, 1967)

Lecture I. Introductory

These notes are addressed more to the teachers than to the pupils. Since, however, each member of the class is both teacher and pupil, it is addressed to all and the demands that each person, who is to lead a class, has to read these notes and the relevant material before the session begins. The notes are hardly more than indications of where to look for the problem. There are no "illusions." At best they hope to lead to a conception of method which one can *practice.*

The great difficulty of plunging into Hegel directly make it necessary to establish the historical points of departure, not only for Hegel but for our life and times. We have, in fact, four points of departure: (1) the French Revolution, which formed Hegel's point of departure, although he most often would refer to the writings in philosophy during that period rather than to the period "in and for itself." There is no doubt, however, both in his historic writings and in the *Phenomenology of Mind* that it is the historic event that he considered the greatest and the measure of philosophy itself. (2) The 1848 revolutions and the 1871 Paris Commune which were the great historic events of Marx's time. (3) From World War I to 1924, the decade from the time Lenin began to re-read Hegel's *Science of Logic* until his death. And, (4) our own post-World War II world.

A good way to prepare ourselves for both the historic periods and Lenin's notes as well as Hegel himself is by way of reading the following sections in *Marxism and Freedom*:

(1) "The Philosophers and the Revolution: Freedom and the Hegelian Dialectic" (pp. 33–37), which relates Hegel to the French Revolution and cites Marx on Hegel's *Phenomenology of Mind.*

(2) "Hegel's Absolutes and our Age of Absolutes" (pp. 37–43), especially the references to Russian Communism's 1947 revisions on the dialectic and its 1955 attack on Marx's Humanist Essays.

(3) "Lenin and the Dialectic: A Mind in Action" (pp. 168–172), dealing with the break in Lenin's thought caused by the outbreak of World War I and the collapse of the Second International.

(4) "The Irish Revolution and the Dialectic of History" (pp. 172–176) which is the historical instance where Lenin applied his new conceptions of the dialectic to an actual revolution and formed the center of his theories on self-determination of nations, that is of the essence for our own age.

(5) Above all, you must read through, as a whole, without stopping to see whether you "really" understand, Lenin's Notes on Hegel's *Science of Logic* as they are abbreviated in the first edition of *Marxism and Freedom* (pp. 327–355).

The two-fold reason for reading through the whole Abstract without questioning one's understanding of any single point in it is this: (1) to have at least a glimpse of the whole, it is important to get the *rhythm*, to follow the *movement.* (2) Since all of the rest of the month or six weeks will be taken up in the detailed studying of Lenin's Philosophic Notebooks, alongside the actual passages in Hegel, to which Lenin referred in his Commentary, it does not matter, in a first reading, that we have let many undigested passages pass us by. The important thing is to hold on to some reality, to the concrete as one works his way through the underlying philosophy, not to let oneself get bogged down by the Hegelian "language." Remember, always, that it was not an abstruse philosopher but a practicing revolutionary who felt the *compulsion* to go to the original sources of Marxism in Hegel's own works at the very moment when the world was collapsing all about him in the holocaust of World War I.

When Lenin asked the editors of *Under the Banner of Marxism* to constitute themselves as a "Society of Materialist Friends of the Hegelian Dialectic" and to print excerpts from Hegel's own works, he did not mean anything as simple as the vulgar explanation of the necessity for standing Hegel "right side up." The materialist reading of Hegel, the need to stand him "right side up" meant to Lenin that Hegel, although he had been standing on his head, had so great and objective a validity in and for himself that he simply must be read, must be allowed to speak for himself, no matter how difficult he sounds, but the editors could help this process, must help because, as he put it, "dialectics is the theory of knowledge of (Hegel and) Marxism."

Let us round out this very crowded evening of discussion by grappling with three quotations from Hegel's Preface to the *Science of Logic*. The first is a challenge to the structure of logic to reorganize itself:

> The complete transformation which philosophical thought has undergone in Germany during the last five-and-twenty years and the loftier outlook upon thought which self-conscious mind has attained in this period, have hitherto had but little influence on the structure of Logic.[2]
>
> SLI, p. 33

The reference to the 25 years refers to Kant's work on the eve of revolution and after the revolution, but in fact he is referring, as is clear from the following, to all of the philosophic writings:

> ... there are no traces in Logic of the new spirit which has arisen both in Learning and in Life. It is, however (let us say it once for all), quite vain to try to retain the forms of an earlier stage of development when the inner structure of spirit has become transformed; these earlier forms are like withered leaves which are pushed off by the new buds already being generated at the roots.
>
> SLI, p. 35

Hegel then spells out that a philosophical meeting of the challenge of the times demands a totally new method:

> ... this movement is the Absolute Method of knowledge and at the same time the immanent soul of the Content of knowledge. It is, I maintain, along this path of self-construction alone that Philosophy can become objective and demonstrated science.
>
> SLI, pp. 36–37

2 In these notes, "Hegel" will always stand for *Science of Logic*, Volumes I and II, and "Lenin" will always refer to his Philosophic Notebooks which constitute Vol. 38 of his *Collected Works*.

The *movement,* the immanent or inherent, and what we will get to know as "the path of self-construction" will from now on form the pivot of all that we will study in the rest of the course.

Lecture II. The First Book of the Science of Logic: *The Doctrine of Being*

It is necessary to establish the *limitation* of this course on the relationship of Philosophy to Revolution. It is, of course, impossible to deal with Hegel's work in so brief a time as we have allotted ourselves. Therefore, instead of dealing with it in terms of its own development, we are, in fact, limiting ourselves to reading only those passages which Lenin singled out, and even these in very abbreviated form. Lenin, in turn, gave very unequal space to the various books (the two volumes of *Science of Logic* constitute three books, the Doctrine of Being, the Doctrine of Essence and the Doctrine of the Notion).

Thus, Lenin's Notes *plus* the quotations from Hegel constitute 159 pages, whereas the two volumes of Hegel number nearly one thousand pages, especially when you consider that Lenin included also certain quotations from what is known as the "Smaller Logic" (Hegel's *Logic* in the *Encyclopedia of the Philosophical Sciences*). Lenin gives 15 pages to the prefaces and introduction, which are some 45 pages. Yet the whole of Book I, 325 pages, takes up only 25 pages of Lenin. To Book II (190 pages), are given 40 pages of Lenin; while to Book III (275 pages) Lenin devotes as much space as to all the others combined, 70 pages. Clearly, not every section was of equal importance. What is most important to us of the twentieth century is that Lenin devoted the most time to the Doctrine of the Notion, or what I have called the method, the way in which a new society is born. Since the last section of that book, the Absolute Idea, will be the point of concentration in the new book, *Philosophy and Revolution,* it is as well that we begin with a quotation from Part 2—"Why Hegel? Why Now?":

> The structure of the *Science of Logic* shows no straight line to the Absolute. It is a circle in which each realm—Being, Essence, Notion—has its own absolute, and each starts afresh on new ground. What is of the essence is that each group of categories "perished" because it could not express the concrete totality. Thus new "names" weren't merely superimposed upon them. Rather they emerged out of the objective pull of history. Insofar as Hegel is concerned, to accept any category at face value is an "uninstructed and barbarous procedure." Conceptually, the absolute that arises for any period has a relative in it even as there is an absolute in every relative. This is so, *not* because the absolute in, say, the Doctrine of

Being is of a rather lowly kind—Absolute Indifference—which, though a transition to Essence, "does not attain to Essence." Even when we have done with the categories of Being—Quality, Quantity, Measure—and reach the Doctrine of Essence, there too the absolute is relative. The new categories—Identity, Difference, Contradiction, Ground, Appearance, Existence, Actuality—no doubt express the essential nature, as against what we may call a market appearance, nevertheless the Absolute here can, again, not just be "taken over" by the Doctrine of the Notion. And this despite the fact that the final section, Actuality, begins and ends with Absolute, it is not this Absolute which "carries over" into the Doctrine of Notion, "the realm of Subjectivity or Freedom."

Without understanding why this is so, the tendency would be to dismiss Hegel's Absolutes either as being no more than a "natural" for each "pinnacle" reached, or to consider that the movement to the Absolute is no more than a regression to the absolute idealism of philosophers who hide from reality. The truth is that, precisely because it is the pull of objective history, toward real freedom, each subsequent age reads Hegel differently.[3]

We are finally ready to turn to Hegel himself, beginning with where we ended in the first lecture on the movement and the path of self-construction that Hegel himself underlines as critical and that Lenin singles out as the quintessential directly after Hegel's statement, "It is the nature of the content and that alone which lives in philosophic cognition" (SL I, p. 36). When Hegel writes that "It is along this path of self-construction alone that Philosophy can become objective, demonstrative science," and talks about the movement of consciousness "like the development of all natural and spiritual life," Lenin writes:

> Turn it around! Logic and the theory of knowledge must be derived from 'the development of all natural and spiritual life.'
>
> LCW 38, p. 88

In the preface to the second edition of Hegel's work—two full decades separate the first preface from the second, written at the end of his life—he speaks about the rise of philosophy presupposing "a long stretch of road already traversed by the mind of man" so that, on the one hand, "those interests are hushed which move the lives of people and individuals" and that, on the other

3 Compare pp. 19–22 of *Philosophy and Revolution.* "Why Hegel? Why Now?" became Part I of the completed book. —Editors.

hand, these categories of logic are indeed "abbreviations," words that epitomize "the endless multitude of particulars of external existence." This universalism of a category stirs Lenin's mind and will bring forth the first reference to what is concrete for Lenin: Marx's *Capital*, expanding Hegel's expression of the relationship of the universal to the particular, and stressing:

> A beautiful formula: "not merely an abstract universal, but a universal which comprises in itself the wealth of the particular, the individual, the single" (all the wealth of the particular and single!)!! *Très Bien*!
>
> LCW 38, p. 99; M&F, p. 328

Lenin had already summarized to himself the first "definition" of what a category is:

> Logic is the science not of external forms of thought, but of the laws of development "of all material, natural and spiritual things," i.e. of the development of the entire concrete content of the world and of its cognition, i.e., the sum-total, the conclusion of the *History* of knowledge of the world.
>
> LCW 38, pp. 92–93; M&F, p. 327

In a word, in studying the categories, the principles of logic, we are, in fact, studying also the objective movement of history itself, and Hegel himself keeps talking about the "strong knots," the "foci of arrest and direction" that are formed in the mind out of whole web. Lenin asks himself:

> How is this to be understood? Man is confronted with a *web* of natural phenomena. Instinctive man, the savage, does not distinguish himself from nature. Conscious man does distinguish, categories are stages of distinguishing, i.e., of cognizing the world, focal points in the web, which assist in cognizing and mastering it.
>
> LCW 38, p. 93; M&F, p. 327

Where the significance of categories preoccupied Lenin as he read the preface to the second edition, the question of what Hegel called "the necessity of connection" and "the immanent emergence of distinctions" is what appears to him most important in the Introduction:

> Very important!! This is what it means, in my opinion:
>
> 1. *Necessary* connection, the objective connection of all the aspects, forces, tendencies, etc. of the given sphere of phenomena;

> 2. The "immanent *emergence* of distinctions"—the inner objective logic of evolution and of the struggle of the differences, polarity.
>
> LCW 38, p. 97; M&F, pp. 327–328

Riding becomes much tougher for Lenin as he approaches the specific sections of the Doctrine of Being than when he read the more generalized prefaces and introduction. But he keeps being very pleasantly surprised, after the many notations to himself that he is reading Hegel "materialistically," that he finds germs of this materialism in Hegel himself. It is Hegel who writes: "What is first in science has had to show itself first, too, historically." And it is Lenin who writes: "It sounds very materialistic."

There are passages when it would seem that Lenin already knew the whole of the Logic since what will appear at the end—that is to say, if one had to summarize the dialectic in a single sentence, it would be sufficient to say it is the unity of opposites—is said right here:

> *Dialectics* is the teaching which shows how *Opposites* can be and how they happen to be (how they become) *identical,* under what conditions they are identical, becoming transformed into one another—why the human mind should grasp these opposites not as dead, rigid, but as living, conditional, mobile, becoming transformed into one another.
>
> LCW 38, p. 109; M&F, p. 328

And yet, it would be totally wrong to think that he had grasped all the ramifications of what he had written. We are, after all, only [in] the realm of Being which, translated in terms of economics, would be the "market" or commodity exchange rather than in production. He himself realized that, despite the "correct definition" of the dialectic as the unity of opposites, he had then not worked out all the implications of this. This is why he had written to the editor of the Russian Encyclopedia, *Granat*—to whom he had just submitted the essay "The Three Sources and Three Component Parts of Marxism," which had, indeed, been the first time that a popularization of Marx contained so much on the philosophy of Marxism—asking the Encyclopedia editor whether they could not return the essay to him for some new additions on dialectics. And it is indeed only when he comes to the realm of Notion that he will insist that it is impossible to understand Marx's *Capital* "especially Chapter 1 without understanding the *whole* of the *Logic*."[4]

What is comprehensively grasped in this first section of Book I is movement and all-sidedness of the dialectic:

---

4 This is a paraphrase. See below, p. 93. —Editors.

> Hegel analyses concepts that usually appear to be dead and shows that there *is* movement in them. Finite, that means *moving* to an end! Something, means *not that* which is Other. Being in general, means such indeterminateness that Being = not-Being. All-sided, universal flexibility of concepts, a flexibility reaching to the identity of opposites, that is the essence of the matter. This flexibility, applied subjectively = eclecticism and sophistry. Flexibility, applied *objectively*, i.e., reflecting the all-sidedness of the material process and its unity, is dialectics, is the correct reflection of the eternal development of the world.
>
> LCW 38, p. 110; M&F, p. 329

The most important new "discovery" that Lenin made in this section is the relationship of the ideal to the real. We must remember that Lenin is reading this at the outbreak of World War I, when the betrayal by the Second International made it clear that it just wasn't enough to be "materialists," that something was very wrong in having concentrated on the "economics" of Marxian doctrine and to have acted as if idealism is purely "subjective" rather than a unity of the subjective and objective. Indeed, in a certain sense, it could be said that it was the new appreciation of the significance of the ideal that had sent Lenin to read Hegel's *Logic*. Thus, it is not only the history of man but the history of thought which has significance for Lenin, and he notes how many "Observations" Hegel makes after he has stated a certain position in order to relate that position to all of the other thinkers. The first chapter of this book, for example, has only three short paragraphs, called Being, Nothing, Becoming, after which Hegel makes no less than five observations, stretching over 25 pages, tracing philosophy from the Orient to the Greeks to Spinoza and Kant. In Chapter 3, Being For Self, which happens to be where we are now, it is the observation on the Ideality of Leibnitz (SLI, pp. 173–176) that makes Lenin speak out both for the profundity of the transformation of the ideal into the real and against vulgar materialism:

> The thought of the ideal passing into the real is *profound:* very important for history. But also in the personal life of man it is clear that this contains much truth. Against vulgar materialism. NB: The difference of the ideal from the material is also not unconditional, not inordinate.
>
> Obviously, Hegel takes his self-development of concepts, of categories, in connection with the entire history of philosophy. This gives still a *new* aspect to the whole *Logic.*
>
> LCW 38, p. 114

(I should also add, since we are doing a great injustice to Hegel by skipping so much in this book and by not going into the categories themselves, that I do have complete outlines of each of the major works of Hegel[5] and it will be possible for those who wish to study the work in greater detail *after* finishing this course to consult these notes. In the case of *Science of Logic*, the outline was made on January 26, 1961.)

The final section of Book I, Measure, is where Lenin makes the greatest leap forward. I am not copying Mao but Lenin himself, who, in this section as he approaches the Observation on Nodal lines, writes the word "Leaps!" repeats it three times, further stresses it by writing: "interruptions in gradualness," and further surrounding these with all sorts of intricate lines I cannot describe (look them up yourself in Lenin, p. 123) and the essence is contained in the following quotations:

> It is said *natura non facit saltum* [nature does not make leaps]; and ordinary imagination when it has to conceive an arising or passing away, thinks it has conceived them (as was mentioned) when it imagines them as a *gradual* emergence or disappearance. But we saw that the changes of Being were in general not only a transition of one magnitude into another but a transition from the qualitative to the quantitative and conversely....
>
> SLI, p. 369

Here what we should hold in mind is that the *leap* is where quantity reveals that it is just quality superseded and absorbed but not annihilated even as, to use words we know better, abstract labor degrades the concrete laborer but cannot destroy him, for he is "Subject," that is to say, the active human being whose "quest for universality" is only the more intense by this degradation of the capitalist process of production. The point is that even before you come to the essential process of production (or what in Hegel is the Doctrine of Essence), the dialectic of development, the transformation of quality into quantity and quantity into measure (which is on the very threshold of essence) is present.

You will see Lenin get along swimmingly as soon as we reach Essence, and so, I hope, will we.

---

5 These were published in Raya Dunayevskaya, *The Power of Negativity: Selected Writings on the Dialectic in Hegel and Marx* (Lanham, Maryland: Lexington Books, 2002), Chapters 3–5. —Editors.

Lecture III. Book II: The Doctrine of Essence "or" Actuality and the Theory of Knowledge

I decided to put a subtitle that is not in Hegel because Lenin keeps stressing the relationship of the theory of knowledge to actuality. It is characteristic of Hegel that, where others would have considered that, with Essence, they have reached what is "behind" appearance, Hegel not only emphasizes the relationship of the two, but the one flowing out of the other *on the way* to a still further *self*-development:

> Essence is midway between Being and Notion: it is the mean between them and its movement constitutes the transition from Being to Notion... Essence first *shows into itself*; or is Reflection; next it *appears*; thirdly, it *manifests* itself.
>
> SLII, p. 17

In a word, every stage, even unessential show, is not to be disregarded. Or as Lenin explains, Hegel's statement that "Show then is the *phenomenon* of skepticism" (SLII, p. 22):

> i.e. the unessential, seeming, superficial, vanishes more often, does not hold so "tightly," does not "sit so firmly" as "Essence." Approximately, the movement of a river—the foam above and the deep currents below. *But even the foam* is an expression of essence!
>
> LCW 38, p. 130

And again:

> This N.B. Hegel is for the "objective validity" (if it may be called that) of Semblance, "of that which is immediately given" (the expression *that which is given* is generally used by Hegel). The more petty philosophers dispute whether essence, *or* that which is immediately given should be taken as basis (Kant, Hume, all the Machists). Instead of *or,* Hegel puts *and,* explaining the concrete content of this "and."
>
> LCW 38, p. 134

The profundity of Hegel lies precisely in this, that even when he dealt with what is unessential, what is mere show, he disclosed its *objectivity*. Appearance is a higher stage than show but at that point, too, we are yet to get to Essence. One of the most pregnant sentences in Essence is that, despite the distinctions and even oppositions between Appearance and Essence, the crucial is not the opposition between the two, but the fact that Essence, too, must *appear*. In a word, no stage can be "skipped." Each of the stages is a necessary "moment," an element of the very development of the essential, of the *contradictory* development. In Hegel, far from opposites never meeting, it is the ceaseless meeting of opposites that is the essential movement in life, in theory, in practice. Hegel has nothing but scorn for "the law of the excluded middle," whereupon Lenin comments:

> Hegel says wittily—it is said that there is no third. *There is* a third in this thesis itself. A itself is the third, for A can be both + A and –A. "The Something thus is itself the third term which was supposed to be excluded." (SLII, p. 65)—This is shrewd and correct. Every concrete thing, every concrete something stands in multifarious and often contradictory relations to everything else, ergo it is itself and some other.
>
> LCW 38, p. 138

The real leap, as we have known for some time and have constantly quoted, comes with the reading of the section on the Law of Contradiction:

> Movement and "*self-movement*" (this NB! Arbitrary (independent), spontaneous, *internally-necessary* movement), "change," "movement and vitality," "the principle of all self-movement," "impulse" (Trieb) to "movement" and to "activity"—the opposite of "*dead Being*"—who would believe that this is the core of "Hegelianism," of abstract and abstruse (ponderous, absurd?) Hegelianism?? This core has to be discovered, understood, rescued, laid bare, refined, which is precisely what Marx and Engels did.
>
> LCW 38, p. 141

From now on, Lenin shows the highest appreciation of the idealism in dialectical philosophy. The thought has its own dialectic and what is crucial here is that Lenin is not merely saying: Let's read Hegel materialistically. Let's never forget that for Marxists, for revolutionaries, the highest contradiction is that between capital and labor, the class struggle. By now he has taken that for granted philosophically as well as in life, and instead stresses that the *idea* of universal movement came first with Hegel, then in Marx and finally with Darwin:

> The idea of universal movement and change (1813 *Logic*) was conjectured before its application to life and society. In regard to society it was

> proclaimed earlier (*Communist Manifesto*) than it was demonstrated in application to man (*Origin of Species*).
>
> LCW 38, p. 141

He will not develop this thought, in full, until the third book, which deals with Notion, and we, too, do not want to rush ahead. Instead, it is important to show how all the Stalinists' and, later, the Maoists' revisions, centered precisely around contradiction. That is to say, the counterpart to their class compromisist actions in life was the revisions introduced into the Hegelian law of objective contradictions. By claiming that there no longer were any classes in "socialist lands," they concluded that "therefore" there were no contradictions. When Mao introduced the concept that there were no contradictions among "people," that in China, "therefore," what differences that there are can be handled by a "correct policy." The headlines throughout the world that he earned with that speech on how to handle contradictions among people, happen to have been uttered just as the first edition of *Marxism and Freedom* went to press and here is the footnote (#17) that I added:

> The lowest of all today's sophists is the head of the Chinese Communist Party and State, Mao Tse-tung, who recently (June 18, 1957) caused a world sensation with his speech, "On Contradiction," in which he proclaimed, "Let a hundred flowers bloom. Let a hundred schools of thought contend." Mao has ridden this single track, which he calls "Contradiction," ever since 1937. At that time, he directed his attack against "dogmatists" who refused to reduce all contradictions in the anti-Japanese struggle and submit to "the leadership of Chiang Kai-shek." In 1952, he introduced a new set of definitions into "Contradictions," this time applying it to those who opposed the Chinese Communist Party taking sole power in China. By June 18, 1957, after editing with a heavy hand the speech he delivered on February 27th to the Supreme State Conference, he reduced the struggle of class against class to a contradiction *among* "the people" while he became the champion, *at one and the same time,* of the philosophy of a hundred flowers blooming *and one and only one Party, the Chinese Communist Party, ruling.* Outside of the exploitative class relations themselves, nothing so clearly exposes the new Chinese ruling class as their threadbare philosophy.

The concrete that Lenin has in mind, the one that he refers most often to, is Marx's *Capital.* He will soon be saying on the whole relationship of Ground to Condition, or the relationship of history to thought: "and purely logical elaboration? It coincides. It must coincide, as induction and deduction in *Capital.*" (LCW 38, p. 146)

The point is that Lenin, throughout this first section, "Essence as Reflection in Itself," is stressing the critical importance of contradiction, without which it is absolutely impossible to understand any development. Anyone who blunts contradiction to either the point of mere difference or to not seeing the *transition* from one to the other has no conception of what Hegel means by negativity or the inherent self-movement:

> NB[6]
> (1) Ordinary perception grasps the difference and the contradiction, but not the transition of one to the other, *but this is the most important.*
> (2) Intelligent reflection and mind. Reflection grasps the contradiction, *expresses* it, brings things in relation to one another, compels the "concept to shine through the contradiction" but does not *express* the concept of things and their relation.
> (3) Thinking reason (Mind) sharpens the blunted differences of variety, the mere manifold of imagination, to the *essential* difference, to *Opposition.* Only when the contradictions reach the peak does manifoldness become regular and lively in relation to the other—acquire that negativity which is the *inner pulsation of self-movement and life.*

Again, the stress is both on life and thought. Hegel himself concludes the section, not with the law of contradiction but with the movement from that first to Ground, then to Condition, which could be translated as history itself. It is impossible to develop at length these quintessential points in so brief an outline. For the time being, it will have to suffice to stress two things. One, that Lenin here brought in, as we already quoted, the relationship between inductive and deductive method in *Capital.* And, two, to keep in mind that what Hegel is arguing for is the need to get rid of the concept of Ground as a *substratum* and to know that when you have got rid of this concept of something being "behind" the immediate, the apparent, you have by no means gotten rid of the fact that the immediate, too, is the result of a *mediating* process. Hegel relentlessly restates his thesis that "The Fact Emerges Out of Ground" (SL II,

6 I have used my own translation (*M&F,* pp. 331–332) because the "official" translation (LCW 38, p. 145) uses here non-philosophic terminology in the question of perception, reflection and mind. There are other places it is equally "loose" in its translation, but for uniformity's sake, I have used their translation generally.

p. 106). And that "When all the Conditions of a Fact are present, it enters into Existence" (SLII, p. 105), whereupon Lenin comments:

> Very good! What has the Absolute Idea and Idealism to do with it?
>
> LCW 38, p. 147

Also let us not forget that when Lenin referred to *Capital,* he at one and the same time stressed what was great about Hegel's concept of Ground and Condition—"the universal, all-sided, *vital* connection of everything with everything and the reflection of this connection in human concepts." And then pointed to the direction in which both the work of Hegel and Marx must continue:

> Continuation of the work of Hegel and Marx must consist in the *dialectical* elaboration of the history of human thought, science and technique.
>
> LCW 38, pp. 146–147

We are, first, now, in Section 2, Appearance, which, in turn, is divided into Existence, Appearance, and Essential Relation. Though we can, by no means, claim to have dealt with it in the few references we made to it in the first section, we nevertheless must here limit ourselves to but two questions, that of the Law of Appearance and the world of appearance. If you wish to *practice* dialectic by going off into your own analysis in the real world, let me give you a hint: Lenin's "playing down" of the importance of law is due to his underlying critique of the economism; thus, on the one hand, he shows that law is "the enduring (the persisting) in appearances" but is not beyond appearance; and, on the other hand, that "Appearance is now *r i c h e r* than law" (LCW 38, p. 152). Let Lenin sum it up for us:

> The essence here is that both the world of appearance and the world in itself are *moments* of man's knowledge of nature, stages, *alterations*, or deepenings (of knowledge). The shifting of the world in itself further and further *from* the world of appearances—that is what is so far still not to be seen in Hegel. N.B. Have not Hegel's "moments" of the concept the significance of "moments" of transition?
>
> LCW 38, p. 153

The most exciting part in the Doctrine of Essence is Section III, Actuality, which Hegel defines as the "*Unity of Essence and Existence*" (SLII, p. 160) Unity is not, however, "synthesis"; it is the very apex of contradiction.

The greatness of Hegel is that he wrote *Logic* freed from anything concrete and yet it contains the essence of all concrete. Thus, if you are an economist, a Marxist economist, think of Actuality as capitalist crises and you will discern some absolutely magnificent developments and truths and think it couldn't possibly mean anything else. But if you think of philosophic terms, say like a [Herbert] Marcuse, the concrete that preoccupies you is that you are finally freed from being enmeshed in phenomena, tied only to "observable facts," are capable of grasping reality as a totality and you would be just as right as when you thought Actuality applied only to capitalist crises.

When you'll be flying on your own, and will have to trace a development, be it in literature, the self-determination of nations, or a general strike, you will at once recognize that the conflict is no longer a question only of opposition between the existent and the as yet non-existent forces, but between two *co-existing* antagonistic forces that simply cannot continue to co-exist endlessly. And of course you'll be right—and in all fields.

The point is that you simply cannot limit the "uses of this self-movement through contradiction." Lenin himself began to free himself from all residue of taking the empiric fact as the actual. You see Actuality first as contingency, then substance and when you come to cause and think you "really" get it this time, Hegel first tells you that effect and cause are not poles apart at all. Let us therefore follow Lenin and note also that at this point he goes back to the "Smaller Logic" where "the same thing is expounded very often more clearly, with concrete examples" (LCW 38, p. 157) and he quotes from it (p. 262) the paragraph on Possibility:

> Whether a thing is possible or impossible depends altogether on the subject matter: that is, on the sum total of the elements in Actuality which, as it opens itself out, discloses itself to be Necessity.
>
> *Encyclopedia of the Philosophical Sciences,* ¶143

Lenin comments:

> *The sum-total of the elements in Actuality,* which in its unfolding discloses itself to be Necessity. The unfolding of the sum-total of moments of actuality NB—essence of dialectical cognition.
>
> LCW 38, pp. 157–158

(One thing is sure, it is much easier to read the "Smaller Logic" than the *Science of Logic* and you now deserve to make it a bit easier for yourself, so start reading, especially the section on Actuality.)

Lenin singles out the expression, "necessity is blind only insofar as it is not understood." When Lenin reaches the section analyzing the relationship of Substantiality to Causality, he sums it up two ways:

> On the one hand, knowledge of matter must be deepened to knowledge (to the concept) of Substance in order to find the causes of phenomena. On the other hand, the actual cognition of the cause is the deepening of knowledge from the externality of phenomena to the Substance. Two types of examples should explain this: (1) from the history of natural science, and (2) from the history of philosophy. More exactly: it is not "examples" that should be here—comparison is not proof—but the *quintessence* of the history of both the one and the other + the history of technique.
>
> LCW 38, p. 159

And again:

> When one reads Hegel on causality, it appears strange at first glance that he dwells so relatively lightly on this theme, beloved of the Kantians. Why? Because, indeed, for him causality is only *one* of the determinations of universal connection, which he has already covered earlier, in his *entire* exposition, much more deeply and all-sidedly: *always* and from the very outset emphasizing this connection, the reciprocal transitions, etc., etc. It would be very instructive to compare the "*birth-pangs*" of neo-empiricism (respective "physical idealism") with the solutions or rather with the dialectical method of Hegel.
>
> LCW 38, p. 162

You can actually *feel* Lenin bursting forth, on his own, prepared to engage the real world as he approaches the end of the Doctrine of Essence and Hegel states that Book III, the Doctrine of the Notion, is "the realm of Subjectivity or of Freedom" (SLII, p. 205). Lenin writes joyously:

> NB Freedom = Subjectivity
> ("or")
> End, Consciousness, Endeavour
> NB
>
> LCW 38, p. 164

Lecture IV. Book III: Subjective Logic or the Doctrine of Notion

With the Notion, we reach, at one and the same time, that which, in philosophic terms, is oldest, most written about, and purely intellectualistic; and from a Marxist point of view, least written about, most "feared" as idealistic, unreal, "pure" thought, in a word, a closed ontology.

And yet, it is the Doctrine of the Notion that develops the categories of Freedom and, therefore, should mean the objective and subjective means whereby a new society is born. It is true that, *consciously* for Hegel, this was done only in thought, while in life all contradictions persisted. But what Hegel did "consciously" does not explain away the objective pull of the future on the present, and the present as history (the French Revolution for Hegel), and not just as the status quo of an existing state. Be that as it may, let's follow Hegel himself. A sweeping and concrete historic sense saved Hegel from both the introspection and empty absolutes of his philosophic contemporaries and from Kant's Critique that, nevertheless, kept object and subject worlds apart:

> It will always remain a matter for astonishment how the Kantian philosophy knew that relation of thought to sensuous existence, where it halted, for a merely relative relation of bare appearance, and fully acknowledged and asserted a higher unity of the two in the Idea in general, and, particularly, in the idea of an intuitive understanding; but yet stopped dead at this relative relation and at the assertion that the Notion is and remains utterly separated from reality; so that it affirmed as true what it pronounced to be finite knowledge, and declared to be superfluous and improper figments of thought that which it recognized as truth, and of which it established the definite notion.
>
> SLII, p. 226

On the relationship of Hegel to Kant, Lenin wrote:

> *Essentially*, Hegel is completely right as opposed to Kant. Thought proceeding from the concrete to the abstract—provided it is *correct* (NB) (and Kant, like all philosophers, speaks of correct thought)—does not get away *from* the truth but comes closer to it. The abstraction of *matter*, of a *law* of nature, the abstraction of *value*, etc. in short *all* scientific (correct, serious, not absurd) abstractions reflect nature more deeply, truly and *completely*. From living perception to abstract thought, *and from this to practice*,—such is the dialectic path of the cognition of *truth*, of the cognition of objective reality. Kant disparages knowledge in order to make way for faith: Hegel exalts knowledge, asserting that knowledge is knowledge of God. The materialist exalts the knowledge of matter, of nature, consigning God, and the philosophical rabble that defends God, to the rubbish heap.
>
> LCW 38, p. 171

On the very next page, Lenin again shows that the concrete he had in his mind in reading Hegel was *Capital* and its economic categories. Thus:

> Here, too Hegel is essentially *right*: *value* is a category which dispenses with the material of sensuousness, but it is *truer* than the law of supply and demand.
>
> LCW 38, p. 172

Indeed, where, in the Doctrines of Being and Essence, Lenin had two references to *Capital*, here in the Doctrine of Notion he has no less than 13 references. Not only that, the references move from seeing parallelisms between *Logic* and *Capital* to the break with *all* (including himself) previous interpretations by Marxists. It is here that Lenin will write the categoric aphorism:

> Marxists criticized (at the beginning of the twentieth century) the Kantians and Humists more in the manner of Feuerbach (and Büchner) than of Hegel.
>
> LCW 38, p. 179

> It is impossible completely to understand Marx's *Capital* and especially its first chapter, without having thoroughly studied and understood the *whole* of Hegel's *Logic*. Consequently, half a century later none of the Marxists understood Marx!
>
> LCW 38, p. 180

But we are forcing Lenin to run ahead of himself, so we better retrace our steps to the end of the Introductory section, "On the Notion in General," as he enters Section I, Subjectivity. The first thing, he meets the specific categories in Book III—Universal, Particular, Individual—and notes: "These parts of the work should be called: a best means of getting a headache!" But he no sooner said it than he began developing all sorts of new concepts:

> Obviously, here too the chief thing for Hegel is to *trace* the *transitions*. From a certain point of view under certain conditions, the universal is the individual, the individual is the universal. Not only (1) *connection,* and inseparable connection, of all concepts and judgments, but (2) *transitions* from one into the other, and not only transitions, but also (3) *identity of opposites*—that is the chief thing for Hegel. But this merely "glimmers" through the *fog* of extremely abstruse exposition. The history of thought from the standpoint of the development and application

> of the general concepts and categories of the Logic—that's what is so needed!
>
> LCW 38, p. 177

By the time he has reached the third chapter (the Syllogism) in that section where Hegel could be said to have broken down the division between objectivity and subjectivity, it is as if a whole new world has opened up before Lenin. He reads Hegel's statement: "All things are a Syllogism, a universal which is bound together with individuality through particularity; but of course they are not wholes consisting of three propositions" (SLII, p. 307). Lenin not only draws the parallel between *Capital* and Marx, and rejects previous interpretations of Hegel, insisting that (as we quoted previously) it was impossible to understand *Capital* without understanding the whole of the *Logic*, but he also gets a new appreciation of the Logic as something that can be used for his age:

> NB: to be inverted, Marx *applied* Hegel's dialectics in its rational form to political economy.
>
> The formation of (abstract) notions and operations with them *already in*cludes idea, conviction, *consciousness* of the law-governed character of the objective connection of the world. To distinguish causality from this connection is stupid. To deny the objectivity of notions, the objectivity of the universal in the individual and in the particular, is impossible. Consequently, Hegel is much more profound than Kant, and others, in tracing the reflection of the movement of the objective world in the movement of notions. Just as the simple form of value, the individual act of exchange of one given commodity for another, already includes in an undeveloped form *all* the main contradictions of capitalism, so the simplest *generalizations*, the first and simplest formation of *notions* (judgments, syllogisms, etc.) already denotes man's ever deeper cognition of the *objective* connection of the world. Here is where one should look for the true meaning, significance, and role of Hegel's *Logic*. This NB.
>
> LCW 38, pp. 178–179

For us to be able to see those objective world connections, we must tarry a bit more with those categories—Universal, Particular, Individual. They characterize not only the movement of the Logic as a whole and in its individual parts; they also characterize the movement of all development in theory and in life.

If you write, for Universal, Socialism; and for Particular, you assume a specific historic period in which, say, the Russian Revolution took the form of nationalized property; and for Individual, that is to say the concrete realization of a Universal, you write the self-activity of man which makes the population "to a man" the controllers of their own destiny in production and in the State; you can see what a very big gap there is between not only the Universal and the Individual, but between the Particular and the Individual, so big a gap, in fact, that the Particular may never reach the Individual, may get transformed into its very opposite. That is why Lenin, even before he summarized the dialectic as the unity of opposites, paid so much attention to *transitions:*

> The *transitions* from the syllogism of analogy (about analogy) to the syllogism of necessity,—from the syllogism of induction to the syllogism of analogy—the syllogism from the universal to the individual—the syllogism from the individual to the universal—the exposition of *connection* and *transitions* (connection is transition) that is Hegel's task. Hegel actually *proved* that logical forms and laws are not an empty shell, but the *reflection* of the objective world. More correctly, he did not prove, but *made a brilliant guess.*
>
> LCW 38, p. 180

It is not as easy to follow through the transitions, to work out the relationships of Universal, Particular, and Individual as it appears when someone else has worked out something that has already been proven by history. A revolutionary like Leon Trotsky "got stuck" in that Particular form because it was a necessary form and the actual historic appearance in the Russian Revolution. It is this which has us by the throat or rather had Leon Trotsky by the throat, and he never did return to test *what* the Individual was either logically or in the concrete life of the population; he merely took for granted the Universal and concluded that "therefore" it was also so in the concrete, or was on the way to being so.

Measure your comprehension of the logical development against a concrete subject. For example, we consider the question of self-determination of nations now, related to what Lenin wrote about it *after* he had gone through the *Logic* (read those articles either in the *Selected Works*, Vol. V, Part 4, or in the *Collected Works,* Vol. XIX.) And then reread it all, after you have completed the *Logic*, always keeping before you Hegel's statement in the Absolute Idea, "the self-determination in which alone the Idea is, is to hear itself speak."

Now return to Lenin on the *Logic* as he comes to Section II, Objectivity. You must read for yourselves pages 167 to 188 since this is one of the times when he divides a page in two and on one side writes directly what Hegel says, and on the other side, "translates" it into Materialist Dialectics. I can only quote one phrase from it:

> At the beginning, man's ends appear foreign ("other") in relation to nature. Human consciousness, science ("*der Begriff*" [the Notion]), reflects the essence, the substance of nature, but at the same time this consciousness is something external in relation to nature (not immediately, not simply, coinciding with it.)
>
> LCW 38, p. 188

Which again gets translated into:

> In actual fact, man's ends are engendered by the objective world and presuppose it,—they find it as something given, present. But it *seems* to man as if his ends are taken from outside the world, and are independent of the world ("freedom").
>
> (NB All this in the paragraph on "The Subjective End." NB)
>
> SLII, pp. 381–383; M&F, p. 342; LCW 38, p. 189

The point throughout Section II, Objectivity, is that, in his "translations," Lenin, far from stressing that he must read Hegel "materialistically," now emphasizes that "the germs of historical materialism" are *in Hegel*. Thus, Lenin capitalized and boldfaced and wrote "Hegel and Historical Materialism" alongside the statement from Hegel: "In his tools man possesses power over external nature, even although, according to his Ends, he frequently is subjected to it" (SLII, p. 388). Once again he relates the categories of Logic to human practice:

> When Hegel endeavors—sometimes even huffs and puffs—to bring man's purposive activity under the categories of logic, saying that this activity is the "syllogism" (*Schlub*), that the subject (man) plays the role of a "member" in the logical "figure" of the "syllogism," and so on, THEN THAT IS NOT MERELY STRETCHING A POINT, A MERE GAME, THIS HAS A VERY PROFOUND, PURELY MATERIALISTIC CONTENT. It has to be inverted: the practical activity of man had to lead his consciousness to the repetition of the various logical figures thousands of millions of times *in order that* these figures *could* obtain the significance of *axioms*. This nota bene.
>
> LCW 38, p. 190

And again:

> Remarkable: Hegel came to the "Idea" as the coincidence of the Notion and the object, as *truth, through* the practical, purposive activity of man. A very close approach to the view that man by his *practice* proves the objective correctness of his ideas, concepts, knowledge, science.
>
> LCW 38, p. 191

This does not mean, as Mao has interpreted, that all that remains is practice. Quite the contrary. Lenin no sooner reaches the third section, the Idea, when he stresses that (1) this section contains "the very best of the dialectic," and (2) that not only for Hegel does practice refer to practice *in the theory of cognition*, but for Marxists the theoretic has an objective validity all its own: indeed, without it, the practice would be insufficient to bring about a successful revolution. (Be sure to read pages 304 to 308, "The Philosophy of the Yenan Period: Mao perverts Lenin" in *Marxism and Freedom*.)[7]

Although we will leave the last chapter of this section to a separate lecture, it is clear here that Lenin no longer counterposes subjective and objective as the twain that never meet:

> Logical concepts are subjective so long as they remain "abstract," in their abstract form, but at the same time they express also the Things-in-themselves. Nature is *both* concrete *and* abstract, *both* phenomenon *and* essence, *both* moment *and* relation. Human concepts are subjective in their abstractness, separateness, but objective as a whole, in the process, in the sum-total, in the tendency, in the source.
>
> LCW 38, p. 208

Because of this profound grasp of the interpenetration of objective and subjective, Lenin makes the leap to recognizing the creativity of consciousness: "Alias: Man's consciousness not only reflects the objective world, but creates it" (LCW 38, p. 212), which he further extends to the transformation of reality: "that the world does not satisfy man and man decides to change it by his activity" (LCW 38, p. 213). Again and again, he relates activity to transformation and on that note will approach the Absolute Idea:

> The activity of man, who has constructed an objective picture of the world for himself, *changes* external actuality, abolishes its determinateness

---

7 See Chapter 13 of this volume, p. 361. —Editors.

> (=alters some sides or other, qualities, of it), and thus removes from it the features of Semblance, externality and nullity, and makes it as being in and for itself (=objectively true).
>
> LCW 38, p. 218

Lecture v. The Absolute Idea

A full lecture is being devoted to a single chapter, the last in the *Logic*, because the working out of this is the task of our age and not only the task of the book, *Philosophy and Revolution*. This separates us from others, *all* others, including even Lenin. It is true, of course, that we could not begin to carry out this task had Lenin not left us all those stepping stones. It is true that we must first internalize what Lenin had done with the chapter before we can make any steps on our own. But it is equally true that no one can work out the problem of another generation. That task has remained for us.

Speaking strictly philosophically, the working out of this chapter in 1953[8] is what led, on the one hand, to the split in the State-Capitalist Tendency, and, on the other hand, to the extension of that analysis into Marxist-Humanism. In a word, even though we ourselves were not conscious of it at the time (as can be seen from the fact that the Letters on the Absolute Idea of May 12 and May 20, 1953, were addressed to a co-leader in the State-Capitalist Tendency), it is, in fact, this grappling with the Absolute Idea which led to our singling out the Humanism of Marxism as the emblem of ourselves as a theoretically independent tendency, and as the unique expression of the age. Therefore, it will be important for you to consider these letters as part of these notes. If you still find it too difficult to follow that paragraph by paragraph interpretation of the Absolute Idea (as well as the chapter on Absolute Knowledge from the *Phenomenology of Mind*) then study only those paragraphs which are the subject of Lenin's notes.

Hegel begins the chapter with this sentence:

> The Absolute Idea has now turned out to be the identity of the Theoretical and the Practical Idea; each of these by itself is one-sided and contains the Idea itself only as a sought Beyond and an unattained goal; each consequently is a synthesis of the tendency, and both contains and does not contain the Idea, and passes from one concept to the other, but failing to combine the two concepts, does not pass beyond their contradictions.
>
> SLII, p. 466

---

8 This refers to Dunayevskaya's Letters on Hegel's Absolutes of May 12 and 20, 1953, which have been published as Chapter 2 of *The Power of Negativity*. —Editors.

And in the next paragraph, Hegel has a statement which we singled out last as the underlying thought which should guide your study of self-determination: "The self-determination therefore in which alone the Idea is, is to hear itself speak." Despite all that Lenin, in 1916, that is to say, the year after completing Hegel's *Science of Logic*, had written on self-determination of nations, it was not this sentence that he singled out in 1915. What he was concerned with was the dialectic summarized by Hegel. As he was to express it at the end:

> It is noteworthy that the whole chapter on the "Absolute Idea" scarcely says a word about God (hardly ever has a "divine" "notion" slipped out accidentally) and apart from that—*this NB*—it contains almost nothing that is specifically *idealism*, but has for its main subject the *dialectical method*. The sum-total, the last word and essence of Hegel's logic is the *dialectical method*—this is extremely noteworthy. And one thing more: in this *most idealistic* of Hegel's works there is the *least* idealism and the *most materialism*. "Contradictory," but a fact!
>
> LCW 38, p. 234

It is this dialectical method, which at this point Hegel calls the Absolute Method, which preoccupies Lenin throughout the chapter, and which allows him to summarize it for himself in 16 points, that stresses the *totality* as well as *objectivity*, unity as well as struggle of *opposites*, co-existence and causality as well as *transition* from one to its opposite until the whole *self-movement* appears to be but a return to the old, but is, in fact, the *negation of the negation*. Studying the whole 16 points very carefully (LCW 38, pp. 221–222, or in *Marxism and Freedom*, pp. 349–350), he is then ready to summarize all of the 16 points into a single one: "In brief, dialectics can be defined as the doctrine of the unity of opposites. This embodies the essence of dialectics, but it requires explanations and development."

It is necessary, once again, to return to those categories: Universal, Particular, Individual, keeping in mind also the definition Hegel gives of Individuality in his final work, the *Philosophy of Mind* [para. 481]:[9] "individuality… purified of all that interferes… with freedom itself." In the *Science of Logic* he wrote:

9 *The Philosophy of Mind* is Volume III of the *Encyclopedia of the Philosophical Sciences*, of which Volume I was published as Hegel's *Logic*; Volume II, the *Philosophy of Nature*, has never been translated into English [the *Philosophy of Nature* has since been translated]; and Volume III, or the *Philosophy of Mind*, is published separately.

> In the absolute method, however, the universal does not mean the merely abstract but the objectively universal, that is, that which is *in itself* the concrete totality, but not as *posited* or *for itself*. Even the abstract universal considered as such in the Notion (that is, according to its truth) is not only the simple: as abstract it is already posited as affected with a negation. For this reason there is neither in actuality nor in thought anything so simple and abstract as is commonly imagined. Such a simple entity is a mere illusion which is based on ignorance of what in fact is given.
>
> SLII, p. 471

Once again, Lenin keeps stressing to himself that there is here a "clear, important *sketch of the dialectic*," singling out the following Hegelian principle:

> To hold fast the positive in its negative, and the content of the presupposition in the result, is the most important part of rational cognition; also only the simplest reflection is needed to furnish conviction of the absolute truth and necessity of this requirement, while with regard to the examples of proofs, the whole of Logic consists of these.
>
> SLII, p. 476

Upon which Lenin comments:

> Not empty negation, not futile negation, *not skeptical* negation, vacillation and doubt is characteristic and essential in dialectics,—which undoubtedly contains the element of negation and indeed as its most important element—no, but negation as a moment of connection, as a moment of development, retaining the positive, i.e., without any vacillations, without any eclecticism.
>
> LCW 38, p. 226

The next two pages in Hegel, Lenin copies pretty nearly in full, stressing constantly that it is "the kernel of dialectics, the criterion of truth (the unity of the concept and reality)." What he is referring to especially is Hegel's description of the second negativity as the *turning point* of the whole movement, and yet the self-movement and the objectivity predominates in Lenin so that when he comes to the sentence in Hegel that we have reached the transition of the Logic to Nature, Lenin notes "it brings one within a hand's grasp of materialism... this is not the last sentence of the Logic but what comes after it to the end of the page is unimportant." (LCW 38, p. 234) We will be retracing our steps to the second negativity just as soon as I show what it is that I wrote in my letter on the Absolute Idea under Lenin's above quoted remarks:

> But, my dear Vladimir Ilyitch, it is not true; the end of that page *is* important: we of 1953, we who have lived three decades after and tried to absorb all you have left us, we can tell you that.
>
> Listen to the very next sentence: "But this determination is not a perfected becoming or a *transition*..." Remember how transition was everything to you in the days of Monopoly, the eve of Socialism. Well, Hegel has passed *beyond* transition. He says this last determination, "the pure Idea, in which the determinateness or reality of the Notion is itself raised to the level of Notion, is an absolute *liberation*, having no further immediate determination which is not equally *posited* and equally Notion. Consequently there is no transition in this freedom.... The transition here therefore must rather be taken to mean that the Idea freely releases itself in absolute self-security and self-repose." (Letter dated 5/12/53)[10]

Now then, let us return to the second negative as Hegel expresses it:

> The negativity which has just been considered is the turning point of the movement of the Notion. It is the simple point of negative self-relation, the immediate source of all activity, of living and spiritual self-movement, the dialectic soul which all truth has in it and through which it alone is truth; for the transcendence of the opposition between the Notion and Reality, and that unity which is the truth, rest upon this subjectivity alone.
>
> The second negative, the negative of the negative which we have reached, is this transcendence of the contradiction but is no more the activity of an external reflection than the contradiction is: it is the innermost and most objective moment of Life and Spirit, by virtue of which a subject is personal and free.
>
> SLII, pp. 477–478

Where Lenin stressed the objectivism, we added emphasis on "personal and free." Where Lenin had next emphasized the materialism, we stressed that "the *transcendence* of the opposition between Notion and Reality... rest upon this subjectivity alone." And where Lenin stopped a paragraph short of the end of the Logic, we proceeded to show that Hegel's anticipation of Volumes II and III

---

10 This can be found in *The Power of Negativity*, p. 22, quoting SLII, pp. 385–386. —Editors.

of the *Encyclopedia* was similar to Marx's anticipation in the "General Law of Capitalist Accumulation" in Volume I of *Capital*, of the movement of the law of motion of capitalism in Volumes II and III. We concluded that what Hegel is showing in the movement from the Logic to Nature to Mind was this: "The movement is from the logical principle or theory to nature or practice *and* from practice not alone to theory but to the new society which is its essence." (Letter, dated 5/20/53 [*The Power of Negativity*, p. 28])

It is this discovery that there is a movement from *practice* to theory as well as from *theory* to practice upon which the whole of *Marxism and Freedom* is built. No wonder that, though *Marxism and Freedom* was only an idea in my head in 1953, I had written:

> I am shaking all over, for we have come to where we part from Lenin. I mentioned before that, although in the *approach* to the Absolute Idea, Lenin had mentioned that man's cognition not only reflects the objective world, but creates it, nevertheless *within the chapter* he never developed it. Objective world connections, materialism, dialectical materialism, it is true, is what predominates, not the object and subject as one fully developed.
>
> *The Power of Negativity*, p. 22

And it is why I had also written, in that letter: "Now stand up and shout, Personal and Free, Personal and Free, Personal and Free, as Lenin had shouted, Leap, Leap, Leap, when he first saw dialectical development" as the development of both the objective and subjective world [*The Power of Negativity*, p. 20]. It is true that Lenin, too, had written: "This NB: The richest is the *most concrete* and most *subjective*" alongside Hegel's statement: "The richest consequently is also the most concrete and *subjective*, and that which carries itself back into the simplest depth is also the most powerful and comprehensive" [LCW 38, p. 232].

But the subjectivity, the self-activity of the proletariat first became *concrete and predominant* when Lenin prepared himself for the November revolution as the February had broken out. It was never to leave him again. There was not a single important writing of his that did not breathe the spirit of freedom, population *to a man*, worker as *subject*, *masses* as subject, from then until the day of his death. Since this meant not only "in general," as against capitalism, but concretely even against his co-leaders, it is of the utmost importance that this lecture be concluded with: (1) the sections on the Trade Union debate (pp. 194–209 [of *Marxism and Freedom*]), which includes also Lenin's *Will*; (2) the debate against Bukharin, that is to say the pamphlet, *State-Capitalism and Marxist Humanism, or Philosophy and Revolution*. Finally, (3) you should now be able to get along swimmingly with the chapter "Hegel's Absolutes as New Beginnings" in "Why Hegel, Why Now?" [in Dunayevskaya's draft of *Philosophy and Revolution*].

In fact, why not practice all you have learned and more by writing *Philosophy and Revolution*?

∵

Hegelian Leninism *Telos Conference,* (October 10, 1970)

> The group of editors and contributors of the magazine *Under the Banner of Marxism* should, in my opinion, be a kind of "Society of Materialist Friends of Hegelian Dialectics."
>
> *LENIN*, 1922

During the disintegration of the entire world and of established Marxism in the holocaust of World War I, Lenin encountered Hegel's thought. The revolutionary materialist activist theoretician, Lenin, confronted the bourgeois idealist philosopher Hegel who, working through two thousand years of Western thought, revealed the revolutionary dialectic. In the shock of recognition Lenin experienced when he found the revolutionary dialectic in Hegel, we witness the transfusion of the lifeblood of the dialectic, the transformation of reality as well as thought: "Who would believe that this—the movement and 'self-movement'... spontaneous, internally-necessary movement... 'movement and life' is the core of 'Hegelianism,' of abstract and abstruse (difficult, absurd) Hegelianism??"[11]

"The Dialectic Proper"

Lenin the activist, Party man and materialist underwent "absolute negativity." While reading "The Law of Confrontation" he concluded his new appreciation of the dialectic by saying:

---

11 The first English translation of Lenin's Abstract of *Hegel's Science of Logic* appeared as Appendix A of my *Marxism and Freedom* (New York, 1958). This translation will hereafter be referred to as *M&F*. I will also cite parallel passages in the Moscow translation (Lenin, *Collected Works*, Vol. 38, 1961). Here, see *M&F*, p. 331; LCW 38, p. 141.

> the principle of all self-movement: The idea of universal movement and change (1813 *Logic*) was conjectured before its application to life and society. In regard to society it was proclaimed earlier (1847) than it was demonstrated in application to man (1859).[12]

The illumination cast here on the relationship of philosophy to revolution in Lenin's day is so strong that today's challenges become transparent and reveal the ossification of philosophy and the stifling of the dialectics of liberation. Russian philosophers refuse to forgive Lenin for this. Their underhanded criticism of his *Philosophic Notebooks* continues unabated even on the hundredth anniversary of his birth. They have blurred the distinction between the vulgar materialist photocopy theory of *Materialism and Empirio-Criticism* (1908) and Lenin's totally new philosophical departure in 1914 toward the self-development of thought.

In the *Notebooks*, Lenin wrote: "Alias: Man's cognition not only reflects the objective world, but creates it."[13] B.M. Kedrov, director of the Institute of History of Science and Technology, reduces Lenin's new appreciation of "idealism" to philistine semantics:

> What is fundamental here is the word "alias," meaning otherwise or in other words, followed by a colon. This can only mean one thing, a paraphrase of the preceding note on Hegel's views… If the meaning of the word "alias" and the colon following it are considered, it will doubtless become clear that in that phrase Lenin merely set forth, briefly, the view of another, not his own.[14]

Professor Kedrov's zeal to deny Lenin's 1914 *Notebooks* "are in fundamental contravention of *Materialism and Empirio-Criticism*" has led him to such cheap reductionism that "in defense" of Lenin, Kedrov can only attribute to Lenin his own philistinism: "Lenin categorically rejects and acidly ridicules the slightest slip by Hegel in the direction of ascribing to an idea, to a thought, to consciousness the ability to create the world"[15] With this single stroke, Kedrov

12 *Ibid.* In this quotation, the date 1847 refers to the writing of *The Communist Manifesto,* which, however, was published only in 1848. The date 1859 is the date of the publication of Darwin's *Origin of the Species.*

13 *M&F*, p. 347; LCW 38, p. 212.

14 B.M. Kedrov, "On the Distinctive Characteristics of Lenin's *Philosophic Notebooks," Soviet Studies in Philosophy* (Summer, 1970).

15 *Ibid.*

deludes himself into believing he has closed the philosophic frontiers Lenin opened.

The West's deafness to Lenin's break with his philosophic past (in which cognition had only the role of "reflecting" the objective or the material) has produced an intellectual incapacity to cope with Communist emasculation of Lenin's philosophy.[16] However, anyone who invokes Lenin's name "favorably" should at least remember either "the objective world connection" to which Lenin incessantly referred or men's "subjective" aspirations, the phrase by which Lenin "translated" his concept of consciousness "creating the world": "the world does not satisfy man and man decides to change it by his activity."[17] Even independent Marxists have been sucked into the theoretical void following Lenin's death and have lazily avoided the rich, profound, concrete *Notebooks*. They bemoan the "jottings" which make the *Notebooks* seem so "scanty" that any attempt to understand them could only be "idle speculation." Sticking to "provable" politics as if that were sufficient, they call for "application" of the dialectic. No doubt, the proof of the pudding is always in the eating, and Lenin's "application" of the *Notebooks* was in politics. But were we to begin there and dwell on politics apart from Lenin's new comprehension of the dialectic, we would understand neither his philosophy nor his politics. It is the interaction of the two which is relevant today.

During the critical decade of war and revolution between 1914 and 1924, Lenin did not prepare the *Notebooks* for publication. However, his heirs had no legitimate reason to delay their publication until six years after his death. When they were published in 1929–1930, neither Trotsky, Stalin, Bukharin, nor "mere academicians" (whether mechanists or "dialecticians") took them seriously.[18] A new epoch of world crises and revolutions and the birth of the

16 Professor David Joravsky senses that Lenin's comments on Hegel's *Science of Logic* are "tantalizingly suggestive of a new turn in his thought" in *Soviet Marxism and Natural Science, 1917–1932* (New York, 1961), p. 20. He exposes Stalin's transformation of Lenin's alleged "partyness" in the field of philosophy into pure Stalinist monolithism. Nevertheless, by excluding from his own work a serious analysis of Lenin's *Philosophic Notebooks*, Joravsky leaves the door wide open for lesser scholars to write as if there were a straight line from Lenin to Stalin instead of a transformation into opposite. As for Lenin's *Materialism and Empirio-Criticism*, Lenin himself was the one who stressed its political motivations. He wrote in his letter to Gorky, "The Mensheviks will be reduced to politics and that is the death of them." See the chapter "Lenin and the Partyness of Philosophy" in Joravsky's work.

17 LCW 38, p. 213.

18 The first publication of the *Philosophic Notebooks* was edited by Bukharin, who, however, had nothing to say about it. The Introduction of 1929 by Deborin and that of 1930 by

Black dimension in Africa and the U.S. finally compelled an English publication in 1961.

Lenin began reading Hegel's *Science of Logic* in September, 1914, and finished on December 17. Even from his comments on the Prefaces and the Introduction, it is clear that Lenin's concrete concerns (to which he referred in his "asides" as he copied and commented on quotations from Hegel) were "the objective world connections," the Marxists and the Machists, and above all Marx's *Capital*. Reading Hegel's Introduction, in which he speaks of logic as "not mere abstract Universal, but as a Universal which comprises in itself the full wealth of Particulars" [SLI, p. 69], Lenin wrote:

> cf. *Capital*. A beautiful formula: "not a mere abstract universal, but a universal which comprises in itself the wealth of particulars, individual, separate (all the wealth of the particular and separate)!!" *Trés Bien!*[19]

No matter how often Lenin reminded himself that he was reading Hegel "materialistically," no matter how he lashed out against the "dark waters" of such abstractions as "Being-for-Self" and despite the fact that in his first encounter with the categories of the Doctrine of Notion (Universal, Particular, Individual) he called them "a best means of getting a headache," Lenin grasped from the outset not only the deep historical roots of Hegel's philosophic abstractions but also their historical meaning for "today." Therefore, Lenin sided with Hegel's idealism against what he called the "vulgar materialism" of his day:

> The idea of the transformation of the ideal into the real is *profound*. Very important for history—Against vulgar materialism. NB. The difference of the ideal from the material is also not unconditional, not excessive (*überschwenglich*).[20]

The significance of Lenin's commentary is that he made it while he was still reading the Doctrine of Being. To all Marxists after Marx, including Engels,[21]

Adoratsky appeared only in the Russian edition. See *Leninski Sbornik* (Moscow), Vol. XII. It is also worthwhile to consult Joravsky, op. cit., pp. 97ff., regarding Bukharin and Trotsky on the *Philosophic Notebooks*.

19 *M&F*. p. 328; LCW 38, p. 99.

20 *M&F*, p. 329; LCW 38, p. 114.

21 The two letters of Engels to Conrad Schmidt dated November 1, 1891, and February 4, 1892, are most applicable: Engels cited "a good parallel" between the development of Being into Essence in Hegel and the development of commodity into capital in Marx.

the Doctrine of Being had meant only immediate perception, or the commodity, or the market, i.e., the phenomenal, apparent reality as against the essential exploitative relations of production. Even here, Lenin escaped "vulgar materialism," which sought to erect impassable barriers between the ideal and the real. In Lenin's new evaluation of idealism, however, there was neither "sheer Hegelianism" nor "pure" Maoist voluntarism.[22] Instead Lenin's mind was constantly active, seeing new aspects of the dialectic at every level, whether in Being or in Essence. Indeed, in the latter sphere Lenin emphasized not the contrast between Essence and Appearance, but instead *self*-movement, *self*-activity, and *self*-development. For him it was not so much a question of essence *versus* appearance as it was of the two being "*moments*" (Lenin's emphasis) of a *totality* from which even cause should not be singled out: "It is absurd to single out causality from this. It is impossible to reject the *objectivity* of notions, the objectivity of the *universal* in the particular and in the individual."[23] Reading the Doctrine of Notion, Lenin broke with his philosophic past. The break began in the Doctrine of Essence, at the end of Causality, when he began to see new aspects of causality and of scientism, which could not possibly fully explain the relationship of mind to matter. Therefore, he followed Hegel's transition to the Doctrine of Notion, "the realm of Subjectivity, or Freedom" which Lenin immediately translated as "NB Freedom = Subjectivity ('or') End, consciousness, Endeavor, NB."[24]

Lenin was liberated in his battles with the categories of the Doctrine of Notion, the very categories he had called "a best way of getting a headache." First, he noted that Hegel's analysis of these categories is "reminiscent of Marx's imitation of Hegel in Chapter 1."[25] Second, Lenin no longer limited objectivity to the material world but extended it to the *objectivity of concepts*: freedom, subjectivity, notion. These are the categories through which we gain knowledge of the objectively real. They constitute the beginning of the transformation of objective idealism into materialism. By the time he reached Hegel's analysis of the relationship of means to ends, he so exulted in Hegel's genius in the dialectic, "the germs of historical materialism,"[26] that he capitalized, boldfaced,

---

22 The pretentious French Communist Party philosopher Louis Althusser is working hard to kill the dialectic and at the same time to present himself as a "Leninist." But such absolute opposites cannot coexist, not even when one is inventive enough to add Mao and Freud to the hodgepodge. See especially his lecture to bourgeois French philosophers, since reproduced as a pamphlet, *Lenine et la Philosophie* (Paris, 1968).

23 *M&F*, p. 339; LCW 38, p. 178.

24 *M&F, loc. cit.;* LCW 38, p. 164.

25 *M&F, loc. cit.;* LCW 38, p. 178.

26 *M&F*, p. 342; LCW 38, p. 189.

and surrounded with three heavy lines Hegel's statement that "in his tools man possesses power over external Nature even though, according to his ends, he frequently is subjected to it."[27] In reaching that conclusion, Lenin had projected his new understanding of objectivity by writing:

> Just as the simple value form, the individual act of exchange of a given commodity with another, already includes, in undeveloped form, *all* major contradictions of capitalism,—so the simplest *generalization*, the first and simplest forming of *notions* (judgments, syllogisms, etc.) signifies the ever-deeper knowledge of the *objective* world connections. It is necessary here to seek the real sense, significance, and role of the Hegelian Logic. This NB.[28]

Thirdly, Lenin began striking out not only against Hegel but against Plekhanov and all Marxists including himself. Although Moscow's English translator omitted the emphasis in "Marxists," there is no way to modify Lenin's conclusion that

> none of the Marxist*s* understood Marx. It is impossible fully to grasp Marx's *Capital*, especially the first chapter, if you have not studied through and understood the *whole* of Hegel's *Logic*.[29]

Naturally, like the aphorism on "cognition creating the world," this cannot be taken literally. Long before Lenin seriously studied the *Logic*, no one had written more profoundly on economics, especially on Volume II of *Capital*, both as theory and as the concrete analysis of *The Development of Capitalism in Russia*. Nevertheless, the world had changed so radically by the outbreak of World War I and the collapse of the Second International that Lenin became dissatisfied with everything Marxists had written before 1914 on economics, philosophy, and even revolutionary politics. These writings lacked the sharpness and the necessary absolutes of his dictum, "Turn the imperialist war into a civil war." Of course, Lenin did not bring a blank mind to the study of *Science of Logic*. Even as a philosophical follower of Plekhanov, who never understood "the dialectic proper,"[30] Lenin was a *practicing* dialectician. The actual contradictions in Tsarist Russia prepared him for these new conceptions of the dialectic, the

27 SLII, p. 338.

28 *M&F*, p. 339; LCW 38, p. 179.

29 *M&F*, p. 340; LCW 38, p. 180.

30 *M&F*, p. 354; LCW 38, p. 277. Cf. "On Dialectics," in Vol. 38.

"algebra of revolution," which he now began to spell out as "subject" (masses) reshaping history. As Lenin prepared himself theoretically for revolution, dialectics became pivotal and ever more concrete to him. He had begun the study of the *Logic* in September, 1914, at the same time he completed the essay "Karl Marx" for the *Encyclopedia Granat*. Lenin was not fully satisfied with what he had written when he *finished* the *Logic* on December 17, 1914. On January 5, 1915, with the world war raging, he asked Granat if he could make "certain corrections in the section on dialectics.... I have been studying this question of dialectics for the last month and a half, and I could add something to it if there was time...."[31] By pinpointing the time as a "month and a half," Lenin indicated the specific book, *Subjective Logic*, which had opened his mind to new philosophical frontiers. The *Notebooks* themselves, of course, make clear beyond doubt that it was while reading the Doctrine of Notion, directly after the section of the Syllogism, that Lenin exploded with criticism of turn-of-the-century Marxists for having made their philosophic analyses "more in a Feuerbachian and Buchnerian than in a Hegelian manner," and with the realization that it was "impossible fully to grasp Marx's *Capital*, especially the first chapter, if you have not studied through and understood the *whole* of Hegel's *Logic*."[32]

The Russians ignore that Lenin not only concentrated on *Subjective Logic* as a whole but also devoted fifteen pages to the final chapter, the Absolute Idea. But they have to acknowledge that "Lenin evidently assigned great significance to Hegel's *Subjective Logic*, since the greater part of his profound remarks and interesting aphorisms are expressed during the reading of this part of the *Logic*."[33] But in the three decades since the first publication of the *Notebooks*, Russian philosophers have not drawn any conclusions from this fact; much less, in their favorite phrase, have they "applied" it. Instead, they have taken advantage of Lenin's philosophic ambivalence and have refused to see his philosophic break in 1914 with his Plekhanovist past. Certain facts, however, are stubborn. One such fact is that whereas Plekhanov, *the* philosopher of the Second International, reverted to the materialists of the seventeenth and eighteenth centuries, Lenin eventually came to concentrate on Hegel. Lenin regarded Hegel as crucial to the task of the Russian theoreticians. Lenin saw the need to "arrange for the systematic study of Hegelian dialectics," which, though it was to be done from a materialist standpoint, was not to be reduced

31 *The Letters of Lenin* (New York, 1937), p. 336.

32 *M&F*, p. 340; LCW 38, p. 180.

33 *Leninski Sbornik, op. cit.*, Introduction by Deborin to Vol. IX.

to mere interpretation. Also, it was necessary to "print excerpts from Hegel's principal works."[34]

Another stubborn fact is that Lenin's advice to Russian youth to continue studying Plekhanov cannot alter the task he set for himself:

> Work out: Plekhanov wrote probably nearly 1,000 pages (Beltov + against Bogdanov + against Kantians + basic questions, etc. etc.) on philosophy (dialectic). There is in them *nil* about the Larger Logic, *its* thoughts (i.e., dialectic proper, as a philosophic science) nil![35]

The third stubborn fact which Communist philosophers disregard is the significance of Lenin's swipe (which included Engels) at "inadequate attention" to dialectics as the unity of opposites. "The unity of opposites is taken as the sum total of examples ('for example, a seed,' for example, primitive Communism)."[36] Lenin forgave Engels this defect because he wrote deliberately for popularization. However, this cannot touch the deeper truth that, although he always followed Marx's principle that "it is impossible, of course, to dispense with Hegel," Engels considered that "the theory of Essence is the main thing."[37] Lenin, on the other hand, held that the Doctrine of Notion was primary because, at the same time that it deals with thought, it is concrete. It is subjective, not merely as against objective but as a unity in cognition of theory and practice. Through the Doctrine of Notion, Lenin gained a new appreciation of Marx's *Capital*, not merely as economics but as logic. Lenin now called *Capital* "the history of capitalism and the analysis of the notions summing it up."[38] Lenin, and only Lenin, fully understood the unity of materialism and idealism present even in Marx's strictly economic categories.

Marx founded historical materialism and broke with idealism. But he credited idealism rather than materialism for developing the "active side" of "sensuous human activity, practice."[39] On the road to the greatest material (proletarian) revolution, Lenin likewise saw the indispensability of the Hegelian

---

34 Lenin, *Selected Works* (New York, 1943), Vol. IX, p. 77.

35 *M&F*, p. 354; LCW 38, p. 277.

36 Lenin, *Selected Works, op. cit.,* Vol. XI, p. 81. "On Dialectics" also appears both in Vol. 38 of the *Collected Works* and in *Selected Works,* Vol. XIII (1927), as an addendum to *Materialism and Empirio-Criticism.* It is also wrongly attributed there to "sometime between 1912 and 1914."

37 Engels to Conrad Schmidt, November 1, 1891.

38 *M&F*, p. 353; LCW 38, p. 320.

39 I have used the latest Moscow translation of the "Theses on Feuerbach" in *Marx and Engels—The German Ideology* (1964), pp. 645 and 647.

dialectic. He summarized in an article what he had just completed in the *Notebooks*: "Dialectics *is* the theory of knowledge of (Hegel and) Marxism. This is the 'aspect' of the matter (it is not 'an aspect' but the *essence* of the matter) to which Plekhanov, not to speak of other Marxists, paid no attention."[40] Having reestablished continuity with Marx and Hegel, Lenin fully grasped what was new in Marx's materialism: its human face. He was not, of course, familiar with the *Economic and Philosophic Manuscripts of 1844,* in which Marx defined his philosophy as "a thoroughgoing naturalism or humanism."[41]

At the opposite pole stand the official Russian philosophers. There is, of course, nothing accidental about this situation: it has deep, objective, material roots. It is outside the scope of this article to discuss the transformation of the first workers' state into its opposite, state-capitalism.[42] What must be stressed is the new quality which Lenin discerned in the dialectic. Because he lived in a historical period entirely unlike Engels', Lenin did not stop at essence versus appearance but proceeded to the Doctrine of Notion. Because the betrayal of socialism came *from within* the socialist movement, the dialectical principle of transformation into opposite, the discernment of *counter*revolution within the revolution, became pivotal. The uniqueness of dialectics as self-movement, self-activity, and self-development was that it *had* to be "applied" not only against betrayers and reformists but also in the criticism of revolutionaries who regarded the subjective and the objective as separate worlds. Because "absolute negativity" goes hand in hand with dialectical transformation into opposite, it is the greatest threat to *any existing* society. It is precisely this which accounts for the Russian theoreticians' attempt to mummify rather than develop Lenin's work on the dialectic. They cannot, however, bury Lenin's panegyric to the dialectic: "the living tree of living, fertile, genuine, powerful, omnipotent and absolute human knowledge."[43]

The contradictory jamming up of the opposites, "absolute" and "human," is *true.* Toward the end of *Science of Logic,* Lenin stopped shying away from "Absolute" and grasped that the true "Absolute" is "absolute negativity." Absolute lost its godlike fetishism and revealed itself as the unity of theory and practice. The dialectical development through contradiction, which is an

---

40 LCW 38, p. 362.

41 [From "Critique of the Hegelian Dialectic," as translated by Dunayevskaya] *Marxism and Freedom,* p. 313.

42 See Chapter 13, "Russian State Capitalism vs. Workers' Revolt," *M&F.* For the development of the state-capitalist theory from its birth in 1941 until the present, see the Archives of Labor and Urban Affairs, Raya Dunayevskaya Collection, Wayne State University.

43 LCW 38, p. 363.

"*endless* process, where *not* the first but the *second* negativity is the 'turning point,' transcends opposition between Notion and Reality." Since this process "rests upon subjectivity alone,"[44] Lenin adds, "This NB: The *richest* is the most *concrete* and *most subjective*."[45] These are the actual forces of revolution, and we will now turn to the dialectics of liberation just as Lenin turned then to the practice of dialectics.

Dialectics of Liberation

Until 1915, Lenin was satisfied with Marxist economic studies of the latest stage of development of capitalism, which had first been analyzed by the bourgeois liberal economist Hobson in his 1902 book, *Imperialism.* The first Marxist study of the new phenomenon was *Finance Capital* by Hilferding (1910). It was praised for singling out a new feature, bank capital, and for asserting that this highly developed stage of capitalism made it easier for the dictatorship of the proletariat "to take over" the organization of industry. Like the categories of Essence, the new economic categories all led to Absolute Substance. Hilferding's analysis disclosed *no new beginning, no self-developing Subject that would determine its own end.* No Marxist noted this deficiency, however. There seemed to be no need of any deeper awareness of the dialectic, of an awareness that the jamming up of opposites is far more complex and more concrete than the general counter- position of labor against capital.

In 1913, Rosa Luxemburg published *Accumulation of Capital,* concentrating on the relationship of capitalism to non-capitalism, that is, on colonialism. What began as a supplement to Marx's *Capital,* an updating of "primitive accumulation of capital" to comprehend the actual ongoing accumulation of capital, ended as a *revision* of Marx's greatest theoretical work.[46] Lenin opposed Luxemburg's underconsumptionism and wrong counterposition of theory to reality. However, what concerns us here is that despite claims by Paul Sweezy and youthful exponents of the "Third World" that colonial people are "the only revolutionaries," Rosa Luxemburg denied that she had unearthed a new subject either in theory or in fact. She insisted that "long before" capitalism could exhaust itself by running out of non-capitalist areas to exploit, the proletariat would overthrow it.

---

44 SLII, p. 447.

45 LCW 38, p. 232.

46 My 1941 study of Luxemburg's work has been republished as an appendix to the pamphlet *State-capitalism and Marxist Humanism* (Detroit, 1967). [Dunayevskaya developed this analysis further in *Rosa Luxemburg, Women's Liberation, and Marx's Philosophy of Revolution.* —Editors].

In 1915, Bukharin published *Imperialism and World Economy.* Lenin was very satisfied with this updated study, which lashed out against the betrayers and their apologetic Kautskyan theory of "ultra-imperialism" as merely "bad policy" instead of as the actual stage of world economy. He wrote an introduction for Bukharin's book without realizing that it treated the proletariat like an "object" or, as Bukharin expressed it, a "substitute" for "finance capital." As with Hilferding, for Bukharin it was merely a question of "taking over" capitalist economy instead of totally uprooting it.

Suddenly, Lenin became dissatisfied with all other studies of imperialism. His uncompromising stand against betrayers and reformists extended even to his Bolshevik co-leaders. He decided to embark on his own dialectical study. Empiricists without method cannot recognize method in others. They still consider the economic analyses of imperialism so similar in all Marxist studies that to them the dispute during the same period on national self-determination seems "only political." In fact, the first thing disclosed in Lenin's *Notebooks on Imperialism* (begun immediately after completion of the *Philosophic Notebooks*) is that they are by no means limited to the economic study of the latest phase of capitalist development but also include outlines of articles on the war, on the National Question, and on "Marxism and the State" (which later became *State and Revolution*). Even an inspection of the "strictly economic" work alone, which was published by itself in 1916 as *Imperialism, A Popular Outline,* shows that methodologies of Lenin and Bukharin are poles apart. As opposed to Bukharin's concept of capitalist growth in a straight line, or via a quantitative ratio, Lenin was fiercely loyal to the dialectical principle of transformation into opposite. Tracing the self-development of the *subject* (not an "objective" mathematical growth) makes it possible to see transformation into opposite both in the transformation of competitive capitalism into monopoly capitalism *and* of a part of the labor force into a labor aristocracy. *Also,* such a study makes clear that this transformation is only the "first negative." The development through *this* contradiction compels analysis toward the "second negative" or, as Marx expressed it, "lower and deeper" into the masses, to find the *new* revolutionary forces. Thus, Lenin held that *just when* capitalism had reached this high stage of "organization," i.e., monopoly (which extended itself into imperialism), the time had grown ripe for new national revolutionary forces to act as "bacilli" for proletarian revolutions.[47] Whereas Lenin saw in imperialism a new urgency for national self-determination, Bukharin vehemently opposed the latter as "impossible of achievement" and "reactionary." Nothing short of a *direct* road to socialism was acceptable to him. This plunge from concretely developing

47 LCW 19, p. 303.

revolutionary forces to abstract revolutionism, which Hegel would have considered a jump into the "absolute like a shot out of a pistol" and which politicos called "ultra-leftism," was to Lenin "*nothing short of imperialist economism.*"[48]

On the surface, it seems fantastic for Lenin to apply that designation to a Bolshevik co-leader. Yet Lenin continued to use it against revolutionaries including "the Dutch" (Pannekoek, Roland-Holst, Gorter), whom he characterized in the same breath as the "best revolutionary and most internationalist element of the international Social Democracy." Long before the National Question emerged as his final battle with Stalin, whom Lenin accused of "Great Russian Chauvinism" and whose removal as General Secretary he demanded in his *Will*,[49] long before Lenin thought that a proletarian revolution would succeed in backward Russia and that national and world revolutions would become questions of the day, and at a time when the horrors of imperialist war were everywhere and no emergent proletarian revolution was in sight, Lenin became uncompromising in his struggles with Bolsheviks on self-determination. He saw it *not only* as a "principle" (to which all Bolsheviks agreed) but as "the dialectic of history," the revolutionary force which would be the "bacillus" of socialism: "The dialectics of history is such that small nations, powerless as an *independent* factor in the struggle against imperialism, play a part as one of the ferments, one of the bacilli, which help the *real* power against imperialism to come on the scene, namely, the socialist proletariat."[50] The word *dialectic* kept springing up because Lenin recognized an old enemy, "Economism," which had never understood mass revolutionary struggle. All revolutionaries had fought Economism when it first appeared in Russia in 1902. It had been easy to recognize it as the enemy of revolution then because the Economists openly tried to limit the activities of the workers to economic battles on the ground that, since capitalism was "inevitable," "therefore" political struggles should be left to the liberal bourgeoisie. Yet in 1914, during an imperialist war, revolutionaries rejected the national struggles of colonial and oppressed peoples on the ground that self-determination was "impossible" and "therefore," as

---

48 *Ibid.*, pp. 213–263. See Gankin and Fisher, *The Bolsheviks and the World War* (Stanford, 1940), pp. 222–223.

49 Lenin's *Will* was first published by Trotsky as "The Suppressed Testament of Lenin" (New York, 1935). Khrushchev quoted it in his famous "De-Stalinization Speech" in 1956. When it finally appeared in English in Lenin's *Collected Works*, Vol. 36, in 1966, it was called "Letter to the Congress" (pp. 593–611) and included much more than the *Will*: there are the final battles between Lenin and Stalin on the Nationalities Question and on "Autonomisation," i.e., the structure of the state. There is also a difference in the translations. On this dispute see Moshe Lewin, *Lenin's Last Struggle* (New York, 1968).

50 LCW 19, p. 303.

Bukharin put it, "utopian and reactionary." They would only "divert" the struggle for "world revolution." This super-internationalism proved to Lenin only that the world war had "suppressed reason" and blinded even revolutionaries to the fact that "all national oppression calls forth the resistance of the *broad masses* of people...."[51] Not even the great Irish Rebellion changed the abstract revolutionism of these internationalists, who were concerned with "imperialist economy" instead of the self-mobilization of the masses. Lenin fought them and branded their thinking "imperialist economism" *not* because they were against revolution but because they were so undialectical that they did not see in the throes of imperialist oppression the new revolutionary force which would act as a catalyst for proletarian revolution. Lenin extended his constant emphasis on the dialectical transformation into opposite to the transformation of imperialist war into civil war. The defeat of one's country became the "lesser evil." Whereas other revolutionaries including Luxemburg[52] and Trotsky[53] still thought of the struggle for "peace without annexations" as the "unifying force," Lenin was preparing for socialist revolution and for "the day after," when the population "to a man" would run society.

When the Russian proletariat smashed Tsarism and created a still newer form of self-mobilization, the Soviets, Lenin further concretized his revolutionary perspective: "No police, no army, no officialdom. *Every* worker, *every* peasant, *every* toiler, *everyone* who is exploited, the whole population *to a man*" must run production and the state; otherwise, no new society could be created. With the new concrete universal "to a man," Lenin completed his theoretical preparation *to be there.* As he phrased it when he found himself without time

51 *Ibid.*, p. 248.

52 *Ibid.* See "The Pamphlet by Junius" and, of course, Luxemburg's own illegal pamphlet *The Crisis in German Social Democracy,* which she signed "Junius."

53 The full collection of Trotsky's articles on the war *before* the Russian Revolution appears only in the Russian edition *War and Revolution* (Moscow, 1923), Vol. 1. The essays are concentrated against social patriotism, of course, but they are also hostile to Lenin's counterposing of "defeatism" ("Turn the imperialist war into civil war") to the "struggle for peace": "Comrade Lenin adequately revealed, especially at the preliminary conference, as earlier in his essays and articles, that he personally has an entirely negative attitude to the slogan of the struggle for peace." English readers can see this to some extent in Gankin and Fisher, *op. cit.*, pp. 170–171, which quotes Trotsky's reply to the Bolshevik call for a special conference of Russian revolutionaries: "Furthermore, under no condition can I agree with your opinion, which is emphasized by a resolution, that Russia's defeat would be a 'lesser evil.' This opinion represents a fundamental connivance with the political methodology of social patriotism... What is necessary is a rallying of all internationalists, regardless of their group affiliation or of the tinge of their internationalism."

to finish *State and Revolution,* "It is more pleasant and useful to go through the experience of the revolution than to write about it."

According to Lenin, the smashing of the old state between October, 1917, and February, 1918, was the easiest part of the job. The difficult, decisive task followed. The population "to a man" must run the state and manage the economy, and thus it was "necessary to abolish the distinction between town and country as well as the distinction between manual workers and brain workers."[54] That, Lenin said, is the goal of genuine communism. The formula of genuine communism differed from the pompous phrase-mongering of Kautsky, the Mensheviks, and the Social Revolutionaries and their beloved "brethren," in that it reduced everything to the *conditions* of labor.[55] To further stress that the role of labor was *the* proof of a workers' state, Lenin maintained that even the smashing of the old state, which marked the proletarian revolution, did not distinguish it: "The petty bourgeoisie in a frenzy may also want as much."[56] What did distinguish the socialist revolution was its accomplishment from below. "We recognize only one road, changes from below, we want workers themselves to draw up, from below, the new principles of economic conditions."[57]

If the Communist party did not become bureaucratized and did not begin thinking it could do for the masses what only the masses could do for themselves, then, *and only then,* people could progress to socialism. "Every citizen to a man must act as a judge and participate in the government of the country, and what is most important to us is to enlist all the toilers to a man in the government of the state. That is a tremendously difficult task, but socialism cannot be introduced by a minority, a party."[58] There is not one critical question, from the National Question and the dominant role of workers in a workers' state to his own unique contribution on organization, the "Vanguard Party,"[59] that is not tested by the dialectics of liberation.

The aspect that concerns us most is Lenin's development of the relationship of the National Question to internationalism, where he set forth new theoretical points which are relevant today and where he fought his final battle with Stalin. Indeed, his declaration of "war to the death on dominant

54 Lenin, *Selected Works,* Vol. IX, p. 433.

55 *Ibid.,* p. 439.

56 *Ibid.,* Vol. VII, p. 337.

57 *Ibid.,* p. 277.

58 *Ibid.,* Vol. VIII, p. 439.

59 I have stressed this point at length in Chapters 11 and 12 of *Marxism and Freedom* stressing the many changes Lenin introduced into the concept during 1902–1923. Here, I limit the discussion to the last two years of his life.

national chauvinism"[60] was based not only on the Russian situation but on the state of world revolution. When the first German revolution was beheaded in 1919, Lenin wondered if world revolution could become a reality through Peking. Later, he reminded the white world that "in the last analysis, the outcome of the struggle will be determined by the fact that Russia, India, China, etc., account for the overwhelming majority of the population of the globe."[61] Lenin projected a totally new departure in theory[62] when he developed the dialectic of world revolution and said that Russia, although it had experienced a successful revolution, must be ready to subordinate its interests *if* it were possible to overthrow world capitalism through colonial revolutions.

> Petty bourgeois nationalism declares the recognition of the equality of nations, and nothing else, to be internationalism, while preserving intact national egoism... proletarian internationalism demands, firstly, the subordination of the interests of the proletarian struggles in the country to the interests of the struggle on a world scale...[63]

---

60 It took over fifteen years to make public this letter of Lenin to Kamenev. See Moshe Lewin, *op. cit.*, p. 52. Trotsky reproduced some of these letters in *The Stalin School of Falsification* (New York, 1937). But the official texts and some fuller ones did not appear in English until 1966, in 36, p. 606. See especially the note on "The Question of Nationalities or 'Autonomisation'": "the apparatus we call ours is, in fact, still quite alien to us: it is a bourgeois and tsarist hodgepodge and there has been no possibility of getting rid of it in the course of the past five years... unable to defend the non-Russians from onslaughts of that really Russian man, the Great-Russian chauvinist, in substance a rascal and a tyrant, such as the typical Russian bureaucrat is."

61 "Better Fewer but Better," in Lenin, *Selected Works*, Vol. IX. I prefer the translation in Lewin, *op. cit.*, p. 172.

62 "Theses on National and Colonial Questions," in Lenin, *Selected Works*, Vol. X.

63 Lenin *Selected Works*, Vol. X, p. 235. The Black dimension first appeared in Lenin's work in 1912 in "New Data on the Laws of Development of Capitalism in Agriculture." See Lenin, *Selected Works*, Vol. XII, pp. 190–282. This work was often cited in the disputes in the United States among Communists, Trotskyists, and others as to whether the "Negro Question" was a National Question and whether there was a relationship between U.S. slavery and serfdom in Russia. In 1915, in *Notebooks on Imperialism*, Lenin had referred to the fact that the I.W.W. had a more correct position on the Negro Question than did the Socialist Party which, Lenin stressed, "Built separate locals for Negroes and whites in Mississippi!!" The question arose a third time in Lenin's debates with Bukharin, whose reference to the Hottentots he criticized; finally, it was made into a new category which combined nationalism and internationalism in the "Theses on National and Colonial Questions." See *Selected Works*, Vol. VIII, pp. 311–367; and Vol. X, pp. 231–244. See also Claude McKay's speech to the Fourth Congress of the Communist International.

Impatient academic Marxists like Marcuse notwithstanding, *the* theoretical departure for the dialectic of world revolution was laid down in 1920, nearly half a century before Marcuse. Trying to dispense with Marx's concept of proletarian revolution, such Marxists contend that Lenin saw national revolutions as only "auxiliary" whereas today, with the rise of the Third World, we can see matters "globally."[64] It is essential, dialectically and historically, in tracing Lenin's "Hegelianism" to grasp his philosophical and national heritage, part of which erupted spontaneously and part of which grew out of organization, and which he extended all the way to leadership and organization.

It was not only the Asian majority that became a new dimension of world revolutionary development. The Black dimension and minority problems in general became *moving* forces. Thus, in the "Theses on National and Colonial Questions," Lenin listed as revolutionary forces the Negro in the United States and the Jew in Poland.[65] The appearance of the Garvey movement gave new urgency to the Black dimension (which Lenin had long studied) just when the German revolution was falling. The central point in Lenin's new relationships of theory to practice had nothing to do with the old concept of practice as "the carrying out of a line" elaborated by the party leadership. Instead, the relationships involved the leadership listening to and *learning from mass practice:* theoretical advances must come *from* the one source of theory which is also its soul.

One thing the Lenin Institute did provide in their empty introductions to Lenin's *Philosophic Notebooks* is the list of Lenin's request for books.[66] Clearly, he had not stopped studying the Hegelian dialectic once the revolution succeeded. Nor was this study "academic" or limited to his asking "the theoreticians" who edited the new theoretical organ *Under the Banner of Marxism* to act as "Materialist Friends of the Hegelian Dialectic" and to continue publishing

---

64 Herbert Marcuse, "Re-examination of the Concept of Revolution," *New Left Review,* 56 (July–August, 1969).

65 Lenin, *Selected Works,* Vol. x, p. 231.

66 The 1966 English publication of LCW 38, although it claims to be more complete than the early Russian editions, does not repeat in its Introduction the listing of books Lenin requested. Therefore, see Adoratsky's Introduction to the first Russian edition (1930) of *Leninski Sbornik, op. cit.* "Despite the fact… [of] the extreme situation and the necessity to give all attention and all energy to practical questions, Lenin continued to interest himself in questions of philosophy. This is evident from his readings…. On June 24, 1921, he asked [for]… a Russian translation of Hegel's *Logic* and *Phenomenology* (see *Notes of the Lenin Institute,* Vol. III, pp. 94–95)…. Lenin not only read but wrote in that period on the questions of philosophy. Nine-tenths of the remarks on Bukharin's *Economics of the Transition Period* concern the question of method."

Hegel's works. Lenin applied the dialectic in life, in theory, in battles with his co-leaders, and in his revolutionary perspectives.

Death of the Dialectic

There is no more tragic document in history than Lenin's *Will*. His criticism of his Bolshevik co-leaders was directed not only against Stalin, whom he asked to be "removed," and against Zinoviev-Kamenev, who by "no accident" published in the bourgeois press the date of the planned seizure of power, and against Trotsky's "administrative mentality"; also damning was Lenin's criticism of Bukharin.

> Bukharin is not only the most valuable and biggest theoretician of the party; but also may legitimately be considered the favorite of the whole party; but his theoretical views can only with the very greatest doubt be regarded as fully Marxian, for there is something scholastic in him. (He has never learned, and I think never fully understood, the dialectic).[67]

Writing the *Theses* and the *Will*, Lenin summed up a lifetime in revolution just as that movement was achieving the greatest proletarian revolution in history. In his last struggle, dialectics became the *pons asini* of Lenin's philosophical thought. It was no small, abstruse matter that the major theoretician of the party did "not fully understand" the dialectic, nor was it unimportant that *if* factional struggles reflected actual class divisions then nothing whatever could prevent the collapse of the proletarian state.[68] And nothing did. When the Russian revolution failed to extend even to Europe, world capitalism gained more than a breather. The isolation and bureaucratization of the workers' state led to its transformation into its opposite. The young workers' state based itself not on the creativity of the masses but on its authority over them; the determinant was not labor but the state plan. The state party and the monolithic state became isolated from the masses, and the party was not checked by the

---

67 Compare this passage from the English edition of the *Will* published in 1935 by U.S. Trotskyists, to the corresponding passage from the Moscow translation (1966) in LCW 36, p. 595: "Bukharin is not only a most valuable and major theorist of the Party; he is also rightly considered the favorite of the whole Party, but his theoretical views can be classified as fully Marxist only with great reserve, for there is something scholastic about him (he has never made a study of dialectic and, I think, never fully understood it)."

68 Trotskyism makes it necessary to say that if the factional struggle between Trotsky and Stalin had been a *class* question, it would have meant nothing as simplistic as Stalin "representing" the peasantry and Trotsky the proletariat.

"non-party masses,"[69] but was impelled by world production. The state had achieved a new stage of world capitalism: state-capitalism. Lenin feared this movement "backwards to capitalism," and in his last speech to the Russian Party Congress he warned that history had witnessed many retrogressions and that it would be "utopian to think we will not be thrown back."

Because of this awareness, Lenin did not limit his critique of his Bolshevik co-leaders to the "politicians" but extended it to the "major theoretician," Bukharin. Lenin lay withering not only in physical pain but in agony over early bureaucratization of the workers' state and its tendency to move "backwards to capitalism." He felt that Bukharin's theoretical positions on the National Question, the trade unions, and the economics of the transition period would stifle rather than release the creative powers of the masses. Lenin sensed "a passion for bossing" in revolutionaries who wielded state power. Unfortunately, in this state-capitalist age the New Left, when it does not support the Russian state power, supports the Chinese. But uprisings, especially those in Eastern Europe, have shown that people hunger for freedom *from* the state party, *from* the state plan, *from* the state; what they hunger *for* is decentralization of rule as in workers' councils, intellectual councils, and youth councils.

Mao Tse-tung has always been terrified of the *objectivity* of the "Hegelian" contradiction, the actuality of Left opposition to the communist state. Thus, in 1937 during the heroic Yenan period when he made his major contribution to dialectics (or, more accurately, to its revision), Mao invented a new distinction between *the* "principal" and *a* "principal aspect" *of* contradiction which neither Marx nor any Marxist had perceived. From this distinction he drew the conclusion that *class* conflict need not be the decisive contradiction. "When the superstructure—politics, culture, and so on—hinders the development of the economic foundation, political and cultural reforms become the principle and decisive factors."[70] The practical reason for the invention was to

69 Lenin, *Collected Works,* Fourth Russian Edition, Vol. 26, p. 475. "We are badly executing the slogan: arouse the non-party people, check the work of the party by the non-party masses." In English, the concept of the importance of the non-party masses checking the party is found in *Selected Works,* Vol. IX, pp. 253–254. The same volume contains Lenin's final speech to the Eleventh Party Congress (pp. 324–371), in which he invents words to describe his disgust for the party leadership and its "passion for bossing" and *"Communlies"* (communist lies). See also "What Happens After," in *Marxism and Freedom,* p. 205, where I summarize Lenin's attitude on vanguardism. It was valid *only if* the party reflected "the actual spontaneous movement of the masses. *Outside of that relationship* the Party would become anything its worst enemies could think of. It did."

70 Mao Tse-tung, "On Contradiction," in *The Political Thought of Mao Tse-tung,* Stuart Schram, trans. (New York, 1963), p. 133.

fight "dogmatism" in the anti-Japanese struggle and to foist upon the masses "the leadership of Chiang Kai-shek." In 1957, Mao gave another twist to this philosophical contribution. This time, he drained contradiction of its class content in order to advise Khrushchev to crush the Hungarian revolution and to tell the Chinese masses that, since the contradictions in China were "non-antagonistic" and "among the people," they could be "handled."[71] Similarly, in 1966, though it was supposedly a "Second Revolution,"[72] the resolution of contradictions depended entirely on the thought of one man, "The Great Helmsman, Chairman Mao." At the same time, although a "war to the end" is directed against "capitalist-roaders" like his co-founder Liu Shao-chi, it is no accident that the "revolution" is not against the actual rulers but is confined to "culture."

A hundred and fifty years ago Hegel pinpointed the inverted relationship of thought to reality which is characteristic of "culture": "Inversion of reality and thought, their entire estrangement of one from the other; it is pure culture."[73] And, "This only led to voluntarism, [for which] 'the world' is absolutely its own will."[74] Mao, of course, has long known that culture is only "the superstructure" as distinct from the determining production relations; thus, he has surrounded his "revolution" with adjectives "Great, Proletarian, Cultural." It is no coincidence that impatient modern Marxists, who talk glibly of revolution, leave out the proletariat. Though they project nothing short of world revolution, their perspective for intellectuals is only "Radical Enlightenment of others."[75]

What we need instead is "seriousness, labor, patience, and suffering of the negative"[76] on two levels. It must start where Lenin left off. That is the indispensable foundation, but not the whole. The new reality of our age cannot be considered a mere updating. Rather, the comprehension of what is new begins by *listening* to new impulses arising from below, from practice. This process, as opposed to the elitist practice of theoreticians "going to the peasants," involves

71 The whole question of "handling contradictions among people" produced the famous "One Hundred Flowers" struggle, for which see Roderick MacFarquar, *The Hundred Flowers Campaign and the Chinese Intellectuals* (New York, 1960). Every issue of *Peking Review* carried documents from the Cultural Revolution, and these in turn were published in separate pamphlets by the millions. Some of the major documents can also be found in A. Doak, *China After Mao* (Princeton, 1967).

72 The expression is from K.S. Karol, *New Statesman* (September, 1966). He has since become so apologetic for Mao that he has hit out against Castro. See *The Course of the Cuban Revolution* (New York, 1970).

73 Hegel, *Phenomenology of Mind* (New York, 1931), p. 549.

74 *Ibid.*, p. 601.

75 Marcuse, *op. cit.*

76 Hegel, *Phenomenology of Mind*, p. 81.

theoreticians *learning from* the masses, at which point they begin to develop theory. For our era, the new reality first erupted in East Berlin on June 17, 1953, and has continued not only in Eastern Europe and throughout the Third World but also in the technologically advanced countries, in the May, 1968, revolt in France and in the new revolutionary forces in the United States.

These new forces of revolution, which begin from and always return to the Black revolution but also include the youth, women's liberation, Chicano, and Indian movements, are not a substitute for the proletariat but are in solidarity with it. The continuous, persistent, never-ending revolt of the Black revolution constantly emphasizes the vital struggle of labor and forms its most militant part.[77] At least verbally, Mao recognizes the role of labor. But what everyone notices is his voluntarism. As if one day could "equal twenty years"! Because so much of the New Left feeds, if not on Maoism, on the American bourgeois philosophy of pragmatism, it is necessary to contrast Mao's dialectics to Lenin's.

> Mao's failure to grasp dialectic logic has nothing whatever to do with "understanding philosophy." Dialectic logic is the logic of freedom and can be grasped only by those engaged in the actual struggle for freedom. Therein lies the key to the fulfillment of human potentialities and therein lies that new relationship between theory and practice which could lessen the birth-pangs of industrialization. Anything else is the type of subjectivism which hides Mao's compelling need to transform the struggle for the minds of men into a drive to brainwash them.... It is sad commentary on our times and exposes how totally lacking in any confidence in the self-activity of the masses are today's claimants to the title "Marxist-Leninist." Their militancy gains momentum only where there is a state power to back it up.... The challenge is for a new unity of Notion and Reality which will release the vast untapped energies of mankind to put an end, once and for all, to what Marx called the *pre*-history of humanity so that its true history can finally unfold.[78]

---

77 See Charles Denby, "Workers Battle Automation," *News and Letters,* 1960. See also his "Black Caucuses in the Unions," which is appended to the *News and Letters* Editorial Board Statement *American Civilization on Trial: Black Masses as Vanguard* [Chicago: News & Letters, 2003]. Along with these statements by a Black production worker, see those of Black, Chicano, and White women theoreticians in "Notes on Women's Liberation: We Speak in Many Voices," News & Letters, 1970.

78 *Marxism and Freedom,* second edition (New York, 1964), pp. 329–330.

Lenin began from this standpoint in 1917 and worked from it until his death in 1924. Mao's *new* revolutionary opposition, Sheng-wu-lien, tried to begin in a similar way in its Hunan Manifesto of 1968. "Contemporary China is the focus of world contradictions.... For the past few months, the class struggle has entered a higher stage.... It is 'to overthrow the newborn bourgeoisie and establish the people's Commune of China'—a new society free from bureaucrats, like the Paris Commune."[79] As the Hunan Manifesto shows, it is impossible to bring about the death of the dialectic simply because the dialectic is not *merely* philosophy. Above all, it is *life,* the extremely contradictory life of *state as well as private* capitalism. The young Chinese and French revolutionaries, and in the United States the anti-Vietnam War movement, the Black revolution, and most recently women's liberation, all give the lie to rumors of the death of the dialectic. Neither Stalinism nor the "de-Stalinized" communists, much less the "vanguardists" who as yet have no state power but hunger for it, can stop the forward movement of the new generation of revolutionaries. It is imperative, therefore, to fill the theoretical void left by Lenin's death. Surely, future generations will marvel at the relentless resistance of today's so-called Marxists against "the dialectic proper" and the dialectics of liberation worked out by Lenin both while gaining power and after power (but not socialism) had been achieved. Lenin concluded that "socialism cannot be introduced by a minority, a party," but only by the population "to a man" taking control of their own lives. Only when this ideal ceases to be merely the underlying philosophy of revolution and becomes its *practice* as well will freedom no longer be "philosophy" but reality.

∵

First English Language Translation[80] of Excerpts from Lenin's "Abstract of Hegel's *Science of Logic*"

79 "The Hunan Manifesto" as well as three other documents of opposition within China, and the attacks upon the young group of revolutionaries by the official leaders of China's "Cultural Revolution," are reproduced in Klaus Mehnert, *Peking and the New Left: At Home and Abroad,* China Research Monographs (Berkeley, 1969).

80 Dunayevskaya's translation of excerpts from Lenin's Philosophic Notebooks appeared as an appendix to the first English language edition of *Marxism and Freedom,* 1957. (New York: Bookman). Dunayevskaya retained the copyright to that edition, so the copyright is with the Raya Dunayevskaya Memorial Fund.

APPENDIX B

First English Translation

of

V. I. LENIN: ABSTRACT OF HEGEL'S *SCIENCE OF LOGIC*

Translator's Note: This *Abstract of Hegel's Science of Logic* is the central part of Lenin's *Philosophical Notebooks.* Lenin wrote these comments as he was reading and copying many sections of Hegel's *Werke* in 1914. The *Abstract* was first published in Russian in the *Lenin Miscellany,* Volume IX, by the Marx-Engels-Lenin Institute in 1929. The *Philosophic Notebooks* were then published as a separate volume and it is from the 1947 edition by the Institute that the present translation is made.

This translation does *not* include the extracts from Hegel. The translator merely indicates alongside which passages in Hegel Lenin wrote his comments. He used the 1883 edition of Hegel's *Werke,* published in Berlin. The pages cited in the present translation, however, refer *not* to the edition Lenin used, but to the pages in the standard English translation of Hegel's *Science of Logic* by W. H. Johnston and L. G. Struthers (New York: The Macmillan Company, 1929 and 1951; London: George Allen & Unwin, Ltd., 1951). The present translator has excerpted the greater part of these comments, and has also included a few excerpts from Lenin's comments on Hegel's other works: *Encyclopaedia,* and the *History of Philosophy.* These were first published in the *Lenin Miscellany,* Vol. XII, 1930, and republished in the above-mentioned 1947 edition. —R. D.

(Volume I, page 45*)

Logic is the doctrine not of external forms of thought but of the laws of development "of all material, natural and spiritual things," i.e., of the development of the total, concrete content of the world and of its knowledge, i.e., the result, sum, conclusion of the *history* of the knowledge of the world.

(Volume I, page 46)

How should one understand this?

Man is faced with a *web* of the phenomena of nature. Instinctive man, a savage, does not separate himself from nature. Conscious man draws out categories, the essence of the steps of separation, i.e., the knowledge of the world, the nodal points in the web, which enable him to understand and master it.

(Volume I, page 66)

Hegel poses two fundamental premises:

1) the necessity of connection

2) the immanent origination of distinctions

Very important!! This is what it means in my opinion:

1) N e c e s s a r y is the connection, the objective connection of all sides, forces, tendencies, etc. of the given sphere of phenomena.

* Unless otherwise stated all volume and page references are to Hegel's *Science of Logic*.

2) "the immanent *origination* of distinctions"—the inner, objective logic of the evolution of the struggle of the distinctions in a polarity.

(Volume I, page 67)

#

Is not this the thought, that appearance is also objective, since it is *one of the aspects* of the objective world? Not only Essence, but also Appearance is objective. Even the distinction between subjective and objective has its limits.

(Volume I, page 69)

// Cf. *Capital.*

A beautiful formula: "not a mere abstract" universal, but a universal which comprises in itself the wealth of particular, individual, separate (all the wealth of the particular and separate) ! ! Tres bien !

(Volume I, page 135)

D i a l e c t i c is the doctrine of the *i d e n t i t y of o p p o s i t e s*—how they can be and how they become—under which conditions they become identical, transforming one into the other—why the mind of man must not take these opposites for dead, but for living, conditioned, mobile, transforming one into the other. *En lisant Hegel . . .*

(Volume I, page 142)

Acute and profound! Hegel analyzes concepts which usually appear dead, and he shows that there *is* movement in them. The finite? That means *movement* has come to an end! Something?—That means n o t w h a t Other is.—Being in general?—That means such indeterminateness that being=Not-Being. All-sided universal flexibility of concepts—flexibility reaching to the identity of opposites.—That is the essence. This flexibility, subjectively applied=eclecticism and sophistry. When this flexibility is *objectively applied,* i.e., reflects the all-sidedness of the material process and its unity, then it is dialectic; it is the correct reflection of the eternal development of the world. *NB*

(Volume I, pages 173-6)

The idea of the transformation of the ideal into the real is *profound.* Very important for history. But also in the personal life of man it is evident that there is much truth in this. Against vulgar materialism. *NB.* The difference of the ideal from the material is also not unconditional, not excessive.

(Volume I, page 182)

Evidently Hegel draws his self-development of concepts, of categories, from the whole history of philosophy. This gives yet a *new* side to the whole of the *Logic.*

(Volume I, pages 386-90)

In the *Observation,* as everywhere, Hegel brings in facts, examples, the concrete (Feuerbach therefore dares once to assert that Hegel reduced *Nature* to *Observation,* Feuerbach, *Works,* p.?)

||| Leaps!

||||||||| Interruptions in gradualness

||| Leaps!

||| Leaps!

Further: Transition of Being to Essence is analyzed doubly obscurely.

End of Volume I.

(Volume II, page 31*)

Thus here also Hegel accuses Kant** of *subjectivism.* This *NB.* Hegel is for the "objective validity" (sit venia verbo) of show, "of the immediate given" (the term, g i v e n, is common with Hegel in general.) The little philosophers dispute whether one should take as basis essence *or* the immediately given. (Kant, Hume, all Machists). Hegel substitutes *"and"* for "o r," and explains the concrete content of this "and".

(Volume II, pages 65-66)

Observation 2. Law of the Excluded Middle.

This is very profound and true. Every concrete thing, every concrete something stands in diverse and often contradictory relation to all others, ergo, it is itself and others.

* Volume II of the English translation includes what Hegel called Book II of Volume I: *Doctrine of Essence.*—Tr.

** The reference is to Kant's *Critique of Judgment.*—Tr.

(Volume II, pages 66-70)

Observation 3 (End of Chapter 2, Part 1, Book II of the *Logic*). Law of *Contradiction.*

Movement and "s e l f-m o v e m e n t" (this *NB!* arbitrary (independent) spontaneous, *internally-necessary* movement,) "change," "movement and life," "the principle of every self-movement," "impulse" (*Trieb*) to "movement" and "activity"—opposite of "d e a d b e i n g."—Who would believe that this is the core of "Hegelianism," of abstract and abstruse (difficult, absurd?) Hegelianism?? It is necessary to reveal, to understand, to save, to release, to purify this kernel —which is precisely what Marx and Engels have done.

The idea of universal movement and change (1813, *Logic*) was disclosed before its application to life and society. It was proclaimed in reference to society (1847)* earlier than in relation to man (1859)**.

NB

(1) Ordinary perception grasps the difference and the contradiction, but not *the transition* of one to the other, *b u t t h i s i s t h e m o s t i m p o r t a n t.*

(2) Intelligent reflection and mind. Reflection grasps the contradiction, *expresses* it, brings things in relation to one another, compels the "concept to

* The reference is to the *Communist Manifesto.*—Tr.

** The reference is to the *Origin of Species.*—Tr.

shine through the contradiction" but does not *express* the concept of things and their relation.

(3) Thinking reason (Mind) sharpens the blunted difference of variety, the mere manifold of imagination, to the *essential* difference, to *Opposition*. Only when the contradictions reach the peak does manifoldedness become regular (*regsam*) and lively in relation to the other—acquire that negativity which is the *inner pulsation of self-movement and life*.

(Volume II, pages 93-94)

The transition from Ground into Condition.

And a "purely logical" working out? It coincides. It *must* coincide as do induction and deduction in *Capital*.

If I'm not mistaken, there is much mysticism and empty pedantry here in the conclusions of Hegel. But the basic idea is magnificent: all-world, all-sided *living* connection of everything with everything else, and of the reflection of this connection—standing Hegel materialistically on his feet—in the concept of man, which must be so polished, broken-in, flexible, mobile, relative, mutually-tied-in, unified in opposition, as to embrace the world. The continuation of the work of Hegel and Marx must consist in the *dialectical* working out of the history of human thought, science, and technology.

(Volume II, page 105)

"When all the Conditions of a Fact are present, it enters into Existence."

> Very good! What have the Absolute Idea and Idealism to do with this?

> Remarkable this "derivation" . . . of existence.

(Volume II, pages 131-132)

NB Law is the persistent (remaining) in appearance.

Law is the identity in appearance.

NB Law=the quiescent reflection in appearance.

NB

> This is remarkably materialistic and remarkably pointed (in a word, "quiescent") determination. Law takes the quiescent—and therefore law, every law is narrow, incomplete, an approximation.

(Volume II, page 140)

> The essence is that both the World of Appearance and the world which is in itself are essentially *moments* of the knowledge of nature by man, steps, *changes* in (or deepening of) knowledge. The shift of the world in itself ever further and further *from* the world of appearance—that is what is not yet visible in Hegel. *NB.* Do not the "moments" of notion with Hegel have the significance of "moments" of transition?

(Volume II, pages 173-187)

Section Three, Actuality

Regarding the question of "Possibility" Hegel notes the emptiness of this category and in the *Encyclopedia** writes:

"Whether a thing is possible or impossible depends altogether on the subject matter: that is, on the sum total of the elements in Actuality which, as it opens itself out, discloses itself to be a necessity."

"The sum total of the elements in actuality, which as it opens itself out, discloses itself to be a necessity."

The unfoldment of the whole totality of moments of actuality NB=essence of dialectic knowledge.

(Volume II, page 192)

On the one hand, we must deepen the knowledge of matter to the knowledge (to the notion) of substance, in order to find the causes of appearance. On the other hand, actual knowledge of causes is the deepening of knowledge from externality of appearance to substance. Two types of examples should explain this: 1) out of the history of natural sciences, and 2) from the history of phil-

* The reference is to *The Encyclopaedia of the Philosophical Sciences,* the English translation of which, by William Wallace, has been published as *The Logic of Hegel,* in 1892 and reprinted in 1931. London and New York: Oxford University Press, page 262. Hereafter all references to the *Encyclopaedia* will be to this edition, which is also known as "The Smaller Logic."—Tr.

osophy. More precisely: not "examples" —*comparaison n'est pas raison*—but the *quintessence* of the one and the other plus the history of technology.

Cause and effect, ergo, only moment of every kind of interdependence, connection (of the universal), the concatenation of events are only links in the chain of the development of matter.

(Volume II, page 193)

NB

All-sidedness and all-embracing character of world connection are only one-sidedly, desultorily and incompletely expressed by causality. *NB*

(Volume II, page 196)

This "inner spirit"—Cf. Plekhanov—is the idealistic, *mystical*, but very profound indication as to the historic causes of events. Hegel *fully* leads up to history under causality and 1,000 times more deeply and richly understands causality than the crowd of the "learned" now.

(Volume II, page 197)

What we ordinarily understand by Causality is only a small part of the universal connection, but (a materialistic addition) the small part is not subjective but the objectively real connection.

(Volume II, page 204)

When you read Hegel on Causality it seems strange at first sight why he stops so comparatively briefly on this theme loved by the Kantians. Why? Because for him causality is only *one* of the determinations of the universal connection, which he has earlier grasped in a much deeper and all-sided manner, in *all* its development, has from the very beginning and *always* emphasized this connection (reciprocal transitions), etc. etc. It would be very instructive to put alongside of the "t r a v a i l" of neo-empiricism (respective* physical idealism) the decisions, more accurately, the dialectic method of Hegel.

(Volume II, page 205)

At the end of Book II of the Logic, before the transition to the Notion, a definition is given: "*the Notion,* the realm of Subjectivity or of Freedom":

NB Freedom=subjectivity
("or")
goal, consciousness, striving *NB*

(Volume II, pages 221-222)

Book Three: Subjective Logic
The Doctrine of the Notion

Hegel is *essentially* completely right against Kant. Thought, emerging from the concrete to the abstract, does not separate—if it is *correct* (NB) (and Kant,

* The word "respective" appears in English in Lenin's text.—Tr.

like all philosophers, speaks about correct thinking)—*from* truth, but goes toward it. Abstraction of *matter,* of natural *law,* abstraction of *value,* etc., in a word, all scientific (correct, serious, not nonsensical, not absurd) abstractions reflect nature more deeply, truly, *fully.* From living observation to abstract thinking, *and from this to practice*—such is the dialectic road to knowledge of *truth,* the knowledge of objective reality. Kant degrades knowledge in order to make place for belief; Hegel elevates knowledge, believing that knowledge is knowledge of God. The materialist elevates knowledge of matter of nature, throwing God and the philosophic rabble defending Him into the dungheap.

(Volume II, page 224)

Here too Hegel is essentially *right; value* is a category which is "devoid of the stuff of sensuality," but it is *truer* than the law of supply and demand. Only Hegel is an idealist; therefore the nonsense of "constitutive," etc.

(Volume II, pages 233-300)

Section One: Subjectivity

The dialectic of movement of "Notion"—from purely "formal" notion at the beginning—to the *Judgment,* then to *Syllogism* and finally to transformation, from subjectivity of notion to its *Objectivity.*

First distinctive characteristic of notion—Universality. NB: Notion came out of *Essence,* which came out of *Being.*

The further development of *Universality, Particularity* and *Individuality* is abstract and *a b s t r u s e* in the highest degree.

En lisant... these parts of the work should be called: a best means for getting a headache.*

Kuno Fischer explains these "abstruse" arguments very poorly, taking the easier examples from the *Encyclopaedia,* adding nonsense (against the French Revolution. Kuno Fischer, Vol. 8, 1901, p. 530), etc., but he does not show the reader *how* to search for the key to the difficult transitions, shades, overflows, ebbs of the Hegelian abstract notions.

Or *all this* is the old, formal logic? Yes! And also the debt—the debt of mysticism = i d e a l-ism

Voilà an abundance of "d e f i n i tions" and of definitions of Notion in this part of the *Logic!*

Apparently here too what is important for Hegel is *to mark* the t r a n s i t i o n s. From a certain point of view, under certain conditions, the universal is the particular, the particular is the universal. Not only (1) the *connection,* and an indissoluble connection, of all notions and judgments, but (2) *transitions* of one into the other, and not only transition, but also (3) *identity of opposites.* This is what is important to Hegel. But this only "pierces through" the *m i s t* of analysis of the "arch-abstruse." The history of thought from the point of view of development and application of universal notions and categories of the *Logic—voilà ce qu'il faut!*

* This sentence is in English in Lenin's text.—Tr.

(Volume II, page 307)

"All things are a Syllogism. . ." NB

Hegel's analysis of the Syllogisms (I-P-U, "individual, particular, universal," P-I-U, etc.) is reminiscent of Marx's imitation of Hegel in Chapter I.

(Volume II, page 309)

The forming of (abstract) notions and their utilization *already include* the presentation, the conviction, the *consciousness* of the law of the objective world connections. It is absurd to single out causality from this. It is impossible to reject the objectivity of notions, the objectivity of the universal in the particular and in the individual. Consequently, Hegel considerably more profoundly than Kant and others, investigates the reflection of the movement of the objective world in the movement of notions.	NB The question of the true significance of Hegel's *Logic*
Just as the simple value form, the individual act of exchange of a given commodity with another, already includes, in undeveloped form, *all* major contradictions of capitalism,—so the simplest *generalization*, the first and simplest forming of *notions* (judgments, syllogisms, etc.) signifies the ever-deeper knowledge of the *objective* world connections. It is necessary here to seek the real sense, significance and role of Hegelian *Logic*. This *NB*.	One must return to Hegel in order to analyze, step by step, every kind of current logic and *theory of knowledge*, of Kantianism, etc. NB: "Conversely": Marx has *applied* the dialectic of Hegel in its rational form to political economy.

Regarding the question of the criticism of contemporary Kantianism, Machism, etc.

Two aphorisms:

1) Plekhanov criticises Kantianism (and agnosticism in general) more from the vulgar materialistic than the dialectic materialistic point of view, *insofar* as he only *a limine rejects* their argumentation and does not *correct* them (as Hegel corrected Kant), by deepening, generalizing, broadening them, showing the *connections* and *transitions* of all and every notion.

2) (At the beginning of the 20th century) Marxist*s* criticized the Kantians and Humists more in a Feuerbachian (and Buchnerian), than in a Hegelian, manner.

(Volume II, page 329)

Aphorism: It is impossible fully to grasp Marx's *Capital,* and especially its first chapter, if you have not studied through and understood the *whole* of Hegel's *Logic.* Consequently, none of the Marxists for the past ½ century have understood Marx! !

Aphorism

Hegel actually demonstrated that the logical forms and laws are not an empty shell, but a *reflection* of the objective world. More precisely, did not demonstrate, but guessed brilliantly.

Very profound and wise! The laws of logic are the reflection of the objective in the subjective consciousness of man.

(Volume II, pages 343-394)
Section Two. *Objectivity.*

(Volume II, page 380)
Materialist dialectic

The laws of the external world, of nature, the subdivisions of *M e c h a n i s m* and *C h e m i s m* (this is very important) are the bases of the *totality* of the activity of man.

In his practical activity man has before him the objective world, depends on it, and his activity is determined by it.

From this point of view, from the point of practical (end-positing) activity of man, the mechanical (and the chemical) causality of the world (of nature) appears as something *external,* secondary, hidden.

2 forms of the *Objectivity* of the process: nature (mechanical and chemical) and *end-depositing* activity of man. The relationship of these forms. The aims of man seem at first alien ("other") in relationship to nature. Consciousness of man, of science ("notion") reflects essence, the substance of nature. But at the same time this consciousness is external in relationship to nature (not at once, not simply coinciding with it).

MECHANICAL AND CHEMICAL TECHNIQUE PRECISELY FOR THIS REASON SERVES THE AIMS OF MEN. ITS CHARACTER (ESSENCE) CONSISTS IN THE FACT THAT IT IS DETERMINED BY EXTERNAL CONDITIONS (LAWS OF NATURE).

(Volume II, pages 381-3)

In reality the aims of man are generated by the objective world and presuppose it, find it as the given, existent. But it *appears* to man that his aims are taken outside of the world, independent of the world ("free").

((NB: All this relates to the "Subjective End" NB))

(Volume II, pages 387-8)

"Insofar as the Means is higher than the finite Ends of external usefulness: the plough is more honorable than are immediately those enjoyments that are procured by it, and are Ends. The instrument is preserved, while the immediate enjoyments pass away and are forgotten. *In his tools man possesses power over external NATURE, EVEN THOUGH, ACCORDING TO HIS ENDS, he frequently is subjected to it.*"*

Hegel and historical materialism

(Volume II, pages 386-394)

All this is in "the Realized End."

Historical materialism is one of the applications and developments of the ideas of a genius which, in seed, in embryo, are to be found in Hegel.

* The emphasis is Lenin's, not Hegel's.—Tr.

When Hegel tries—sometimes even strains himself and worries to death—to subsume the purposeful activity of man under the categories of logic, saying that this activity is the "syllogism," that the subject plays the role of some sort of "member" in the logical "figure" of the syllogism, etc., *then this is not only a strain, not only a game.* There is here a very deep content, purely materialistic. It is necessary to turn this around: The practical activity of man, repeated billions of times, must lead the consciousness of man to the repetition of the various logical figures in order that these can achieve the significance of an *axiom. This nota bene.*

NB

The categories of *Logic* and the practice of man

NB

Remarkable: Hegel goes *through* the practical, end-positing activity of man, to get to the "Idea" as correspondence of the notion with the object, to the Idea as *truth.* A close approach to this, that man by his *practice* demonstrated the objective correctness of his ideas, notions, knowledge, science.

From subjective notion and subjective end to *objective* truth.

(Volume II, pages 395-486)

Section III: The Idea

(Volume II, pages 395-400)

In general the introduction to The Idea of Part II of the *Logic* (Subjective Logic) and the corresponding paragraphs in the *Encyclopaedia* is nearly the very best description of the dialectic.

Here, then, the correspondence, so to speak, of logic and gnoseology is demonstrated in a remarkably inspired manner.

(Volume II, pages 399-400)

Idea (read: knowledge of man) is the correspondence (conformance) of the notion and objectivity ("the universal"). This firstly.

Secondly, the idea is the *relationship* of subjectivity (=man) existing for itself (=as if independent) to objectivity *distinct* (from this idea).

Subjectivity is the *striving* to abolish this separation (of idea from the object).

Knowledge is a *process* of submersion in inorganic nature (of mind) for the sake of subordinating to it the power of the subject and generalization (of the knowledge of the universal in phenomena) . . . Correspondence of thought with the object is a *process.* Thought (=man) must not present to itself thought in the form of a dead repose, in the form of a simple picture (image) of the pale (spent) thought, without impulse or motion, as a genii, a number, as an abstraction.

Knowledge is eternal, infinitite approachment of thought to object. The *reflection* of nature in the thought of man must be understood not in a "dead," not in an "abstract" manner, *not without motion, not without contradictions, but in an eternal process of movement, emergence* of contradictions and their solution.

(*Encyclopaedia,* pages 302-4)

The *t o t a l i t y* of *all* sides of a phenomenon, of actuality and their (mutual) *r e l a t i o n*—this is out of what truth is formed. Relations (= transitions=contradictions) of notions=the main content of logic, *and moreover* these notions (and their relations, transitions, contradictions) are shown as reflections of the objective world. The dialectic of *t h i n g s* creates the dialectic of *ideas,* and not the reverse.

Hegel as a genius *guessed* the d i a l e c t i c of things, phenomena, the world (nature), in the dialectic of notions.#

#One must express this aphorism more popularly, *without* the word, dialectic: thus: Hegel brilliantly *guessed* in change, in the inter-relations of *a l l* notions, in the *identity of opposites,* in the *transitions* of one notion into another, in eternal change, of movement of notions *just such a relation of things, of nature.*

P r e c i s e l y *guessed,* and no more.

= . . . .

interdependence of concepts

< o f a l l >

without exception

transitions of concepts of one into the other < of all > without exception relativity of the opposition between concepts . . . identity of oppositions between concepts.

In what does the d i a l e c t i c consist?

=*NB*

Every concept finds itself in a certain *r e l a t i o n,* in a certain connection with *a l l* t h e rest.

Truth is a process. From the subjective idea man goes to objective truth *through* "practice" (and technique).

(*Encyclopaedia*, pages 352-5)

Idea is "truth" (paragraph 213). The Idea, i.e., *truth* as a process—because truth is a *process*—goes through three steps in its *development*: 1) life; 2) process of knowledge, including *practice* of man and *technique* (see above); 3) the step of the absolute idea (i.e., full truth).

Life gives birth to brain. Nature is reflected in the brain of man. Man, by verifying and applying in practice and in technique the correctness of these reflections, arrives at objective truth.

(*Encyclopaedia*, pages 360-361)

"The inorganic nature which is subdued by the vital agent suffers this fate, because it is *virtually* the same as what life is *actually*."

Conversely=pure materialism. Splendid, profound, true! And also *NB*: demonstrates the extreme correctness of the terms "in itself" and "for itself"!!!

(Volume II, page 429)

The logical notions are subjective so long as they remain "abstract," in their abstract form, and at the same time express also the thing-in-itself. Nature *and* concreteness *and* abstractness *and* phenomenon *and* essence *and* moment *and* relation. Man's cognition is subjective in its abstractness and separateness but objective as a whole, in the process, in the result, in the tendency, in the source.

(Volume II, page 460)

Theoretic cognition must give the object in its necessity, in its all-sided relations, in its contradictory movement in and for itself. But man's understanding "definitively" grasps this objective truth of cognition, discerns it, masters it only when cognition becomes "being for itself" in the sense of practice, i.e., the practice of man and humanity is the verification, criterion of objectivity of knowledge. Is that the thought of Hegel? One must return here.

Hegel about practice and the objectivity of cognition.

All this is in the chapter on "The Idea of Cognition" (Chapter II) in the transition to "The Absolute Idea" (Chapter III), i.e., undoubtedly practice in Hegel stands as a link in the analysis of the process of cognition and precisely as a transition to the objective ("absolute," according to Hegel) truth. Marx, consequently, clings to Hegel, introducing criteria of practice into the theory of knowledge. Cf. *Theses on Feuerbach.*

Practice in the theory of cognition.

Alias:

Man's cognition not only reflects the objective world, but creates it.

(Volume II, page 463)

NB

"Syllogism of action." For Hegel *action*, practice is the *logical conclusion* of the figure of logic. And this is true! Of course, not in the sense that the figure of logic has by its Otherness the practice of man (=absolute idealism) but vice versa: the practice of man, repeated billions of times, fastens itself in the consciousness of man by the figures of logic. The figures have the solidity of a prejudice, an axiomatic character precisely (and only) because of this billion times repetition.

NB

1st postulate: *good End* (subjective aim) *versus actuality* ("external actuality")

2nd postulate: external means (weapon) (objectivity)

3rd postulate: namely, the conclusion: the correspondence of subject and object, the verification of subjective ideas, the criteria of objective truth.

(Volume II, page 465)

NB

The activity of man, composing for itself an objective picture of the world, *changes* the external activity, transcends its determinateness (=changes these or other of its aspects, qualities) and thus takes away from it the traits of show, externality and nullity, gives it being-in-itself and for itself (=objective truth).

(Volume II, pages 466-486)

Chapter III. "The Absolute Idea"

(Volume II, page 466)

The unity of theoretic ideas (cognition) and *practice*—this NB—and this unity *precisely in theory of knowledge* for the result is the "Absolute Idea" (and Idea = "objective truth").

(Volume II, page 473)

We can, if you please, present these elements of the dialectic in a more detailed way, thus:

Elements of the dialectic.

1) The *objectivity* of the analysis (not examples, not digression, but the thing in itself).

2) The whole totality of the manifold *relations* of this thing to the others.

3) The *development* of this thing (respective appearance), its own movement, its own life.

4) The internally contradictory *tendencies* (*and* sides) of this thing.

5) The thing (the appearance, etc.) as sum and *unity of opposites*.

6) The *struggle* respective* the unfolding of these opposites, the contradictions of the impulses, etc.

7) The unity of analysis and synthesis,—disintegration of the particular parts of the totality, the summation of these parts together.

* The word "respective" was in English in Lenin's text.—Tr.

8) The relation of *each* thing (appearance, etc.) is not only manifold but general, universal. Each thing (appearance, process, etc.) is connected with *every* other.

9) Not only unity of opposites but *transitions of every* determination, quality, characteristic, side, feature into *every* other (into its opposite).

10) Infinite process of unfolding of *new* sides, relations, etc.

11) Infinite process of the deepening of man's cognition of things, appearances, processes, etc., from appearance to essence, and from the less profound to the more profound essence.

12) From co-existence to causality and from one form of connection and of mutual dependence to another, deeper and more universal.

13) The repetition at a higher stage of certain features, characteristics, etc., of the lower, and

14) The apparent return to the old (*the negation of the negation*).

15) The struggle of the content with the form and the reverse. The shedding of the form, the transformation of the content.

16) The *transition* of quantity into quality and *vice versa*. ((15 and 16 are examples of 9))

Briefly the dialectic can be defined as the doctrine of the unity of opposites. Thereby is the kernel of the dialectic grasped, but that demands explanation and development.

(Volume II, pages 473-474)

Further there follows an interesting, clear, important *sketch of dialectic.*

(Volume II, page 476)

Not a bare negation, not a random negation, not *a sceptical negation,* vacillation, doubt, which is characteristic and existent in the dialectic—which, undoubtedly, contains in itself the element of negation and as the most important element at that—no, but a negation as a moment of connection, as a moment of development, retaining the positive, i.e., without any vacillation, without any eclecticism.

Here is what is important:

1) the characteristic of the dialectic: self-movement, source of activity, movement of life and spirit; correspondence of notions of the subject (man) with reality;

2) objectivism to the highest degree ("the most objective moment").

NB: In the smaller logic (the *Encyclopaedia*, page 379) the *last* phrase of the book is: "but this Idea which has Being is Nature."

(Volume II, page 485)

This phrase on the *last** page of the *Logic* is extraordinarily remarkable. The transition of the logical idea to *nature*. Stretches a hand to materialism. Engels was right when he said that the system of Hegel is materialism turned upside down. This is not the last phrase of the *Logic*, but what follows to the end of the page is not important.

End of the *Logic*. December 17, 1914.

Supplementary Quotations from the *Encyclopaedia* (pages 364-379)

Plan of the Dialectic (Logic) Contents Page of the Smaller Logic (*Encyclopaedia*)

Cognition (knowledge) in Being (in the immediate phenomena) reveals the essence (law of cause, identity, difference, etc.)—such actually is the *universal course* of all of man's knowledge (of all of science) in general. Such is the course also of *natural science* and *political economy* (and of history). So precisely is the dialectic of Hegel the generalization of the history of thought.

Extremely productive seems to be the task to follow this through more concretely, in greater detail, regarding the *history of individual sciences*. In the

* In the English edition the phrase referred to, "it is *Nature*," is on the page before the last.—Tr.

Logic the history of thought *must,* in general and as a whole, correspond with the laws of thought.

If Marx did not leave a Logic (with a capital letter), he left the *logic* of *Capital,* and this should be especially utilized on the given question. In *Capital,* the logic, dialectic and theory of knowledge of materialism (3 words are not necessary: they are one and the same) are applied to one science, taking all that is valuable in Hegel and moving it forward.

Commodity–money–capital

→ production of absolute surplus value

→ production of relative surplus value

The history of capitalism and the analysis of the *notions* summing it up.

The beginning–the most simple, ordinary, obvious, immediate "being": an individual commodity ("being" in political economy). Its analysis, as a social relation. The analysis is a *dual* one, deductive and inductive,–logical and historical (forms of value). Verification of facts respective* the practice is here in *every* step of the analysis.

---

* The English word "respective" is in Lenin's text.–Tr.

Cf. regarding the question about essence versus appearance
–price and value
–demand and supply versus "value" (="crystallized labor")
–wages and price of labor power

Excerpts from Lenin's Abstract of Hegel's *History of Philosophy*

Intelligent idealism is nearer to intelligent materialism than is stupid materialism.

Dialectical idealism instead of intelligent; metaphysical, undeveloped, dead, vulgar, static, instead of stupid.

NB Work out:

Plekhanov wrote probably nearly 1,000 pages (Beltov + against Bogdanov + against Kantians + basic questions, etc., etc. on philosophy (dialectic).

There is in them *nil* about the Larger Logic, *its* thoughts (i.e., dialectic *proper*, as a philosophic science) nil ! !

NB Arisitotle's critique of "the ideas" of Plato is a critique of *idealism as idealism in general*: because wherever notions, abstractions are, there are also "the law," and "necessity," etc. The idealist Hegel in a cowardly fashion goes around the fact that Aristotle (in his criticism of the Ideas of Plato) undermined the *foundations* of idealism.

Materialism is always the victor when *one* idealist criticizes the foundations of *another* idealist. Cf. Aristotle vs. Plato, etc. Hegel versus Kant, etc.

Hegel, the adherent of the dialectic, was incapable of understanding *dialectically* the transition *from* matter *to* movement, *from* matter *to* consciousness —especially the second.

Marx corrected the mistake (or weakness?) of the mystic.

NB

Not only is the transition from matter to consciousness dialectical, but so is it from feeling to thought, etc.

CHAPTER 2

Dunayevskaya's Changed Perception of Lenin's Philosophic Ambivalence, 1986–87

In 1986–87, as Dunayevskaya was working on a projected book, "Dialectics of Organization and Philosophy," one dimension that emerged was a "changed perception of Lenin's philosophic ambivalence." This changed perception centered on the fact that, despite commenting on the Absolute Idea chapter in his Hegel Notebooks, philosophically *Lenin remained on the threshold of Hegel's Absolutes—in the chapter on the Idea of Cognition, where he was drawn to the Practical Idea. Though she had explored and written about Lenin's "Great Divide in Marxism" on many occasions since first translating Lenin's 1914–15 Philosophic Notebooks on Hegel's* Science of Logic *in 1949, her 1986–87 changed perception meant a new vantage point for analyzing Lenin's thought and action.*

Dunayevskaya recognized that Lenin remained on the threshold of the Absolute Idea and was beginning to ask what the impact was on aspects of his political practice, particularly with regard to a failure to fully rethink the question of revolutionary organization (including his Bolshevik Party) in the same way she had seen Lenin reorganize other dimensions of his political practice after his Hegel Notebooks.

Dunayevskaya did not write a draft chapter or complete essay on her changed perception. However, she did express ideas on the direction she was intent on developing in several of her writings. Below are excerpts from several documents that take up this theme. As Prologue, an excerpt from her May 12, 1953, Letter on Hegel's Absolutes expressed "where we part from Lenin" at an early moment of her Lenin studies.

Prologue: Lenin as Seen in Excerpts from Dunayevskaya's May 12, 1953 Letter on Hegel's Absolutes

... I am shaking all over for we have come to where we part from Lenin. I mentioned before that, although in the *approach* to the Absolute Idea Lenin had mentioned that man's cognition not only reflects the objective world but creates it, but that *within the chapter* he never developed it. Objective world connections, materialism, dialectical materialism it is true, but not the object and subject as one fully developed—that's what he saw. Then he reaches the last paragraph:

> For the Idea posits itself as the absolute unity of the pure Notion and its Reality, and thus gathers itself into the immediacy of Being; and in doing so, as totality in this form, it is Nature.
>
> SLII, p. 485

There Lenin stops—it is the *beginning* of the last paragraph—and he says: "This phrase on the *last* page of the Logic is exceedingly remarkable. The transition of the logical idea to *Nature*. Stretching a hand to materialism. This is not the last phrase of the *Logic*, but further till the end of the page is unimportant" [M&F, p. 352; LCW 38, p. 233].

But, my dear Vladimir Ilyitch, it is not true; the end of that page is important; we of 1953, we who have lived three decades after you and tried to absorb all you have left us, we can tell you that.

Listen to the very next sentence: "But this determination is not a perfected becoming or a *transition*... ." [SLII, p. 485]. Remember how transition was everything to you in the days of Monopoly, the eve of socialism. Well, Hegel has passed *beyond* transition; he says this last determination,

> the pure Idea, in which the determinateness or reality of the Notion is itself raised to the level of Notion, is an absolute *liberation*, having no further immediate determination which is not equally *posited* and equally Notion. Consequently there is no transition in this freedom.... The transition here therefore must rather be taken to mean that the Idea freely releases itself in absolute self-security and self-repose.
>
> SLII, pp. 485, 486

You see, Vladimir Ilyitch, you didn't have Stalinism to overcome, when transitions, revolutions seemed sufficient to bring the new society. Now everyone looks at the totalitarian one-party state, *that* is the new that must be overcome by a totally new revolt in which everyone *experiences* "absolute liberation." So we build with you from 1920–23 and include the experience of three decades.

∵

Letter to Non-Marxist Hegel Scholar Louis Dupré

July 3, 1986

Dear Louis Dupré:

Suddenly I remembered when we first met at Yale University, where I talked on *Philosophy and Revolution.* We continued the dialogue after the formal talk. I believe it set the ground for my paper on "Hegel's Absolute Idea as New Beginning," which was accepted for the 1974 Hegel Society of America conference. Don't you think that in a way we have had a continuing dialogue since? At any rate, I consider you a *very* good friend. I hope you agree. Or do you think that the sharpness of my critique of Hegel scholars who are non-Marxists goes beyond their critique of Marxism? I seem always to get friends—Marxist as well as non-Marxist—who consider me a friendly enemy rather than a friend. That friendly enemy relationship continued, for example, with Herbert Marcuse for three long decades, and we still never agreed, specifically on the Absolutes. That's where I want to appeal to you, even though we do not have the same interpretation either.

Along with the battle I'm currently having with myself on the Absolutes (and I've had this battle ever since 1953, when I first "defined" the Absolute as the new society), I am now changing my attitude to Lenin—specifically on Chapter 2 of Section 3 of [the Doctrine of the Notion in] the *Science of Logic,* "The Idea of Cognition." The debate I'm having with myself centers on the different ways Hegel writes on the Idea of Cognition in the *Science of Logic* (hereafter referred to as *Science*), and the way it is expressed in his *Encyclopedia* (Smaller Logic), ¶225–235, with focus on ¶233–235. The fact that the Smaller Logic does the same type of abbreviation with the Absolute Idea as it does with the Idea of Cognition, turning that magnificent and most profound chapter of the *Science* into ¶236–244, and that ¶244 in the Smaller Logic was the one Lenin preferred[1] to the final paragraph of the Absolute Idea in the *Science,* has had me "debating" Lenin ever since 1953. That year may seem far away, but its essence, without the polemics, you actually heard at the 1974 Hegel Society of America conference.

Whether or not Lenin had a right to "misread" the difference in Hegel's two articulations in the *Science* and in the Smaller Logic, isn't it true that Hegel, by

1 All the references to Lenin are to his "Abstract of Hegel's *Science of Logic,*" as included in Vol. 38 of his *Collected Works,* pp. 87–238. Concretely the subject under dispute here is on the Doctrine of the Notion, Section Three, Chaps. 2 and 3, "The Idea of Cognition" and the "Absolute Idea."

creating the sub-section ß, "Volition," which does not appear in the *Science*, left open the door for a future generation of Marxists to become so enthralled with Chapter 2, "The Idea of Cognition"—which ended with the pronouncement that Practice was higher than Theory—that they saw an identity of the two versions? These Marxists weren't Kantians believing that all contradictions will be solved by actions of "men of good will."

There is no reason, I think, for introducing a new subheading which lets Marxists think that now that practice is "higher" than theory, and that "will," not as willfulness, but as action, is their province, they do not need to study Hegel further.

Please bear with me as I go through Lenin's interpretation of that chapter with focus on this subsection, so that we know precisely what is at issue. Indeed, when I began my talking to myself in 1953, objecting to Lenin's dismissal of the last half of the final paragraph of the Absolute Idea in the *Science* as "unimportant," preferring ¶244 of the Smaller Logic—"go forth freely as Nature"—I explained that Lenin could have said that because he hadn't suffered through Stalinism. I was happy that there was one Marxist revolutionary who had dug into Hegel's Absolute Idea.

Now then, when Lenin seems to have completed his *Abstract*, and writes "End of the *Logic*. 12/17/1914" [M&F, p. 352; LCW 38, p. 233], he doesn't really end. At the end of that he refers you to the fact that he ended his study of the *Science* with ¶244 of the Smaller Logic—and he means it. Clearly, it wasn't only the last half of a paragraph of the Absolute Idea in the *Science of Logic* that Lenin dismissed. The truth is that Lenin had begun seriously to consult the Smaller Logic at the section on the Idea, which begins in the Smaller Logic with ¶213. When Lenin completed Chapter 2, the "Idea of Cognition," he didn't really go to Chapter 3, "The Absolute Idea," but first proceeded for seven pages with his own "translation" (interpretation). This is on pp. 212–219 of Vol. 38 of his *Collected Works*.

Lenin there divided each page into two. One side, he called "Practice in the theory of Knowledge"; on the other side, he wrote: "Alias, Man's consciousness not only reflects the objective world, but creates it." I was so enamored with his "Hegelianism" that I never stopped repeating it. Presently, however, I'm paying a great deal more attention to what he did in that division of the page into two, with these "translations." Thus: (1) "Notion = Man"; (2) "Otherness which is in itself = Nature independent of man"; (3) "Absolute Idea = objective truth." When Lenin reaches the final section of Chapter 2, "The Idea of the Good," he writes, "end of Chapter 2, transition to Chapter 3, 'The Absolute Idea.'" But I consider that he is still only on the *threshold* of the Absolute Idea. Indeed, all that follows p. 219 in his Notes shows that to be true, and explains why Lenin proceeded on his own after the end of his Notes on the Absolute Idea, and returned to the Smaller Logic.

Thus when Lenin writes that he had reached the end of the Absolute Idea and quotes ¶244 as the true end, because it is "objective," he proceeds to the Smaller Logic and reaches ¶244, to which he had already referred.

Although he continued his commentaries as he was reading and quoting Absolute Idea from the *Science*, it was not either Absolute Idea or Absolute Method that his 16-point definition of the dialectic ends on: "(15) the struggle of content with form and conversely. The throwing off of the form, the transformation of the content. (16) the transition of quantity into quality and vice versa. (15 and 16 are examples of 9)" [M&F, p. 350; LCW 38, p. 222]. No wonder the preceding point 14 referred to absolute negativity as if it were only "the apparent return to the old (negation of the negation)."

Outside of Marx himself, the whole question of the negation of the negation was ignored by all "orthodox Marxists." Or worse, it was made into a vulgar materialism, as with Stalin, who denied that it was a fundamental law of dialectics. Here, specifically, we see the case of Lenin, who *had* gone back to Hegel, and *had* stressed that it was impossible to understand *Capital*, especially its first chapter, without reading the *whole* of the *Science*, and yet the whole point that Hegel was developing on unresolved contradiction, of "two worlds in opposition, one a realm of subjectivity in the pure regions of transparent thought, the other a realm of objectivity in the element of an externally manifold actuality that is an undisclosed realm of darkness" (Miller translation, p. 820 [SLII, p. 462; *Hegel's Science of Logic* (New York: Humanities Press, 1969), p. 820]), did not faze Lenin because he felt that the objective, the Practical Idea, is that resolution. Nor was he fazed by the fact that Hegel had said that

> the complete elaboration of the unresolved contradiction between the *absolute* end and the limitation of this actuality that *insuperably* opposes it has been considered in detail in the *Phenomenology of Mind.* (The reference is to pp. 611 ff. of the *Phenomenology*, Baillie translation.)

In the original German the above sentence reads:

> Die vollständige Ausbildung des unaufgelösten Widerspruchs, jenes *absoluten* Zwecks, dem die Schranke dieser Wirklichkeit unüberwindlich gegenübersteht, ist in der *Phänomenologie des Geistes.*
>
> 2 AUFL., S. 453ff

Nothing, in fact, led Lenin back to the Idea of Theory and away from dependence on the Practical Idea, not even when Hegel writes:

> The practical Idea still lacks the moment of the theoretical Idea.... For the practical Idea, on the contrary, this actuality, which at the same time confronts it as an insuperable limitation, ranks as something intrinsically worthless that must first receive its true determination and sole worth through the end of the good. Hence it is only the will itself that stands in the way of the attainment of its goal, for it separates itself from cognition, and external reality for the will does not receive the form of a true being; the Idea of the good therefore finds its integration only in the Idea of the true.
>
> SLII, p. 463; Humanities Press edition, p. 821

In German this sentence reads:

> [D]er praktischen Idee noch das Moment der theoretischen fehlt.... Der praktischen Idee dagegen gilt diese Wirklichkeit, die ihr zugleich als unüberwindliche Schranke gegenübersteht, als das an und für sich Nichtige, das erst seine wahrhafte Bestimmung und einzigen Wert durch die Zwecke des Guten erhalten solle. Der Wille steht daher der Erreichung seines Ziels nur selbst im Wege dadurch, dass er sich von dem Erkennen trennt und die aüsserliche Wirklichkeit für ihn nicht die Form des wahrhaft Seienden erhält; die Idee des Guten kann daher ihre Ergänzung allein in der Idee des Wahren finden.

I'm certainly not blaming Hegel for what "orthodox Marxists" have done to Hegel's dialectic, but I still want to know a non-Marxist Hegelian's viewpoint on the difference of the two articulations on the Idea of Cognition and the Absolute Idea in the *Science* and in the Smaller Logic. What is your view?

To follow out this question we need, in one respect, another journey back in time—to 1953 when, in parting from Lenin on the vanguard party, I had delved into the three final syllogisms of Hegel's *Philosophy of Mind*. You may remember that in my paper to the Hegel Society of America in 1974, where I critique Theodor Adorno's *Negative Dialectics*—which I called "one-dimensionality of thought"—I said that he had substituted "a permanent critique not alone for absolute negativity, but also for 'permanent revolution' itself." I had become so enamored with Hegel's three final syllogisms that I was searching all over the "West" for dialogue on them.

Finally, in the 1970s, after Reinhart Klemens Maurer had published his *Hegel und das Ende der Geschichte*, which took up those final syllogisms, I tried to get him involved, his sharp critique of Marcuse notwithstanding. Maurer was anxious to establish the fact, however, that he was not only non-Marxist, but not wholly "Hegelian." In any case, he clearly was not interested in any dialogue with me, and he told a young colleague of mine who went to see him that "I am not married to Hegel." But as I made clear at the 1974 Hegel Society of America conference, I do not think it important whether someone has written a serious new study of those final three syllogisms because of a new stage of scholarship, or because the "movement of freedom surged up from below and was followed by new cognition studies."

The point is that as late as the late 1970s, A.V. Miller wrote me calling my attention to the fact that he had not corrected an error in William Wallace's translation of ¶575 of the *Philosophy of Mind*. He pointed out that Wallace had translated *sie* as if it were *sich*, whereas in fact it should have read "sunders" not *itself*, but *them*.[2] That, however, was not my problem. The sundering was what was crucial to me; the fact that Nature turns out to be the mediation was certainly no problem to any "materialist"; the form of the transition which was departing from the course of necessity was the exciting part.

In introducing those three syllogisms in 1830, Hegel first (¶575) poses the structure of the *Encyclopedia* merely factually—Logic-Nature-Mind. It should have been obvious (but obviously was not) that it is not Logic but Nature which is the mediation.

¶576 was the real leap as the syllogism was the standpoint of Mind itself. In the early 1950s I had never stopped quoting the end of that paragraph: "Philosophy appears as subjective cognition, of which liberty is the aim, and which is itself the way to produce it." It justified my happiness at Hegel's magnificent critique of the concept of One in the Hindu religion, which he called both "featureless unity of abstract thought," and its extreme opposite, "long-winded weary story of its particular detail" (¶573). In the following ¶574 we face Hegel's counterposition of what I consider his most profound historic concept—and by history I mean not only past, or even history-in-the-making, the present, but as future—"SELF-THINKING IDEA."

My "labor, patience, and suffering of the negative"[3] those 33 years hasn't exactly earned me applause either from the post-Marx Marxists, or from the Hegelians, who are busy calling to my attention that the final syllogism (¶577)

---

2 Wallace's translation of this part of ¶575, one of the "three final syllogisms" in the *Philosophy of Mind*, is: "Nature, standing between the Mind and its essence, sunders itself, not indeed to extremes of finite abstraction, nor itself to something away from them and independent...." —Editors.

3 Hegel's *Phenomenology of Mind* speaks of "the seriousness, the suffering, the patience, and the labor of the negative." —Editors.

speaks about the "eternal Idea," "eternally [setting] itself to work, engenders and enjoys itself as absolute Mind," fairly disregarding what is just a phrase in that sentence: "It is the nature of the fact, the notion, which causes the movement and development, yet this same movement is equally the action of cognition."

It is here that I'm in need of your commentary both on Absolute Idea in the *Science of Logic* and on Absolute Mind in the *Philosophy of Mind*. The "eternal Idea" to me is not eternality, but ceaseless motion, the movement itself. Far from me "subverting" Hegel, it is Hegel who made Absolute Method the "self-thinking Idea." George Armstrong Kelly, in his book *Hegel's Retreat from Eleusis*, said that

> for the complex linkage of culture, politics and philosophy, within the matrix of the "Absolute Idea," Mme. Dunayevskaya proposes to substitute an unchained dialectic which she baptizes "Absolute Method," a method that "becomes irresistible... because our hunger for theory arises from the totality of the present global crisis."
>
> P. 239, quoting *Philosophy and Revolution*, p. 7

The "eternal Idea" in the *Philosophy of Mind* not only reinforced my view of Absolute Method in the *Science of Logic*, but now that I am digging into another subject for my work on "Dialectics of Organization," which will take sharp issue with Lenin, both on the Idea of Cognition and on the Absolute Idea, I consider that Marx's concept of "revolution in permanence" is the "eternal Idea."

∴

Excerpts from Presentations, Letters, Notes

In Lieu of Minutes of News and Letters Committees Resident Editorial Board Meeting of August 5, 1986, on Executive Session (Raya Dunayevskaya Collection 10665)

... Take the one reference at the Executive Session 1985–86 [of News and Letters Committees] to what I listed as the Dialectic of the Party. For heaven's sake, what way of hiding the really new and making it appear as if it is the 1987 answer to 1902–03. Believe me, I am not writing a new *What Is to Be Done?* and taking that ground to answer the "opposite" to the elitist party. In a fundamental way the one who did the best rejection to 1902–03—and that for twelve long years—is Lenin. [This is most likely a reference to the Preface to the Collection *Twelve Years* that Lenin wrote in September, 1907. The Collection was to include a selection of Lenin's articles and pamphlets from 1895 through 1905. In the Preface Lenin discussed the circumstances and writing of *What Is to Be Done?*] Why he didn't listen to his own critique, especially when 1905 showed so new a form of organization from spontaneity to Soviets, that it changed his very principle as to *who* brings socialism to *whom*, the intellectuals or the proletariat. Lenin didn't generalize his whole twelve-year critique but turned back to *What Is to Be Done?* [and] let it be reprinted. All "Leninists," including Trotsky, then declared that 1903 form a Universal. This is what we have rejected and this concept of the elitist party will be totally uprooted in the new book on the Dialectics of Organization.

∴

Presentation by Dunayevskaya to the Resident Editorial Board on December 1, 1986 (Raya Dunayevskaya Collection 10678)

The nub of what has been the philosophic need of the age that began in the post-World War II world... was to see that as great a divide as Lenin's *Philosophic Notebooks* had made, the practice that followed *State and Revolution* was so historic, so world-shaking, so great, that no one had stopped to ask either: what happens after the revolution, OR what *in thought* (if they knew dialectic thought at all) do we develop now as the next step?

The Dialectic of Thought demands that our age finally get down to the concretization of that pivotal, climactic Idea of Cognition. In the penultimate chapter of the whole *Science of Logic,* I found a difference in Hegel himself as to how the concept of self-determination of the Idea [was expressed] in the *Science* and how he had shortened it in the Logic in the *Encyclopedia.*

... what really was urgent for the book [*Dialectics of Organization and Philosophy*] was where we are as Marxist-Humanists in relation to Lenin.

Where we appear publicly to differ from Lenin only politically-organizationally, i.e., ever since 1950 we rejected the concept of the vanguard party to lead and constantly developed that (preceded in the '40s by being so passionately for the national liberation movements and insisting that they are a new world stage), philosophically our translation of and digging deep into Lenin's return to Hegelian dialectics in 1914 made it appear that that Great Divide in Marxism still held for the post-World War II world. Now, on the other hand, we further develop what in 1953 seemed only the difference of half a paragraph of the Absolute Idea which Lenin in his *Philosophic Notebooks* had asked to be disregarded. We are now expanding it to be one of the pivots of the book-to-be:

First, we point to the fact that Lenin's dating of the end of his *Philosophic Notebooks*, 12/14/14, is actually not the end, as he continued for four other pages, which showed his preference for the Smaller Logic rather than the *Science of Logic*. The difference is that Hegel himself had made a category in the Smaller Logic of "Will, Volition, of action" which "proved" to Lenin that Hegel considered Practice as Higher than Theory. In truth, that was only the end of the penultimate chapter, the Idea of Cognition, *not* the Absolute Idea. Put differently, the phrase he singled out from Hegel: "cognition not only reflects the world, but creates it," was left at the state of an abstract conclusion. It was never concretized. This is what we are trying to concretize in the book on "Dialectics of Organization and Philosophy"....

"The Year of Only 8 Months," Jan 3, 1987 (Raya Dunayevskaya Collection 10690)

III New Perceptions of Lenin's Philosophic Ambivalence as They Developed during the Preparatory Work for the Biweekly *News & Letters*

... From the first, whether it be only the translation of Lenin's *Philosophic Notebooks* in 1948–49 or the 1953 Letters on the Absolute Idea, where I separated myself not only from Lenin's rejection of the last half-paragraph of Hegel's Absolute Idea, but from his impatience when he reached the Absolute, I was always precise on the points of divergence. As I put it back in the letter of May 12, 1953:

> I am shaking all over for we have come to *where we part from Lenin*. I mentioned before that, although in the *approach* to the Absolute Idea Lenin had mentioned that man's cognition not only reflects the objective world but creates it, but that *within the chapter* he never developed it.

He then began quoting the Smaller Logic; and now I see what I didn't see then in Lenin's brief contents page of that work. That is to say, Lenin's outline of the Smaller Logic first begins with Being, which is p. 103 of Hegel's book. Lenin had entirely left out Attitudes to Objectivity as well as the Introduction. Yet these are the very sections added to the Smaller Logic after the larger *Logic* [*Science of Logic*] was written—a full decade after. Add to this new discovery, my latest exchange of letters with non-Marxist intellectuals,[4] as well as reports and discussions at the REB [Resident Editorial Board of News and Letters Committees] itself. The fact that our critique of Lenin becomes very much sharper than it had been....

The exact phase we are facing now insofar as Lenin and the Party is concerned is this: we had rejected the elitist party so many years before we ever started developing philosophy in any concrete sense that it led too many times to taking the question for granted, as though the Organization question were "solved." The result is that when it comes to the rigors of philosophy, you begin using the word, "dialectic," as if you were already in the Absolute. The dialectic as second negativity doesn't appear fully until the Absolute itself.

The nub of the question is that the discussion on what new discoveries I had made dealt with the dialectic in the Doctrine of the Notion, specifically the final two chapters—the Theory of Cognition, being on the threshold, *on the threshold only*, of the Absolute, and the Absolute Idea itself.... [Lenin] hadn't grasped the dialectic in the Doctrine of the Notion, specifically in the final chapters that we were most excited about, and that we are working so hard to concretize for our age.

I should also add that by this I mean further that Hegel's *Philosophy of Mind*—which Lenin didn't touch at all, especially its final three syllogisms—and all the prefaces, introductions, attitudes to objectivity of the Smaller Logic, were written *after* the *Science of Logic* had already been completed and Hegel was re-examining his whole life's work. Thus, the 1830–31 writings of Hegel are as critical as those of Marx's last decade.

The point now is that Lenin's statement in his *Testament*—that Bukharin, though he was a great theoretician, hadn't fully understood the dialectic[5]—couldn't remain anything but an abstraction. Instead of ever publishing his *Philosophic Notebooks*, Lenin republished his old vulgarly materialist *Materialism and Empirio-Criticism*, even as, instead of developing all the individual

4 See letter to Louis Dupré above in this chapter, and *Raya Dunayevskaya Collection* #11215-50. —Editors.

5 Because Lenin kept his Hegelian writings private, the first time that philosophy appears openly in the movement is in Germany in 1919 and the early 1920s—first, with Lukacs using the Hegelian dialectic as a revolutionary element vs. Social Democratic economic determinism; second, with Korsch. Both unfortunately capitulated organizationally, one to Stalinism, the other out of the movement. We have nothing original from them by the 1930s when Marx's Humanist Essays were published in Germany.

critiques in his [Preface to] *Twelve Years* regarding the 1903 concept of the Party, he had *What Is to Be Done?* republished.

This question first manifested itself, mysteriously enough, at Lenin's very highest political-philosophic achievement on the eve of November 1917, in *State and Revolution*, by the absence of a Dialectic of Organization, the Party. Instead, *What Is to Be Done?* became very nearly a Bible.

The most difficult of all tasks that confronts us, indeed, that has confronted all post-Marx Marxists who have tried to get out from under some form of stratification—and none more so than those like us who have been hewing a road back to Marx's Marxism—is to project that it is not the Party or the leader or leadership, but *philosophy*, the body of ideas, the dialectic of ideas and organization, as against the Party as well as distinct from forms of organization born out of spontaneity. While these, of course, are correct, as against the elitism and ossification of the Party, the truth is that these forms also search for an organization different from their own in the sense that they want to be sure that there is a totality of theory and practice against the establishment of a power that has stopped dead with its conquest of state power—in short, altogether new beginnings.

Talking to Myself Document, January 21, 1987 (*Raya Dunayevskaya Collection 10848*)

... The focus is on the May 12, 1953, Letter on the Absolute Idea. The point is to catch the dialectical flow of the Self-Determination of the Idea, paragraph by paragraph.

[A page of this Letter] calls attention to p. 483 of the *Science of Logic* [Vol. II], which shows how the stage of "exteriorization" is also that of intensification, i.e., "interiorization," i.e., *objective* manifestation makes the inward extension more intense.

The paragraph [on this page], which attacks impatience in "*an absolutely uncompromising Bolshevik*" manner, I attribute to Hegel, after which I quote from p. 484 of the *Science of Logic*:

> That impatience whose only wish is to go beyond the determinate... to be immediately in the absolute, has nothing before it as object of its cognition but the empty negative... or else a would-be absolute, which is imaginary because it is neither posited nor comprehended.

The dialectic flow of this quotation... even if said unconsciously, has everything to do with what I follow the Hegel quotation with:

> I am shaking all over for we have come to *where we part from* Lenin. I mentioned that, although in the *approach* to the Absolute Idea Lenin had mentioned that man's cognition not only reflects the objective world but creates it, but that *within the chapter* he never developed it. Objective world connections, materialism, dialectical materialism, it is true, but not the object and subject as one fully developed.

Stop for a moment. Hold tightly to the fact that ever since 1948–49, when I first translated Lenin's Abstract of the *Science of Logic,* I have done nothing less than extol Lenin philosophically, specifically on the *Science of Logic.* There is no question about the fact that it was Lenin who created the great divide in Marxism in 1914–17. Our present *changed* perception of Lenin's philosophic ambivalence shows here that I actually did have some philosophic differences as far back as the early 1950s.

The fact is that it was not only Lenin who, by keeping the *Philosophic Notebooks* to himself, separated philosophy from politics. When we broke politically with the concept of the vanguard party, we kept philosophy and politics in two separate compartments. What this 1953 Letter shows now is that embedded in it was a sharper critique of Lenin's philosophic ambivalence than shown in *Marxism and Freedom.* In 1953, on the other hand, as we saw above, I had stressed that in the chapter on the Idea of Cognition Lenin had not concretized the *objectivity* of cognition....

[In the 1953 Letter] I began arguing with Lenin because he had asked the readers to disregard the last half paragraph of the chapter on the Absolute Idea while I insisted that had he suffered from Stalinism for three long decades he would have seen the relevance of following Hegel's Absolutes to the end. (This of course is taken up in the May 20, 1953, Letter, where I deal with the three final syllogisms [of Hegel's *Philosophy of Mind*], but for the present what is compelling is to trace the many ways of the development of the Self-Determination of the Idea.)

Here is how the May 12, 1953, Letter manifested the dialectical flow [on the page quoted above], *from* exteriorization/interiorization it lapsed into a would-be "absolute" which led Lenin to remain at the "approach to," i.e., on the threshold of, the Absolute Idea. This is the reason why Lenin preferred to let the Absolute Idea stop at *Nature* (Practice), crediting Hegel with "stretching a hand to materialism," instead of following Hegel to the last part of that paragraph when Hegel insists that the Absolutes had not been completed with the Absolute Idea, and must still go through the *Philosophy of Nature* and *Philosophy of Mind* before completion is reached with Absolute Mind. Put another way, in place of any *self-criticism*, or *objectivity*, Lenin left future generations without full illumination of what may befall them—Stalinism. It is the generation that followed, our age, that suffered through those three decades of Stalinism, that had to face the reality of what happens after. It is *this* point, *this* objectivity, *this* concreteness, that emboldened me not to stop where Lenin stopped at the approach to the Absolute Idea, but to follow Hegel to the *Philosophy of Mind*. The Absolute Method opened new doors already in the Absolute Idea, which Hegel defined as:

> The pure Idea, in which the determinateness or reality of the Notion is itself raised to the level of Notion, is an absolute *liberation*, having no further immediate determination which is not equally *posited* and equally Notion. Consequently there is no transition in this freedom.... The transition here therefore must rather be taken to mean that the Idea freely releases itself....
>
> SLII, pp. 485–486

Now stand up and shout: "The Idea freely releases itself." Shout this while a flashing light illuminates Reality and its meaning, philosophy and revolution.

Instead of placing a "No Entrance" sign over organization as "pure politics," we finally are in the process of working out dialectics of philosophy *and* organization.

Presentation on the Dialectics of Organization and Philosophy, June 1, 1987 (Raya Dunayevskaya Collection 10737)

.... [E]ven the one post-Marx Marxist revolutionary who *did* reach deeply into philosophy—Lenin—nevertheless did not do so on the question of organization. In truth, he never renounced his position on the vanguard party set out in 1902 in *What Is to Be Done?* though he often critiqued it himself. He profoundly extended his new breakthrough in philosophy to a concretization of the dialectics of revolution, and yet never changed his position on the need for the "thin layer of Bolsheviks" [LCW 33, p. 257] as a vanguard party organization. In 1982 in *Rosa Luxemburg, Women's Liberation, and Marx's Philosophy of Revolution*, we critiqued Lenin politically. To fully work out the dialectics of philosophy and organization for our age, it is now clear that that critique must dig deep philosophically....

Lenin... never raised philosophy directly in relationship to organization. It was at most a phrase, like the famous reference in the Trade Union Debate, where he brings in, in a general way only, dialectics and eclecticism (see page 65 of Volume IX of Lenin's *Selected Works*, on "glass cylinder") ["Once Again on the Trade Unions, the Current Situation and the Mistakes of Trotsky and Bukharin," LCW 32, pp. 90–100]....

Lenin did return to Marx's roots in Hegel, and did see that the *Critique of the Gotha Program* had never really been concretized as the smashing of the bourgeois state, without which you could not have a revolution. In a word, he certainly worked out the dialectics of revolution, and made it be in Russia. But, but, but—he... didn't touch the question of the party. On the contrary, it didn't even go as far as his own varied critiques of *What Is to Be Done?* once the Bolsheviks gained power....

PART 2

On the Meaning of Lenin's "Great Divide in Marxism"; Contrast with Trotsky, Bukharin, Luxemburg

CHAPTER 3

Lenin on Self-determination of Nations and on Organization After His *Philosophic Notebooks*

From the vantage point of her translation and study of Lenin's Philosophic Notebooks, *Dunayevskaya examined and wrote about Lenin's political practice in the period of the First World War through his* State and Revolution *on the eve of October. Below are excerpts from her* Marxism and Freedom *and* Philosophy and Revolution *with focus on: (1) her commentaries on Lenin's concept of self-determination of nations in contrast to Bukharin's dismissal of self-determination in the age of imperialism; and (2) her view of Lenin on "the Relation of the Masses to the Party."*

The Break in Lenin's Thought

Marxism and Freedom

There is no major work of Lenin's, from the *Philosophic Notebooks* until his death, that is not permeated with the dialectic. It is the very warp and woof of all his works from *Imperialism* to the *Split in the International*; from the *National Question* to *State and Revolution*; from the famous *Trade Union Debate* to his *Will*. It is in the *Will* that Lenin says he thinks Bukharin never quite grasped the dialectic and, *therefore*, cannot be considered "fully a Marxist." Thus we see that the great divide in Marxism, that set an unbridgeable gulf between the Second International, and the tendency that would become the new Third International, did not exhaust itself there. On the contrary, the new philosophic foundations already contained in germ the *next* division of Marxism. For this is the battle of reason and if one hasn't changed his *method* of thought, he can be sure to collapse at the next great crisis. The supreme example of that, during the war, was one who would become a leader of the Russian Revolution—Nikolai Bukharin. The question was that of Self-Determination of Nations on which Lenin suddenly found himself isolated even among the Bolsheviks.

Prior to World War I there was no difference among the Bolsheviks on the question of the self-determination of nations. All agreed to the liberation of nations "in principle." But where, with the outbreak of war, Lenin saw a new urgency in the question, Bukharin elaborated an entirely new thesis:

> The imperialist epoch is an epoch of the absorption of small states.... It is therefore impossible to struggle against the enslavement of nations otherwise than by struggling against imperialism ... *ergo* against *capitalism* in general. Any deviation from that road, any advancement of "partial" tasks, of the "liberation of nations" *within* the realm of capitalist civilization, means diverting of proletarian forces from the actual solution of the problem.... The slogan of "self-determination" is first of all *utopian* and *harmful* ... as a slogan which *disseminates illusions*.[1]

And, blaming the masses, he also wrote:

> The collapse of the Second International is recognized as a fact. This collapse is explained not so much by the treason of the leaders as by the objective cause of chauvinist conduct of the masses. [p. 222]

Lenin called this nothing short of "Imperialist Economism," saying it is clear Bukharin had permitted the war "to *suppress*" his thinking: "The scornful attitude of 'imperialist economism' toward *democracy* constituted one of these forms of *depression*, or *suppression*, of human reasoning by the war." [p. 223]

Lenin hit as hard against Bukharin's co-leader, Pyatakov:

> The real source of all his curious errors in logic is that his thinking *has been depressed* by the war and because of this depression the position of Marxism toward democracy in general has been basically distorted. [p. 225]

It is true, Lenin continued, that "capitalism in general and imperialism in particular transforms democracy into an illusion." But it "at the same time generates democratic tendencies among the masses...."[2] As opposed to Bukharin's

1 Quoted by O.H. Gankin and H.H. Fisher, *The Bolsheviks and the World War*, p. 219.

2 *Ibid.* p. 226. This is even more true in our epoch of state capitalism. It is this which compelled Mao Tse-Tung to try to hide his totalitarianism under the slogan, "Let a hundred flowers bloom, let a hundred schools of thought contend." In admitting the existence of contradictions in the "Peoples' Republic," he said that to do otherwise would be "to fly in the face of objective reality." That, most certainly, is true. But this precisely is the supreme manifestation of the class character of the Chinese regime. The one thing this "haughty vassal ... in the interests of state-power" (to use a Hegelian phrase) forgot is that 600,000,000 human beings will not long be bottled up in contradictions. They are sure to find their way *out of* "contradiction" to the true revolutionary solution. (For an objective analysis of Chinese economy, see: *An Economic Survey of Communist China*, by Yuan-Lu Wu, Bookman Assoc., N.Y., 1956.)

and Pyatakov's counter-posing the existence of imperialism and the non-existence of democracy, Lenin stress the *co-existence* of imperialism and the democratic tendencies among the masses.

On Easter Day, 1916, the Irish masses acted.... [Dunayevskaya here described the Irish rebellion of 1916.]

Lenin hailed the rebellion and accepted it as the real test of his thesis. In summing up the discussion on self-determination he concluded:

> The dialectics of history is such that small nations, powerless as an *independent* factor in the struggle against imperialism, play a part as one of the ferments, one of the bacilli, which help the *real* power against imperialism come on the scene, namely, the socialist proletariat.[3]
>
> To imagine that social revolution is *conceivable* without revolts by small nations in the colonies and in Europe ... means *repudiating social revolution*.[4]

Bukharin was entirely blind to the fact that the dialectics of the revolution itself was at stake in the theoretical debate. Where he was looking for some integral picture of the collapse of imperialism and capitalism, *Lenin was searching for new beginnings which would determine the end*, and he found these in two directions: (1) the struggle of national grouping for independence, and (2) the very stratification of the working class. Far from finding the working class *as a class* "chauvinist," he was searching for lower and deeper strata in it to release the creative energies of millions.

If Hegelian phraseology may be permitted, what Lenin was saying to Bukharin was that he who does not see a new "subject" emerge out of a great crisis is compelled to run to the "Absolute" (read: "Socialism") like a bolt out of the blue, instead of living through the birth-throes of an actual developing revolution or living history. Long ago Marx had castigated the "abstract materialist" for not seeing "the process of history." Now Lenin became intolerant of the "economist." The *logic* of self-determination, in theory as in fact, showed that *just when* there was the growing "internationalization," i.e., imperialist suppression, *that is when* there was also revolt. He was asking Bukharin to get away from "causality" to explain the relation between the idea and the real, and instead to be where the "notion" of freedom and subjectivity are, that is to say, the free creative power of the masses.

3 "Discussion on Self-Determination Summed Up," is part of Lenin's *Collected Works*, Vol. XIX, which contains the best material on the National Question available in English.

4 Lenin, *Selected Works*, Vol. V, p. 303.

Thus, the great divide in Marxism was not alone with those who betrayed, but with those who, in thought, are near the dialectic, but never quite make it and thus cannot be considered "fully Marxist." The slightest slip off the dialectic of revolution—that is, the strictest *relationship* of the revolutionary activity of the mass to the specific economic epoch—and the Marxist theoretician ends by anticipating the next stage of *bourgeois* development. What Bukharin only theorized about, Stalin was ruthless enough to put into effect. We shall see, when we deal with Stalin, how prophetic Lenin was when he wrote:

> The necessity of solidarity of forces against the international West which defends the capitalist world is one thing.... It is another thing when we ourselves fall into something like imperialistic relations toward the oppressed nationalities.[5]

It remains the most devastating commentary on present-day Russia.

∴

What Was New on the Party Question in the Great Divide and After: The Relationship of the Masses to the Party

Marxism and Freedom

> Actuality and thought (or the Idea) are often absurdly opposed.... Thought in such a case is, on the one hand, the synonym for a subjective conception, plan, intention or the like, just as actuality, on the other, is made synonymous with external and sensible existence....
>
> For on the one hand ideas are not confined to our heads merely, nor is the Idea, upon the whole, so feeble as to leave the question of its actualization or non-actualization dependent on our will. The Idea is rather absolutely active as well as actual. And, on the other hand, actuality is not so bad and irrational as it is supposed to be by the practical men, who are either without thought altogether or have quarreled with thought and have been worsted in the contest.—Hegel[6]

5 From the Trotsky Archives at Harvard College Library, as quoted in Richard Pipes, *The Formation of the Soviet Union, Communism and Nationalism, 1917–1923*.

6 A slight variation from this first translation appears in Wallace's second edition of *Science of Logic*, p. 258.

Prior to 1914, the contradiction in Lenin between the practicing revolutionary dialectician and the thinking Kautskyan reflects the contradiction in Russian society whose singular development from the feudal monarchy to the bourgeois monarchy was through proletarian methods of struggle. It was the extreme contradiction in the development of the Russian economy, and the manifold but *concrete* struggles of political tendencies, which prepared Lenin for the break in thought which the collapse of the Second International signified in life. As he returned to the philosophic foundations of Marx and Hegel, he went there with all this rich and contradictory experience behind him.

The break in thought, the battle of reason, now was to break up the rigidity to which Kautskyan understanding had reduced everything. Prior to 1914, Lenin had accepted a series of abstractions—party, mass, revolution. *Except for Russia,* he never contrasted these with the struggles of the revolutionary masses, even as he had previously failed to analyze the latest phase of world capitalism and had failed to see the connection of the Second International with it. It is only now that he saw that not only had capitalism changed. So had the labor organization *because* so had the labor living off the super-profits of capitalist imperialism. Now that he fully analyzed the objective reasons for the collapse of the International, he questioned the Social Democratic Party's very use of the phrase—mass organization. He denied it was a mass organization.

On a much higher, that is, more complex, historical scale, Lenin's problems and views here parallel the position of Marx in his struggle with the British trade unions whose leadership began to take flight from the First International during the Paris Commune. According to the protocol of Marin, during the September 20, 1871 conference on trade unions, Marx stated

> that the trade union represents an aristocratic minority. The poorly paid worker cannot belong to it; the great mass of workers whom the economic development daily drives from the country to the city remain outside of the trade union for a long time, and the most poverty-stricken mass does not go into it at all. The same is true of workers born (and raised) on the East End of London, among whom only one out of ten belongs to the trade union. The peasants never join these societies.
>
> Trade Unions by themselves are impotent; they remain a minority. They have no authority over the mass of the proletarians while the International shows a direct influence among these people.[7]

7 *London Conference of 1871,* pages 49–59 (Russian edition, 1936).

It is first now that Lenin "discovered" Marx's and Engels' analysis of the "bourgeoisification" of the British proletariat. Lenin first now sensed the emphasis on the need to go *"deeper and lower"* into the working class. Although the founders of modern socialism had carried on this fight all the way from 1858 to 1892 he saw it for the first time. He saw it with the eyes of one who had just gone through the collapse of the Second International. He called this, *just this,* going "deeper and lower" into the working class, *"the quintessence* of Marxism."[8]

After questioning the German Social Democracy's claim to being a proletarian mass organization, he concluded that, above all, a Marxist would have to answer: organization of proletariat *for what purpose*?

His mind working dialectically, Lenin now approaches the problem from two levels: (1) the real, and (2) the ideal springing from the real. The betrayal of the proletariat by the Second left no doubt that, far from being an ideal organization, it had become the enemy of the purpose for which it was formed—to organize the revolutionary activity of the masses. No doubt the corruption, of the Second was unavoidable under the growth of monopoly capitalism and imperialism. But having traced its objective basis, that is to say, the economic roots, his mind found it all the more necessary to see it philosophically, and to go forward from the *recognition* of the contradiction in every single thing, to its *resolution:* If the unity of opposites is not limited to the two fundamental classes in society, if the duality extends to labor itself, then one must speak out the truth—the labor party itself is *bourgeois.* It is thus necessary to *drive a wedge between the opposites in labor itself.* It was the deeper and lower layers, in *and* outside the party that would have to restore labor to its revolutionary being. The masses would do more than regain their self-activity when they finally destroyed the *bourgeois labor party.* In overcoming that barrier, the working class will finally find itself undivided against itself. Its "knowing," its consciousness, will be reunited with its "being," its creative activity. The type of party it creates would not shirk *taking power.*

What was still not clear was what type of organization the spontaneous workers' revolt would form. Lenin did not think of the Soviet. It was now January, 1917. He had long since broken with the Second International; he had called for the formation of a new, Third International. He had long since said that the only way out of the war was to turn the imperialist war into a civil war. The imperialist slaughter had now been going on for nearly three years. He did not know that he would live to see the revolution, but he was sure the youth would, and it was the Swiss youth he addressed in January, 1917, on the Russian

8 *Selected Works,* Vol. XI, *The Split in the International.*

Revolution of 1905. He singled out, not the Soviet, but the mass strike as the outstanding feature.

The following month, the February (March) Revolution broke out. In eight days, the monarchy which had maintained itself for centuries and had withstood the Revolution of 1905 was overthrown. When he heard of the February Revolution he sent his co-leaders a telegram which showed that his mind was still operating within old categories. Combine legal and illegal work, read his first telegram. The very next day, the *newness,* the truth dawned upon him, finally. The Russian workers had, *on their own,* recreated that "peculiar organization," the Soviet, and now it had spread through the length and breadth of the whole land. There were Soviets of Workers, Soviets of Soldiers, Soviets of Peasants. The Russian workers alone had remembered. Not a single theoretician—including Lenin—had thought of Soviets or told the workers to build them. The workers' own creative energies had built this alternative form of government. It continued to stand there challengingly, though the Tsar was overthrown and there was now a Provisional Democratic Government headed by Kerensky, Socialist.

Now that Lenin finally comprehended the Soviet fully he realized that he never had really seen it before, not as *the* form that would supersede the Paris Commune and become the workers' state itself.

Lenin's mind leapt forward with the surge of the spontaneous movement of the workers which revealed what Engels had long since called their "latent socialism." Lenin now wrote his colleagues from his exile as he prepared to return to Russia,

> I'm afraid that the epidemic of "sheer" enthusiasm may now spread in Petrograd, without a systematic effort towards the creation of a party of a *new* type, which must *in no way* resemble those of the *Second International.*
>
> *Never again* along the lines of the Second International!

And again:

> Our immediate problem is organization, not in the sense of affecting ordinary organization by ordinary methods, but in the sense of drawing in large masses *and* embodying in this organization, military, state, and national economic problems.[9]

9 *Collected Works,* Vol. XX, Book I, p. 55.

What was to become the famous April Thesis was taking shape. Heretofore, the break had been against Kautsky, then against Bukharin. Now, the big break was to be with *his own past.* The contradictions had been *in himself.* The workers had broken out of all old shackles and were creating a truly new way of life for millions. He must now break with all that stood in the way of this elemental surge for freedom, for peace, for bread, for land.

The first thing he did was to discard the old slogan, "the democratic dictatorship of the proletariat and peasantry." The democratic revolution, he now said, *has been completed.* An entirely new, unforeseen situation has arisen, that of a *Dual Power:* on the one hand stood the Provisional Government which was still carrying on the war; on the other, stood the Soviets themselves which wanted peace. Had the creative impulse of the Russian masses not created the Soviets, the Russian Revolution would have been hopeless. But now, with "socialism looking out of all windows," *all* politics stemmed from that. Only the Soviets could create a new order.

What was needed now was the arming of the proletariat, strengthening and broadening and developing the role *and* power of the Soviets: "All the rest is mere phrases and lies and the self-deception of politicians of the liberal and radical stamp." It was not that the workers must support the Government. It was that the Provisional Government must support the workers. "All Power to the Soviets!"

His Bolshevik colleagues, no less than the Mensheviks, thought that Lenin had come home from another planet altogether, and *Pravda* published his thesis as an "individual" viewpoint.

Where to the others it seemed as if he forgot about "the role of the party," to Lenin a vanguard party now was such *only because* in April, 1917, it represented the revolutionary masses. As he was to tell his co-leaders and his party in the next few months as he mobilized them for just this purpose of reflecting the will of the revolutionary masses, the ranks of the party are ten times more revolutionary than the leaders, and the masses *outside* are ten times more revolutionary than the ranks. He told them if they would not place the question of *workers' power* on the order of the day, he would "go to the sailors!" "I am compelled *to tender my resignation from the Central Committee* which I hereby do, reserving for myself the freedom to agitate among the rank and file of the Party and at the Party congress."[10] But he didn't have to go to that extreme before the party finally did become "the vanguard," that is to say when they finally saw that without the spontaneity, the creative energies of millions, the "masses as reason," which meant *concretely* their form of organization to have *power,* the Marxist party would indeed be nothing but an elite.

---

10 *Selected Works,* Vol. VI, p. 232.

The method of winning his party was this total concept which he now had. Not only were economics, politics and philosophy *not* three separate constituent parts. The point was that unless all, as a totality, are taken *in strict relationship to the actual class struggle, the activity of the masses themselves,* it would be nothing but "project-hatching."

The foundation was, of course, economics, and the *new,* the *concretely* new was that "Monopoly had evolved into state-monopoly." That meant that planlessness has ceased. There is no such thing, however, as "pure plan"; the *class* character of the plan must now be fought relentlessly. To the Government's Plan he counterposed "Workers' Control." Control and accounting by workers, he warned, "must not be confused with the question of a scientific educated staff of engineers and agronomists, etc." Nationalization without workers' control meant nothing:

> The workers must sweep aside high-sounding phrases, promises, declarations, projects evolved in the center by bureaucrats, who are always ready to draw up the most ostentatious plans, rules, regulations, and standards. Down with all this lying! Down with all this hullabaloo of the bureaucratic and bourgeois project-mongering that has everywhere collapsed with a crash. Down with this habit of procrastination! The workers must demand *immediate* establishment of control *in fact* to be exercised by the *workers themselves.*

The workers became the center of everything in Lenin's mind. Everything else was subordinate to it:

> I "calculate" *solely* and *exclusively* on the workers, soldiers, and peasants able to tackle better than the officials, better than the police, the *practical* and difficult problems of increasing the production of foodstuffs and their better distribution, the better provisions of soldiers, etc. etc.

Lenin now sat down to work out his theory. As he had "lived" with the *Science of Logic* in the writing of *Imperialism, so now he re-created Marx's Civil War in France, for his country and his epoch, as State and Revolution.* Basing himself on Marx's concept that "centralized state power, with its ubiquitous organs of standing army, police, bureaucracy, clergy and judicature—are organs wrought after the plan of a systematic and hierarchic division of labor,"[11] Lenin now saw that the need of his time was *to destroy bureaucratism.* There is no other way to wither away The State. Even the workers' State cannot wither away *unless* the

11 *Civil War in France,* (included in Marx's *Selected Works,* Vol. II, p. 495).

workers, "organized as the ruling class," *are* to become the basis for the end of all class rule. That now became the key to his theory and his practice. It was a new organization of thought in the true Hegelian-Marxian manner.

In his book, Lenin writes against Kautsky's conceptions, *not* only in the period when he became a traitor to the workers' cause, *but when he was the established Marxist theoretician.* He explains that even in his most "revolutionary" works, *Social Revolution,* and *The Road to Power,* Kautsky had developed ideas that "certain enterprises cannot do without a bureaucratic organization," and even Marxists could not do "without officials in the Party and the trade unions."

This, Lenin now says, "is the *essence* of bureaucracy and until the capitalists are expropriated *even* proletarian officials will be bureaucratized to some extent." For Lenin, democracy under capitalism is mutilated by wage slavery. "This is why, and the only reason why.... This is the essence of bureaucracy." The only way to have genuine democracy is to have proletarian democracy, to suppress bureaucracy and give all powers to the workers.

That is why it is important to establish from the start "immediate introduction of control and superintendence by *all* so that *all* shall become 'bureaucrats.'" The essence of a commune-type of government is that "the *mass* of the population will rise to *independent* participation, not only in voting and elections, *but also in the everyday administration of affairs."*

The population *"to a man"* must manage production and the state. That is the Ideal which must become the reality.

There have been self-avowed Marxists whose own narrow vision led them to the conclusion that Lenin's *State and Revolution* was "nothing but a re-write" of Marx's *Civil War in France.* They fail to see that "to re-write" *Civil War in France,* on the eve of a Revolution in Russia, is a creative act. It meant cleansing the concept of superseding the bourgeois State of its Second Internationalist perversion, which was not a literary perversion but a perversion of a working class movement and aspiration. In counterposition, Lenin put his theoretical emphasis on the concept of all, "to a man" to run their own lives. *"No police, no army, no officialdom. Every* worker, *every* peasant, *every* toiler, *everyone* who is exploited, the whole population to a man."

That was Lenin's vision and that is what he aimed at in practice. The masses, to Lenin, were not a "means" to reach an "end," socialism. Their self-activity *is* socialism. All of this sharpened sense of self-movement as the inner core of the dialectic: all of this sharpened sense of the opposition of dialectics to eclectics as the central philosophic concept of revolution was, of course, not a "study" of past revolutions. It was the preparation for the coming one in Russia. As Lenin approached the section of the book which was to deal with the Russian scene, the actual November Revolution broke out. Such an "interruption," he wrote in the Postscript to the unfinished *State and Revolution,* "can only be welcomed." And, having led the first proletarian revolution to victory, Lenin addressed the Congress of Soviets on January 24, 1918:

> In introducing workers' control we knew it would take some time before it spread to the whole of Russia, but we wanted to show that we recognized only one road—changes from below; we wanted the workers themselves to draw up, from below, the new principle of economic conditions.[12]

The greatest test of all was now at hand: practice.

∴

The Shock of Recognition and the Philosophic Ambivalence of Lenin

Philosophy and Revolution

... Lenin was fighting not only the betrayers, but also Menshevik internationalists and Rosa Luxemburg and "the Dutch" (Pannekoek, Roland-Holst, Gorter) *and* the Bolsheviks abroad. And he had to do it on a subject upon which the Bolsheviks previously had agreed "in *principle*"—self-determination of nations. Furthermore, it had begun with the economic subject of imperialism, and he had just appended his signature to the Introduction of Bukharin's work on the subject. Why did he then embark on his own study?

It is ironic indeed that the very philosophers who try to confine Lenin to "economics," "the philosopher of the concrete," do not bother at all to grapple with the Leninist *methodology*[13] of these "concretes," Imperialism, Self-Determination of Nations. It is to these subjects we must turn also to illuminate the new dialectic appreciation of Marx's *Capital,* not just as economics, but as logic—defining the work now as, "The history of capitalism and the analysis of the *notions* summing it up."[14]

Empiricists who have no method are incapable of recognizing method in others. To this day they consider all the "Marxist" economic analyses of

---

12 Lenin, *Selected Works,* Vol. VII, p. 277.

13 See my 1951 answer to the Trotskyist analysis of that subject, "The Revolt of the Workers and the Plan of the Intellectuals," in the Raya Dunayevskaya Collection.

14 Vol. 38, p. 318.

imperialism so similar that they deem the dispute on national self-determination that was going on during the same period as "only political." In truth, the very first thing that Lenin's *Notebooks on Imperialism*[15] (begun directly after completion of his *Philosophic Notebooks*) discloses is that it is by no means limited to the economic study of the latest phase of capitalist development, but includes also the outline of articles on the war itself, on the National Question—and on "Marxism and the State," which later became *State and Revolution.*

Even when one looks only at the "strictly economic" as published by itself in *1916—Imperialism, A Popular Outline*—the methodologies of Lenin's and Bukharin's works show that they are poles apart. Thus, as opposed to Bukharin's concept of capitalist growth in a straight line, or via a quantitative ratio, Lenin's own work holds on tightly to the dialectical principle, "transformation into opposite." The key point in tracing the *subject's* self-development instead of an "objective" mathematical growth is that you thus see the simultaneity of the transformation into opposite, of competitive capitalism into monopoly, *and* part of labor into an "aristocracy of labor." Above all, you become conscious that this is but the "first negative." The development through *this* contradiction compels finding the "second negative," or as Marx expressed it, going "lower and deeper" into the masses to find the *new* revolutionary strata.

Thus, Lenin held that *just when* capitalism had reached this high stage of "organization," monopoly (which extended itself into imperialism), was the time to see new, national revolutionary forces that would act as "bacilli" for proletarian revolutions as well.[16] Where Lenin saw in the stage of imperialism a new urgency for the slogan of national self-determination, Bukharin vehemently opposed the slogan as both "impossible of achievement" and "reactionary." Nothing short of a *direct* road to socialist revolution would do for him. This plunge to abstract revolutionism in place of working with the concretely developing revolutionary forces, which Hegel would have considered a manifestation of jumping to the "absolute like a shot out of a pistol," and which politicos called "ultra-leftism," Lenin called nothing short of "imperialist economism."[17]

---

15 Lenin's notes on Hegel's *Phenomenology of Mind* never appeared, but the *Notebooks on Imperialism* show that he read it while he was preparing the pamphlet on Imperialism. The *Notebooks* are a massive 739 pages as against the short pamphlet that was actually published.

16 *Collected Works,* Vol. 19, p. 303. This volume contains major writings on National Self-Determination.

17 Gankin and Fisher, *The Bolsheviks and the World War,* quote also Bukharin's theses (see especially pp. 219–223). But the latest and one of the finest discussions on the battle against national chauvinism during the period after the Bolsheviks gained power is to be found in Moshe Lewin's *Lenin's Last Struggle.*

On the surface that designation sounds absolutely fantastic since it is directed against a Bolshevik co-leader. Since, however, Lenin continued to use it against Bukharin and against all revolutionaries, including "the Dutch" (whom he in the same breath characterized as the "best revolutionary and most internationalist element of international Social Democracy"), we must here probe deeper into the dispute.

Long before Lenin's final battle with Stalin, whom he accused of "Great Russian Chauvinism" and for whose removal he asked from the post of General Secretary,[18] Lenin became uncompromising in his struggles with Bolsheviks. His point was that the right of self-determination was *not only* a "principle" (to which all Bolsheviks agreed), but "the dialectic of history," a force of revolution which would be the catalyst for socialism:

> The dialectics of history is such that small nations, powerless as an *independent* factor in the struggle against imperialism, play a part as one of the ferments, one of the bacilli, which help the *real* power against imperialism to come on the scene, namely, the socialist proletariat.[19]

That little word, dialectic, kept springing up also because Lenin recognized an old enemy, "Economism," which never understood the mass revolutionary struggle. All revolutionaries had fought Economism when it first appeared in Russia in 1902. It had then been easy to recognize as the enemy because the Economists openly tried to circumscribe the activities of workers, limiting these to economic battles, on the ground that since capitalism was "inevitable," "therefore" political battles were to be left to the liberal bourgeoisie. But here they were in 1914, in an imperialist war, and revolutionaries were rejecting the national struggles of colonial and oppressed peoples on the ground that self-determination was "impossible" of achievement and "therefore," as Bukharin put it, "utopian and reactionary," and would only "divert" from the struggle for "world revolution."

---

18 Lenin's *Will* was first published by Trotsky in 1935, as *The Suppressed Testament of Lenin* (Pioneer Publishers). Khrushchev quoted it for the first time in his famous 1956 De-Stalinization Speech. In 1966 it finally appeared in Lenin's *Collected Works,* Vol. 36, pp. 593–611, where it was titled "Letter to the Congress." The new volume contains a great deal more than just the *Will.* It includes the final battles of Lenin with Stalin on the Nationalities Question and on "Autonomization," i.e., the structure of the state. There is also a difference in translations.

19 *Collected Works,* Vol. 19, p. 303.

This super-internationalism, as far as Lenin was concerned, only proved that the World War had "suppressed reason," blinding even revolutionaries to the fact that "All national oppression calls for the resistance of the broad masses of people...."[20] Not even the great Irish Rebellion changed the abstract revolutionism of these internationalists who were busy looking at "imperialist economy" instead of the self-mobilization of masses. Lenin fought them, branded their thinking as "imperialist economism," *not* because they were not "for" revolution, but because they were so undialectical that they did not see that out of the very throes of imperialist oppression a new revolutionary force was born which would act as a catalyst for proletarian revolution.

Dialectics, that "algebra of revolution,"[21] has been on many great adventures since Hegel created it out of the action of the French masses and thereby revolutionized metaphysics. What had been, in Hegel, a revolution *in* philosophy, became, with Marx, a philosophy *of* revolution, a totally new theory of liberation—the proletarian revolutions of 1848 culminating in the Paris Commune of 1871. Lenin's rediscovery of dialectics, of self-activity, of Subject versus Substance at the very moment of the collapse of the Second International, simultaneously disclosed the appearance of counter-revolution from *within* the Marxist movements and the new forces of revolution in the national movements. Moreover, these new forces were present not only in Europe, but throughout the world as well. What Lenin's economic study of imperialism revealed was that capitalism had gorged itself on more than a half billion people in Africa and Asia. This was to become a totally new theoretic departure *after* the Bolshevik conquest of power, expressed as the Thesis on the National and Colonial Question presented to the Third International in 1920. Even while the holocaust was most intense and Lenin stood alone, he refused to retreat an inch to abstract internationalism. The outbreak of the Easter Rebellion in 1916, while proletarians were still slaughtering each other, showed the correctness of his position on the self-determination of nations.

In 1914–15 Lenin turned to the study of Hegel, the "bourgeois idealist philosopher." Whatever the reason, it certainly was not in order to discover the driving forces of revolution. Yet Hegelian dialectics was more useful in making sense out of the action of the masses' taking fate into their own hands in Ireland in 1916 than the debates on the National Question with his Bolshevik colleagues.[22]

---

20 *Ibid.*, p. 248.

21 *Alexander Herzen, Selected Philosophical Works* (Moscow, 1960), p. 524.

22 "I do not attribute significance to the desire to hold onto the word, 'Bolshevism,'" Lenin wrote in his reply to Bukharin, "for I know some 'old Bolsheviks' from whom may God preserve me" (Gankin and Fisher, *The Bolsheviks and the World War*, p. 235).

In 1917 the opposition to national self-determination should have ended. In fact, it only took on a new form. This time Bukharin contended that it was no longer possible to admit the right of self-determination since Russia was now a workers' state, whereas nationalism meant bourgeois and proletarian together, and "therefore" a step backward. In his admission that in some cases he would be for it, he listed the "Hottentots, the Bushman, and the Indians." To which Lenin replied:

> Hearing this enumeration I thought, how is it that Comrade Bukharin had forgotten a small trifle, the Bashkirs? There are no Bushmen in Russia, nor have I heard that the Hottentots have laid claim to an autonomous republic, but we have Bashkirs, Kirghiz.... We cannot deny it to a single one of the peoples living within the boundaries of the former Russian Empire.[23]

---

23 Lenin, *Selected Works* (New York: International, 1943), Vol. VIII, p. 342. The whole of Part IV, "The Party Program (1918–19)," is very valuable for the theoretic points in dispute, and has the advantage of being cast more in a theoretical frame than the factional bite of the Trade Union Dispute, which can be found in Vol. IX.

CHAPTER 4

On Trotsky

As noted in the Introduction, Dunayevskaya (Rae Spiegel) had been one of Leon Trotsky's secretaries during his exile in Mexico. She wrote numerous times on Trotsky and Trotskyism. Her most comprehensive analyses include "Leon Trotsky as Theoretician," Chapter 4 of Philosophy and Revolution, *and "Trotsky's Theory of Permanent Revolution," Afterword to Chapter 11 of* Rosa Luxemburg, Women's Liberation, and Marx's Philosophy of Revolution. *Below is her essay "Leon Trotsky as Man and as Theoretician." Included is an exchange with the Trotskyist theoretician Ernest Mandel.*

Leon Trotsky as Man and as Theoretician

Studies in Comparative Communism Vol. X, Nos. 1 & 2, with a Comment by Ernest Mandel

Leon Trotsky at no time let subjectivism enter into an analysis of a situation, whether he was a creator of that situation or its victim. Because of the high tragedy of Trotsky's murder at the hands of an NKVD assassin who drove a pick-axe into the skull of the "Man of October"—so called because the day of his birth coincided with the date of the successful Bolshevik Revolution, October 25—the last years of his life seem to have provided a field day for psychological approaches even on the part of political analysts.[1] The reason the present study is of Trotsky As Man and As Theoretician is not to add to the myriad writings about him which claim "subjectivism." By relating his behavior during the crucial period of the Moscow Trials, when all the "General Staff" of the Revolution was killed off by Stalin, and Trotsky himself was accused of the most heinous

1 Isaac Deutscher's massive three-volume biography of Trotsky notwithstanding, there is yet to appear an objective biography worthy of the man and his times. This is no place to review *The Prophet Armed, The Prophet Unarmed,* and *The Prophet Outcast,* but two matters cannot be left unsaid. One concerns Deutscher's many adjectives in praise of Trotsky, but he ends with a Stalinist apologia: "By a feat of history's irony, Stalinism itself *malgré lui* broke out of its national shell" (Vol. III, p. 516). The second and truly damning point is that the last volume is devoted to the worst and pettiest type of gossip, with hardly a whiff of the life Trotsky lived: Trotsky the founder of the Fourth International, devoting his life to the Trotskyist parties at the expense of all else, is submerged by Trotsky the faithful lover of Natalia.

crimes, I hope, instead, to clear the air of such trite characterizations as "great egotist," "dictatorial and exacting," "arrogant and conceited." The inadequacies of his theories, unrooted as they are in philosophy, are far too deep to sink into such subjectivism.

In these *Gulag Archipelago* publicity days it may seem unnecessary to talk of such truisms as Stalin's monolithism, the nightmarish terror of Lubyanka and torture. But the Gulag Archipelago is both 37 years beyond the period which I'm describing, and it, too, is neither the whole truth nor objective history. It is necessary, instead, to return to the year 1937, when a lonely exile of the heroic mold of the former Commissar of War is suddenly confronted with the results of the whole decade of Stalin's victory over Trotsky; when Russia uses its state power, its Army, its brutality, its total disregard for history to fabricate the greatest frame-up in all of history; and when it is only through the sympathy of President Cardenas of Mexico that the Mexican press does hold open two columns of space for a few hours of time for Trotsky to answer the charges that it took the Stalinist bureaucracy a decade to fabricate.

Trotsky didn't know either what the accusation would be, or the year he was alleged to have done this or that. Moreover, the Trials had come at a time of the greatest personal grief in the Trotsky family, for the long arm of the GPU had reached out to kill the only living son of Trotsky, Leon Sedov. It was a predetermined, insidiously planned feat of a master intrigant, calculated to give Trotsky the blow that Stalin hoped would render him incapable of answering the accusations against himself. The lapse between the two events was but two short weeks.

The death of Leon Sedov did indeed inflict the deepest wound, and in the most vulnerable spot. Lev Davidovich and Natalia Ivanovna locked themselves in their room and would see no one. For a whole week they did not come out of their room, and only one person was permitted in—the one who brought them the mail, and food, of which they partook little.

Those were dismal days for the whole household. We did not see either L.D. or Natalia. We did not know how they fared, and feared the consequences of the tragedy upon them. We moved typewriters, the telephone, and even doorbells to the guard house, out of sound of their room. Their part of the house became deathly quiet. There was an oppressive air, as if the whole mountain chain of Mexico were pressing down upon this house.

The blow was the harder not only because Leon Sedov had been their only remaining living child, but also and especially because he had been Trotsky's closest literary and political collaborator. When Trotsky was interned in Norway, gagged, unable to answer the monstrous charges levelled against him in the First Moscow Trials (August 1936), Sedov had penned *Le Livre Rouge*, which, by brilliantly exposing the Moscow falsifiers, dealt an irreparable blow to the prestige of the GPU.

In the dark days after the tragic news had reached us, when L.D. and Natalia Ivanovna were closeted in their room, Trotsky wrote the story of their son's brief life. It was the first time since pre-revolutionary days that Trotsky had written by hand.

On the eighth day, Leon Trotsky emerged from his room. I was petrified at the sight of him. The neat, meticulous Leon Trotsky had not shaved for a whole week. His face was deeply lined. His eyes were swollen from too much crying. Without uttering a word, he handed me the handwritten manuscript, *Leon Sedov, Son, Friend, Fighter*, which contained some of Trotsky's most poignant writing.

One passage read: "I told Natalia of the death of our son—in the same month of February in which, 32 years ago, she brought to me in jail the news of his birth. Thus ended for us the day of February 16, the blackest day in our personal lives... Together with our boy has died everything that still remained young within us..."

The very next morning, the morning papers carried the announcement of the Third Moscow Trials (March 1938).

Trotsky labored late into the night. One day he was up at 7 a.m., and wrote until midnight. The next day he arose at 8 a.m. and worked straight through to 3 a.m. the following morning. The last day of that week, he did not go to sleep until 5 in the morning. He drove himself harder than any of his staff.

Leon Trotsky wrote an average of 2,000 words a day. He gave statements to the North American Newspaper Alliance, the UP, the AP, Havas Agency, France, the London *Daily Express*, and to the Mexican newspapers. His declarations were also issued in the Russian and German languages.

The material was dictated in Russian. While I transcribed the dictation, the other secretaries checked every date, name, and place mentioned at the Moscow Trials. Trotsky demanded meticulous, objective research work, for the accusers had to be turned into the accused.

So unused to subjectivism was this revolutionary that, at the very moment of the Moscow Trials, he was deeply incensed when the papers printed "rumors" that Stalin had at no time been a revolutionist but had always been an agent of the Tsar and was now merely wreaking vengeance.

When I brought L.D. the newspapers that carried this explanation of the blood purge, he exclaimed, "But Stalin was a revolutionist!"

"Wait a moment," he called to me as I was leaving the room, "We'll add a postscript to today's article." He dictated:

> The news has been widely spread through the press to the effect that Stalin supposedly was an *agent-provocateur* during Tsarist days, and that he is now avenging himself upon his old enemies. I place no trust whatsoever in this gossip. From his youth Stalin was a revolutionist. All the facts about his life bear witness to this. To reconstruct his biography *ex post facto* means to ape the present bureaucracy.

No, Trotsky was not guilty of any subjectivism. This does not mean he did not suffer from theoretical deficiencies, but these stemmed not from any subjectivism, a failure to be "dispassionate." Rather, the analysis of the *objective* situation, including *objectively grounded reason* of the proletarian forces of revolution, was without philosophic roots, and thereby lacked a unifying objective-subjective vision. Since all of Marx's revolutionary theories flowed dialectically from his philosophy of liberation, and since the first appearance of Revisionism in Marxian theory (Bernstein) by no accident arose with the demand to have done with "Hegel's dialectic scaffolding" and to return to "facts"—Bernstein's demands—revolutionary Marxists felt the strong need to reassert their "allegiance" to dialectics and rejection of "Kantianism." Insofar as not being guilty of any departure from the class struggle, or being guilty of a concept of the dependence on "men of good will" to resolve class contradictions, this certainly held true of Trotsky the revolutionary. Unfortunately, this did not lead to deep digging into the philosophic origins of Marxism in the Hegelian dialectic. It is here, and not in subjectivism, where dualism emerged in Trotsky's theory at its highest point of development—his most original theory, the Permanent Revolution.

I The Permanent Revolution and "Conciliationism"

> It will always remain a matter for astonishment how the Kantian philosophy knew that relation of thought to sensuous existence, where it halted for a merely relative relation of bare appearance and fully acknowledged and asserted a higher unity of the two in the Idea ... but stopped dead ... so that it affirmed as true what it pronounced to be finite knowledge, and declared to be superfluous and improper figments of thought that which it recognized as truth, and of which it established the definite notion.
>
> HEGEL, *Science of Logic*, Vol. II, p. 226.

Surely no more brilliant prognostication has ever been made of an historic event. When no Marxist, let alone other theoreticians, projected for Tsarist Russia anything but a "bourgeois democratic revolution," Trotsky—at the time he was a young man of 26, and already the head of the St. Petersburg Soviet of 1905—elaborated a theory which stated that the revolution in Russia would continue "in permanence," that is, go over from the bourgeois to the proletarian or socialist stage. Here are the main theses as Trotsky wrote them:

> In a country economically more backward the proletariat may come to power sooner than in a country capitalistically advanced... Marxism is above all a method of analysis—not an analysis of texts, but an analysis of social relations...
>
> We have shown above that the objective premises of socialist revolution have already been created by the economic development of the advanced capitalist countries...
>
> It is the purpose of every Socialist party to revolutionize the minds of the working class in the same way as development of capitalism has revolutionized social relations... The colossal influence of the Russian revolution manifests itself in killing party routines, in destroying Socialist conservatism, in making a clean contest of proletarian forces against capitalist reaction a question of the day...[2]

Despite the sweeping prediction made with Parvus[3] in 1904 and elaborated into the specifically Trotskyist theory, 1905–6, the theory underwent no "suffering, seriousness, patience, labor of the negative,"[4] that is to say, was not fleshed out either as to the actually developing forces for revolution or deepening of theory to meet the new reality. It was still-born throughout the period 1906–1917, as well as after Lenin's death when Trotsky began claiming it was "proved." It remained like a bolt out of the blue, not only when it was written, not only in the period between the 1905 and 1917 Revolutions, but also in the period of actual workers' power.

---

2 See Leon Trotsky's *Our Revolution* (New York: Henry Holt and Co., 1918). Also see *The Permanent Revolution* (New York: Pioneer Publishers, 1931) and "Historic References on the Theory of Permanent Revolution," which is Appendix Three to Vol. II of *The History of the Russian Revolution* (New York: Simon and Schuster, 1937).

3 For a biography on the life of Parvus as well as his role in the elaboration of the theory of permanent revolution, see *The Merchant of Revolution* by Z.A.B. Zeman and W.B. Scharlau (London: Oxford University Press, 1965). Also see Deutscher's *The Prophet Armed* (New York: Oxford University Press, 1954), p. 104, ff.

4 G.W.F. Hegel, *The Phenomenology of Mind*, trans. by J.B. Baillie (London: George Allen & Unwin, 1931), p. 81.

Above all—and that is the most telling and authentic manifestation of its failure to undergo objective-subjective dialectical development, that is, meet the challenge of new times and new problems—the theory of permanent revolution was never used as foundation for the establishment of an independent political tendency, grouping or party. That was true when Trotsky was a Menshevik, when he considered himself "above" all "factions," and tried to "unify" all tendencies, when he became a Bolshevik in 1917, and even when he finally did call for the creation of a new Fourth International against the Stalinized Third International. When he lost out to Stalin the struggle for the mantle of Lenin, and wrote *My Life* on the island of Prinkipo, he said:

> Finally, I never endeavored to create a grouping on the basis of the theory of the permanent revolution. My inner-party stand was a conciliatory one and when in certain moments I strove for groupings, then it was precisely on this basis. My conciliationism was derived from a certain Social Revolutionary fatalism. I believed that the logic of the class struggle would compel both factions to pursue the same revolutionary line...[5]

He quoted and accepted Lenin's characterization: "Conciliationism was represented most consistently by Trotsky, who, almost alone, endeavored to lay a theoretical foundation for this current."[6]

Was the dualism then only between the decisive, "correct" theory and "derivative," "organizational" questions? Didn't it rather characterize the theory of revolution? Lenin's remarks on conciliationism were limited to the organizational question, were written before World War I, while the pivotal, objective, shocking, all-determining question became philosophic: why did the Second International collapse at the very moment when the imperialist war broke out? The simultaneity of the two events could not be answered only by pointing to the all-too-obvious betrayal of established Socialism. They demanded a re-examination of the very mode of thought which led those who did *not* betray not to have anticipated such a development, much less prepare in a totally new way *now* (1914) "to meet destiny," that is, to assure the transformation of the imperialist war into a civil war.

Or so Lenin, who felt a compulsion to return to the origins of Marxism in the Hegelian dialectic, thought. As not only the *Abstract of Hegel's Science of Logic*[7] but all that he wrote and did between 1914–1924 showed, Lenin had singled

5 Leon Trotsky, *The Permanent Revolution*, p. 20.

6 V.I. Lenin, *Selected Works*, Vol. IV (New York: International Publishers, 1943), p. 93.

7 I was the first to translate this into English and it appears as Appendix B to *Marxism and Freedom*, first edition (New York: Bookman, 1958). In 1961 it finally appeared in "official"

out two dialectical principles—"transformation into opposite," and "Cognition not only reflects the world but creates it"—to theoretically prepare himself for revolution as he worked out a new relationship of the movement from theory to the movement from practice, the experiences of the masses. This is not the place to deal with what I consider the Great Divide in Marxism[8]—Lenin's break not only with the Second International but with his own philosophic past and philosophic preparation for both the Russian Revolution and the world revolution, to enlist "all the toilers to a man in the government of the state" since "socialism cannot be introduced by a minority, a party."[9]

Here what is of concern are the consequences of Trotsky's failure to do any re-examination, *or* application for that matter, of his theory of permanent revolution. This was so in 1914–17, and 1917–24. In 1919 (and again in 1923) when his *Collected Works* began being published in Russia, and *1905*, which included of course the theory of permanent revolution, was reproduced, the volume also included his wild 1909 attack on Bolshevism: "While the anti-revolutionary aspects of Menshevism are already expressed in full force today, the anti-revolutionary features of Bolshevism threaten to be of great danger only in the event of revolutionary victory." This was footnoted as follows: "As is known, this didn't take place for Bolshevism, which under the leadership of Lenin (though not without internal struggle) accomplished ideological re-armament in this most important question in Spring of 1917, that is, before the seizure of power."[10]

It is true that except for Lenin, the Bolsheviks were found wanting on the question of putting the struggle for proletarian power on the order of the day in October, that Lenin had to "re-arm" the Party and did so from the moment he returned to Russia in April, 1917. It is not true that Trotsky's theory of permanent revolution was "proven correct" or that the rearming was "belated" because Lenin was not armed with the theory of permanent revolution. What Lenin was "armed" with, and Trotsky was not, was having faced the reality of 1914 with a totally new concept of Hegelian dialectics as self-developing "Subject." Naturally Lenin at once "translated" Subject as the masses—proletarian and peasant.

---

translation as "Conspectus of Hegel's Book The Science of Logic" in Lenin's *Collected Works*, Vol. 38, pp. 85–238.

8 Elsewhere I have developed this fully. See Ch. 3, "The Shock of Recognition and the Philosophic Ambivalence of Lenin," in *Philosophy and Revolution* (New York: Dell, 1973) pp. 95–120.

9 V.I. Lenin, *Selected Works*, Vol. VIII, p. 320.

10 Leon Trotsky, *Collected Works*, Vol. I, "War and Revolution," second Russian edition, Moscow, 1923.

Where Lenin called for "transformation of the imperialist war into a civil war," Trotsky called for "a struggle for peace," "peace without annexations." Where Lenin called for the approval by name of Liebknecht who alone voted against granting war credits to the Kaiser, Trotsky led the "internationalists" at Zimmerwald to reject that as "a personification of tactical evaluations, conformable to German conditions alone" as "inappropriate in the given documents." And where to Lenin "self-development of the Idea" imparted a new urgency to the "principle" of self-determination of nations by the "dialectic of history" which makes is possible for small nations to become "the bacilli" for proletarian revolution, Trotsky concentrated his fire on calling for an "end to circle exclusiveness," "factional insulation."

Now, even if we were willing to "skip over" the differing theories as to how to fight against the imperialist war as not necessarily related to any preconceived theories of revolution, and held that what counts is 1917 and 1917 alone, how does that "prove" Trotsky's conclusion that the November Revolution "liquidated" all differences between him and Lenin?

Much later he was to claim "correctness" for his theory, not only as it concerned Russia, 1917, but China, 1927: "The conception of the permanent revolution was confirmed once more, this time not in the form of a victory, but of a catastrophe."[11] The defeat of the 1925–27 Chinese Revolution by Chiang Kai-shek's counter-revolution was related to Stalin's mistakes vs. Trotsky's "correct" estimation of the peasantry as incapable of "an independent role and even less a leading one." This integrality of the lowly role of the peasantry in his concept of the theory of the permanent revolution was so all-pervasive that as late as 1937 Trotsky continued laughing at Mao's claim of having established peasant Soviets.

Up to the very end (1940) he reiterated: "I repeatedly returned to the development and the grounding theory of the permanent revolution...the peasantry is utterly incapable of an *independent* political role."[12] We cannot but conclude that it is not only a question that Trotsky's words speak louder than any of

---

11 Leon Trotsky's Preface to the original 1938 edition of Harold Isaacs' *The Tragedy of the Chinese Revolution.* Mr. Isaacs, who eliminated this from subsequent editions, also took liberties with later editions of his own work.

12 Leon Trotsky, *Stalin,* (New York: Harper & Bros., 1941), p. 425. For that matter, directly in *The History of the Russian Revolution* and directly after Trotsky himself shows that the Land Committees were being transformed "from chambers of conciliation into weapons of agrarian revolution," he still repeats "This fact that the peasantry as a whole found it possible once more—for the last time in their history—to act as a revolutionary factor testifies at once to the weakness of the capitalist relations in the country and to their strength," Vol. 1, p. 407.

Stalin's allegations about Trotsky's "underestimation of the peasantry," but, above all, that a theory so far removed from the realities of the age of imperialism and state-capitalism had to collapse of its own hollowness.[13]

Dialectics takes its own toll of theory and theoreticians: the dualism in the theory of permanent revolution resides not alone in the artificially impenetrable division between proletariat and peasantry, nor between theory and organizational "conciliationism," but in uniting at one moment what the previous moment had been declared impossible of unification. At the same time, the lack of a dialectical unifying force is best seen within the theory, precisely on the level which gave it the greatest authority—world revolution vs. nationalism. I'm not here referring to the struggle against Stalin's concept of "socialism in one country," but to the National Question *within* the context of the U.S.S.R.-to-be-created as outpost of world revolution which totally preoccupied Lenin on his deathbed.

Clearly, by now "conciliationism" was not the issue. Quite the contrary, Lenin had called Trotsky "the best Bolshevik," and Trotsky himself, now that he accepted the 1903 concept of the vanguard party, did so without any of the modifications Lenin had introduced through the two decades 1903–23.[14] It had become a veritable fetish. Moreover, Lenin had fully entrusted him to conduct the fight against Stalin who acted the Great Russian chauvinist against the Georgians. Lenin was too ill to appear at the Congress and Trotsky was asked to act out for him, as Lenin put it:

> I am declaring war against Russian chauvinism ... It is said we need a single apparatus. From where comes such assertions? Is it not from the same Russian apparatus...borrowed from Tsarism and only barely anointed with a Soviet chrism?[15]

To Lenin, the National Question was inseparable from internationalism, from proletarian internationalism, and what he was writhing in agony about was that now that the Communists were in power, they were acting as imperialists:

---

13 See the *Raya Dunayevskaya Collection* at the Wayne State University Library of Labor History and Urban Affairs, Detroit, Michigan. [Available on the internet at rayadunayevskaya.org].

14 *Marxism and Freedom*, Ch. XI, "Forms of Organization: The Relationship of the Spontaneous Self-Organization of the Proletariat to the 'Vanguard Party,'" pp. 177–193.

15 The latest edition of Lenin's *Collected Works*, Vol. 45, as well as Vol. 36, finally have reproduced both the *Will* and the disputes on the National Question. The original information and reproduction of these documents were first published by Trotsky in *The Stalin School of Falsification* (New York: Pioneer Publishers, 1937).

"scratch a Communist and you'll find a Great Russian chauvinist." This bomb he was going to release against Stalin, and indeed it formed the very ground for which, in his *Will*, he was to ask for "the removal of Stalin," once again ended in "conciliationism," that which Lenin feared and warned against most—"a rotten compromise." Here is Trotsky's explanation:

> I do agree with Lenin in substance. I want a radical change in the policy on the national question, a discontinuance of persecutions of the Georgian opponents of Stalin... The last thing I want is to start a fight at the congress for any changes in organization. I am for preserving the status quo ... I am against removing Stalin... There should be no more intrigues, but honest co-operation.[16]

Whether that fatal compromise was bound in part, as Professor Lewin holds, by "magnanimity,"[17] or was the inescapable result of the dualism in theory not grounded in philosophy, will be put to the severest test at the time of the Hitler-Stalin Pact after "Trotskyism" reached its peak both in the proclamation for world revolution and the establishment of the Fourth International, and yet also clung to the defense of Stalin's Russia as a workers' state! Thus had Trotsky, who proclaimed the "higher truth" to be world revolution, stopped dead, as Kant had on a different level, at bare appearance—the very "socialism in one country" he fought so bitterly and correctly for two long decades.

II The Fourth International and Leadership, Leadership, Leadership

Whether Trotsky could not or did not wish to fathom the phenomenon of the workers' state being transformed into its opposite—a state-capitalist society[18] —the point is that his theory, unrooted as it was in philosophy, had him face reality stuck in the fixed particular of nationalized property, as if that equaled socialism. In any case, he denied the fact. Yet, clearly, just as everything had changed in the private capitalist world once the Depression caused its collapse and it had to accept state intervention, state planning (be it in the form of the so-called "combined development" as New Dealism or as total statism as in Nazi Germany), so had it in Stalin's Russia. Though he himself entitled his most comprehensive economic analysis of Russia *The Revolution Betrayed*; though

16 Leon Trotsky, *My Life* (New York: Charles Scribner's Sons, 1931), pp. 485–486.

17 Moshe Lewin, *Lenin's Last Struggle* (New York: Vintage, 1970), pp. 140–141.

18 I was the first to analyze the three Five Year Plans in my study of state capitalism in *The New International*, 1942, This series of articles has since been reproduced as *Russia as State-Capitalist Society* (Detroit: News & Letters, 1973).

he knew of the most oppressive conditions of labor, including forced labor; though he had written against Stalin's fantastic scheme of "liquidating" the peasantry; though he fought the Moscow Trials, 1936–38,[19] which had decapitated the whole "General Staff of the Revolution" as the greatest frame-up trials in all history; and though with a non-existent "socialism in one country" and existing Big Power politics, Stalin had reduced the Third International to nothing but outposts of defense of *national* Bolshevism, still Trotsky denied any change in the class structure of Russia. He denied the very theory: "The first concentration of the means of production in the hands of the state to occur in history was achieved by the proletariat with the method of social revolution, and not by capitalists with the method of trustification."[20] The role of the totalitarian bureaucracy was defined as that of policeman arrogating to himself a greater share of wealth.

And because to Trotsky Stalinist Russia was still considered to be a workers' state, he held that the Moscow Trials had weakened Stalinism. Actually, they consolidated that rule. But to Trotsky the macabre Kremlin purges only proved that "Soviet society organically tends toward the ejection of the bureaucracy"! Like all fetishisms, the fetishism of state property blinded Trotsky from following the course of the counter-revolution in the relations of production. The legitimization of the counter-revolution against October—the Stalinist Constitution of 1936—Trotsky viewed merely as something that first "created the political premise for the birth of a new possessing class." As if classes were born from political premises!

The struggle against Stalinism had the air of self-defense, not because he was subjective, but because, *objectively*, he saw nothing totally new in world capitalist development except that it continued to be in "death agony." Nothing had changed since Lenin's death except leadership. Stalin was the "organizer of defeats"—and he, Trotsky, could organize victories, if the proletariat followed him. This is not meant sarcastically. He certainly was a leader of the only victorious proletarian revolution in history. Whether as Chairman of the Military Revolutionary Committee, which had planned the actual insurrection, builder of a Red Army out of raw peasant recruits that withstood all counter-revolutionary attacks from Tsarist generals as well as all foreign militarists who

---

19 See *The Case of Leon Trotsky* (New York: Harper & Bros., 1937) and *Not Guilty: Report of the Commission of Inquiry into the Charges Made Against Leon Trotsky in the Moscow Trials* (New York: Harper & Bros., 1938).

20 Leon Trotsky, *The Revolution Betrayed* (Garden City: Doubleday, Doran & Co., 1937), pp. 247–248.

attacked the newly born workers' state; whether as Commissar of War or Foreign Minister or fighter against Stalin, History will not deny him his victories.

But that is *not* the mark of a revolutionary Marxist theoretician whose philosophic perspective charts the course of actual historical development on the basis of the most profound analysis of the objective situation, in strict relationship to the subjective development, the new form of workers' revolt, and on the basis of the objective and subjective, working out dialectically of a new relationship of theory to practice, in a way that the philosophy of revolution and the actual forces of revolution do not get separated. But Trotsky, since he never moved away from that fixed particular, nationalized property (any more than Kant from the thing-in-itself), stated in nothing less fundamental than "The Imperialist War and Proletarian Revolution," the manifesto of a new Fourth International: "To turn one's back on the nationalization of the means of production on the ground that, in and of itself, it does not create the well-being of the masses, is tantamount to sentencing the granite foundation to destruction on the ground that it is impossible to live without walls and a roof."[21]

The man of October couldn't have fallen any deeper into the mire of the ideas and methodology of the Russian bureaucracy which, instead of theory, was presenting an administrative formula for minimum costs and maximum production—the true gods of all class rulers. Empiricism does indeed wreak its greatest vengeance on Marxist revolutionaries whose universalism sinks to abstract revolutionism disconnected from the self-developing Subject, and they get stuck in a fixed particular like nationalized property. Ever since the rise of Nazism and the capitulation to Stalin of the greatest (except, of course, Trotsky himself) Left opposition theoretician, Christian Rakovsky, Trotsky faced a historic What Next? but answered it as if what is required is "five years of uninterrupted work to insure succession."[22]

---

21 *The Founding Conference of the Fourth International,* published by the Socialist Workers Party, New York, 1939.

22 Leon Trotsky, *Trotsky's Diary in Exile, 1935* (Cambridge: Harvard University Press, 1958), pp. 46–47, states "After his [Rakovsky's] capitulation there is nobody left...and still I think that the work which I am engaged in now, despite its insufficient and fragmentary nature, is the most important work in my life. More important than the period of the Civil War, or any other. For the sake of clarity I would put it this way: Had I not been present in 1917 in St. Petersburg, the October Revolution would have taken place on the condition that Lenin was present and in command. The same can, by and large, be said of the civil war period...Thus I cannot speak of the indispensability of my work even about the period from 1917–21. But now my work is indispensable in the full sense of the word...There is

If only Trotsky had developed a theory to measure up to the challenge of the times, even if the "cadre" had not. But, no, as the world crises moved from Depression to War and the Hitler-Stalin Pact signaled a green light for that holocaust, Trotsky operated on the basis of the Fourth International Manifesto, once again reducing the whole question to a matter of leadership: "The world situation as a whole is chiefly characterized by a historical crisis of the leadership of the proletariat." And again: "The historical crisis of mankind is reduced to the crisis of the revolutionary leadership." And once again, for the last time in his lifetime, the organization he founded was not founded on the theory of permanent revolution, either as he conceived it in 1905–06, or without further development, he had seen it "proven" in 1917 in victory and in 1927 in defeat, or throughout the struggle against Stalin's "socialism in one country," or when he finally broke away from being a "Left oppositionist" to something as total as founder of the Fourth International.

The duality between the concept of world revolution and that of defense of Stalinist Russia; between socialism as a classless society that can only realize itself as a world society, and socialism = nationalized property isolated from the world economy; between workers as the vanguard and workers who need to submit to "the militarization of labor"; between "Party" as leader of the proletarian revolution and "Party" as ruling *over* workers' own instincts and demands—all these dualities were compounded by, but not limited to, the contradiction between the dialectics of the revolution and the specific Subject who constituted the majority of "the masses," when they happened to be peasant rather than proletarian. No wonder Trotsky ended up by tailending Stalinism both on the question that he himself first articulated—the State Plan—and on the "vanguard party to lead."

The greatness of Leon Trotsky as revolutionary, as historian and pamphleteer will far exceed his conceptual perceptions, the cognition which gives action its direction. Leon Trotsky as man will tower above Leon Trotsky as theoretician.

Studies in Contemporary Communism *submitted the preceding essay on Trotsky to Ernest Mandel for his critique, which is printed below with Raya Dunayevskaya's rejoinder.*

Ernest Mandel: Mrs. Dunayevskaya's contribution touches on some key questions. She does it from the standpoint of a particular shibboleth ("Trotsky was theoretically wrong, because he didn't study Hegelian philosophy"), which,

now no one except the 2nd and 3rd Internationals. I need at least five years of uninterrupted work to insure the succession."

to say the least, is rather peculiar. Needless to say, I cannot agree with her assessment.

I will single out a series of points, where, it seems to me, most students of Marxist thought, or at least of the writings of Trotsky and Lenin, will agree with me that she is wrong.

She holds against Trotsky (and against his theory of the permanent revolution, which is his main theoretical achievement) his statement that "the peasantry is utterly incapable of [playing] an independent political role." She adds to that that "Trotsky's words speak louder than any of Stalin's allegations about Trotsky's underestimation of the peasantry," and above all, "that a theory so far removed from the realities of the age of imperialism and state-capitalism had to collapse of its own hollowness."

To this I would reply (besides the point that "state-capitalism," in Mrs. Dunayevskaya's sense, far from being a "reality," is a concept which doesn't correspond to any social reality anywhere in the world; where you have capitalism, it isn't state capitalism; and where you have statified planned economy, you don't have capitalism, as the present world slump should again convince anybody who is not blinded by prejudice):

1. That Trotsky, in his theory of permanent revolution, explicitly states that the peasantry will play the major role qua number of combatants in any revolution in a backward country, which isn't exactly "underestimating the peasantry";
2. That his point about the impossibility of an independent political role of the peasantry means simply that there have never existed, will never exist or cannot exist in the bad world in which we live since the capitalist system spread globally, any "peasant state" or "peasant government," and that therefore, whenever the working class and (or) its revolutionary party does not establish hegemony over the rebellious peasant masses, even the broadest peasant uprisings and revolutions will only lead to *capitalist* counter-revolution and to a bourgeois state.

Now far from this being a "hollow" theory "far removed from the realities of the age of imperialism," I would contend that it explains what happened in all revolutions in all backward countries in the 20th century, positively and negatively. And I would cap my argument by reminding Mrs. Dunayevskaya that Lenin, who supposedly in opposition to Trotsky had understood Hegelian dialectics, came to exactly the same conclusion at the end of his life as Trotsky had formulated on the "independent political role of the peasantry." He wrote in his speech to the transport workers congress of March 27, 1921:

"Notre expérience nous a appris—et nous en trouvons la confirmation dans le développement de toutes les révolutions du monde, si l'on considère la nouvelle époque, disons les 150 dernières années—que partout et toujours il en a été de même: toutes les tentatives faites par la petite bourgeoisie en général, et les paysans en particulier, pour prendre conscience de leur force, pour diriger à leur manière l'économie et la politique, ont abouti à un échec. Ou bien ils doivent se placer sous la direction du prolétariat, ou bien sous celle des capitalistes. Il n'y a pas de milieu. Ceux qui rêvent d'un moyen terme son des rêveurs, des songe-creux" (*Oeuvres Choisies* en deux volumes, p. 839, Moscou, Editions en Langues étrangères, 1947).

Mrs. Dunayevskaya holds against Trotsky that he "equaled nationalized property with socialism." Nothing was further from his mind. He thought (correctly so) that the suppression of private property of the means of production was a *necessary but insufficient* prerequisite for a socialist society. But he never for one minute defended the idea that you had "socialism" in Russia; that was one of the main contents of his fight against Stalin, to deny strongly any such utopia. For Trotsky Russia was a society in transition between capitalism and Socialism, which could fall back towards capitalism (if private property was restored and a new class of buyers of labor power would become a ruling class) or advance towards socialism (if the revolution spread towards large parts of the world and the monopoly of power of the bureaucracy in state and economy was abolished). Mrs. Dunayevskaya, by eliminating all these nuances, eliminates transition, i.e. mediation, from her thinking, which is not very suitable for a student of Hegel, who, after all, saw in mediation one of the key characteristics of dialectics.

Mrs. Dunayevskaya takes up against Trotsky the slander of his being in favor of "militarization of labor," whereas the concrete measures this refers to were taken by a unanimous decision of the Bolshevik Central Committee in 1919, in the midst of a civil war (including the vote of the later "workers opposition" leaders). She then goes on to make Trotsky's defense of the *Leninist* theory of organization equivalent with the defense of the "party ruling *over* workers' own instincts and demands," without explaining: (1) why Lenin who in opposition to Trotsky had studied Hegelian dialectics, clung to these concepts till the end of his life; (2) why workers, in innumerable massive revolutions throughout the 20th century, showed themselves unable to overthrow capitalism through spontaneous actions, "basing themselves on their own instincts and demands."

Two of the most difficult problems of contemporary Marxism, if not sociology and social sciences in general, the problem of the *formation* of proletarian class consciousness in a society hostile to socialism and dominated by the enemies of the workers, and the problem of bureaucracy, beginning with that of the bureaucratization of the workers' organizations, are dismissed with the sleight of hand as nonexistent or irrelevant, and all evil is brought back to the wrong ideas of a single person. This doesn't sound very "dialectical," not to say "materialist" or "Marxist," to me.

***

Raya Dunayevskaya: Ernest Mandel has devised several straw men, grouped under a single wifely designation, *Mrs.*, whom he accuses of slandering Trotsky: "Mrs. Dunayevskaya takes up against Trotsky the slander of his being in favor of 'militarization of labor' whereas the concrete measures this refers to were taken by a unanimous decision of the Bolshevik Central Committee in 1919, in the midst of civil war..." In the process of his expose of "Mrs. Dunayevskaya" as "blinded by prejudice," Mandel achieves some remarkable feats:

One, the revolutionary role of the peasantry does a disappearance act, first by being reduced "qua number of combatants," then by claiming that Trotsky's thesis of the impossibility of the peasantry's playing a political role "means simply that there have never existed, will never exist...any 'peasant state' or 'peasant government,'" and, finally, by proclaiming that "Mrs. Dunayevskaya" needs "reminding that Lenin came to exactly the same conclusion at the end of his life as Trotsky had formulated..." If even we leave aside the fact that this flies in the face of Trotsky's own pronouncement that, on the question of the peasantry, he was Lenin's "pupil," how could we disregard the irony of Mandel's choice of speeches from which to quote? It was the speech delivered to the very union that initiated the fight against Trotsky's "militarization of labor," demanding the return of the union to their own control, and Lenin referred to the disagreement by citing the fact that the Ninth RCP Congress had dealt with "the mistakes that required rectification" and did so "by subordinating the upper ranks to the lower ranks." That part of Lenin's speech Mandel does not quote; what he does quote was not the point at issue between Lenin and Trotsky for some two decades.

Two, "the slander." It was not I, but Trotsky, who used the expression, "militarization of labor." He held that each worker must feel himself "to be a soldier who cannot freely dispose of himself... That is the militarization of labor."[23] The "concrete measures" this referred to were not what the CC approved; rather

23 I had not footnoted the phrase, but this and all other quotations cited here can be found in *The Stenographic Report of the 9th RCP*; the English quotations (which include the Lenin speech Mandel quotes) can be found in Lenin's *Selected Works*, Vol. IX.

it referred to the merging of the trade unions into the state which not only the CC but the whole Congress rejected. It was not proposed "in the midst of civil war," but at the end of it. The Congress, instead, approved Lenin's Resolution because it agreed with his analysis: "Taken as a whole, Trotsky's policy is one of bureaucratically nagging the trade unions... There is valuable military experience, heroism, zeal, etc. There is the bad experience of the worst elements of the military: bureaucracy and conceit."

Three, "the particular shibboleth" attributed to "Mrs. Dunayevskaya": "Trotsky was theoretically wrong, because he didn't study Hegelian philosophy." Although Mandel enclosed the sentence in quotation marks, I not only never made any such ludicrous assertions, I was taking issue with Trotsky's concept of "belated" (April, 1917) "rearming of the Party," with its underlying assumption that by then it was somehow anchored in Trotsky's theory of the permanent revolution. In arguing that "what Lenin was armed with and Trotsky was not, was having faced the reality of 1914 with a totally new concept of Hegelian dialectics as self- developing Subject... 'translated' as the masses—proletarian and peasant," I held that the decisive test came after 1917, at a time when Lenin launched his last struggle against "great Russian chauvinism" (Stalin), asked Trotsky to present it to the Congress he himself was too ill to attend, warning against any "rotten compromise." I wrote: "Whether the fatal compromise was bound, in part, as Professor Lewin holds, by 'magnanimity,' or was the inescapable result of the dualism in theory not grounded in philosophy will be put to the severest test at the time of the Hitler-Stalin Pact after 'Trotskyism' reached its peak in the proclamation of the world revolution...and yet also clung to the defense of Stalin's Russia as a workers' state!"

Now, Ernest Mandel, evidently not totally satisfied with his economic-political-sociological feats, wanders also into the philosophic field where he is at his most ambitious. At one and the same time, he empirically reduces Hegel's concept of mediation to transition and ties "transition" to that totalitarian state-capitalist monstrosity, Russia, which he calls "a society in transition" as if the concept of Stalin's Russia as a "workers' state, though degenerated," which had split the Trotskyist party into smithereens during World War II, had never existed. Of what use is all that when one can point a finger at "Mrs. Dunayevskaya [who] by eliminating all these nuances ["society in transition between capitalism and socialism"], eliminates transition, i.e., mediation, from her thinking, which is not very suitable for a student of Hegel..."

Whether or not Ernest Mandel will ever stoop to becoming "a student of Hegel," I do hope he will grapple with Marx's concept of mediation, specifically on the question of Communism, specifically when Marx discovered his own unique continent of thought and revolution, and wrote: "Only by the transcendence of this mediation (Communism) ...does there arise *positive* Humanism beginning from itself."

It is, after all, a question of nothing short of a totally new, classless society, which alone can also re-establish the greatness of Trotsky as revolutionary, if not as great theoretician.

CHAPTER 5

On Bukharin

Dunayevskaya's writings on Nikolai Bukharin were almost always in relation to Lenin: to their differing attitudes to the dialectic as methodology, and to the political consequences of those differences in areas such as self-determination of nations in the age of imperialism. Below is one commentary. For others see her Marxism and Freedom *and* Philosophy *and* Revolution.

Lenin vs. Bukharin: The Dialectic and Its Methodological Enemy, Abstract Revolutionism

Excerpt from "State-Capitalism and Marx's Humanism, or Philosophy and Revolution," News & Letters, *December 1966*

Because the transformation of reality is central to the Hegelian dialectic, Hegel's philosophy comes to life, over and over again, in all periods of crisis, and transition, when society is shaken to its foundations as the world reaches a new turning point. Hegel himself lived at just such a turning point in history—the French Revolution; the dialectic has rightly been called "the algebra of revolution."[1] What seems almost beyond comprehension is this: *just when* the Russian Revolution made real "the algebra of revolution," and smashed bourgeois state power, *just when* "workers organized as the ruling class" was concretized as Soviet power, and the workers finally organized national trade unions, and *just when* the Party that led the revolution was establishing the first workers' state in history, that Party became embroiled in arguments over, of all things, state-capitalism.

The two debates most relevant to us are the vocal one on the trade unions and the silent one—Lenin's Notes on Bukharin's *Economics of the Transition Period.* Elsewhere[2] I have analyzed the three major positions in that famous

---

1 Alexander Herzen, *Selected Philosophical Works*, p. 521. (Foreign Language Publishing House, Moscow, 1956.).

2 See Chapter XII, *Marxism and Freedom.* Those who can read Russian will find the major positions included in *The Party and the Trade Unions,* edited by Zinoviev, and the major proponents speaking for themselves—Lenin, Trotsky, Shlyapnikov—in the *Stenographic Minutes of Ninth Congress of the Russian Communist Party.* When Lenin was alive, no one thought that theoretical disputes are won through concealing the opponents' views. The English

trade-union debate, 1920–21, including that of Shlyapnikov of the Workers' Opposition who opposed both Lenin and Trotsky-Bukharin and who called for an "All-Russian Congress of Producers." The position of Lenin—that the workers must maintain the independence of their trade unions (and all other organizations) *from* the state, although that state be a workers' state—was opposed by Bukharin, this time in coalition with Trotsky. They maintained that, "since" Russia was a workers' state, the workers had nothing to fear from it, and "therefore" should dissolve their trade unions into the state apparatus. Here, where we are concerned with methodology, the trade union debate concerns us only as it illuminated, theoretically, the role of workers in a workers' state and as this, in turn, was related to the theory of state-capitalism. In a word, Bukharin's *theory* underlying his argumentation in the trade union debate is of greater relevance to us than the debate itself, which, of necessity, bears the marks of factionalism. It will clarify matters if we concentrate, therefore, on his *Economics of the Transition Period*, and, along with it, Lenin's commentary on it.[3]

Bukharin's theory of state-capitalism, the obverse side of his theory of economic development under a workers' state, is that of a continuous development, a straight line leading from "unorganized" competitive capitalism to "organized" state-capitalism. On a world scale, it remains "anarchic," subject to the "blind laws of the world market." Anarchy is "supplemented by antagonistic classes." Only the proletariat, by seizing political power, can extend "organized production" to the whole world. The fact that Bukharin believes in social revolution does not, however, seem to stop him from dealing with labor, *not as subject, but as object*.

Quite the contrary. 1917 notwithstanding—and despite the fact that Bukharin played no small role in that revolution—his *concept* of revolution is so abstract that all human activity is subsumed under it. Thus, he is inescapably driven to preclude self-movement. Which is exactly why labor remains an object to him. As object, the highest attribute Bukharin can think of assigning labor is its becoming an "aggregate." Indeed, Bukharin uses the word, subject,

---

reader is limited to Lenin's views arguing against the other positions. Lenin, *Selected Works*, Vol. IX (International Publishers, NY, 1943) is indispensable both for the trade union debate and the Report to 11th Congress of RCP where Lenin warned of a "return backwards to capitalism."

3 Unfortunately neither Bukharin's *Economics of the Transition Period*, nor Lenin's *Commentary* on it is available in English. (I've used the Russian texts.) [Now available in English, *The Politics and Economics of the Transition Period*] However, other works by N. Bukharin are available in English. These are: *The World Economy and Imperialism*, *Historical Materialism*, and individual essays are included in other works, those against self-determination in *The Bolsheviks and the World War* (edited by Gankin and Fisher, Stanford U. Press, 1940) and elsewhere.

not to denote the proletariat, or living man, but just "consciousness," "single will" so that, despite his contention that only the proletariat can plan on a world scale, state-capitalism "has become a rational organization from an irrational system; from a subject-less economy, it has become an economic subject." To this economic form of "the future" the proletariat must submit; in a workers' state he becomes the "smallest cell." Thus: "The statification of the trade union and factual statification of all mass organizations of the proletariat is the result of the very inner logic of the process of transformation..., The smallest cell of the workers' apparatus must become transformed into a bearer of the general process which is planfully led and conducted by the collective reason of the working class which finds its material embodiment in the highest and most all-embracing organization, in its state apparatus. Thereby the system of state-capitalism is dialectically transformed into the state form of workers' socialism." Everything here stands topsy-turvy as if indeed people were nothing but "human machines."[4]

For a revolutionary intellectual to have become so entrapped in the fundamental alienation of philosophers in a class society, identifying men with things, is a phenomenon that laid heavy on Lenin's mind as, he wrote his *Will*, but in his Notes on Bukharin's book, Lenin moved cautiously in drawing any conclusions. Yet he began his criticism with Bukharin's very definition of political economy as "the science of social economy based on production of *commodities*, i.e., the science of an *unorganized* social economy." Lenin comments: "Two untruths: (1) the definition is a step backward from Engels; (2) commodity production is *also* 'organized' economy."

By stressing that not only state-capitalism, but even simple commodity production is "*also* 'organized' economy," Lenin is rejecting the counter position of "unorganized" to "organized" as any sort of fundamental criterion for the determination of a workers' state. By pointing out that Engels had, as far back as 1891, held that, with trustification, planlessness ceases, Lenin has in mind his *State and Revolution* where he first developed not only his theory of state-capitalism (based on Engels' thesis) but also his theory of proletarian revolution.

Or, to put it differently, what Lenin is saying is that the days when plan and planlessness were considered absolute opposites, are gone forever. What is now on the agenda is listening to the voices from below not only for the theoretical preparation for revolution, as he had done in *State and Revolution*, but for reconstruction of society on new beginnings. The point at issue now, 1920, is this: Russia is not a theoretical or "abstract" workers' state. It is a workers' and

---

4 *Draft CI Program*, included in *Ataka*, p. 121, Collection of Theoretical Articles by N. Bukharin (May, 1924, Moscow, Russian).

peasants' government that is "bureaucratically deformed." The workers are demanding an end to State interference in their trade unions: "We, the ordinary rank and file, the masses, say that we must renovate, we must correct, we must expel the bureaucrats; but you pitch us a yarn about engaging in production. I do not want to engage in production with such and such a bureaucratic board of directors."[5]

So totally did Lenin disagree with Bukharin's *method* of presentation that even when he agreed with the specific points, he felt it necessary to criticize. Thus, he singled out for praise Bukharin's restatement of Marx's "*two* essential moments: *centralization of means of production and socialisation of labor* which bloomed together with the capitalist method of production and inside it." But here is how he phrased his agreement: "Finally, thank god! Human language instead of 'organized' babbling. All is well that ends well."

But "all" didn't end well, not even when there was no disagreement. Thus, there was certainly no disagreement about the major achievement of the Russian Revolution—the destruction of bourgeois production relations. But the minute Bukharin tried to make an abstraction of that, tried to subsume production relations under "technical relations," it became obvious to Lenin that Bukharin simply failed to understand the dialectic. Thus, when he quoted Bukharin to the effect, that, "Once the destruction of capitalist production relations is really given, and once the theoretic impossibility of their restoration is proven," Lenin hit back with: "'Impossibility' is demonstrable only practically. The author does not pose *dialectically* the relationship of theory to practice."

Practice to Lenin was *workers practicing. To the Marxist theoretician, this is where all theory must begin.* Without having been aware of Marx's Humanist Essays—they had not yet been discovered and published—Lenin developed a "new universal" for his age, that the population, *to a man,* was to run production and the state—or it could not be considered a new social order. He wrote this in *State and Revolution*, and he tried practicing it after conquest of power. What worried him about his Bolshevik co-leaders was that, now that they had power, they themselves either displayed "a passion for bossing," or, at best, were ready with an administrative solution where only the self-activity of the masses could solve the crisis.

In the fires of revolution and, again, when under the threat of counter-revolution, all may have been forgiven. On his death-bed, however, Lenin showed he had not forgotten. As he lay writhing in agony—not just physical agony, but agony over the early bureaucratization of the workers' state and its tendency "to move backwards to capitalism"—Lenin took the measure of his

5 Lenin, *Selected Works*, Vol. IX, p. 19.

co-leaders in his *Will*. In it, Lenin warns that Bukharin, despite the fact that he was the Party's "most valuable and biggest theoretician," "never learned and, I think never fully understood the dialectic."[6]

It sounds like the kind of abstraction that Lenin considered his methodological enemy, the kind of abstraction that Lenin criticized in Bukharin. Once, however, one remembers that the *Will* is both concrete and the summation of a whole decade of theoretical disputes, the realization begins to dawn that this is a generalization based on what had started with the beginning of the new, monopoly stage of capitalist production which had brought about the collapse of the Second International. At the turn of the century, the new development of capitalism had the leading Marxists searching for answers to new problems. The results of the new research and analyses can be seen in the following major works: Rudolf Hilferding's *Finance Capital* (1910), Rosa Luxemburg's *Accumulation of Capital* (1913),[7] Nikolai Bukharin's *The World Economy and Imperialism* (1915), and Lenin's *Imperialism* (1916). Because Lenin had also introduced Bukharin's work, and took no issue with it, the impression created when the two disagreed sharply on the question of national self-determination during the same period, was that the point at issue was "only political."

In truth, the methodology of the two works shows they are poles apart. Thus, as opposed to Bukharin's concept of capitalist growth in a straight line, or via a quantitative ratio, Lenin's own work holds on tightly to the dialectical principle, "transformation into opposite." The key point in tracing the subject's self-development instead of an "objective" mathematical growth is that the former not only makes it possible to see transformation into opposite of both competitive capitalism into monopoly *and* part of labor into an aristocracy, *but also* makes you conscious that this is but the "first negative," to use an expression of Hegel's. The development through *this* contradiction compels finding the "second negative," or as Marx expressed it, going "lower and deeper" into the masses to find the mew revolutionary forces. Thus, Lenin held that, *just when*, capitalism had reached this high stage, of "organization," monopoly (which extended itself into imperialism), is the time to see new, national revolutionary

---

6 Lenin's *Will* has been published in various papers since Khrushchev's deStalinization speech in 1956. I've used the text as first published by Trotsky, *The Suppressed Testament of Lenin* (Pioneer Publishers, NY, 1935.).

7 Insofar as Luxemburg's theory of accumulation deviated from Marx's and anticipated that of Keynes on the question of "effective demand," Luxemburg was suddenly nailed by academic economists, particularly Joan Robinson. Nothing, however, could have been further from Luxemburg's mind than the uses to which her theory is put.

forces that would act as "bacilli" for proletarian revolutions as well.[8] Where Lenin saw, in the stage of imperialism, a new urgency for the slogan of national self-determination, Bukharin vehemently opposed the slogan as both "impossible of achievement" and "reactionary." Nothing short of a *direct* road to socialist revolution would do for him. This plunge to abstract revolutionism in place of working with the concretely developing revolutionary forces, which Hegel would have considered a manifestation of jumping to the "Absolute like a shot out of a pistol," and which politicos called "ultra-leftism," *Lenin called nothing short of "imperialist economism."*[9]

Such a characterization of a Bolshevik co-leader whose work *The World Economy and Imperialism* he had introduced less than a year before, wasn't something that came out only because of the heat of a factional debate. *In the heat of a factional debate what became clear to Lenin was that "the failure to understand the dialectic" meant the failure to see self-activity of the masses. To think that anything short of sensing blindness to the self-activity of the masses would have caused Lenin to describe a Bolshevik co-leader in words that would characterize a class enemy is to close the only avenue open to marching with "the masses as reason."*

The dialectic obviously meant something different in 1917 than it had in 1914–16 when the problem was to relate the betrayal of the Second International to the objective development of capitalism. Then "the transformation into opposite"—competition into monopoly—meant also the transformation of a part of labor into its opposite, the aristocracy of labor that gained from capitalism's imperialist adventures. By 1917 the administrative mentality began to permeate Bolshevism itself, once it assumed power. Lenin discerned the tendency to substitute an administrative solution to problems which can only be resolved by the self-development of the proletariat precisely because he stood firmly on the ground of the historic achievements of the Russian Revolution. For this reason and for this reason alone he could be so uncompromising in his criticism of the Bolsheviks who led the revolution.

Where the dialectic became the *pons asini* for Lenin who was witnessing the barest emergence of bureaucratization of the early workers' state, can the dialectic mean less for us who have seen its full development—the transformation of the workers' state into its absolute opposite, a state-capitalist

---

8 Vol. V of Lenin's *Selected Works* and Vol. XIX of his *Collected Works* contain the major articles on the question of national self-determination.

9 See "Lenin and the Imperialist Economism of the Bukharin-Piatakov Group" (pp. 22–247), in *The Bolsheviks and the World War*, edited by Gankin and Fisher, where Bukharin's analyses are likewise published.

society? Where the debates on the class nature of Russia in the late 1930's and early 1940's could revolve around political forms and economic relations, can we continue to escape the integrality of philosophy with revolution in the 1950's? Once the workers have revealed new revolutionary impulses in the 1950's, shouldn't this, of necessity, have also created a new vantage point for the debates on state-capitalism?

CHAPTER 6

On Luxemburg

Dunayevskaya wrote extensively on Rosa Luxemburg, beginning in the 1940s with a critical analysis of her Accumulation of Capital. *This continued in* Marxism and Freedom, *and briefly in* Philosophy and Revolution. *In the 1970s, the rise of the Women's Liberation Movement became the catalyst for Dunayevskaya's return to Luxemburg not alone as theorist of capital accumulation, but in the fullness of a revolutionary activist-thinker, including "unearthing Luxemburg's unknown feminist dimension"—a category she felt the modern women's movement had disregarded. The result was her third major philosophic work,* Rosa Luxemburg, Women's Liberation, and Marx's Philosophy of Revolution—*which comprehensively presented Luxemburg's legacy in the context of Marx's philosophy of revolution. While appreciating Luxemburg as a revolutionary and thinker, Dunayevskaya would note: "But the totality of Marx's philosophy of revolution, which never separated the philosophy of revolution from actual revolution, was nevertheless missing, even in Rosa Luxemburg"* (Women's Liberation and the Dialectics of Revolution, *p. 57*).

Below are two selections from Rosa Luxemburg, Women's Liberation, and Marx's Philosophy of Revolution*: "Luxemburg and Lenin: Anti-War Internationalism; Contrasting Views on National Self-Determination," and on Luxemburg's view of the Russian Revolution.*

Luxemburg and Lenin: Anti-war Internationalism; Contrasting Views on National Self-Determination—The "Junius" Pamphlet

Rosa Luxemburg, Women's Liberation, and Marx's Philosophy of Revolution

In her dark and dreary prison, Luxemburg—isolated from everything that was going on outside, even though she had worked out a network for getting some news in and smuggling her writings out—at once set out to write the first comprehensive antiwar pamphlet to come out of Germany. *The Crisis in the German Social-Democracy* has retained its fame to this day, known by the signature she used as *Junius.*[1]

1 This is included in several collections. The page citations in the following text are to the translation in *Rosa Luxemburg Speaks,* ed. by Mary-Alice Waters, pp. 257–331.

It raised high the banner, not only for internationalism and against imperialist war, but also against the official Social-Democracy: "Shamed, dishonored, wading in blood and dripping with filth, thus capitalist society stands ... And in the midst of this orgy a world tragedy has occurred: the capitulation of the social democracy" (p. 262).

Far from being only agitation, the pamphlet traced capitalism's historical development for the past fifty years, that is to say, ever since it had destroyed the Paris Commune, and started on its imperialist course. Luxemburg had always felt that the Chinese-Japanese War of 1895 had signaled a shift in global power, which indeed led up to the First World War. Her main stress, however, was on German imperialism, from the "Morocco incident" on: "Whole peoples are destroyed, ancient civilizations are levelled to the ground, and in their place profiteering in its most modem forms is being established... The present world war is a turning point in the course of imperialism..." (p. 325).

As against the "stinking corpse" of the SPD, Luxemburg pointed to the revolutionary nature of Marx's Marxism and the revolt of the workers themselves:

> The theoretical works of Marx gave to the working class of the whole world a compass by which to fix its tactics from hour to hour, in its journey toward the one unchanging goal... Historic development moves in contradictions, and for every necessity puts its opposite into the world as well. The capitalist state of society is doubtless a historic necessity, but so also is the revolt of the working class against it (pp. 263, 324–325).

It is on these two grounds that the "Theses on the Tasks of International Social Democracy," which followed the Junius pamphlet, were based, as they propounded the following principles:

> The class struggle against the ruling classes within the boundaries of the bourgeois states, and international solidarity of the workers of all countries, are the two rules of life, inherent in the working class in struggle and of world-historic importance to it for its emancipation (pp. 330–331).

At the same time, Luxemburg repeated her opposition to national self-determination on the ground that it would be a return to "nationalism":

> In the present imperialistic milieu there can be no wars of national self-defense. Every socialist policy that depends upon this determining historic milieu, that is willing to fix its policies in the world whirlpool from the point of a view of a single nation, is built upon a foundation of sand (p. 305).

This first great antiwar pamphlet—which was, at one and the same time, propagandistic in the bravest sense, seriously theoretical, and straight out of Germany itself—was more than just a breath of fresh air for isolated antiwar Marxists the world over. It was the genuine opening of a new epoch, of a new path to revolution. Lenin was among those heaping praise upon the pamphlet for its courage, but he felt strongly that it was worked out in isolation. He did not know that "Junius" was Rosa Luxemburg when he wrote:

> Junius' pamphlet conjures up in our minds the picture of a *lone* man who has no comrades in an illegal organization accustomed to *thinking* out revolutionary slogans to their conclusion and systematically educating the masses in their spirit...[2]

Marxists from the day of Marx had always felt that criticism was pivotal to clarification and development of ideas. Just as Luxemburg had felt it important to criticize the Russian Revolution while hailing it as the greatest event, so Lenin, in introducing his criticism, wrote:

> It would be a very deplorable thing, of course, if the "Lefts" began to be careless in their treatment of Marxian theory, considering that the Third International can be established only on the basis of unvulgarized Marxism (p. 207).

We have dealt previously with his criticism, especially on the National Question, both as principle and as it related to one of the struggles against imperialism. He felt that unless one was most specific—that is to say, *named* the betrayers like Kautsky—Luxemburg's magnificent expose of the imperialist war would sound merely agitational, instead of becoming a call to transform this imperialist war into a civil war. That, of course, was not her slogan.

Whereupon Lenin singled out what he considered her greatest error, hitting at it in the same manner in which he attacked his own Bolsheviks on the same question in the same period of 1916:

> ...when Junius lays particular emphasis on what to him is the most important point: the struggle against the "phantom of national war, which at present dominates Social-Democratic policy," we cannot but agree that his reasoning is correct and quite appropriate. But it would be a mistake to exaggerate this truth; to depart from the Marxian rule to be concrete; to apply the appraisal of the present war to all wars that are possible

2 Lenin, *Collected Works,* 19:213. The page citations in the text following are to this edition.

> under imperialism; to lose sight of the national movements *against* imperialism... (p. 202).

As we saw in the previous chapter, Lenin accused Junius of applying Marxist dialectics

> only halfway, taking one step on the right road and immediately deviating from it. Marxist dialectics call for a concrete analysis of each specific historical situation... Civil war against the bourgeoisie is *also* a form of class struggle ... (p. 210).

∴

Luxemburg's View of the Russian Revolution

Rosa Luxemburg, Women's Liberation and Marx's Philosophy of Revolution

Into the dark dungeon came a most brilliant and inspiring light—news of the March 1917 Revolution in Russia. So historic was the achievement, so great was the overturn of the tsarist regime, so magnificent was the first revolution to emerge out of the imperialist war, that it lighted up Luxemburg's life. As she put it in April in a letter to Marta Rosenbaum:

> Of course the marvels in Russia are like a new lease on life for me. They're a saving grace for all of us. I only fear that you all do not appreciate them enough, do not recognize sufficiently that it is our own cause which is winning here. It *must* and *will* have a salutary effect on the whole world, it must radiate outwards into the whole of Europe; I am absolutely certain that it will bring a new epoch and that the war cannot last long.

In her pamphlet on "The Russian Revolution," Luxemburg's praise went hand in hand with her opposition to anything that would infringe on democracy: "Socialist democracy begins simultaneously with the demolition of class rule and the construction of socialism."[3]

A new epoch was indeed dawning. 1917 was not only March, it was November as well. And it included not just the overthrow of the tsar, but the conquest of power by the Bolsheviks. Luxemburg was absolutely and firmly for it. "Yes,

---

3 In *Gesammelte Werke*, 4:363.

dictatorship! But this dictatorship consists in the *manner of applying democracy,* not in its *elimination,*" she wrote in "The Russian Revolution." So anxious was she to stress that it was "a first proletarian revolution of *transition,* world-historical in significance," that she had written to Luise Kautsky on 11 November 1917, that if the Russians "will not be able to maintain themselves in this witches' sabbath," it would not be "because statistics show that economic development in Russia is too backward, as your clever husband has figured out, but because the social democracy in the highly developed west consists of pitifully wretched cowards who, looking quietly on, will let the Russians bleed themselves to death..." Her point was that it must be supported, extended by the world proletariat, especially the German proletariat. As she was to put it in "The Russian Revolution," "In Russia the problem could only be posed, it could not be solved." In a word, it was the first step in the world revolution and could be saved only if it became the world revolution.

On one point in that pamphlet she seemed to support the SPD: "It is a well known and indisputable fact that without a free and untrammeled press, without the unlimited right of association and assemblage, the rule of the broad masses of the people is entirely unthinkable." This critique of the dismissal of the Constituent Assembly in Russia was a few months later seen differently in her own revolution. There she declared the national assembly to be a "bourgeois assembly," "a counter-revolutionary stronghold" against the genuine democracy contained in her slogan "All power to the Workers, Soldiers and Peasants Councils."

***

For both Luxemburg and Lenin, once the revolution became actual all other disputes faded into the background. Just as the 1905 Revolution towered high above the 1904 dispute [on organization], so the 1917 Revolution once again brought them close together, Luxemburg declaring:

> The Russian Revolution is the most overwhelming fact of the World War. Its outbreak, its unparalleled radicalism, its enduring action best give the lie to the catch phrases with which official German Social-Democracy, eager to be of service, at first ideologically cloaked German imperialism's campaign of conquest: phrases about the mission of German bayonets to overthrow Russian tsarism and liberate its oppressed peoples.[4]

4 This and the following quotations from Luxemburg's *The Russian Revolution* can be found in her *Gesammelte Werke,* 4:332–365.

She continued to stress that "Freedom only for the supporters of the government, only for the members of one party—however numerous they may be—is no freedom at all. Freedom is always and exclusively freedom for the one who thinks differently." On the other hand, nothing could be more wrong than to think—or more correctly put, to try to make others think—that Luxemburg's criticisms meant opposition to the Russian Revolution.[5] The very opposite was the case:

> Everything that is happening in Russia is comprehensible and an inescapable chain of causes and effects, whose point of departure and keystone are the abdication of the German proletariat and the occupation of Russia by German imperialism. It would be demanding the superhuman of Lenin and his comrades to expect them, under such circumstances, to also conjure up the most beautiful democracy, the most exemplary dictatorship of the proletariat, and a flourishing socialist economy. Through their resolutely revolutionary stand, exemplary energy, and inviolable loyalty to international socialism they truly have accomplished enough of what could be accomplished under such diabolically difficult conditions. The danger begins when they make a virtue of necessity, when they wish henceforth and in all points to theoretically fix the tactics forced upon them by these fateful circumstances and to recommend them for imitation by the international [proletariat] as the model of socialist tactics.

Luxemburg herself gave the best summation of her position:

> The question is to distinguish the essential from the non-essential, the core from the coincidental in the politics of the Bolsheviks ... In this connection, Lenin and Trotsky with their friends were the *first* to set the example before the world proletariat, and so far they are still the *only ones* who can proclaim with Hutten: I have dared!... In Russia the problem could only be posed. It could not be solved in Russia, it can only be solved internationally. And *in this sense,* the future everywhere belongs to "Bolshevism."

All the divisive questions became unimportant once the Russian Revolution broke out. What mattered was the revolution. Luxemburg's criticism of some

5 Luxemburg never finished the draft of her pamphlet on *The Russian Revolution,* which she had begun in her prison cell, nor did she attempt to publish it. It was published posthumously by her associate, Paul Levi, when he broke with Lenin.

of the features, especially what she considered insufficient democracy, took secondary place to her hailing the Russian Revolution as the greatest world event and praising the Bolsheviks as the only ones who dared, and who therefore should serve as the beacon light for all.

Within a year came the overthrow of the Kaiser and the beginning of the German Revolution. Her commitment to the revolution being total, once action became *the* determinant, Luxemburg plunged in to lead the January 1919 Spartacist revolt, although she had soberly advised against it as both ill-timed and ill-prepared. There was certainly no time to talk of any other organization but the newly created Communist Party of Germany—not when the counterrevolution was moving so murderously fast that in two short weeks it would behead the German Revolution, murdering Luxemburg, Liebknecht, and Jogiches.

CHAPTER 7

On Women Revolutionaries in Russia

Dunayevskaya's relationship with Natalia Sedova Trotsky began when she went to Mexico in 1937 to be Leon Trotsky's Russian language secretary and lived in the same household as Natalia. After Trotsky's assassination, the relation continued with correspondence and a visit with Natalia in 1947. Below, an in memoriam written in 1962 discusses Natalia Trotsky in the context of revolutionary women in Russia as exemplified by Vera Zasulitch. A second document "Russia, February 1917; Germany, January 1919; and Rosa Luxemburg" describes the role of women in the February 1917 overthrow of the Czar, and Luxemburg as theoretician-activist before and during the German Revolution, 1919.

In Memoriam: Natalia Sedova Trotsky. Role of Women in Revolution

News & Letters, *February 1962*

The death of Natalia Sedova Trotsky marks the end of the generation that achieved the greatest, and only successful proletarian revolution in history—the Russian Revolution in 1917. It has brought into sharp focus that other unique phenomenon—the unusual role of women in the original Russian Marxist movement.

One has only to compare an opportunist like Furtseva, the only woman to reach, for a single year, the Political Bureau of the Russian Communist Party, with a Vera Zasulitch—one of the three founders of the Russian Marxist movement—to see the class abyss that divides one from the other.

I mention Zasulitch rather than the one woman in the world Marxist movement that has made her mark as an original theoretician—Rosa Luxemburg—because, in memoriam of Natalia, I wish to speak of those women who had not gained theoretical leadership and therefore were very nearly disregarded except as faithful wives and mothers.[1] Vera Zasulitch, though a leader, was

1 To this day the American Trotskyists maintain this type of bourgeois attitude. In the February 5, 1962 issue of *The Militant*, the article that is supposed to praise Natalia's life is, in actuality, derogatory of her role as revolutionary and as an independent thinker. Their condescension reaches its most paternalistic hue in a reference to disagreements between them: "But this (period of political disagreements) never altered the respect or affection or material support

known for her bravery and emotions rather than for any theoretical contributions, although it was her letter to Karl Marx that had produced his answer on the special role that the *mir* (old Russian agricultural commune existing even in Tsarist days) might play *if* Russia could find a way "to skip" capitalism in her path to industrialization.

Vera Zazulitch was only 16, in 1861, when she was first arrested. She was in and out of jails when she gained prominence for shooting the most hated Tsarist Governor General of St. Petersburg, Trepov, for the flogging of an imprisoned fellow student. The exciting thing was that she had turned her trial into such an expose of the horrors of Tsarism that even in those days (1878) the jury acquitted her! She was then smuggled out to exile and it is to her place that all who escaped from Tsarism found their way—Martov, Lenin, Trotsky. She was Plekhanov's colleague when he broke with the populists, attacked terrorism, and founded Russian Marxism.

Natalia told me that even though they were all convinced Marxists, that is to say, believing that only the mass movement can overthrow Tsarism or capitalism, and writing heated articles against terrorism, they would all feel so elated when some particularly hated Tsarist official was shot, that they would quietly drink to the daring terrorist who had made that attempt.

When, on January 23 the air waves from France carried the news of the death of Natalia, there came over me both extreme sadness and yet a warmth and the kind of good feeling that comes from having witnessed intellectual daring and never-ending revolutionary optimism. For the tragic news of death followed on the heels of the last letter from her, addressed to the French press that I received, in which she hit back against the misrepresentations of the French press that had quoted her as saying that Leon Trotsky was allegedly "the spiritual father of Mao Tse-tung" She fired back:

> These words-don't belong to me at all. They were introduced by the writer of the interview...A great revolutionary like Leon Trotsky could not in any way be the father of Mao Tse-tung who won his position in direct struggle with the Left Opposition (Trotskyist) and consolidated it by the murder and persecution of revolutionaries just as Chiang Kai-shek did...

---

which the movement tended her." While they fail to publish her letter breaking with them, they do go out of the way to slander her by innuendos which imply that, if it were not for the wisdom of "the leaders of the SWP" (Socialist Workers Party), Natalia would have fallen into the trap of the, House Un-American Committee. Wouldn't it have been more honest if they, at least, had published her last statement denouncing Khrushchev and Mao, which showed how totally different her method of fighting Stalinism is from their shadow-boxing!

> I don't expect anything from the Russian party nor from its fundamentally anti-communist imitators. All de-Stalinization will prove to be a trap if it doesn't lead to the seizure of power by the proletariat and the dissolution of the police institutions, political, military and economic, based on the counter-revolution which established Stalinist state-capitalism.[2]

This was the first time that Natalia Trotsky had used the designation of state-capitalism in her reference to *established* Communism, in China or in Russia "or all others based on the latter model." Never before had Natalia developed a position beyond that developed by her famous husband. Because of this, I must confess that when, in 1947, I had come to visit her, I still thought that her theoretical development had been willingly stifled because she had subordinated everything in her life to that of Leon Trotsky.

I had asked her what about her Diary (to which Trotsky refers and quotes in his *My Life*.) She said she had undertaken it only to help Trotsky remember certain events in periods when he was so preoccupied that he couldn't pay attention to them, and that Trotsky had exaggerated the diary's value. I felt that in no case would she publish it if she thought any views she had might differ from those of Trotsky. But both 1951, when she broke with the American Trotskyists, and 1961, when she exposed Khrushchev's de-Stalinization as a fraud "based on the counter-revolution which established Stalinist state-capitalism" proved me wrong.

Natalia Sedova Trotsky first came in contact with the revolutionary movement in Tsarist Russia when she was only 15. When still in her teens she emigrated to Europe to study, and there joined the small Russian émigré group around the paper *Iskra*. This modest self-effacing young woman had been assigned to get a room for a new and promising young theoretician who had just escaped from Siberia and whose name she had not been told. It turned out to be Lev Davidovitch Trotsky, and she was asked to make sure that he was not wasting time but preparing for his first lecture in Paris. This was the only incident of her personal life that Natalia ever told me during the years (1937–38) that I was in Mexico as Trotsky's secretary. She said that she just couldn't get herself to enter Trotsky's room and deliver the message of the need to concentrate on the lecture. She therefore told the older comrade that she thought he was preparing since she had heard him whistling. Her interpretation of the whistle, however, was not accepted and she was sent back to knock on the door and speak to him. She was blushing and walking slowly toward the room when Lev Davidovitch burst out of it, almost knocking her over.

---

2 For the full text, see January, 1962 issue of *News & Letters*.

It was love at first sight. She was then almost 21. She remained his life-long companion: through the exile from Tsarism, and in Tsarist prisons, through the tidal wave of revolution and in power, in exile from Stalin till the tragic murder parted them.

I shall never forget the only time I ever saw Natalia cry. News came of the death of her son, Leon Sedoff, in Paris. I happened to have been the first to have gotten the tragic news when I answered the phone while we were all at the table eating lunch. I did not dare face anyone with that news. Stalin had persecuted her other son whose whereabouts we didn't know. He had persecuted Trotsky's daughters by his first wife as well as the wife herself until death by suicide or torture. And now this—I just sat through lunch, pretending that it was a wrong number, and at the end of the lunch the secretariat got together to figure out who should break the news to Leon Trotsky and who to Natalia. We all decided that only Leon Trotsky could be the bearer of such news to Natalia.

They departed to their rooms and in a moment came her scream. We did not see them for eight days. The blow was the harder not only because Leon Sedoff had been their only living child, but also because he had been Trotsky's closest literary and political collaborator. When Trotsky was interned in Norway, gagged, unable to answer the monstrous charges levelled against him in the first (August, 1936) Moscow Trials, Sedoff had penned *Le Livre Rouge*,[3] which, by brilliantly exposing the Moscow falsifiers, dealt an irreparable blow to the prestige of the GPU (Russian Secret Police).

In the dark days after the tragic news had reached us, when Leon Trotsky and Natalia were closeted in their room, Trotsky wrote the story of their son's brief life. It was the first time since prerevolutionary days that Trotsky had written by hand.

On the eighth day Leon Trotsky emerged from his room. I was petrified at the sight of him. The neat, meticulous Leon Trotsky had not shaved for a whole week. His face was deeply lined. His eyes were swollen from so much crying. Without uttering a word, he handed me the hand-written manuscript, *Leon Sedoff, Son, Friend, Fighter*, which contained some of Trotsky's most poignant writing. My eyes set first on this statement,

> I told Natalia of the death of our son—in the same month of February in which, 32 years ago, she brought to me in jail the news of his birth. Thus ended for us the day of February 16th, the blackest day in our personal

3 First appeared in Russian as special issue of the *Opposition Bulletin* (organ of the Russian Bolshevik-Leninists), edited by Sedoff in Paris.

> lives; ... Together with our boy has died everything that still remained young within us.

The pamphlet was dedicated "to the proletarian youth." The following morning the papers, carried the announcement of the Third (March 1938) Moscow Trials, scheduled to open within two short weeks of the death of Leon Sedoff.

One day shortly after this Natalia went for a walk with me in the woods and there she began to cry quietly and asked me not to let Leon Trotsky know since he more than anyone needed all his strength and our help to answer these fantastic, slanderous charges from the man in the Kremlin who was bent on murdering the one man (Trotsky) who could still lead a revolution against the bureaucracy and restore the Russian, and thereby the international movement to its Marxist path of liberation.

With the beginning of the Third Moscow Trials we had to forget everything else and concentrate on fighting the fantastic charges. Stalin, backed up by the might of Russian state and military power, had been preparing the stage for these monstrous frame-ups for a full decade. Leon Trotsky had only two hours in which to answer—and that only because the Mexican press would tell him what charges came over the teletype and held the presses open for him to answer.

Two years after the Trials had been exposed not only by Trotsky himself, but by the Commission of Inquiry, headed by the late John Dewey, as the greatest frame-up in history, a GPU agent drove an ice-axe into the head of Leon Trotsky. In the lonely, hectic decade that followed, Natalia also found that she had to separate herself from the Fourth International her husband had founded.

When I had visited Natalia in 1947, she had asked me about my writings. Although I had broken with Trotsky over the class nature of Russia and its defense, she not only treated me as a colleague because of my past association with Trotsky, but was very interested in finding out what were the theoretical reasons for the break. She had me translate for her, word for word, the articles on the Russian revisions of Marx's theory of value.[4]

She refused, however, to take a position on the designation of Russia as state-capitalist. She said that it was implicit in Trotsky's fight against the bureaucracy, that she felt he himself would have reached that position had he lived through to the end of the war and seen the Stalinist exploitation of Eastern Europe. But she insisted that she simply did not know enough theory to venture out on her own when Trotsky had died before coming to such a conclusion.

---

4 "A New Revision of Marxism" in *The American Economic Review*, September 1944, September 1945.

In 1951, however, she felt she had to speak out against the American Trotskyists for falling into the trap created by Tito's break from Stalin as well as the Korean War. She wrote to the Political Committee of the Socialist Workers Party in unflinching Bolshevik language.

A decade passed before we saw from her pen her final conclusion that Russia was a state-capitalist society. It came during the 22nd Russian Communist Party Congress where that obedient Stalinist in Stalin's lifetime—Nikita Khrushchev—dared to picture himself as an anti-Stalinist as if his suppression of the Hungarian Revolution in 1956 had not been in the true counter-revolutionary tradition of Stalin. The Trotskyists, not having learned anything from these counter-revolutionary actions, were now tending to accept the ground rules that Mao was laying down on war and revolution.

Again Natalia refused to follow. This time she hit out against both Khrushchev and Mao. She did not limit her attack to an attack of "bureaucracy." She rose to her full stature and declared both countries state-capitalist, warning that all "de-Stalinization will prove to be a trap if it doesn't lead to the seizure of power by the proletariat, and the dissolution of the police institutions, political, military and economic..."

Shortly thereafter she fell ill. On January 23 she died. The last words of this frail 81-year-old Bolshevik had all the revolutionary vigor and the optimism of a new, youthful adherent to Marxism. She leaves this generation a great heritage of heroism, independent thought, and devotion to world liberation that gives the appearance of a lack of any personal life. But I shall never forget the one moment of tears when her son died.

I shall remember Natalia in that one moment when she let the tears rain down, but reminded me not to tell Trotsky about it, and not to let it interfere with the needs of the movement—to expose the Moscow Frame-Up Trials. It so clearly expressed the combination of personal tragedy and worldwide concern, the discipline old Bolsheviks imposed on themselves not to let anything interfere with the liberating movement that presses ever forward.

I shall remember Natalia as the great revolutionary whose thoughts were as majestic as her devotion and her daring in speaking out even against those who had led the movement her husband had founded because nothing at all could stay in the way of principles.

I shall remember Natalia as the mother who had brought up her children in the midst of all these hardships to be revolutionaries in their own right, men of character who knew how to stand up to might and not flinch.

I shall remember Natalia for the legacy she has left us of a generation that made a revolution, saw the first workers' state transformed into its opposite—state capitalism—and yet wavered not either in its principledness or its optimism.

I shall always remember the tenderness that shone through the hard-as-flint attitude toward the rulers of the world who are now leading us to a nuclear holocaust.

Death here becomes a beacon to the future—the intercommunication between the ages will continue until a new, liberated world is born.

∴

Russia, February 1917; Germany, January 1919; and Rosa Luxemburg

Excerpted from a Lecture given in 1976 Women's Liberation and the Dialectics of Revolution

Now let's turn to the 20th century and see, firstly, what can we learn from women as masses in motion, initiating nothing short of the overthrow of that reactionary Russian colossus, Tsarism—the dramatic, creative, empire-shaking five days in February, 1917; and, secondly, let's turn to the 1919 German Revolution and its greatest theoretician, Rosa Luxemburg.

That first day, Feb. 23, in Russia, appeared simple enough as a celebration of International Women's Day by the textile workers in Petrograd. But was it that simple, when they insisted it become a strike, despite a raging world war in which their country was doing very badly? Was it that simple when all revolutionary parties—Bolsheviks, Left Mensheviks, Social Revolutionaries, Anarchists—were telling them that they were courting a massacre, and they shouldn't go out on strike? Was that first day of the revolution, when 50,000 women marched despite all advice against it, a "male-defined" revolution? Was the letter they addressed to the metal workers, which the metal workers honored by joining the strike—and 50,000 grew to 90,000: men and women, housewives as well as factory workers—a proof of the fact that they didn't really "know" what they were doing?

When the Bolsheviks did join the women textile workers and the strike turned into political opposition to the imperialist war and the Cossacks did open fire, it was too late to save the Russian empire. By then the soldiers also joined the masses in revolt, and "spontaneously" the whole rotten empire toppled.

It is true that those five historic days that crumbled the might of Tsarism led, in turn, to the Revolution of Oct. 25, and that certainly was led by the Bolshevik Party. That, however, can no more detract from what the women workers initiated on Feb. 23, than the October Revolution can be blamed for its transformation into opposite under Stalin a decade later.

What had happened in action, what had happened in thought, what had happened in consciousness of the mass participants—all this is ground on which we build today. Or should be. But even if some still insist on playing down women *both* as masses in motion and as leadership, let them consider the German Revolution, January 1919, led by Rosa Luxemburg. None questioned that she was the leader.

From 1898 when she fought the first appearance of reformism in the Marxist movement, through the 1905 Revolution in which she was both a participant and out of which she drew her famous theory of the Mass Strike; from 1910–13 when she broke with Karl Kautsky—four years in advance of Lenin's designation of Kautsky as not only opportunist but betrayer of the proletariat—and when she first developed her anti-imperialist struggles and writings, not only as political militant but carving out her greatest and most original theoretical work, *Accumulation of Capital,* to the 1919 Revolution; she made no division between her theory and her practice.

Take her *Reform or Revolution* against Bernstein, who demanded that "the dialectical scaffolding" be removed from Marx's "materialism." Talking of Bernstein, she wrote:

> When he directs his keenest arrows against our dialectic system, he is really attacking the specific mode of thought employed by the conscious proletariat in its struggle for liberation ... It is an attempt to shatter the intellectual arm with the aid of which the proletariat, though materially under the yoke of the bourgeoisie, is yet enabled to triumph over the bourgeoisie. For it is our dialectical system that shows to the working class the transitory character of this yoke, proving to the workers the inevitability of their victory, and is already realizing a revolution in the domain of thought.[5]

The next great historic event—the Russian Revolution of 1905—again reveals her as theorist and activist-participant who did not stop at oratory but, with gun in hand, made the proprietor-printer print a workers' leaflet. What she singled out, however, from the great experience, what she made ground for other revolutions, what she created as a theory also for the relationship of spontaneity to party, was *The Mass Strike, the Political Party and the Trade Unions:*

> The revolution is not an open-field maneuver of the proletariat, even if the proletariat with social democracy at its head plays the leading role, but it is a struggle in the middle of incessant movement, the creaking,

5 Rosa Luxemburg, *Reform or Revolution (New York: Three Arrow Press, 1937) p. 47.*

> crumbling and displacement of all social foundations. In short, the element of spontaneity plays such a supreme role in the mass strikes in Russia, not because the Russian proletariat is "unschooled," but because revolutions are not subject to schoolmastering.[6]

It is this concept and this activity and this perspective that led, in 1907, to Luxemburg's joining with Lenin and Trotsky to amend the resolution at the Stuttgart meeting of the International that declared socialist opposition to war and the imperative need to transform it into revolution.

At the time when Luxemburg recognized the non-revolutionary character of Karl Kautsky, when all other Marxists, Lenin included, were still acknowledging him as the greatest theoretician of the Second International, she embarked on the most hectic point of activity outside of a revolution itself.

She felt very strongly that the German Social Democracy had been hardly more than a bystander instead of militant fighter against Germany's imperialist adventures. It was this, and not mere "organizational" questions, which made her return to her original analysis of mass strike which had always meant to her that "the masses will be the active chorus, and the leaders only 'speaking parts', the interpreters of the will of the masses."

Luxemburg was not only involved in lecturing and developing an anti-imperialist struggle over the Morocco crisis which would, in turn, lead to her greatest theoretical work, *Accumulation of Capital*,[7] but she also turned to work on the "Woman Question,"[8] which heretofore she had left entirely to Clara Zetkin, who was editing the greatest German women's magazine, *Die Gleichheit*, from 1891 to 1917.

The magazine's circulation rose from 9,500 in 1903 to 112,000 in 1913. Indeed, by the outbreak of the war, the female membership in the German Social Democracy was no less than 170,000. It is clear that, as great a theoretician as Rosa Luxemburg was, and as great an organizer as Clara Zetkin was, they were not exceptions to the alleged apathy of German women. On the contrary, it would be more correct to say that there wouldn't have been as massive and important

6 Luxemburg's pamphlet on *The Mass Strike* is included in *Rosa Luxemburg Speaks*, Mary-Alice Walters, ed. (New York; Pathfinder Press, 1970) pp. 144–218.

7 I happen to disagree seriously with her theory in *Accumulation of Capital*, because I consider it a deviation from Marx. This cannot, however, detract from the important contribution it made in the struggles against imperialism in her day. See my *State-Capitalism and Marx's Humanism or Philosophy and Revolution*. (Detroit: News & Letters, 1967).

8 See Rosa Luxemburg's speech on "Women's Suffrage and Class Struggle" at the Stuttgart Second Social Democratic Women's Rally, May 12 1912, included in *Selected Political Writings of Rosa Luxemburg*, Dick Howard, ed. (New York. Monthly Review Press, 1971), pp. 216–222.

a revolution in Germany were there not that many women involved in the revolution. Naturally none could compare with Rosa Luxemburg as theoretician. That is certainly true of genius whether that be woman or man. As one of the very few persons who has written on the subject put it, were it not for the proletarian women, "there might have been no revolution in Germany."[9]

Despite all the misrepresentation of her position on the Russian Revolution, Luxemburg had hailed it as the greatest proletarian revolution ever, insisting that the Russian Bolsheviks alone had dared and dared again. It was exactly for such a daring act that she was preparing herself from her jail cell, from which she was not freed until Nov. 9, 1918, when the German masses in revolt had driven the Kaiser from the throne. Anyone who tried to use her criticism of the Russian Revolution as the German Revolution unfolded got from her the following: Where did you learn the ABCs of revolution? Is it not from the Russians? Who taught you the slogan, "All power to the soldiers, workers, and peasants"? Isn't it the Russians? This is the dialectics of revolution: that is what Spartakus wants; this is the road we are taking now.

Rosa Luxemburg lived only two and a half months after being let out of jail. Two and a half months in which the upsurge of the masses led to the establishment first of the Spartakus League and then the independent Communist Party in Germany. Two and a half months in which to call for all power to the soldiers' and workers' councils. And then the counterrevolution caught up with her, shot her, bashed in her head, and threw her body into the Landwehr Canal.

Does the beheading of the German Revolution—Liebknecht and Jogiches were murdered along with Luxemburg—mean that we're not to learn from a revolution because it was "unsuccessful"? Has the Women's Liberation Movement nothing to learn from Rosa Luxemburg just because she hasn't written "directly" on the "Woman Question"? Outside the fact that the latter doesn't happen to be true, should not the corpus of her works become the real test of woman as revolutionary and as thinker and as someone who has a great deal to tell us as Women's Liberationists today? Are we to throw all that into the dustbin of history because she had not written on the "Woman Question"?

---

9 A good beginning on this subject has been made by William A. Pelz in his unpublished thesis, "The Role of Proletarian Women in the German Revolution, 1918–19," presented at the Conference on the History of Women, College of Ste. Catherine, St. Paul, Minn., Oct. 24–25, 1975.

PART 3

What Happens After?—Lenin 1917–1923

CHAPTER 8

The Trade Union Debate and Lenin's *Will*

The category "What Happens After," that is, what happens after the revolution takes power, was developed by Dunayevskaya in her examination of Russia after the October Revolution (November, new style) until Lenin's death (January, 1924). Central to the development of this category in relation to Lenin were: (1) the Trade Union Debate of 1920 on the role of workers and their trade unions in a "workers' state"; (2) Lenin's struggles with a growing bureaucracy within the new Soviet state and its Bolshevik (Communist) Party, and (3) Lenin's assessment of his fellow Bolshevik leaders in what became known as his Will *(written in the last weeks of 1922 and the first week of 1923).*

Dunayevskaya subsequently saw this category as being crucial to other revolutionary moments, including African, Asian and Latin American movements, that is, Third World Revolutions in the post-World War II world. The category has a dialectical relation to seeing social revolution as having a dual rhythm: the uprooting of the old (first negation) and the construction of a human society as new beginnings (second negation):

> *"[B]efore, during and after the social revolution the problem of the conquest of power and the problem of the new society is one and the same. Its axis is the relationship to the masses."* R.D.

For this reason, though "What Happens After" is here present as only a single chapter, it is as well presented as a separate part of this book. The documents below are drawn from an analysis Dunayevskaya wrote for the mimeographed newspaper Correspondence, *and from* Marxism and Freedom.

The Trade Union Debate

The Famous Trade Union Debate that Took Place in Russia in 1920 Excerpt from Mimeographed* Correspondence*, Vol. 4 No. 2, April 16, 1953: The Raya Dunayevskaya Collection, #2186

I The Facts

The Railroads and the Military

At the end of the First World War and the civil war that followed it in Russia, railroad transportation was in utter chaos. No modern country can exist without transportation, and here at the birth of a new society, the first workers state in history, the railroads weren't running and the whole transportation system was still plagued with sabotage from the defeated counter-revolutionary forces. Something drastic had to be done. A committee was established called the *Cectran*—that is, the Central Executive Committee of Transportation. It was a merger of the railroad workers' and water transport workers' unions and a non-union man was put at the head of it—Leon Trotsky, the Commissar of War. He and his Committee were granted extraordinary military powers in order to cope with the disastrous situation. Within a year not only were the railroads running again and on time but the railroad trackage had been much expanded. The country was beginning to breathe again. It was then that the water workers union, which had been merged with the railroad workers and put under this special commission called the *Cectran* headed by Trotsky, spoke up. They said that they had fully approved the extraordinary military measures needed to restore transportation, but now that the job was done, they demanded "our normal trade union democracy be given back to us." Trotsky reacted violently. He said it wasn't the special commission that had to be abolished. It was the trade union leaders that "had to be shaken up."

That is how the famous trade union debate began. Before it ended, the subjects in dispute ranged far and wide: (1) What is a workers' state? (2) What is the role of trade unions in a workers' state? (3) What is the relationship between workers at the point of production and the political party in such a state? (4) What is meant by an administrative attitude and how is that distinguished from the old propagandist attitude? (5) How is it possible for a Communist to display "a passion for bossing"? (6) What is the relationship between leaders and ranks, the party and the masses? (7) Where do we go from here?

Here they had just overthrown the hated Tsarist autocracy and the feeble bourgeois democracy. Yet, already, *within* the revolutionary party itself, the Bolsheviks, different political tendencies were arising of such a serious nature that it was clear that *class attitudes* were involved. How could that be since the capitalists had been gotten rid of and the workers held power? As the debate unfolded, every conceivable political tendency unfolded. The three most important ones were those of Lenin, Trotsky, and Shlyapnikov, the head of the Workers Opposition Group.

The Debate Proper: A Preliminary Statement

Lenin rose to the defense of the trade unions. "Taken as a whole," he said, "Trotsky's policy is one of bureaucratically nagging the trade unions." "There is valuable military experience: heroism, zeal, etc.," he continued, "There is the bad experience of the worst elements of the military: bureaucracy and conceit."

He criticized the *Cectran* for its "bureaucratic excesses," for ordering people about instead of spreading the knowledge of what the workers themselves were doing. Then he turned to his co-leader, Trotsky, and said that the trouble with him was that he had approached the problem as an *administrator* where he should have been a *propagandist.*

When *Trotsky* pontificated, "Workers democracy knows no fetishism. It knows only revolutionary expediency," Lenin answered sharply that the workers would be right in saying,

> We, the ordinary rank and file, the masses, say that we must renovate, we must correct, we must expel the bureaucrats; but you pitch us a yarn about engaging in production. I do not want to engage in production with such a bureaucratic board of directors, chief committee, etc., but with another kind.

Shlyapnikov opposed both Lenin and Trotsky. Now that there was a workers state he could not grasp the role of the Communist party—that is of political leadership—although he himself was a Bolshevik leader. It was as if all problems had faded away with the conquest of political power. He called for the convocation of a "producers' congress."

Once again, Trotsky, Shlyapnikov, Lenin; the Essence of the Debate

In their various ways the three leading positions contain embryonically the problems of today; what *is* the relationship between these three social formations—the trade unionist, the politicos, the masses. Posed in terms of relations in a workers state, here is how the three leaders symbolically expressed them:

(1) *Trotsky* contended that since Soviet Russia was a workers state, the workers had nothing to fear from it and hence you could incorporate the trade unions into the state and *militarize labor*; establish

> such a regime under which each worker feels himself to be a soldier of labor who cannot freely dispose of himself; if he is ordered transferred, he must execute that order; if he does not do so, he will be a deserter who would be punished. Who will execute this? The trade union. It will create a new regime. That is the militarization of the working class.

Trotsky's callousness to the dissatisfaction of the workers with the functioning of his special commission, the *Cectran*, showed itself especially clearly in the attention he concentrated upon the trade union leadership. He said this must be "shaken up." According to him, it was not the extraordinary political commission with its extraordinary military powers which was at the root of the crisis. Rather, it was the trade union leadership which had failed to create a proper "production atmosphere."

To Lenin, on the other hand, the bureaucracy, petty tyranny, red tape of the *Cectran* was as oppressively real as it was to the workers themselves. He begged Trotsky to put away his "intellectual trick words (like), production atmosphere" and recognize that the workers not only had a right to fight bureaucratism but that that was the *only concrete path to the establishment of new social relations*:

> It is wrong to look only to the cited persons, only to the organizers, the administrators, etc. These after all are only a minority of prominent people. We must look to the rank and file, to the masses.

But there was no way to dissuade Trotsky from his stubborn persistence in defense of the *Cectran*, his refusal to see that it had been guilty of any "bureaucratic excesses," his drowning himself in abstractions on the workers' state.

(2) Interestingly enough, *Shlyapnikov* too began and ended with the abstraction of a workers' state. Since that was already established, he asked, what is the necessity for the political leadership to hold a primary place? To him it was all a simple matter—all that was needed in the chaotic conditions of 1920—was to turn over the industry to the corresponding trade unions. His call for a "producers' congress" disregarded at one and the same time the class realities of Russia and its relationship to the capitalist world outside.

Lenin was the supreme realist. He asked both Trotsky and Shlyapnikov what was the use of talking about "a" workers state when the reality of the *specific Russian Soviet state* disclosed that the dictatorship of the proletariat existed in a country where workers were a tiny minority *surrounded by a sea of peasants*. To talk of "a producers' congress"—a term used by Marx and Engels for a classless society—in the specific circumstances where the defeated counter-revolution was looking for ways to get back into power was to play right into its hands. *At this moment* in our history—Lenin turned sharply to Shlyapnikov—you and your "Workers Opposition" are the greatest danger to our continued existence. Just look about you, look at the Kronstadt mutiny and see how quickly the White Guards have grabbed on to the anarchistic, syndicalistic talk of "freedom," "freedom from political leadership" and, *with guns in their hands*, are threatening the new workers state. Under these *actual* conditions for you to propose a "producers' congress" means for you to ask the workers state to commit suicide.

Then Lenin turned to Trotsky and told him he must never forget that the Soviet Russia is a workers state, yes, but it is a workers state "with bureaucratic distortions" Every other word on Lenin's lips these days was *bureaucracy*. The Soviet Union was a workers state with "bureaucratic distortions." Any attempt to plan that did not involve the masses themselves was nothing but "bureaucratic project-hatching." Anyone who desired to "shake up the trade union leadership" displayed "a bureaucratic concentration on the loading strata." In fact, any political tendency that did not concentrate the whole weight of the argument on the question of working out a relationship to the masses betrayed "bureaucratic tendencies."

According to Lenin "*The whole point is the method of approach to be adopted toward the masses, the method of winning the masses, of contact with the masses*" (Our emphasis.)

If talking about a "producers' congress" as Shlyapnikov had done, could aid no one but the *class enemy*, Trotsky's kind of talk about "production atmosphere" could do nothing but alienate the workers who must be protected from their own state. Lenin insisted that the workers were absolutely right when they demanded the return to ordinary trade union democracy.

> We must understand the significance of this slogan in the present political situation when the bureaucracy is confronting the masses in a form they can understand and they have put the question of bureaucracy in the agenda.

That is just the point Trotsky could not grasp.

The Logic of the Trade Union Debate

What is at issue in a theoretical debate is which side expresses which class's political line. The point is that, just as in life, so in thought, there is only one fundamental division in society—*the class division*. When a revolutionary begins to deviate *theoretically* he is expressing fundamental class forces pulling at him. The simple truth is that not only does the man on the production line *act* one way and the foreman another, an opposite way; the *thinking* of the two is as wide apart.

Marx was the first to show the relationship of the intellectual representatives of a class to the class it represents:

> Just as little must one imagine that the democratic representatives are all shopkeepers or enthusiastic champions of shopkeepers. According to their education and their individual position they may be separated from them as widely as heaven from earth. What makes them representatives of the petty bourgeoisie is the fact that in their minds they do not go beyond the limits which the latter do not go beyond in life, that they are constantly driven theoretically to the same tasks and solutions to which material interests and social position practically drive the latter. This is in general the relationship of the *political and literary representatives* of a class to the class they represent.

Marxists have always been acutely aware of the fact that a theoretical position is not accidental. That is why Lenin tried *to correct Trotsky*. He begged him to stop and look and take note of where his theoretical position was leading him to. Why not face the simple facts first? he pleaded. The *Cectran* which Trotsky headed was guilty of bureaucratic excesses. Why not admit the error and rectify it? To *persist* in it can mean only one thing: it is beyond the control of the individual's will precisely because an objective force is pulling in a direction over which the individual has no control. That is what is meant by "the objective logic of a theoretical position."

It is objective–outside of the subjective will and consciousness of the person holding it. It is solidly rooted in the stage of development of the economy and the relations of men at the point of production. Thus in Russia in 1920 the economy was in chaos and the question was what to do. Would the worker on the line or the administrator in the office decide what constitutes labor discipline?

Lenin said that, the only correct position was that of the trade union thesis:

> Introduction of genuine labor discipline is conceivable only if the whole mass of participants in production take conscious part in the fulfillment of these tasks. This cannot be achieved by *bureaucratic methods and orders from above.*

Trotsky, on the other hand, contended that

> We suffer not so much from the bad sides of bureaucracy, as chiefly from the fact that we have not assimilated its many good sides.

It did Lenin no good to remind Trotsky that they had all voted for the New Program of the Russian Communist Party which directly *after* gaining power recognized that the new enemy was bureaucratism, that:

> In the struggle against bureaucratism there will be gradual inclusion of the whole toiling population to a man in the work of running the state.... This plus simplification of the functions of the government will lead to the abolition of state authority.

Trotsky went his own way. He refused to recognize the administrator as the *new enemy*. Quite the contrary. He accused a Leninist of approaching

> very practical questions too much from the propagandist point of view, and forgets that here we not only have *material* for agitation but a problem which must be solved administratively.

Lenin, on the other hand, shouted loudly and clearly that the *bureaucracy* was the new enemy, and that Trotsky's administrative approach made him weakest where he should be strongest: as a *propagandist*. That was precisely what was wrong with his whole thesis, that through...them "there runs, like a red thread, the administrative approach."

II The Propagandist vs. The Administrative Approach

Where Lenin put the workers' attitude in the center of all his thoughts, Trotsky put the administrative plan. Where Lenin's every other word was an attack on bureaucracy, Trotsky worried over their not yet having mastered "the many good sides." Where Lenin said that what was *new*, what was so shocking was "passion for bossing" on the part of Communists now that they had power, Trotsky was shadow-boxing with "the old trade unionist concepts."

There was no meeting half-way because this was a leadership divided against itself on the very solid ground of *its relationship to the masses*.

"We must not fear to admit the disease"—the disease of bureaucratism, Lenin warned, lest we ourselves develop an administrative mentality. When you come down to rock bottom, there is one way, only one way, to arrive at new social relations for *ever new millions of toilers* and that is "gradually to draw the whole toiling population to a man in the work of running the state."

"The toiling population to a man." "To a man!" That is to say all those on the production line, *every single* man and woman from cook to bottle washer, from machinist to handyman, from intellectual to washerwoman. Then, *only then* will new social relations be established.

No planning from above, or what Lenin called "bureaucratic project-hatching" could establish the new. Only the masses *from below, to a man*. This total conception, and totally new attitude, was the very conception that Lenin first elaborated in his *State and Revolution* as the only true meaning of a social revolution. Now it had assumed new flesh and blood for now it was *not only theory but the practice* and not only the practice in "making" revolutions but in working out truly human relations.

Lenin was so concrete in his understanding of *propagandist* because his over-all conception was so magnificent. He said all that the leadership can do, all that Trotsky should do if he is to remain a propagandist and not the administrator ordering people about, is to shout from the Kremlin walls, the *Pravda* offices, what the workers themselves are doing. *Their* initiative, *their* activity, *their* attitude must become the basis of all *your* (the intellectuals) theory.

Lenin never moved from his position, not even after he won and the Russian Communist party had adopted his theses and rejected those of Trotsky and Shlyapnikov. On the contrary, he continued to hammer away: "History knows all sorts of degeneration to depend upon conviction, devotion and other spiritual qualities in politics, that is not all a serious thing."

Trotsky, on the contrary, beginning with that fateful year of 1920 when he proposed the militarization of labor, persisted in an administrative approach. It did not matter what the economic conditions were—his concept was administrative. Always it was the concept of Plan and the workers' initiative being circumscribed by that Plan.

He *never* admitted his error of 1920. On the contrary, he insisted that "this mistake was not in the demand for stratification but in the fact that the economic policy did not correspond to the economic conditions." But it was *not* the economic conditions, either in 1920, nor in 1921, nor in 1923, that made Trotsky write as he did. It was his *attitude, his attitude to the broad masses*. That is why it did not matter whether the year was 1920 and his program was one of the "Single Plan"; nor whether it was 1921 and his program was "stratification of the trade union"; nor 1921–2 when the "New Economic Policy" (modified commercial capitalism) was established and he still held that the concrete conditions "excluded the possibility of practical inclusion of trade unionist in the management of the economy." He never changed his position, not even after he was expelled and his arch-enemy Stalin put into operation the Five Year Plan which moved to its own gory conclusion in 1932. Trotsky still wrote: "The role of factory committees remains important, of course, but in the sphere of the management of industry it has no longer a leading but an auxiliary position."

If he did not "mean" what he wrote, this great revolutionary journalist wrote for two decades without finding the words necessary to express what he *did* mean. Yet he always found words, thousands and thousands of words, to express the opposite of what he "did mean."

There was always a different "reason" for the administrative approach. In 1920 it was the disorganization of the economy. In 1921 it was the inefficiency of the trade union personnel. In 1922 it was "the market economy." In 1928, 1932, 1940, it was the Plan. But whatever the "reason" the conclusion was always the same: Planning by specialists, Planning from above, workers control, yes, if it were heavily detailed by planners. By whatever name you wish to label it, this precisely is the administrative approach to workers' self-activity strictly subordinated to the Plan.

That is precisely why Trotsky, despite all his revolutionary ardor and devotion, could not fight the counter-revolutionary Stalin. Their *theoretical basis* was the same. The Plan. It happened, as it so often happens in history, that in the 1920 debate Stalin, a man who appreciated what majority means, supported Lenin who then had the majority behind him. But in his *concept* of plan and administration he was with Trotsky. And he had the complete brutality needed to *carry through* the Plan to the bitter end and establishing the greatest tyranny on earth. How right Lenin was with his prediction "History knows all sorts of degenerations..."

The uniqueness of 1920 is this: it disclosed that *before, during and after* the social revolution the problem of the conquest of power and the problem of the new society is one and the same. *Its axis is the relationship to the masses.* It is this which 1920 posed: the relationship of the masses to the trade unions and the political parties. This relationship has yet to be worked out. It remains the problem today. We hope in future issues of the paper to show *how* we are trying to work out this triangular relationship as it is reflected in our own small organization.

Postscript

There is no need for our readers to think that because they know only English while the books on the trade union debate are mainly in Russian, thereby they must miss a single important point of the debate. The truth is that Volume IX of Lenin's *Selected Works*, especially the first three articles, contains not alone the summation of all positions but an analysis of the various attitudes as they changed in the course of the debate.... It is the most remarkable book in the great library of Marxism.

Lenin and His New Concept: Party Work to Be Checked by Non-party Masses

Marxism and Freedom

Lenin's enemies are legion nowadays. There is always a lot of talk about his having been a "democrat" and an exponent of "workers management from below" only "in theory," but that as soon as *State and Revolution* was put away as a book, the practice of governing made him a "dictator." Attempts have been made to give the impression that the young workers' state forbade strikes. If it did, it surely failed to enforce the edict. In the year of the trade union debate, Tomsky, the head of the trade unions, reported that there were, in Moscow alone, between thirty and forty strikes a month. Naturally, the Party thought the trade unions ought to function so well that workers' grievances are acted upon as they arise, and not let dissatisfactions accumulate and cause walkouts. But, not only were strikes permitted, Tomsky and other Communist leaders were complaining that Communists were losing influence because some were stupid enough not to walk out when the workers in their shops went on strike!

Tomsky severely rebuked "the *chinovnik* (petty bureaucrat) attitude" underlying the proposals that strikes be allowed only in privately-owned plants, and not in state enterprises. Lenin's insistence on trade unions as "schools of communism" was *not* to enforce discipline, which he insisted only the workers themselves can enforce, but to stress that production problems cannot be solved "for" the workers—*if* the transitional state was to be transitional to socialism and *not* to a "return backwards to capitalism."

One of the "conclusive" proofs of Lenin's "dictatorship," cited by his enemies, is that it was he who introduced the Resolution on Party Unity which forbade factions. It is true that at the Tenth Congress—when the economy lay in ruins, and the Kronstadt mutiny threatened the very existence of the new state, and forced a return backward to limited capitalism (The New Economic Policy)—Lenin asked that all differing positions within the Communist Party be expressed to the Party directly rather than through caucuses. But: (1) this was done after the discussion was over, after delegates had been elected on the differing platforms, and after the duly convoked Congress had come to majority decisions and voted, (2) Shlyapnikov, against whom the Resolution was aimed, was not only *not* removed from his post, but representatives of his position were taken into the Central Committee; (3) the Platform of the Workers' Opposition had appeared in the central organ of the Party in no fewer than 250,000 copies; and (4) even after the elimination of caucuses, a Discussion Sheet was established so that opposing views could continue to be expressed.

The Kronstadt mutiny compelled sharp measures which are certainly no model for a workers' state to follow. But, to draw a parallel between Lenin's Resolution and Stalin's monolithism is to fly in the face of facts as well as of theory, and to make a complete hash of historic periods.

The truth is, precision such as Lenin's, in the 1920 debate, can come only from a man who lives by his theory, or more precisely, by the vision of the future society. To put it dialectically, Lenin had a clear "Notion" in his head—it was the new absolute, *"to a man"*—and he judged the truth of reality *by* its relationship to the truth of the "Notion."

"The toiling population to a man." *To a man.* That is to say, *every single* man, woman, and youth, from cook to bottle washer, from machinist to handyman, from intellectual to washer-woman, *especially* "the unskilled laborers who are living under *ordinary, i.e., very hard* conditions."[1] (Emphasis is Lenin's.) Lenin was most insistent, in his writings in those early years, that, just as Marx, in *Capital* counter-posed the workers' struggle for the shortening of the working day to all the grandiloquent and empty phrases of the "Declaration of Rights," so must they now, in Russia, have "fewer pompous phrases, more plain, *everyday* work, concern for the pood of grain and the pood of coal!"[2] Genuine communism, he wrote, differs from phrase-mongering in that it *"reduces everything to the conditions of labor."* (Emphasis is Lenin's.) This total conception—that only the masses, *from below,* "to a man," can create a new way of life for millions—he elaborated in *State and Revolution* as theory. It was the guiding line in his every-day practical work.

The tragedy of the Russian Revolution is that this was *not* achieved. Even with a correct approach to the masses, as exemplified in the trade union resolution incorporating Lenin's views, the young workers' state could not lift itself by its own bootstraps, particularly as it didn't have any boots. A retreat to the NEP (the New Economic Policy which permitted operation of certain capitalist enterprises) had to be undertaken. None of the Bolshevik leaders thought they could hold out for long in isolated backward Russia without the aid of the European revolution. In explaining the policy of the NEP to the Third Congress of the Communist International, Lenin stressed their dependence on the international revolution:

> We quite openly admit, we do not conceal the fact that concessions in the system of state capitalism mean paying tribute to capitalism. But we gain time and gaining time means gaining everything, particularly in the

1 Lenin, *Selected Works,* Vol. IX, p. 429.

2 Lenin. *Selected Works,* Vol. IX, p. 440.

epoch of equilibrium when our foreign comrades are preparing thoroughly for their revolution.

With the defeat of the German Revolution of 1923 (after the beheading of the German Revolution of 1919) the proletarian revolution in Russia was completely isolated. Lenin, who made no fetish of the workers' state, watched like a hawk the further development of the NEP *and* of his party. He knew very well that the dictatorship of the proletariat was a transitional state which could be transitional "either to socialism or to a return backward to capitalism," depending upon the historic initiative of the masses and the international situation. He knew that the Party, especially now that it had power, was not immune to the circumstances under which it operated. The whole 1920–1921 debate showed that the same great formations in society—trade unionists, politicos, masses—were reflected in the leadership of the party. He depended on the ranks, who were closest to the masses outside, to set the party straight.

Party work must be checked by the *non-party* masses. He wrote:

> Of course we shall not submit to everything the masses say, for the masses also yield to sentiments that are not in the least advanced, particularly in years of exceptional weariness and exhaustion resulting from excessive burdens and suffering. But in appraising persons, in determining our attitude to those...who have become "commissarised," "bureaucratised," the suggestions of non-party proletarian masses and in many cases of the non- party peasant masses, are extremely valuable. The toiling masses have a fine instinct for the difference between honest and devoted Communists and those who arouse revulsion of feeling in one who obtains his bread by the sweat of his brow, who enjoys no privileges, and who has no "open door to the chief."[3]

This "Party man," in his last appearance before the Communist Party Congress,[4] spoke about how "mortally sick" he was of "*Communlies*"[5] (Communist lies).

---

3 *Selected Works.* Vol. IX. pp. 253–54. See also, Lenin's *Collected Works,* Rus. Ed., Vol. XXVI: "To put life into the Soviets, to attract the non-party people, to have the work of the party people checked by non-party people.... We are badly executing the slogan: arouse the non-party people, check the work of the party by the non-party masses." (p. 474, 475.).

4 Because Lenin, at that Congress, spoke of a "state capitalism that is not written about in books," that "exists under Communism," some Marxists have denied that Russia is an "ordinary" state capitalist society. The Russian Communists are banking on just such a misreading of Lenin's warning about "a return backwards to capitalism."

5 *Selected Works,* Vol. IX, p. 346.

This Communist leader *invented* words to express his severe criticism of the young workers' state and of the Party that led the Revolution. Precisely because he *stood on the great achievements of this Revolution,* his criticism was more devastating than that of any of its enemies. "History proceeds in devious ways," he kept warning. Making no fetishism out of the workers' state, he spoke of "the simple class truth of the class enemy" who say that the Soviet state "has taken the road that will lead to the ordinary bourgeois state."

> It is very useful to read this sort of thing, which is written not because the Communist state allows you to write some things and does not allow you to write others, but because it really is the class truth, bluntly and frankly uttered by the class enemy.[6]

What he warned about, in a word, is of the inevitable coming of state capitalism if the bureaucratization and isolation of the Soviet state continued:

> If we take that huge bureaucratic machine, that huge pile, we must ask: Who is leading whom? I doubt very much whether it could be said that the Communisis were guiding this pile. To tell the truth, it is not they who are leading, they are being led.[7]

Just as he made no fetishism out of the workers' state, neither did he of the Bolshevik Party which he founded. We have followed the development of his views on that since 1902, and *especially* the period of 1917, when he told his Party that if they would not put the question of workers' power on the agenda, he would "go to the sailors." He, at all times, not only said so but *acted* on the principle that in revolutionary situations the masses are far in advance of the Party, and the Party ranks far in advance of the Party leadership. Of course, that did not mean that he did not assign a very fundamental role to the Party he founded; but it was *in strict relationship* to the actual spontaneous movement of the masses. *Outside of that relationship* the Party would become anything its worst enemies could think of. It did.

∴

6 *Selected Works.* Vol. IX, p. 347.

7 *Selected Works.* Vol. IX, p. 348.

Lenin's *Will*

Marxism and Freedom

There is no greater indictment of the Party leadership that led the only successful revolution in history than Lenin's *Will.* In it he was concerned with his own colleagues, leaders of the Bolshevik Revolution in Russia in November 1917, who had themselves given birth to a new bureaucracy.

There is no more amazing document in the annals of politics than this brief, two-page *Will.*[8] It deals, in the concrete, with the leaders of the Russian Communist Party in a manner which leaves no division between politics and economics, history and philosophy, theory and practice, revolution and counter-revolution.

Lenin states boldly that, if the *dual* nature of the Russian state—that of being a state of workers and peasants—is at the root of the dispute between the principal combatants—Trotsky and Stalin—then no force on earth could stop the class division from bringing down the workers' state. Its fall is inevitable. However, the trends implicit in the dispute are *not yet* a reality. With that in mind, says Lenin, let's take a look at the general staff which made the revolution:

(1) *Stalin.* He is "rude and disloyal." *He must be removed.*
(2) *Trotsky.* His "non-Bolshevism," writes Lenin, does not in any way detract from the fact that he is "the most able man in the present Central Committee," but he is *"far too much attracted by the purely administrative side of affairs."* (My emphasis.)
(3) *Zinoviev and Kamenev.* They publicized the date of revolution in the capitalist press, at the very moment when the workers were trying to take power. This was "no accident," Lenin reminds us. That is to say, at every critical moment, they can be expected to do the same.

What stands out in the rest of the *Will* is that it was not alone the older men who would look for administrative, instead of human, solutions to complex problems, but the younger men. Take Bukharin:

> (4) Bukharin is not only the most valuable and biggest theoretician of the party, but also may legitimately be considered the favorite of the whole party; but his theoretical views can only with the very greatest doubt be regarded as fully Marxian, for there is something scholastic in him (he never learned, and I think never fully understood, the dialectic).

8 First published in 1932 by Leon Trotsky. See *The Suppressed Testament of Lenin.*

Lenin once said that the one word which could characterize the whole of the Marx-Engels Correspondence was "dialectics." This is no less true of Lenin in the period since his *Philosophic Notebooks.* This, again, is the central feature of all of Lenin's disputes with Bukharin, beginning with the National Question during World War I and ending with the *Will.* That was so not only in his public debates but in his commentary on Bukharin's theoretical works which Lenin did not publicly criticize. We have Lenin's Notebooks of 1920[9] in which he commented on Bukharin's *Economics of the Transition Period.*[10] The book puts forward the theory of an allegedly classless force, "a third group," (neither capitalist nor worker that is) which Bukharin calls "the technical intelligentsia," whose mission it seems to be to establish "economic equilibrium." According to Bukharin, the "technical intelligentsia" was born "to replace the blind laws of the market." The development from industrial to finance capital was a development from an unorganized, anarchic commodity economy "to an organized, planned economy." The organizing force of that is the technical intelligentsia. This is the new absolute for state capitalism *and* for the dictatorship of the proletariat, "the transition period." No wonder Bukharin found himself alongside Trotsky in the Trade Union debate. As Lenin put it, in his "Remarks on Bukharin's *Economics of the Transition Period,*" when he reached a passage where Bukharin finally remembered the two fundamental laws of capitalist production—centralization of capital and socialization of labor—"Finally, thank god, Human language instead of 'organized' babbling. All is well that ends well."[11] But two pages later he is hitting out against Bukharin again. He quotes Bukharin: "Once the destruction of capitalist production relations is really given and once the theoretic impossibility of their restoration is proven." Then Lenin comments: "'Impossibility' is demonstrated only practically. The author does not pose *dialectically* the relationship of theory to practice."[12]

Now, in his *Will,* Lenin is summing up his analysis of Bukharin the theoretician, and again, the criticism is all concentrated in the word, "dialectic." It is evident that, to Lenin, one cannot be regarded as a Marxist though one is "the biggest theoretician of the party" *if* one has "never fully understood the dialectic."

---

9 *Leninski Sbornik,* No. 11. Russian ed. [Available in English as appendix to Bukharin's *Economics of the Transition Period.*].

10 [Available in English, Routledge] There are some Marxists who first now wish to take that work as a new point of departure. Evidently anything is good enough to avoid working out for oneself an analysis of one's own epoch!

11 *Leninski Sbornik* (Lenin's Miscellany), No. 11, p. 360.

12 *Ibid.,* p. 362.

Far from making the *Will* a new point of departure, the whole leadership of the Bolshevik Party agreed not to publish the founder's *Will*.

After Trotsky was exiled he published it. His commentary does not shed much illumination on it. Because Trotsky was closest to Lenin in that year, he tried to play down the seriousness of the 1920–21 debate, although it is clear Lenin had that debate in mind when he spoke of Trotsky's administrative attitude. Far from admitting his error, Trotsky insisted in all his later writings that "the mistake was not in the demand for statification, but in the fact that the economic policy did not correspond to the economic conditions."[13] He maintained that it was the economic conditions which made him propose free trade a year before the NEP and when the Political Bureau rejected his proposal, then he proposed statification of the union and "in the end" Lenin and he agreed. The truth, however, is that though all did vote for the NEP, Trotsky did so administratively once again and *therefore* he spoke of the concrete conditions which now "excluded the possibility of practical inclusion of trade unionists in the management of the economy."

It was not the economic conditions, neither in 1920, nor in 1921, nor in 1923, that made Trotsky write as he did. It was his attitude to the broad masses. Whether his program was for "free trade" or for the "Single Plan," his attitude to the masses was the same. The proof is in his theories *after* he was expelled from Russia and his arch-enemy, Stalin, put into operation the Five Year Plan which moved to its own gory conclusion in 1932. Trotsky still spoke the same language: "The role of factory committees remains important, of course, but in the sphere of the management of industry it has no longer a leading but an auxiliary position."

If Trotsky did not "mean" what he wrote, this great revolutionary wrote for two decades without finding the words to express what he did mean. Yet he always found words, thousands and thousands of words, to express the *opposite* of what he "did mean." It is impossible to arrive at any other conclusion than the fact that even Lenin's closest colleagues—and none was closer than Trotsky in that last period when Lenin appealed to him for a joint struggle against Stalin—had been treating Lenin's philosophic concepts as the Marxists before World War I had treated Marxian philosophy—as some rhetorical adjunct to "the great economic theories."

13 See *The Stenographic Report of the Tenth Congress of the R.C.P.*, Russian. The essence is repeated in almost all of Trotsky's criticisms of the "tempo" of the Five Year Plans. See also his "Letter to the Bureau of Party History," in *The Stalin School of Falsification*, especially pp. 28–30 and 64–65.

Nothing could be further from the truth. Without the Humanism of Marx, and later, of Lenin, the economic theories of both are meaningless. Leaders are not classless creatures floating between heaven and earth. They are very much earth men. When they lose close connection with the working class, they begin to represent the only *other* fundamental class in society—the capitalist class.

What was not yet a reality when Lenin wrote this, became a reality very soon when Stalin consolidated his power and introduced the Plan. It is true that even Lenin did not see Stalin as representing an alien class. But he was prophetic in this: he stated that *if* the differences within the leadership *did* reflect outright class differences, then nothing could save the workers' state. Nothing did. It became transformed into a State Capitalist society.

As we shall see later, once a new class, that of state capitalism, emerged in Russia, not only did the Russian Communist Party become its victim, so too did the Third International. Where Lenin, with characteristic precision, moved from the strict conditions he laid down for joining the International to an admission that the "language" of its Resolutions was "too Russian," Stalin imposed monolithism upon the Russian Communist Party and made it the ukase for the entire International.

The totalitarian dictators who now rule Russia have, after more than a quarter of a century of silence, during which the State and the Party have been entirely transformed, and all the people mentioned in the *Will* are dead, "suddenly" decided to admit its existence, subordinating it to their contrived myth of "the cult of personality." Nothing could have been stranger to Lenin. The "rude and disloyal" characterization of Stalin had nothing to do with any "cult of personality." What Lenin was saying was: it is the masses and only they who can smash the old and create the new, while the leaders who made such great contributions to the success of the Revolution, are, *as individuals,* impotent to change the course of history. *Worse yet,* there is nothing in the philosophy and politics of the leaders that can keep the passions that stirred in their breasts from being as "base and mean" as those that stirred the capitalists to their mission.

What was not a reality in January, 1924, soon became a reality. It is not alone Stalin whom Lenin characterized, it is his progeny, the present rulers whom Stalin brought up in his own image. The one and only way for them to carry out Lenin's *Will* is to remove themselves from power.

Lenin *summed up* a lifetime spent in the revolutionary movement and concluded that if the Party dispute reflected actual class lines, nothing on earth can close up those divisive lines. The proletarian state would collapse. *So it did.*

PART 4

Russia's Transformation into Opposite: The Theory of State-Capitalism

CHAPTER 9

The Development of State-Capitalist Theory in the 1940s

> *... the shock of the Hitler-Stalin Pact in 1939, followed by the outbreak of World War II and Trotsky's call for the defense of Russia, signaled the beginning of the end of world Trotskyism. The many tendencies that sprang up within Trotskyism questioned the very nature of the Russian state and the Russian economy, rather than just the political bureaucratization that Stalin introduced and that Trotsky had fought.*
>
> *I plunged into the study of all the Russian Five-Year Plans. (The most valuable research work was done in the Slavic Division of the New York Public Library, the Library of Congress, and Hoover Institute in California.)... [A]t the same time I was engaged in research on the Russian economy of 1928–39, I was translating for myself philosophic works of Marx, those that were listed by Ryazanov as "Preparatory Works for The Holy Family" and which we now know as the famous Humanist Essays, as well as Lenin's Abstract of Hegel's Science of Logic... In a word, the relationship between philosophy and economics was intensified. Indeed, by the 1940s I saw philosophy as inherent in new revolutionary forces—labor, Black, women, youth...*
>
> —DUNAYEVSKAYA, *Introduction to Volume XII of the Raya Dunayevskaya Collection*

Dunayevskaya's 1940s writings on the theory of state-capitalism, initially begun independently, were developed while she was co-leader with C.L.R James of the State-Capitalist Tendency (Johnson-Forest Tendency) within the Trotskyist movement. Her analyses—demonstrating Stalin's Russia to be a state-capitlist society—not only took issue with Trotsky's continued defense of Russia as a workers' state, but critiqued the beaucratic collectivist analysis of Max Shachtman and others.

As Dunayevskaya noted above, these economic studies were unseparated from probing the philosophic writings of Marx and Lenin on Hegel, and finding "philosophy as inherent in new revolutionary forces." Thus, the origins of her Marxist-Humanism are found in State-Capitalist theory.

Several key documents of Dunayevskaya's state-capitalist analysis are presented in this chapter. Additional documents on state-capitalism can be found in Volume I of the Raya Dunayevskaya Collection.

The Union of Soviet Socialist Republics is a Capitalist Society

February, 1941, Written under the Pseudonym "Freddie James" Published by the Workers' Party in Mimeographed form in an Internal Discussion Bulletin of March, 1941

> And even when society has got upon the right track for the discovery of the natural laws of its movement—and it is the ultimate aim of this work, to lay bare the economic law of motion of modern society—it can neither clear by bold leaps, nor remove by legal enactments, the obstacles offered by the successive phases of its normal development. But it can shorten and lessen the birth pangs.
>
> KARL MARX, Preface to *Capital*, Vol. I[1]

I Political and Social Rule

It was the contention of Comrade [Leon] Trotsky that the existence of statified property in Russia was sufficient to characterize it as a workers' state, regardless of the political regime in power. The counter-revolutionary Stalinist bureaucracy, therefore, could and did (though badly) defend the social rule of the proletariat. To thus epitomize the constituent elements of a workers' state is at wide variance with the views held by Marx and Lenin. Let us look at the birth of the Soviet Republic for a verification of their views.

In establishing itself as the ruling class, the Russian proletariat not only expropriated the capitalist and landlord but also guaranteed power to the poor; *political* power (a state controlled by them through their own organs—the trade unions, the Soviets, the Bolshevik Party), and *social* power, which Lenin defined as the "practical participation in the management" of the state. Lenin emphasized that it was the aim of the Soviet state "to attract every member of the poor class to practical participation in the management."[2] In the same pamphlet, *Soviets at Work*, he further elaborated this view: "The proximity of the Soviets to the toiling masses creates special forms of recall and other methods of control by the masses."[3] He called for the development "with

1 Unless otherwise noted, all notes in this document are by the editors. Karl Marx, *Capital*, Vol. I (New York: Vintage, 1977), p. 92; see also *Capital*, Vol. I (Chicago: Charles H. Kerr, 1906), pp. 14–15.

2 See V.I, Lenin, "The International Position of the Russian Soviet Republic and the Fundamental Tasks of the Socialist Revolution," in *Collected Works*, Vol. 27 (Moscow: Progress Publishers, 1965), p. 273.

3 *Ibid.*, pp. 274–275.

specific diligence" of these special forms of recall and diverse methods of mass control. By means of "practical participation in the management" of the state the political and social rule of the proletariat are merged and that guaranteed power in the hands of the proletariat. The diverse forms of mass control would paralyze "every possibility of distorting the Soviet rule," remove "the wild grass of bureaucratism." That was his practical interpretation of his theoretical elaboration of the state in his *State and Revolution*, to wit: (1) Control by the workers cannot be carried out by a state of bureaucrats but must be carried out by a state of armed workers, (2) In a proletarian state all must be "bureaucrats" so that no one could be a bureaucrat. (3) The state should be so constituted that it begins to wither away and cannot but wither away.

In 1918, Lenin stressed the fact that the expropriation of the capitalists was a comparatively simple problem when contrasted to the more complex one of "creating conditions under which the bourgeoisie could neither exist nor come anew into existence."[4] In the further development of the Soviet state, Lenin once again realized the practical meaning of the dictum of Marx that a society could "neither clear by bold leaps, nor remove by legal enactments, the obstacles offered by the successive phases of its normal development." But he knew that so long as the Soviet state "guaranteed powers to the workers and the poor" that it need not be fatal to it to "implant" state capitalism.

Not even the most pious worker-statist would contend that the workers had any power in the present Soviet state. He would merely reiterate that so long as there was statified property, etc., etc. But I deny that the social conquests of October [1917]—the conscious and active political and practical participation of the masses in liberating themselves from the yoke of Tsarism, capitalism and landlordism—are to be narrowly translated into mere statified property, that is to say, the ownership of the means of production by a state which in no way resembles the Marxian concept of a workers' state, i.e., "the proletariat organized as the ruling class."[5]

II State Capitalism or Bureaucratic State Socialism?

Comrade Shachtman[6] asks: "If the workers are no longer the ruling class and the Soviet Union no longer a workers' state and if there is no private property

4 *Ibid.*, p. 245.

5 This expression of Marx is from *The Communist Manifesto.*

6 Max Shachtman (1903–72) was a leader of the Workers' Party who argued that Stalinist Russia was a form of "bureaucratic collectivism."

owning capitalist class ruling Russia, what is the class nature of the state, and what exactly is the bureaucracy that dominates it?" And he answers: bureaucratic state socialism, because, among other things, the new term elucidates the "distinction from capitalism" characteristic of the class nature of the Soviet state.

But how does the mode of production differ under bureaucratic state socialist rule from that under capitalist rule? What is the economic law of motion of this presumably new exploitative society? These crucial points Comrade Shachtman fails to discuss. Let me examine the alleged "distinction from capitalism" characteristic of the Soviet Union and see whether it isn't a distinction from a certain stage of capitalism rather than from capitalism as a whole. The determining factor in analyzing the class nature of a society is not whether the means of production are the private property of the capitalist class or are state-owned, but whether the means of production are capital i.e. whether they are monopolized & alienated from the direct producers. The Soviet Government occupies in relation to the whole economic system the position which a capitalist occupies in relation to a single enterprise. Shachtman's designation of the class nature of the Soviet Union as "bureaucratic state socialism" is an irrational expression behind which there exists the real economic relation of state-capitalist-exploiter to the propertyless exploited. Shachtman correctly emphasizes that: "The conquest of state power by the bureaucracy spelled the destruction of the property relations established by the Bolshevik revolution." Yet he does not see that the "new" production relations are none other than the relations under capitalism. He does not even consider the possibility that the "new" exploitative society is state capitalism. Comrade Trotsky did consider that variant interpretation but violently opposes defining the Stalinist bureaucracy as a class of state capitalists. Let us see whether he was justified in his opposition.

State capitalism, Trotsky contended, does not exist in Russia since the ownership of the means of production by the state occurred in history by the proletariat with the method of social revolution and not by the capitalist with the method of state trustification.[7] But does the manner in which a thing is accomplished determine the use to which it is put by its usurpers any more than each test to be accomplished determines the group to execute it. "The bourgeois character of a revolution," wrote Trotsky in polemicizing against the Menshevik thesis that since the Russian Revolution was a bourgeois revolution the proletariat ought to renounce power in favor of the bourgeoisie, "could not answer in advance the question as to which class would solve the tasks

7 See Leon Trotsky, *The Revolution Betrayed* (New York: Doubleday, 1937), p. 248.

of the democratic revolution."[8] In further expounding his theory of the permanent revolution, Trotsky, wrote: "Socialization of the means of production had become a necessary condition for bringing the country out of barbarism. That is the law of combined development for backward countries." Precisely! But is it necessary among Marxists to stress the fact that socialization of the means of production is not socialism but as much an economic law of capitalist development as is monopoly. The weak Russian bourgeoisie was incapable of accomplishing either the democratic tasks of the revolution or the further development of the productive forces. "Its" task was accomplished by the masses with the method of social revolution. However, the task of the young proletarian rulers was greatly complicated by the backwardness of Russia; and the treachery of the Social-Democracy left them unaided by the world proletariat. Finally, the Stalinist counter-revolution identified itself with the state. The manner in which the means of production were converted into state property did not deprive them of their becoming capital.

To prove that the particular state-monopoly capitalism existing in Russia did not come about through state trustification but by methods of social revolution explains its historic origin but does not prove that its economic law of motion differs from that analyzed by Karl Marx, Engels and Lenin. It is high time to evaluate "the economic law of motion of modern society" as it applies to the Soviet Union and not merely to retain for statified property the same "superstitious reverence" the opportunists entertained for the bourgeois state.

III No Defense of the Capitalist Society Existing in Russia

Because we did not clearly understand the class nature of the present Soviet state, the Soviet Union's integral participation in the Second Imperialist World War came as a monstrous surprise.[9] The Red Army march on Poland, the bloody conquest of part of Finland and the peaceful conquest of the Baltic States proved that the Stalinized Red Army had no more connection with the spirit, purpose and content of October than has the Stalinist state, whose armed might it is. What an abhorrent relapse from the conquests of October are the Stalinist conquests! Long before the outbreak of World War II the Russian masses bore the brunt of this "abhorrent relapse." The worker had a first premonition of it when as a Left Oppositionist he fought the Thermidorians[10]

8 Leon Trotsky, *The Permanent Revolution* (New York: Pioneer, 1931), p. xxvii.

9 This refers to the signing of the Hitler-Stalin Pact of August 1939, which was followed within a month by the joint Russian and German carving up of East Europe.

10 The "Left Opposition" refers to the political opposition against Stalin grouped around Trotsky from 1923. "Thermidor" was the month in the calendar adopted by the French

who deprived him of his job along with his Communist Party membership card. The glimmer of hope that he had when the Stalinist bureaucracy nevertheless adopted the Opposition plank for industrialization and collectivization, faded as soon as he realized that the development of the productive forces did not raise his standard of living. He learned quickly enough that the "socialist fatherland" knew how to accumulate for other purposes. He would have felt the grind of Stakhanovism[11] if the name had not been russified for him but had the original Ford-Taylor speed-up insignia. To call the piece work system which is best suited to capitalist exploitation "socialist working norms" does not lighten the degree of exploitation of the bricklayer who has to lay 16,000 bricks per day, or for a typist (if I may be permitted a petty-bourgeois interest in my own trade) to type 45 pages of 30 lines each and 60 strokes in each line per day[12] Decreeing "universal, free and equal suffrage" does not make it possible for the 14-year-old to vote "no" to being conscripted in the labor reserves, "educated" (read: taught a trade), and at the end of the two year training program, being put to work on state enterprises for four consecutive years—even if this newly educated 16-year-old is guaranteed "the established wage rate." It is not only that the income of the factory worker is 110 rubles a month, and that of the director 1,200 a month, but that the whole mode of production produces and reproduces the capitalist production relations. State capitalism, it is true, but capitalism nevertheless. Could we have forgotten that state property forms (and it is only *form*, not *relation*, for it is without control by the masses) are the aim of proletarian revolution only as a *means* to achieve the quicker the fullest development of the productive forces the better *to satisfy the needs of man?*

No, the existence of statified property in Russia does not make its defense imperative even were the Soviet Union attacked by other imperialist nations for purposes of abolishing statified property (which is less likely just now than the Stalinist state joining the "new order" of Hitler)—unless we are to

---

Revolution, in which Robespierre was overthrown by a reactionary wing of the revolution. Trotsky often used the term to describe those grouped around Stalin after 1923.

11 "Stakhanovism" was a system of speedup of production introduced in Russia in 1935, which led to a rise in income differentiation. It encountered much resistance by the workers. For Dunayevskaya's analysis of this phenomenon, see *The Marxist-Humanist Theory of State-Capitalism* (Chicago: News and Letters, 1992), pp. 61–62 especially.

12 The norms must be higher now. The above norms were effective up to June 26, 1940, at which time the working day was changed from 7 to 8 hours. This decree was supplemented by a law interpreting this lengthening of the work day by instructing the various institutions "to raise the norms of production and lower piece prices in proportion to the lengthening of the working day."—RD.

change our policy and call for the defense of, say, France because the work of the German fascists in dividing the country is of a decidedly retrogressive character. It is the irrationality of Shachtman's characterization of the class nature of the Soviet Union as "bureaucratic state socialism" that leads him to expound conditional defense of the present Soviet state. It is the real economic relations behind that irrational expression that leads to: *no defense of the capitalist society existing in Russia.*

∴

An Analysis of Russian Economy[13]

Written under Pen Name of Freddie Forest, *The New International,* Dec.1942, Jan. 1943, Feb. 1943

***The New International,* December, 1942**

I *The Approach*

In this study of Russian industrialization, 1928–1941, a period encompassing the First and Second Five Year Plans and that part of the Third Plan which preceded the present war, my fundamental purpose is to analyze the direction in which Russian economy has proceeded during that period. Is the direction of its growth—the preponderance of means of production over means of consumption, the high organic composition of capital and the rapid deterioration of the living standards of the masses—merely an accidental tendency, or is it the inevitable consequence of the law of motion of its economy?

First of all it is necessary to analyze the progress of Russian economy during the entire period covered by this study. I'm not concerned primarily, however, with a mere statistical measurement of this development because the degree to which the goals established under the plans were or were not achieved have no direct relevance to my thesis. But so extravagant has been the publicity which the proponents of the Soviet have given these data that the view is widely held that the allegedly phenomenal rate of industrial growth in Russia is the criterion of a unique form of economy. Therefore, in order to clear the decks for a basic approach to the subject, it is necessary to deal with this contention.

13 Dunayevskaya preferred the name "Russia" rather than "USSR" (Union of Soviet Socialist Republics) because in her view it was neither socialist nor run by actual soviets, and was dominated by Russia.—Editor.

Russian economists refer to the purported 650 per cent increase in the value of all industrial production from 1928 to 1938 as a phenomenon that could not be surpassed, or even matched, except under socialism. They point with pride to that record as one far exceeding the accomplishments of the great capitalist nations in their balmiest days: the highest increase of industrial production in England was 29 per cent for the decade 1860–70 and for the United States it was 120 per cent for the decade 1880–90. It should be obvious, however, that the rate of economic development of a nation inevitably depends upon a number of circumstances:

(1) The level world-wide technological development when the nation embarks on industrialization. Russia in 1928 need not await the tedious process of discovery and invention, as did other nations at the dawn of the industrial revolution, but could draw upon the accumulation of centuries of industrial capitalism.
(2) The extent of the natural resources available to the nation. Russia, one of the most favored of all lands in natural resources, containing in its borders all the essential materials of industry, is at a decided advantage compared to the nations less well favored by nature, as, for example, Japan.
(3) The base from which the achievements are calculated. Clearly, it is easier to attain an annual rate of increase of 100 per cent when the base is one automobile or fifty than when it is one million or fifty million. Furthermore, the sheer bulk of capital goods in an advanced industrial society impedes the rate of technological progress because of the enormous expense and difficulty of replacing obsolete equipment.
(4) And, the measure of control which may be exerted over the component parts of the economy.

Russian statisticians and their apologists have a "preferred" method of proving Russia's unprecedented rate of development: they use as their base the year 1929—on one hand, the year of world prosperity, preceding the depression and, on the other hand, the first year of the Five Year Plan when the Soviet Union had just regained the pre-war levels of production. Thus they more easily can show a sharp upward trend in Russian production and an equally sharp decline in world production.

Presumably, it was because Japan was not among the highly industrialized nations that Russian statisticians, who so impartially compared the Russian growth to that of the advanced nations of the capitalist world, did not include "feudal" Japan in their comparison. We must, however, pause here and note that not only "socialist" Russia but also "feudal" Japan showed a tremendous rate of growth during that period. If we take a comparable period of development, say 1932–37, we find that the total value[14] of the output of Soviet heavy industry was 23.2 billion rubles in 1932 and 55.2 billion in 1937, the value at the end of the Second Five Year Plan thus being 238 per cent of that in 1932.

Japan,[15] also passing to a more rationalized economy, had an index of 97.9 for heavy industry in 1932 and 170.8 in 1937, or 176 per cent of the 1932 figure. Moreover, Japan, poor in materials of industry, was compelled to travel long distances to import 85 per cent of its iron ore and 90 per cent of its crude oil and was far short of being self-sustaining in copper, lead, zinc, tin and other essential industrial metals. Furthermore, were we to take Japan's high point of industrialization August, 1940, as the criterion, we would see that Japan had achieved a 253.5 per cent growth in the means of production, as compared to the index of 1931–33. Such a comparison then robs much from the contention that the rate of growth in Russia is either completely unprecedented or evidence of "socialism."[16] In and by itself the rate of economic growth in Soviet Russia, as compared with rates of economic growth under other forms of economy, is not of definitive importance. To a Marxist the criterion of transcendent importance in investigating the nature of an economy is the intrinsic law of motion of the economy. With that criterion as our guide, let us review the achievements of Soviet industrialization.

II *A Statistical Abstract of the USSR*

The only available index of total production in the USSR is that of the ruble value of all industrial output. Although the value of the ruble is fixed by the Soviet State bank at 19 cents ($1.00 equals five rubles and thirty kopeks), it is utterly useless as an index of production or purchasing power in the internal economy. (See section on turnover tax in next installment.) Neither has it any value on the international market.

---

14 Measurement of growth by value of output, is of course, an entirely spurious method, althought, for reasons best know to themselves, very commonplace with Soviet statisticians. Since later sections treat the subject of the inflated ruble at length, I shall leave criticism of this method aside for the moment.

15 For studies of Japan, see: *Industrialization of Japan and Manchukuo, 1930–1940*, by Schumpeter, Allen, Gordon and Penrose; *The Economic Strength of Japan*, by Isoshi Asahi, and *Industrialization of the Western Pacific*, by Kate L. Mitchell, 1942.

16 Colin Clark, a bourgeois economist sympathetic to the Soviet Union, estimates that the most rapid advance in economic porgress, from the turn of the century to 1940, was made by Japan. Cf. his *The Conditions of Economic Progress* (London; McMillan, 1940).

An index of total industrial production which carefully weights each element in the economy in order to arrive at a statistically valid index of the volume of production has never been prepared by the Russian economists. This task, never easy under ordinary circumstances, is especially difficult in the case of Soviet statistics, which are concealed or perverted to prove the correctness of "the general line." Under these circumstances the best available gauge is that of comparing physical output of selected sections of both heavy and light industry as well as agricultural production, against a background of statistics on population and national income. Below is an abstract of the USSR prepared by me to illustrate the course of development of the whole economy from Czarist times through 1940. Figures for the year 1922 have been included in order to show the accelerated pace of the growth of production from the year of ruin following the end of counter-revolution and famine to the eve of the First Five Year Plan. All data are from official state documents in the original Russian: 1913, 1922 and 1928 figures from *Gosplan: State Planning Commission for the Development of the National Economy of the USSR: The Five Year Plan*; 1932 and 1937 figures from *Gosplan: Results* (of respective plans); 1940 figures from reports to the eighteenth conference of the Russian Communist Party, appearing in *Pravda*, February 18–21, 1941:

Statistical abstract, 1913–1940

Heavy industry	**Unit**	**1913**	**1922**	**1928**	**1932**	**1937**	**1940**
Electricity	Billion kilowatt hours	1.9	1.0	5.0	13.0	36.4	39.6*
Coal	Million tons	28.9	11.0	35.4	65.4	127.9	164.6
Petroleum	Million tons	9.3	5.0	11.7	21.3	30.4	38.0
Pig iron	Million tons	4.2	–	3.3	6.2	14.5	14.9
Steel	Million tons	4.2	–	4.0	5.9	17.7	18.4
Metal working lathes	Thousands	1.5	–	3.8	18.1	36.1	53.9*
Tractors	Thousands	0.0	0.0	1.3	51.6	80.0	176.0
Combines	Thousands	0.0	0.0	0.0	10.0	43.9	–
Length of railroads	Thousand Kilometers	59.0	71.0	77.0	83.4	84.9	93.0
Freight Traffic	Million tons	132.4	58.0	156.2	267.9	517.3	536.6

Light industry	**Unit**	**1913**	**1922**	**1928**	**1932**	**1937**	**1940**
Cottons	Million meters	2224.0	0.6	2742.0	2417.0	3447.0	3491.0
Woolens	Million meters	95.0	22.0	96.6	88.7	108.3	114.0
Linen	Million square meters	219.0	93.0	165.0	135.0	285.2	272.2
Paper	Thousand tons	197.0	–	284.5	479.0	831.6	834.0
Sugar	Thousand tons	1290.0	211.0	1340.0	828.2	2421.0	2530.0
Leather footwear	Million pairs	60.0	29.6	60.0	84.7	164.3	–
Agriculture and livestock	**Unit**	**1913**	**1922**	**1928**	**1932**	**1937**	**1940**
Total area sown	Million hectares	105.0	77.7	112.9	134.4	135.3	141.2
Amount grain harvested	Million quintals	801.0	503.1	733.2	698.7	1202.9[17]	–
Yield of crop	Per hectare	8.5	7.6	7.9	7.0	10.4[18]	–
Horses	Million head	35.8	24.1	35.9	19.6	16.7	17.5**
Cattle	Million head	60.6	45.8	70.5	40.7	57.0	64.6**
Sheep and Goats	Million head	121.2	91.1	146.7	52.0	81.3	111.6**
Pigs	Million head	20.9	12.1	26.0	11.6	22.8	32.5**
Population and national income	**Unit**	**1913**	**1922**	**1928**	**1932**	**1937**	**1940**
Total Population	Millions	139.3	133.3	152.3	165.7	[19]	170.5**

17 This is not based on the unit which was used for previous years since, in 1933, for reasons best known to the Russian state and unrevealed to the public, a measure known as the "biological yield" was adopted. This standard of measurement meant the grain is estimated on the stalks in the field before harvesting, and a 10 per cent deduction is allowed for waste. All agricultural economists, with the exception of the Stalinists, of course, agree that such an estimate does not account for actual waste. Prof. Prokopovitch discounts an additional 10 per cent, or a total of 20 per cent, for waste; other bourgeois economists discount as high as 30 to 40 per cent. However, this abstract reports official figures only.

18 See footnote 15.

19 1937 census was destroyed and data were not made available to public.

Population and national income	Unit	1913	1922	1928	1932	1937	1940
Worker and employees[20]	Millions	11.2	–	11.5	22.8	27.0	30.4
National income, of which	Rubles, per capita	52.0	–	56.0	95.0	198.0	–
Nominal wages							
Real Weekly Wages	Rubles, per week	6.0	–	14.0	–	–	78.0***
In percentage of 1913:[21]	Rubles, per week		125.0				62.4

*1938 figure; **1939 figure; ***approximate, computed from 18th party conference report.

There is one other factor in the development of the Russian economy—a most essential effect of its evolution—to be the considered and which the Abstract did not deal with: the relationship between the production of means of production and the production of the means of consumption. Since it is purely for the purpose of contrast and the same basis is used in both instances, the estimates may be made in terms of rubles. The value of gross industrial production (in billions of rubles, fixed 1926–27 prices) reveals the following proportional development between the means of production (Group A) to the means of consumption (Group B) since the initiation of the First Five Year Plan:

	1928		1932		1937		1940	
	Value	Pct	Value	Pct	Value	Pct	Value	Pct
Group A	7.0	44.3	23.2	52.3	55.2	57.5	83.9	61.0
Group B	8.7	55.7	20.3	46.7	40.3	42.5	53.6	39.0

Here we note a phenomenon characteristic of the whole contemporary world: the preponderance of the means of production over means of consumption.

20 Russian statistics lump workers and employees in one category; or when they separate them into two categories they lump rural and urban workers in one category and rural and urban employees in another; the above figure represents urban workers and employees.

21 Author's own estimate; cf. section on Standard of Living, 1940.

Was the manner in which the economy developed bureaucratically desired? Was a different course open to it? In order to be able to answer these questions and fully to understand the Abstract, it is necessary to analyze the data in the Abstract, not so much from the point of view of mere volumetric increase, but, again, from the perspective of the law of motion of the economy. The volumetric comparisons will be considered only because they offer a clearer view of the direction in which the economic structure was evolving. With this as our perspective, we turn to an analysis of the individual Plans.

III *Plans and Accomplishments*

1 First Five Year Plan, 1928–32

The Gosplan brazenly proclaimed, whilst a famine was raging in the country, that the First Five Year Plan was 93.7 per cent fulfilled—just that precisely 93.7 per cent. That much publicized figure was based upon the *value*, and not upon the volume of production, and furthermore was derived in the following manner: (1) by using the worthless standard of the inflated ruble to measure the value of industrial output; and (2) by vulgarly computing an "average" between the "103 per cent" overfulfillment of Group A to the "89 per cent" fulfillment of Group B industries. There is, of course, no doubt whatsoever about the tremendous strides made in heavy industry during that period but in no case does the value of output present a true picture of industrial production, as can be seen from the following table of actual physical output of major items of heavy and light industry:[22]

Means of production	**Unit**	**Planned**	**Accomplished**	**Pct.**
Electrification	Million kilowatt hours	22.0	13.1	59.5
Petroleum	Million tons	22.0	21.3	96.8
Coal	Million tons	75.0	65.4	87.2
Iron	Million tons	10.0	6.2	62.0
Steel	Million tons	10.4	5.9	56.7
Tractors	Thousands	55.0	51.6	93.8
Length of railroads	Thousand kilometers	90.0	83.4	92.7

22 1928 figures: *Gosplan*, State Planning Commission for the Dev. of Nat. Eco., 1930; 1932 figures: *Gosplan*, Results of the First Five Year Plan, 1933, both in Russian. The results are also published in English.

Means of consumption	Unit	Planned	Accomplished	Pct.
Cotton materials	Million meters	4700.0	2417.0	51.4
Woolens	Million meters	270.0	88.7	32.8
Linen	Million square meters	500.0	135.7	27.1
Paper	Thousand tons	900.0	491.2	54.6
Sugar	Thousand tons	2600.0	828.2	31.9
Leather footwear	Million pairs	145.0	84.1	58.4
Rubbers	Million pairs	75.0	64.8	86.4

As we can see from the above table, the actual production, based on volume, is far short of the 93.7 claimed as accomplished, based on the value of production. Even the percentages of accomplishment in the above table, however, are an overestimate because, although we have changed the basis from value to physical output, we still have retained the Soviet method of including the level of past production as part of the present accomplishment.[23]

To illustrate what we mean, let us take the example of what happened to the railroads. Seventy-seven thousand kilometers of railroads were in operation in 1928 and ninety thousand were planned for the end of the First Five Year Plan. Actually, 83.4 thousand kilometers were in operation in 1932. Since the seventy-seven thousand kilometers in operation before the plan was included in the "accomplishment," the plan was "92.7 per cent" completed. Obviously there is something wrong with a method that considers performance before the Plan as part of the accomplishment under the Plan. The correct method of computation is to determine the percentage of actual increase to planned increase for the years covered by the Plan, and none other. The planned increase is thirteen thousand kilometers, of which only 6.4 thousand were actually laid. Thus the Plan regarding the railroads was 49 per cent, not 92.7 per cent, accomplished. Carrying this method through, we find the following to be the true percentages of actual increase compared to the planned increase:

23 The credit taken for past performance is particularly ludicrous in the instance of the railroads. This was the only item which, for the year of ruin, 1922, revealed a tremendous growth. This was due to the effective work of Trotsky, who was charged with responsibility for restoring railroad transportation. Cf. Part Two, section on trade union dispute.

Means of Production	Unit	1928 Level	Planned Incr.	Accd. Incr.	Pct. Accd.
Electricity	Billion kilowatt hours	5.0	17.0	8.1	47.6
Petroleum	Million tons	11.7	10.3	9.6	93.2
Coal	Million tons	35.4	39.6	30.0	75.7
Iron	Million tons	3.3	6.7	2.9	43.3
Steel	Million tons	4.0	6.4	1.9	29.7
Tractors	Thousands	1.3	53.7	50.3	93.7
Length of railroads	Thousand kmts.	77.0	13.0	6.4	49.0

Means of Consumption	Unit	1928 Level	Planned Incr.	Accd Incr.	Pct. Accd.	Pct. Decr.
Cottons	Million meters	2742.0	1958.0	-325.0		-11.8
Woolens	Million meters	96.6	173.4	-7.9		-8.2
Linen	Million square meters	165.0	335.0	-29.3		-27.9
Paper	Thousand tons	284.5	615.5	206.7	33.6	
Sugar	Thousand tons	1340.0	1260.0	-521.8		-39
Leather footwear	Million pairs	60.0	85.0	24.7	29.0	
Rubbers	Million pairs	37.0	38.0	37.8	73.2	

The above tables are a true balance sheet of the accomplishments of the First Five Year Plan. Particularly poignant is the record of how the production of means of consumption not only failed to meet its goals, not only showed no increase in production, but starkly reveals a decrease from even the 1928 levels. Moreover, the annual curve of production reveals that light industry was progressively deteriorating:

	1928	1929	1930	1931	1932
Cotton, million meters	2742.0	3068.0	2351.0	2272.0	2417.0
Woolens, million meters	93.2	100.6	114.5	107.9	88.7

It should also be remembered that neither the annual curve nor the percentage of fulfillment takes cognizance of the extremely large amount of "defectives," admitted to be as high as 30 per cent in many instances. Although disposed of as trash, they are nevertheless quantitatively counted toward the "fulfillment" of the Plan.

The best proof of the worthlessness of the standard of value output is that it not only fails to reveal the downward curve, but, by inflation, makes the reverse seem true. Thus the gross output of articles of consumption is valued as follows (in billions of rubles):

1928	1929	1930	1931	1932
8.7	10.8	12.5	14.9	16.3

Needless to say, the drastic slaughter of livestock (greater than the decrease due to war, revolution, civil war and famine in 1914–20) was likewise not taken into account in arriving at the glorious "93.7 per cent" completion of the Plan. After all, the decrease in livestock was "no part" of the Plan.

Neither was it part of the Plan—and this is of the essence of things—to achieve the relationship of production of means of production to articles of mass consumption which resulted. As a matter of fact, the bureaucracy had planned an increase in production of articles of mass consumption. However, the manner in which heavy industry developed forced a different course upon the economy. For instance, 4.4 billion rubles was planned as capital investment in the production of means of consumption. However, only 3.5 billions was expended. This failure is even greater than appears on the surface because, in the intervening years, 1928–32, the ruble experienced further inflation. For the moment we leave that feature aside in order that our attention will not be diverted from the actual course of the development of the means of production. There was the necessity of producing machinery with the most modern technique. The low productivity of Russian labor conflicted with the high productivity of international labor. Consequently, the reality of the world market and world prices constantly forced the state to increase the amount of capital investments going into the production of means of production. At the end of the period, planned capital investments for this end, which were to have been 14.7 billion rubles and were to have achieved a "balance" between the production of means of production and that of means of consumption, were actually

21.3 billion rubles, with a concomitant reduction in capital investments in the production of means of consumption. This resulted in a complete reversal in the planned relationship between Group A and Group B industries. This relationship was to be further aggravated by the progress of the Second Plan, although the announced purpose of the Plan was "to achieve a yet better improvement in the living standards of the masses."

2 The Second Five Year Plan, 1932–37

In the final year of the Second Five Year Plan, the controlled press published no announcement from the *Gosplan* in regard to the state of completion of the Plan. The press was busy in describing in glowing language the witch-hunt the state was staging; the infamous Moscow Frame-up Trials. It took two years for the *Gosplan* to regain its voice. In 1939 it pronounced the Second Five Year Plan to have been successfully—and timely—accomplished. The "timely" referred to the year 1937, although no explanation was made of the overly-belated pronouncement. Let us scan the results, comparing the actual with the planned increase:[24]

Means of production	**Unit**	**1932 Level**	**Planned Incr.**	**Accd. Incr.**	**Pct. Accd.**
Electricity	Million kilowatt hours	13.0	25.0	23.4	93.6
Petroleum	Million tons	21.3	26.2	9.1	34.7
Coal	Million tons	65.4	87.1	62.5	71.8
Iron	Million tons	6.2	11.8	8.3	70.3
Steel	Million tons	5.9	13.1	11.8	90.0
Combines	Thousands	10.0	240.0	190.0	79.2
Tractors	Thousands	51.6	124.8	115.1	92.2
Length of rrds.	Thousand kmts.	83.4	10.4	1.5	14.4

24 Planned figures computed from: *Gosplan*, The Second Five Year Plan for the Development of Nat'l Eco. of the USSR; accomplished figures computed from *Gosplan*, Results of the Second Five Year Plan, 1939; both in Russian. There is no English edition of the results; there is one of the Plans, but it varies considerably from the figures in the Russian edition.

Means of consumption	Unit	1932 Level	Planned Incr.	Accd Incr.	Pct. Accd.
Cottons	Million meters	2417.0	3833.0	1030.0	26.9
Woolens	Million meters	88.7	181.9	19.6	10.8
Linen	Million square meters	135.0	465.0	148.8	32.0
Paper	Thousand tons	479.0	521.0	352.6	67.0
Sugar	Thousand tons	828.2	1971.8	1592.8	80.7
Leather footwear	Million pairs	84.7	165.3	84.4	51.0

The lamentable showing in the production of articles of mass consumption was, again, contrary to the original Plan. The Seventeenth Congress, which approved the Second Plan, specified that there should be "a more rapid rate of development in the production of manufactured articles of mass consumption, not only in comparison with the First Five Year Plan… but also in comparison with the rate of development of the production of means of production during the Second Five Year Plan period." However, the high organic composition of capital on a world scale *imposed*[25] this law of motion on the Russian economy. Even the more rapid development of the means of production at the expense of the means of consumption did not gain for the Soviet Union an illustrious place in a setting of the production of the advanced capitalist countries:

Per capita world production in 1937[26]

Item	Unit	USSR	USA	Germany	Japan
Electricity	Kilowatt hour	215	1160	735	421
Coal	Kilo	757	3429	3313	643
Pig iron	Kilo	86	292	234	30
Steel	Kilo	105	397	291	62

25 That the bureaucracy became the wiser because of this "imposition" will be seen in the section on "Ending Depersonalization and Creating Stakhanovism."

26 Table by Molotov [Chairman of the People's Commisars] in speech to the 18th Congress, RCP [Russian Communist Party], March, 1939, with exception of starred figure, which is from *Problems of Economics*, No. 3/39, in Russian.

Cement	Kilo	32	156	173	60
Paper	Kilo	5	48	42	8
Soap	Kilo	3	12	7	–
Sugar	Kilo	14	12	29	17
Cottons	Sq. meter	16	58	–	57*
Leather footwear	Pair	1	2.6	1.1	–

As we see from the above table, the Soviet Union, at the end of the Second Five Year Plan, "when the first phase of communism, socialism, was irrevocably established," had not only not outdistanced but was a long way from "catching up" with the capitalist world and compares not too favorably with "feudal" Japan.

It was in the year 1939, after the results of the Second Year Plan were first published, when the Third Five Year Plan[27] was officially approved and had supposedly been in operation for over a year, that Molotov "suddenly" remembered that it was not so much the rate of growth, or even the volume of output, as the per capita production that defined the real state of development of a national economy. In presenting the Third Five Year Plan, he stated:

> People here and there forgot that economically, that is, from the point of view of the volume of industrial output per capita of the population, we are still behind some capitalist countries.... Socialism has been built in the USSR but only in the main. We have still a very great deal to do before the USSR is properly supplied with all that is necessary...before we raise our country economically as well as technically to the level not only as high as that of the foremost capitalist countries but considerably higher.

Thus the slogan of the First Five Year Plan, "To catch up with and outdistance the capitalist lands," still remained as the task of the Third Plan.

3 The Third Five Year Plan and Labor Productivity

The press followed up Molotov's discovery that in the matter of *per capita production*, Russia was still far behind the advanced capitalist countries by systematic "revelations" of the low productivity of Russian labor. *Industry*, the

27 Those who wish to see the Third Plan can consult: *Gosplan*, The Third Five Year Plan for the Dev. of the Nat. Eco. of the USSR, 1939 (Russian); no English edition was published.

organ of the Commissariat for Heavy Industry, reported in its issue of March 24, 1939, that for a capacity of 1,000 kilowatt hours the USSR employs eleven people but for a similar capacity in Europe and America only 1.3 people are used. The official organ proceeded to say that the example cited is not the exception but the rule; that, for instance, when an electric plant in South Amboy, N.J., is compared with a similar plant in the USSR, it is found that whereas in America 51 people are used to run the plant, 480, or 9.5 as many people, were used in Russia. *Planned Economy*, in its issue of December, 1940, emphasized that, despite Stakhanovism, a Russian coal worker produces 370 tons, whereas in Germany the worker averages 435 tons and in the USA 844 tons. Likewise, whereas production in a U.S. coal mine is three times as great as that in a comparable Russian mine, the latter uses eleven times as many technicians, twice as many miners, three times as many office workers and twelve times as large a supervisory staff! The official organ of the State Planning Commission concludes that Russian labor productivity amounts to only 40.5 per cent of American labor productivity!

Despite high mechanization, labor productivity on the agricultural front[28] shines no brighter. The January, 1941, issue of *Problems of Economy*, issued by the Academy of Sciences and the Institute of Economy, carried an article on labor productivity in Agriculture in the USSR and the USA which included the following table:

Number of times the productivity of agricultural labor in the USA exceeds that of the Russian kolkhoz.

Wheat	6.7 times
Oats	5.7 times
Corn	4.1 times
Cotton	1.8 times
Sugar beet	8.1 times
Average for Agriculture	3.1 times
Milk	3.1 times
Wool	20.1 times
Average for livestock	6.7 times
Aggregate agricultural average	4.4 times

In 1937, the article continues to sum up, the *per capita* value output of the Russian worker was $166, or only one-seventh the value of output in the USA.

28 Cf. Section on collectivization for more detailed treatment of agricultural front.

Previous attempts to relate labor productivity to *per capita* production had resulted in an article in *Planned Economy* for October, 1940, which included the following table:

Relationship of industrial level in the development of Russia and capitalist countries; per capita production of Russia in percentages as compared to the USA and Germany

	USA	Germany
Industrial production as a whole	24.8	28.4 [*later corrected to 46.2%*]
Of which:		
Heavy Industry		
Electricity	18.5	28.4
Machine Building	31.6	56.4
Ferrous metals	27.6	36.3
Sulphuric acid	25.6	32.3
Cement	20.6	18.6
And automobile which are less than 1 percent of U.S production		
Light Industry		
Cotton	27.6	–
Wool	21.4	–
Leather footwear	38.5	90.9
Paper	104	11.9
Soap	25.0	–
Sugar	116.6	–
Gramophones	89.0	–
Agricultural production as a whole	54.4	123.4

The above *official* table reveals that, instead of being in the position of one of the most economically advanced countries, *Russia is still a backward country industrially.* It is interesting to note that for the period 1929–40, when, in Russia, Group B industries (means of consumption) fell from 55.6 per cent to 39 per cent of total production, while Group A industries (means of production) increased from 44.4 per cent of total production to 61 per cent, Japan's heavy industry like-wise increased from 33.7 per cent of total production in 1929 to 61.8 per cent in 1939, while light industry declined from 55 per cent to 38.2 per cent of the total economy. The fact that is of utmost importance is that, despite the comparative backwardness of both Russia and Japan, both countries reflect the high organic composition of capital characteristic of all important industrially developed countries. The Russian rulers were neither blind to this development nor undecided about which road they would follow in order to expand their industries. Listen to the chairman of the State Planning Commission [Voznessensky]:

> The plan for 1941 provides for a 12 per cent increase in the productivity of labor and a 6.5 per cent increase in wages per worker. This proportion between the increase in labor productivity and average wages furnishes a basis for lowering production costs and increasing socialist accumulation and constitutes the most important condition for the realization of a high rate of extended socialist reproduction.

We have followed the direction of Russian industrialization and arrived at "socialist accumulation." Voznessensky hid nothing from us when he mapped the main road for achieving "socialist reproduction." Besides the chief sources of life—the relationship of wages to labor productivity, more commonly known as exploitation—"socialist accumulation" grew fat on other fare. Let us discover what kind of manna that was, for it will help us considerably in understanding Russia's economic structure.

***

The New International, January, 1943

"Socialist Accumulation"

> Upon what meat hath this our Caesar fed
> That he has grown so great?
>
> SHAKESPEARE: *JULIUS CAESAR*

The manner of swelling the State Treasury appeared in an innocent enough guise. On December 5, 1929, the Central Committee of the RCP passed the following resolution: "To instruct the Peoples Commissariat of Finance and Supreme Council of National Economy to draw up a system of taxation and government enterprises on the principle of a single tax on profits."[29]

29 Along with all other "original documents," this bill of goods was passed on to the Webbs at face value, with the result that in their 1,100 pages on *Soviet Communism* the Webbs find

"The single tax on profits" turned out to have two sections: (1) a tax on profits which comprised 9–12 per cent of the state budget and (2) a turnover tax which comprised 60–80 per cent of the state budget. It is the latter tax which is crucial—sufficient to finance all industrialization and militarization. Let us examine it in detail.

I *The "Socialized" State Budget, or Turnover*

The turnover tax is a tax applied to all commodities at the point of production or immediately upon acquisition of the goods by the wholesaler. The wholesaler pays the tax direct to the State Treasury before selling goods to the retailer, who, in turn, pays the tax before selling it to the consumers. However, there is absolutely no doubt that the burden of the tax is passed on to the consumer masses since the law obliges the retailer to include the tax in the sales price of the commodities.

Contrary to the usual sales tax, which is a fixed percentage of the base price of the commodity, the turnover tax is a fixed percentage of the total sales value of merchandise, including the amount of tax. This means that whereas a 90 per cent sales tax raises the price of merchandise 90 per cent, a 90 per cent turnover tax increases the sales price tenfold. Here is how the turnover tax affects the sales price in various instances:

> With a tax of 20 per cent, the price increases by 25 per cent.
> With a tax of 40 per cent, the price increases by 66.7 per cent.
> With a tax of 50 per cent, the price increases two-fold.
> With a tax of 75 per cent, the price increases four-fold.

To get the full significance of the turnover tax, as contrasted with an ordinary sales tax, we need to consider how it affects a single commodity. Let us take bread—the staff of life of the masses—upon which the tax is 75 per cent. This means that the proletarian, in paying a ruble for his kilo of black bread, pays 25 kopeks for the actual cost of the bread, including production, distribution, transportation and delivery, and 75 kopeks of that ruble goes to the state as turnover tax.

---

room for but one sentence on the tax, reading: "The principal (tax) is a tax on the output or turnover of all industrial enterprises of any magnitude which are now all state-owned." How the State Budget can keep on expanding from taxing its own state-owned enterprises, instead of the "non-state-owned" masses, the Webbs fail to explain. [Cf. Sidney and Beatrice Webb, *Soviet Communism: A New Civilization* 2 vols. (London: Longmans, Green and Co., 1935), 1:116].

The tax is very unevenly spread, falling light on means of production and heavy on articles of mass consumption, which are the very "meat" of the tax. The tax on essential products of heavy industry seldom goes as high as 10 per cent. Contrast this with the average rate of 82.8 per cent on agricultural products and recall that a turnover tax of that percentage will increase the sales price nearly sixfold! On food industries the average rate of turnover tax is 50 per cent and doubles the cost to the masses—and on spirits the rate of tax is 82.1 per cent! The tax on light industry is 20.3 per cent. If we once again take individual commodities, the disparity is even more shocking. The tax on coal is .05 per cent and on machinery 1 per cent. But on textiles it is 25 per cent, thus increasing the cost of clothing one-third. Moreover, the tax on light industry is not without its fine discriminations: while women of the "intelligentsia" are taxed 68 per cent for their perfume, the peasant woman is taxes 88 per cent for her kerosene. The Stakhanovite pays 21–37 per cent of the price of her silk garment in the form of turnover tax but the working class woman pays a tax of 48 per cent on her calico!

Biggest of all taxes is the turnover tax on bread and agricultural produce. When the turnover tax was first introduced in 1930, a considerable increase in the state revenue immediately resulted. But it emerged as nothing short of a "socialist victory" in 1935 when rationing was abolished[30] and the price of foodstuffs leaped up. Thus the turnover tax from all agricultural produce sold to the population rose from 4.340 billion rubles in 1930 to 24 billion rubles in 1935.[31] By 1940 it was 35 billion, or 20 per cent of the entire budget!

Marx once said that "The only part of the so-called national wealth that actually enters into the collective possessions of modern peoples is their national debt." Never was this truer than in the case of Russia, where the whole cost of industrialization and militarization has been borne by the people through that ingenious scheme known as the turnover tax, which provided 79 per cent of the total state revenue in l937. Of the 178 billion rubles in the state budget in 1940, 106 billions came from the turnover tax—a "socialized" form indeed of financing the Plans! The "national wealth" grew from 19 billion rubles in 1931 to 178 billion in 1940;[32] the per capita national income increased from 52 rubles in 1928 to 198 in 1937. But the real wages of the proletariat decreased to half of what they were in 1928![33]

30 Cf. section on ending rationing.

31 Cf. article by Baykov in *The Economic Journal* (London), December, 1941.

32 Due consideration should, of course, be given the inflation of the ruble.

33 Cf. section on proletariat.

II *Fight for Profit, or the Modus Operandi of a Soviet Undertaking*

On June 30, 1935, *Izvestia* proclaimed: "Ahead of us are struggles for profit, for elimination of subsidies." Thereafter steps were taken to create a private incentive for making a profit and achieving industry's capacity to avoid complete state subsidization. By April 19, 1936, a decree established what was known as a directors' fund, to be at the disposal of the management and to provide for paying premiums to the administrative staff and workers. It is a secret to no one that these funds are used mainly as premiums for directors and Stakhanovites and not for rank and file workers. This fund is made up of 4 per cent of the "planned profits" plus 50 per cent of profits achieved by the enterprise in excess of those planned for it by the state. But how are profits planned and how is it possible to have, besides, "surplus" profits? We can find the answer if we examine the *modus operandi* of a Soviet enterprise.

A Five Year Plan or an annual plan is elaborated which allows for a planned profit to accrue to each enterprise. The prices of commodities, as we have seen in the section of the turnover tax, are pegged considerably above the cost of production and the cost of production is measured by the cost of labor power and raw materials and by the depreciation of fixed capital which includes amortization charges. The planned profit is likewise included as part of "the cost of production." Each individual undertaking has considerable discretion in the manner of executing the plan. For instance, the management can make profits over and above those "planned" for it by economizing on the cost of labor. The minimum wage law—and that has been in effect only since 1937—the management has to obey. But the minimum is low enough, 110 to 115 rubles a month—and between that and the highest wage—2,000 rubles monthly—there is sufficient room for maneuvering.

When the First Five Year Plan was launched, capital expenditures came wholly out of the national budget. There was then an automaticity in granting credits to all Soviet enterprises. However, since 1930 by the Credit Reform Act and subsequent banking legislation[34] in 1931, particularly the Act of June 25, 1931, automatic credits to industrial and commercial enterprises were stopped. There was introduced what was known as the "ruble control," that is to say, the undertakings were to be conducted on principles of cost accounting, as in any money economy. A working capital was given them and they were to function

34 Cf. *Soviet Money and Finance*, by L.E. Hubbard, and *Bank Credit and Money in Soviet Russia*, by A.Z. Arnold. The latter is evidently a Stalinist but if the rationalization is thrown out, the banking legislation is there in full. In Russian the legislation (as well as all decrees mentioned in this article) can be found in Compendium of Laws, 1929–40: also, the daily press generally carries decrees the day after enacted.

unassisted by bank credit. Where credit was necessary it was extended only to those whose credit was good. Thus there was created an incentive "to fight for profit," and a control was established over the industrial and commercial enterprises by the banks, which saw to it that the slogan "fight for profit" was achieved—with the threat of having the enterprise declared "bankrupt" and taken out of the hands of the management.

By February, 1941, Voznessensky could report to the Russian CP conference: "The profits of socialist industry are increasing from year to year. The net profit of the plants of industry rose to nearly 14 billion rubles in 1940." The *gross* profits were considerably above that figure of 14 billion as the profits tax to the State Treasury for that year amounted to 21.3 billion. The achievement of these profits was in turn helped not a little by the mode of functioning of the enterprises. Since it is state owned, a Soviet enterprise is considered to be "socialist property." However, the worker in it does not "share the profits," whereas the "enterprise," that is, the management, is permitted to accumulate funds both from the planned profits and from the amortization charges. In 1940, 32.5 [percent] of capital outlays[35] came from these sources. This permitted the diversion of the state budget for national defense, without upsetting the funds for industrialization. Defense expenditures jumped from 3.5 billion (or 8.9 per cent of the entire budget) in 1933 to 56.1 billion, or 32.4 per cent of the entire budget in 1940! Although state investments in the national economy more than doubled in volume since 1933 (they were only 25.1 billion in 1933 and were 57.1 billion in 1940), they dropped, in ratio to total expenditures, from 60.8 per cent in 1933 to 33 per cent in 1940.

Not only have the industrial enterprises achieved this miraculous "elimination of subsidies" and not only do the individual members of the management of the enterprises receive a salary considerably above the 110 minimum rubles but the managers are able to up their 2,000 rubles monthly salary by various means. It is [Gregori] Malenkov, the secretary of the RCP, who reveals one of these methods to the 18th party conference, which had been told so much of "socialist accumulation." Malenkov relates the following incident: the Middle Ural Copper Mills in the Sverdlovsk region sold plumbing materials to the Non-Ferrous Metals Supply Trust for 100,000 rubles and had them carted to the Trust. The responsible agent, who did not know about this transaction but saw the materials when he visited the Trust, bought these materials for 111,000 rubles and had them carted back to his own plant. Malenkov remarks, after he

35 Cf. Aron Iugov, *Russia's Economic Front for War and Peace, An appraisal of the Three Five-Year Plans* (New York: Harper & Brothers, 1942).

awaits the peals of laughter from his audience:[36] "Since it is the State Treasury that bears the expense of such twofold transactions, the director and the responsible agent must have each gotten a bonus, one for making such a smart sale and the other for such a smart purchase." After the laughter subsides, he adds that this was the reason for promulgating the decree of February 10, 1941, forbidding the sale and/or exchange of machinery materials. And—we might add in a serious vein—that this is only one more reason why it is difficult to estimate the exact income of a factory director. His basic salary of 2,000 rubles monthly is merely the *first* contrast to the 110 to 115 rubles monthly minimum salary of the factory worker, before the former's is swollen by bonuses, premiums, exemptions from income tax, once he has succeeded in obtaining the title "Hero of Labor." That title can be gained not only when fulfilling the Plan by having the factory show a profit but also when one "proves" his particular tasks have been accomplished "honorably," although the factory he manages has not fulfilled the plan. No wonder details of the latest income taxes revealed such unbridgeable "differentiations" as earnings above 300,000 rubles a year when the "average" annual income is 3,467 rubles![37]

The Economics of Russian Agriculture, 1928–41

Thus far we have been on the industrial front only, where we have been led from industrialization to extended reproduction and have seen how two handmaids (the turnover tax and profit motive) helped socialist accumulation grow fat. What about the agricultural front? Are the same factors at work here? What is the economy of Russian agriculture and what is its law of motion? Let us study the development of Russian agriculture since the initiation of the First Five Year Plan.

By the end of the Second Five Year Plan the Russian state declared the land was collectivized to the extent of 99.6 per cent and the peasantry to the extent of 93.6 per cent. Socialism was indeed "irrevocably established." Percentages and labels, however, are deceiving, as we shall see when we analyze the *economy* prevalent on these collectivized farms (*kolkhozy*) and amidst the collectivized peasantry (*kolkhozniki*). The Russian state would have us believe that the millions transported to the Far Northern territories during the execution of the First Five Year Plan had indeed liquidated the kulak "as a class." It may be possible that the newly-created, hot-house fashion, Lubyanka method *kolkhozniki*

36 Report in *Pravda*, along with stenographic notes of the conference, February 18–21, 1941.

37 Cf. Boris M. Stanfield, "Private Property Rights in Russia," *in International* Conciliation No. 375, December, 1941.

were made of a different psychological mold than were the kulaks—but the *economic* demand was the same: a free market. That demand was granted them in 1932. In 1935 the permanent usufruct of the land was likewise bestowed upon them. And finally, and of most recent vintage, is the appearance and the publicity attendant upon the birth of the millionaire *kolkhozy*. Does this prosperity embrace the whole "socialist agricultural front"?

I *The World Crisis and the Russian Famine*

1 The World Market and the Russian Agricultural Crisis

"Enrich yourself!" had been the slogan while the NEP was still in effect. This slogan the *kulak* rightly adopted as his own. Since the state did not pay him sufficient for his grain to achieve this enrichment, there was no inducement to produce a large marketable surplus. Eighty per cent of the grain output in 1927 was consumed by the peasantry and only 20 per cent was left to feed the urban population. This contrasted poorly with the period prior to World War I (1909–14) when the peasantry consumed 63 per cent of the grain and 37 per cent of the total constituted the marketable surplus.[38] Therefore, although the urban population was growing, there was less for it to eat. Moreover, 60 per cent of the marketable surplus in 1927 was concentrated in the hands of the *kulaks*, who constituted a mere 6 per cent of the peasant population. While Stalin proclaimed that it was "nonsense"[39] to call the NEP capitalism and Bukharin declared that it was possible to reach socialism "at a tortoise pace," the *kulak* had concentrated the greater part of the marketable surplus and refused to turn that over to the state. Forced collectivization was resorted to.

Forced collectivization achieved 78.2 per cent collectivization of the total area under crops by the end of the First Five Year Plan, instead of the 17.5 originally envisaged by the Plan.[40] Forced collectivization wrought such havoc that the harvest declined from 83.5 million tons in 1930 to 70 million tons in 1931. The attempt of the bureaucracy to erase all past mistakes in encouraging NEPist accumulation as a "step toward socialism" by an absolutely dizzy speed in "collectivization" found its match in the equally terrific thoroughness with which the peasantry proceeded to slaughter its animals. When the Plan was officially declared "completed," here is what had happened to the livestock:

38 Cf. L.E. Hubbard: *Economics of Soviet Agriculture*.

39 Cf. *Minutes of the 14th Congress of the RCP*, page 493 (in Russian).

40 Cf. *Gosplan, The First Five Year Plan*.

In millions of head[41]	1928	1932
Horses	35.9	19.6
Large horned cattle	70.5	40.7
Sheep and goats	146.7	52.0
Pigs	26.0	11.6

If we take the 1928 figure as 100, we get the following indices for 1932: for horses, 54.6 per cent; cattle, 57.7 per cent; sheep and goats, 35.4 per cent; pigs, 44.6 per cent!

The havoc on the agricultural front was aggravated by the reality of the world market, which would not permit Russia to tear itself out of the vortex of world economy and build "socialism in one country." The world crisis adversely affected the price Russian agricultural produce could command on the world market. If we take 1928 to be 100, prices on the world market dropped to 67.2 and on agricultural produce, which is what Russia wished to sell in order to buy machinery, they dropped to 45.5. Tractors, which were not manufactured rapidly enough in Russia to take the place of the draft animals slaughtered, could not be bought in sufficient quantity because of lack of capital. The disorganization on the agricultural front was accompanied by a famine that stalked throughout the Soviet land. Millions died.

2 The Effect of the Russian Famine on the Population

Despite the fact that, on the one hand, their own statistics of decline in harvest and slaughter of cattle point to catastrophic conditions; and, on the other hand, the fact that the bourgeois journalists in Russia saw to it that the world heard of the famine, the state has denied the existence of famine in 1932–33. Apparently even the bureaucracy did not know what a toll of lives the famine had taken for by 1937 they ordered a census taken to prove that "life had become gayer." According to the Plan, the census should have proved the existence of a population of 180.7 millions. But the data the census takers brought back told a vastly different story. Despite the fanfare that heralded the census, the data were never made public. The census was declared "defective" and another census was ordered for January, 1939, to find the missing millions. The 180.7 millions "planned" for 1937 were based on the three million yearly growth in population characteristic of the period 1922–28. On that basis the 1939 census should have recorded a population of approximately 186 million. However,

41 First officially revealed in 1934 in Stalin's Report to the 17th Congress of the RCP.

the accepted 1939 census revealed the population to be 170.5 million. No explanation was made as to the discrepancy in the figures, but much publicity was given to the 15.9 per cent increase over the 1926 census disclosed by the 1939 census. No explanation was made of the discrepancy between the planned figures and those found actually living. This 15.9 per cent increase, however, is not reflected in each age group and thereby hangs a tale of confirmatory evidence of the famine in 1932.

The age group up to seven years does not reflect the general 15.9 per cent increase. Instead it records a 1.6 per cent decrease! Moreover—and this makes the decrease even more appalling—the age group in the 1926 census to which this age group is compared was itself an abnormally small part of the population since the birth rate was below normal and infant mortality above normal in the period 1919–22. Some demographic catastrophe must have occurred in the years when "socialism was irrevocably established" to result in a decline in an age group that is contrasted to one born in the period of civil war and famine! The Stalinist statisticians, for reasons best known to themselves, did not deign to break this age group into single years and we cannot, therefore, tell whether the decree was due to infant mortality or to an abnormally low birth rate. But what is absolutely clear from the official statistics is that the "socialist" year 1932–33 stands out in black relief even against the famine year 1919–20!

That the regime was able to survive such a catastrophe is in no small measure due to the reality of the world crisis. Whereas the world crisis, on the one hand, aggravated the internal situation in Russia by upsetting its financial plans, it had, on the other hand, likewise induced such combustible situations in each of the capitalist countries that none of these governments dared take advantage of the internally weak Soviet Union to the extent of attacking its borders.

In the Soviet Union itself the powers that be felt the discontent of the village. The tops accused the rank and file of being "dizzy from success" (Stalin). Retreat was the order of the day. The village was granted the open market. Never having had the courage of its own convictions, the bureaucracy gave the free market its benediction (April, 1932, edict of the CC of the RCP and of the Presidium of the Soviet Government) and the free market was pronounced to be a "collective farm market." Thus was the exchange process made "kosher" by a ukase of the "socialist state."

II *The Free Market on the Countryside*

Forty per cent of the grain output goes to the state in the form of compulsory deliveries or purchases, at a price fixed by the state. Another 20 per cent of the grain crop is given for the use of the MTS (Machine Tractor Stations) and to tractor drivers. Over half of the remaining 40 per cent is consumed by the peasant population itself, leaving 15–20 per cent of grain production as the marketable surplus. Variations in the price of grain, depending upon the buyer, were tremendous. For example, 100 kilograms of rye sold in 1933 at these widely different prices:[42]

Delivery price to the state	6 rubles and 5 kopeks
Rationed price (rye flour)	25 rubles
Commercial price (rye flour)	45 rubles
Kolkhoz price (January)	58 rubles (Moscow region)

The open market price, which is some ninefold that of the state price, is inducement enough to the *kolkhozniki*. Though the free market it called the collective farm market, the collectives supply only 15 per cent of the agricultural commodities on the market whereas 85 per cent is supplied by the peasants, collectivized, or individual, thus:

Produce of *kolkhozy* sold by *kolkhozy*	15%
Produce of *kolkhozy* sold by *kolkhozniki*	45%
Produce of *kolkhozniki's* own livestock and allotments	30%
Produce of independent peasants	10%
	100%[43]

An insight into both the prohibitively high prices on the market and of the inflation of the ruble can be gained from the fact that in 1934 the open market turnover was valued at 14,000 million rubles in current prices whereas the country's total agricultural produce that year, calculated in 1926–27 prices, was valued at 14,600 million rubles! It is therefore not surprising that in 1935 the sale on the open market of less than 20 per cent of the marketable surplus yielded a greater sum of money than the sale of 60 per cent of the marketable surplus to the state and state organizations:

42 Ct. article by Baykov in *Economic Journal*, London, December, 1941.

43 Development of Kolkhoz Trade in 1936. In Russian.

	In millions of rubles
Income from compulsory deliveries to state	7,370
Income from decentralized collections	1,344
Income from open market sales	10,783

Because of this extreme difference between open market sales and sales to the state, 25 per cent of the whole money income (10,783 million rubles out of 43,646 million rubles) of the *kolkhozniki* (and the whole means not only what they earned in the *kolkhoz* but also outside earnings in factories off-seasons) was derived from open market sales.[44] Moreover, the *kolkhozniki* need not submit any turnover tax to the state.

At the 18th Congress of the RCP held in March, 1939, it was stated that the free market turnover of foodstuffs in 1938 was valued at 24,399 million rubles, or 15 per cent of the total value of all retail trade, including public feeding. However, this does not mean that the actual commodities sold approached that percentage. Because the prohibitively high prices on the open market and the inflated rubles, the value output, as we have seen above, give no indication of the physical output, small wonder that the newly-created *kolkhozniki* jealously guards an old institution: the free market!

III *Private Property in the Kolkhozy; Millionaires and Paupers*

The free market was not the only conquest of the village. In 1935 the *kolkhozy* were granted the permanent use of the land and the *kolkhozniki* the following private property rights: their dwelling, one-half to two and one-half acres of land (depending upon the region) and the following livestock:[45] one cow, two calves, one sow and its litter, up to ten sheep or goats, unlimited poultry and rabbits and up to ten bee-hives. The slogan for industry, "fight for profit," had its parallel in the countryside: "Make all *kolkhozniki* prosperous." Since all produce of his private property was his and the sale of it on the open market was unencumbered by a turnover tax, the *kolkhoznik* began to pay a lot of attention to the care of his own small plot of land, where he carried on diversified farming. *Planned Economy*, in its December, 1938, issue carries a report which reveals that the *kolkhozniki* spend 30 to 45 per cent of their

44 *Problems of Economy*, No. 6, 1936, In Russian (as are all official magazines and newspapers mentioned in this article).

45 It is considerably higher in nomad regions.

time on their own homesteads while the women spend most of their time on their own plot. The reports to the 18th Conference in February, 1941, related the fact that farming on their own homesteads "overshadowed farming in the collective"!

Despite the trumpeted 99.6 per cent collectivization, here is the extent to which private property has developed: although the *kolkhozy* own 79.2 per cent of the area under crops, they own only 17.6 per cent of all cows, 30.4 per cent of sheep and goats. On the other hand, the *kolkhozniki*, who own a mere 3.3 per cent of the area under crop, own as high as 55.7 per cent of all cows and 40 per cent of all sheep and goats. Individual (private) peasants cultivate only 5.2 per cent of the land under crops but own 12.1 per cent of draught horses, 16.9 of cows and 13 per cent of the sheep and goats. Contrast to this the *sovkhozy* (state farms which are owned and managed by the state like the factories) which control 12.3 per cent of the area under crops but own only 9.8 per cent of the cows and 16.6 per cent of the sheep and goats. The *sovkhozy* possess only as many productive cattle as are owned by the workmen and employees who live in the country and are responsible for sowing only 1.1 million hectares of land![46]

Besides these legitimate claims (that is, those recognized by the state) the People's Commissar of Agriculture reported in May, 1939, that the following surplus allotments were found to exist illicitly as private property:

778,000 hectares among kolkhoz members
203,000 hectares among private peasants
432,000 hectares among workers and employees and other non-members living in agricultural districts

The Commissar failed to inform us as to the degree of concentration of these surplus allotments. Surely they were not divided some one-tenth of an acre evenly among all homesteads or there would have been no necessity for promulgating the May 27, 1933, decree forbidding the sale or transfer of *kolkhoz* property. That decree also made it obligatory for *kolkhoz* members to work a minimum of sixty to a hundred days a year, depending upon the region, in order to be entitled to *kolkhoz* membership. *Kolkhoz* membership, however, does not mean being an equal among equals. No, among the *kolkhoz* members there are millionaires and there are paupers. That is a fact, notwithstanding

46 *Quarterly Bulletin of Soviet Russian Economics*, No. 1–2, 1939, Prague; Prokopovicz is the editor of this and it is translated into English; excellently documented.

the praise of the millionaire *kolkhozy* in the Russian press as if their existence signified the realization of the slogan, "Make all *kolkhozy* prosperous."

Far from eliminating the poverty of the village, the millionaire *kolkhozy* have so accentuated it that the "differentiation" in social composition parallels the Czarist village. There are small, medium-sized and vast *kolkhozy*, and the crops grown on them and the tractor drivers available to them vary greatly. The "fortunate" ones are those which possess high grade soils, produce industrial and medicinal crops for the state, have comparatively large area in proportion to the number of members, have a great many more than the average number of tractor drivers at their disposal. *Pravda* of January 14, 1939, reported that on November 15, 1938, 5,000 MTS still owed their drivers 206 million rubles. The report reads that, naturally, the tractor drivers left the *kolkhozy* serviced by these MTS. The *kolkhozy* that could afford to pay well and on time got the best tractor drivers. Besides having the best soil and the best tractor drivers, the *kolkhozy* were able to work into the millionaire class by having had a larger surplus to put away for the further improvement of the *kolkhozy*. A certain percentage continually grew richer and richer. To be precise, the millionaire *kolkhozy* comprize *one-third of one per cent* of all *kolkhozy* (610 *kolkhozy* out of 2,424 thousand *kolkhozy* in the USSR!)[47]

In extreme contrast to this handful of millionaire *kolkhozy* are the PAUPER *kolkhozy*, which are twenty times as numerous as the millionaire ones. They constitute 6.7 per cent of the *kolkhozy* and earn annually 1,000 to 5,000 rubles. The overwhelming majority, 75 per cent, of the *kolkhozy* are medium-sized and earn about 60,000 rubles annually. This means only 172 rubles per member.[48]

Enormous extremes prevail in the distribution of farm products as compensation for labor, as well as in farm wages. In 1937, 8 per cent of all *kolkhozy* allotted less than 1 ½ kilograms of grain per labor day to each worker, over 50 per cent gave up to three kilos, 10 per cent distributed seven to fifteen kilos and, again, one-third of one per cent allotted over fifteen kilos.

It must be emphasized that the labor day is not a calendar working day but a piece rate unit accorded the various categories of skilled and unskilled labor. A field hand's working day is "worth" one-half a labor day and a tractor driver's day is worth five labor days! Moreover, a labor day does not command the same price in all regions, as can be seen from the following table:[49]

---

47 *Socialist Agriculture of the USSR Statistical Yearbook*, for 1939, in Russian.

48 Cf. *Russia's Economic Front for War and Peace*, by Yugow.

49 *Income, Savings and Finance in Collective Farms*, in Russian.

District	Income from days in rubles
Vangerovsky	0.52
Slaviansky	1.37
Vannovsky	0.42
Shpoliansky	0.67
Korunsky	0.34
V. Khavsky	0.45
Bazhetsky	1.18

Thus, even for the same work, the *kolkhozniki* might have been paid either 34 kopeks or 1 ruble and 37 kopeks—*a four-fold difference per labor unit!*

In 1939 the Central Administration of National Economy Statistics reported that 25 per cent of the *kolkhozniki* had earned 300 labor days, the average being 150 labor days a year, while 3.5 per cent had not earned a single labor day. The other extreme to this polarization of wealth is told in *Pravda* of January 17, 1939, which reports that a single collective peasant family in the Soviet cotton growing region of Uzbekistan had earned 22,000 rubles. These "differentiations," we must bear in mind, are *within the kolkhoz*. It is not from amongst the three million individual peasants that the "millionaires" arise but from amongst the 75 million collective farmers, out of those that have the largest tracts of land and are favored by the state with "contracts," that is, produce industrial and medicinal crops for the state. As we have seen, the state gets approximately 40 per cent of the gross crops of the *kolkhozy* through obligatory deliveries, taxes and payments for use of tractors and combines. Of the surplus reverting to the *kolkhozy* and *kolkhozniki* there is economic base for both millionaire and pauper members.

IV *Mechanization and Unemployment in the Countryside*

Unemployment has been officially declared abolished ever since 1930. However, such a bourgeois agronomy specialist as Sir John E. Russell, director of the Rothamsted Experimental Station, declared after his visit to Russia in 1937 that the number of workers per hectare of land was some two to four times as many as would be used in England and that, most probably, only half of the agricultural population of Russia was necessary to run production efficiently. That, despite the fact that between 1928 and 1938, 22.8 million individuals left the farms and the peasant population declined by 20 per cent. That Russia is still overwhelmingly a peasant country (67.2 per cent of the total population is still rural) was revealed by the 1939 census. Of the 114.6 million rural inhabitants

78.6 million are peasants. Are all these millions still necessary to agricultural requirements, despite the extent of mechanization?

The Russian state prided itself on the tremendous development of mechanization on the agricultural front, yet denied the existence of unemployment and continued to deny it until 1939. The mop-up operations against the remaining revolutionists in the 1937 Trials and the anti-labor legislation in 1938 resulted in a mass flight of labor. Industry once again found itself without sufficient help. It was then that "The Leader" indirectly revealed the existence of unemployment in the countryside. At the 18th Congress of the RCP in March, 1939, Stalin appealed to the *kolkhozniki* for their surplus labor: "The *kolkhozy* have the full possibility," he stressed. "to satisfy our request inasmuch as abundance of mechanization in the *kolkhozy* frees part of the workers in the country and these workers, if they were transferred to industry, could bring about a great benefit to the whole national economy." Since that appeal was issued, it became the vogue in Soviet periodicals to speak of the "balance of labor" (a euphemistic enough name for the unemployed!) on the *kolkhozy*. Here is one table officially published to show the effects of mechanization:

Amount of Man-days per hectare of land under grain crops	
1922–25	20.82
1933	12.30
1937	10.55

Here we see a full 50 per cent decrease in the need for manpower on the farm.

Still more directly, unemployment is attested to in the December, 1938, issue of *Planned Economy*, which publisher the following interesting table regarding the portion of labor resources that took part in *kolkhoz* work:

	January	July
Men	68.2%	84.8%
Women	21.2%	68.2%

This reveals that even in the busiest month of the year, July, about 15 per cent of the men and 30 per cent of the women were surplus to labor requirements in the *kolkhozy*, regardless of whether they were officially declared to be among the unemployed or not. In the January, 1941, issue of the *Problems of Economy* there appeared an article called "Labor Productivity in Agriculture in the USSR and USA" (an article we have already discussed in the section on labor productivity on the industrial front), in which the writer comes to the conclusion that, although the Russian worker put in an average 152 labor days per year, the American farmer works 258.6 days, and that Russia has three times as many farmers as the USA: 36.6 million against 12.1 million.

However, no amount of discussions about the "balance of labor" in the *kolkhozy*, no scientific proof that much of labor was surplus to agricultural requirements, not even the appeal of "The Leader" himself, proved powerful enough to move the peasant off from his half acre plot of land and willingly give himself over to the factory regime. It was then that the state enacted the October 2, 1940, decree creating the state labor reserves. The decree made is obligatory for the *kolkhozy* and city Soviets to give up to one million youths between the ages of 14 and 17 for compulsory vocational training. After two years of training for the 14 and 15 year olds and a bare six months for the 16 and 17 year olds, the youths had to work for the state for four years at the prevailing rate of wages. The irony of this decree lies in its being officially predicated on the fact that it was made necessary "as a consequence" of the "abolition of unemployment and the fact that the poverty and ruin of the village and city are forever done away with" and "therefore" there were no people "quietly forming a constant reserve of manpower for industry"! The truth of the matter is that unemployment, poverty and misery continue to exist in the country but even under his unhappy lot the peasant will not turn to industry because conditions in the factory, especially after 1938, are well known to him and he prefers unemployment in the country instead.

And what about the proletariat who cannot escape the factory regime? What is the factory regime like? What are the production relations at the point of production?

***

The New International, February, 1943

"Social Classes in Russia"

Our study of the Russian economy would be barren of any social significance were we not to examine the production relations characteristic of the mode of production. Stalin said that there were no classes in the Soviet Union "in the old sense of the word." Let us see. Social classes are defined by the role they play in the process of production. What places do the "classless" groups known as the proletariat and the intelligentsia occupy in the economic system that still retains the name of the Union of Socialist Soviet Republics? Who runs the economy? Whose life-blood cements and expands it? Who benefits from it? In order of their origin, let us analyze the evolution of the "social groups" during the Five Year Plans.

I The Proletariat

1 *The Worker and the Law*

Throughout the life of the First and Second Five Year Plans labor fluidity was great. The trial of the "Trotskyist-Bukharinist fascist wreckers" only served to heighten the workers' restlessness and not merely the fluidity of labor (labor turnover) but the actual flight of labor away from the city assumed disastrous proportions. To try to check this development a decree of December 28, 1938, introduced labor passports. This decree had no teeth in it because the worker was not the least intimidated by the threat of being fired for a day's absence. Since he could always get another job but could not quit his job without giving a month's notice, the worker very often took advantage of the fact that coming late twenty minutes made him a truant and caused his dismissal. On June 26, 1940, "as a consequence of the current international situation," the 1938 decree was greatly "elaborated." It forbade the worker to leave his job. Truancy and other infractions of the law were punishable by six months' "corrective labor"—labor in the factory, that is, with a 25 per cent reduction in pay. Furthermore, the workers' hours were increased from seven to eight, with a proportionate increase in the "norms" of work but no increase whatever in pay. Toward the end of that year, on October 2, 1940, the State Labor Reserves were created, which, as we saw, gave the worker free training of from six months to two years and made it obligatory for him to work for the state for four years "at the prevailing rate of wages." But even these Draconian anti-labor laws did not succeed in making of the Russian wage slave a slave of old, an integral part of the means of production. The Russian worker found all manner and means to circumvent the legislation.

Reviewing six months of operation of the law of June 26, 1940, the *Pravda* of December 26, 1940, had to report that in many enterprises, especially coal mines, truancies were greater in October than in the months prior to the enactment of the barbarous anti-truancy laws. The reports to the eighteenth conference of the RCP in February, 1941, complained of the fact that the workers still absented themselves "particularly after pay day." And on April 16, 1941, two short months before the invasion by Germany, Shvernik, head of the so-called trade unions, reported to the eleventh plenum of the Central Executive Committee of the Trade Unions that 22–32 per cent of the workers still do not accomplish their minimum "norms"; that, furthermore, workers of the same category get different wages in different factories, sometimes even in the same factory, and, worst of all "evils," some factories continue to pay on the basis of experience rather than on the basis of the piecework system.

However, the fact that the Russian worker has been able in great measure to circumvent anti-labor legislation does not mean that he is the proletarian of the high morale of the days of his *own* dictatorship. It is sufficient to counterpose the hero of those days to the "hero" of today to bring out the change in morale in striking relief. Simply contrast to the *Subbotnik*, who gave his Saturday services without pay to his state, the Stakhanovite, whose pay envelope is twenty times that of the rank and file worker! The *Subbotnik* neither complained nor boasted of his economic conditions—they were bad but the movement of the economy which he ruled over was such that he gained by the progress of the state. When, by 1928, production had gained its pre-war level, the workers' wages were 125 per cent of that level. The Stakhanovite boasts of his pay envelope and complains to the state of the disrespectful attitude toward him on the part of the "ignorant" (read: rank and file) workers who "preen themselves of their proletarian origin."

When the First Five Year Plan was launched the enthusiasm of the workers for the Plan was so high that during the first year all norms set by the Plan were over-fulfilled. The bureaucracy saw the blue in heaven and raised the slogan: The Five Year Plan in Four. But then the trade unions and shop committees were still functioning and collective labor agreements were in force both in state institutions and at those private concessionaires that still existed, such as the Lena Gold Fields. Rulings made by the Workers Conflict Commissions generally favored the workers in their fight with the management. On January 5, 1929, for example, *Economic Life*, the organ of the Council of Labor and Defense, emphasized that piece work rates are subject to the approval of the Workers Conflict Commission but that the responsibility for fulfilling the financial program rests exclusively with the management. That issue of the publication reports also that it is an ordinary occurrence for a worker dismissed by the management to be reinstated by the labor inspector.

When the worker, however, found that agricultural prices had soared so high that his salary could not even cover the purchase of sufficient food, his enthusiasm subsided and production lagged far behind the Plans. Immediately the state struck out against him. On January 24, 1929, a decree was promulgated making workers responsible for damaged goods. In 1930 it became obligatory for a factory director to insert into the worker's paybook the reasons for his dismissal. That same year the labor exchanges were instructed to put the workers who left their jobs on their own initiative on a "special list" (read: blacklist) and deprive them of unemployment compensation.

Of food there was such scarcity that rationing had to be introduced in 1930. For the manual worker the rations were: twelve pounds and five ounces of black bread a week, and the following items, in quantities, per month: two and a half pounds ten ounces of herring, thirteen ounces of sugar and two and a half ounces of tea. Soon tea disappeared from the meager diet and we read of the workers having a *kipyatok*, which is plain boiled water, without either sugar or tea. Meanwhile, unemployment had been declared officially to be nonexistent and unemployment insurance was actually abolished. The worker's ration card was transferred into the hands of the factory directors.

The workers became restless. The rate of labor turnover in 1930 was 152 per cent. But the slogan of "The Five Year Plan in Four" was not changed. The controlled press voiced criticism of the trade unions and blamed them for not seeing to it that the workers fulfilled their "norms." In 1932 it was decreed that the worker could be fired for a single day's absence without permission. Moreover, the factory director thereupon could deprive him not only of his food card but also of the right to occupy the premises owned by the factory, that is, the worker's living quarters. To stifle the expression of dissatisfaction on the part of the workers, it was decided to deprive the worker of any form of redress through his trade unions by "statification" of the latter. In 1933 the liquidation of the Council of Labor and Defense into the Economic Council was decreed. Thus, while the factory director had control over the worker's food and lodging, the worker had no trade unions independent of the state to take up his grievances. But it was impossible to *decree* slavery. So long as industry was expanding and workers were necessary to man the machines, the workers took advantage of that one fact and continued to shift from job to job.

The 1938 law was no harsher than the 1932 law but no more effective. The barbarous 1940 law was likewise found inadequate. Shvernik proposed that, instead of bare decrees, the state use the indirect method to get the most out of labor. Shvernik raised the slogan "To liquidate to the end equalitarianism in pay." In other words, piece work should be the rule not only in 70 per cent of the enterprises, as heretofore, but be 100 per cent prevalent. "Petty bourgeois equalitarianism" and "depersonalization" must be "liquidated." The Leader had been wise when, as far back as 1931, he had said that there should be an end to depersonalization. It was high time to realize that slogan.

What, precisely, does "putting an end to depersonalization" mean?

2 *Ending Depersonalization and Creating Stakhanovism*

Although the state, as the owner of all means of production, is the overall employer, every state enterprise must procure its own labor force and there is keen competition between individual enterprises because (1) there is a shortage of experienced labor; (2) productivity is so low that there is a constant need for more labor than theoretically is necessary according to the Plan. For instance, the First Five Year Plan called for an increase of laborers to 15.7 million. Actually, 22.8 million laborers were used even to achieve the unattained production plans. Living quarters in the city became unbearably overcrowded but the famished peasants continued to flock to the city in millions so that a large reserve army of labor was finally created. In 1933 passports had to be introduced to restrain the peasants' search of employment in the city. In tune with the times. *Industry*, the organ of the Commissariat of Heavy Industry, in its issue of March 16, 1933, informs managers who had not fired their "poor" workers because heretofore there had been severe shortage of labor that now they have a "trump card: there are *more workers* in the shops than is necessary according to plans." (Emphasis in original.) In analyzing the excessive turnover the writer of this front page article has the gall to attribute it to the "enthusiasm" of the Don Basin miners for collectivization, which made them leave their work and "themselves" put through collectivization in the village! "But, why," he continues, "is there still excessive labor turnover?" One of the reasons he admits to be "In the communal dwellings, which have been built in the past months it is filthy, uncomfortable, boring." But the biggest cause for labor turnover is the search for better wages. He asks management to stop bidding against management for workers. Neither this appeal nor the anti-labor legislation that was enacted nor the fact that the proletariat was deprived of the use of the trade unions which had become part of the administrative machinery of the state accomplished the trick of straight-jacketing labor. The 1931 slogan, "Let there be an end to depersonalization," needed a big stick to enforce it. So the state arranged for a "gift from heaven"[50] to be sent them in the form of Stakhanovism.

Here is [Valeri] Mezhlauk's (the then chairman of the State Planning Commission) explanation of this "gift from heaven":

> A plain miner, the Donetz Basin hewer, Alexei Stakhanov, in response to Stalin's speech of May 4, 1935, the keynote of which was the care of the human being and which marked a new stage in the development of the USSR, proposed a new system of labor organization for the extraction of coal. The very first day his method was applied he cut 102 tons of coal in one shift of six hours instead of the established rate of seven tons.

So this "gift from heaven" came on August 31, 1935, "in response to Stalin's speech of May 4." In the four months that elapsed between the two events a

50 Stalin's expression; see his speech on November 25, 1935.

lot was done by the state to set the stage for "the miracle," so that the press, the photographers, the wires of the world immediately heard of "the gift from heaven." Contrast the hullabaloo about Stakhanov with the silence as to the hothouse conditions created for Stakhanovites who get the finest tools and spoil them at the fastest pace without the necessity of paying for them as the workers have to pay for damaged goods, and the silence as to the brigade of helpers who do all the detail work but get no Stakhanovite recognition either in fame or in money! These record-breakers for a day do not repeat their records but retire behind swivel chairs while the mass of workers are now told that the "miracle" should really be their regular "norm"!

Armed with Stakhanovism, the state was able to revive the 1931 slogan, for now they had the wherewithal to enforce it. Piecework was made the prevailing system of work in Russia. In the state of Lenin-Trotsky, where the *Subbotnik* was the hero, the range of pay was one to three; in the Stalinist state, where the Stakhanovite is the hero, the range of pay is one to twenty!

3 *Ending Rationing and Producing Luxury Goods*

Ending depersonalization and creating this extreme differentiation in pay had its corollary in ending rationing and producing luxury goods, for the rise in pay would have meant nothing to the Stakhanovites if they could not put it to use. It is interesting, therefore, to note that whereas production of articles of mass consumption kept little pace with the demand for them, the production of luxury goods leaped almost to the miraculous heights achieved in the production of means of production goods. The tremendous increase in realized output of luxury goods contrasts sharply to the very slight increase in articles of mass consumption. Let us look at the luxury goods first:[51]

	1932	1936
Watches	65,000	558,000
Gramophones	58,000	337,000
Cameras	30,000	557,000
Silk (million meters)	21.5	512,000

51 Cf. L.E. Hubbard: Soviet *Trade and Distribution*.

Even the Perfumery Trust, headed by the cultured Mme. Litvinoff, showed a great increase.[52] Contrast the 270 per cent increase in "production" of perfumes to the measly 44 per cent in the production of cotton goods for the period of the Second Five Year Plan!

Even so the Stakhanovite was dissatisfied, for it was irksome to him to be favored only in the matter of luxury goods, whereas in the articles of first necessity the manual worker with his ration card was still favored by the state stores. And the prosperous *kolkhoznik* who was not entitled to a ration card, of what good was his prosperity to him? Clearly, the status of these two groups contradicted the reality of rationing. The state took steps to end this contradiction.

On November 15, 1935, the first All-Russian Conference of Stakhanovites was called to order. It was addressed by the Leader himself and *Pravda* waxed editorially enthusiastic about the "salt of the Soviet earth." It initiated a campaign to teach the people "to respect those leaders of the people." It tried to counteract the detestation of the rank and file workers toward these unsocial speed-demons. That hatred had no bounds and it was not altogether an unheard-of event that individual Stakhanovites were found murdered. The press hushed down the occasional murder and played up the state praise. These Stakhanovites, the masses were told, were "non-party Bolsheviks." The Stakhanovites themselves were favored with something more practical than the label "non-party Bolshevik": *rationing was abolished!*

The abolition of rationing made it possible for the Stakhanovite to reap full advantage of his high salary. The abolition of rationing benefited the prosperous *kolkhoznik* who had heretofore not been entitled to a ration card. The abolition of rationing worsened the conditions of the mass of toilers.

The state, however, pictured the abolition of rationing as a boon to the workers. A lot was said about the "rise in the consumption of the masses." What they cited as "proof" of that was the increase in gross (not net) retail turnover. The State Treasury does not divide its revenue from turnover tax into that obtained from articles of mass consumption and those from heavy industry, but we know, through the manner in which it taxes individual items, that in no case could the percentage of turnover tax from heavy industry have been higher than 10 per cent. Hence, if we examine the gross retail turnover, we will see that there was not so much an increase in the turnover of goods as in the money turnover:[53]

---

52 Cf. N. Mikhailov: *Land of the Soviets.*

53 Table abstracted from *Quarterly Bulletin of Soviet-Russian Economics*, No. 1–2, November, 1939.

	Gross Ret. Turnover	Turnover Tax	Net Ret. Turnover	Incidence of Tax
1930	19,915.5	6,735.1	13,180	51.1
1931	27,465.2	10,607.8	16,863	62.9
1934	61,814.7	37,615.0	24,200	155.4
1935	81,712.1	51,900.0	29,812	174.4

Thus the effect of the turnover tax was "a rise in consumption of the masses" (*read: a rise in the incidence of the tax*) from 51.1 per cent in the first year of its adoption to 174.4 per cent in 1935, when rationing was abolished. According to the table above, that is according to the value of goods, production of articles of mass consumption more than quadrupled from 1930–35. But we know that, at best, production only doubled (that is, even if we take the Soviet economist's gauge of value output and exclude only the turnover tax). Clearly, no more commodities could be consumed than were produced. But even if we accept the doubling in production of articles of mass consumption, we can still, by no stretch of the imagination, conclude that that meant a rise in the consumption of the masses. The high prices in effect after rationing made it difficult for the ordinary worker to buy even the few commodities he had bought during the rationing period. The rise in "mass" consumption meant a rise in the consumption of the labor and *kolkhoz* aristocracy and a *decrease* in the consumption of the rank and file workers, as we shall soon see.

The Russian statisticians would have us believe that there was a decrease in the prices of articles of mass consumption after rationing. As proof of that, they place parallel the prices in effect before and after rationing was abolished. However, what they place alongside of one another is not the rationed and non-rationed price *but* the *open market prices*, which were completely beyond the reach of the rank and file workers, and the *commercial* prices, that is, the state store prices *after* rationing was abolished and the prices were *raised*. As the table below will show, the reduction in the open market price (the single uniform price) was a *tremendous increase* nevertheless over the rationed price, which the worker had heretofore been entitled to:[54]

54 1928 prices abstracted from *Statistical Handbook* (In Russian); 1932 prices from Prokopovicz's *Bulletin*, No. 1–2; 1935 prices from *American Quarterly for the Soviet Union*, April, 1940. Starred items are 1939 prices.

Item	Rationed prices		Open market	Single uniform
	1928	1932	1935	1935
Black bread	.09	.12½	1.00	.85
Wheat flour	.22	.19	2.25	1.80
Beef	.70	2.12	11.76*	5.80
Potatoes	.07	.25	.50	.40
Sugar	.65	1.25	4.50	3.80
Sunflower oil	.49	–	–	13.50*
Butter	2.21	4.05	–	16.50

Thus the "victorious reduction in prices" reveals a *ten-fold* rise in prices since the initiation of the First Five Year Plan. The change from the open market price to the single uniform price benefited only those who were not entitled to a ration card and had to buy in the open market. But for the mass of workers the abolition of rationing meant such a rise in price as must *considerably decrease* his standard of living. This deserves more detailed treatment, for his standard of living has deteriorated even more since then, as we shall see in examining his real wages at the outbreak of the Russo-German war.

4 *The Worker's Standard of Living at the Outbreak of War*

The above table was the first official glimpse we have had of the rising cost of living since the discontinuation of the publication of the food index in 1930. Further data in regard to the rise in retail prices in government stores in Moscow in 1939 and 1940 were gathered by the American Embassy and published in the November, 1939, and May and August, 1940, issues of the *Monthly Labor Review*. In addition to reporting the prices of food, the *Review* also records the fact that, although there were 129 items of foodstuffs in state stores in 1936, there were only 88 on January 1, 1939, only 83 on June 1, 1939, and only 44 items on January 1, 1940. Further, that such essential commodities as milk, butter, eggs, sugar and potatoes which were listed as available, are available very irregularly. The prices quoted have been disputed by no one.[55] The only subterfuge left to

55 Confirmatory evidence of the validity of these prices appeared in the *Pravda* of October 21, 1940, which announced that potatoes have been "reduced from one ruble and twenty kopeks to ninety kopeks" and "bread raised from eighty-five kopeks to a ruble per kilo." The only place that had quoted the ruble and twenty kopeks as the price for potatoes was the *Monthly Labor Review* article; the last the outside had had of the official figures was the quotation of potatoes at fifty kopeks a kilo in 1935.

the Soviet apologists is that it is insufficient merely to show the rise in cost of food without knowing the Russian worker's preference in food—he may prefer herring to caviar. But our method of measuring the worker's standard of living takes away even that shabby subterfuge since the goods used are those found by an official study in Moscow in 1926 to be those consumed by the masses.[56]

Cost of food in the czarist times and before and after the five year plans[57]

Foodstuffs consumed weekly in Moscow in 1926 (*in rubles per kilo, except milk in liters and eggs in units*)		**1913**	**1913**	**1928**	**1928**	**1940**	**1940**
	Quantity	**Price**	**Cost**	**Price**	**Cost**	**Price**	**Cost**
Black bread	2.46	0.07	.1722	0.08	.1968	0.85	2.0910
Wheat flour	0.79	0.12	.0948	0.22	.1738	2.90	2.2910
Potatoes	3.04	0.05	.1520	0.09	.2736	1.20	3.6480
Beef	0.92	046	.4232	0.87	.8004	12.00	11.0400
Mutton	0.17	0.34	.0578	0.79	.1343	14.00	2.0080
Sugar	0.45	0.34	.1530	0.62	.2790	3.80	1.7100
Milk	1.24	0.11	.1364	0.06	.0774	2.10	2.6040
Butter	0.11	1.15	.1265	2.43	.2673	17.50	1.9250
Eggs	1.60	0.03	.0480	0.20	.3200	0.85	1.3600
Sunflower Oil	0.12	0.15	.0180	0.53	.0636	15.65	1.8780
			1.3819		2.5832		30.6270

56 Furthermore, the benefit of the doubt In each case goes to the state. For example, of the eleven items listed in the 1920 budget, we have listed only ten because the eleventh, rice, was unavailable and rather than guess at a substitute we have simply taken for granted that the worker did without rice. Again, when the 1926 list did not mention the quality of food, we In each case put down the cheaper quality, thus the price for beef is that of beef for soup, not either roast beef or beefsteak; the prices of butter and wheat flour are second quality, etc.

57 The 1918 figures are from Prokopovlo's *Bulletin*, No. 1–2; 1928 prices as in note 51; 1940 figures for beginning of year from *Monthly Labor Review*. The 1928 study, including quantities, reproduced in *International Labor Review*.

Using 1913 as 100, the index of the cost of food for 1928 is 187 and for 1940 it is 2,248. The weekly wages for those years were: 1913, six rubles; 1928, fourteen rubles, and 1940, 83 rubles. Again using 1913 as our base for nominal weekly wages, we have an index for 1928 of 233, and for 1940 of 1,383. We can now construct our index of real wages by dividing the nominal weekly wage into the real cost of food, thus obtaining 125 *as the index of real wages* in 1928 and 62.4 per cent for 1940, when compared to Czarist times, we must not forget! Had we considered the further rise in food prices by October, 1940, it would have been a mere 55 per cent of 1913! And even that appallingly low figure, which so glaringly proves the deterioration in the worker's standard of living, does not picture the situation at its worst for we have considered the single uniform price in 1940 and not the open market price (to which the worker sometimes had to resort because few foods were available in state stores). On the average, the open market prices are 78 per cent higher than the state store price! There is supposed to be no black market in Russia but in the officially recognized free market beefsteak sold for seventeen rubles a kilo when the state stores sold the same commodity at ten and a half rubles!

The full significance of the miserable living standards of the Russian worker first fully dawns upon one when he reads the Stalinist publicity of the "socialized" wage—that is, the free medical care, education and reduced rent that the Russian worker is supposed to count as part of his "wages" and of which he was deprived during Czarist times. First of all, even that would not bring the worker's real wages to more than 70.8 per cent of Czarist time, which is not much to boast of for a "socialist" land. But more than that, the point as to the "socialized" wage *does not affect our comparison with 1928.* All of the beneficial legislation was enacted in the first years of the workers' state. Both in relation to education[58] and health[59] the worker fares worse, not better, after three Five Year Plans than before their initiation. And *in comparison to his 1928 standard of living his 1940 standard is but one-half!* His standard of living deteriorated not only in regard to the main basis, food, but also in regard to his four square meters of living space and his clothing (in rubles):

58 He now has to pay for his education above the first year of high school.

59 Consider, for example, the pregnancy laws. In the first years of the workers' state the working woman got eight weeks before and eight weeks after pregnancy; now she gets paid for a total of only 35 calendar days. Moreover, she does not get that unless she has worked seven months in a single enterprise; and that, when you consider the extent of the labor turnover, does not often happen!

Article of clothing	1928	1939	Increase
Calico, meter	.50	3.50	7-fold
Woolens, meter	6.50	180.00	28-fold
Men's Leather Shoes	9.35	175.00	19-fold
Women's Leather Shoes	6.89	85.00	12-fold
Galoshes	3.60	19.65	5.5-fold

We see here a *fourteen-fold* increase in the cost of clothing as compared to 1928. If, because of the paucity of data, we have not included rent and cost of clothing in computing the worker's standard of living and real wages, that, too, was in favor of the state. The inescapable conclusion is that even from the *most optimistic view* the worker's standard has decreased 20 to 30 per cent from Czarist times and by half since 1928! Neither should it be forgotten that we took the *average* weekly wage; the minimum weekly wage of 25–30 rubles would have been insufficient to pay for his food alone, much less consider clothing and rent! Contrast to this deterioration the fact that the per capita income has increased from 52 rubles in 1928 to 196 in 1937 and that the "national wealth" leaped from six billions in 1928 to 178 billions in 1940, and you have the most perfect polarization of wealth in an "industrially advanced" society!

We have traced the development of the "social group known as the proletariat"; let us now scan the social physiognomy of the "classless intelligentsia," which is not a class "in the old sense of the word" (Stalin), but nevertheless performs the function of ruling production and the state.

II The Intelligentsia: The Social Physiognomy of the Ruling Class

Stalin was addressing the Eighteenth Party Congress of the RCP in March, 1939:

> Notwithstanding the complete clarity of the position of the party on the question of the Soviet intelligentsia—the Leader complained—there are still within our party those who have views hostile to the Soviet intelligentsia and incompatible with the position of the party. Those who hold such incorrect views practice, as is known, a disdainful, contemptuous attitude toward the Soviet intelligentsia, considering it as a force foreign, even hostile, to the working class and the peasantry... incorrectly carrying over toward the Soviet intelligentsia those views and attitudes which had their basis in old times when the intelligentsia was in the service of the landowners and the capitalists....

> Toward the new intelligentsia a new theory is necessary, pointing out the necessity of a friendly relation to it, concern over it, respect for it and collaboration with it in the name of the interests of the working class and the peasantry.[60]

The following day the press waxed enthusiastic not only of the Leader but of the group he extolled, the intelligentsia. *Izvestia* assured us that "these leaders of the people" were "the salt of the earth." Stalin, being a practical man, said that these "cadres" should be valued as "the gold fund of the party."

Molotov, addressing the same congress, was very specific as to who constituted the intelligentsia. He listed 1.7 million directors, managers, *kolkhoz* heads and "others"—that is, the politicians—who constituted the "most advanced people." When to the "most advanced" he added the rest of the intelligentsia, he got a total of 9.5 million who, with their families, constituted 13–14 per cent of the population.[61]

[Andrei] Zhdanov, the secretary of the party, drew some practical conclusions from the Leader's "theory" and Molotov's statistics. It was true that since there were "no exploiting classes" there could not be any bosses. But there were factory directors and they were a part, a most essential part, of the intelligentsia, the very part whom it was necessary "to respect and obey." Therefore, he, Zhdanov, elaborated a plan by which to pave the way for smooth collaboration of these "classless" groups. The plan boiled down to a proposal to change the statutes of the party in such a way as to erase all distinction of class origin.[62]

In arguing for the change, Zhdanov fairly wreaked tears of pity from his listeners when he told them the sad tale of a certain Smetanin who at the time that he was a worker at the factory Skorokhod had become a candidate for party membership. Before action was taken upon his application for membership he turned, first, into a Stakhanovite and immediately thereafter into the director of the factory, whereupon, according to the statutes of the party, he was placed in Category 4, for alien class elements. He protested: "How am I worse now that I am made a director of the factory?" The Eighteenth Congress of the CP—not the factory Skorokhod—"unanimously decided" that he was no "worse," and the old statutes of the party were thrown overboard. The party,

60 *Problems of Economy*, No. 3, 1939.

61 The 1939 census was not yet published. Molotov based his figures on the 1937 census, which was not made public because it was "defective."

62 When the NEP was introduced, the party of Lenin decided to keep careerist elements out of the party by establishing three categories, in the order of the accessibility of entrance into the party: the worker, the peasant and the employees.

at any rate, toed the "theoretic" line of Stalin and decided that there were no classes in Russia and the "vanguard" party therefore need have no class distinctions in its statutes.

But the course of the economy which proceeded upon its way more along the line of the world market and less along Stalin's rationalizations, the production process which gave birth to a class and was in turn determined by it clearly revealed the social physiognomy of the rulers. Much as the Central Administration of National Economy statistics tried to give the 1939 census a "classless" physiognomy, and incomprehensive as the data were, there is much we can learn from them in regard to the actual existence of classes from it. Here is how the Central Administration of National Economy grouped its population statistics:

Social Group	Number	Pct. of Total
Workmen in towns and villages	54,566,283	32.19
Employees in towns and villages	29,738,484	17.54
Kolkhoz members	75,616,388	44.61
Individual peasants	3,018,050	1.78
Handicraft workers in organized in cooperatives	3,888,434	2.29
Handicraft workers outside cooperatives	1,396,203	0.82
Non-Working Population	60,006	0.04
Individuals without indication of social standing	1,235,279	0.75
Total	169,519,127[63]	100.00

These percentages were further reshuffled in order to compare the social composition of the land of "socialism" with the land of Czarism:

Social group	1913	1939
Workers and Employees	16.7	49.73
Collective farmers and cooperative handicraftsmen	–	46.9
Bourgeoisie (landlords, merchants, *kulaks*)	15.9	–

63 One million in the Far Northern territories was unavailable for analysis.

Individual farmers and non-cooperative handicraftsmen	65.1	2.6
Others (students, pensioners)	2.3	–
Non-working population	–	0.04
Not listed	–	0.73
Total	100.0	100.00

Note that the *whole* population is accounted for by using the family as the unit. That helps hide both child labor and dependents on wage earners. Note, further, that the population is practically one homogeneous mass of "classless" toilers: almost 50 per cent of the population are workers and employees and the collective farmers constitute practically all of the other 50 per cent. And where are the intelligentsia we heard so much about? The reader will search in vain for them. Yet every "academician" who set out to analyze the above figures in the official periodicals had much to say about the rise of the intelligentsia. Who are they? What do they do? In order to find them and learn their social physiognomy, we shall have to break up the single category of "workers and employees," which hides the ruling class under its broad wings. Let us turn to the occupational classifications and find out how Russians earn a living. The headings of the following groupings are mine, but the categories are from official statistics:

Aristocracy of labor[64] (thousands)	
Heads of tractor brigades	97.6
Heads of field brigades	549.6
Heads of livestock brigades	103.1
Tractor drivers	803.1
Combine operators	131.2
Skilled laborers in industry, including metal workers, lathe operators, welders and molders	5,374.4
Total	7,059.0

"Employees" (thousands)	
Economists and statisticians	822*
Legal personnel (judges, attorneys)	46

64 Stakhanovites are not listed separately; they are spread among the aristocrats of labor and "advanced" intelligentsia.

Engineers, architects (excluding those acting as directors)	250*
Doctors and middle medical personnel	762
Middle technical personnel	836
Agro-technical personnel	96*
Teachers	1,207
Cultural and technical workers (journalists, librarians, club directors)	495
Art workers	46
Bookkeepers, accountants, etc.	1,769
Total	6,451

"The advanced intellegentsia"	
Factory directors and mgrs., *kolkhoz, sovkhoz,* and MTS presidents	1,751*
Agronomists	80
Scientific wkrs. (incl. supvrs, professors of higher education institutions)	93
Others (incl. the army intelligentsia)	1,550*
Total	3,174

*Starred figures are those given by Molotov; I could find no later figures.

We thus get a total of 16.9 million, or only 10.02 per cent of the total population who are considered a part of the "classless intelligentsia" in the broader sense of the word. The "most advanced" of the intelligentsia, "the genuine creators of a new life," as Molotov called them—those, that is, who are the real masters over the productive process—constitute a mere 3.4 million or 2.05 per cent of the total population. (We are not here considering the family unit since we are interested only in those who rule over the productive process, not their families who share in the wealth their husbands extract). The remaining eight per cent share in the surplus value and sing the praises of the rulers, but it is clear that they leave to the latter the running of the economy and the state.

The Central Administration of National Economy statistics, needless to say, did not reveal the exact share of surplus value appropriated by this "advanced" intelligentsia. But at least we now know who this group is and what it does. The part it plays in the process of production stamps it as clearly for the ruling class it is as if indeed it had worn a label marked "Exploiters." Just as the Russian state could not "liquidate Category 4" merely by writing it off the party statute books, so it could not hide the social physiognomy of the ruling class merely by choosing for it the euphemistic title of "Intelligentsia."

∴

Labor and Society

1942 or 1943, Raya Dunayevskaya Collection, #87

> ... the key to the understanding of the whole history of society lies in the historical development of labor.
>
> F. ENGELS, *Ludwig Feuerbach and the End of Classical German Philosophy*[65]

I The Concept of Labor

Labor has been decisive in the evolution of man.[66] Historical materialism traces a progressive development in the course of human ascendancy from the lower to the higher stages, which has asserted itself through all seeming accidents and temporary retrogressions. The driving forces of history have not been great men, but great masses of people, who were set into motion by the incongruity between productive forces and production relations, that is to say, by the antagonism between the development of the material means of production and the relations of people in production. They liberated the new productive forces fettered by the outlived mode of production and production relations, created the conditions for a new method of production and thus laid the basis for a new social order.

The evolution of man from lower to higher stages takes place by means of the developing process of labor. Labor has transformed the natural conditions of human existence into social ones. In primitive communism labor was a mode of self-activity, the creative function of man, which stemmed from his

65 Frederick Engels, *Ludwig Feuerbach and the Outcome of Classical German Philosophy* (New York: International Publishers, 1941), p. 61. Also see Marx-Engels, *Collected Works*, 26:398.

66 "... to socialist man *all of history* is nothing else than the production of man through human labor." Marx: *Private Property and Communism*, in *Archives of Marx and Engels*, Vol. III, in Russian; also in German: *Gesamtausgabe*, Abteilung I, Band III. [See Marx's "Private Property and Communism," in his *Economic and Philosophic Manuscripts* of 1844, in *Collected Works* (New York: International Publishers, 1975), 3:305.].

natural capacities and further developed his natural talents. In his contact with nature, primitive man, despite the limitations of his knowledge, exercised not only his labor power but his judgment as well. He thus developed himself and nature. The method of increasing the productivity of nature through human activity resulted in the further development of man. But freedom and historic initiative of man could not further the progress of mankind until man had learned to *master* nature. It is true that under primitive communism the producers were masters of production and of the products of their labor, but production was carried on in such narrow limits as merely to procreate barely self-subsisting units. So limited a production could not thrust humanity forward. The social division of labor was the necessary prerequisite in molding nature to man's will and creating new productive forces. However, this undermined the collective nature of production and appropriation. Producers no longer consumed directly what they produced, and they lost control over the products of their labor.

1) *Labor in Class Societies*

With the division of labor—the most monstrous of which is the division between mental and manual labor—class societies arose. The separation of intellectual and physical labor stands in the way of man's full development. Hence labor in class societies—whether that be slave, feudal, or capitalist order—no longer means the free development of the physical and intellectual energy of man. The product of his labor is alienated from the laborer, and his very mode of labor becomes an alien activity. Labor is no longer voluntary but compulsory. It has ceased to be "the first necessity of living" and has become a mere *means* to life. It has become a drudgery man must perform to earn a living, and not a mode of activity in which he realizes his physical and mental potentialities. He is no longer interested in the development of the productive forces, and, in fact, the productive forces seem to develop independently of him. Labor has become a means of creating wealth and "is no longer grown together with the individual into one particular destination."[67]

Labor in class societies has taken the form of one of three types of servitude: (a) outright slavery, (b) serfdom, and (c) wage slavery. The mode of labor corresponds to the mode of production. Slave labor used the rudest and heaviest implements and wasted the soil. Improved methods of cultivating the land led to the substitution of serf for slave labor. However, both under slavery and serfdom the development of the productive forces was on a low level,

---

67 Marx, *Critique of Political Economy* (Chicago: Charles Kerr, 1904), p. 299. [Marx-Engels, *Collected Works* (New York: International Publishers, 1976), 28:41].

the economy was stagnant, and the mode of activity of the direct producer was limited by a crude instrument of production. Hence, any liberation achieved by an individual slave or serf could not emancipate him from the limitation of that crude instrument of production. Even in freedom they remained bound by the restricted mode of activity imposed by that crude instrument. Each man's particular labor and necessary tools of his craft became his own property but the necessity to protect the laboriously acquired skill led to the formation of guilds. Hence the social relations in the city where the refugee serfs escaped imitated the feudal form of organization prevailing in the country. "Their instrument of production became their property," Marx sums up, "but they themselves remained determined by the division of labor and their own instrument of production."[68]

The multitude of productive forces available to men determines the nature of their society. Man is essentially a tool-making animal and the process of the production of his material life, the process of labor, means the process of the growth of the productive forces and his command over nature. "Industry," explained Marx in his *Private Property and Communism*, "is the *actual* historical relation of nature, and consequently of the science of nature, to man." The industrial revolution, the progress of natural science and the general technological advance so revolutionized the mode of production that finally there arose a basis for a true freedom, not only freedom from exploitation, but freedom from want. Tremendous progress has been achieved, but the productive forces which have been developed by the bourgeois mode of production have also been harnessed and fettered by bourgeois production relations which have resulted in labor's enslavement to capital. Technology has progressed so far that general want does not reign out of the nature of production but because of the *production relation*. It becomes necessary to put an end to that relationship to make it possible for the *nature* of production to assert itself.

2) *Labor in Socialist Society*

Production is no longer limited by a crude instrument, nor does a crude instrument restrict the activity of man as it did in pre-capitalist societies, even when it was his property. Were man to appropriate the modern machines of production, that would open up limitless vistas for the development of man himself, for it would be on such a high material base that the intellect of the masses could combine with their physical powers and truly lay the basis for a new mode of life. Thus, the appropriation of the totality of the instruments of

68 Marx, *The German Ideology* (New York: International Publishers, 1939), p. 67. [Marx-Engels, *CW*, 5:88].

production "is nothing more than the development of the individual capacities corresponding to the material instruments of production. The appropriation of a totality of instruments is for this very reason, the development of a totality of capacities in the individuals themselves."[69] That is the heart of the problem, because the development of man's capacities means the re-establishment of self-activity on a gigantically higher historical scale and the "abolition" of labor.

Because of the class content of the word, labor, Marx, in his early works, never used the term to describe the mode of activity in socialist society. He wrote, not of the emancipation of labor, but of its "abolition." In the historical circumstances of the complete separation of manual from mental labor, he stressed, man can become master of himself, not through the development of labor, but through its abolition. Hence the proletarian revolution is not only the revolutionary appropriation of the totality of the instruments of production, but is directed against the very mode of activity under capitalism, and "does away with labor."[70]

Marx did not abandon this concept of labor when he abandoned the use of the philosophical term, self-activity, and began, in his later works, to speak of the emancipation of labor. For labor in a socialist society was in no manner whatever to be the type of activity as under capitalism where man's labor is limited to the exercise of his physical labor power. No, labor in socialist society would be the *type* of activity as in primitive communism. The division between mental and manual labor would be abolished and the two aspects of labor thus united would make it possible for "freely associated men"[71] consciously to plan production, and what would assert itself would be the "free individuality of the laborer himself."[72]

The emphasis placed by Marx on the individual rather than on society in his late works thus consistently follows and develops the theoretic scope of his early works where he sketched the pattern of the social order to follow capitalism. It is true that the new mode of production does not appear full-blown on the morrow the bourgeoisie is overthrown. But whether the dictatorship of the proletariat will be transitional from capitalism to socialism will be judged by whether the socialized means of production serve social needs to an ever greater and greater degree. Marx had warned us, in his *Civil War in France*, that

69 Marx, *The German Ideology*, p. 66. [CW, 5:87].

70 Marx, *The German Ideology*, p. 69. [CW, 5:52].

71 Karl Marx, *Capital* (Chicago: Charles H. Kerr, 1906), 1:92. Also see the Marx Library edition, translated by Ben Fowkes (New York: Vintage Books, 1977), 1:173. Hereafter, the editions are cited as "*Capital*, Kerr" and "Vintage," respectively.—Editor's Note.

72 Marx, *Capital* (Chicago: Charles Kerr, 1906), Vol. 1, p. 835. [Vintage, 1977, 1:173.].

if cooperative production were not to prove to be a delusion, it must be under the proletarians' own control. And in his earlier writings he had written significantly enough: "It is especially necessary to avoid ever again to counterpose 'society' as an abstraction, to the individual."[73] This prophetic statement will be analyzed in greater detail in the section, "Is Russian Society Part of the Collectivist Epoch." [See this essay below.] Here we are only interested in tracing the general Marxian concept of labor, which, in primitive communism, was synonymous with the self-activity or the creative function of man but which has undergone a deterioration in class societies.

On the basis of a production of abundance, for which the highly developed productive forces have laid the groundwork, the further development of the productive forces means the all-rounded development of the greatest productive force, the laborer. Labor then will mean the unrestricted development and exercise of man's physical and mental faculties. That is the basis for what Engels calls "humanity's leap from the realm of necessity to the realm of freedom."[74]

That is not Utopia. That is not the hereafter. That road has to be taken on the morrow the bourgeoisie is overthrown and the dictatorship of the proletariat established *if* the socialized means of production are to serve any better end than the privately owned means of production. *For it is not the means of production that create the new type of man, but the new type of man that will create the means of production*, and the new mode of activity will create the new type of human being, socialist man.

II The Concept of Property

> All science would be superfluous if the appearance, the form, and the nature of things were wholly identical.
>
> —KARL MARX, *Capital*, Vol. III[75]

A great advance in the evolution of political economy as a science was made when the source of wealth was recognized to be not in objects outside of men—precious metals or the earth—but in the function of man, that is, the result of man's labor was the source of private property. How is it, then, that that living embodiment of labor, the laborer, continues to remain poverty-stricken

---

73 *Archives of Marx and Engels*, Vol. III, Russian edition. Also *Gesamtausgabe*, Abteilung I, Band III. [Marx, CW, 3:299].

74 Frederick Engels, *Herr Eugen Duhring's Revolution in Science* (*Anti-Duhring*) (New York: International Publishers, 1939), p. 310. [Marx-Engels, *Collected Works*, 25:270.].

75 *Capital*, Kerr, 3:951; Vintage, 3:956.—Editor's Note.

and the products of his labor are not his "private property?" Here the classical economists could offer no answer and merely tried to pacify the laborer by stating his condition was "temporary," and pointing to his "freedom." They were limited by their bourgeois horizon and labored "to purify economic relations from their feudal blemishes."[76]

"When one speaks of private property, one thinks of something outside man," wrote the young Marx in 1844. "When one speaks of labor, one has to do immediately with man himself. The new formulation of the question already involves its solution."[77] But, as we saw, that new formulation of the question involved the solution not when the bourgeois economists tackled the problem, but when the revolutionist Marx did. The difference between the science of economics "as such," as a science of objective elements, wages, value, etc., and the Marxian science of economics is that for Marxism, all economic categories are social categories and thus in the science of economics it incorporates the subjective element, the receiver of wages, the source of value, in other words, the laborer. You cannot dissociate property forms from production relations. The laborer, whose function, labor, creates bourgeois wealth and his own impoverishment, is opposed to his predicament of being dominated by a product of his own labor. He rebels against the mode of labor and thus becomes the gravedigger of bourgeois private property. Private property thus contains within itself the seed of its own disintegration. It is for that reason that the classical economist, limited by the concepts of his class which blurred his vision as to the *historic* nature of the capitalist mode of production, could not probe the problem to the end, and failed to see that the living embodiment of the source of wealth, the laborer, would bring to a head and to an end all the contradictions inherent in private property.

In actual fact, wrote Marx, bourgeois private property is not private property at all, but is based on "the expropriation of the peasants, artisans, in general on the abolition of the method of production *resting on private property of the direct producer, on his conditions of production*" and "develops to the degree that this private property and the method of production based on it is abolished."[78] Thus the very basis of capitalist production is expropriation of the self-earned private property of the direct producer. It is the "free," the

---

76 Marx, *Poverty of Philosophy*, p. 134. [CW, 6:176].

77 *Archives of Marx and Engels*, II (VII), p. 263. [Marx, "Alienated Labor," in *Economic and Philosophic Manuscripts of 1844*, in *Collected Works* (New York: International Publishers, 1975), 3:281].

78 *Archives of Marx and Engels*, II (VII), p. 263. [Marx, "Results of the Immediate Process of Production," in *Capital* (New York: Vintage, 1977), 1:1083].

propertyless laborer that creates the "private property" of the capitalist and it is he who sharpens the inherent contradictions of capitalist private property that will rend it asunder.

The machine age demanded the abolition of private property; the full development of the productive forces will achieve the true abolition of property, although, "in the first instance"[79] this has taken the contradictory form of capitalist private property. The juridical notion that this is really private property is at complete variance with the bourgeois production relations.

The legal concepts of private property, which sprawl across diverse societies, are as heterogeneous as the societies where they exist. Under capitalism, furthermore, every phase in the development of industry has altered the legal concepts of private property. The manufacturer thinks of it as the legal title he has to the factory he runs. The financier thinks of it as "a bundle of expectations which have a market value."[80] It is not the legal concepts, not the *appearances* of property that interests us. It is the nature of private property, which scientific socialism has investigated to the end, that is of primary importance. In reducing private property to labor and labor to man, Marx got behind the legal fiction of property ownership to the hard reality of the activity of man and the relations of men in production.

The Marxian concept of property stresses the fact that from the very outset the *division of labor* has meant the division of the conditions of labor, of the tools and materials. From the moment that the product of his labor did not belong to the direct producer, man became an "object" for himself. That is to say, the object which he himself has created by his activity was something outside of him because it was appropriated by another who had power over him. As long as there exists "power *over* individuals," wrote Marx in *The German Ideology*, "private property must exist."[81] Property is the power of disposal over the labor of others. Private property has developed so diversely under capitalism that one's property is only "a bundle of expectations" in the form of stocks and bonds, yet *power* is still the power of disposing, or sharing in the disposition of, the labor of others.

It is impossible for a Marxist to discuss property forms, or even production relations without knowing the state of production. Marx attributed such great importance to the multitude of productive forces accessible to man

79 Marx, *Private Property and Communism*, to be found in *Gesamtausgabe*, Abteilung I, Band III and in the Russian *Complete Works of Marx*, III. [Marx, CW, 3:294].

80 Adolph Berle and Gardiner Means, *Modern Corporation and Private Property* (New York: MacMillan, 1932).

81 Marx-Engels, *Collected Works*, 5:64.—Editor's Note.

that he practically discounted the forms of property ownership. In and of itself, that is to say, without a high stage of industrial development, a change from private to communal ownership would be barren of historic significance. "Lacking any material basis and resting on a purely theoretical foundation, it would be a mere freak and would end in nothing more than a monastic economy."[82]

So insistent was Marx in stressing that the mode of production was crucial, not the form of property, that he spoke of "communal private property" when he described ancient state ownership, for it was "only as a community that the citizens hold power over their laboring slaves, and on this account alone, therefore, they are bound to the form of communal ownership."[83] Thus communal ownership in and of itself does not denote a new, non-private property epoch.[84] It is only when collectivist property arises under highly developed industrial conditions that it can denote the new collectivist epoch where society will not be counterposed to the individual and the totality of the instruments of production will be controlled by all and made "subject to each individual."[85]

For Marx the abolition of private property was not an end in itself but a means toward the abolition of the alienated mode of labor. He did not separate one from the other. He never tired of stressing that what was of primary importance was not the form of property but the mode of production; every mode of production creates a corresponding form of property. "But to see mystery in the origin of property; that is to say, to transform the relations of production into a mystery—is that not," asked Marx of Proudhon, "to renounce all pretensions to economic science?... In each historic epoch, property is differently developed and in a series of social relations entirely different. Thus to define bourgeois property is nothing other than to explain all the social relations of bourgeois production."[86]

∴

82 *The German Ideology*, p. 18 ftn. [This footnote does not appear in the edition of *The German Ideology* published in Marx's *Collected Works*, 5].

83 *The German Ideology*, p. 9. [CW, 5:33].

84 This will be dealt with in greater detail in "Is Russian Society Part of the Collectivist Epoch."

85 *The German Ideology*, p. 67. [CW 5:88].

86 *Poverty of Philosophy*, pp. 129–130. [CW, 6:197].

Is Russia Part of the Collectivist Epoch of Society?

1942 or 1943, The Raya Dunayevskaya Collection, *#8888*

The Fetishism of State Property

The revolutionary movement has lost Marx's capacity to keep his fingers on the pulse of human relations, that is, social relations of production, and gets lost in the world of objective things. It keeps its eyes glued on the phenomena, property and politics, instead of keeping them focused on the essence: labor and production. It took the genius of Marx to extract political economy from its fetishism of commodities. Has the revolutionary movement freed itself from the fetishism of a *form* of a product of labor (a commodity) only in order to create a new fetishism of a *form* of property (statified property)?

In his preface to *Capital* Marx warned us that in the analysis of *economic forms*, "neither microscopes nor chemical reagents are of use. The *force of abstraction* must replace both."[87] However, abstractions have no value viewed apart from history. Bourgeois economists were incapable of separating the theoretical potentialities of a relation from its historical starting point because of their bourgeois limitations in judging their own historic period. Their horizon was bounded by "the personification of things and reification of people";[88] they tried to turn the historicity of the particular period in which they lived into a theoretical abstraction; thus there was past history but there is no longer history. On the other hand, they tried to turn a *historic form of labor such as "free labor" into a theoretical abstraction.* In both instances, the human content was lost sight of behind the historic form.

The confusion in the minds of even the best bourgeois economists, said Engels in his review of Marx's *Critique of Political Economy*, is due to the fact that "economics deals not with things, but the relations between persons and in the last resort between classes; these relations are, however, always *attached to things and appear as things.*"[89] For example, exchange of commodities seems to mean exchange of things. In reality, however, the product appearing in exchange is a commodity "solely because a *relation* between two persons or communities attaches to the *thing*, the product."[90]

---

87 All footnotes in this document are by the editor. Karl Marx, *Capital* (Chicago: Charles H. Kerr, 1906), 1:12. Also see the Marx Library edition, translated by Ben Fowkes (New York: Vintage Books, 1977), 1:90. Hereafter, the editions are cited as "*Capital*, Kerr" and "Vintage."

88 *Capital*, Kerr, 1:128; Vintage, 1:209.

89 Marx-Engels, *Collected Works*, 16:476.

90 *Ibid.*

In his famous chapter on the "Fetishism of Commodities," Marx demonstrates most clearly how "a definite social relation between men, that assumed the fantastic form of a relation between things."[91] And to the question, "Whence, then, arises the enigmatical character of the product of labor, so soon as it assumes the form of commodities?" Marx replied, "Clearly from the form itself."[92] Clearly, the fetishism of state property arises from the fact that the *form* of state property appeared in history as *workers'* state property and was thus identified with a *new production relation*, which became attached to the *thing*, statified property.

First, there was the abstraction, workers' state. When Trotsky failed to check the abstraction, workers' state, against the reality, the Soviet Union, the mistake, in a practical sense, was a minor one because it concerned the viable workers' state of Lenin and Trotsky which was still a workers' state, though bureaucratically distorted. But when Trotsky carried over his mistaken conception of the workers' state to the state of Stalin, the mistake was fatal.

1 *Trotsky's Concept of Workers' State and Statified Property*

Watch how Trotsky turns the abstraction, workers' state, into the fetish, statified property:

> The nationalization of the land, the means of industrial production, transport and exchange, together with the monopoly of foreign trade, constitute the basis of Soviet social structure. Through these relations, established by the proletarian revolution, the nature of the Soviet Union as a proletarian state is for us basically defined.[93]

Which relations, production relations or property relations? They are *not* one and the same thing. A property relation is the legal expression of the production relation. It expresses that relationship, sometimes correctly, sometimes incorrectly, depending upon whether the production relationship has been validated by law. In itself, without reference to the actual production relations, state property is a form of property or property relation, not a relation of production. It is a derivative, not a fundamental relation. In periods of revolution and counter-revolution, when the actual production relations undergo a transformation while the legal expressions are still retained in the laws, production

91 *Capital*, Kerr, 1:83; Vintage, 1:165.

92 *Capital*, Kerr, 1:82; Vintage, 1:164.

93 Leon Trotsky, *The Revolution Betrayed*, translated by Max Eastman (New York: Pioneer Publishers, 1945), p. 248.

relations cannot be equated to property relations without equating revolution to counter-revolution! Fetishisms, whether of commodities or of state property, have ever obscured the economic relations between men.

Trotsky never comprehended what making a fetish of statified property *could* lead to. He always spoke of the recession in the workers' state as something that *might* consolidate, or as something that *would* happen, but not as a process that was evolving before his very eyes. When confronted with the familiar features of private property capitalism of the New Economic Policy (NEP), he correctly warned that an unbridled development of the NEP would lead to the Soviet Union's acquiring "capitalism on the installment plan." But in 1927–28 when the "principle" of industrialization and collectivization was adopted, the abstraction, the workers' state, was transformed into the fetish, statified property. Yet he mercilessly criticized the Left Oppositionists who were led to capitulation through equating workers' state to statified property. He subscribed to [Christian] Rakovsky's correct analysis of the capitulators:

> The capitulators refuse to consider what steps must be adopted in order that industrialization and collectivization do not bring about results opposite to those expected.... They leave out of consideration the main question: what changes will the Five-Year- Plan bring about in the *class relations in the country?*
>
> *Russian Bulletin of the Opposition*, No. 7, Nov.–Dec., 1929[94]

Rakovsky saw that the conquests of October would not remain intact if economic laws were permitted to develop "spontaneously" or through state planning, that is, any plans other than that of the proletariat itself. Trotsky, in the early years, warned prophetically that a ruling class other than the proletariat was crystallizing "before our very eyes. The motive force of this singular class is the singular form of private property, state power" (*Russian Bulletin of the Opposition*, No. 17–18, Nov.–Dec., 1930).

In the analysis of the counter-revolution we saw that the fetishism of state property blinded Trotsky from analyzing correctly the development of that "singular form of private property, state power" and thus from discerning the *social* character of the counter-revolution when it came. Trotsky continued to employ the same terminology and gave it the same content when he spoke of

94 Christian Rakovsky, leader of the Left Opposition and former president of the Soviet of People's Commissars of the Ukraine, was tried in Stalin's last great frame-up trial in 1938, and imprisoned. On the *Russian Bulletin of the Opposition*, see *The Raya Dunayevskaya Collection*, #2342.

the state property characteristic of the dictatorship of the proletariat where the proletariat is the ruling class, as when he deals with state property characteristic of the Stalinist state where the working class is not the ruling class but the class in subjection! He thus substituted a *property form* for the *class content*. At the time of the Moscow Trials "the production relations established by October" were still in existence! He saw (the Trials) merely as a gory *political* spectacle, as a sort of palace counter-revolution without social root, an excrescence of the rotten political super-structure but one that lacked an economic base nevertheless. But that is precisely what it did not lack. The Moscow Trials did not culminate merely a political counter-revolution in which the social foundations were left intact. Rather it was a counter-revolution in the relations of production. Apropos of "purely" political revolutions we must not forget Marx's emphasis that they have merely *perfected the existing state machinery.*[95] In other words, since they involved a change of political rulers, and not a *social* change, the bourgeois political revolutions perfected, not distorted, the bourgeois state machine and thus the domination of the bourgeoisie as a class. Surely that cannot be said of the Stalinist "political" revolution in its relation to the social foundations of October. The analogy not only does not hold, but has led Trotsky to defend the actions of the Red Army at the outbreak of war.

It is high time to discard this suicidal policy, and that can be done only on the basis of re-examination of the class nature of the Soviet Union. The first prerequisite for that is to overturn Trotsky's method of judging which class is in control. [...] It is a fetishism which has led part of the revolutionary movement to align itself with one of the imperialist camps in an imperialist war!!

2 *Shachtman's Concepts of Collectivist Property*[96]

"Under a social system of bureaucratic collectivism," states the [Workers'] Party's Russian thesis, "... in the field of property ownership *all* classes are equal—hence none of them owns social property" (emphasis in original).[97] But whether or not all classes are "equal" in a property sense (in the bourgeois "eyes of the law" all classes are also "equal") no one—whether proletariat, collectivist commissar or capitalist coupon clippers—can gain a livelihood except out of the proceeds of *production*. Hence it is the *relationships of production*, not merely the legal aspects or the property relations which are the

95 *See Marx's* "The Eighteenth Brumaire of Louis Bonaparte", *in Marx-Engels, Collected Works, 11:86.*

96 Max Shachtman, a founder of American Trotskyism.

97 See the Workers' Party resolution on the "Russian Question," written by Max Shachtman, published in *The New International*, October, 1941, p. 238.

essence of things. To say that in Russia all classes are equal because none owns, is to take the legal fiction of ownership at face value. In her polemic against reformism, Rosa Luxemburg deals most profoundly yet succinctly with the property versus production theory:

> By capitalist Bernstein does not mean a category of production but the right to property. To him, a capitalist is not an economic unit but a fiscal unit. And "capital" is for him not a factor in production but simply a certain quantity of money.[98]

When Marx analyzed the process of *capitalist* production, he probed deeper than its legal outer covering. That is why he concluded that it was not the ownership but *function* of capital that produced surplus value. Even when one analyzes a "new" order, one should not forget our Marxist ABC's which tells one that it is the productive process, wherein labor is exploited, which is creative of surplus-value. Marx's *Capital* says,

> If, therefore, the capitalist is the owner of the capital, which he employs, he pockets the whole profit, or surplus value. It is immaterial to the laborer, whether the capitalist pockets the whole profit, or whether he has to pay over a part of it to some other person, who has a legal claim to it. The reason for dividing the profit among two kinds of capitalists thus turns surreptitiously into reasons for the existence of surplus-value to be divided, which the capital as such draws out of the process of reproduction, quite apart from any subsequent division.[99]

Does this not apply to a bureaucratic collectivist society? What then, in that society, is the function of capital (or whatever you call the means of production alienated from the direct producers and those exploiting them)? Again we quote from Luxemburg's *Reform or Revolution*:

> By transferring the concept of capitalism from production relations to property relations, and by speaking of simple individuals instead of speaking of entrepreneurs, he (Bernstein) moves the question of socialism from the domain of production into the domain of relations of

---

98 *Rosa Luxemburg,* "Social Reform or Revolution", in *Selected Political Writings*, edited by Dick Howard (New York: Monthly Review Press, 1971), p. 96.

99 *Capital,* Kerr, 3:448; Vintage, 3:504.

> fortune; that is, from the relation between capital and labor to the relation between rich and poor.[100]

Luxemburg was polemicizing against reformists who did not accept Marx's description of *capitalist* production. We are dealing with comrades who accept Marx's analysis of capitalist production—then apply none of his general criteria to the "new" social order just because they have given it a new name. Look at Russia and tell me what the proletariat lacks in order to be ruler in that state. It is not the title of ownership. On the contrary, the Constitution of that country defines state property as property "belonging to the whole people." The legal title notwithstanding, the profits that come out of the Soviet industry go partly to the enterprises and partly to the state. The worker does not share in it, not because he does not "legally" own it, but because his role in the process of production is such that he labors and gets paid for his labor power at its value, which is at a probably low level—110 rubles per month. The worker does not "share the profits" because his relation to the means of production is such that when he has finished using the instruments, the product created (a commodity) through the union of that labor power with the means of production, belongs not to himself, but to the enterprise for which he works.

Now keep in mind the Russia of Lenin when the legal title was the same but the *production relations* were different. In Lenin's time, before the worker entered the factory, he had his production conference, where he decided upon the plan. While he applied his labor power to the instruments of production in the factory, there were his trade union and party representatives to contest any bossy conduct on the part of the factory director. When he got his pay envelope, he once again had recourse to his trade unions and once again had discussed production results. He might have been told that he cannot get a further raise in pay because although his industry made a "profit," still the whole benefit should not revert to him because his state needed to produce steel and that didn't cede a profit yet. He would *know* then that he did not directly benefit by his industry's growth but that his *class* did.

Does Shachtman know what the railroad worker did when he was dissatisfied with the regime? Why, the rank-and-file workers, in one single year, brought pressure to bear so that the *Glavpolitput* (the political superintendence over the economic programs) was abolished; the composition of the *Cectran*[101]

---

100 Rosa Luxemburg, *Reform or Revolution*, pp. 96–97.

101 The *Cectran* was a body created through the merger of the Central Committees of the Railway and Water Transport Workers Unions, established in order to facilitate the

was changed; all went back to their respective trade unions and functioned through normal democratic procedures.

Yes, Comrade Shachtman, the rank-and-file workers had that power not because they had the legal title, which they likewise have now, but because of the production relations (which were the opposite of what they are now). In this case the vanguard political party followed the lead of the workers. "Every political superstructure in the last analysis serves production, and in the last analysis is determined by the production relations prevailing in the given society" (Lenin).[102]

Further our thesis reads: "With the new mode of distribution, the bureaucracy developed a new mode of production, production for the swelling needs of the bureaucracy."[103] Thus the party thesis perverts a basic Marxian concept in order to lay the basis for a rather original (for a Marxist) position on Soviet economy. Or have we forgotten our Marxist ABC's that (1) distribution is merely the "expression of the historically determined conditions of production";[104] and (2) that before distribution can become distribution of production, it is the distribution of the means of production. Here is how Lenin expresses the difference between scientific and vulgar socialism:

> Marx contrasted vulgar socialism to scientific socialism, which does not attach great importance to distribution and which explains the social system by the organization of the *relations of production* and which considers that the given system of relations of production includes a definite system of distribution. This idea runs like a thread through the whole of Marx's teachings.[105]

And this idea applies not only to capitalist society but to all societies, particularly to all class societies, including, we should think, bureaucratic collectivism.

It is not as Shachtman puts it, "the equality of poverty" which was responsible for the type of distribution prevailing during the period of the workers' state of Lenin and Trotsky, but the fact that the workers were the rulers of, masters over, the productive process. Lenin wrote:

---

restoration of railroad transportation at the conclusion of the Russian Civil War. The functioning of this body figured prominently in the Trade Union dispute of 1920–21 between Lenin, Trotsky-Bukharin, and the Workers' Opposition. See Chapter 8 for Dunayevskaya's discussion of Trade Union dispute.

102 Lenin, *Collected Works*, 32:81.

103 "Our thesis" refers to the Workers' Party resolution; see note 95.

104 *Capital*, Kerr, 3:1028; Vintage, 3:1022.

105 Lenin, "The Economic Content of Narodnism" [1894], *Collected Works*, 1:442.

> Having overthrown the bourgeoisie and conquered political power, the proletariat has become the ruling class; it holds the power of the state; it has the disposal of the means of production which have now become social.[106]

In other words, when the means of production are collective property of the workers, there "naturally" (Marx) results a different distribution, not merely of commodities produced, but *primarily*, of the means of production. For what is crucial regarding the subject of distribution is: which class determines production?

Contrasting the young workers' state to capitalist lands, Lenin wrote,

> But see how things have changed since the political power is in the hands of the working class, since the political power of the exploiters is overthrown and since all the means of production (except those which the workers' state voluntarily gives to the exploiters for a time, in the form of concessions) are *owned* by the working class.[107]

Thus when the proletariat owned the means of production, the relationship of the means of production to the means of consumption was 44.6% to 55.4%, and by the time industry reached its pre-war level, the standard of living not of Shachtman's propertyless proletariat but Lenin's property-owning proletariat was 125% of that level. But when the appropriating class differed from the direct producers, then the relationship of the means of production to the means of consumption moved in such a direction that by 1940, the means of production constituted 61% of the total economy, and the means of consumption but 39%, and, most important of all, the standard of living *decreased to half of what it was in 1928* whilst the "collectivist" wealth of the "whole people" jumped from 6 billion to 178 billion rubles! The distribution of the means of consumption was due, in the first place, not to the fact that one class had the wherewithal to buy these products and others did not, but because one class, as the owner of the means of production, or, more correctly, the agent of a definite mode of production, determined the *direction* of the state economy.

Shachtman looks at the deterioration of the workers' standard of living and says that bureaucratic collectivism is nearer to capitalism than to socialism. Then he looks at the collectivist *forms* of property and the "equality" of all

---

106 Lenin, "Economics and Politics in the Era of the Dictatorship of the Proletariat" (Oct. 30, 1919), *Collected Works*, 30:115.

107 Lenin, "On Co-Operation" (Jan. 6, 1923), *Collected Works*, 33:474.

classes in a *property* sense and these two words so overawe him that he comes to the conclusion that the 178 billion rubles of collectivist wealth is worthy of being called part of the "collectivist epoch." Along with Trotsky, Shachtman turns statified property (collectivist) into a fetishism. In Trotsky's case it led him to call for the unconditional defense of the "workers' state" which was integrally participating in an imperialist war. We recoiled. In Shachtman's case, it left an open way for the conditional defense of the same Stalinist state which is now called "bureaucratic collectivism" and because the defense is in the theoretic realm only, the Party accepted this straddling position.

3 *Carter's Species of Collectivist Property*[108]

Along with Comrade Shachtman, Comrade Carter has discovered a new society which he likewise dubs "bureaucratic collectivism." However, he differently interprets this "new social order." Comrade Carter grants that the Stalinist bureaucracy collectively *owns* the means of production but he insists that such ownership does not turn the means of production into "private property," which is what distinguishes the capitalist epoch. We beg to differ. The *differentia specifica* of capitalist production is not that the means of production are privately owned in the sense that they are private property, but that the means of production are *capital*. Under feudalism and under slavery there was likewise private property; neither must we forget that Marx also called tribal ownership "communal private property."[109]

Under the concept of property, we saw over the variety of class societies private property has sprawled. What precisely does Carter mean by private property? Surely the capitalist private property of the present monopoly imperialist epoch is not the individual private property of Adam Smith's era. The five million IT&T (International Telephone & Telegraph) stockholders may be owners of "private property" (surely stocks are calls upon surplus value to be produced), but in no way do they control, and Marx has stated that the formation of stock companies signified "the abolition of capital as private property within the boundaries of capitalist production itself."[110] But the abolition of capital as "private property" is not the abolition of capital, and it is *capital* which signifies that labor in that society is wage labor, and it is the capital-labor relation which determines the class structure of society as capitalistic.

---

108 Joe Carter was a leader of the Workers' Party who developed his own version of bureaucratic collectivism.

109 Marx-Engels, *The German Ideology*, in *Collected Works*, 5:33.

110 *Capital*, Kerr, 3:516; Vintage, 3:567.

Marx wrote that all conditions of capitalist society were reduced to two: private property, which he defined as accumulated labor, and living labor. So long as accumulated labor dominates over living labor there will be "private property" for "property turns out to be the right, on the part of the capitalist, to appropriate the unpaid labor of others or its product and to be the impossibility on the part of the laborer of appropriating his own product." Capitalist private property is the materialized unpaid labor of the laborer.

It was precisely this thorough understanding of contemporary society, the profound analysis of its law of motion, that enabled Marx *not only to foresee but warn against* being taken in by mere change in form of ownership, specifically, of the statification of the means of production. Listen to the collaborator of Marx in a book read by Marx before its publication. In *Anti-Duhring* Engels stressed that the statification of the means of production

> does not deprive the productive forces of their character as capital.... The modern state, whatever its form, is essentially a capitalist machine; it is the state of the capitalists, the ideal collective body of all capitalists. The more productive forces it takes over as its property, the more it becomes the real collective body of all the capitalists, the more citizens it exploits. The workers remain wage-earners, proletarians. The capitalist relationship is not abolished; it is rather pushed to an extreme. But at the extreme it changes into its opposite. State ownership of the productive forces is not the solution of the conflict, but it contains within itself the technical conditions that form the elements of that solution.[111]

Instead of analyzing how the technical conditions became, not the elements to the solution of the capital-labor relation, but the means to more brutal, totalitarian exploitation, Carter has used the existence of state property as a cloak to hide the real relations of production, which in no way differ from those under capitalism.

Slave or Forced Labor

It is unnecessary again to repeat our Marxist fundamentals, to show that what distinguishes various forms of labor is the manner in which surplus labor is extracted; nor to show that the manner in which it is extracted in Russia parallels that in the rest of the capitalist world. The whole discussion regarding "free" labor—free "in the double sense that neither they themselves form part

111 Frederick Engels, *Anti-Duhring*, (New York: International Publishers, 1939), pp. 304–305; Marx-Engels, *Collected Works*, 25:266.

and parcel of the means of production, as in the case of slaves, bondsmen, etc., nor do the means of production belong to them, as in the case of peasant-proprietors"[112]—has been given a putridly liberal tinge by the exponents of bureaucratic collectivism, both of the Shachtman and Carter species.

It is a prime necessity to capitalist production that the worker be "free," for where he has not been entirely separated from the means of production, he does not readily offer his labor power for sale to the owner of the means of production. We had an example of that in the 19th century when the Russian serf was first freed but was not fully separated from his means of production, with the result that he refused to sell his labor power. Here is Marx's comment:

> The Russian farm laborer, owing to the communal property in land, has not been fully separated from his means of production and hence is not yet a "free wage worker" in the full capitalist meaning of the word.[113]

In the 20th century, history re-enacted an analogous scene in Russia. After the State granted the *kolkhozniki*[114] certain private property rights, it found that there was not sufficient labor for industry. The *kolkhozniki*, certainly not having been separated fully from the means of production and hence not being a "free wage worker" in the full capitalist meaning of the word, refused to offer his labor power to city industry. In order to have a constant reserve army of "free" labor, the State decreed the creation of State Labor Reserves.

The worker must be "free" for capitalist production to be a fact, not in the sense that Kent[115] interprets it of being "personally free" but in the sense of being free from the instruments which would put his labor power in action. That is why Marx placed the word free more often in quotations than in italics. Or he would refer to the free worker as a wage-slave—and other times simply speak of all forms of slavery, "direct and indirect."[116]

Will the bureaucratic collectivists please tell me when slave labor became an inherent feature of the Russian economy? Was it in 1932 when both his

---

112 *Capital*, Kerr, 1:785; Vintage, 1:874.

113 *Capital*, Kerr, 2: 40–41; Vintage, 2:117.

114 The *kolkhozniki* are the collectivized farm peasantry. For Dunayevskaya's analysis of the impact on them of forced industrialization, see "An Analysis of the Russian Economy," in this Chapter.

115 Kent, proponent of bureaucratic collectivism in the Workers' Party.

116 See Marx's letter, Dec. 28, 1846, to P.V. Annenkov, Marx-Engels, *Collected Works*, 38:101, where he writes: "We are not dealing with indirect slavery, the slavery of the proletariat, but with direct slavery, the slavery of the Black races in Surinam, in Brazil, in the Southern States of North America."

ration card and his right to living space were given into the hands of the factory director who had the right to fire him and evict him from the premises he occupied as living space for so little a misdemeanor as a single day's absence? 1932, however, has never been referred to by them; more often it is 1938 and 1940 laws. Pray tell, how the law, which seems to have such omnipotence in your eyes, could not make of the worker a slave in 1932 but could do so in 1938 when the same laws were restated with much more publicity attending the decree? Or was it in 1940 when criminal penalties were attached to the Order regarding the restoration of railroad transportation back in 1920! They might answer: it is not in the law but in the economic conditions. We will agree that it is the economic conditions, not the law, that carries the greater weight, but it is precisely when you weigh the economic conditions, that you see the Russian worker is as "free" as the German worker where the economy is still capitalist, not bureaucratic collectivist. Any serious study of the German economy will reveal that the labor market is more efficiently controlled in Germany than in Russia, that the laborer is less able to break through the anti-labor legislation because, among other things, there is no extensive agricultural industry where the laborer can keep from being "free" by hiding himself on his 1/2 acre plot of land. That, however, is not the issue; the dispute is about the time when he is "free," free from land and free from the instruments of labor.

The Russian worker has been so ingenious in circumventing the anti-labor legislation which tried to harness him to a single enterprise that the latest pre-war conference stressed the fact that absenteeism and truancy were in many instances more prevalent than before the enactment of these decrees. Voznessensky[117] complained that the Russian worker, alas, still absented himself "particularly after pay day." It takes more than legislation to make of the wage slave a slave of old, a slave in body, and an integral part of the means of production!

It is a sad commentary on our movement that we have suddenly discovered that when Engels used the expression the proletariat is a "slave of no particular person but of the whole property owning class" he used it "metaphorically." Evidently what needs emphasis (in this period of fetishism of the state), according to our bureaucratic collectivists, is that the wage slave is "personally free" in all countries (where, in Germany?) except in Russia where he is "literally" not "metaphorically," a slave. Since "free labor" is a specific feature of capitalist production, and since it is nonexistent in Russia, therefore, say

117 Nikolai Voznessensky was Chairman of the State Planning Commission during the implementation of the First Five Year Plan. Also see Dunayevskaya's critique of Voznessensky's *The Economy of the USSR During World War II*, in *The Raya Dunayevskaya Collection*, #1322.

Shachtman and Carter, it is in Russia, where (slave) labor is an inherent feature of the Russian economy, that we have a new non-capitalist social order. They are adamant on the point of slave labor, though they have failed to prove that the Russian worker has sold himself "rump and stump."[118] Furthermore, Shachtman thinks that the collectivist epoch in Russia has created a superior form, a higher rate of production, than under capitalism.

What dangerous contradictions! Slave labor exists, is an inherent feature of the new order; alongside it exists a superior form of production. The idea that a superior form of production can coexist with slave labor destroys the entire Marxist conception of the development of labor in society. If Shachtman has not found out yet, Stalin has: forced labor is not conducive to high productivity necessitated by a highly industrialized economy. The state economy must have highly productive labor "to catch up with capitalist lands"[119] and thus the management of the plants found that it must bid against each other for the labor power of the worker. The worker continues to be "free," that is, the wage slave continues to be obliged to sell his labor power on the market, and being "personally free," he finds he can force a few concessions while industry needs his labor power. That is why the state found that the worker was not afraid of being fired. That is why the state, realizing that it could not straight-jacket labor by threatening to fire him, thought it could force him to work through enacting criminal statutes, requiring the laborer to work at 25% reduction in pay. That is why it has now granted amnesty to all labor offenders.

∴

A New Revision of Marxian Economics

American Economic Review, *Vol. 34:3, September 1944*

The article from *Pod Znamenem Marxizma* (*Under The Banner of Marxism*), which is published in this issue [of *American Economic Review*], appears to be merely a criticism of the old methods of teaching political economy in the

118 See Marx's statement in *Capital*, Kerr, 1:186; Vintage, 1:271: "...for if he were to sell it (labor power) rump and stump, once for all, he would be selling himself, converting himself from a free man into a slave..."

119 This refers to the slogan of the First Five Year Plan. See "The Nature of the Russian Economy," in this Chapter.

"curricula and textbooks" of the higher Soviet schools.[120] Actually it is no mere reproof of pedagogical error. Its raison d'être is contained in the argument that the law of value, in its Marxian interpretation, functions under "socialism." This is a clear departure from the former economic doctrine which prevailed not merely in the schools but in the most authoritative and scholarly publications as well as throughout the Soviet press. That this treatise appears now is an indication of the lines along which Soviet political economy may be expected to develop in the post-war period.

Foreign observers who have carefully followed the development of the Soviet economy have long noted that the Soviet Union employs almost every device conventionally associated with capitalism. Soviet trusts, cartels and combines, as well as the individual enterprises within them, are regulated according to strict principles of cost accounting. Prices of commodities are based upon total costs of production, including wages, raw materials, administrative costs, amortization charges and interest plus planned profit and the various taxes imposed as revenue for the maintenance of the state. Essential to the operation of Soviet industry are such devices as banks, secured credit, interest, bonds, bills, notes, insurance, and so on. As the present document explains it, "denial of the law of value created insurmountable difficulties in explaining the existence of such categories under socialism."

The article, "Some Questions of Teaching of Political Economy," contends that although the law of value operates in Russia, it functions in a changed form, that the Soviet state subordinates the law of value and consciously makes use of its mechanism in the interest of socialism. In order to show that the operation of the law of value is consistent with the existence of socialism, the article cites those passages from the *Critique of the Gotha Program* in which Marx states that in a socialist society, "as it emerges from capitalist society," the laborer will receive in return for a given quantity of work the equivalent of such labor in means of consumption. The present authors reject, however, the formula that flows from these passages, namely, that labor will be paid by "the natural measure of labor": time. This, the document states, is not in

---

120 Published in the *American Economic Review*, Vol. 34:3, September 1944, pp. 531–537, Dunayevskaya's "A New Revision of Marxian Economics" accompanied and critiqued "Teaching of Economics in the Soviet Union," the article she had translated from the Russian theoretical journal *Pod Znamenem Marxizma* (*Under the Banner of Marxism*). Her critique provoked great controversy, reaching the front page of The *New York Times* in October 1944, and drawing responses in *American Economic Review*from Oscar Lange, Leo Rogin and Paul Baran. For Dunayevskaya's rejoinder to her critics, see *American Economic Review*, September 1945; also see *The Raya Dunayevskaya Collection*, 213.—Editor's Note.

consonance with the experience of Russia, where labor is highly differentiated according to degree of skill and as regards intellectual and physical differences. The authors therefore propose a new slogan: "distribution according to labor." They consider that they have thus translated the law of value into a function of socialism. It should be noted that they thereby completely identify "distribution according to labor" with distribution according to value.

There is incontrovertible evidence that there exists in Russia at present a sharp class differentiation based upon a division of function between the workers, on the one hand, and the managers of industry, millionaire *kolkhozniki*, political leaders and the intelligentsia in general, on the other. It is this which explains certain tendencies which began to appear after the initiation of the Five Year Plans and have since become crystallized. The juridical manifestation of this trend culminated in 1936 in the abolition of the early Soviet constitution. The constitution which was adopted in its place legalized the existence of the intelligentsia as a special "group" in Soviet society. This distinction between the intelligentsia and the mass of workers found its economic expression in the formula: "From each according to his ability, to each according to his labor." This formula should be compared with the traditional Marxist formula: "From each according to his ability, to each according to his need." "Each according to his need" has always been considered a repudiation of the law of value. The document, however, states that "distribution according to labor" is to be effected through the instrumentality of money. This money is not script notes or some bookkeeping term but money as the price expression of value. According to the authors, "the measure of labor and measure of consumption in a socialist society can be calculated only on the basis of the law of value."

The whole significance of the article, therefore, turns upon whether it is possible to conceive of the law of value functioning in a socialist society, that is, a non-exploitative society.

Marx took over from classical political economy its exposition of the law of value in the sense that labor was the source of value, and socially necessary labor time the common denominator governing the exchange of commodities. Marx, however, drew from this labor theory of value his theory of surplus value. He criticized classical political economy for mistaking the apparent equality reigning in the commodity market for an inherent equality. The laws of exchange, Marx contended, could give this appearance of equality only because value, which regulates exchange, is materialized human labor. When the commodity, labor power, is bought, equal quantities of materialized labor are exchanged. But since one quantity is materialized in a product, money, and the other in a living person, the living person may be and is made to work beyond the time in which the labor produced by him is materialized in the means of consumption necessary for his reproduction. To understand the nature of capitalist production, it is therefore necessary, Marx contended, to leave the sphere of exchange and enter the sphere of production. There it would be found that the dual nature of commodities—their use-value and value—merely reflects the dual nature of labor—concrete and abstract labor—embodied in them. For Marx the dual character of labor "is the pivot on which a clear comprehension of political economy turns."[121]

Marx called the labor process of capital the process of alienation. Abstract labor is alienated labor, labor estranged not merely from the product of its toil but also in regard to the very process of expenditure of its labor power. Once in the process of production, the labor power of the worker becomes as much a "component part" of capital as fixed machinery or constant capital, which is, again, the workers' materialized labor. According to Marx, Ricardo

> sees only the quantitative determination of exchange value, that is, that it is equal to a definite quantity of labor time; but he forgets the qualitative determination, that individual labor must by means of its alienation be presented in the form of abstract, universal, social labor.[122]

In its Marxian interpretation, therefore, the law of value entails the use of the concept of alienated or exploited labor and, as a consequence, the concept of surplus value. Hitherto all Marxists have recognized this fact. Hitherto Soviet political economy adhered to this interpretation. In 1935 Mr. A. Leontiev, one of the present editors of *Pod Znamenem Marxizma*, wrote: "The Marxian doctrine of surplus value is based, as we have seen, on his teaching of value. That is why it is important to keep the teaching of value free from all distortions because the theory of exploitation is built on it."[123]

[You are saying that the ruling class in Russia "owns" the means of production. What you are saying in reality is that the ruling class is in such a productive relation to the working class that the means of production thereby become capital. That is what Marx meant by saying that capital was conditioned on wage-labor. If you don't want that, then back to the old degenerated workers' state conception.] And again: "It is perfectly clear that this division of labor into concrete and abstract labor exists only in commodity production.

121 *Capital* (Charles Kerr, 1909), 1:48. [Also see Vintage, 1:132.].

122 *Teorii Pribawchnoi Stoimosti,* T II, 2, c. 183–184. [Also see *Theories of Surplus Value* (Moscow: Progress Publishers, 1968), 2:504; cf. Marx-Engels, *CW*, 32:135.].

123 *Political Economy, A Beginner's Course* (New York: International Publishers, 1935), p. 38.

This dual nature of labor reveals the basic contradiction of commodity production."[124]

The new article contradicts this theory and its past interpretation. It recognizes the existence in Russia of concrete and abstract labor but denies the contradiction inherent in the dual nature of labor. It recognizes the pivot upon which political economy turns, but denies the basis of exploitation which to all Marxists as well as to opponents of Marxism has hitherto been the essence of the Marxist analysis. This is the problem the article must solve. It is interesting to watch how this is done.

In place of the class exploitation, which was the basis of the Marxist analysis, the new theoretical generalization proceeds from the empirical fact of the existence of the USSR, assumes socialism as irrevocably established, and then propounds certain "laws of a socialist society." These are (1) the industrialization of the national economy, and (2) the collectivization of the nation's agriculture. It must be stated here that both these laws are not laws at all. Laws are a description of economic behavior. The "laws" the article mentions are statements of fact. What follows the laws as a manifestation of the "objective necessity of a socialist society"—"distribution according to labor"—does partake of the character of a law. "Objective necessity," it must be remarked, does not arise from the economic laws; the economic laws arise from objective necessity; it may, of course, manifest itself differently in the Soviet Union, but the manifestations the present authors cite are precisely the ones that emanate from capitalist society.

The document fails to make any logical connection between the new basis, "socialism," and the law characteristic of capitalist production—the law of value. The implication that the state is really "for" the principle of paying labor according to needs, but is forced by objective necessity to pay according to value is precisely the core of the Marxist theory of value. The supreme manifestation of the Marxian interpretation of the law of value is that labor power, exactly as any other commodity, is paid at value, or receives only that which is socially necessary for its reproduction.

This startling reversal of Soviet political economy is neither adventitious nor merely conciliatory. That is the real significance of the article. It is a theoretical justification of social distinctions enshrined in the Soviet constitution. That this elaborate theoretical justification is made is proof that the Russian people are being prepared for the continuance of a social relation which had no place in the conceptions of the founders of communism or the founders of the Soviet state. The article argues that the law of value has operated not only

124 *Ibid.*, p. 58.

in capitalism but also has existed from time immemorial. As proof, its present existence in the Soviet Union is cited and a reference is made to Engels' statement that the law of value has existed for some five to seven thousand years. Engels' statement, however, is contained in an article in which he deals with the law of value only in so far as commodity prices reflect the exact value of commodities.

The Marxian thesis is that the more backward the economy, the more exactly do prices of individual commodities reflect value; the more advanced the economy, the more commodity prices deviate; they then sell at prices of production though in the aggregate all prices are equal to all values. In that sense, Engels states, the law of value has operated for thousands of years, that is, ever since simple exchange and up to capitalist production.[125]

That Engels did not in any way depart from value as an exploitative relation characteristic only of capitalist production can best be seen from Mr. Leontiev's own preface to that little booklet, *Engels on Capital.* There the Soviet economist says:

> Whereas at the hands of the Social-Democratic theoreticians of the epoch of the Second International, the categories of value, money, surplus value, etc., have a fatal tendency to become transformed into disembodied abstractions inhabiting the sphere of exchange and far removed from the conditions of the revolutionary struggle of the proletariat, Engels shows the most intimate, indissoluble connection these categories have with the relations between classes in the process of material production, with the aggravation of class contradictions, with the inevitability of the proletarian revolution.[126]

Value, Engels has written, is "a category characteristic only of commodity production, and just as it did not exist prior to commodity production, so will it disappear with the abolition of commodity production."[127] It would be sheer absurdity, argued Engels, "to set up a society in which at last the producers control their products by the logical application of an economic category

125 Cf. *Engels on Capital* (New York: International Publishers, 1937), p. 106. [Also see *Capital,* Vintage, 3:1037].

126 *O Kapitale Marksa,* pp. xi-xii. (*Engels on Capital.*) The English translation does not carry this preface, issued by the Marx-Engels-Lenin Institute under the supervision of the Central Committee of the Russian Communist Party.

127 *Sochineniia Marksa-Engelsa, T.* XXVII, c. 408. (Works of Marx-Engels, Russian ed., 1928–41.).

(value) which is the most comprehensive expression of the subjection of the producers by their own product."[128]

In the last theoretic writing we have from the pen of Marx, a critique of A. Wagner's *Allgemeine oder theoretische volkswirtschaftslehre*, Marx castigates "the presupposition that the theory of value, developed for the explanation of bourgeois society, has validity for the 'socialist state of Marx.'"[129]

In the opinion of this writer nothing in the article contradicts this firmly established coexistence of the law of value with capitalist production.

The radical change in theoretical interpretation that the article presents not unnaturally brings with it important methodological consequences. The authors propose that in the future the structure of *Capital* be not followed and state that the past textbooks which followed the structure violated the "historic principle." Obviously, this is a very grave departure. Engels explains Marx's rejection of the method of the "historical school" by the fact that history proceeded by jumps and zigzags and that, in order to see its inner coherence, it was necessary to abstract from the accidental. The structure of Marx's *Capital* is a logical abstraction seen in its evolution and constantly checked and rechecked and illustrated by historical development.

Marx's dialectic method is deeply rooted in history. However, it utilizes history not as a chronological listing of events but "divested of its historic forms and fortuitous circumstances."[130] Thus the abstract method of Marx does not depart from the "historic principle." On the contrary, the theoretical development of the commodity is in reality the historical development of society from a stage when the commodity first makes its appearance—the surplus of primitive communes—to its highest development, its "classic form"—in capitalism. Where a commodity existed accidentally or held a subordinate position as in primitive, slave or feudal societies, the social relations, whatever we may think of them, were at any rate clear. It is only under capitalism that these social relations assume "the fantastic form of a relation between things."[131]

That is why Marx analyzes the commodity "at its ripest." He is separating its theoretical potentialities from its historic starting point. Where Marx

---

128 *Herr Eugen Dühring's Revolution in Science* (New York: International Publishers, 1939), p. 347.

129 *Arkhiv Marksa-Engelsa*, T.V., c.59. (*Archives of Marx-Engels*, Vol. v, p. 59, edited by Adoratsky.) [See Marx: *Texts on Method*, edited by Terrell Carver (New York: Barnes & Noble Books, 1975), p. 208.].

130 Frederick Engels on the Materialism and Dialectics of Marx, included in *Ludwig Feuerbach and the Outcome of Classical German Philosophy* (London: Martin Lawrence, 1934), p. 99.

131 *Capital*, Kerr, 1:83. [Also see Vintage, 1:165.].

analyzes a commodity in order to discern the law of its development, the Soviet economists now merely proclaim the arrival of the commodity in a "socialist society."

Hence when the authors propose that the structure of *Capital* be not followed in the future, it is not because past Soviet textbooks, patterned on it, violated the "historic principle." It is because of their need to divest the commodity of what Engels called "its particular distinctness" and to turn it into a classless, "general historic" phenomenon applicable to practically all societies.

The ideas and methodology of the article are not accidental. They are the ideas and methodology of an "intelligentsia" concerned with the acquisition of "surplus products." What is important is that this departure from "past teaching of political economy" actually mirrors economic reality. The Soviet Union has entered the period of "applied economics." Instead of theory, the article presents an administrative formula for minimum costs and maximum production. It is the constitution of Russia's post-war economy.

∴

The Nature of the Russian Economy

Written under Name of F. Forest,* The New International, *December 1946, January 1947

The New International, December 1946

In Analysis of Russian Economy,[132] *which was made after an exhaustive study of all available data on the dynamics of the Five Year Plans, it was shown that the law of value dominated the Russian economy. This law expressed itself in two ways: (1) The production of means of production outdistances the production of means of consumption. (2) The misery of the workers increases, along with the increase in capital accumulation. No one has challenged this study based on official Russian documents, which, however, did not draw the inescapable conclusions. It is necessary, therefore, to draw fully and explicitly the conclusions implicit in the statistical analysis, which this author has always considered as Part 1 of her study of the Nature of the Russian Economy.—Freddie Forest* [*Raya Dunayevskaya*]

132 Published in *The New International,* Dec. 1942, Jan. and Feb. 1943. This series will hereafter be referred to as Part 1.

Introductory—"A Single Capitalist Society"

The profound simplicity of Marx's method of analysis of capitalist society revealed that, given the domination of the law of value, which is the law of the *world* market, a *given* society would remain capitalist even if one or all of several conditions prevailed: (1) the exchange between the sub-divisions of the department producing means of production were effected *directly,*[133] that is, without going through the market; (2) the relationships between the department producing means of production and the one producing means of consumption were planned so that no ordinary commercial crises arose; and, finally, (3) even if the law of centralization of capital would reach its extreme limit and all capital were concentrated in the hands of "a single capitalist or ... a single capitalist society."[134]

Precisely because Marx analyzed a pure capitalist society which has never historically existed, his analysis holds true for *every* capitalist society, *but only* for capitalist society. What Marx was primarily concerned with was not the abstraction, "a single capitalist society." His concern was with the fact that this extreme development would in no way change the law of motion of that society. He made this abstraction a point of analysis because by it the limitations of any individual capitalist society could be seen more clearly. The only basic distinction from the traditional capitalist society would be in the method of appropriation, and not in the method or laws of production.

Russian State Capitalism: A Given Single Capitalist Society

I The Mode of Appropriation

Since under the specific Russian state capitalism legal title to the means of production as well as the competitive market for such means have been abolished, how is appropriation achieved?

Inasmuch as private property in the means of production has been abolished in Russia, it is a deviation from the juridical concept to permit accumulation within any enterprise since the state aims to increase only "national capital." Nevertheless, with the establishment of "ruble control," enterprises were permitted to accumulate internally. In fact, incentives towards that interest in capital accumulation were created through the establishment of the

---

133 "In a given society, this limit [extreme centralization] would be reached if all social capital were concentrated into the same hands, whether those of an individual capitalist or those of a single capitalist society."—Karl Marx, *Capital,* Vol. 1, p. 692, Eden and Cedar Paul translation; in the Kerr edition this appears on p. 688.

134 Cf. "Analysis of Russian Economy," *N.I.,* Jan. 1943. This series, published in Dec. 1942, Jan. and Feb. 1943, will hereafter be referred to as Part 1.

Director's Fund. In 1940 internal accumulation comprised 32.5 per cent of capital investment.

Because these agents of state capital do not have title to this accumulated capital, however, is production thereby governed by a different motive force?

1 *Planning vs. the Average Rate of Profit*

The Stalinists, in denying that Russia is a capitalist society, insist that the best proof of that is that Russia is not subject to "the law of capitalism: the average rate of profit."[135]

"The law of capitalism" is not the *average* rate of profit, but the *decline* in the rate of profit. The average rate of profit is only the manner in which the surplus value extracted from the workers is divided among the capitalists.[136] It is impossible to jump from that fact to the conclusion that "therefore" Russia is not a capitalist country. It is for this reason that the Stalinist apologists, with great deliberation, perverted "the law of capitalism" from the decline in the rate of profit to the achievement of an average rate of profit. With this revision of Marxism as their theoretic foundation, they proceeded to cite "proof" of Russia's being a non-capitalist land: Capital does not migrate where it is most profitable, but where the state directs it. Thus, they conclude Russia was able to build up heavy industry, though the greatest profits were obtained from light industry. In other words, what the United States has achieved through the migration of capital to the most profitable enterprises Russia has achieved through planning.

Profit, moreover, does not at all have the same meaning in Russia as it does in classical capitalism. The light industries show greater profit not because of the greater productivity of labor, but because of the state-imposed turn-over tax which gives an entirely fictitious "profit" to that industry. In reality, it is merely the medium through which the state, not the industry, siphons off anything "extra" it gave the worker by means of wages. It could not do the same

135 cf. "Teaching of Economics in the Soviet Union," *American Economic Review,* Sept. 1944, p. 526.

136 "A single capitalist, as is well known, receives in the form of profit, not that part of the surplus value which is directly created by the workers of his own enterprise, but a share of the combined surplus value created through the country proportionate to the amount of his own capital. Under an integral 'state capitalism,' this law of the equal rate of profit would be realized, not by devious routes—that is, competition among different capitals—but immediately and directly through state bookkeeping."—L. Trotsky, *Revolution Betrayed.*

things through the channel of heavy industry because the workers do not eat its products. That is why this "profit" attracts *neither* capital *nor* the individual agents of capital. That is the nub of the question.

Precisely because the *words*, profit and loss, have assumed a different meaning, the individual agents of capital do not go to the most "profitable" enterprises, even as capital itself does not. *For the very same reason* that the opposite was characteristic of classic capitalism: The individual agent's share of surplus value is greater in heavy industry. The salary of the director of a billion dollar trust depends, not on whether the trust shows a profit or not, but basically upon the magnitude of the capital that he manages.

State capitalism brings about a change in the mode of appropriation, as has occurred so often in the life span of capitalism, through its competitive, monopoly and state-monopoly stages. The individual agent of capital has at no time realized directly the surplus value extracted in his particular factory. He has participated in the distribution of national surplus value, to the extent that his individual capital was able to exert pressure on this aggregate capital. This pressure in Russia is exerted, not through competition but state planning. But this struggle or agreement among capitalists, or agents of the state, if you will, is of no concern to the proletariat whose sweat and blood has been congealed into this national surplus value.[137] What is of concern to him is his relationship to the one who performs the "function" of boss.

2 *Private Property and the Agents of Capital*

It is neither titles to property nor motives of individuals that distinguishes different exploitative economic orders, but their method of production, or manner of extracting surplus labor. If it was the legal title to property that were basic, the Stalinists would be right in assuming, "Since there is no private property in Russia, there is no exploitation of man by man."

Behind the imposing façade of the "socialist economy," however, stands the "classless intelligentsia."[138] The specific weight of the upper crust, as we saw in Part I, comprises a mere 2.05 per cent of the total population!

137 "It is immaterial to the laborer, whether the capitalist pockets the whole profit, or whether he has to pay over a part of it to some other person, who has a legal claim to it. The reason for dividing the profit among two kinds of capitalists thus turns surreptitiously into reasons for the existence of surplus value to be divided, which the capitalist as such draws out of the process of reproduction, quite apart from any subsequent division."—Marx: *Capital*, Vol. III, p. 448.

138 Cf. Part I, *New International*, Feb. 1943.

The individuals who act as agents of the state and its industry are, of course, theoretically free to refuse to participate in the process of accumulation, just as a capitalist in the United States is free to sign away to the workers in his factory his legal title to the means of production. In the United States he would retire to Catalina Island or, at worst, be sent to an insane asylum. In Russia he would be "liquidated." But he does not refuse. He acts exactly as the agent of capital that he is, as agent of the dead labor alienated from the worker and oppressing him. The class difference between the two, which the Russians euphemistically call "functional," is expressed outwardly, too, in no different manner than under traditional capitalism, where the one lives in luxury and the other in misery. It is true that in Russia the agent of capital does not "own" the factory. But personal property is recognized in the unlimited right to purchase interest-bearing bonds, sumptuous homes, *datchas*, and personal effects. State bonds, no matter how large the amount, are not subject to inheritance or gift tax. All forms of personal property can be left to direct descendants. Institutions of higher learning, the tuition fees of which make them inaccessible to the proletariat, welcome the children of these property-less factory directors, and this assures their offspring of good positions as befits the sons and daughters of the ruling class. This, however, is entirely incidental to the relationship in the factory.

It is not the caprice of the bureaucracy nor the "will" of the individual capitalist in competitive capitalism that sets the wages of the workers. It is the law of value which dominates both.

The law of value, i.e., the law of motion, of the Russian economy has led to the polarization of wealth, to the high organic composition of capital, to the accumulation of misery at one pole and the accumulation of capital at the other. This is *a* given single capitalist society, an economy governed by the laws of world capitalism, originating in the separation of the laborer from control over the means of production.

But how could that arise when not only private property was abolished, but the capitalists were expropriated?

II The Counter-Revolution (Emphasis 1935–1937)

Given, on the one hand, the environment of the world market, and, on the other hand, the failure of the advanced proletariat of Europe to make its revolution and thus come to the aid of the Russian proletariat, it was inevitable that the transitional stage between capitalism and socialism perish, and the law of value reassert its dominance. It is necessary, Lenin warned the last party congress at which he appeared, to examine squarely "the Russian and international market, to which we are subordinated, with which we are connected and from which we cannot escape."

The counter-revolution did not make a "formal" appearance, with arms in hand, and therefore it was hard to recognize it. Along with the bureaucratization of the apparatus and loss of political control over the state by the proletariat, the relations of production were undergoing a transformation. It was, in fact, the changing relations of production which laid the basis for the eventual consolidation of the bureaucracy as a class.

The initial changes in the relations of production appeared imperceptibly. The labor inspector failed to defend the workers' interests because, with the adoption of the First Five Year Plan, all enterprises became state enterprises and automatically were labelled "socialist." The leaders of the trade unions who displaced, first the Left Oppositionists, and then the Tomsky leadership, were all too ready to speak out against any "right wing unionistic tendencies" of those who put their welfare above those of the "socialist" economy. When, in 1931, the state told the worker he could not change his job without permission of the director of the plant in which he worked, the trade unions had to acquiesce. When the worker's ration card and his right to living space were placed in 1932 in the hands of the factory director, the trade unions hailed the step as a necessity for establishing "labor discipline." The Workers' Production Conferences, established by the early workers' state so that every worker "to a man" might participate in the management of the economy, seldom convened. In 1934 the trade unions were made part of the administrative machinery of the state.

But the final divorce of labor from control over the means of production could not be achieved merely by legal enactment, any more than the constitutional dictum that the means of production belonged to the "whole nation" could give the workers automatic control over them. Stalin saw early that the dual nature of the economy violently shook his rule, now to one extreme, now to the other. In his address to the directors of industry, he issued the slogan: "Let there be an end to depersonalization." This, translated in industrial terms, read, "Better pay for better work." "Better pay for better work" needed a foundation, a piecework system that could gain momentum only with such a momentum as Stakhanovism, which arose in 1935.[139]

1 *Stakhanovism and the Stalinist Constitution*

The high organic composition of capital in advanced capitalist countries, which makes necessary a comparable technical composition in any single society, demands sacrifice in the sphere of the production of articles of mass

139 Cf. Part I (section on "Ending Depersonalization and Creating Stakhanovism"). *N.I.*, Feb. 1943, pp. 53–54.

consumption. That the resulting distribution of the scarce means of consumption is at the expense of the proletariat is only the "natural" result of value production. This, in turn, engenders a certain relationship which gives the impulse to the capitalistic movement of the economy. The "underconsumption" of the workers in a capitalist society is not merely a moral question. It is of the essence of Marxism, that once the workers are in that situation, the relationship of constant to variable capital moves in a certain direction. This is the hardest point for the petty bourgeois to understand.

The piecework system was declared by Marx to be best suited to the capitalist mode of production. The Stakhanovite piecework system was best suited to the mode of production prevalent in Russia. These record-breakers-for-a-day soon entered the factory—not through the back door, but through the front office—because they themselves occupied that front office. The politician bureaucrat found an "heir apparent" in this "production intelligentsia." Both groups soon fused to comprise the new "classless intelligentsia."

Stakhanovism made possible the development of a labor aristocracy. But not merely that. A labor aristocracy meant a better prop for the ruling clique. But not merely that either. No, as master over the production process, with Stakhanovism as a base and nourishing soil for "heirs" to bureaucrats, the bureaucracy began to feel the stability of a class. Feeling the stability of a class and having a source of reinforcement from the managers of industry, the bureaucracy moved headlong toward the juridical liquidation of the dictatorship of the proletariat. To legitimize the counter-revolution against October, the new class needed a new constitution.

The Stalinist Constitution of 1936 recognized the intelligentsia as a special "group," distinct from workers and peasants. With this juridical acknowledgement of the existence of a new ruling class went the guarantee of the protection of state property from "thieves and misappropriators."

Moreover, the Constitution raised into a principle the Russian manner of payment of labor. The new slogan read: "From each according to his abilities, to each according to his labor." This seemingly senseless slogan is in reality only a method of expressing the valid capitalist law of payment of labor according to value. To guarantee the free functioning of this truly economic law, it became necessary to exterminate the remnants of the rule of October, even if it were only in the memory of some men.

2 *The Moscow Trials*

The Moscow Trials of 1937 were the culminating point to the counter-revolution that we saw developing in the changed relations of production. A hangman's noose, rather than arms in hand, sufficed because only one of the parts of this conflict was armed. The October Revolution was exterminated and the proletarian state overthrown not only by the execution of the Old Bolsheviks who led it, but by clearing a place in the process of production for the new class. That place could have been cleared for that "classless intelligentsia" only when there *existed* such a class, only where the method of production called it forth.

The Russian worker knows that the job of factory director is not, as the Russians put it euphemistically enough, merely "functional." The factory director behaves like a boss because he *is* a boss. The state bears no more resemblance to a workers' state than the president of the U.S. Steel Corp. does to a steel worker just because they are both "employees" of the same plant. The Counter-Revolution has triumphed.

Yet it was not the laws that caused the triumph of the counter-revolution. The accumulation of these laws only bears witness to the accumulation of changes in the role of labor in the Soviet state and in the process of production.

The Counter-Revolution is not the child, not even an illegitimate one, of "Bolshevism." The Counter-Revolution is the legitimate offspring of the "new" mode of production, out of Stalinism and fired by the imperialist world economy. It is this method of production, and not the legal enactments, that needs, above all, to be investigated. In this investigation we will find that, as in any capitalist economy, the two major contending forces are capital and labor.

III Labor

> *The economic laws of such a regime (state capitalism) would present no mysteries.*
>
> LEON TROTSKY[140]

The inner essence of the Marxian theory of value, and hence of surplus value, is that labor power is a commodity bought at value.

Up until 1943, the Soviet theorists had denied that the law of value, the dominant law of capitalist production, functioned in Russia where socialism had been "irrevocably established." In 1943, however, a startling reversal of this position was published in the leading theoretical journal of that country, *Pod Znamenem Marxizma*.[141] The authors of this article state that the teaching of political economy is being resumed after a lapse of several years, and offer the teachers rules to follow in their "teaching" of political economy. Even a

140 *Revolution Betrayed*, p. 245.

141 *Under the Banner of Marxism*, No. 7–8, 1943. Russian. For English translation see "Teaching of Economics in the Soviet Union" in the *American Economic Review*, Sept. 1944.

superficial glance at the article reveals, however, that it is not the teaching that is being reversed, but the political economy taught.

The Stalinist ideologists affirm that the denial of a law of value in Russia has "created insurmountable difficulties in explaining the existence of such categories [as money, wages, etc.] under socialism." Now the admission that the law of value operates must bring with it the further admission that the law of surplus value operates. Like all apologists for ruling classes, this admission they refuse to make. This then, is their dilemma, which does not concern us here.[142] What does concern us here is the admission that the law of value does in fact function in Russia, and that money is therefore the "price expression of value."

1 *Value and Price*

As in all capitalist lands, so in Russia, money is the means through which prices and wages are equated in the supply and demand for consumption goods, that is to say, the value of the worker is equal to the socially-necessary labor time that is incorporated in the means of subsistence necessary for his existence and the reproduction of his kind. So long as the production of means of consumption is only sufficient to sustain the masses, prices will irresistibly break through legal restrictions until the sum of all prices of consumption goods and the sum of wage payments are equal. Price-fixing in Russia established neither stabilization in prices of goods nor of wages. The abolition of rationing in 1935 brought about so great an increase in prices that the worker who had eked out an existence under the very low rationed prices, could not exist at all under the "single uniform prices." The state was therefore compelled to grant general increases in wages, so that by the end of the Second Five-Year Plan wages were 96 per cent above that planned.

The erroneous concept that because prices are fixed by the state, they are fixed "not according to the law of value, but according to government decision on 'planned production,'"[143] fails to take into consideration the *economic* law that dominates prices. Even a casual examination of any schedule of prices in Russia will show that, giving consideration to deviations resulting from the

---

142 For an analysis of how they attempt to solve their dilemma, see commentary of Raya Dunayevskaya to the above article published in same issue of *A.E.R.*, under the title "A New Revision of Marxian Economics." The attacks upon this from the Stalinist apologists in this country were published by that journal in the following three issues, and Dunayevskaya's rejoinder, "Revision or Reaffirmation of Marxism," appeared in the Sept. 1945 issue.—Editor's Note.

143 Cf. Kent in the *New International*, Oct. 1941.

enormous tax burdens on consumer goods, *prices are not fixed capriciously and certainly not according to use-values*, but exhibit the same differentials that prevail in "recognizably" capitalist countries, i.e., *prices are determined by the law of value*.[144]

2 *Labor: "Free" and Forced*

Time is of the essence of things in a society whose unit of measurement is socially-necessary labor time, whose mode of existence is enveloped in technological revolution, and whose appetite for congealed surplus labor is from its very nature insatiable. The machine age has therefore passed this wisdom to its trustee, the bourgeoisie: Use "free labor" if you wish the wheels of your production to turn speedily.

As if to prove that they are not "really" capitalists, the Russian rulers ignored this elementary wisdom and attempted to turn wage slaves into outright slaves through legislative enactment. At the lowest point of production in 1932 when the whole régime was tottering and labor was turbulently restless, a law was enacted which transferred the worker's ration card into the hands of the factory director who had the right to fire the worker and evict him from his home for even a single day's absence. This statute failed to fulfil the desired end. Labor would not come to industry and when it did come, it left soon, after producing as little as possible. Since industry needed labor the factory director "forgot" to fire the worker for absence and slow-ups in production. By 1933 the crisis in agriculture and consequent unemployment and actual famine caused such an inflow of labor to the city as to permit the managers of industry to discipline labor through "natural" bourgeois methods. What the reserve army of labor accomplished in 1933, the speed-up and piecework system of Stakhanovism accomplished in 1935.

These "natural" methods brought about natural results: the class struggle. The simmering revolt among the workers, which was ruthlessly crushed during the staging of the Moscow Trials, only produced further chaos in production and a mass exodus of workers from the city. In 1938 the state grew desperate. The 1932 law was revived and "improved upon." This still proved fruitless. In 1940 came the creation of the State Labor Reserves, and with it came the

144 This has finally been admitted by the Stalinists. In the above cited thesis, they write: "Cost accounting, which is based on the conscious use of the law of value, is an indispensable method for the human management of the economy under socialism. Value of the commodities in a socialist (*sic!*) society is determined not by the units of labor expanded in its production, but upon the quantity of labor socially necessary for its production and reproduction."

institution of "corrective labor": workers disobeying the laws were made to work six months with 25 per cent reduction in pay.

Because the state is in their power, the rulers think that it is within their power to coerce labor by non-economic means to obey the needs of value production. Statification of production has resulted in restricting the free movement of workers. It has not achieved the increase of labor productivity required by constantly expanding production.

There is this constant pull and tug between the needs of production for highly productive labor which means "free" labor, and the resort to legislative enactment to bring about this in hot-house fashion. On the one hand, several million workers end up in prison camps as forced laborers. On the other hand, many are released back to join the "free" labor army. The phenomenon of "corrective labor" is the result of a compromise between the resort to prison labor, and the need to get some sort of continuous production right within the factory.

Labor, too, has shown ingenuity. Where it cannot openly revolt, it either "disappears," or so slows up production that in 1938 production was lower than in 1935! There have been periods when the *rate* of increase has been at a practical standstill, and all the while labor turnover continues to be very high.[145] So widespread were the labor offenses during the war that the state has found that it must disregard its own laws if it wishes to have sufficient labor to begin to put the Fourth Five-Year Plan in effect. It has therefore declared a general amnesty for all labor offenders.

Thus while the state has found that it cannot by legal enactment transform wage slaves into outright slaves, the worker has found that he has the same *type*[146] of "freedom" he has on the capitalist competitive market: that is, he *must* sell his labor power if he wishes to get his means of subsistence.

3 *Unemployment and the Growing Misery of the Workers*

Just as labor power being paid at value is the supreme essence of the law of value, so the reserve army of labor is the supreme essence of the law of the preponderance of constant over variable capital. The greater expansion of production, it is true, has meant an *absolute* increase in the laboring army, but that

---

145 See Part I (section on "The Workers and the Law"), *New International*, Feb. 1943, pp. 52–53. [Document can be found earlier in this Chapter.].

146 The same *type* of "freedom," Franz Neumann shows, existed for the German worker, in Nazi Germany. Cf. his *Behemoth*. [*Behemoth:The Structure and Practice of National Socialism*, by Franz Leopold Neumann, c. 2009 with new introduction by Peter Hayes, published in association with the National Holocaust Museum].

in nowise changes the fact that the law governing the attraction and repulsion of labor to capital is that of the *decrease* of living labor as compared to constant capital. It is for this reason that Marx called the unemployed army "the general absolute law of capitalist production."

In Russia unemployment has officially been abolished since 1930. In 1933, however, it was revealed, as the Russians so delicately put it, that "there are *more workers* in the shops than is necessary according to plans." The influx from the famished countryside was, in fact, so great that labor passports had to be introduced and anyone without a passport was not permitted to live in the large cities. Stakhanovism in 1935 and the gory Moscow frame-up trials in 1937 changed the picture in the opposite direction. There was a mass exodus from the city to the country. The 1939 census revealed that 67.2 per cent of the total population was rural, and that of the 114.6 million rural dwellers 78.6 millions were peasants. To find so overwhelming a percentage of the population in agriculture in the United States we would have to go back to a period before the American Civil War!

Russia is backward, but is it that backward? The productivity of labor there is very low, but is it that low? Or is it rather that the unemployed army hides out in the countryside? That the latter is the true situation was revealed by the "Great Leader" himself when, in announcing the creation of State Labor Reserves, he appealed to the *kolkhozy* for their surplus labor. "The *kolkhozy* have the full possibility," said Stalin, "to satisfy our request inasmuch as abundance of mechanization in the *kolkhozy* frees part of the workers in the country ..."

It has been impossible for Russia, as it has for traditional capitalism, to avoid unemployment over a historic period, because this single capitalist society is straining every nerve to bring its plants to the level of the more advanced productive systems and the only way to do this is to use as little living labor as possible to produce as much value as possible. It is for this reason that Russian state capitalism has had to base its entire calculation, not on the amount of labor time, as in a transitional society, but basically on wages, that is to say, upon the value of the worker. This has been further aggravated by the backwardness of the Russian economy so that we meet there the extreme condition to which Marx pointed to in Volume III of *Capital*.[147] In order to obtain sufficient surplus value to increase production, part of the agricultural population receives payment as a family unit.[148]

147 p. 273.

148 Earning statistics are "per peasant household." Population statistics "per family unit" help hide child labor. Cf. Part I, *New International*, Feb. 1943.

The conditions of the workers have constantly deteriorated. Since the initiation of the Five-Year Plan, the real wages of the workers, as I have shown in Part 1, have declined by half! That is not at all accidental. It is the inevitable consequence of the law of motion of that economy which had resulted in so high an organic composition of capital. Accumulation of misery for the class that produces its products in the form of capital necessarily flows from the accumulation of capital.

IV Capital

Capital, said Marx, is not a thing, but a social relation of production established through the instrumentality of things. The instrumentality which establishes this exploitive relationship is, as is well known, the means of production alienated from the direct producers, i.e., the proletariat, and oppressing them. The capitalist's mastery over the worker is only the "mastery of dead over living labor." The material manifestation of this greater preponderance of constant over variable capital is the preponderance in the production of means of production over means of consumption. In capitalist society it cannot be otherwise for the use values produced are not for consumption by workers or capitalists, but by capital, i.e., for productive consumption or expanded production. The greater part of the surplus value extracted from the workers goes back into this expanded production.

The Russian exploiters are so well aware of the fact that surplus value, in the aggregate, is uniquely determined by the difference between the value of the product and the value of labor power, that the Plan for 1941 stipulated openly that the workers are to get a mere 6.5 per cent rise in wages for every 12 per cent rise in labor productivity.

"This proportion between labor productivity and average wage," brazenly proclaimed Voznessensky, "furnishes a basis for lowering production cost and increasing socialist (!) accumulation and constitutes the most important condition for the realization of a high rate of extended production."[149]

1 *The Production of Means of Production at the Expense of the Production of Means of Consumption*

The huge differential between labor productivity and labor pay goes into expanded production at a stupendous rate. According to Voznessensky, the Chairman of the State Planning Commission, 152.6 billion rubles were invested in plant and capital equipment from 1929 to 1940. Of the entire national income in 1937, 26.4 per cent was expanded in capital goods. The plan for 1942

149 Cf. *The Growing Prosperity of the Soviet Union*, by N. Voznessensky.

had called for an estimated 28.8 per cent of the national income to be invested in means of production. Some idea of the rate at which production goes into capital goods in Russia may be gained from the fact that in the United States, during the prosperous decade of 1922–1932, only 9 per cent of the nation's income was utilized for expansion of means of production.

At the time the Plans were initiated, the production of means of production comprised 44.3 per cent of total production, and production of means of consumption 55.7 per cent. By the end of the First Plan, this was reversed, thus: means of production 52.8 per cent; means of consumption, 46.7 per cent. By the end of the Second Five-Year Plan, the proportions were 57.5 per cent to 42.5 per cent. By 1940 it was 61 per cent means of production to 39 per cent means of consumption. This is true of contemporary world capitalism.

The slogan "to catch up and outdistance capitalist lands" was the reflection of the compelling motive of present world economy: who will rule over the *world* market? Therein lies the secret of the growth of the means of production at the expense of means of consumption. Therein lies the cause for the living standards of the masses growing worse despite the "state's desire" for what it called "the still better improvement of the conditions of the working class."

The fundamental error of those who assume that a single capitalist society is not governed by the same laws as a society composed of individual capitalists lies in a failure to realize that what happens in the market is merely the consequences of the inherent contradictions in the process of production. A single capitalist society does not have an illimitable market. The market for consumption goods, as we showed, is strictly limited to the luxuries of the rulers and the necessaries of the workers when paid at value. The innermost cause of crisis is that labor, in the process of production and not in the market, produces a greater value than it itself is.

But wouldn't it be possible to raise the standard of living of the workers (not of some Stakhanovites, but of the working class as a whole) if all capital is concentrated in the hands of the state?

What a grand illusion! The moment that is done, the cost of production of a commodity rises above the cost of the surrounding world market. Then one of two things happens: Production ceases because the commodity cannot compete with the cheaper commodity from a value-producing economy, or, even though the society insulates itself, temporarily, it will ultimately be defeated by the more efficient capitalist nations in the present form of capitalist competition which is total imperialist war.

Our specific single capitalist society has achieved some highly modern factories, and a showy subway, but it has not stopped to raise the living standards of the masses of workers. It cannot. Capital will not allow it. Because of this the economy is in constant crisis.

2 *Crises, Russian Brand*

The value of capital in the surrounding world is constantly depreciating which means that the value of capital inside the capitalist society is constantly depreciating. It may not depreciate fully on the bureaucrats' books. However, since the real *value* of the product can be no greater than the value of the corresponding plant on the world market, the moment the Ford tractor was put alongside the Stalingrad tractor, the state had to reduce the price of its own brand. This was the case in 1931 when Russia, while importing 90 per cent of the world's production of tractors, sold its own below cost.

However, of greater importance—and therein lies the essence of Marx's analysis of all economic categories as social categories—is the fact that, no matter what values may appear on the books, the means of production *in the process of production* reveal their true value in their relationship to the worker. That is to say, if an obsolescent machine was not destroyed but continued to be used in production, the worker suffers the more since the overlord of production still expects him to produce articles at the socially-necessary labor time set by the *world* market.

As long as planning is governed by the necessity to pay the laborer the *minimum* necessary for his existence and to extract from him the *maximum* surplus value in order to maintain the productive system as far as possible within the lawless laws of the world market, governed by the law of value, that is how long capitalist relations exist, no matter what you *name* the social order. It has thus been absolutely impossible for Stalin, Inc. to guide the productive system without sudden stagnation and crises due to the constant necessity of adjusting the individual components of total capital to one another and to the world market. He has avoided the ordinary type of commercial crises. But, on the other hand, when the crises came, they were more violent and destructive. Such was the case in 1932. Such was the case in 1937. And one is brewing now.

The Fourth Five-Year Plan is being initiated in the midst of a new purge wave, at a time when the country has suffered a loss of 25 per cent of capital equipment on the one hand, and of 25 million homes on the other. And, towering above all these now that "peace" has arrived, is the need to keep up with the latest and greatest discovery of atomic energy. All this keeps the Russian economy in a constant state of turmoil. Behind this turmoil is the law of value, and hence of surplus value, which cause world capitalism in decay to writhe.

If this law, in its essence and in its essential manifestation, is *dominant* also in Russia, what kind of society can it be but capitalist?

***

The New International, *January 1947*

Part II

Trotsky dismissed the idea that Russia might be a state capitalist society on the ground that, although *theoretically* such a state was conceivable, in reality: "The first concentration of the means of production in the hands of the state to occur in history was achieved by the proletariat with the method of social revolution and not by the capitalists with the method of trustification."[150]

It is true, of course, that *historically* state property appeared as *workers'* state property, but that is no reason to identify the two, and in no way justifies Trotsky's transformation of that historic fact into a theocratic abstraction.

1 *History and Theory*

In the early years of existence of the Soviet state, Lenin fought against those who, instead of looking at "the reality of the transition," had tried to transform it into a theoretic abstraction. In the trade union dispute with Trotsky[151] Lenin warned the latter not to be "carried away by ... abstract arguments" and to realize that it was incorrect to say that since we have a workers' state, the workers primary concern should be about *production.* Lenin insisted that the workers had a right to say: "... you pitch us a yarn about engaging in production, displaying democracy in the processes of production. I do not want to engage in production in conjunction with such a bureaucratic board of directors, chief committee, etc., but with another kind"[152]

We must not forget, Lenin continued, that

> All democracy, like every political superstructure in general (which is inevitable until classes have been abolished, until a classless society has been created) in the last analysis serves production and in the last

150 *Revolution Betrayed*, pp. 247–248.

151 Trotsky's position does not, unfortunately, exist in English. It can be found in Russian, along with all other participants in the dispute, including Shlyapnikov, in: *The Party and the Trade Unions*, ed. by Zinoviev. Lenin's position has been translated into English and can be found in his *Selected Works*, Vol. IX, to which work we refer.

152 *Ibid.*, p. 19.

> analysis is determined by the production relations prevailing in the given society.[153]

This stress on the primacy of production relations in the analysis of a social order runs like a red thread through all of Lenin's writings, both theoretically, and in the day-to-day analysis of the Soviet Union. In his dispute with Bukharin on the latter's *Economics of the Transition Period,* he strenuously objected to Bukharin's assumption that the capitalist production relations could not be restored and therefore his failure to watch the actual *process of development* of the established workers state. Where Bukharin had written: "Once the destruction of capitalist production relations is really given and once the theoretic impossibility of their restoration is proven ..." Lenin remarked: "'Impossibility' is demonstrable only practically. The author does not pose *dialectically* the relation of theory to practice."[154]

So far as Lenin was concerned, the dictatorship of the proletariat, since it was a transitional state, could be transitional "either to socialism or to a return backwards to capitalism," depending upon the historic initiative of the masses and the international situation. Therefore, he held, we must always be aware that (1) *internally* there was "only one road ... changes from below; we wanted the workers themselves to draw up, from below, the new principles of economic conditions";[155] and (2) *externally,* we must not forget "the Russian and international markets with which we are connected and from which we cannot escape." All we can do there is gain time while "our foreign comrades are preparing thoroughly for their revolution."

After the death of Lenin, Trotsky himself was the first to warn against the possibility of the restoration of capitalism. Not only did he insist that an unbridled continuance of the NEP would bring about the restoration of capitalism "on the installment plan," but even after private concessions were abolished and national planning instituted, he mercilessly castigated the Left Oppositionists who used this as a reason to capitulate. He subscribed to Rakovsky's statement:

> The capitulators refuse to consider what steps must be adopted in order that industrialization and collectivization do not bring about results opposite to those expected ... They leave out of consideration the main

153 *Ibid.,* p. 52.

154 Lenin's "Remarks on Bukharin's *The Economics of the Transition Period*" (in Russian, in his *Leninski Sbornik,* No. 11).

155 *Selected Works,* Vol. VII, p. 277.

> question: what changes will the Five-Year Plan bring about in the *class relations in the country*.[156]

Rakovsky saw that the conquests of October would not remain intact if economic laws were permitted to develop by any other plan than one in which the workers themselves participated, for only the proletariat could guide it into a direction advantageous to itself. That is why he warned prophetically that a ruling class other than the proletariat was crystallizing "before our very eyes. The motive force of this singular class is the singular form of private property, state power."[157]

This clarity of thought, and method of analysis were buried in the process of transforming statified property into a fetishism.

2 *The Fetishism of State Property*

Trotsky continued to speak of the possibility of a restoration of capitalist relations, but it was always something that *might* or *would* happen, but not as a *process* evolving "before our very eyes." The reason for this was two-fold: Firstly, the counter-revolution in Russia did not come in the manner envisaged by the founders of the proletarian state. That is, it came neither through military intervention, nor through the restoration of private property. Secondly, the victory of fascism in Germany presented a direct threat to the Soviet Union. Thus precisely when history demonstrated that statification of production can occur by counter-revolutionary methods, the concept of statified property = workers' state was transformed into a fetishism!

We did call for the formation of new proletarian parties everywhere, including Russia. But our break from the past was not clean-cut. Our turn was stopped short by the elaboration of a new theory, to wit, that the building of a proletarian party aiming for power in Russia aims, not for *social*, but only for *political* power.

Like all fetishisms the fetishism of state property blinded Trotsky from following the course of the counter-revolution in the relations of production. The legitimization of the counter-revolution against October, the Stalinist Constitution, Trotsky viewed merely as something that first "created the political premise for the birth of a new possessing class." As if classes were born from political premises! The macabre Kremlin purges only proved

156 *Opposition Bulletin*, No. 7, 11–12/29. Russian. [Christian Rakovski was a Bolshevik and a collegue of Trotsky.].

157 *Ibid.*, No. 17–18, 11–12/30.

to Trotsky that "Soviet society organically tends towards the ejection of the bureaucracy!"[158] Because to him Stalinist Russia was still a workers' state he thought that the Moscow Trials weakened Stalinism. Actually, they consolidated its rule.

The dilemma created by continuing to consider Russia a workers' state is not resolved by calling the bureaucracy a caste and not a class. The question is: what is the role of this group in the process of production? What is its relationship to the workers who operate the means of production? Calling the bureaucracy a caste and not a class has served as justification for remaining in the superstructural realm of property. This has only permitted exploiters to masquerade as mere plunderers. How far removed is that from the petty bourgeois concept that the evils of capitalism come not from the vitals of the capitalist system, but as a product of "bad capitalists"?

In her struggle against reformism, Luxemburg brilliantly exposed what the transformation of the concept of capitalists from "a category of production" to "the right to property" would lead to:[159]

> By transporting the concept of capitalism from its productive relations to property relations, and by speaking of simple individuals instead of speaking of enterpreneurs, he [Bernstein] moves the question of socialism from the domain of production into the domain of relations of fortune—that is, from the relations between Capital and Labor to the relation between poor and rich.

Trotsky, on his part, substitutes for analysis of the laws of production, an analysis of the distributive results. Thus he writes: "The scarcity in consumers goods and the universal struggle to obtain them generate a policeman who arrogates to himself the function of distribution."[160]

But what produces the "scarcity of consumers goods"? It is not merely the backwardness of the economy since the same backwardness has not prevented Russia from keeping, approximately, pace with advanced capitalist lands in the production of means of production. The relationship of means of production to the means of consumption, characteristic of capitalism generally, including Russia, is: 61:39. That and not the "scarcity of consumers goods" is the decisive relationship. That is so because this relationship is only the reflection of the

158 *In Defense of Marxism*, p. 13.

159 *Reform or Revolution*, pp. 31–32.

160 *In Defense of Marxism*, p. 7.

capitalist's domination over the laborer through the mastery of dead over living labor.[161]

To Trotsky, however, the existence of nationalized property continued to define Russia as a workers' state because, to him, "the property and production relations established by October" still prevailed there.

Which relations: production or property? They are not one and the same thing. One is fundamental, the other derivative. A property relation, which is a legal expression of the production relation, expresses that relationship, sometimes correctly and sometimes incorrectly, depending on whether the actual production relationship has been validated by law. In periods of revolution and counter-revolution, when the actual production relations undergo a transformation while the legal expressions are still retained in the laws, production relations cannot be equated to property relations without equating revolution to counter-revolution!

The Marxian law of value is not merely a theoretic abstraction but the reflection of the actual class struggle. The correlation of class forces in Russia in 1917 brought about the statification of production through the method of proletarian revolution. But, as Engels long ago noted, statification in and by itself, "does not deprive the productive forces of their character of capital":

> The more productive forces it [the modern state] takes over, the more it becomes the real collective body of all the capitalists, the more citizens it exploits. The workers remain wage-earners, proletarians. The capitalist relationship is not abolished; it is rather pushed to an extreme. But at the extreme it changes into its opposite. State ownership of the productive forces is not the abolition of the conflict, but it contains within itself the technical conditions that form the elements of the solution.[162]

Neither the particular method of achieving statification—socialist revolution—nor the creation of the "technical conditions which form the elements of the solution" to the conflict of capital and labor could assure the real abrogation of the law of value, once the Russian Revolution remained isolated. However, the isolation of the Russian Revolution did not roll history back to 1913. Just because the bourgeois revolution was accomplished by the proletariat

161 The whole dispute on Marxist fundamentals within our party has centered precisely on this relationship. Cf. the following *Workers' Party Bulletin*: "Production for Production's Sake" by J.R. Johnson; "The Mystification of Marxism" by J. Carter; and "A Restatement of Some Fundamentals of Marxism" by F. Forest.

162 *Anti-Dühring*, pp. 312–313.

who proceeded to make of it a socialist revolution, the bourgeois revolution, too, was accomplished with a thoroughness never before seen in history. It cleared away centuries-old feudal rubbish, nationalized the mean of production and laid the basis for "the technical conditions" for socialism. Hence the power of Russia today.

However, socialism cannot be achieved except on a world scale. The socialist revolution is only the beginning. The greater and more arduous task of establishing socialist relations of production begins *after* the conquest of power. That task, as the leaders of October never wearied of stressing, cannot be accomplished within the confines of a single state. Without the world revolution, or at least the revolution in several advanced states, the law of value reasserts itself. The new "technical conditions" began to dominate the Russian laborer, once he lost whatever measure of control he had over the process of production. *In this unforeseen manner, Marx's theoretical abstraction of "a single capitalist society" became a historic reality.*

Since then Germany had achieved the statification of production through fascist methods; Japan through totalitarian methods began its Five-Year Plans. Both these methods are more recognizable capitalist methods of achieving the extreme limit of centralization. Since World War II Czechoslovakia has achieved statification through "democratic" means. No one, we trust, will call it a "workers' state," degenerate or otherwise. What then happens to the identification of statified property with workers' statism? It falls to the ground. So false to the roots was that method of analysis of the nature of the Russian state and the policy of unconditional defensism which flowed from it that it led the Man of October to call for the defense of Russia at a time when it was already participating in an imperialist war as an integral part of it!

3 *Bureaucratic Imperialism and Bureaucratic Collectivism*

The counter-revolutionary role of the Red Army in World War II has shaken the Fourth International's theory of Russia. A break with the policy of unconditional defense was made inevitable. But how explain the imperialist action of the Army of a "workers' state," though degenerate it be? Daniel Logan searches seriously for the answer. He writes:

> However the Stalinist bureaucracy manages the Soviet economy in such a way that the yearly fund of accumulation is greatly reduced ... Thus, the bureaucracy finds itself forced, lest the rate of accumulation fall to a ridiculously low level or even become negative, to plunder means of production and labor power, everywhere it can, in order to cover the cost that its management imposes on Soviet economy. The parasitic character

> of the bureaucracy manifests itself, as soon as political conditions permit it, through imperialist plundering.

His explanation has all the hallmarks of confinement within Trotsky's theory of Russia as a workers' state bureaucratically managed. The error in it reveals most clearly that it is not so much an error of fact as an error in methodology. It is not true that the yearly fund of accumulation is greatly reduced; on the contrary, despite usual periods of stagnation, it is growing. Within the stifling atmosphere of degenerated workers' statism, however, it was natural to identify the decrease in the *rate* of accumulation with the decrease in the yearly fund because to grasp clearly the distinction between the two would have meant to be oppressively aware of the fact that decrease in the rate of accumulation is characteristic of the whole capitalist world. It is a result, not of the bureaucratic management of the economy, but of the law of value and its concomitant tendency of the rate of profit to decline.

It is not "the parasitic character of the bureaucracy" that causes the decline any more than the growth in the rate of accumulation in the early stages of world capitalism was caused by the "abstinence" of the capitalists. The present world decline, which is the reflection of *the falling relation of surplus value itself to total capital,* is a result of what Marx called "the general contradiction of capitalism." This general contradiction, as is well known, arises from the fact that labor is the only source of surplus value and yet the only method of getting ever greater masses of it is through the ever greater use of machines as compared to living labor. This causes at one and the same time a centralization of capital and a socialization of labor; a decline in the rate of profit and an increase in the reserve army of labor.

The decline in the rate of profit brings to the overlords of production the realization that the method of value production carries with it the germ of its own disintegration and sends them hunting for "counter-acting measures." They plunge into imperialism, go laboriously into statification of production, or into both. Imperialist plundering is just as much caused by the objectives of value production.

Trotsky left the Fourth International a dual heritage: the Leninist concept of the world proletarian revolution and a Russian position which contained the seeds of the present dilemma and disintegration. The Fourth International, trapped in his Russian position, wishes to escape its logical political conclusions, but wishes to do so without breaking with Trotsky's premises. That, it will find, is impossible.

Trotsky always insisted that the virtue of the nationalized economy was that it allowed the economy to be planned. The adherents of Trotsky's defensism continue to see in the perpetual degeneration some progressive element of planning. Others who have broken with defensism (including both those who expound the theory of bureaucratic imperialism on the one hand, and bureaucratic collectivism on the other), still remain prisoners of Trotsky's basic method of analysis. This method, in fact, paved the way for bureaucratic collectivism, although Trotsky himself considers it a theory of "profound pessimism."

Basing itself upon Trotsky's characterization of nationalized property as progressive, the Workers' Party has labelled Russia a bureaucratic collectivist society, a part, though mongrelized, of "the collectivist epoch of human history."[163] To this collectivism has now been added the concept of "slave labor" as the mode of labor characteristic of the bureaucratic collectivist mode of production.

What is the relation of this "slave labor" to the economic movement of this "new" society? What social development would lead these "slaves" to revolution? What distinguishes them from capitalist proletarians, in, say, a fascist state? What are the problems (if any), of accumulation?

All these questions remain unanswered, and indeed it would be difficult to make any coherent theory of a social order which is part of the collectivist epoch of human society but rests on slave labor. Beginning with their theory as applicable only to Russia, some of the proponents of bureaucratic collectivism now threaten to cast its net over the whole of modern society. This could only end, as Trotsky pointed out, in the recognition that the "socialist program, based on the internal contradictions of capital-society ended as a Utopia." Bureaucratic collectivism has forced those Fourth Internationalists who have broken with defensism to hold on nevertheless to the concept of degenerated workers' statism, on the ground that out of the monstrous society "nothing

163 The official Party position on bureaucratic collectivism, along with the Carter-Garrett position on it, as well as the Johnson position on state capitalism, are all included in The Russian Question, a documentary compilation issued by the Party's Educational Department. The Party thesis, written by Shachtman, states: "Bureaucratic collectivism is closer to capitalism so far as its social relations are concerned, than it is to a state of a socialist type. Yet, just as capitalism is part of the long historical epoch of private property, bureaucratic collectivism is part—an unforeseen, mongrelized, reactionary part, but a part nevertheless—of the collectivist epoch of human history. The social order of bureaucratic collectivism is distinguished from the social order of capitalism primarily in that the former is based upon new and more advanced form of property, namely, state property. That this new form of property—a conquest of the Bolshevik revolution—is progressive, i.e., historically superior, to private property is demonstrated theoretically by Marxism and by the test of practice." (This resolution has also been printed in *The New International*, October 1941, p. 238.).

new or stable has yet come out." It is true that nothing "new and stable" has yet come out of the Stalinist society but that is not because it is still a degenerated workers' state, but because Stalinist Russia is part of decadent world capitalism and is destined for no longer life span than world capitalism in its death agony.

Our analysis has shown that Soviet planning is no more than a brutal bureaucratic consummation of the fundamental movement of capitalist production toward statification. As Johnson wrote in the International Resolution presented to the last convention of the Party in the name of the Johnson Minority, with which this writer is associated:

> The experience of Stalinist Russia since 1936 has exploded the idea that planning by any class other than the proletariat can ever reverse the laws of motion of capitalist production. Planning becomes merely the statified instead of the spontaneous submission to these laws ... Stalinist Russia, driven by the internal contradictions of value production, i.e., capitalist production, has defeated Germany only to embark upon the same imperialist program, reproducing in peace the economic and political methods of German imperialism, direct annexation, looting men and material, formation of chains of companies in which the conquering imperialism holds the largest share.[164]

The only section of the Fourth International that has been able clearly to emerge from Trotsky's method of analysis of the Russian state has been the Spanish section in Mexico. G. Munis, the leader of that section, has come out in his recent pamphlet,[165] squarely for the analysis of Russia as a capitalist state. His economic analysis may not be adequate, but in his attempt to grapple with the problem of planning in terms of the categories, *c*, *v*, *s*, and the social groups which control them, he has made the decisive step of breaking with the concept of degenerated workers' statism and initiating within the Fourth International the development of a theory adequate to the analysis of Stalinist totalitarianism and the present stage of world development.

The Johnson Minority has successfully corrected the false Russian position of Trotsky by revising it in terms of the Leninist-Trotskyist analysis of our epoch. For us the Russian experience has made concrete the fundamental

---

164 Cf. *Bulletin of the Workers Party*, Vol. 1 No. 11, April 27, 1946. It contains also the official Party position on the International Situation.

165 Cf. *Los Revolucionarios ante Rusia y el Stalinismo Mundial*, published by Editorial Revolucion, Apartado 8942, Mexico, D.F.

truth of Marxism, that in any contemporary society there can be no progressive economy, in any sense of the term, except an economy based on the emancipated proletariat. Proletarian democracy is an *economic* category, rooted in the control over production by the workers. So long as the workers are chained by wage slavery, the laws of capitalism are inescapable.

The Fourth International does grievous harm to the very doctrine of socialism when it teaches that a society can be progressive with labor enslaved. It handcuffs itself politically as well as organizationally in the task of gaining leadership of the European proletarian movement.

Statified property equals workers state is a fetishism which has disoriented the whole Fourth International. If in the early stages of the war when the impulse of revolution *seemed* to come from the march of the Red Army, there was some shred of excuse for a political policy which disoriented the movement and led to its being split, by what rhyme or reason can the Fourth International justify the position that revolutionists must "tolerate the presence of the Red Army"[166] at a time when Stalinism proved to be the greatest counter-revolutionary force in Europe? To tolerate the presence of the Red Army in Europe is to doom the European revolution to be still-born!

The recent turn in the position of the Fourth International, calling for the withdrawal of all occupation armies, including the Red Army,[167] is the first necessary step in the right direction. But it is only the first, and a very halting and belated step it is, precisely because it has been arrived at empirically and not through a fundamental understanding of the class nature of the Russian state. It is high time to take stock, to reexamine not merely the policy flowing from the false theory of the class nature of the Russian state, but to reexamine the theory itself. It is the urgent pre-requisite for rearming the Fourth International and making it possible for it to take its rightful place as the vanguard of the world revolutionary forces.

---

166 *Fourth International,* June 1946.

167 *Ibid.,* Aug. 1946.

PART 5

From State-Capitalist Theory to Marxist-Humanism, 1950s–1980s

INTRODUCTION

From the State-Capitalist Tendency to the Birth of a Marxist-Humanist Organization—New Stage of Production, New Stage of Cognition, New Kind of Organization

In 1980, Dunayevskaya began to write a short history, 25 Years of Marxist-Humanism in the U.S.—A history of worldwide revolutionary developments, *which was published serially in several issues of* News & Letters. *Its Prologue, "New Stage of Production, New Stage of Cognition, New Kind of Organization" (reproduced below) traced the political-philosophic differences that developed within the State-Capitalist Tendency (C.L.R, James, Dunayevskaya, and Grace Lee Boggs) in the context of a new stage of production—automation; Dunayevskaya's exploration of Hegel's Absolutes—a new stage of cognition; and which, together with immediate political differences, would lead to a split and the founding of a new kind of organization, a Marxist-Humanist one—News and Letters Committees.*

In the context of discussing a proposed pamphlet on the importance of the Miners' General Sriike of 1949–50 (http://rayadunayevskaya.org/ArchivePDFs/15977.pdf) in the development of Marxist-Humanism, Dunayevskaya elaborated on the relation of a new stage of production and a new stage of cognition:

> What we have to ask is what is the relation between [a] new stage of production and [a] new stage of cognition? Here is what I see: (1) The workers are raising the question, "What *kind* of labor?"—and by the way they ask, they are telling you the answer they expect. (2) There is a new point in cognition when R[aya] D[unayevskaya] says that there question means they are challenging the division of mental/manual. (3) When they call the continuous miner a "man-killer" you have to ask yourself what is the relationship between that question and your theory of state-capitalism? Here is the root of the division between RD and CLR J[James]. (4) When you study Lenin's return to Hegel you hear what he discovered about the relation of philosophy to economic and philosophy to politics.

New Stage of Production, New Stage of Cognition, New Kind of Organization

Prologue to 25 Years of Marxist-Humanism in the U.S. News & Letters, *August–September, 1980*

Ever since I began preparing for the celebration of May 5 as the birth-time of history—Marx's new continent of thought—I have been rethinking the birth of Marxist-Humanism in the US. There was no way to sum up 25 years of the birth and development of the News and Letters Committees, as well as *News & Letters* as paper, without taking account of the *philosophic* breakthrough on the Absolute Idea as containing a movement *from practice* as well as from theory. That occurred in 1953. Once the split in the State-Capitalist Tendency, known as Johnson-Forest,[1] was complete in 1955, our very first publication reproduced my May 12–20, 1953 Letters on the Absolute Idea along with the first English translation of Lenin's *Philosophic Notebooks.*

In a word, while 1955 saw the birth of News and Letters, both as Committees and as our paper, 1953 saw, at one and the same time, the emergence, in. the Johnson-Forest Tendency, of open divergences towards objective events (be it Stalin's death, the East German revolt, the Beria purge, or McCarthyism), as well as towards the subjective idea of what type of paper *Correspondence* was to be and what was its relationship to Marxism.

It is important that we look at the new, stage of production, Automation, and the form of the workers' revolt against it—the 1949–50 Miners' General Strike—in the same way as, in 1953, we looked at the first revolt against state-capitalism and its work-norms in East Berlin. The point is that both stages of production and both forms of revolt were every bit as crucial for the re-emergence of Marx's Humanism in our age, as had been the outbreak of World War II for the birth of the State-Capitalist Tendency...

We were experimenting with a decentralized form of organization and a new form of paper—*Correspondence*—but only in mimeographed form. By 1953, it was decided to come out with a printed, public paper, and towards that end were preparing for the first (and what turned out to be the last) convention of what had been the united Johnson-Forest Tendency. *Everything changed with the death of Stalin on March 5, when suddenly, it wasn't only the objective situation that had so radically changed, but divergences appeared between Lee*

1 Johnson (C.L.R. James) broke with Forest (Raya Dunayevskaya), co-founder of the State-Capitalist Tendency, in March, 1955. News, and Letters Committees began functioning at once as Marxist-Humanists.

and me within the Tendency. Let us look at the sequence of events that followed Stalin's death.

That very same day I wrote a political analysis which stressed that an incubus had been lifted from the minds of both the masses and the theoretician; and that, therefore, it was impossible to think that this would not result in a new form of revolt on the part of the workers. Secondly, when Charles Denby (the Black production worker who was to become the editor of *News & Letters* after the split) called me upon hearing of Stalin's death, I asked him to inquire about other workers' reactions to the event. When he reported these conversations, I suggested a second article that would reproduce the 1920–21 Trade Union debate between Lenin and Trotsky within the context of both Russia and the U.S., 1953. Denby not only approved both ideas but the very next day brought me a worker's expression: "I have just the one to take Stalin's place—my foreman." It was that expression which became the jumping-off place for my analysis of the 1920–21 debate, on the one hand, and Stalin's death in 1953, on the other. The article was called "Then and Now."

Lee (who was then on the West Coast and acting as editor that month) had a very different view of what kind of analysis of Stalin's death was needed, because—far from seeing any concern with that event on the part of American workers—she made her point of departure the fact that some women in one factory, instead of listening to the radio blaring forth the news of Stalin's death, were exchanging hamburger recipes. She so "editorialized" my analysis and so passionately stressed the alleged indifference of the American proletariat to that event, that the article became unrecognizable. It was included in the mimeographed *Correspondence* of March 19, 1953 (Vol. 3, No. 12) as "Why Did Stalin Behave That Way?"

As we know, the subjective movement—*not* of intellectuals debating, but of millions of masses in motion—transforms the objective scene totally. In this case, the June 17, East German Revolt which erupted was followed, within two weeks, by a revolt from inside Russia—the slave labor camp of Vorkuta. Both events so electrified the world that this time there was no way to narrow the question to an "internal matter"...

In my analysis of the Beria purge, though I called attention to the fact that when thieves fall out, the one who was "not to be forgotten, although little known at present" was Khrushchev, my main point was:

We are at the beginning of the end of Russian totalitarianism. That does not mean the state-capitalist bureaucracy will let go of its iron grip. Quite the contrary. It will shackle them more...what it does mean is that from the center of Russian production, from the periphery of the satellite countries oppressed by Russia, and from the inside of the Communist Parties, all contradictions are moving to a head and the open struggle will be a merciless fight to the end.

What I stressed was: "There is no getting away from it, the Russian masses are not only ill-fed, ill-clad, and ill-housed. *They are rebellious*."

There was no way of keeping this article out of the Lead of the first issue of the printed *Correspondence*, because that was what was happening in the objective world and we were now public. That did not, however, mean that Johnson and Lee greeted it enthusiastically. Quite the contrary. It was met with the same hostility as was my analysis of Stalin's death, and the critique of it by followers of Johnson and Lee continued for several issues.

The analyses of both Stalin and Beria were written while McCarthyism was raging in the country. All three events brought about a sharp conflict between Johnson and Lee on the one side, and me on the other. It was clear that in the two years between leaving the SWP and the appearance of *Correspondence* there had developed in the followers of Johnson a great diversion from Marxism as well as from the American revolution. Just as Lee said Marxism was Europe's responsibility, not ours, so now Johnson said that the stewards' movement in Britain rather than the American workers here could dissipate the war clouds over Formosa.

The truth is that they were not prepared to fight McCarthyism, once the war clouds began to form and we were listed [on the Attorney General "subversive" list] in December 1954. When Johnson could not win a majority of the organization, he broke it up.[2] War and revolution have always constituted the Great Divide between Marxist revolutionaries and escapists.

Within a short month, we held our first Conference, which decided that our new publication, *News & Letters*, would appear on the second anniversary of the June 1953 East German revolt; that it would be edited by a production worker; and that I should complete the work on Marxism, now known as *Marxism and Freedom—From 1776 Until Today*. At the same time that we singled out the four forces of revolt—rank and file labor, Blacks, women and youth—we projected the calling of a Convention within a year to create, for the first time, a Constitution for the committee form of organization we were working out as against a "vanguard party to lead." In November, 1955, we published as our first pamphlet the translation of Lenin's *Abstract of Hegel's Science of Logic*, along with my Letters on the Absolute Idea.

2 See "Johnsonism: An Appraisal" by O'Brien, a 1956 Bulletin which is included in the *Archives*.

CHAPTER 10

On Stalin

*Dunayevskaya's commentaries on Stalin can be found in her analysis of Russia as a state-capitalist society, and in some of her writings on Trotsky. Her response to Stalin's death (March 5, 1953) was an important moment in the development of Marxist-Humanism (Raya Dunayevskaya Collection # 2193). Her analysis provoked a sharp dispute within the State-Capitalist Tendency (which by then had left Trotskyism and formed an organization and mimeographed newspaper—*Correspondence*), on the meaning of Stalin's death. The dispute was one indication of the differences within the Tendency that would in less than two years lead to a split and the formation of News and Letters Committees.*

Dunayevskaya's most extensive analysis of Stalin was her chapter in Marxism and Freedom *reproduced below.*

Stalin

Marxism and Freedom

Upon what meat hath this our Caesar fed
That he has grown so great.
SHAKESPEARE

Stalin had once been a revolutionary, a Bolshevik, which meant an uncompromising fighter for the overthrow of Tsarism. There was a time when Bolshevism was a doctrine of liberation. Today, everyone knows Russian Communism as the greatest barbarism on earth. Stalin is the name which symbolizes this.

It was this one-time revolutionary who initiated, and carried through, with unmatched brutality, the greatest *counter*-revolution in all history. But Stalin is only the Russian name for a phenomenon that is *world-wide.*

Two questions stand out: (1) Why does any individual behave like that? *What objective movement in the economy, what class impulses, necessitate such brutality?* (2) What specific characteristics in a man enable him to become the receptacle and the executor of class impulses from an alien class—the very one he either challenged or actually helped overthrow?

When the energies of the million-headed masses smashed the old and created the new, those who led the Russian Revolution could and did make great contributions to the greatest single fact of world history: the creation of the workers' state.

However, when the Russian working-class was itself in a crisis, these intellectual leaders, as individuals, did not stack up very high. At a critical juncture in world history their will reflected the movement of the working-class. But, as Lenin pointed out in his *Will*, "A seriously false turn at that juncture could unloose the disintegrative forces at work in a dual worker-peasant state which is surrounded by world capitalism, from which it cannot fully free itself without the help of the advanced European working-class."

As Lenin lay dying, the German Revolution failed, and in Russia's exhaustion Stalin flourished.

Stalin's outstanding trait was a bureaucratic attitude to the masses. He claimed to be a leader of the workers, but to him it meant to make the workers do as the leader wanted and told them to do. He spoke of the party as "the vanguard of the proletariat," but to him this meant that just as the leaders of the party were *to tell the ranks* what to do, so the party was *to order the masses about.* This was true of him as an individual even when he was a revolutionary fighting in the underground. Once the Communist Party got into power his passion for bossing came out in full bloom. It showed itself clearest of all in his attitude to the many nationalities which constitute the Soviet Union.

In overthrowing the Tsarist monarchy, the Russian workers had fought not only to overthrow the capitalists and the landlords, but to overthrow as well the Great Russian overlordship of the many nationalities in Russia. One of their first acts upon getting into power was to grant freedom to all the different nationalities that lived in Russia. But Stalin, though himself a Georgian, ran roughshod over the aspirations of his native Georgia, displaying a chauvinism and a national arrogance that was as rabid as that of any Tsarist official.

Lenin drew back in horror. "Scratch a Bolshevik," he wrote, "and you will find a Great Russian chauvinist." It remains the most precise commentary of the totalitarian personality-in-the-making.

Lenin's last appeal to Trotsky reads: "I am declaring war on Great Russian chauvinism.[1]" His last theoretical contribution on the National Question continued:

> It is said we need a single apparatus. From where come such assertions? Is it not from the same Russian apparatus, which, as I have pointed out in

1 Trotsky often spoke of this, I know, but neither in 1923 nor when he formed the Left Opposition and was expelled had he revealed the full text. This is from the Trotsky archives at Harvard College Library and is quoted in *The Formation of the Soviet Union, Communism and Nationalism, 1917–1923* by Richard Pipes.

> one of the previous numbers of my diary, was borrowed from Tsarism and only barely anointed with the Soviet chrism?

When Stalin began his struggle for power, as Lenin lay dying, he moved quite empirically. The road to power seemed obvious: it was to get control of the Party which was the State which was the Economy. To get the Party which was *in power* meant to get control of its functionaries, those people who displayed a "passion for bossing," and whom Lenin had fought. These, Stalin embraced. He knew them and knew how to talk to them. Where Lenin appealed to the *non-party masses* to help him expose the vain Communist bureaucrat, Stalin was later to appeal to the *non-party careerists* to flood the Party and help defeat Trotsky. It wasn't, as Trotsky thought, because the new members didn't know the *issues* in dispute. It was that they *chose* what Stalin represented.

No one, however, at that time conceived Stalin as a *class* enemy, not even Lenin who had asked for his removal from the post of General Secretary. Although Stalin was crafty enough, there is no point to assigning omniscience to him either. He didn't know what strong objective forces were pulling for him. He didn't have a *theory* about that. He let Bukharin carry the ball here while he shied away from fundamental theoretical questions. That does *not* mean that theory didn't matter to him, but as yet he didn't know *what* theory he would espouse. He was nowhere the mediocrity Trotsky made him out to be—he was capable enough when he wanted to win that way. It was *he* who made Trotsky argue on *his* ground, *his* fantastic notion of "socialism in one country." It was *he* who made Trotsky's "permanent revolution" appear as an immediate adventuristic scheme that was out of all bounds for exhausted Russia in the 1920's. He wasn't playing intellectual games. He was playing for power. He maneuvered with one faction, then with another. He played the modest man who didn't hunger for Lenin's mantle and portrayed Trotsky as one who did. Thus he defeated both the Left and Right Oppositions and became the undisputed leader of the Party.

The first problem that confronted him when he won the victory of Party power was that the kulak refused to turn grain over to the Soviet State. That decided the sudden zigzag for the abolition of "the kulak as a class," just as the resulting chaos made him turn backwards with his "Dizzy With Success" speech. There wasn't a zigzag, however, that didn't rhyme with the strong pull of an objective force.

Once the Russian people, "to a man," did not run the economy and the state; once the German Revolution too was defeated; once world capitalism regained its breath and the vortex of the world market had full sway, the logic of the Russian development was startling, unforeseen, but inevitable. The Revolution then found the really serious counter-revolution *inside itself.* Stalin was the perfect representative of that counter-revolution, not only because his personality suited the task so well, but, above all, because he did come *from* the Revolutionary Party and did have command of the Marxist "language." So corrupt and outlived is capitalism that it cannot hope to win except by pretending to be other than it is. Hitler too knew how to call his fascism National *Socialism.* Stalin was Hitler's superior by far, because his functionaries came from the working-class.

In Stalin's zigzags and lack of theoretical acumen was the straight line of development of the newly-emergent world phenomenon of state capitalism. It now had a personality, a totalitarian personality, armed with a theory of totalitarianism called "the monolithic Party."

Nor was the "liquidation of the kulak as a class" as ludicrous as Trotsky made it appear. It is true a class cannot be liquidated by fiat. A class is such by virtue of its role in production and production would have to be entirely differently motivated to overcome a class. That is certainly not a job to be done in a day or a year. But, *objectively,* this is not what Stalin meant. Objectively, the kulak couldn't stand up to the *combined* might of State and industry. That was true even under "ordinary capitalism"—agriculture lost out to industry in the long run. Stalin saw that it happened in an enormously accelerated fashion. State power enforced collectivization so rapidly that he could dream of "liquidating the kulaks as a class." He first now became conscious of representing a new force—State power, the *State* Plan, the *State* economy, the *State* Party. There was going to be no "withering away" of *his* State. His rule was absolute and so was his theory and ideology.

In 1931, Stalin's slogan, "End Depersonalization," got nowhere. By 1934, however, when there was sufficient means of production built up, and insufficient means of consumption to go around, there were enough opportunists to create a "mass" base for the ruling bureaucracy. Again, the creation of Stakhanovism was done in hothouse fashion. This time, however, as opposed to the time of liquidating kulak resistance, there was but one purpose—to appropriate the wealth created by the workers. No ghost come from the grave was needed to tell him of this. Stalin concluded it was time to legitimize the new class called "the classless intelligentsia." The new Stalin Constitution likewise had no need for ghosts from the past. It was then that he planned the macabre Moscow Trials to kill off, at one and the same time, what was left of the "General Staff of the Revolution," *and* the workers who resisted the norms set by the Plan.

Stalin acted that way to the Russian *people.* He acted that way to *Hitler.* He, Stalin, set the conditions for the Nazi-Soviet pact. His share of Poland was one, *only one,* of the territories he wanted. What he didn't get from Hitler, namely, all of Eastern Europe, he got from the *Allies.* When the war was over in 1945, and he was victor over his immediate enemy, he wanted to move straightway toward world conquest—especially if he could get others, Chinese and North Koreans, to do the fighting.

Hitler used to rave and rant to his lieutenants of his envy and appreciation of the genius of Stalin who had the perspicacity and audacity to get rid of the general staff of the Red Army before launching a world war. He knew whereof he spoke, for totalitarian economics has no room for a command divided between political and military needs.

But by 1948, after two decades of undisputed power, topped by a military victory, Stalin, to use a phrase of his own on another occasion, was "dizzy with success." This is not used here as a psychological epithet. His exhilaration from success was a sign that he no longer was responsive to the *objective needs* requisite for a struggle for world power. The bureaucracy whom Stalin had so long and so fully represented began to find him inadequate to the new situation created by the end of a world war which no one really won but which left each of the two state capitalist giants so exhausted that a halt had to be called. Stalin failed to grasp the new situation. He had won a war, a mighty one, over Nazi Germany, yes. But he had yet to face the real contender for world power—the United States.

Economists like Varga[2] were saying that if Plan means "no general crisis," then there will be no general crisis in the private capitalist world. Plan, said Varga, is no longer a monopoly of "socialism." The war showed that the Allies also planned and meant to continue to plan, and not to let a depression follow the war.

One top economist, Maria Natanovna Smit, spoke of state capitalism in the spirit in which Lenin had analyzed it:

> The book—she began, referring to Varga's work—lacks an analysis of the great new changes connected with the transition from simple monopoly capitalism to state monopoly capitalism, as Lenin understood this transition.... During the war, world capitalism took a step forward not only toward concentration in general, but also toward state capitalism in even a greater degree than formerly.
>
> LENIN's *Collected Works,* Russian edition, Vol. XXX, p. 300.

2 See Varga's *Changes in the Capitalist Economy as a Result of World War II,* 1946; in Russian only.

> Where Lenin unites the concept of "state" and of monopoly, Com. Varga seems to separate them: each exists by itself, and meanwhile in fact the process of coalescence of state with monopolists manifests itself quite sharply at the present time in such countries as the U.S.A. and England.

This, for Stalin, was "dangerous cosmopolitanism." It had to be fought—not in Varga nor in Maria Natanovna Smit, who had no power and could easily be made to sing another song—but among those closest to him, the Politburo members who were "deviating." The first to go was Voznessensky, Chairman of the State Planning Commission.

How pyrrhic was Stalin's victory could be seen in the unrest in the national republics which constitute Russia. By a ukase of the Supreme Soviet, five autonomous republics were liquidated. Russia had suffered the greatest devastation and was in crying need for a labor force to rebuild the country. It could not hope to have that force enlarged by the return of slave laborers in Hitler's Germany—too many had willingly escaped from the prison which was Stalin's Russia. Anyone who was in Germany at the end of the war knows that long before Koje, the Korean War and the massacre of P.O.W.'s, a veritable civil war was going on in the Russian displaced persons camps. But the Allies forced the Russians to return to their "homeland."

The restlessness of the Russian masses knew no bounds. If they were merely to go on in the same old way, keeping their noses to the grindstone, then at least it would not be in the godforsaken Urals. The totalitarian Russian bureaucracy had all the power and all the force and all the laws it needed to enforce labor discipline, but absolutely nothing could stem the tide of resistance of returning Russians. The tide invalidated all laws. To have a labor force at all, the Planners were compelled to make an unplanned declaration—an amnesty for all labor offenses committed during the war.

So catastrophic, however, had been the decline of the labor force during the war years (a drop from 31.2 million in 1940 to 27.2 million in 1945 with more than a third of these unskilled new women workers) that even the amnesty was insufficient to create the labor force necessary. Thereupon occurred one of the speediest demobilizations of an army anywhere in the world; no fewer than ten million were demobilized between 1945 and 1947.

By 1948, Stalin had only one colleague fully with him in the headlong rush to World War III and he, Zhdanov, was assassinated without the "Great Leader" knowing. This was the beginning of the end of Stalin's power.

By 1950, the Russian economy had about got back to normal when Stalin had a brainstorm. It was known as the "Stalin Plan for the Transformation of Nature." To put the scheme into effect Stalin brought to Moscow one

N. Khrushchev from the Ukraine, where he had been Premier. This man had been ruthless enough to put down actual armed insurrection, and now he was given the job to announce the most fantastic scheme yet—the creation of *agro-gorods* (agricultural towns). Just like that—decree them, and they shall arise, and abolish the centuries old distinction between city and country. Instead of "abolishing" the distinction between city and country, this scheme brought such chaos to the countryside that even in this land of monolithic planning, the idea had to be shelved in a few months. It was easy enough to have songs written about this irrigation which would soon produce enough food to feed 100 million people. It was something quite different to convince the peasant to transport, at his own expense and his own time, his little hut in the collective farm to the agro-town which was yet to be created, while the apartment house in which he was to live like a worker had not only not been built, it had not even been planned.

But if Stalin had to be satisfied with something less than the "abolition" of the difference between city and country, he was going full speed ahead towards a head-on collision with the United States—at least where he could get the Koreans and the Chinese to do the fighting for him. There was no breathing spell, let alone peace. Yugoslavia had defected.[3] The iron-fisted Stalin was clearly becoming a millstone around the neck of the bureaucracy which yearned for a truce between wars.

Stalin may have read the handwriting on the wall; he certainly took no chances with his too-eager heirs. Though he let Malenkov read the main address at the nineteenth Congress, he made his greatest bid to remain *the* immortal theoretician with his 1952 magnum opus, "Economic Problems of Socialism."

This, which we may call Stalin's "Last Testament," is the most pathetic document that ever a tyrant left his fighting heirs. After a quarter of a century of Plans, and what he assured them was the actual transition "from socialism to full communism," Stalin's mighty labors brought forth only the need to merge

---

3 Tito's defection did not signify any fundamental change in production relations *in* Yugoslavia. True to his Russian model, the trade unions had been liquidated into the State, the guiding principle of factory directors was to sweat the workers *"by thoroughly utilizing working hours."* This Article (14) of the Five Year Plan, introduced in 1947, was not changed after the break with Russia and the introduction of a "New Law on Peoples Committees." Tito's nationalism is Stalinism in Yugoslav dress. The fact that Tito's country is very small and very backward, and independent of Russia, does not make his "socialism" any different so far as the Yugoslav workers are concerned. They continue to labor under the same state capitalist exploitative conditions. The break from Russia, however, was a blow to that pole of world capital. That America recognized this at once is seen in the aid granted Yugoslavia.

the peasant's private allotment adjoining the collective farm into the collective itself. Upon this private garden, rightly called in this country "an acre and a cow", evidently depends the building of "full communism." This, plus the "gradual abolition" of the collective farm market, and substitution of "products exchange" for money exchange, will bring them to "communism in a single country."

That was little enough of a legacy to leave his bureaucratic heirs. But the Russian masses, who know that Stalin doesn't go in for theory unless he *plans to apply it,* made one grand rush to transform their money into manufactured products (consumer goods), and the peasants at the same time withheld farm products. This does not mean that it was the Stalin thesis and not the actual difficulties, particularly in agriculture and particularly since Korea, that created the crisis. Nevertheless it is true that it was the closest to panic Russia had been since forced collectivization took its toll in 1932.

The minute Stalin was buried, the bureaucracy ran from his last testament like rats from a sinking ship. This absolute tyrant who, when alive, could command the adulation, "Sun of the Himalayas," was forgotten ere a single sundown. This does not mean that his battling heirs fundamentally changed a single part of the state capitalist structure they inherited, either before or after "De-Stalinization." They continue "Communism" as a system of the most sweated labor in a modern industrial society, buttressed by a vast complex of spies and counter-spies. The counter-spies are not "foreign agents." They are "Party men" who spy on the police who spy on the Party men and both spy on the people. This does not mean the death of Stalin brought about the new conflicts in Russia. It would be far more correct to say that the continuous, inner crisis in Russia had produced Stalin's death. It does mean that the death of Stalin symbolizes the beginning of the end of totalitarianism, not on the part of his heirs, but from the forced labor camps in the wilds of Siberia that buttress the Russian regime. But before the challenge from Vorkuta, the bell of freedom sounded in East Berlin in the heart of Europe.

CHAPTER 11

The Beginning of the End of Russian Totalitarianism

In her writings on Russia as a state-capitalist society, Dunayevskaya's analysis was not alone an economic one. Her "economics" were rooted, at one and the same time, in Marx—in his analysis of capitalism's socially necessary labor time with its law of value, as well as its absolute opposite, freely associated labor—and *in the resistance she discerned within the Russian working class, who of necessity had often to express it in secretive, underground ways. In* Marxism and Freedom *this was expressed in Chapter 13, titled "Russian State Capitalism vs. Workers' Revolt."*

With Stalin's death early in 1953, the revolt broke out into the open both in the satellite states under Russia's bootheel and within the slave labor camps in Russia itself. In this chapter are three documents from Dunayevskaya on the early revolts—in East Germany, June 17, 1953, the Vorkuta prison camps uprising the following month, and the 1956 Hungarian Revolution. After the Hungarian Revolution, Dunayevskaya continued writing on the resistance to Russia's rule, including Czechoslovakia's Prague Spring in 1968, and the Poland of Solidarność in the 1980s.

East Germany, June 17, 1953

Marxism and Freedom

The myth that the Russian totalitarian State is invincible was suddenly and strikingly shattered. On June 17, 1953, the workers in the East German satellite took matters into their own hands on the questions of speed-up. They moved speedily, confidently, courageously and in an unprecedented manner to undermine the puppet state. Heretofore, absenteeism and slowdowns were the only weapons used by the workers against the intolerable conditions in the factories. But the struggle reached a new and higher stage of opposition in late spring of 1953. Here is a brief chronicle of the events leading up to June 17th and the days that followed:

Beginning with May 18th, the Communist government announced a new increase in work hours. The German workers broke out in open strikes. In one effort to stop the strikes the Communist government, on June 10th, offered concessions on all points *except* speed-up.

On June 16th, construction workers organized a protest march against speed-up from the Stalin Alee housing project. The government sent its supporters to join the marchers, apparently hoping to appear as sponsor. But as the marchers approached the government, joined en route by swelling numbers of demonstrators, the cry had become, "Down With the Zones—Down With the Government." The government then admitted it had been doing "wrong" and issued an order revoking the speed-up. It was too late.

By the evening of June 16th, the workers had turned the streets of East Berlin into political centers. On block after block, hundreds of people assembled and discussed what to do next. Early on the morning of June 17th they acted.

Columns of strikers charged the main government buildings where the government bureaucrats cowered. Reluctant police moved into pre-arranged positions. Youth and workers tore down the symbols of Communist power—flags, posters, pictures of Communist leaders. Despite rifle shots, one young man clambered up the famous Brandenburg Gate and tore down the Communist banner. Dispersing on one street and surging up another, the swelling ranks of strikers chanted, "We will not be slaves." *For four hours the only power in East Berlin belonged to the workers.* They, in fact, overthrew the East German government. They destroyed the police power, burning barracks, throwing policemen out of windows, and forcing them to flee to the West or to come over to the side of the workers.

At 1:00 P.M. the Russian command marched into Berlin with ten thousand troops and decreed martial law. Street gatherings of more than three people were forbidden. The people laughed at the order.

At the same time, in Jena, strikers from the Zeiss optical factory stormed the Communist Party and Communist Youth offices and hurled books, papers, typewriters out of the windows and burned them.

At the Kodak supplies plant, the workers took over and put strikers in charge.

State railway workers walked out, crippling zonal intercommunications and halting the shipment of reparations into Russia.

Construction workers cut power cables of both elevated and subway lines and blocked the tracks.

Twenty-five thousand workers at the Leuna Chemical plant (formerly I.G. Farben) at Halle set the plant afire. The workers at the Buna synthetic rubber plant burned it down. These plants were the chief suppliers of gas and tires to the occupation army.

The hard coal area at Zwickau was damaged beyond estimate. The demonstrators set fire to huge piles of coal between Halle and Magdeburg. They destroyed uranium mining facilities.

They opened prisons and concentration camps to set free the political prisoners. At Gera, an industrial city about the size of Cincinnati, near the Russian-operated uranium mines of Saxony, thousands of workers struck and marched on the city prison demanding release of its political prisoners.

Later in the day, five thousand uranium miners from nearby Ronneburg joined the Gera workers. They threw German police from the windows of their barracks. Russian reinforcements were called, this time they came with tanks.

The workers concentrated their anger against the German Communist officials who acted as agents of the government. At Rathenow they killed a factory guard when he tried to stop the strikers from entering the plant. At Erfurt they hanged two Red policemen from lamp posts.

By Saturday, June 20th, the Russians had sent twenty-five thousand troops to Berlin from their three-hundred-thousand-man occupation force at nearby Potsdam. In every major city, Russian power supplanted East German puppet police power. The Minister of Justice was purged. One half of the German police were demobilized as unreliable and sent into the plants to work.

In small but significant numbers Russian soldiers defected to the workers of East Germany, as became apparent when the demonstrations subsided and eighteen Russian soldiers were speedily executed for mutiny.

Twenty to thirty thousand strikers were jailed; untold dozens were executed; families of convicted strikers were driven from their homes and sent to concentration camps. But on June 22, the city of Leipzig, showplace of East German Communism, was still paralyzed by a general strike.

Strikes by the workers in the rest of Eastern Europe followed. The Russian bureaucracy slept uneasily and Beria, who was directly in charge of the satellites, was to feel it most keenly for it was the beginning of *his* end.

Above all, it was the regaining of the workers' confidence in the struggle for freedom. The East Germans wrote a glorious page in this struggle for they answered, in an unmistakable affirmative, *Can* man achieve freedom out of the totalitarianism of our age?

Even the slave laborers in Vorkuta heard this answer. Whereupon they wrote the second page in the new struggle for freedom.

∴

The Revolt in the Slave Labor Camps in Vorkuta

News & Letters, ***July 8, 1955***

Today marks the second anniversary of the most unprecedented strike in the world—the revolt in Russian slave labor camps in Vorkuta. The outstanding part of the strike is that it ever took place at all. No one on the inside or outside of the Kremlin, the seat of Russian Government in Moscow—nor even the prisoners themselves who were to organize this strike—thought such a thing possible in their wildest dreams. Yet, a few short weeks after the East German revolt on June 17, 1953, these same prisoners were inspired to strike out on their own.

Myth of Invincibility Destroyed

Nothing so shows the uncertainty and insecurity of these totalitarian rulers, armed to the teeth and with all the power and terror in their hands, as the caution with which the Government at first dealt with the strike. They sent a commission, headed by General Derevyanko, to fly down to the camp. When he tried to harangue the prisoners and failed, the commission returned to Moscow with the demands of the prisoners for a review of all their cases and the removal of the barbed wires. In the end, the Kremlin did what the Tsar had done back in 1912: they opened fire on the unarmed strikers and killed some 200. *But they could not put up what the strikers had destroyed: the myth of invincibility.*

These prisoners without any rights had dared to strike. They held out for weeks, shaking the Kremlin to its very foundations. Despite total censorship, the workers in Leningrad knew at once of the strike. A few months after, students from the Leningrad Mining Institute, working in the pits in Vorkuta, told the prisoners how everyone had talked of the strike in Leningrad:

> We soon got to know you were on strike. The drop in coal was noticeable at once. We don't have any reserves. There's just the plan, that's all. And everyone knows how vulnerable plans are. It destroyed the myth that the system was unassailable.

The Silence of "The West"

A meeting "at the summit" is being ballyhooed now and a meeting, of the Big Four Ministers, took place then. The upshot of it was, that they achieved as total a silence on the question of the revolt during that conference in West Berlin as in Moscow. Dr. Joseph Scholmer tells us that story in a most remarkable book called *Vorkuta*.[1]

Dr. Scholmer was one of thousands of slave laborers released during the Big Four Ministers Conference in 1953. He has this to say of the Western "experts" on Russia:

---

1 *Vorkuta* (Holt, 1955)—Editor.

> When I first mentioned the word, "civil war" to these people they were appalled. The possibility of a rising lay outside their realm of comprehension. They had no idea that there were resistance groups in the camps...
>
> I talked to all sorts of people in the first few weeks after my return from the Soviet Union. It seemed to me that the man in the street had the best idea of what was going on. The "experts" seemed to understand nothing.

On Both Sides of the Iron Curtain

It was not for lack of understanding that the Western rulers acted as they did. Quite the contrary. I remember that when Stalin died, one worker in Flint said: "What is the use of all this talk against Russia when Eisenhower sends the Russian leaders his sympathy?"

Over at the other end of the world from Flint, in the Russian slave labor camps, the same disgust with Western leaders swept the Russian resistance movements. For years there have been underground resistance groups, mainly Ukrainian. Prior to June 17th, all the preparations for resistance to the totalitarian rulers were based on the eventuality of war and looked to the Western rulers. When Stalin died in March, 1953, hope spread through the camps. But all that came from the Eisenhowers and Churchills were condolences to the Russian leaders who continued the Stalin regime. Gloom spread throughout the slave labor camps until the June 17th revolt in East Germany showed that liberation can be achieved only by the workers themselves. The Russian political prisoners followed up with their revolt.

The strike in July, 1953, could not have occurred without the previous underground formation of resistance groups within the camps. But the strike as it occurred was entirely different from the action planned when they looked to "the West." June 17th had changed all that.

The sabotage and treachery of the West seemed to astound some. But one of the Russian resistance leaders put it in a nutshell:

> Those radio stations are controlled by the various governments, aren't they? Well, on June 17 they had to ask the government officials what they were to do. And the government officials have a professed dislike of popular uprisings, wherever they take place.

Spontaneity of Action and Organization of Thought: In Memoriam of the Hungarian Revolution

Weekly Political Letter, September 17, 1961

Don't talk to me about space ships, a trip to the moon or Marx, about life in the atomic age...

We live like this. In darkness, in mud, far away...

Don't tell me it is worse in Africa. I live in Europe, my skin is white. Who will embrace me to make me feel that I am human?

KAROLY JOBBAGY, *Budapest, April 1956*

On October 23, 1956 the Russian puppet regime in Hungary fired on a student youth demonstration in Budapest. Far from dispersing the young students, these were soon joined by the workers from the factories in the outlying suburbs. The Revolution had begun in earnest. During the following 13 days, ever broader layers of the population revolted. From the very young to the very old, workers and intellectuals, women and children, even the police and the armed forces—truly the population to a man-—turned against the top Communist bureaucracy and the hated, sadistic AVO (secret police).

The Communist Party with more than 800,000 and the trade unions allegedly representing the working population just evaporated. In its place arose Workers' Councils, Revolutionary Committees of every sort—intellectuals, youth, the army—all moving *away from* the Single Party State. Overnight there sprung up 45 newspapers and 40 different parties, but the decisive force of the revolution remained the Workers' Councils.

When 13 days of armed resistance was bloodily crushed by the might of Russian totalitarianism, the new form of workers' organization—factory councils—called a general strike. It was the first time in history a general strike *followed* the collapse of the revolution. It held the foreign imperialist as well as the "new" government at bay for five long weeks. Even a Janos Kadar had to pretend he was listening to the demands of the Workers' Councils for control over production and even the possible abrogation of the single party rule.

As late as November 21, 1956, the Appeal of the Central Workers' Council of Great Budapest stated: "We protest against the attitude of the newly-formed 'Free Trade Unions' which are ready to accept the workers' councils merely as economic organs. We declare that in Hungary today the Workers' Councils represent the real interests of the working class, that there is no stronger political power in the country today than the power of the Workers' Councils."[2] And on November 30th the Bulletin of the Central Workers' Council reported a meeting with Kadar at which they demanded a daily press organ: "Our position is that the Workers' Councils are in absolute need of a press organ so that the workers may receive uniform and true information...We also raised the question of the multi-party system."[3]

It was the attempt to publish the *Workers' Journal* without state permission that made Kadar realize that "the government was simply ignored. Everyone who had a problem to settle came to us (Central Workers' Council)."[4] That made the Kadar Government, with the help of the Russian Army, move in and dissolve the Councils, on December 9th, long after armed resistance had been crushed and the exodus of refugees had reached 200,000 or a full 2% of the total population.

Although the Revolution had been sparked by the intellectuals, not only had the workers borne the main brunt of the fighting, but it was they who had shown the greatest creativity and given the Revolution its historic direction. Even their support of Imre Nagy was dependent on his acceptance of the workers' control over production, a multi-party system of government, and a new type of socialism.

Central to it was an independent Hungary, but this demand for self-determination had nothing in common with narrow bourgeois nationalism. As Imre Nagy himself recognized—it was this fact that brought him to the leadership of a revolution he did not desire—"They want a People's Democracy where the working people are masters of the country and of their own fate, where human beings are respected, and where social and political life is conducted in the spirit of humanism...An atmosphere of suspicion and revenge is banishing the fundamental feature of socialist morality, humanism."[5]

This Marxist humanism was in the air since 1955. Because the Communist intellectual caught this in the air, he was assured of leadership of a revolution against Communism. When the fight against the Stalinist, Rakosi, had

---

2 *The Review* (published by the Imre Nagy Institute, Brussels) #4, 1960. *Ibid.* East Europe (New York) April 1959 also carries an "Eyewitness Report of How the Workers Councils Fought Kadar."

3 *Ibid. East Europe* (New York) April 1959 also carries an "Eyewitness Report of How the Workers Councils Fought Kadar."

4 "My Experiences in the Central Workers' Council of Greater Budapest" by Miklos Sebestyen, *The Review*, Vol. Ill, #2.

5 Imre Nagy on *Communism: In Defense of "The New Course,"* pp. 49, 56.

first begun and he called these intellectuals "outsiders," Tador had replied that the ruling circle "is not the party. The party is ourselves, those who belong to the other current, who fight for the ideas and principles of humanism, and whose aims reflect in ever-increasing measure those of the people and of the country."[6]

But though the intellectuals had caught the humanism in the air and set off the revolution, they did not reveal themselves as leaders and organizers at the moment of crisis. The best, the young, however, did recognize that the spontaneity which produced the revolution will see that it does not die. "As a true Marxist I believe in the inevitability of the historic processes. We know perfectly well that a wave of terror and Stalinist repression will be let loose on us...You know how the revolution broke out—spontaneously, without any kind of preparation. When the police fired on our students, leadership and organization sprung up overnight. Well, we'll scatter now just as spontaneously as we came together.... The revolution can't die; it will play dead and await its moment to rise again."[7]

Today, when the world stands on the brink of nuclear holocaust, sparked by Russian state-capitalism calling itself "Communism" and American private capitalism calling itself "Democracy," the page of freedom opened by the Hungarian Revolution shows the only way out of the crisis-wracked capitalist order. When the 1917 Russian Revolution put an end to the first betrayal of established Marxism, Lenin never wearied of reminding us that without "the dress rehearsal" of 1905, there could have been no successful 1917.

Because of the maturity of our age, marked, on the one hand, by the African revolutions which broke from Western capitalism, and, on the other hand, by the East European Revolutions against Russian totalitarianism, the Hungarian Revolution of 1956 is more than a dress rehearsal for a new European Revolution. It is the dress rehearsal for a world revolution that is out to reconstruct society on new, truly human beginnings and in that way finally bring to an end that which Marx called the pre-history of mankind.

---

6 *Behind the Rape* of Hungary by F. Fejto. See also my *Marxism and Freedom*, pp. 62, 255–256 on the Russian debates on Marx's Humanist Essays, and my *Nationalism, Communism, Marxist Humanism and the Afro-Asian Revolutions* on the Polish debates.

7 From a report by Peter Schmid quoted in *The Hungarian Revolution*, edited by Melvin J. Lasky.

CHAPTER 12

Post-Stalin Russia

Following the death of Stalin, Dunayevskaya continued to examine ongoing events in state-capitalist Russia. These included the revolts both within Russia and in East Europe, the Cold War rivalry between the two nuclear-armed superpowers (including the Cuban missile crisis), and the emergence and deepening of the Sino-Soviet split. As well, she wrote of the maneuvering of the leadership within Russia, from Khrushchev's so-called de-Stalinization campaign, to leaders such as Brezhnev and Gorbachev. Some of these developments are covered in the documents below. Others are taken up in Chapters 14, 15 and 16.

Without a Past and Without a Future [On Khrushchev]

News & Letters, ***March 30, 1956***

The 20th Congress of the Russian Communist Party, which met on February 15, 1956 in Moscow, was the first to be convened since Stalin's death in 1953. It wasted no time in launching a campaign against him. The First Deputy Premier, Anastas Mikoyan, perfunctorily dismissed the heretofore sacred Stalin['s] *History of the Communist Party of the Soviet Union*, and asked, "How can you justify our lack of an accepted history of the party for two decades?"

A Tragic Farce

"So the Russians are rewriting history yet once again," I heard one Russian specialist say, "I understand that they now publish their Encyclopedia in loose-leaf form."

These vainglorious bureaucrats, without a past and without a future, rule over a land of 200 million, are armed with the H-bomb and are reaching out for world domination. Let us see what is new and what is old in their latest rewrite of history. The last two decades evidently need "correction." Mikoyan specifies the period to go back "about 20 years."

"About 20 Years"

Lenin died not "about 20 years" ago, but 32 years ago. He left a *Will* in which he called Stalin "rude and disloyal" and asked that he be "removed from his post of General Secretary."

Instead of removing Stalin, the present leadership collaborated in hiding the *Will*, which to this day has never been published in Russia. To talk only of "about 20 years" means the bureaucracy is anxious somehow to skip a decade. *It is the decade in which they helped Stalin not alone to maintain his post but to transform it into one of dictatorial power.*

Above that struggle for power that followed Lenin's death, was the struggle against the newly-established workers state itself. Indeed, the struggle for power among the bureaucracy was only *the reflection of the counterrevolution that took from the Russian workers their rights and freedom, and instituted bureaucratic planning. In a word, established a relationship between worker and management that in no essential respect differs from that in Western countries.*

"About 20 years" correctly sums up the basis on which they mean to begin their rewrite. No one who had not participated in the counter-revolution, following the death of Lenin, is included. Trotsky is therefore excluded. Indeed, their present establishment of "collective leadership" is only a farcical imitation of Stalin's struggle for power against Trotsky on the basis of a collective leadership against alleged one-man rule. Not only that, with the sole exception of Tito, there is not a living person whom they are "rehabilitating." Not only are those to be "rehabilitated" dead, they are those who, in the first place, made their peace with Stalinism. As for Tito, he has power in his own right, rules over a country which is strategically placed, is flirting with "the West" and the Russian, bureaucracy *needs him. He is of the same cloth as they.*

When to Struggle for World Domination

As we can see, the truth is that the entire "collective leadership" lives by virtue of Stalin's leadership which brought them to power.

It is the only foundation for all exploitation: the rulers continue to sit in the seats of power and rule while the workers continue to slave the harder and produce the more.

This does not mean that there have been no changes initiated at this congress. Tito is one of those changes. Stalin had, in fact, lost power long before he died. Not that any one dared challenge him. But he ceased to *represent* the bureaucracy which wanted a breathing spell between wars, while he was so drunk with power that he was in a mad rush for world domination the day after World War II concluded. The bureaucracy that dared not challenge his rule openly, "collectively" plotted to hasten his natural death. He no sooner was dead than the Korean War came to a conclusion, on the one hand, and some internal changes occurred within Russia.

Although they "collectively" agreed that Stalin was in their way when he was alive, Stalin was no sooner dead than a new struggle for power began. But by now the regime is too crisis-ridden to dare public trials. That, and *not* the "collectivity" of leadership, is the reason why Malenkov was not "liquidated" when he lost out to Khrushchev.

Greater and more terrifying than the "myth of Stalin" is the present identification of revolutions with counterrevolutions under the gigantic fraud of an alleged return to Leninism. The only way the present "collective leadership" could follow out the Leninist principle is to remove themselves from power.

If Khrushchev, the heir, is not all that Stalin was, his ambitions and appetites are just as insatiable. It was merely a question of *when* to fight for world power. History, however, will not give the new pretenders to world rule another period of "about 20 years."

After the 20th Congress of the Russian Communist Party: Where is Russia Going?

News & Letters, ***March 30, 1956***

Since the recent 20th Congress of the Russian Communist Party, the capitalist press and spokesmen of the West have been so busy publicizing what the Russian Communists wanted publicized—the destruction of the so-called Stalin myth—that they failed completely to see what is new in the present Russian situation.

The Russian people never believed in the Stalin myth in the first place, or in "the cult of personality," as the present Russian rulers call it.

The millions in forced in labor camps testify to more than mere disbelief in the myth of Stalin "the miracle worker." These imprisoned millions are proof of the continuous revolt of the Russian people against the tyrant, Stalin, and against his heirs who are now his detractors.

Contrast the big noise in the press, about the Stalin myth, to the matter-of-fact knowledge of the Russian peasant who, when asked by reporters for the name of his collective farm, answered, "Up to now it was called the Stalin Collective."

The Agricultural Crisis

To the Russian peasant it matters little whether it was Stalin or is Khrushchev; or whether it is Khrushchev alone or Khrushchev plus a dozen other bureaucrats who rule "collectively." What does matter—and what is new, is that the newest Plan demands nothing less than 100 per cent increase in agricultural productivity per person.

Since the Russian peasant has resisted the rate of output set by *all* previous plans and intends to continue his resistance to totalitarian planning, this new, impossible demand can have but one meaning:

A new move against him that will be more ferocious and more charged with terror than even the forced collectivization of the 1930s.

In the depth of the internal crisis of Russia, can be seen the reality and nonreality of the "collectivity" of the Russian leaders. Khrushchev, the leader, dares not openly stand forth as such. He tries to cover himself against the wrath of the Russian people, first by attempting to divert their anger to the dead Stalin and then, by surrounding himself with the collective approval of the leadership. He does not, for one moment, fool himself about any approval by the Russian people.

World Crisis and Colonial Revolts

What does give Khrushchev his confidence is the world crisis. The Russian masses know the Communist system for the tyranny it is. So does Eastern Europe that has fallen under its domination. But the gigantic Communist bureaucracy has no vested interests in the countries suffering under British and French imperialism. The Asian and African people have also come to know what is attached to the American dollar. It is this which gives Khrushchev a free hand in demagogy.

He hopes to reap a rich harvest from the hatred of the colonial peoples against British and French imperialist rule to which American dollar-diplomacy and "brink of war" strategy is tied.

By casting away from himself the name of Stalin, Khrushchev hopes to parade under the unsullied banner of liberation, of Marxism.

To counter this, the American Government can think of nothing better than a junket for that "brink of war" strategist Dulles, to be followed by that spokesman for "people's capitalism," labor bureaucrat Walter Reuther. But Reuther is no match for the Russian appeal for a "popular front for peace" which will travel from Nehru's India to Western Europe and back again, not excluding America.

The majority of the world's population lives in the oppressed colonial portion of the earth. The Russian bureaucracy has shown how brave they can be with other people's lives, as they were with the lives of the Chinese and Koreans during the Korean War.

Khrushchev can now dream of starting the next world war from the East and enjoying the luxury, which America has always enjoyed heretofore, of not having the battle fields in his own country.

At the same time, Russian power has grown mighty enough so that its Defense Minister, Eisenhower's "old friend" Zhukov, can threaten America with the "mighty guided missiles" he has at his disposal and can hurl at American cities.

Internal Crisis in Russia

If the American capitalists and their State Department have freed Russia's hand, the Russian working class has not.

(1) Out of 12 million industrial workers in Russian enterprises, no fewer than 2.8 million left their jobs in 1954.

(2) 1.45 million workers in the building industries simply left the building sites altogether. In an attempt to counteract this movement, Bulganin [Premier of the Soviet Union under Khrushchev] proposed to promise building trades workers that ten per cent of all the living space they construct will be for their own use.

The Russian worker cannot strike, but he has managed to resist the labor bureaucracy's demands for continuous and heightened production by labor turnover and slow down on the job.

Resistance of Labor

The Russian bureaucrats are now breaking their heads on how to solve the problem of the resistance of labor and the *shortage* of labor.

Just as, at the end of World War II, the Russian rulers had to grant a general amnesty for all labor offenses, to gain some kind of labor force, now, they hope to gain some more production from labor by promising a shorter working day.

The Russian workers have just been promised a 7-hour day, 6-day week. First of all, this promise doesn't give the Russian worker something "new." He had a 7-hour day before the war which was never restored to him when the war was over. Secondly, the "new" 42-hour week is not promised as of now, but, presumably, by 1960 when this newest—the sixth—Five Year Plan ends. For now, all the Russian worker got was a reduction of two hours a week. Instead of 48 hours, they now need work only 46 hours.

The joker is in the decree which announced this "new" reduced work-week without pay cut. The decree also states; "Managers are instructed to see to the carrying out of the decree and are also responsible for the unconditional fulfillment of the set assignments for the volume of production."

In a word, the Russian workers are required to produce as much in 46 hours as they did in 48 hours.

That is the favorite underhand trick of wage-cutting in Russia. They don't ever announce a wage cut, but they constantly revise the production norms, *always upward.*

The latest Plan calls for a 50 per cent increase in labor productivity.

Technology and More Technology

The bureaucracy hopes to overcome the workers resistance by automation. No private property capitalist has ever dreamed more fantastic dreams of push-button factories without workers, than the present dreams of the Russian state capitalists.

Bulganin laid the basis last summer, when he told the plenary session that

> some economic managers have lost their feeling for the new... Great harm is caused to technical progress in our country by underestimating the achievements of technology abroad... The main thing is not to discover first but to introduce first... Industry must be redesigned to provide proper incentive to technical innovation.

"Decentralizing Planning"

Some Western writers have been completely confused by the new stress the Russian rulers have put on "decentralizing planning." Like Ford's present "decentralization plans," *it is not* to give the worker any voice in production—but to give the director, that is the manufacturer, a freer hand and more power over the workers as to hiring and firing and intimidation to extract more production.

The increase in managerial powers is to be backed up by an increase in the percentage of profits that is at the disposal of the factory director. It was between 15 to 45 per cent. It is now to be no less than 50 per cent and as high as 70 per cent.

The totalitarian rulers place no reliance in the Russian working people. "Specialists," said Premier Bulganin, "are our gold reserves. We are proud of them and we value them." This privileged intelligentsia—the engineers, technicians and speed-demons, whom they call "innovators"—are to be wooed with even higher wages than they already receive, which is no less than 20 times more than the average worker gets.

The Struggle for the Minds of Men

The Russian tyranny is the exact opposite, in theory and in practice, of the theory of liberation of Marxism-Leninism. In its gigantic effort *to force an identity between the two opposites—Marxism and Russian Communism—it gets its greatest help from the American Administration.*

The struggle for the minds of men cannot be won under the banner of "free enterprise." Empty talk about "American democracy" will not do. The majority of the world's population is colored and none is as backward as Eisenhower or Stevenson that he does not know the truth of the situation in the South, which shows in concentrated form the situation in the North.

Russia is winning battles without fighting only because it can pretend to march under the banner of Marxism. There is no way to "expose" that except through an appeal to—*and the realization of*—actual freedom. The only thing that will stay the hand of Russian state capitalism, reaching out for world domination, is the Russian working class in alliance with the working people of the world.

American capitalism hopes to use the American workers' detestation of Russian Communism, in order to keep them from going to Marxism. Their hope is in vain. Marxism is not in Russia. It is in the daily life of people, the world over, striving to break out of the chaos of capitalism and war to a new society.

The only thing that American capitalism will have achieved by its attempted identification of Marxism with Communism is to identify *itself* with Communism as the other pole of world capital striving for world power.

Tito's Turnabout

News & Letters, ***Oct. 1961***

Russia's atomic blastoff scattered to the winds filled with radioactive fall-out, the pie-in-the-sky promises in the Draft Program of the Communist Party which is to convene in Moscow October 17th. But it succeeded in pulling Tito back into the Russian orbit. His break from Stalin had never, of course, been a fundamental departure from the state-capitalist fold. I do not mean that Stalin's order for Tito's expulsion from the Cominform [Communist Information Bureau was the name for the Information Bureau of the Communist and Workers' Parties] wasn't real. It assuredly was. Enthusiastic mass support by a country that had won over the Nazi juggernaut propelled Tito to take the daring step away from Stalin's Russia. But what the Yugoslav people aimed at in their break from Stalin and what Tito aimed at in his derived from two different *class* sources.

"Different Paths to Socialism"

Tito's break with Stalin produced a new crop of theories on "different paths to socialism." The crop was a sufficiently alluring one to win Trotskyist world support, despite the fact that Tito had come to head the Yugoslav Party because he had dutifully followed through with the Moscow Frame-Up Trials, and beheaded not only the Yugoslav Trotskyists but also Spanish Trotskyists who stood in way of Stalin's aim to dominate the Spanish Revolution. The "objective" reason for this unasked-for Trotskyist support was based on Tito's "struggle" against the bureaucracy and alleged return to the Marxist-Leninist theory of the withering away of the state. The only trouble was that the struggle was directed, not against his own Single Party Bureaucratic State, but only against Russia.

Nevertheless it would be wrong to think of Tito's break as merely a "nationalist" one, anymore than Stalin's theory of "socialism in one country" was proof of his "nationalism," though Trotsky died thinking so. *"Socialism in one country" is only secondarily nationalist. Primarily it is a euphemistic expression for state capitalism—a state exploitative system that aims to become a "world system" which, at the point of production, preserves the relation of manager to worker which characterizes private capitalism.*

The "giving up" of the pursuit of "world revolution" is true only where it involved the release of spontaneous action from below; it is not true where it meant the establishment of world domination by arms, a coup, or the undermining of the self-activity of the masses. Indeed, just as "socialism in one country" called upon the workers of the world to defend Russia, so the Yugoslav "new path to socialism" was declared "a new universal."

And there was never any doubt that Tito was building in a single, small country the same system Stalin built in a single, vast land. In December 1946 Tito revealed that as far back as 1944 the Anti-Fascist Council of National Liberation had so strengthened the state apparatus that it would be a mere question of "taking over," not of reconstructing from below:

> Nationalization was well prepared organizationally... All enterprises in the entire country were taken over on the same day (of liberation) and almost at the same time *without the stopping of production.* (My emphasis.)

The same held true on the day of Tito's break with Stalin. The bureaucratic state mentality ruled undeviatingly: the managers continued to order the workers about, and the workers had to produce ever more. As Article 14, entitled "Work and Cadres," of the Five Year Plan of 1947, had put it, it was necessary "to ensure a steady increase in productivity of work by introducing the greatest possible mechanization, and *by thoroughly utilizing working hours*." (My emphasis.)

The Dialectic of "Revisionism"

What is instructive in Tito's "revisionism" is its own dialectical development. The changes introduced into the State Plan to appease mass pressure produced startling theoretic insights into *Russia's* revisionism. For example, Yugoslavia abandoned forced collectivization in favor of a combination of state farms, co-operative, and private farming. From this experience Milovan Djilas, who had not theretofore been distinguished by any profound comprehension of Marx's third volume of *Capital*, now characterized Russia's agricultural policy as "a struggle with the collective working peasantry for absolute rent."

Kardelj [a political leader in Tito's Yugoslavia; main creator of a system of so-called "workers' self-management"] gained as penetrating an insight into Russia's industrial set-up from the changes introduced in Yugoslavia's decentralized planning accompanied by establishment of "workers' councils." (How totalitarian rulers torture words to transform them into their opposite!) *Although these so-called workers' councils were not born of revolution and could not therefore signify any "withering away of the state," nevertheless the cracks in the iron wall revealed new life, like grass that suddenly shows through between stones. And Kardelj came through with a priceless description of Russian Communism as "a pragmatic statist revision of Marxism."*

No wonder there was no end to the screaming about Tito's "apostasy" at the 21st Congress of the Russian Communist Party on February 6, 1959. The following year, however, after the U-2 spy flight, a new wooing of the "apostate" began. Tito held back. While condemning the U-2 flight, he insisted that it "should not and must not" be used to heat up the cold war. Tito proceeded with his own plans to convene the "non-aligned" nations as a "third force" between the two contending blocs of powers.

The Nearness of War

On the very eve of his success, as the heads of nations gathered in Belgrade, when Khrushchev seemed openly to slap their collective two-facedness, Tito suddenly announced that he understood the "reasons" behind Russia's unilateral action in resuming nuclear testing. What changed between the time of the openly provocative U.S. spy flight deep into Russia and the equally provocative *Russian* atomic explosions that poisoned the whole world's atmosphere to have caused Tito's turnabout?

We can discount the arrogant stupidities of the American bourgeois press, which attribute to all but themselves obeisance to superior force. A country like Yugoslavia that fought Nazism at the staggering cost of a full 10 per cent of its population, and then stood up to Stalin, needs to produce no "credentials" of its bravery to the well-paid press pounding typewriters in the comfort of their sheltered ivory towers. No, the struggle such a people is sure to carry on against its leadership for catapulting it to another war will be due to mightier convictions than those of "Western democracy with all its imperfections." The masses are well aware of *what* has changed: *It is the nearness of actual war.*

For Tito, the nearness of war that may spell the doom of the Single Party State and its "world system" of state-capitalism is sufficient to make him praise his chief opponent in the Communist world: Mao Tse-tung. Tito's "path to socialism," it is true, lasted a good deal longer than Mao's violently aborted call to "Let 100 flowers bloom. Let 100 schools of thought contend." But it was bound to come to an end with the approach of war. Now that the nearness of war may inspire the Yugoslav masses to find a truly independent class road away from state and private capitalism, their joint chaos leading to world wars, Tito must realign himself to save his rule. *Therefore* he accepts Russia's substitute for the class struggles at home—the designation that the struggle between the two nuclear blocs for world domination is "the class struggle of today."

For Tito that is a "must" choice. For the Yugoslav masses the war-charged transformation of the Marxist theory of liberation into the Communist practice of enslaving is something they are experienced in fighting.

∴

Andropov's Ascendancy Reflects Final State of State-Capitalism's Degeneracy

Political-Philosophic Letter,* News & Letters, *December 1982

The death of Brezhnev, which the mass media and the so-called scholar-specialists on Russia are writing up as if it were a turning point in history—"the end of an era" and the "beginning of a new age"—has nothing new about it. Far from signifying anything historically new, Andropov's ascendancy reflects the final stage of state-capitalism's degeneracy. Never before has a man who has spent 15 years of his life heading the most hated of secret police, the KGB, become the ruler of Russia, though that country had, under the totalitarian

Stalin, been transformed from the first workers' state into its opposite—a state-capitalist society calling itself "Communist."

When the head of that secret police at the time of Stalin's death—Beria—thought he could achieve such a feat because he had dossiers not only on dissidents but on each Politburo member, Khrushchev knew how to put to his own use the hatred of the masses for this executioner, by having Beria executed, instead. *The one thing that has never changed—until now—is the fact that the Party has always remained the "vanguard," the monolithic institution which gave orders to all other institutions, including the Army and especially the secret police.*

Nothing is more illusory in the current analyses than the indulgence of the American "spets" on how technologically backward Russia is supposed to be, how unknowledgeable of computers and electronics, and how "on its last legs" is the Russian economy—as if the global recession resides only in Russia and not in the U.S. Nothing better gilds the equally reactionary Reagan Administration. Russia is no "basket case." Have the "Western" ideologues forgotten that it was Russia, not the U.S., which sent up the first Sputnik? Russia has by now extended itself not only to outer space but right on this earth, from Africa, Latin America and the Mediterranean to the Gulf region and most of the oceans of the world.

It is precisely Russia's "high technology"—when directed, as it has been, to militarization—which is the ground Reagan is rushing "to catch up with" in the hope of surpassing it, if only he, too, can achieve the destruction of unionization and high wages. And in the kind of technology represented by microchips and robotics, among other things, isn't it Japan which has outdistanced the "West," be it in autos or steel or whatever?

"Unemployment Within Factory Gates" and Martial Law

No, it is not in "high technology" that one can find the great contradictions wrecking capitalism, private as well as state. One needs, instead, to dig deep into the basic capital/labor relationship. Though the Russians, too, don't know how to overcome it, they do have a name for the current "low productivity" of Russian labor: "unemployment within the factory gates." Jaruzelski's answer is to militarize labor [he imposed marshal law in Poland in December 1981]—which gives us a clue to Andropov, to whom we'll turn later.

Here, however, all eyes must return to the period from August, 1980 through December, 1981, when state-capitalism confronted an impossible contradictory duality. On the one side, the Polish workers created *Solidarity*, that elemental new form of a genuinely independent trade union movement, within the Russian orbit, which raised political demands of such an indivisible nature as

Freedom. On the other side, the totalitarian State turned to the Army when they saw that *Solidarity* had inspired even some in the Communist Party to solidarize with it. The *shock* to the rulers, in Poland as in Russia (who recognized in *Solidarity* a veritable "dual government"), was so overwhelming that they decided the Communist Party, too, must be put in its place. The decision was made to launch martial law on Dec. 13.

Do Western ideologues need to see the actual Minutes of the last meeting the Russian "eminence grise," Suslov, [chief ideologue of the Soviet Communist Party] had with the Polish rulers he still could trust, in order to understand what has happened in the new stage of state-capitalism? Wasn't that made clear enough once *General* Jaruzelski was elevated to be the leader also over the Party? *The subordination of the Party to the Army and the ZOMOS* [paramilitary police used to attack protests] *has proved to be an actual anticipation of what would happen in Russia.* But, because that is hardly the focus of the Western ideologues, the current events in Russia have diverted them, instead, to talking of Andropov's "culture."

The truth is that Andropov's coming to power, far from revealing a new era of "culture," reveals the state of degeneracy of state-capitalism as a whole. It was anticipated at its weakest point—in a satellite where the masses were in revolt and therefore the military had to be given power almost on a par with Big Brother himself. What needs to be seen as the pivot is not the degeneracy at the top, but the truth that the revolts against Communist totalitarianism for fully three decades have been so deep that the rulers have had to resort to the military over the heretofore sacrosanct Party machine.

The Continuous Revolt

Consider what Russia had to do, itself, to put down the East German revolt of June 17, 1953, the Hungarian Revolution in 1956, the Czechoslovak Spring in 1968—whereas, in Poland, 1981, it was a native Pole, General Jaruzelski, who did it by himself. Any nuance of difference between the State and Production and the Military is gone. Marx is the only one who was right about the ultimate in capitalism—state-capitalism: there is nothing between the hierarchy in the factory at the point of production, and the State. As Marx put it, the State is the "excrescence" of capital's domination.

Even under martial law the workers in Poland have continued their revolt. When Jaruzelski "abolished" *Solidarity* on Oct. 8, the shipyard workers in Gdansk, Gdynia and Sopot refused to wait for a General Strike called for Nov. 10 and struck immediately. And when the government militarized the shipyards, drafting all those workers, men and women in Wroclaw and Nowa Huta walked out of their mills and plants. Yet, instead of reporting the thousands who did come out again on Nov. 10, the Western media reported these tremendous demonstrations a "failure" and the General Strike a "fizzle"—as if anyone could actually execute a general strike under martial law.

The greatness, newness and continuity of the Polish revolt lies deep in the creative recesses of spontaneous mass uprisings. For the first time ever in the three-decade-long revolt in East Europe, the workers had found a way, paved for them by a small, unique combination of workers and intellectuals known as KOR [Workers' Defence Committee, which developed into the Committee for Social Self-defence], who had developed the concept of a totally independent trade union movement far out of the confines of trade unionism in any other country in the East or in the West. When *Solidarity* became an actuality, the union did not leave matters only at the production line but demanded political freedoms as well. Indeed, it was because *Solidarity* had reached the stage of challenging state authority and winning legal status that the Communist ideologues, in Russia and at the top echelons of the military in Poland, feared they were confronting a veritable "dual government."

When the martial law, the imprisonments, and the hated ZOMOS still could not succeed in crushing the revolt, they added their version of "Roman circuses." To encourage the Church's continued undermining of what the Underground Resistance was working for (and the masses were, indeed, undertaking actions independent of Church advice), the State granted the Church a promise for a June visit by the Pope. Walesa's freedom was conditional on his "prudence"—a prudence that they (Jaruzelski, the Army, the ZOMOS, and Russia) will judge.

The question that must now be asked is what about the true independents, the politicos who weren't separating freedom from workers' control of production, the initiators of that unique worker-intellectual combination that laid the ground for *Solidarity*—KOR? What about those who are now risking their lives in continuing Underground activity? *What about Kuron, Modzelewski, Michnik, Litynski, Lipski, Wujec, Frasyniuk? Are the rulers preparing their execution to balance the Roman Circuses?*[1] The last word has by no means yet been said!

State-Capitalism and the "Hungary Road"

Not even that possibility has stopped the Western ideologues from their empty speculations about the Andropov phenomenon in Russia. Added to

---

1 An important letter, "The Danger in Poland," by George Konrad, has brought out the historic fact that in the Hungarian Revolution the leaders had also been promised that there would be no executions once "order is restored." But in fact Nagy and his colleagues were executed. (See *New York Review of Books*, Dec. 2, 1982, p. 6.).

descriptions of Andropov's "culture" and "shrewdness" is speculation, not about the Hungarian Revolution, but about what they call the "Hungary road"—freer trade and some private property. We are now reminded that Andropov, who was Russian Ambassador to Hungary when Russia brought in its tanks to crush the revolution, had chosen Kadar as "his man"—and, since Kadar opposed the Russian overlordship when revolution first broke out, we are supposed to think of him as a socialist when he came to preside, over the counter-revolution, especially since it then evolved as a "new Hungary road."

What is this "Hungary road"? Does allowing some "free trade" and relaxation of collectivization of agriculture change the class nature of the State? Does any of this make Andropov a veritable "closet liberal"? Total nonsense. Worse than that, such analysis discloses how totally ignored is the whole phenomenon of what has happened to the *world* economy ever since the Depression caused the total collapse of private capitalism. *The truth is that the only way capitalism could save itself, and then launch into World War II, was to bow to the State Plan. It isn't Plan, Plan, Plan, but State, State, State that marked the new, the ultimate stage of capitalism.* By whatever name it went—whether Roosevelt's "New Deal," or Japan's "co-prosperity sphere," or, after World War II, DeGaulle's constitutional authoritarianism—state intervention was here to stay. It achieved total control in its Russian form—Stalinism—only because it was easier to do it there since the revolution had destroyed Tsarism.

In Russia, though Stalin called it "socialism," what the world witnessed in fact was a *transformation into opposite*—of a workers' state into a state-capitalist monstrosity. Old capitalism, in the West and in the East, had what its ideologues call "a mixed economy," while aiding Stalin by gilding Russian state-capitalism as "socialism." The language could not possibly change the facts: Plan from above, State Plan, with its destruction of the workers' attempts to control production, spells out the State as sole decision-maker. *This is what Marx called "barracks discipline"—and he was applying the expression not just to the Army but to the relations of capital and labor at the point of production in the factory.* Which is why the State remains the excrescence of that exploitative relationship. In the nuclear age, it has reached its ultimate as both Goliaths, Russia and the U.S., are preparing for the Apocalypse with the Grand Illusion that nuclear war is "winnable" and that only the "Other" will suffer total annihilation.

Finally, Andropov—And the Russia-Chinese Feelers

Lest the phenomenal haste with which Andropov assumed full power before ever Brezhnev was buried gives us the impression of a well-oiled machine that never runs astray and of an uncheckered rapid road to power, it is necessary to look carefully and objectively at Andropov's long road to becoming General

Secretary of the Russian Communist Party in the 30-year period which was never free of the impossible dualities of exploitation, racism, sexism and brutal repression, on the one hand, and never ending revolts in Russia's Empire in East Europe, on the other.

As a young man, at the head of the Young Communist League, Andropov was sent to aid in the amputation of Finland during World War II. Thus, at the very beginning of his high-rising career, the simultaneous task of repression and giving the appearance of maintaining independence was first witnessed in Finland. In 1951 he was brought to Moscow. No sooner had the very first workers' revolt from under Communist totalitarianism erupted and been crushed in East Germany in 1953, than Andropov was sent to Hungary in 1954. He was to crush the revolution there in 1956, and supervised the rise of Kadar.

Whatever it was that Andropov learned from Khrushchev's rise *and* fall after putting missiles in Cuba at a time when Russia's nuclear might could not match the U.S. Goliath's, it was Khrushchev's "reforms"—so inseparable from state-capitalism's savagery—that molded Andropov's "new" regime as he came to head the KGB in 1967. He "liberalized" Stalin's treatment of the intellectuals by sending them to the new horrors called psychiatric hospitals.

The following year Brezhnev dared to call the counterrevolutionary assault on Czechoslovakia by Russian tanks—"internationalism." The infamous "Brezhnev Doctrine" is actually Russian chauvinistic imperialistic intervention into all "socialist countries." Stalin's "socialism in one country" has gone abroad to roost. In the half century since Stalin's usurpation of power developed into state-capitalism and reached a climax in the "Great Russian Patriotic War," what the world has witnessed is what Lenin sensed on his dying bed as he warned against Stalin. Lenin correctly spelled out Stalin's relations with fellow Communists in Georgia as: "Scratch a Communist and you find a Great Russian chauvinist." This rising tide of nationalism-chauvinism is now armed with nuclear power, as is the U.S., and both nuclear Titans are driving toward a single country's total global power.

It is in this context, and not in the 90-minute long talk between Gromyko and Huang, that one needs to see whether there is anything new in Chinese-Russian relations since Andropov's ascendancy to power. The relations between so-called "socialist countries" were starkly revealed in their true nationalistic context in the mid-1960s, when the turbulence was world-wide and the Nixon Administration, in its sphere, carried out the height of the counter-revolution against Vietnam abroad and against the anti-war Youth, the Black Revolution and Women's Liberation at home.

It was then that Andropov came to head the KGB and was followed by the "Brezhnev Doctrine." The Sino-Soviet orbit which split at the beginning of the 1960s, from an "unbreakable friendship" to a great conflict, reached its climax in Mao's "Cultural Revolution" when China subordinated Vietnam's life-and-death struggle with American imperialism to declare Russia as "Enemy No. 1." Deng's post-Mao China has not only continued that line but intensified it. Just as Mao sacrificed his "closest-comrade-in-arms," Lin Piao, when he dared to object to Mao's rolling out the carpet for Nixon, so Deng was concretizing Russia as "Enemy No. 1" by saying Russia was the worst of the imperialistic super-powers, and flirting with outright collaboration with U.S. imperialism against Russia.

But, just as U.S. imperialism never gave up its "national interests" in the preservation of the Chiang Kai-shek connection and protection of Taiwan even after the U.S. "alliance" with Deng, so Deng never gave up its stake in Russia—not when U.S. imperialism seems to disregard *China's* "national interests." Anyone, however, who seriously thinks that Andropov's putting out feelers to China means Russia's forgetting China's defection needs to take a deeper look at the *capitalistic* interests of each of these "socialist countries."

Just when we were confronted with a pre-revolutionary situation in Iran and the mass movement against the Shah was gaining a momentum of its own, both Russia and China, for their own national interests, were still embracing the Shah! Ever since the Hitler-Stalin Pact gave the green light to World War II, neither Stalin's Russia nor Mao's China (even when it was only in Yenan and pursued by Chiang Kai-shek's Army) has ever fundamentally departed from its inherent Stalinism, that is to say, its state-capitalist nature.

The overriding question for capitalist-imperialism the world over is how to force labor to produce and produce and produce for "production's sake"—that is, how to enforce "labor discipline." For Russia, which has already tried "barrack discipline" in the factory as in the military—and still faces the continuous labor revolts in its East Europe, the question is: what else is left to try? It is here we need to have one more look at Andropov.

The "newness" of the present stage of state-capitalism, its full degeneracy, lies, not in its foreign relations, but strictly in the internal conflict, and that does include Russia's East Europe Empire. Let's return to Suslov's last visit to Poland on the eve of Dec. 13 (and, as it turned out, the eve of his death)—this time not to see what it signified for Poland, but for Russian succession. Suslov was Russia's preeminent ideologist, recognized as "the dogmatist" but at least somewhat apart from a direct economic-political-military identity, especially its secret police demands. Andropov, the KGB man, nevertheless moved rapidly to take over that portfolio after Suslov's death. That was the beginning of the year 1982.

As the conflict between Russia and the U.S. is heating up with Reagan's revival of the Cold War, and Russia is no longer that lesser nuclear might of the 1962 Cuban Missile crisis when Khrushchev had to bow to Kennedy, there seems to be no area which Andropov seems willing to leave out of his totalitarian hold. By taking over also all ideology, state-capitalism has "coordinated" political and military and ideology. And let's not forget that Weinberger has met his match in Russia's Defense Minister as Ustinov was the first to vote for Andropov, and declared that anyone calling for military cuts was committing an "unpardonable mistake."

Andropov has summed it all up himself in his first major speech to the Supreme Soviet—not when he talked the same language as Reagan against "the other," but when he talked of the crisis *within* the Russian economy. It is clear that the 1975–76 economic global crisis has not abated in 1982. The tough words are directed against Russia's 80 million work force for its lack of "labor discipline," its "shoddy work, inactivity and irresponsibility." Then comes still another warning against insufficient "labor productivity" which, says the new ruler and ideologist, should result in "an immediate and unavoidable effect on earnings."

Yes, the Russians have a word for it: "unemployment within factory gates." No, the Russians do not have the answer to the continuous resistance to "labor discipline" and the endless revolts. Here, too, Marx had the answer: The deeper the economic crisis the more does capitalism create its own "grave-diggers": the proletariat. In Russia, as in Poland, the gravediggers of capitalism are preparing. No, the last word has not yet been said, and Andropov's ascendancy will not stifle the massive opposition from all over its empire, beginning at home.

Detroit, Mich. Nov. 26, 1982

∴

Reagan, Gorbachev in Iceland: All Things Fall Apart

Political-Philosophic Letter,* News & Letters, *November 1986

The collapse of the hastily-called Reagan-Gorbachev "pre-summit" in Iceland—which turned out to be the real summit—is the most ominous happening in this changed world. It actually opens up the race to the nuclear holocaust, meticulously prepared for. It is this precisely—the need for highly technological preparations on the level of who can be superior in space—that is making the bi-polar nuclear behemoths walk so softly, making sure that the blaming of each other for the collapse of the summit is shrouded in a note of hope.

I The Negotiations and the Trap

As against the flim-flam man in the White House, who has been called the Great Communicator, and the head man in the Kremlin, who has passed himself off as from a totally new generation, it becomes necessary to examine what did happen at Reykjavik. Why was the collapse such a total surprise not only to observers, but to Reagan himself?

So confident was Reagan that he was going to have another Geneva-type summit capitulation from Gorbachev, who he felt was nowhere as sophisticated as he, that Reagan came to the summit empty-handed. On the other hand, Gorbachev came well prepared, precisely because he had taken the measure of Reagan's immovable stance on Star Wars at the Geneva summit.

It began with bringing his beautiful wife, Raisa, with him for public relations chores. After all, Iceland, where the U.S. has a nuclear installation, is much closer to Russia's border than to the U.S.'s, and is a country with which Russia wants to have very good relations.

At the summit itself Gorbachev read a prepared, collective statement from the Politburo. One more thing was left. He convinced Reagan to have unscheduled meetings of their respective arms control specialists, who worked through the night to 6:30 a.m. Statements were coming from both sides that made it clear that arms control was the *issue, and that they were getting so far on that, that all other issues from Afghanistan to human rights were forgotten.*

It was at this point that Gorbachev sprang the trap that would make Reagan responsible for the break-up of this "pre-summit." That is to say, he made it clear that all the radical things they had agreed upon concerning reductions in intermediate and intercontinental ballistic missiles were all a "package" which depended on leaving Star Wars at the laboratory stage. Down came Reagan's Great Illusion, down came Gorbachev's package, down came whatever hopes the masses of the world had that we weren't headed for nuclear holocaust. Indeed, in this week that was, all things fell apart. This included those which had no direct connection with the summit, as was seen when the U.S. C-123 cargo plane, with arms for the Nicaraguan counter-revolutionaries, was shot down over Nicaragua.

As if that were not enough, the natural disaster of the El Salvador earthquake—which the U.S. certainly could not be blamed for—still revealed how deadly is the U.S. embrace of a colonial country. The devastation was so great that the guerrilla rebel army unilaterally declared it would not attack and asked for similar action on the part of the government. Whereupon, both the U.S.-backed army and the U.S.-chosen President Duarte gave a resounding "No" as their answer. Indeed, Secretary of State Shultz went there not merely to announce U.S. aid, but to "warn" against the revolutionaries "taking advantage" of this disaster.

II The Aftermath: First Reactions and the Whiteout

Whatever shock and rage Reagan displayed to his close entourage on his way from the Hofdi House Summit to the U.S. airbase was well wrapped in a mixture of superpatriotism and light jokes by the time he addressed the assembled airmen, uttering words about being so glad to be "at home."

As against this utter subjectivism, Gorbachev's first statement was objectively framed and full of internationalism. He even used the Chernobyl nuclear disaster to show not only the lessons they themselves had learned from it, but what Russia had as well learned from the International Atomic Energy Agency in Vienna, which resulted in the establishment of international machinery on nuclear safety: "We must take steps away from the nuclear abyss...we were guided by the motive of freeing the European peoples from nuclear catastrophe..." Whereupon he proceeded to talk of the summit and how the Russians were for "on-site verification," as against the U.S. attempt to actually replace the Antiballistic Missile Treaty (1972).[2]

Gorbachev concluded that it "was not just a matter of reducing arms as was the case with SALT I and II and other treaties. But here we were speaking about the actual elimination of nuclear weapons in a relatively short time."

And it is this message that he had his "diplomats" present not only to the Third World, who he takes for granted will support him, but within the NATO nations as well.

That his framework will go far could be seen right in Washington, D.C., with the visit of West Germany's Chancellor Helmut Kohl, who spoke of the necessity of resuming the negotiations with Gorbachev,

So insoluble is the contradiction between trying to present the collapse as both a great victory for Reagan and as a non-collapse for the West as a whole—a veritable "whiteout," not only for what actually had happened, but of the orders to Weinberger at the Pentagon for a helter-skelter rush with Star Wars—that there has been as well a return to the old theme of the alleged backwardness of Russian technology, which cannot possibly catch up with the U.S.

III The Backwardness of Russia or of Science?

In the deluge of articles on just how backward the Russians are on computers, the indispensable tool for space wars, there has been but one article disputing the alleged backwardness by Daniel Greenberg, the editor and publisher of the Washington-based newsletter, *Science and Government Report*, who wrote for *U.S. News and World Report* (10/20/86). Mr. Greenberg stressed that we better not forget that Russia beat us into space with Sputnik. (At that time

2 See Tom Wicker, "Origins of the Collapse," *New York Times* 10/19/86, which deals with article 5 of the ABM treaty which is being given a "reinterpretation" by the Reagan administration.

Khrushchev was having a good time at the U.S.'s expense, saying that they had sent a Volkswagen into space while the U.S. had only sent a grapefruit.) Greenberg notes that right now the Russians are "building the biggest ever atom smasher, and it is clear that their theoretical mathematicians and physicists rank with the world's finest."

But even Greenberg is so busy pointing to the backwardness of Russia in agriculture that he does not seem to recognize that the superior technology of U.S. agriculture has not stopped it from having a total crisis that has brought the family farmer back to Depression days.

In Russia, what had suddenly brought mathematics into the center of everything at the end of the 1920s was the fact that what they thought would bring them everything, would bring them "socialism"—the Plan—*brought them a crisis as big as the 1929 Great Depression had brought to private capitalism. Bureaucratic planning was no more than a moment of the chaos of the market. In the 1930s, in the middle of the first 5-Year Plan, they suddenly "discovered" Marx's Mathematical Manuscripts. Instead of seeing the genius of Marx in defining Plan as "despotic plan of capital"—the barrack discipline over the workers on the production line—they embraced the law of value. The mathematicians' clinging to the formalism of Newton flowed from Stalin's christening the law of value as "socialism."*[3]

IV More Big Power Maneuvers

The most ominous part of that summit collapse is that Russia and the U.S. are so much alike that these two nuclear titans are twins. Though one is state-capitalist and one is private capitalist, both practice exploitative capital/labor relations. Though not identical, both are creating some loopholes that seem to contain a ray of hope one moment, to be dashed apart the next moment. Witness the fantastic new expulsion of 55 Russian diplomats (added to the 25 who were just expelled). Whereupon Gorbachev has now expelled not only five Americans, but ordered all Soviet employees in the American Embassy in Russia not to work there any longer.

Much more serious is the search on the part of both Russia and the U.S. to more closely align science with its "application" on the production line.

What has followed the Reagan-Gorbachev summit is that on Oct. 16 the leading Soviet mathematician and science administrator, the Ukrainian Gury I. Marchuk, was elected president of the Academy of Sciences. What is interesting about Marchuk is that back in 1964 he organized the computer center and was then transferred to what they devoted a whole city (*Akademgorod*) to, the

---

3 See *The Fetish of High Tech and Karl Marx's Unknown Mathematical Manuscripts*, *News & Letters*, 1984.

research center in Novosibirsk. That far back he became the deputy director. Now this mathematician, computer-wise, is the head of it all.

The whole so-called reforms of Gorbachev are all directed to making inseparable scientific research and the production line. In a word, we are back at sweated labor and how much unpaid labor you can get from any worker depending on the speed of the machine.

The mad dream is that Reagan with his computers is sure the U.S. can get "there" first and destroy Russia before the Russian laggard can reach the U.S.

Each nuclear Behemoth is aiming for superiority, for single mastery of the world. *This helter-skelter unabated "computerized" arms race must be stopped now! The stakes are nothing short of humanity itself.*

—October 22, 1986

CHAPTER 13

On Mao's China

Dunayevskaya wrote extensively on China from the 1950s into the 1980s. Topics included Mao's history as revolutionary before coming to power, "The Hundred Flowers Campaign," the Great Leap Forward, the Sino-Soviet Split, the "Great Proletarian Cultural Revolution," as well as post-Mao China. Her major writings on Mao include two chapters added to editions of Marxism and Freedom, *"The Challenge of Mao Zedong" (Chapter 17) and "Cultural Revolution or Maoist Reaction?" (Chapter 18), as well as "The Thought of Mao Zedong," Chapter 5 of* Philosophy and Revolution.

The documents presented below include discussion of Mao's philosophical writings, writings on China in the mid-1950s and on the Sino-Indian War, as well as Maoism's outreach to Indonesia. For Dunayevskaya's writings on the Sino-Soviet split, see Chapter 14.

Only Freedom Can Solve the Crisis

News & Letters, ***July 16, 1957***

According to late reports, it seems likely that the State Department will finally allow American newsmen to travel to China so that the American public may at last receive "first hand" reports about what goes on there.

At the same time, Chiang Kai-Shek, writing from his crisis-torn island of Formosa, has just published a book in America, in which he makes what amounts to a last plea to be restored to power on the Chinese mainland, "in the interests of democracy."

Nothing and no one can whitewash the corruption and oppression of Chiang Kai-Shek's regime. The truth of Communist China's totalitarianism cannot be learned from him, nor from those who speak for him. But it can be glimpsed from an examination of the conflicts within China itself. It can further be approached by an analysis of what Communist Boss, Mao Zedong, revealed in his speech on "Contradictions," that was released to the world on June 18.

State-Capitalist

The Chinese Communist regime is a state-capitalist society. It was born out of the revolution against the corrupt feudal-capitalistic society under Chiang

Kai-shek. There is no doubt that when Chiang and his Guomindang regime were overthrown, a much wider base was created for the new state-capitalist regime. Chinese capitalism was finally stripped of its feudal trappings and its corrupt warlords. Honest or otherwise, however, state-capitalism is an exploitative society. Exploitation of man by man has its own consequences.

3 Characteristics

The three primary characteristics of this development in China are:

(1) Forced labor to build water conservation projects, highways and railways. Forced labor for excavation and construction of defense works, and timber felling. This mass labor army was supposed to consist mainly of "counter-revolutionaries." But it was soon clear that there were not enough "bureaucrat capitalists" and "imperialists" to fill the mass labor projects, and the rebellious workers were its actual base.

(2) Under state-capitalism, the function of free, or trade unionized labor, is not to increase its material benefits, but to fulfill the production quotas set by the State. Indeed, the Constitution openly boasts that the function of the trade unions is to increase production, raise labor productivity, and achieve the production plans of the State.

(3) Since 80% of the work, in a country as underdeveloped as China, is agriculture, the State must ask for what it calls "voluntary cooperativization." That is to say, instead of outright confiscation of the land from its landlords, or its collectivization, only the land of those landlords who did not cooperate with the Chinese Communist government was confiscated.

Otherwise, as in industry, so in agriculture, there are private farms as well as State farms, as well as joint private-State farms. The lot of the Chinese peasant is still the bowl of rice, and no more.

"Let 100 Flowers Bloom"

The internal crisis, in this limited state capitalism, has produced dissatisfaction among all layers of the population, including the intellectuals. The totality of the crisis produced Mao Zedong's sensational speech, which ordered "Let a Hundred Flowers Bloom, Let a Hundred Schools of Thought Contend."

From this abstract freedom, however, Mao's particular totalitarianism was showing badly. Despite the many "flowers," it seems that one, *and only one*, party, the Chinese Communist Party, must rule. Mao rejected the two-party system as a bad capitalist plot. It is clear that the so-called democratic, that is, capitalist, parties can exist only insofar as they do not contend for power by any test of vote, much less of mass strength. Thus has forced labor produced its own type of forced brain work.

Mao "Discovers" Contradiction

Mao Zedong, ruler of China, Chairman of the Chinese Communist Party, and leader of its Army, caused a world sensation with his speech, "On the Correct Handling of Contradictions Among the People." The speech was made to a closed session of the Supreme State Conference, on February 27th. It was not released until June 18th, after substantial "editing."

It would seem, from the unofficial version of the speech, which appeared in Poland, that Mao had claimed to be the discoverer of contradictions. He stated that "Marx and Engels did not know about these problems! Lenin mentioned them but did not enlarge upon them."

In the officially released text, Mao toned down the "originality" of his discovery by attributing it to "Marxist philosophy." He magnanimously stated that "Lenin gave a very clear exposition of this law" (of contradiction).

The official text might as well have made him the sole discoverer of the law of contradiction, since there is no doubt whatever that, in the manner in which Mao expounds this law of development, *it is neither Marxist nor Leninist. It is revisionist.*

Not by accident, there isn't a single mention of the whole philosophy of which contradiction is a part: *Dialectics.* Marxian dialectical philosophy *centers* around contradiction as the motive power of development, but it *does not stop there.* The contradictions of capitalist society are resolved only through the attainment of freedom.

Marxist-Humanism

It is the *solution* of contradiction which distinguishes Marxism. At one and the same time, Marx took contradiction out of its all-too-general context, concretized it as the law of development of *capitalist* society, and showed that the class struggle, in overcoming the antagonism between worker and capitalist, will *thereby* abolish the class structure of society. *This specific contribution characterizes Marxian dialectical philosophy,* or *Humanism,* as *the theory of liberation.*

Mao, on the other hand, trying to pass off Chinese state-capitalism as something that is socialist, is compelled to tread along two diversionary paths: (1) the objectively-based antagonism between exploiter and exploited, he transforms from an antagonistic contradiction into a contradiction which, "if properly handled, can be transformed into a non-antagonistic one and resolved in a peaceful way"; (2) out of the differences within the capitalist class, he creates a new antagonism between bad capitalists, whom he calls "bureaucrat capitalists" and "imperialists," and good capitalists, whom he calls "the national bourgeoisie."

To deny that contradictions exist in China, says Mao, "is to fly in the face of objective reality." That most certainly is true, but it is this, precisely, which is the supreme manifestation of the class character of the Chinese regime.

Because he tries to reconcile the restless Chinese masses to the existence of capitalism, Mao has been compelled to redefine everything, including the concept, "the people."

Who are "People?"

It seems that the people are not the working people, but all those who accept the Chinese Communist regime, which Mao defines as the leadership of the Communist Party *and* its Army. That is how he smuggled the capitalists into the concept, "the people." Mao says: "In our country, the contradiction between the working class and the national bourgeoisie is a contradiction among the people. The class struggle waged between the two is, by and large, a class struggle within the ranks of the people."

That fits neatly into the concept that the National Association of Manufacturers and the Administration, as well as Reuther, in this country call "a people's capitalism." Just as what we need to redefine in this country is not capitalism, but the class character of the labor leadership, so what needs redefining in China is not "the people," but the class nature of Chinese Communism.

Contradictions—With and without Mao

Mao warns: "Certain people in our country were delighted when the Hungarian events took place. They hoped that something similar would happen in China, that thousands upon thousands of people would demonstrate in the streets against the People's Government."

He thinks that by admitting contradictions, which he says is facing up to objective reality to the extent of recognizing limited strikes, he will thereby avoid open revolution. That accounts for his pride in "discovering" the law of contradiction. Mao thinks that the translation of the law of contradiction into Chinese will make everybody happy as if to recognize the crisis is to solve it.

Now, it is not Mao, in the year 1957, who discovered the law of contradiction. Nor is it Marx who did. Marx recreated it from the great bourgeois philosopher, Hegel, who in the period 1807 to 1831 gave this law its most profound interpretation in *The Phenomenology of Mind, Science of Logic,* and *The Encyclopedia of Philosophical Sciences.*

What Marx did that was *new* was to show that it summed up the law of capitalist development, all of which he proved in the three volumes of *Capital.* In brief, Marx held that, whereas all class societies developed through contradiction, *only* under capitalism does it reach the intensity whereby it can be transformed into its opposite—freedom from capitalist wage slavery. Capitalism, he maintained, produces its own gravedigger in the working class.

Transformation into Opposite

Just as Marx concretized this law for capitalism, so Lenin concretized it for the working-class organization itself. At the outbreak of World War I, when the Second (Socialist) International betrayed the working class, Lenin demonstrated that it was due to the fact that a part of the working class had become transformed into its opposite—the aristocracy of labor that profited from the super-profits of imperialism, and thereby undermined the working class nature of the Second International.

In a different historic period—World War II—this is what happened to Communism, which became transformed from its Marxist liberating base into its opposite, a state capitalist, totalitarian philosophy.

Chinese and Russian Revisions

Mao admits that, just as under ordinary private capitalism, the basic contradictions in Chinese society "are still those between the relations of production and the productive forces, and between the superstructure and the economic base." This is precisely the Achilles' heel upon which Mao's father superiors—the Russian theoreticians—also fell, when, in 1943, they were compelled to revise Marx's economic theory of value.

No matter by what name it is called, capitalistic relationships, at the point of production, reveal their exploitative nature. Why Russia "chose" to revise Marx's *economic* theories, and why China "chose" to revise Marx's *philosophy*, is due both to the totality of the *world* crisis and to the important industrial differences between the two countries.

Russia has become an important industrial land, a country that *possesses* values. China is a vast underdeveloped land, whose main possession is not the machine, but the human being.

600,000,000 Humans

It is precisely this backwardness which has pushed China forward to pose—only to pose but not to solve—its crisis is *human* terms. Six hundred million human beings will not long be bottled up in contradictions. They are sure to find the true revolutionary solution.

"Let 100 Flowers Bloom...But Only One Party Rule"

News & Letters, *August 1957*

A reader of my article on China and Mao Zedong's perversion of Marxian philosophy (see "Only Freedom Can Solve the Crisis," *News & Letters*, July 16, 1957) writes: "I fail to see how you can class Mao's speech on Contradictions as the same species of totalitarianism as Stalin's speeches on monolithism. Where Stalin's word was law, Mao invites disagreement with his proclamation: 'Let 100 flowers bloom. Let 100 schools of thought contend.'"

Communist Double-talk vs. Totalitarian Reality

I will not take time out to tell the reader what he can hear daily on the radio—how short-lived was this invitation of Mao's and how the official Chinese Communist press has now reversed itself. Claiming that "counter-revolutionaries" were taking advantage of the freedom of the press, the Communists put a stop to it.

Anyone acquainted with Communist double-talk should have been able to foresee this development, since the very speech which allegedly granted freedom to "100 schools of thought" also proclaimed that *one Party, and only one Party, the Communist Party*, may rule China.

Transformation into Opposite

There is no doubt that at one time the Chinese Communist Party was a workingmens' party, and that Mao Zedong had been a revolutionary who, for two full decades, had fought for the overthrow of the feudal-capitalistic regime of Chiang Kai-Shek. But once the party won power, it was not long before it became transformed into its opposite.

It is not the old moral question of "power corrupts and absolute power corrupts absolutely." *But State power, when it becomes one with economic power at the point of production, of necessity becomes the boss over production.* That is what Lenin saw at the *birth* of Communist State power and he warned his colleagues, the former revolutionaries, against "a passion for bossing." It was in vain—in vain not alone for Stalin, the bureaucrat, but for the *whole* Russian Communist Party.

The same transformation into opposite—of a one-time working-class party becoming the ruling Party which plans production—is taking place in China. *The Chinese working people refuse to accept this counterfeit. It is this which compelled Mao to admit that contradictions exist in China.* To do otherwise, he says, would be to "fly in the face of reality." That most certainly is true, and as I pointed out in the last issue, "it is this precisely which is the supreme manifestation of the class character of the Chinese regime."

The Fetishism of One-Party Rule

The fascists were the first *openly* to proclaim One-Party rule, but the Communists *practiced* that before the rise of Nazism. One learned from the other during the Depression which shook the world to its foundations. Thus, to win workers, the fascists named their philosophy "National *Socialism*." The deceit was only in the name, for no one could mistake the anti-Semitic, anti-union, anti-democratic Nazi writings for anything written by Karl Marx, the founder of modern socialism.

In the case of Russia and China, on the other hand, the whole State power is mobilized to shroud the name and works of Marx in its Communist (more truly state-capitalist) vise. *That is to say, Communism tries to keep the theory of liberation known as Marxism imprisoned in its own perverse philosophy that State property equals socialism.* In truth, it is the State property which has transformed what was once a working-class party, the Communist Party, into its complete opposite, the *One Party State Power. Therein lays the whole corruption of Communism, that is to say, the full exploitation of the working class by the totalitarian State power.*

The Haughty Vassal of State Power

As a social type, the state-capitalist individual who calls himself a Communist has one thing in common with the "self-estranged spirit" that the great German philosopher, Hegel, described. It is his relationship to state power. Hegel wrote, "Such a type is the haughty vassal. He is active in the interests of the state power, and thus completes the inversion of reality and thought, their entire estrangement the one from the other...What is found out in this sphere is that neither the concrete realities, state power and wealth, nor their determinate conceptions, good and bad, nor the consciousness of good and bad...possess real truth; it is found that all these moments are inverted and transmuted the one into the other, and each is the opposite of itself."

This, dear reader who sees a difference between Stalin and Mao, includes *both* Mao and Stalin. The one thing both failed to see in "contradictions" in "each being the opposite of itself," is that it *included* them above all. For just as the supreme manifestation of the capitalistic law of value is the worker paid at minimum, so the supreme manifestation of totalitarianism is the One-Party rule: Mao or Stalin, fascist or Communist.

The "Philosophy" of the Yenan Period: Mao Perverts Lenin

Excerpt from "The Challenge of Mao Zedong," *Marxism and Freedom,* 1964 Edition

> We are opposed to the die-hards in the revolutionary ranks...We are opposed to the idle talk of the 'left.'
>
> MAO ZEDONG

The drastic change from the first "Soviet" period (1928–34) to the second (Yenan) period (1935–1945) was naturally questioned by many Communists. When some in his "Red Army" called the merger with the Chiang Kai-shek regular Army "counter-revolutionary," Mao replied that they were "dogmatists." This political struggle underlies the period of Mao's alleged original contribution to the philosophy of Marxism.

Objective research has since cast considerable doubt as to the date (1937) when the essays "On Practice" and "On Contradiction" were written; they weren't published until 1950–52.[1] We, however, are willing to accept the official date for their writing at face value because they are objectively, subjectively, for yesteryear and for today, so very Maoist that it does not matter that Mao may have back-dated them to make them appear prescient or re-written them to suit his present style. The point is, in order to sell the policy of class collaboration, Mao evidently thought a frontal attack on "dogmatists" would be insufficient. Hence he chose the form of "Philosophic Essays." These are so filled with empty abstractions that it is difficult to discover either his subject or his aim.

In "On Practice," Mao writes, "The epistemology of dialectical materialism... regards human knowledge as being at no point separable from practice." If knowledge is at no point separable from practice, he would have done well to tell us what practice he is talking about. But, no, Mao is anxious to make this reduction of theory to "practicality" appear to be based on nothing less authoritative than Lenin's *Philosophic Notebooks.* Mao quotes Lenin's sentence, "Practice is more than cognition (theoretical knowledge)." He fails to tell us, however, that Lenin was only restating Hegel's analysis of the relationship of the Practical Idea to the Theoretical Idea before the two are united, as Lenin puts it, "precisely in the theory of knowledge."

---

1 "How Original Is 'Maoism'?" by Arthur A. Cohen in *Problems of Communism,* November, December, 1961.

Far from theory being reduced to "practicality," Lenin asserts, in the very section from which Mao quoted one sentence, the following: "Alias: Man's consciousness not only reflects the objective world, but creates it." Since this preceded the quotation Mao used, it would have seemed impossible for even a Confucian like Mao so totally to have misunderstood its meaning—unless, of course, he had set out deliberately to pervert Lenin. In any case, the world the sophist Mao created was for such a low purpose—to compel obedience to a new united front with Chiang—that one hesitates to dignify the writing as "philosophy."

Only because this state-capitalist tyrant rules over no less than 650 million souls is one compelled to attempt an analysis of his "original contribution to Marxism."

Evidently, Mao failed to convince his hearers or his readers (we are not told which) because he soon followed with still another "philosophical essay," once again directed against the "dogmatists," and this time called "On Contradiction." We are told that it was delivered as a lecture at the Anti-Japanese Military and Political College in Yenan, August, 1937.

In "On Contradiction" Mao used some "practical" examples. This has at least one virtue: it shows exactly how he has to rewrite his own previous period of rule in order "to balance" the mistakes of "dogmatists" against those of the Guomindang. It turns out that only "*after* 1927 (my emphasis—R.D.), the Guomindang turned in the opposite direction" from the "revolutionary and vigorous" period of united front in 1925. The defeat of the Chinese Revolution is now laid at the door of "Chen Duxiuism," that is to say, the revolutionary Trotskyist leader, Chen Duxiu! Even the loss of "Soviet China" (now called merely "revolutionary bases") is blamed, not on Chiang's extermination campaigns, but on the "mistakes of adventurism."

"Since 1935," Mao pompously continues amidst a great deal of pretentious phrase—mongering on the philosophic meaning of "Contradictions," "it (the Communist Party) has rectified these mistakes and led the new anti-Japanese united front." It follows that after "the Sian Incident in December, 1936, it (the Guomindang) made another turn," obviously in the "right revolutionary direction" since they are once again in a united front. In "On Contradiction," this demagogic class collaborationist says benignly, "We Chinese often say: 'Things opposed to each other complement each other.'"

So permeated to the marrow of his bones is Mao with Confucianism that it is doubtful he is even conscious that he is thereby perverting in toto the Hegelian-Marxian theory of development through contradiction. Seen in all its profundity for the first time by Lenin, in 1915, as he re-read and commented upon Hegel's *Science of Logic,* this development through contradiction, transformation into opposite, helped Lenin get to the root of the collapse of established Marxism, the Second International. Blind to the developing oppositions, contradictions, antagonisms, Mao on the other hand invented a "truly original" division in the concept of contradiction, which he called "Principal Aspect of the Contradiction." This division between "the principal contradiction" and "the principal aspect of contradiction" permits Mao to make as complete a hash of philosophy as he has previously made of history. Thus it turns out that under certain conditions, "even principal contradictions are relegated temporarily to a secondary, or subordinate, position" and, because of "uneven developments" and "mutual transformations," the economic basis becomes "subordinated" while "political and cultural reforms become the principal and decisive factors." Trying to make up for this insipid subjectivism, Mao proceeds to tell his readers that Communists "of course" remain materialists since, "as a whole," they see that "material things determine spiritual things." All one can say of such a hodgepodge is what Kant said of "the cosmological proof," that it was "a perfect nest of thoughtless contradictions."

A recent traveler to China cited what a local party secretary from Shensi said: "Through the study of theory, I clearly understood the principles of uninterrupted revolution and of revolution by stages and put them into concrete application in pig breeding." Senseless as the local party secretary's statement is, it is only the logical conclusion of "The Leader's" reduction of theory to "practice" compelling the Chinese to follow his dictum that "dogmas are more useless than cow dung."

Before, however, we flee in disgust from the vulgarities that pass for "philosophy," and become too anxious to dismiss what totalitarian China lovingly calls "Mao's thought," let us bear in mind his present power. Let us remember, also, that when Mao made the Chinese Communist Party accept the new united front with Chiang and initiated his "three-thirds" principle—that one-third Communist Party members, one-third Guomindang, and one-third non-party people constitute the administration in Communist areas—the fight against Japan stiffened. This was the period when visiting foreign journalists, whose cultural standards were greater than those of Mao's cohorts, were impressed with his "exciting speeches on culture." Wearied of the Guomindang corruption and its ineffectualness in fighting Japan, they were impressed by the Communists, not only in the fight against Japan, but in the dedication "to go to the people," i.e., to establish schools among the peasants in remote areas, and proceed with agricultural reforms. Still others, including many of the bourgeoisie and landlords, were attracted by the moderate agricultural program, and hence many anti-Communists began accepting the Chinese Communists as mere "agrarian reformers." Mao contributed nothing to Marxian philosophy, and denuded its politics of its class content. But he certainly carved out an original road to power.

∴

Sino-Indian War Reveals Relationship of Ideology to State-Capitalist Imperialism

Political Letter, **December 8, 1962**

The sudden, spontaneous unity of the Indian people, born out of opposition to China's invasion of their borders, has no doubt been instrumental in staying the hand of Mao, at least temporarily. The fact that this may have coincided also with his original military plans to invade on two fronts, one for bargaining *and* gaining support from "the uncommitted nations," and the other front for keeping as part of China, can in no way diminish the significance of the *new* factor of Indian unity *from below, unled, and emerging despite the attempted brainwashing by the Nehru-Menon apologetics for Mao's China, over the entire period since independence.*

In *The Christian Science Monitor* (11/27/62), Sharokh Sabavala writes: "Contributions to the defense fund in cash, gold, and work continue uninterrupted. On this front, it is interesting to note that it is the poorest in the land, the outcasts, the dispossessed, and the underemployed who lead the queues of contributors, giving, in many cases, all their meagre savings to prove that freedom, *even without bread,* is a most precious heritage." (My emphasis.)

This very love of freedom compels the drawing of a balance sheet of 15 years of Indian independence, during which bourgeois India has proceeded in its plodding way (as China has proceeded with "leaps") without regard for the creativity of the masses which made independence from imperialist rule possible, and is presently saving India from the collapse upon which Mao counted.

I do not mean immediate and utter collapse—not even Mao could consider a border war to cause a whole subcontinent to buckle under; I mean the kind of chaos and confusion which would have made possible "very fruitful work," *within* India, for the Maoist wing of the Indian Communist Party.

Instead, it brought about a national unity not seen except in the struggle for independence from British imperialism, and so popular a revulsion against China and a self-sustaining resistance, "even without bread," that not only Menon had to resign, but Nehru remains in power on the condition that, instead of laying down (and erratically at that) Congress Party policy, he now follows it.

In a word, it may consolidate capitalist India, bring it into the Anglo-American imperialist orbit, have a prolonged war with China, which, whether victorious or otherwise, would once again change nothing fundamental in the relations within the country, so that neither freedom nor bread will be the possessions of the courageous Indian people.

Whether in the American orbit, or the Chinese, *or* "neutral," India must answer the question: What happens after? Why did independence from British rule not lead to a non-exploitative society in India and fraternal international relations with the *peoples* of the world, instead of resulting in continued class rule and a "neutrality" that acquiesced in China's conquest of Tibet and all its consequences, ideologically and militarily. That has now made it possible for Mao to claim Ladakh as needed "defense" for his new road linking Tibet with China, not to mention the propaganda theme against India for "tying itself to the war chariot of United States imperialism."

The obvious aspects of the China-India war—the fact that China did the invading, and that India was compelled to go to "the West" for military aid (even as she is still trying to get some from Russia) cannot change the objective fact that *the entry of American imperialism means that the Sino-Indian relations will never be the same whether or not the war is resumed.*

The point at issue, however, is the class nature of India itself.

India since Independence

India was the first country to gain its independence from British imperialism and thus, in 1947, open a new Third World that was to stretch from Asia to the Middle East, and from Africa to Latin America. Since all newly independent countries born in the next decade, or 13 years, had all emerged out of *national* movements striving to free themselves from Western imperialism, the unifying link predominated over the divisions *within* this post-war world and seemed indeed capable of forging a new path for all mankind.

Both because it was one of the richest in culture and past traditions, and the first to gain its independence, India seemed destined to play a central role on the Asian continent. As the African continent also sought to use Gandhism,[2]

2 Gandhism means both much more, and much less, than passive nonviolent mass resistance. From Gandhi's first introduction of *santughara* and the resulting British massacre at Amritsar in 1919, which coincided in world affairs with the Russian Revolution and the attempts in India to start a Marxist movement which he fought, to Gandhi's role in the post-World War II movement he finally led to victory and thus became the prototype of the new nationalist revolutionary in Africa—there lies a quarter of a century in need of analysis. This is not the place to attempt it.

or the non-violent mass resistance method, to gain freedom, India's world role shone so brightly that it dimmed the *other truth, that no fundamental change in human relations followed independence.* The dominant Congress Party,[3] which had succeeded in uniting all classes in the struggle against foreign domination, first began showing its true *class* nature by leaving production relations, in the city or the country, basically unchanged.

India continued to be the land of villages, with an outmoded agriculture, overladen with an entrenched landlord class, and a halting, partial industrialization that was grafted on top of the semi-feudal relations. It was further both overburdened and undermined by the Hindu caste system that has remained changeless through the millennia. Back in the 19th century, Hegel designated it as "the philosophy of unfreedom."

It is true that, politically, there was *both* independence from Britain *and* a parliamentary democracy established so that, in law, caste is not "recognized." In life, unfortunately, it remains dominant so that slums in the city, with their countless unemployed; the hungry villages, with their sacred cows and unsacred disregard for human lives, remain the most characteristic features of "the Indian way of life."

Every leader in the new Third World seems to consider himself a "socialist"—from Menon to Nasser, from Mao to Nkrumah, not to mention the "Marxist-Leninist-till-the-day-I-die" Castro. But, obviously, it is not the *human* difference these leaders are concerned with, but the State Plan and some statistics about the "rate of economic growth." Even that admirer of the Indian way of life, Barbara Ward, admits that "large programs of public investment under the Plans...have given Indian private enterprise the best decade in its history."[4] But the standard of life remains the lowest in the world—$60 per capita per annum; the average span of life is a mere 26 years, and the unemployed are countless. Even with the lush profits, Indian investment is only about half of the Chinese rate of investment (10% as against 20% of national income).

China after Independence

It is here that the entry of China, two years after India's independence, quickly took away from India its status as a "beacon for the underdeveloped lands." It is

3 One other role for which Gandhi will go into history is hardly ever mentioned, and yet it will endear him more to future generations than the role he is famous for. This "hidden" role is his recognition that "The Party" in power is corruptible. Though he passed on his mantle of leadership to Nehru, he himself refused to take a position of power, and urged that others too must stay out of power and look at the ruling Congress Party, their own, with "outside" eyes.

4 Barbara Ward, "The Rich Nations, the Poor Nations."

true that in Mao's China, the state, *and not the people*, rules over production, in agriculture as in industry. But once it drove out Chiang Kai-shek, China did experience an agricultural revolution, and did not have to compete with private vested interests when it established its Five Year Plans. Above all, it had what the Indian rulers did not and would not have—a usurped banner of Marxist liberation. Up to the "Great Leap Forward," which turned out to be state regimentation in forced barrack-like "communes"—or, more precisely put, up to the *failure* of the great Leap Forward in 1959, there was no doubt that on every front, from agricultural reform to rapid industrialization, from the prestige of its own hard-won victory through guerrilla war to encouragement of national liberation movement, stretching from Algeria to Cuba, armed with the banner of Marxist liberation, China was winning as against India, both the struggle for the minds of men and actual adherents in this new Third World.[5]

We need not stop here to demonstrate how false is the claim of Mao to any "Marxism." Friends should reread the special supplement on "Mao Zedong, From the Beginning of Power to the Sino-Soviet Dispute"[6] to get new insights into the present war with India as well. All I want to say here is that, despite China's setback, she does not fear, at this moment, economic competition from India. Those who think that, if it were not for the defeat of the fantastic attempt to leap to 20th-century industrialism in a single year, Mao would not have embarked on his present imperialist adventure, will once again be caught blindfolded *both* as to the expected fair harvest this year *and, above all, the possible breakthrough in the nuclear field in 1963*.

Once India acquiesced in China's conquest of Tibet, the road linking Tibet to China, which caused the latter to cross Indian territory to build, seemed a "natural." Nehru disputes that they had crossed Indian territory to build it, but the truth is that, following the old line of imperialist secrecy, the seemingly endless correspondence between himself and Zhou Enlai, over the years, on that one point remains hidden from the masses, Whatever the truth, it was done behind the backs of the masses, Chinese and Indian, and Nehru's illusions about Mao's intentions have nothing to do with objective reality.

Takashi Oka, writing about the "Paradox in the Himalayas,"[7] compares Mao's present Chinese empire to that existing "1300 years ago, in the spacious days of the Tang dynasty...The Chinese Communist armies have already filled out the boundaries of Imperial China at its zenith, except Outer Mongolia and Siberian and Trans-Pamir areas lost a century ago to Russian Tsars."

---

5 *Nationalism, Communism, and the Afro-Asian Revolutions.*

6 *News & Letter*, January, 1962.

7 *Christian Science Monotor,* Nov. 26, 1962.

The Sino-Soviet Dispute

Offhand, it may appear that the Sino-Soviet dispute has no relationship to the China-India war. Or, if it has, Russia is "on the side of India." Nehru is not the only one that wishes to leave that impression. President Kennedy's special emissary to India, Averill Harriman, appeared on NBC this Sunday, and approved of the role Nehru is trying to play. This is not only a question of "tactics." Ever since the Sino-Soviet dispute started, many "specialists" have seen a possible realignment of all "advanced industrial countries" against Chinese pretensions.

Indeed, everyone from de Gaulle to Toynbee has had such contradictory "reasons" as West Europe "extending to the Urals" and Communism being "part of Western Christendom," for clinging to the view that Russia and China will be in opposing war camps at the final showdown. Mao, for his part, has, ever since the "Great Leap Forward," presented himself as "the true Leninist" against "the revisionist" Khrushchev. This has reached its own type of climax during the Cuban crisis, when Beijing's analysis of Russia's withdrawal of missiles amounted to an accusation of betrayal and acting the role of "an appeaser" of American imperialism.

Nothing could be further from the truth. We will limit ourselves here to those three critical points in the Sino-Soviet dispute which affected India. The first is the 20th Congress of the Russian Communist Party, the so-called de-Stalinization congress, which first elaborated the "peaceful co-existence" policy calling attention to "the emergence in the world arena of a group of peace-loving European and Asian states which have proclaimed non-participation in blocs as a principle of their foreign policy," thus creating "a vast peace zone."

Mao acts as if "peaceful co-existence" was a "revisionist" invention of Khrushchev. In fact, however, both the policy of "peaceful co-existence" and its underlying class collaborationism—"the unity of four classes"—was in effect throughout the Sino-Japanese war when Mao Zedong and Chiang Kai-shek collaborated in a "national front." When Mao refurbished this policy in 1954 for the Bandung Conference, Khrushchev took notice of it not alone because it was against Western imperialism, *but also because he read it as Mao's declaration that the whole of the Afro-Asian world was now declared to be his "sphere of influence."* Khrushchev's trip to India followed, and the following year Russia elaborated "peaceful co-existence" as its own theory. *Mao, in turn, read it as Russian "interference" into the Afro-Asian world.* Nevertheless, it was through no accident that the two Communist powers came to the same policy of "peaceful co-existence": it was organic to their state-capitalist class-collaborationist nature.

The re-establishment of Sino-Soviet unity later that year in order to put down the Hungarian Revolution, and the launching of Sputnik No. 1 in October 1957, created grandiose illusions in Mao's China, about both its ability "to skip directly into Communism," and its view that Russia was now strong enough to risk all-out nuclear war with that "paper tiger, the United States." Khrushchev's opposition to both proposals makes Mao refurbish the much misused Marist lexicon, tailored to the Afro-Asian-Latin-American worlds. *The power conflict is transformed by Mao into a "theory of revolution" while Khrushchev moves both theoretically and practically to compete with Mao for this Afro-Asian-Latin-American world,* frowning upon Mao's incursions into Indian territory, elaborating a theory of his own on the new "uncommitted world." This Khrushchev presented at the UN in 1960 first, and then as the Party platform. In 1961, he won a seat at the UN for Outer Mongolia.

The period of 1957–61, the period of rivalry within the Communist orbit, however, showed what could, *and always does, unite them*: it is opposition to the United States. The U-2 spy plane incident in 1960 served as the unifying ingredient then, *even as India's acceptance of military aid from the United States will soon become that unifier again.*

The reason it appears otherwise is that the Cuba crisis paralleled the India-China war and was used by Mao as pretext once again to appear the "Marxist revolutionary," placing Khrushchev in the role of "appeaser." The conflict between Russia and China is as real, *and as power-driven,* as is the rivalry within NATO. And, just as the latter unite in any showdown with the state-capitalist orbit, so does the state-capitalist orbit, *calling itself Communist,* unite in showdown of which of the two nuclear titans will dominate the world.

Two Opposing Ideologies?

Strangest of all blindfolds is the one that covers Nehru's vision. Now that his "neutrality" principle lies as shattered as Bandung's "Five Principles of Co-Existence," co-authored by himself and Zhou Enlai, he has suddenly discovered that Mao wishes "to destroy the Indian way of life." He rolls that phrase off his moral lips as if it were some classless phenomenon instead of so class-ridden and contradictory a chain over so unfinished a revolution that the strains and stresses in the Indian body politic gave Mao the illusion he could have as easy a victory within India as the military victory on its borders. *The fact that the invasion, instead, united India as a nation should give no illusions to Nehru that the masses will forever be satisfied with a sham freedom and no bread.*

The truth is that it was not the classlessness but *the sameness of the class*—that of State Planners—which united Mao and Nehru at Bandung. The respect for "sovereignty of nations" and "non-interference in internal affairs" meant no *foreign* interference in class relations within each country *so long as* the Third World could be a single unit against "the West." Mao still thinks that, on that basis, he can get acquiescence in his grab of Indian territory by many of "the uncommitted nations," as indeed he seems to be doing at the Colombo Conference meeting presently in Sri Lanka.

But if his imperialist ambitions are all too clear, do Nehru's lesser ambitions constitute a different *class* phenomenon? The moment of independence was the moment also of the fratricidal war with Pakistan. (That unresolved conflict was another element in the temptation of Mao to attack.)

There is no doubt that British imperialistic maneuvers and their eternal attempt to break up a country at the moment of independence so as to continue its rule over it helped set up the division between India and Pakistan. It is as true, however, that once the countries did separate, each had a right to its own existence. Gandhi became a martyr when he fought to end the "holy war" and build up fraternal relations. Nehru chose Menon as *his* "holy man" to proclaim Pakistan "Enemy No. 1" for all these 14 years, keeping two-thirds of the Army at the Kashmir site while leaving the borders to China unprotected from that "ally."

Despite its "period of glory"—the 1947–48 Kashmir war—Nehru had not allowed the Army any decisive role in the Indian pattern of life. Despite the fact that he allowed the ultra-conservative Sandhurst-educated officer class to have the Army under its command and play some old imperialist roles—in Korea and in the Congo—Nehru's concept of the role of the army made it subordinate to the civil authorities. In this he fundamentally differs from Mao, who even in the Communist (read: state-capitalist) orbit holds to a special militaristic position. The Chinese Constitution is the only one where not only the "Party" but the Army is made synonymous with the state authority.

This one element that would have created at least the semblance of an ideology in opposition to that expounded in China is now itself a question, since the Anglo-American aid will not only come with political strings attached, but inevitably create its own image internally by raising the Indian Army to a new status. Since Nehru's good anti-military instincts were not backed up by a proletarian class position, he will inevitably give way both to the Anglo-American advice and Indian Army ambitions.

It is true that he is still holding out one hope of not completely falling into the orbit of Western imperialism by counting on Russian aid, but insofar as the Indian masses are concerned, *does it really matter whether it is the Russian or the American nuclear orbit?* Even as a foreign policy, a military line is a derivative, rather than a determinant, of the class relations within the country. IN THIS LIES THE DANGER THAT INDIA MAY STILL CAPITULATE EITHER TO COMMUNIST TOTALITARIANISM OR TO A MILITARY CLIQUE.

Nehru's unique authority in India does not stem from his creation of new relations with the great mass of the Indian people who must bend both to his State Plans and to the private capitalist and entrenched landlord interests. He has been a leader of the struggle for independence from Britain, and he has now been attacked by his Communist ally, and the Indian people have saved him from downfall. His desperate attempt first now to search for a new ideological banner and come up with "the Indian way of life" will create no new world apart from both poles of world capital—the Russo-Soviet or Anglo-American orbits—fighting for world domination. To cling to the class-ridden "Indian way of life" is only one more way of saying "the old cannot be changed"—and, by losing the struggle for the minds of men, losing both India and the new Third World.

It was no accident that in the 15 years since independence, in the 13-year alliance with Mao's China, in the seven years of "Afro-Asian Solidarity Conference," plus the innumerable "neutralist" conferences since, Nehru failed to condemn Russia either for its counter-revolutionary role in putting down the Hungarian Revolt in 1956 or for its unilateral breaking of the nuclear moratorium; acquiesced in China's conquest of Tibet, and bowed sufficiently to the UAR's stand on Israel not to open an embassy there, although he had been among the first to hail its independence. The opportunist, the short-sighted, the self-righteous, the ambivalent in foreign and military policies, was the counterpoint to the so-called socialist, but actually capitalist, exploitative relations internally. The Indian people who have pushed him off his "neutrality" for the Sino-Soviet orbit must now see that he doesn't merely shift over to the Anglo-American orbit, leaving production relations and ideological banner as unchanged as the changeless caste system of "unfreedom."

Indonesian Communism: A Case of World Communism's Decomposition

News & Letters, *October 1965, November 1965*

It is impossible at this moment (October 5) to know whether the coup on September 30, and the counter-coup on October 1, were manifestations of nothing more than divisions within the armed forces in Indonesia, or were indicative of class divisions within the population. There is no doubt that the masses are fed up with a government that, in the 16 years of independence, has failed to make any serious dent in the prevailing poverty, or to achieve basic land reforms, much less carry through an agrarian revolution. Nor has there been any serious industrialization, much less any radical change in the conditions of labor.

The fact that both the rebels and the regular armed forces stressed that President Sukarno is "well" shows how non-revolutionary the attempted coup was. Whether or not the Communists were involved in it, it is they whom the masses will rightly hold to blame for the failure to dislodge Sukarno since the Communists too have, ever since the 1950s, always kowtowed to him. *For their one and overpowering desire for state power is based on the concept of "boring from within." This managerial concept of "taking over" power, the root cause of what successes national Communism has achieved, from Stalin to Mao, is here the root cause of its failure.*

The PKI (Indonesian Communist Party) is the proof that (1) when it comes to desiring state power at all costs, there not only is no fundamental difference between the "revolutionary" Beijing line and the "revisionist" Moscow line, but the multiplicity of roads to be embarked upon is very nearly endless; (2) *so capitalistic is their joint mentality that the one and only road that is completely ruled out is that of proletarian revolution*; and that (3) the shift *from* the proletariat *through* the peasantry *to* the army as the motive force of "revolution" has, in the case of Indonesia, led to the end of the very concept of theory, with the resulting eclecticism producing the wild gyrations from the adventuristic, abortive revolt of 1948 to the current policy of "integrating" the Communists into the Sukarno regime.

Aidit's "Five Devils"

D.N. Aidit, Chairman of the PKI, was, characteristically enough, in Beijing at the time of the latest coup. And, characteristically from the Chinese side, the head of the Chinese delegation to the 45th anniversary celebration of the founding of the Indonesian Communist Party—Peng Zhen—neatly skipped 31 years[8] of that period and began his interpretation after Aidit's return from Beijing in 1950: "Since 1951 the PKI has had a Marxist-Leninist nucleus of leadership headed by Com. Aidit at its center...It stands steadfast in the forefront of the fight...against modern revisionism."

And, just to make sure that standing "steadfast in the forefront" means Aidit's choice of Beijing, not only in the Sino-Soviet conflict, but on *all* foreign policy issues, Peng Zhen threw in some anti-Semitism as well: "Comrades,

8 Fundamentally, of course, there is nothing whatever in common between the Communist Party founded in 1920 (under the impact of the Russian Revolution of 1917, and the work done there by the Dutch Marxist, Hendrik Sneevliet, before the Revolution and in the early years after it) which stood for a socialist reconstruction of society, and the present opportunist Communist Party. Peng Zhen, be it noted, is skipping not only this early Leninist period, but also the Stalinist period beginning with 1928. Obviously, history for him begins only when the Communists came to power in China.

the present international situation is excellent...United States imperialism, the chieftain of world imperialism...is using Israel to threaten the security of the Arab countries...*The Indonesian Communists are at once patriots and proletarian internationalists*." (My emphasis.)

Just how patriotic D.N. Aidit is can be gleaned from his speech[9] at that same May 23rd mass rally in Jakarta which began as follows:

> Your Excellency, President of the Indonesian Republic, the great leader of the Indonesian revolution, beloved Bung (Brother) Karno!...If there is still poverty in Indonesia, which I do not deny, it is...because of the existence of the remnants of imperialism and feudalism and the existence of bureaucratic-capitalists as well as village and off-shore devils.

Obviously, though the Communists "were unanimously determined to implement still more resolutely the revolutionary general line...to realize the national and democratic revolution and march forward to Indonesian socialism," they cannot do so until they overcome the "five devils: (1) Malaysia; (2) the seven village evils; (3) world devil, U.S. imperialism; (4) bureaucrat-capitalists, and (5) modern revisionism."

It turns out, not accidentally, that, since one of the "five devils" is a "world devil," the Indonesian masses must continue to work the harder and "launch more frequent and more stubborn struggles against U.S. imperialism, the world devil and ringleader of all imperialists." And, while approving the "steps taken by President Sukarno and the Indonesian Government against the Trotskyite personalities,"[10] the Communist Party, "thanks to its loyalty to the NASAKOM[11]

---

9 "Intensify Revolutionary Offensive and First Oppose 'Five Devils'" appears in *Beijing Review*, June 4,1965, which also printed Peng Zhen's speech as well as excerpts from President Sukarno's address, "Indonesian C.P. Is a Thoroughly Progressive, Revolutionary Party."

10 Tan Malaka, one of the early founders of the PKI, broke with the Comintern in 1928, when he attacked Bukharin's program and was called by him a "Troyskyite." He carried on revolutionary work in Indonesia, building a new revolutionary party. It was strongly suspected by the Trotskyists that the Communists were responsible for his murder. In any ease, the "Trotskyite personalities" Aidit now refers to are probably the banned Murba (Proletarian) Party, for a new attack on genuine Marxists was begun by Sukarno in 1964–65. For Tan Malaka's position at the 4th Congress of the CI, see the Abridged Report, published in Great Britain, 1923.

11 NASAKOM, the "popular front" now in existence, represents "nas" (nationalists), "a" (religious groups), and "kom" (Communists). Since Sukarno has done away with parliament, asking that "all parties be buried," the manner in which this "popular front" operates actually depends on Sukarno and whom he chooses to include in his "inner cabinet."

idea...has good comrades-in-arms among nationalist and religious believers," not to mention the "two-in-one relations between our people and the armed forces."

Having thus well "integrated" the Communists into the ruling power, Aidit elaborated on the PKI's growth, which, from "less than 8,000 members in 1951, the year of its rebirth, now has more than 3 million members. By adding the 3 million Communist youth of the People's Youth League, the number is more than 6 million. There are about 20 million sympathizers of the Indonesian Communist Party throughout Indonesia...The Indonesian Communist Party belongs not only to the Indonesian Communists but also to the entire people and nation."[12]

The Indonesian masses may rightly question what they ever got out of that: 16 years after independence from Dutch rule, food is still rationed; ten years of friendship with "revolutionary" China, but the Chinese *in Indonesia* remain the exploitative landlords and usurious merchants. *No wonder that in May 1963, just when Zhou Enlai was visiting Sukarno and Sukarno was expressing his "undying friendship," the students and youth of Indonesia rose in spontaneous ANTI-Chinese demonstrations! For, while Aidit may attribute class suffering to "devils," and chose one among these—U.S. imperialism—as the supreme manifestation, THEY know the DIRECT oppressors. Aidit's only answer was "politics moves to the left but the stomach to the right."*

Part II

Against the Proletariat with the "Progressive" Elements

Aidit's conception of "left" politics is that which gives the widest room for maneuverability to the Communist Party thirsting for power. In 1953 when PKI backed the strongly nationalist Sasroamijojo cabinet, it not only saddled the SOBSI (central trade union federation) with a no-strike pledge, but it actually expelled Tan Ling Djie, a party functionary and general secretary of SOBSI's largest affiliated trade union, the Plantation Workers' Union, for his opposition to the no-strike pledge. A decade later, when the PKI became Beijing's strongest

12 In the full speech, New Year's 1964, Aidit evidently was concerned arguing against "dogmatists and revisionists who hold that a good communist party cannot possibly exist without a strong proletariat as its basis." He wished to show that the peasantry is more revolutionary than the proletariat. Nevertheless, the only possible conclusion one could draw is that the *proletariat* ("plus revisionism," it is true) constituted "a mighty strength for the bourgeoisie." See two interesting articles on Indonesian Communism, one by Donald S. Zagoria and the other by Ruth McVey, in the January 1965 issue of *Survey* devoted to "International Communism: the End of an Epoch."

backer, Aidit maintained that "the proletariat plus revisionism constitute a mighty strength of the bourgeoisie." Not that Aidit was in a hurry to overthrow the Indonesian bourgeoisie. On the contrary. So long as the bourgeoisie was "national" and "patriotic," it was welcomed into the NASAKOM.

Indeed the "progressive" elements included also the rich peasantry who, though they exploit those to whom they lease their land, and are usurers besides, do perform "some" work and "can also help the struggle against imperialism." This despite the fact that none described better the actual conditions of the poor peasants: "The Indonesian peasants, who comprise 70% of the population, are still in a position of slavery, living a poverty-stricken and backward life under the oppression of the landlords and usurers...The non-participation of the peasants means the non-participation of the majority of the Indonesian people, and this is a very great weakness in our united national front...Because of this, the primary task of the Communists is to...eliminate the survivals of feudalism, to develop the anti-feudal agrarian revolution."

Lest anyone take this agrarian revolution seriously, however, our expert in doubletalk once again reiterated that one must "first" oppose the "five devils," and "above that"..."the world devil." Meanwhile, and for a long while to come, even into the "People's Democratic Government": "The lands and other property of the rich peasants do not come under confiscation; the lands and other property of the middle peasants will be protected by the government."[13]

Only those who have short memories and have conveniently forgotten that this was the road also of Mao to power can possibly think that Aidit will be expelled, and especially so by those fire-breathing Chinese "revolutionaries." *The truth is that ever since Stalin's rise to power and the transformation of the young workers' state of Russia into its opposite—a state-capitalist society—Communism has been a euphemism for a new stage of capitalistic state power.*

With his concept of the "bloc of four classes," Stalin helped kill the 1925–27 Chinese Revolution. Mao, who never knew much about genuine Marxism, took over this Stalinist legacy, adding a perversion of his own: *where Lenin laid the theoretical and practical basis for an alliance of the revolutionary proletariat of Russia in particular and Europe in general with the revolutionary nationalist and peasant forces in the "East," Mao raised the guerrilla army to such primacy that he shattered to smithereens the alliance of proletariat and peasantry and, in the process, debased internationalism to racism.*

It is this racism which has won Mao not only Aidit but Sukarno, who, during World War II, saw nothing wrong in collaborating with the Japanese when

13 Quoted by J.S. Van der Kroef in "Communism in Indonesia" in *Problems of Communism*, Nov.-Dec. 1958.

they occupied what was then the Dutch East Indies, and, tomorrow, may see nothing wrong in choosing to side with his army against Mao.[14] *The overriding truth about Maoism, however, is that it itself is the consequence, not the cause, of the decomposition of world communism into its national component parts.* What began with Stalin when he christened his nationalism "socialism in one country" reached a new low with "Mao's Thought," which anoints racism and wars as internationalism and revolution.

Aidit's "original" contribution to this debasement was the cynicism evident in his use of the word "proximity," when he first explained why he chose the Beijing side in the Sino-Soviet conflict. What Aidit wants, above all else, is state power. *What he distrusts, above all else, is revolution, masses in motion, spontaneity that he neither can anticipate nor control. The class collaborationism this opportunist indulged in in Indonesia has made Khrushchev's goulash Communism look very nearly Marxist.* Since, however, the one and only criterion Mao uses is whether the party in question follows *his foreign* policy—anti-Americanism and anti-revisionism being its two poles—Aidit was pictured as a sterling revolutionary and President Sukarno as "an anti-imperialist fighter" who was very nearly a Marxist. The *Beijing Review* of June 4 put it all in bold headlines: "Great Victories of Indonesian C.P.'s Marxist-Leninist Line."

What Price "Integration"

The tragicomic aspects of "integration," of "boring from within," is seen nowhere more clearly than in *asking* Sukarno to establish a "people's militia" *and also* introducing "political commissars" into the army! Once, however, you eliminate the comic aspects of trying to get the fruits of power without the necessary revolution, the tragedy is unrelieved, totally encompassing the whole of this nation of 100 million that has fought and won its independence from Dutch imperialism only to exude from within itself a gangrenous combination of strident nationalism and unprincipled national-Beijing Communism.

Here was but yesterday the largest mass Communist Party anywhere in the non-Communist world, and second only to Peking and Moscow where

---

14 The confused story of that period led to Sukarno's being first branded by Communists in 1945 as a "fascist collaborationist," but later presented as one who collaborated only with the express agreement of the underground movement. See *Nationalism and Revolution in Indonesia,* by George McT. Kahin. It is the most scholarly work on the subject, and has the advantage also of being an eyewitness report for the critical 1948–49 period. The work was published in 1952, and should therefore be supplemented by a 1965 work, *Mohammed, Marx and Marhaen, The Roots of Indonesian Socialism,* by Jeanne S. Mintz. Neither work deals with theory in a serious way and must therefore be supplemented by "The Challenge of Mao Zedong" in *Marxism and Freedom.*

Communism is the state power and you belong because you have to, not because you want to. To the three million members in the PKI and three more million in the youth movement, you must add that it controlled also the main trade union federation as well as the peasant organization. No less than 22 million voted Communist before voting was abolished, to be substituted by Sukarno's corporative "guided democracy."

All this was used not to move the national revolution into the socialist one, but to go on with endless demonstrations "against U.S. imperialism," direct actions "as such"—like taking over British-owned companies *not* to establish workers' control over them, but to give them over to Sukarno's state—approval of all actions that move toward an axis with Peking, including *persecution of Trotskyists and Socialists, and the banning of the neo-Trotskyist Murba* (*Proletarian*) *Party which opposed becoming a satellite of China.* And just as the Communists helped to discipline labor by using the trade unions only when the policy of struggling for better conditions did not upset Sukarno's "anti-imperialist policy" and erratic balancing of Communists against army and vice versa, so it helped the army and military policy "to maintain law and order" during the "crush Malaysia" campaign. If now—and the situation is changing daily as I write this—Sukarno has failed in his balancing act, and must now bow to the army, where does that leave the masses of Indonesia, except to become the victims of another reactionary axis, with U.S.–British imperialism, now?

***

In the immediate postwar period in Europe when the Communist Parties in Italy had become mass parties, the saying was that all Stalin had to do to get power was to raise his telephone and give the proper order. Only he never picked up that telephone because, while he wanted power, he was as scared as any capitalist ruler of power in the streets, power he could not control with *his* "Red Army," power therefore that might really be in the hands of the masses themselves. Whether, for Indonesia, Mao did finally pick up that telephone or not, for him, too, the masses could not be trusted unless *his* "Red Army" was nearby and the Communist Party *led them*, preferably with Sukarno's aid, *but in no case should a spontaneous revolution develop which might escape their control.*

The result has been precisely that which it was in Western Europe: capitalism has gotten its second wind and is poised for new alignments in World War III. And now not only Indonesia, but all of Asia, will move to the right, unless the masses, once and for all, release themselves from the hold of Parties "out to lead" and take destiny into their own hands.

CHAPTER 14

The Sino-Soviet Split

Dunayevskaya wrote on rifts between Russia and China long before those differences publicly emerged as the Sino-Soviet split. Despite China and Russia's use of Marxist phraseology and putting forth dueling quotes from Lenin and others, she analyzed the rivalry not as two versions of Marxism in conflict, but as a manifestation of "The Non-Viability of State-Capitalism." Both Russia and China were fighting for influence in the international Communist movement that from Stalin's time on had ceased to be a revolutionary alternative to capitalism. At the same time a rising Third World—the Afro-Asian-Latin American movements rejecting colonialist capitalist-imperialism and seeking an alternative of humanism and socialism—became an arena for Sino-Soviet rivalry. Maneuvering between state-capitalist powers within the Communist orbit or over relations with their nominal common enemy the United States led Dunayevskaya to note in 1969: "Russia and China now considered each other as Enemy No. 1."

Dunayevskaya in Marxism and Freedom *and* Philosophy and Revolution, *together with numerous writings in* News & Letters *newspaper, took up ongoing aspects of the split in the context of our state-capitalist world. Below are two documents on aspects of the Sino-Soviet conflict, one from* Marxism and Freedom, *the other from* News & Letters.

Can There Be War between Russia and China? The Non-Viability of State-Capitalism

Marxism and Freedom

1) 1960–62: Preliminary Sparring

In 1960 China took advantage of the 90th anniversary of the birth of Lenin (April 22) to transform the power conflict into a "theory of revolution." It was called "Long Live Leninism," and appeared as an "Editorial" in *Red Flag,* No. 8, 1960 (translated in *Beijing Review,* No. 17, 1960).

This "Editorial" is a full-sized pamphlet of some 40 pages. It is heavily sprinkled with quotations from Lenin, which stress proletarian revolution. While the editorial itself plays down "modem science" (that is, ICBMs, H-bombs, and sputniks) as mere "specific details of technical progress in the present-day world," it unleashes an attack on "modern revisionism" in a way that makes it very easy to read "Khrushchev" where the editorial says "Tito." Since all the proofs of the war-like nature of the United States are drawn from the period *after* Khrushchev's visit with Eisenhower, it is easy to see that "the inevitability of war" is, in truth, not a question of Lenin's theory, but is specifically directed against Khrushchev's policy of peaceful co-existence.

Khrushchev correctly judged that lengthy editorial on Lenin as a new stage, not merely in "Mao's Thought," but in Mao's ambitions for leadership in the Communist orbit, in influence over the underdeveloped areas, and in planning the strategy of any war with the United States. It is rumored that a discussion between Russia and China regarding a joint Pacific Fleet was cancelled by Khrushchev for fear that Mao would push him into a war over the Formosa Straits.[1] The "Editorial," however, was a stillbirth. The May 1, 1960 U.S. U-2 spy plane over Russia made it so. It also gave Khrushchev the opportunity he needed not only to break up the summit conference he had heretofore planned, but also to convoke an international conference of the Communist world to discipline Mao. Khrushchev's appearance at the UN was part of the preparation for this conference. In the well-known shoe-pounding incident at the UN Khrushchev got his opportunity to announce to the whole world that he is not only master of the Communist world, but the only hope of the new world opened up by the African Revolutions.

On Dec. 7, 1960, Khrushchev convened the 81 Communist Parties for a conference in Moscow.[2] There he transformed his UN speech into the new Communist Manifesto which declared Russia to be "the first country in history to be blazing a trail to communism for all mankind." The overwhelming majority of the Communist Parties present in Moscow demanded Mao sign the Declaration so that a "unanimous" Communist front be shown American imperialism. Mao could not refuse to do so without exposing the fact that China considered Russia to be the enemy. Mao signed, but continued his independent road not only in China but throughout the third Afro-Asian-Latin American world.

China's signature to the 1960 Moscow Manifesto did not stop its deviationary road along its own national interests any more than France's signature to

1 See Edward Crankshaw in *The London Observer,* February 12 and 19, 1961.

2 The English translation, released by *Tass* was published in *The New York Times,* Dec. 7. 1960. In view of the fanciful interpretation by Russian "experts," especially Isaac Deutscher (*Reporter,* Jan. 5, 1961) about how the "compromise" between Khrushchev and Mao was achieved at this meeting of the 81 Communist Parties which was supposed to have been "very nearly a revival of the old Communist International," it is important to get "first reactions" and compare them with the present stage of the Sino-Soviet rupture. See my analysis of this "New Russian Communist Manifesto" in *News & Letters,* January, 1961.

NATO stopped de Gaulle from seeking his own glory road. The post-war world of the 1960s is, after all, a very different world from what it was in the late 1940s when both Europe and China lay in ruins, and each had to accept aid and. with it, the "philosophy" underlying the Marshall Plan and the Warsaw Pact respectively. Mao is trying to do with a barrage of revolutionary phrases what de Gaulle is trying to achieve with spoutings about "French grandeur." In both cases, however, the split within their respective orbits is due to national ambitions for world expansion.

The initiative, however, had returned into Khrushchev's hands after the U-2 spy plane discovery. He used it to isolate China further. In 1961 the Draft Program for the 22nd Russian Communist Party Congress relegates the Chinese Revolution to a total of 11 words. This was done, not because it is the program of a national party, the Russian, but because Russia as a world phenomenon began the 20th century with the 1917 Revolution as a new epoch and continued it with the 1957 Sputnik which outdistanced even the United States. Moreover, Khrushchev insisted, this Russian age is not only different as against the United States, but as distinct from China, because the Russians are "building Communism."[3] No wonder Khrushchev at the Congress itself chose to attack Albania (meaning China) and Zhou Enlai chose to walk out after defending Albania (meaning China), and challenging Russia's right to bring such disputes into the open without "prior consultation" with the Communist world. These attacks and defenses are as counterfeit as the "theories" in which Mao and Khrushchev wrap themselves as they carry on their bitter competition.

The October 22, 1962 confrontation of J.F. Kennedy and Nikita Khrushchev over missiles in Cuba, the historic moment when the whole world held its breath for fear of nuclear holocaust, gave Mao Zedong the opportunity to regain the initiative in the Sino- Soviet conflict. The moment Khrushchev backed down when Kennedy made it clear he was ready to plunge the world into nuclear war unless Khrushchev removed those missiles from Cuba, Mao launched the new stage of conflict by accusing Khrushchev of "cowardice in the face of imperialism." Then he moved to take over "leadership" of the "socialist world" by demanding that it come to his support in the Sino-Indian war.

---

3 See the Draft Program of the 22nd Russian Communist Party Congress released by *Tass* July 30, and published in *The New York Times*, Aug. 1, 1961. Consult also "The 22nd Party Congress" by Merle Fainsod, issued as a special supplement of *Problems of Communism*, Nov.-Dec. 1961.

2) New Dateline: Beijing, June 14, 1963: "A Proposal Concerning the General Line of the International Communist Movement"[4]

The new, the qualitative difference in the Sino-Soviet conflict crystallized into an open challenge theoretically as well. It took the form of a "letter" of the Central Committee of the Chinese Communist Party (CC of the CPC) to its Russian counterpart, dated June 14, 1963, and entitled "A Proposal Concerning the General Line of the International Communist Movement." Soon thereafter it was published as a pamphlet in a dozen different languages of East and West.

China's industrial development may lack everything from steel to dams and atomic energy. Its Army, however, has everything from overwhelming numbers to military equipment. In the first instance, it is the largest land army in the whole world, and in the second instance it has the most modern equipment on the Asian continent. Russian humor may have pinpointed Mao's historic image when it says history will record him "as an athletic failure in the broad jump." But he was no failure in the Sino-Indian War. As "Mao's Thought" thrives on military engagements, it has given birth to yet a new crop of "theories." These are developed with much subterfuge and great wordiness in the 61-page June 14th "letter." They add up to a single and total ambition for world mastery.

In five different ways the June 14th "letter" states that "the touchstone of internationalism" (p. 10) should no longer be the defense of Russia. The first reason given for the new thesis is that the defense of the Soviet Union was originally the touchstone of internationalism because it was the only "socialist country" but "Now that there is a socialist camp of thirteen countries" the whole "socialist world" has become that "touchstone of internationalism." "Therefore," reads the second point of indictment against Russia, referred to as "anybody": "If anybody...helps capitalist countries attack fraternal socialist countries, then he is betraying the interests of the entire international proletariat and the people of the world." (p. 10) The accusation of betrayal is obviously aimed at Russia for its failure to support China's invasion of India. The third variation of "Russia no longer" is an appeal for adherents within the country under attack, since the "step back in the course of historic development" is declared to be tantamount to "doing a service to the restoration of capitalism." Yugoslavia is named as the culprit but, clearly, Russia is meant.

The Manifesto of the Central Committee of the Chinese Communist Party is now prepared for the big jump, the shift from proletarian revolutions to national struggles "since" the countries of Asia, Africa and Latin America are

4 Issued in English by *Foreign Language Press*, Beijing, 1963. The page numbers cited here are to this edition. The reply of the Central Committee of the Russian Communist Party on July 15 was published in *The New York Times*, July 15, 1963.

"the storm centers of world revolution dealing direct blows at imperialism." (p. 12) "In a sense, therefore, the whole cause of the international proletarian revolution hinges on the outcome of the revolutionary struggle of the people in these areas." (p. 13)

This shift of pivot—the fourth variation on the theme, "Russia no longer"—is supposed to be based on Lenin's thesis (at the Second Congress of the Communist International, 1920) about the imperative duty of the proletariat of the technologically advanced countries to unite with the peasant masses in the colonial countries struggling to free themselves from imperialism. Lenin's new point of departure in the theory of non-inevitability of capitalist development for backward economies is based on a big "if": *if* "aid of the proletariat of the most advanced countries" is extended unstintingly. Lenin stresses that the only proof of proletarian internationalism, therefore, is for the Russian proletariat to extend this aid along with the theory and practice of revolution. All of this is reduced by Mao to a matter of his competition with Khrushchev as to who will "lead" this new Third World. In the process, Mao moves away from his concept of the division of the world into two camps, "the socialist countries" against "the capitalist countries." Although he had taken great pains to bring this concept in as a substitute for the class struggle in each country, he now disregards it. In order to reintroduce his old, ruinous "four class policy" he broadens the concept of "the people" to include "also the patriotic national bourgeoisie, and even certain kings, princes, and aristocrats who are patriotic." (p. 15)

By the time Chinese Communism reaches the fifth and final theme of its international manifesto of "never, no, never again Russia"—this time directed against Russia being "a state of the whole people building communism"—we are suddenly confronted with the most sinister of all theories of retrogression. Over and over again, "A Proposal Concerning the General Line of the International Communist World" proclaims that "for a very long historic period after the proletariat takes power" (p. 36); "for decades or even longer after socialist industrialization and agricultural collectivization" (p. 37) have been achieved, "the class struggle continues as an objective law independent of man's will." (p. 36) This holds true in all "socialist countries." Now whatever the subjective impulse for concocting this—all too transparently it is meant to lay the foundation for opposition to the 22nd Russian Communist Party Congress which enunciated that Russia was "building Communism"—it is the most serious of all theories of retrogression. We now have not only the retrogression of capitalism to fascism, but the retrogression of socialism, that is to say, a supposedly classless society, to one in which "there are classes and class struggles in all socialist countries without exception." (p. 40) Surely no more deadly deviation has ever been proclaimed "a principle of Marxism-Leninism."

Where the tiny state power of Yugoslavia, in 1948, when it fought the giant, Russia, for national independence, could not allow itself any new glory roads a la de Gaulle in the Western camp, Mao's delusions are as vast as the Chinese continent—and not only as it is now constituted, but as it was at the height of its imperial glory under the Yuan and Ming Dynasties when China conquered Burma, Thailand, the Indochina Peninsula, debarked troops to Indonesia, imprisoned the king of Ceylon and once even imposed annual tribute from the Moslem world, or at least from the Holy City of Mecca. Before 1962 only Nehru had questioned the map included in "A Manual of History," which was published in Beijing in 1954.[5] This shows a great part of the Soviet Far East as well as the Republic of Outer Mongolia, North and South Korea, Cambodia, Thailand, Malaya, Burma, Assam (about 50,000 miles of Indian territory, in fact), Bhutan, Sikkim, Nepal, the island of Sakhalin as well as some islands in the Philippines, as having been part of China.

When, in 1962, Khrushchev dared to quip at Mao's phrase about "cowardice in the face of the imperialists" by saying it ill-behooves Mao to speak so when he is doing nothing presently to drive the imperialists from "his own territory—Taiwan, Hong Kong. Macao," the *People's Daily* and *Red Flag* hit back with: "Certain persons would like us to raise the questions of unequal treaties here and now...Have they realized what the consequences of this might be?" Whereupon the Chinese began explaining "the imperialist encroachments on Chinese territory (1840–1919). Period of the Early Democratic Revolution." And, in expanding themselves on what Tsarist Russia took from "old China," the present Chinese rulers included territories taken from Emirs and Khans who most assuredly did not consider themselves vassals of the Emperor of China. (Nor, for that matter, did Mao's dream of China's past glories stop itself from designating as an "imperialist encroachment" Thailand's becoming independent; that too "belonged" to China of the Emperor and he means "to redress" someday the borders of what the CC-CPC designates only as "old China.")

Mao opts for nothing short of mastery of the world, of the Communist world to begin with. Though, for tactical reasons, and because of the withdrawal of Russian technical aid, China had to fall back on a variation of "the theory of socialism in one country" ("Every socialist country must rely mainly on itself for its construction," (p. 45)), the CC-CPC challenges not only Russia but the

---

5 This map is reproduced in the *New Republic* of 4/20/63 in an article, "China's Borders," the third of a series of articles by J. Jacques-Francillon. The other articles appear in the issues of 3/16/63 and 3/23/63. (See also B. Shiva Rae's article in the *National Observer* of 7/23/63.).

majority of the presently constituted Communist world. It warns that, "One should not emphasize 'who is in the majority' or 'who is in the minority' and bank on a so-called majority." (p. 47) In the place of following majority rule, he proposes the rule of "unanimity," that is to say, China's right of veto over policies formulated by Russia and the majority of other Communist Parties. Thus, the present Sino-Soviet conflict differs fundamentally not only from Yugoslavia's 1948 conflict with Stalin for national independence, but also from Mao's own differences both in 1957 and in 1960 when the conflict could be hushed up because it was fought within the Communist world.

The one and only thing that both Khrushchev and Mao prove, the one and only thing that is beyond the peradventure of any doubt, is the non-viability of their "new" social order. *The non-viability of state-capitalism as a "new" social order is proven by the same laws of development as that of private capitalism, that is to say, the compulsion to exploit the masses at home and to carry on wars abroad.* A shocking question faces us now: *Can* there be a war between two regimes calling themselves Communist?

3) Back to "Wars and Revolutions": Russia and China at War?

The challenge to totalitarian power that was issued by the Hungarian Revolution of 1956 brought Russia and China closer together than they had ever been, either in Stalin's era or in Malenkov-Khrushchev's times. The class content of the counter-revolutionary crushing of the proletarian revolution is crucial to all else that has happened since. Directly after the show of solidarity with Russian imperialism against the Hungarian revolutionaries, China, as we saw, moved toward expanding its own state power.

Despite de Gaulle's derisive question, "The ideological split? Over what ideology?" his display of arrogance at his news conference on July 29, 1963, could not clothe his nuclear ambition as Mao does his. Its death features stood out in all their goriness: "France will not be diverted by Moscow agreements from equipping herself with the means of immeasurable destruction possessed by other powers." By contrast, Mao was enabled to excoriate Khrushchev for "servilely meeting the needs of United States imperialism" by his agreement to a treaty which "undertakes...to refrain from causing, encouraging, or in any way participating in, the carrying out of any nuclear weapon test explosion, or any other nuclear explosion, anywhere." This, said Mao, means "out and out betrayal" of "the socialist countries and all oppressed countries," since it would keep them "from acquiring nuclear weapons" while consolidating the United States' "position of nuclear monopoly." The superiority of arguments, carefully clothed in Marxist garb, however, cannot be maintained when both contestants are so clothed.

For the time being no war is in the offing between Russia and China. From Russia's side, this would make no sense not only because it is the "have" nation, but also because it certainly would break up the international Communist movement that still considers the State Plan as a fundamental division between itself and "the bourgeoisie." From China's side, such a war would be suicidal not only because Mao isn't strong enough to challenge the Russian goliath, but also because he is a firm believer in the infamous Dulles policy of negotiating from "positions of strength." Those he will not have unless he first wins to his side both the West European and the Asian Communist Parties which are in power (North Korea, North Vietnam), and also the African non-Communist world—or that of Latin America.

Moreover this struggle between state capitalist powers is taking place in a nuclear age. Because the opposition of all the peoples of the world to nuclear war is total, Khrushchev would like nothing better than to reduce all his differences with Mao to a disagreement on "peaceful co-existence." As *Izvestia* put it, Russia was not surprised that militarist, reactionary forces in the West were "atom mongers and madmen," but it was most "sadly" surprised to find that the "Chinese comrades should join their voices to the screams of those madmen." Indeed, so total is the opposition to nuclear war that the only two countries which dared openly oppose the Nuclear Test Ban Treaty—Mao's China and de Gaulle's France—had to claim that they did so "in the name of peace." Mao went so far as to offer counter-proposals for nothing short of "complete, thorough, total and resolute prohibition and destruction of nuclear weapons." That did not prevent him from attacking the actual treaty not only as "a big fraud" and "betrayal of the Soviet people," but also as an exposure of "the servile features of those who warmly embrace imperialism." "The exposure," he said, "of these freaks and monsters in their true colors is an excellent thing for the revolutionary struggle of the peoples and the cause of world peace." (*People's Daily,* Aug. 2, 1963) Mao, indeed, is no less scared of a nuclear holocaust than the rest of the world. But he does not allow the question mark this puts over the very survival of civilization to divert him from his feeling that this time the "have" nations—the United States and Russia—will first of all eliminate each other!

There is no doubt that China expounds a global strategy basically different from that of Russia. It alone has the audacity to speak of a time to follow a nuclear war when "socialism will be built on its ruins." Nevertheless, this is not the point in the Sino-Soviet conflict. Nor is that divisive and decisive point to be found in China's recent attempts to exclude Russia from Asian and African meetings on racial grounds. Both points are only the culmination of something that began as Mao strove for power. It had been obvious in all Mao's fights with

Stalin, and as soon as the Chinese Communist Party took power it demanded that "Mao's Thought" become the underlying theory for all conquests of power in "colonial countries."

This theme was muted during the Korean War of 1950–53 and again in the "joint" Khrushchev-Mao 1957 Manifesto against the proliferation of polycentrism. Naturally, every ruling class has found it easy to support revolutions—abroad. But, whereas new ruling classes, when they first come on the historic scene, proved themselves full of vitality because they did have a wider support among the masses than the old ruling classes they overthrew, the State Planners of today feel compelled to embark on wars before ever they have proved their right to historic existence on native soil.

Wars and revolutions are not synonymous. They are opposites. Here, then, are the actual consequences of Mao's revolutionary thunder since he won power against Stalin's advice to maintain his coalition with Chiang Kai-shek: (1) China embarks on wars only when it is sure to win, as against Tibet first, and limited to incursions into borders of India now; (2) When it suits its purpose, China peacefully, or more correctly shrewdly, "co-exists" with European imperialist outposts on its own territory, like Hong Kong and Macao: (3) If Mao, whose "Thought" could exude nothing more original than "a four-class policy," is nevertheless more adept than Khrushchev in the use of Marxist terminology to hide his territorial ambitions, he is no "braver" in facing a challenge from the greatest military power in the world—the United States. Mao has backed down more times, not only on Taiwan, but on Quemoy and Matsu, than did Khrushchev when he saw that Kennedy was actually ready to go to nuclear war over missiles in Cuba; (4) Despite his revolutionary thunder in the abstract, Mao is, in the concrete, an expert in imperialist maneuvering and in dubbing even "fascist regimes" as "peace-loving." Thus, before the Sino-Indian war, Mao called the military regime in Pakistan "fascist," but the moment China was engaged in war with India, Mao lost no time in making a deal with Pakistan, which had suddenly become a "peace-loving nation"; (5) Nor does his "revolutionary defense" of the Afro-Asian world he hopes one day to dominate keep him from excluding other Communist lands whom he calls "revisionist" while including, as we saw, "the national bourgeoisie, and even certain kings, princes, and aristocrats who are patriotic."

The odd mixture of Mao's opportunism and adventurism, the ordinary imperialist power struggle (both within the Communist world and outside, as in the conquest of Tibet, incursions into Indian territory, and covetous glances cast from Burma to Vietnam, and from Nepal to Laos) cannot be separated from the struggle for the minds of men. It is here that the irresponsible abuse of Marxist language—on the question of "revolutions without pause" proceeding in a straight line from State Plans to "Communism"—makes it imperative to show not only the blind alley into which the dialectic of Mao's thought has led and from which it may catapult the world into a nuclear holocaust, but to show also that which is opposite from both the state-capitalist powers and the general global struggle with the United States for world domination. That is to say, it is imperative to illumine the path of freedom.

∵

Splintered World Communism

News & Letters, ***June–July 1969 and August–September 1969***

The two topics—the Sino-Soviet conflict and the Czechoslovak "question"—that were most discussed at the recently concluded Moscow conference were not the ones that are gnawing at the vitals of the 75 Communist Parties. The way in which they were handled will, however, illuminate that peculiar brand of nationalism that, at one and the same time, tears apart and binds together state-capitalism. It is necessary, therefore, to turn to the different attitudes to the points in dispute.

Brezhnev and the "Dissenters" on Mao

Maoism is one question Brezhnev wanted aired and the dissenting Communist Parties wanted to avoid. To get these parties to the conference Brezhnev had to promise that the question of China would not be placed on the agenda. The excuse for the breach of faith was that "a new situation had arisen." Brezhnev claimed that "only two days ago" the Chinese press had issued "the call to prepare both for conventional and big nuclear war against Soviet revisionism... The combination of the Chinese leaders' political adventurism with the sustained atmosphere of war hysteria injects new elements into the international situation and we cannot ignore it."[6]

The truth, however, is that, if even we were to disregard that the Sino-Soviet conflict, begun in 1960, had reached just this high intensity during the 1967 "Cultural Revolution" with its accusation of "Russian collusion with American imperialism," the "new" situation arose no later than January, 1969 with the *absolutely unprecedented identification of "Russian revisionism" as "the enemy" in*

---

6 The most detailed quotations from Brezhnev's speech are in Richard Reston's article in the *Los Angeles Times*, June 8, 1969.

the most basic state document, the Draft Chinese Constitution itself. And finally, at the Ninth Congress of the Chinese Communist Party, called to ratify the new Constitution in April, Lin Biao fleshed out the accusation, thus: "The Soviet revisionist renegade clique had been practicing social imperialism and social fascism more frantically than ever."[7]

Notwithstanding these vituperations, spoken in April, the "dissenters" had Brezhnev reiterate the promise not to deal with China at the preparatory conference held as late as May 23. Moreover, they did so though they were no doubt aware of the equally vituperative accusations against China of the Russian press. Defense Minister Andrei A. Grechko had very nearly called for a preventive war when, after speaking of the "chauvinist-hegemonial aspirations of the Mao Zedong group," he concluded: "Only by a resolute offensive can one defeat the enemy's forces."[8]

It is true that nothing could possibly have happened "only two days ago" that hadn't been happening since the January Draft Constitution and the April Lin Biao speech, on the one hand, and the May statements of the Russian generals and the constantly recurring border incidents, on the other hand. *But Brezhnev was not the only hypocrite at the "world" conference. The dissenters would have had to have been not merely naive, but actually moronic, to have taken his promise at face value after Russia's invasion of Czechoslovakia!*

The Hypocrisy of the "Dissenters"

These East European state powers, and West European aspirants for the same, were far from being naive, much less moronic. Indeed they were so knowledgeable in the ways of Big Brother and had so successfully resisted Khrushchev's attempt to call just such a "unity" conference that he, not they, lost his head. How then did Brezhnev win where Khrushchev lost? And at a time when not only relations with China, which is far, far away, were much exacerbated, but when a country much closer to home base, a country that was engaged not in attacking Russia, but in trying to reform itself, had nevertheless been invaded by Big Brother's troops—500,000 strong!

Therein, precisely, lies one answer. The occupation of Czechoslovakia created terror throughout East Europe.

It is true Rumania had rejected the notorious Brezhnev doctrine of "limited sovereignty," declaring: "Limited sovereignty makes no more sense than limited honesty." Nevertheless, Ceausescu had not, as he had previously done,

7 A full page of official excerpts of Lin's speech appeared in *The New York Times*, April 29, 1969.

8 *Pravda*, May 9; a few excerpts from it can be found in Paul Wohl's article in the *Christian Science Monitor*, June 10, 1969.

walked out when there was a breach of faith. It is true he wished to cut down Russian hegemony: "It is not necessary to have any leading center!"[9] But it was quite obvious that the autonomy of the Communist Parties he was talking about was the very specific nationalism of Rumanian Communism. He did not even mention Czechoslovakia by name!

Another reason—*a more crucial one insofar as the class nature of present-day Communism is concerned*—for Brezhnev's "victory" is that the "dissenters" are themselves either state-capitalist bureaucrats like Rumania, or hoping in some way to become part of a government coalition. Thus, the Italian Communist Party, the largest in Western Europe, expects to do very well in the next general election.

The fact that its representative, Enrico Berlinguer, is the most outspoken critic of Russian monolithism, both as it concerns its "intervention" in Czechoslovakia, and its propaganda against Mao, must therefore be related to these expectations. In a word, there is more opportunism than courage in his criticisms of Russia. This becomes especially clear in his speech on Mao where he, at one and the same time, criticized Chinese Communism and opposed Russia's attempt to "excommunicate" Mao from the world movement. Enrico Berlinguer's speech on Czechoslovakia was the most outspoken one at the Moscow conference.

He may also have been under the illusion that the Italian CP had influenced the delay of this conference from the date it was supposed to have taken place—November 1968—a date altogether too close to the Russian invasion. *The more likely reason, however, is that Brezhnev needed the time to create a handful of Czechoslovak Quislings. Out they strutted just as soon as Berlinguer had finished his speech defending Czechoslovakia's struggle to be autonomous.*

Czech Quislings vs. Mao

Gustav Husak rose to take issue with the speeches attacking the Russian invasion by, first, dutifully repeating what *Rude Pravo* had written about the "wrong attitude" of Communist Parties in the West being based on "distorted facts and false information handed out to them by counter-revolutionary journalists and even by some top party officials." Now that neither the new allegedly undistorted facts, nor the pre-conference appeal that the "comrades" should not discuss this "family affair," halted criticism, this miserable little Quisling dared to speak lovingly about the Russian occupiers of his native land. Czechoslovakia, he ended with a flourish, was bound "by ties of Communist international brotherhood with the Soviet Union and the socialist countries."[10]

---

9 Quoted by Henry Kamm in *The New York Times*, June 10, 1969.

10 *Ibid*, June 12, 1969.

To the disgust and despair of the Czechoslovak people, the Quisling leader thereby embraced "the gravediggers of their short-lived hopes."[11] Not only that; they thereby lay the foundation for the emergence of the next tragedy—the view that Maoism has the answers to those who would fight for their freedom from Russia. For if there is anywhere where the calling of the Russian leaders "the new Tsars" sounds both true and revolutionary, it is surely in occupied Czechoslovakia. *The victory of creating Quislings is Pyrrhic.* To see the dimension of Communism's disintegration, we must now turn to the main absentee from the Moscow Conference: Mao.

Part II

Mao Zedong dominated the Congress of the "world" Communist Parties that met in Moscow without him. The heated border incidents on the Ussnri River that erupted at the time of the June Congress were not the reasons for the absentee's dominance, although Brezhnev tried to make it appear so. Whether these border clashes were provoked by Russia or China does not matter. With or without these strangely-timed outbreaks, there was no way to hide the extreme, the totally new, the absolute shift in world strategy on the part of both giants of world Communism.

Just as the January 1969 Draft of the new Constitution of the Chinese Communist Party had made clear what had been initiated by the "Cultural Revolution," 1966–1968, (and the April, 1969, Congress had been convened to rubber stamp it) so the Kremlin, in initiating and demanding a "world" Congress, had decided to make clear beyond any peradventure of a doubt in the minds of "its" 75 Communist Parties what the new reality was: all talk about U.S. imperialism as "Enemy No. 1" was pure ritual. The new reality was this—*Russia and China now considered each other as Enemy No. 1.*

The very fact, however, that there were dissenters in the Russian orbit, that these dissenters were not Maoist followers, and had different problems, disclosed more than the lack of "homogeneity" in either Communist world. It revealed, albeit indirectly, that, outside of the different *nationalisms* (China included) at stake, there was also a dualism in Maoism. They could not face that reality either. But it is of the essence that we do.

The Dualism of Maoism

Lin Biao, in deifying (or mummifying!) Mao, laid claim to nothing short of Mao's superiority over not only living Communists, but Marx, Engels and

11 For the most knowledgeable analysis of the Quislings, read "Sell-out in Prague," by Kamil Winter. The writer had been Editor of News and Current Affairs for, Czechoslovak TV until the Russian invasion. His article is in the *New Statesman*, June 13. 1969.

Lenin: "Chairman Mao's experience, in passing through many events, is more profound than that of Marx, Engels and Lenin. No one can surpass Mao's rich revolutionary experience."

Moreover, went on the anointed, named, constitutionalized successor to Mao, this superiority is not limited either to "experience," or to a single country: "The world has entered a new epoch—the epoch of The Thought of Mao Zedong."[12] *And,* since it is China which has unfurled this epochal, indeed eternal, banner, the new Constitution sees no contradiction in committing the Party members "to work for the interests of China" and upholding "proletarian internationalism."[13] Surely none of the 1,522 "newly minted delegates" (to use Edgar Snow's phrase)[14] doubted that China is "the world."

How, however, does one make sure that this will appeal to the non-Chinese world? First, of course, is the Marxist language. Thus, Lin Biao assures us that: "From the Marxist point of view, the main component of state power is the Army." The only thing that the General forgot to inform his audience is that Marx said that about a *capitalist* state.

In place of the *class* nature of the state and its army, the ruler of a state capitalism calling itself Communist exudes paternalism: "We must carry out the great tradition of supporting the Government and cherishing the people; of supporting the Army and cherishing the people."

Nevertheless, Marxist language does appeal to rebels when the phrasing concerns "world revolution," "uninterrupted revolution," and endless "transformation." Toward that end, Lin trotted out a new quotation from Mao: "The final victory of a socialist country requires not only the efforts of its own proletariat, it also depends on world revolution." Mao's "purism" shines forth: "The age that is just beginning, that will last about 50 or 100 years, will be a great one. It will bring a radical change in the social system of the whole world. It will be an age of great upheavals, an age without parallel in history," says Chairman Mao.

Meanwhile, "China must consider itself at war. We are threatened and encircled by the two greatest powers in the world and we must be prepared for them to launch a large-scale war on us, either conventional or nuclear." To make sure that the proper patriotic fervor animates the Chinese masses, the "new" Maoist rulers, properly cleansed of "revisionism," produced the most chauvinistic film this side of actual warfare between Russia and China, and entitled it "The Anti-Chinese Crimes of the New Tsars." (Not to be outdone by the Chinese, the

12 Lin's Report was published by *The New York Times* April 29, 1969. The translation is the official CCP translation.

13 The Constitution appeared in *The New York Times*, Jan. 8, 1969; a slightly different, version appears in a translation by Stuart Schram, *China Quarterly*. Jan.-Mar., 1969.

14 "Mao and the New Mandate" by Edgar Snow, *New Republic*, May 10, 1969.

Russian rulers produced their own film version of the border incidents, equally chauvinistic, equally heavily edited, and equally accompanied by actual military build-up at key disputed borders.)[15]

The real shocker is not the rise of "new Tsars" out of "revisionism," The real shocker is cushioned with so much "revolutionary" verbiage that it will hardly be visible to the naked eye. But a close comparison of the ritualism with which Lenin is mentioned (throughout the "Cultural Revolution" Lin Biao assured us that "99% of Marxist-Leninist classics which we study should consist of Mao Zedong's writings"), and the deification with which Mao is being read back into history for a *half-century* (i.e., the whole mature life of Mao), *reveals that 1917 has disappeared from history. World revolutionary history begins, instead, in 1919 with China.*

The rollback of world revolutionary history to China, and not just when the Communist Party gained power in 1949, but back to China's first modern awakening when the Communist Party had not yet been born at all, hardly puts "the universal truths of Marxism-Leninism" on a level with "the concrete practice of revolution." The new Constitution is most specific on the timing: "In the past half century, in leading China in the great struggle to fulfill the new democratic revolution, in leading the great struggle of Socialist revolution and Socialist construction of China...Comrade Mao Zedong has...lifted it (Marxism-Leninism) to a completely new stage."

The shocker didn't influence the dissenters at the Moscow conference half as much as the dualism—the appeals to world revolution within the Sino-centric context. These appeals, as they affected the young revolutionaries of their own countries, are what underlined their whole behavior. They could hardly take issue with the nationalism, since it is what they themselves practice. Nor could these self-centered, nationalistic weak dissenters separate Mao's concept, practice, and passion for "protracted war" which inheres in his view of the "uninterrupted revolution" from the long-range timing of "a century or more." Since, however, there is no other way to attack the *retrogressionist content* of the Maoist form of revolutionary verbiage, neither the Russian rulers nor the fake dissenters succeeded in halting the disintegration of world Communism.

State-Capitalism and "The Struggle against Counter-revolutionary Economism"

The varied nationalisms underlying splintered Communism are neither the ordinary bourgeois type of the 19th century, nor the new revolutionary

15 For a fairly detailed report of the military build-up, see "Will There Be War Between Russia and China?" by Harrison E. Salisbury, *New York Times Magazine*, 7/27/69.

nationalisms either of the Third World against Western imperialism, or of East Europe against Russian imperialism, be that of the Hungarian Freedom Fighters of 1956, or the Czechoslovakian Spring 1968.

We must not forget that Mao *urged* Khrushchev to launch the counter-revolution against the Hungarian Revolution. He opposed the invasion of Czechoslovakia only because by then he had broken with Russia on *other* grounds. Mao wants a third axis for world power created as against the "hegemonies" of the Russian *or* American orbits, *not* because he was for the revolutionaries in Czechoslovakia (whom he bitterly attacked as "revisionists" until the very day of the invasion), but because the class-collaborationist third axis he had counted on, Beijing-Jakarta, collapsed ignominiously.

The varied nationalisms do have a "world" character. but it is not the kind Trotsky predicted would result from Stalin's theory of "socialism in one country," i.e. that each Communist Party would capitulate to the bourgeoisie in its own country—the French CP to France, the American CP to the U.S., etc. No, the national Communisms kept faithful to *their world*, the new stage of world capitalism, state-capitalism, with its State Plan, State Party, "Red Army." Being the highest form of centralization of capital, state-capitalism reaches out for *contiguous* masses of capital. Hitler attempted it with his search for *lebensraum* and in the end failed. Stalin attempted it in East Europe and succeeded. It remains the model for *both* Brezhnev and Mao. *The collision of the two models at a still newer front only proves the non-viability of state-capitalism calling itself Communism. Like private capitalism, state-capitalism has but one way to live luxuriously—the exploitation of "its" masses. It is this which dooms it, with or without the embroidery of Marxist language transformed into its opposite.*

Of all Mao's perversions of "Marxism-Leninism," none is of a more *capitalistic* mentality and nature than that which he calls "the struggle against counter-revolutionary economism." When Lenin first began his battles against the "economists," i.e., the intellectuals who wished to restrict workers' activities to the trade union field only, reserving for themselves the field of politics, he maintained that the backwardness of the Tsarist regime did not mean the workers were backward; that only by mass initiative and all-round political activity could Tsarism be overthrown. When World War I broke out and he found that even some Bolshevik intellectuals, specifically Bukharin and Pyatakov, opposed self-determination instead of seeing that national struggles were a "bacillus" for proletarian revolution, he lashed out against their "imperialist economism." In all cases, the fight against "economism" was a fight against intellectuals, leaders, elitists of all sorts, whose mechanical views on economic development led them to disregard the "sense and reason" of the masses, who alone could transform society.

Lenin held on to his principle that Bolsheviks could prove their "proletarianism" *in one and only one way*—by changing the conditions of labor—after they came to power. He lashed out against the beginnings of Soviet bureaucracy by reminding his co-leaders that Marx had but one way of distinguishing socialism from capitalism, and that is by the change in labor's conditions of labor. "In *Capital*," wrote Lenin,[16] "Karl Marx ridicules the pompous and grandiloquent bourgeois-democratic great charter of liberty and the rights of man... Marx contrasts this pompous declaration of rights to the plain...presentation... by the proletariat: the legislative enactment of a shorter working day."

Lenin drives home the point for Russia: "The 'formulae' of genuine Communism differ from the pompous, involved, solemn phrasemongering of the Kautskys, the Meneheviks and the Socialist Revolutionaries...in that they reduce everything to the *conditions of labor*."[17]

Now contrast this to the pompous phrases of Mao who, at one and the same time, asks the masses "to grasp the revolution and increase production" and, at once, spells out "increase in production" not only as more proletarian sweat, but also "equalized" (*read: lowered*) to peasant wages, at which point Lin-Mao unloose a political barrage against workers who fight the lowering of their wages as "economists." All this is climaxed by an actual military move against workers who dare to strike. This passes for "the struggle against counter-revolutionary economism."

This is not just a perversion of theory, nor merely a rewrite of history. This is class exploitation of the masses, proletariat and peasantry alike.

All you have to do to see that a "mass line," in Mao's China, means mass sweat, is to contrast it to the pampering of private capitalists—not the Party men who are supposed "to have taken the road back to capitalism," but the real, the existing private capitalists—who, 20 years *after* the Communist conquest of power, still get 5% profits on their investments. Where a worker gets barely enough to live, a capitalist like Rong Yeren gets annually 3 million yuan in profit. Not only that; he also has important political posts, which is a great deal more important than money in a country where "politics takes command."

I do not mean to say that these private capitalists have the power of the Party, much less the Army. I do say they exist, and *the only reason they are still permitted to exist is because the opposition of the masses to Mao and his*

---

16 Lenin, Selected Works, Vol. IX, p. 439. (A Great Beginning, dated 6/28/19, can be found both in *Collected Works* and as a separate pamphlet.).

17 *Ibid*, p. 440.

"hereditary" hierarchical heir, Lin Biao, is via slowdown, "low productivity" and what, when it comes to the youth, the Maoists now call "anarchism."[18]

The total hypocrisy of the dissenters in Russia was seen not so much in keeping Mao from getting excluded from "world Communism"—after all, all of the Communist *state powers* from Russia to China, and from Rumania to Albania, rule exactly by such exploitative means. No, the total hypocrisy was to be seen in doing nothing for Czechoslovakian Freedom Fighters, though these same loud-mouthed leaders did, in words, denounce the Russian invasion. The hypocrisy was seen as they closed their eyes to the Tartar demonstration right in Moscow.

The hypocrisy was seen in doing nothing for the brave Russians who demonstrated in opposition to their country's imperialist invasion of Czechoslovakia, and who are now rotting in jail for it. In thus evading the *Russian* dissenters urging help in prevention of the recurrence of "the ominous shadow of Stalin from darkening our future," the 75 Communist Parties meeting in Moscow, including those dissenters, proved they themselves were that "ominous shadow."

Equally ominous a shadow was cast by Mao, who had shown his first hostility to Russia in February 1956 when the 20th Russian Communist Party launched de-Stalinization "without consulting China." Obviously, however, the Central Committee of the Communist Party of China did know what was required of them since, in September 1956, they convened their first Congress since coming to power in 1949, *and* the new Party Constitution they then adopted eliminated the expression "under the guidance of the Thought of Mao Zedong," replacing it with the phrase "under the guidance of Marxism-Leninism." It is the latter phrase which has now been eliminated. The 1969 Constitution both deifies Mao and rolls history back not only from "socialism" but even from capitalism, as it returns to the feudal, monarchical form of having the ruler name his "successor."

This rollback of history is being touted as a "new model of Communism and attracting the interest of a whole generation (sic!), even in Europe and in the U.S."[19] *That some who call themselves the New Left do indeed accept this bizarre happening as "revolutionary" only discloses a "new model" of Communist bankruptcy of thought that vies with the bourgeois bankruptcy of thought that is the seal of decadent capitalism.*

---

18 "Peking Asks Student Discipline," *NYT*, July 27, 1969. For my analysis of the "Cultural Revolution" as a whole, see "Mao's China and the 'Proletarian Cultural Revolution.'" (News & Letters).

19 See K.S. Karol, "Drawn Match at Moscow," *New Statesman*, June 27, 1969.

On the other hand, the Chinese masses are restless, so opposed to Mao as to make his victories Pyrrhic enough. Thus, the time and place of the CCP Congress was not revealed until after it met. Thus, the open attacks on youth opposition that is suddenly declared to be "anarchist." Thus, *mass opposition* to Maoism and outright revolts are first now coming to light but have, in fact, been occurring for years and were the reason that Mao-Lin had called the "Great Proletarian Cultural Revolution."[20]

Will West Germany Suddenly Become the Holder of the Key to World History?

The shift in world strategy within the Communist orbits, of necessity, involves drastic changes in all international relations. At the Moscow Congress Brezhnev accused Mao's China of flirting with "West German revengists." It is true that there has been some detente between China and West Germany. But the greater truth is that a rapprochement of relations between Russia and West Germany has begun on a vaster scale, not only in trade, but in toning down the criticisms of West Germany, including its failure to sign the anti-nuclear proliferation treaty.

So worrisome is this development to France that some have urged that its coming meeting with Germany be especially "open," that is to say, that France itself offers to sign the anti-nuclear proliferation treaty in order to get West Germany to do so. They hope to thwart both Russia, which wants its European frontier "secure" for any possible war with China, and the U.S., which might be tempted actually to provide nuclear arms to West Germany and thus undermine the Franco-German Pact.[21]

There is no way to foresee all the ramifications of the present heated stage of the Sino-Soviet conflict, or to predict the possible shocking international realignments now that world Communism is so splintered. No doubt the double and triple crosses awaiting the masses will pale the Hitler-Stalin Pact. But one thing is sure, predictable, irreversible—the class enemy is always at home; the production relations between exploiters and exploited determine everything else, internally and externally.

---

20 One of the Manifestos of the opposition to Mao by the Hunan Provincial Proletarian Revolutionary Great Alliance Committee was translated in *Survey of China Mainland Press*, Hong Kong, 4190, and appears in *International Socialism*, June/July 1969.

21 "Germany Remains Focal Point" by Andre Fontaine, *Le Monde* (Weekly Selection), July 9, 1969.

There is therefore only one position for Marxist-Humanists to take, and that is to refuse to side with "the lesser evil," no matter what that is declared to be. Nothing short of uprooting the world status quo, of being with the genuine revolutionary forces—proletarians, national minorities, women's liberation, youth—to forge a new relationship of theory and practice will, once and for all, create the foundation of a society on totally new, human foundations.

—*August 7, 1969*

CHAPTER 15

The Cuban Revolution and What Happens After?

Dunayevskaya saw the Cuban Revolution as a great Latin American revolution and a blow against United States imperialism. At the same time, she critiqued Fidel Castro's willingness to be sucked almost immediately into the Russian orbit, despite the fact that the Cubans had made their revolution independently of that state-capitalism that called itself Communism. She wrote on the deep contradictions that followed the Revolution from the Cuban missile crisis, to the tragedy of Che Guevara in Bolivia, as well as taking up the ideology of Fidel's focoism *as put forth in Regis Debray's* Revolution in the Revolution*?*

The Cuban Revolution: The Year After

News & Letters, *December 1960*

In a few weeks the Cuban Revolution will mark the first year of its victory. It is no accident that its enthusiastic and uncritical alliance with the Russian orbit of power is almost as old. Contrary to the claims of the old radicals, who can no longer remember what constitutes principled working-class politics, this was not the only path open to it when it shook off the American imperialist yoke. The revolutions that preceded it—in the Middle East and in Africa—took advantage of the global division into two nuclearly-armed blocs fighting for world power to play off one against the other to its own national advantage. If Cuba chose to disregard this precedent and align itself with but one of these power blocs, the answer cannot lie outside of itself.

Fidelismo

Forget Russia for a moment—it was nowhere around when Fidel Castro marched into Havana at the head of the July 26th guerilla movement. Neither it nor the native Cuban Communists supported that movement during the seven years it hid out in the Sierra Maestra Mountains. The revolutionary petty-bourgeois lawyer who led this movement had been so little concerned with Communist theory that he gained financial help from many a Cuban, and even some American, liberal bourgeois who had had their fill of the corrupt Batista.

The guerilla fighters from the mountains, the peasants in the Oriente province, the proletariat and students of Havana merged to bring the greatest revolution Latin America had ever witnessed. There is no doubt that with the overthrow of the bloody Batista dictatorship, the revolution broke decisively with United States imperialism which had plundered the Cuban economy. In expropriating the American capitalistic owners, it achieved an agricultural revolution and put an end to the feudal relations between the Cuban peasants and the Cuban-American plantation owners. At the same time, however, the power lay not in peasant committees, but in the state who was the new owner.

State-ism

As for Castro's attitude to the industrial workers, from the very start his bossist, administrative mentality stuck out from the very first day of victorious entry into Havana when he demanded that the revolutionary students and workers there put down their arms. He proclaimed his movement alone to be the government, his army alone the army. Nevertheless, the overwhelming enthusiasm for the revolution made the proletariat, despite its reservations, lay down its arms, and willingly tighten its belt even as the unemployed continued to be silent. When it did, in due course, at the first trade union congress question some economic policies of the new government, Castro ran out of the convention, calling it a "madhouse."

It is at this point that a kinship was established between the new regime and the native Communists, for it is they who used their leadership of the trade unions to transform them into a pliant tool of the new armed state. TOGETHER WITH WORLD COMMUNISM FIDEL CASTRO SHARED THE CONCEPTION OF THE "BACKWARDNESS OF THE MASSES" WHO HAD TO BE LED. THE STATE WOULD HENCEFORWARD GIVE THE ORDERS, THE WORKERS AND PEASANTS WOULD CONTINUE TO WORK HARDER WHILE THE LEADERS CONTINUED TO LEAD AND SET FOREIGN POLICY.

Just as the peasant found that, in tilling the soil, he was responsible, not to a committee elected by himself and subject to his recall, but to the state, so the worker found that he too had no organization responsible to him. Despite the lower rents, there has been no change, except for the worse, in the workers' conditions of life and labor. Unemployment continues as do poor wages. Worst of all, there are no Workers' Councils or any other form of free expression, whether in their own organization or in the press. Those who had hailed the revolution had by now as little freedom to criticize any action of the government, least of all its total embrace of all things Russian, Chinese, East European, including the bloody regime of Kadar's Hungary.

The stream of refugees are by no means restricted to "Batista's supporters" or "agents of American imperialism." Everyone from the editor of *Bohemia* to militant trade unionists have attempted to escape, and if the price isn't always the firing squad, it is always silence. When only a Castro—Fidel or Raul—or a Che Guevara have endless voice here and abroad while the masses are made voiceless; when all spontaneity becomes hypostatized into state grooves; when relations with the outside world are not as people-to-people but through arm-state powers; and when all this occurs in a world whose division into two nuclearly-armed powers which threaten humanity's very existence—isn't it time for a new realistic balance sheet to be drawn up? Least helpful in this regard are the old radicals.

Old Radicals

Trotskyists, who have spent years in exposing Russia as "a degenerated workers' state" headed by a counter-revolutionary bureaucracy, now feel that it is necessary to whitewash that regime "in order to fight the main enemy, Yankee imperialism." Even some radicals who have spent many years exposing Russian Communism as just another form of state capitalism feel that it is their "revolutionary duty" to spend all their time attacking American imperialism, and none exposing the other pole of world imperialism—Russian totalitarianism.

What is it that impels such self-imposed blindness to the tragedy of the Cuban Revolution which still has a chance to compel its leaders to follow an independent road? Why should the workers and peasants in Cuba be allowed to think that in the Chinese "commune" the Chinese peasants are any less oppressed than the Cubans were by the American plantation owners? Why should the Cuban workers be kept in ignorance of conditions of labor in totalitarian state capitalistic Russia? Why should the Cuban people know that the Guantanamo base is a threat to their existence and not know that the Russian tanks rolled over the Hungarian Freedom Fighters? Why should they only know of the discrimination against the Negroes in the South but not know of the extermination of nationalities opposed to Stalinism in Russia?

Some Possible Double-crosses

Why should literacy be equated to illiteracy of the realities of a world divided into two, and only two, nuclearly-armed powers out for conquest of the world? Why not allow your *new* hero, Castro, to know some things about Russia—its cynicism in foreign policy—which might easily result in its dropping of Cuba the minute it could get a "peaceful co-existence alliance" with America? Why, for that matter, not make yourself aware that this petty bourgeois lawyer is just as cynical and could as easily slide into alliance with the American State Department if it came to face the only truly independent third force—the masses wishing to mold their own destiny in their own hands sans Fidel Castro, Che Guevara and the newly-arisen state bureaucracy?

There is one reason, and one reason only, behind all this self-imposed blindness to the realities of our state capitalist world. One and all are Planners who fear the spontaneity of the revolutionary masses more than anything else on earth, including state capitalism.

Fidelistas, like Communists, Trotskyists like other radicals who thirst for power, share the capitalistic mentality of the "backwardness of the masses." All are ready "to lead," none to listen.

Who are Doomed?

It has been said of Jesus: "He could save all others. Himself he could not save." It needs now to be said of the old radicals: They could save no one, and now they do not even want to save themselves. The one consoling feature is their impotence. Far from being capable of dooming the revolution, history will show them to be the doomed ones.

∴

Ideology and Revolution: A Study of What Happens After...

News & Letters, ***November 1962***

The sudden transformation of Cuba into a Russian missile base, followed by the even more sudden dismantling of the base, makes it necessary to probe deeply into the matter of what happens after a revolution is won and the heroes from the mountains become the administrators of the state.

This paramount question is not merely a new variation of the old moralistic question about how power corrupts; and how absolute power corrupts absolutely. Rather it is one that concerns the internal dynamics of revolutions in underdeveloped economies that evolved out of small guerilla bands and came to fruition in a nuclear age which has split the whole world into two, and only two, Big Powers—the United States and Russia.

In contrast to the African Revolutions which, after victory, set out on a course of "positive neutralism," the Cuban Revolution was, after a year, sucked into the Russian-Chinese Communist orbit. Fidel Castro now claims that there is no third road. The truth, however, is that Cuban independence was achieved without Communist help and the first year of revolution revealed an original philosophic as well as social transformation.

Between that first year and the present satellite status, the point of transition was caused, *not* by a "foreign agent," but by natural affinity between Fidel Castro, administrator, and *both* the native and world Communists. Let's take a closer look at these three clearly discernible stages that transpired since Fidel Castro came to power nearly four years ago, in January, 1959.

The First Year of Revolution

The first year of revolution unfolded with no dichotomy between philosophy and deed. The banner it unfurled made it as original in ideology as in its indigenous roots. Even Fidel Castro could express it succinctly then. The Cuban Revolution, he wrote was "a humanistic revolution because it does not deprive man of his essence, but holds him as its basic aim. Capitalism sacrifices man; the Communist state, by its totalitarian concept, sacrifices the rights of man."

The Cuban Revolution was a high stage in the development of freedom in the whole of Latin America. It did more than overthrow the cruel and despotic Batista dictatorship, which was both puppet of American imperialism and tyrant over its own nation. It achieved a *revolution in agricultural relations*.

Although the State, and not the agricultural worker, is the owner of these expropriated vast tracts of land, the *feeling* of liberation was exhilarating, and true, when compared with the previous state of servitude to the United Fruit Co.

While no comparable revolution in industrial relations was achieved, the fact that there was little industry in Cuba, and the people had to pull themselves up by their own bootstraps, when they didn't even have boots, also made the workers willingly, though not uncritically, identify themselves with Fidel Castro and his July 26th Movement.

The first point of division came when the workers took issue with the State Plan and wanted to make sure of retaining their trades unions. Fidel Castro attended their trade union congress to urge the election of Communists whom he had found to be the most enthusiastic of State Planners and concerned with "rational investment." When the trade unions balked at electing Communists who had nothing to do with their revolution, and had, in fact, played with Batista, Castro declared the congress "a madhouse."

This kinship with the Communists, an attraction of one bossist attitude to another; this sharing of a conception of "the backwardness of the masses who had to be led;" this ordering about of workers to obey planned production targets and get over their "lack of revolutionary conscience and enthusiasm in their work;" in a word, this substitute of the State Plan for the people's needs marks the first divide between the Cuban state leaders and the Cuban workers.

The Point of Transition

It was the beginning of the end also of the independence of the July 26th Movement and the beginning of domination by the Cuban Communist Party whose general secretary, Blas Roca, began to spout forth *counter*-revolutionary slanders: "The true role of Trotskyism throughout the entire world is well known. In their eagerness to fight the Soviet Union, they went into the ranks of Hitler's apparatus of espionage and provocation and into that of the North American imperialists...Today in Cuba we also have libertarian anarcho-syndicalists."

Such outbursts in Havana and Khrushchev's declaration at the UN prompted us to write in September, 1960:[1]

> Russia is now trying to make it appear that it ended America's domination of Cuba. It isn't true. To the extent that the revolution is due to any other source than the Cuban people themselves, it is due to the *African Revolutions which preceded it.*
>
> By fighting for independence from imperialism and embarking on a new path of development, the African Revolutions also *put an end to the isolation of Latin America in the Western Hemisphere as well as to the loneliness, the feeling of helplessness of any underdeveloped country anywhere in the world.*
>
> The only thing Russia can rightly claim credit for is *hardening* Castro's natural petty bourgeois tendency to solve administratively what can only be solved through the self-activity of the masses. This hardening of the administrative mentality has meant that revolutionary changes notwithstanding, *the single element of not creating a form for the release of the creative energies of the masses, of not allowing any reorganization from below, of doing everything from above, that single element of the administrative mentality, which is the hallmark of our age of state capitalism, was sufficient to begin the rapid descent of Cuba into the quagmire of Russian-Chinese totalitarianism.*
>
> At this point the tragedy is assuming tragically comic aspects. Fidel Castro thinks he is "The Leader." In truth, he is *being led.* He does not even have any comprehension of where in the world's capitalistic complex he is being led to.
>
> That great German philosopher, Hegel, spoke with profundity about just such blabbermouths seeking "self-expression." He said they reflected "an unreflective, incoherent stage of consciousness" characteristic of societies that are no more than a "community of animals."

1 From "On War and Peace," News & Letters.

"An unreflective incoherent stage of consciousness"— what could better describe a Castro?—characteristic of a society as a "community of animals," This is the best *contemporary* description I have yet seen anywhere of state capitalist societies like Mao's China.

Enter Russia

Russia has certainly hit the jackpot in Cuba, and America is eaten up with jealousy. Nowhere, from Alaska to Adenauer's West Germany, does America have so monolithic, anxious, enthusiastic, undivided *and* blithely unsuspecting a collaborator-victim, 90 miles from the shore of its main protagonist, as Russia has in Cuba.

As if sucked into the jet-propelled Ilyushin, the Cuban Revolution has been unable to resist the totalitarian pull of Russian state capitalism, with the administrative mentality running roughshod over the self-activity of the masses. Suddenly we are face to face with the negative element of a world crisis that will not let go of the newly-freed countries.

Castro fancies that his loud *pronunciamentos* against the stupidities of the American State Department "make up" for *his* "incoherent stage of consciousness."

In truth, they only too clearly show that this "haughty vassal"—to use yet another expression of Hegel's—is so bitten by the state capitalistic bug—that is, "a passion for bossing"—that he does not even stop to reflect that he is trying to foist on the Cuban people hands made bloody by their crushing of the Hungarian people's revolt. *Nothing can wash those hands clean. NOTHING...*

This new arrogant administrator may feel sufficiently like a king, now that he has a nuclear power at his side, as to issue invitations to all underdeveloped countries to come to a command performance in Havana. The African countries gave him his first rebuff when they refused to be taken in by this later-comer on the revolutionary scene and his pretensions of "world leadership."

In declining the invitations for a conference in *this* hemisphere, when they have carried on the struggles for freedom decades ahead of him in Africa, they have given him his first lesson in freedom that is *not* dependent on Russia and China who are only using the Cuban Revolution to further their own ends of world conquest.

There is yet time to escape the world holocaust Mao Tse-tung is in such a hurry to unleash today, *not tomorrow but today, IF* Fidel's Cuba will break loose from both poles of capital...

The two years that have passed since this was written have witnessed Castro's irretrievable entanglement in the Communist web, including also his total acceptance of the Communist perversion of Marxism. Fidel Castro is a man who thinks that if he himself drives the last nail into his own coffin, he thereby remains alive, and, if still alive, then certainly he is still the leader!

The Tragedy of the Cuban Revolution

Far from seeing that when the going got tough between the Big Two Powers Khrushchev would find *him* to be expendable, he was busy "proving," on December 2, 1961, that, long before he got power, he had read Marx's *Capital* "up to page 370" and "a text of Lenin" and would remain "a Marxist-Leninist to the end of my life." Misnamed as a speech on "Marxism-Leninism," Castro only proves that he has swallowed hook, line and sinker the Communist perversion of Marxism-Leninism. In any case, both the occasion for, and purpose of, the speech is to excuse the final dissolution of the July 26th Movement into the Communist Party, now renamed the Integrated Revolutionary Organization. He has discovered that the single party state is "the ideal government" and that that single party "is a selective party which leads."

It matters little whether, by the time Castro equated "The Revolution" he had made without any party to "The Party," he was also signing away to Russia the rights to missile bases and their operation. There was little left of Cuba that remained in the hands of the working people themselves. The State Plan reigned supreme and thought control was so total that it not only choked off the philosophy of freedom but overfilled the prisons.

Where "the party to lead" dominates one's every thought, and the masses to be led must have no organizations of their own, there the fulfillment of the State Plan takes the place of the liberation of mankind. Where one is busy with power politics rather than the release of human energies for their self-development, there one stifles both the human needs of a single country and the human aspirations of the forward movement of mankind the world over. Where missile bases have sprouted, and may again, there one has buried the philosophy of Marxist-Humanism.

The leadership complex, itself a by-product of our state-capitalist age and its drive for world domination, blinds Castro totally to the creativity of the masses. That, for him, remains an unopened book. Therein lies the tragedy of the Cuban Revolution.

∴

The Double Tragedy of Che Guevara

First Titled "Che Guevara, Revolutionary" News & Letters, *November 1967*

Che Guevara has joined the ranks of immortal martyrs. What makes his martyrdom unique is that he chose not to remain part of the new state power, although he had been a leader of the successful revolution in Cuba. He gave up his post as head of the economic ministry and embarked anew on the hardships of guerrilla fighting in still another country, Bolivia.

Che's death in Bolivia at the hands of the U.S.-trained-and-led Bolivian Rangers was a case of outright murder. He had been wounded and surrounded by a force of 180, armed with automatic rifles. He was alive. From Quebrada del Yuro, where he had been overwhelmed, he was carried five miles on a stretcher to the town of La Higuera. There the Bolivian army junta was asked what to do with him. Assured of American support, they ordered him shot.

Although Bolivia has no official death penalty, Che was executed within two hours of arrival in La Higuera. Seven bullet holes were clearly visible, including one through the heart, administered after he became a prisoner. His fingers were then cut off to identify his fingerprints, obligingly sent to the Bolivian military by the Argentinean junta. His body, strapped to a helicopter, was then flown to Valle Grande and taken to a Catholic hospital where the body was put on public exhibition.

So afraid was the Bolivian military of even the dead Guevara that, though it is against all custom in Catholic Bolivia, his body was nevertheless cremated. Even that didn't end the macabre ritual. As if that would stop Che from becoming a beacon for all Latin Americans struggling for freedom from their own oligarchy and U.S. imperialism, they then scattered his ashes to the wind. [It was later learned that Che's body was buried in a secret grave.]

When the Time was Ripe

In vain are all these frantic efforts to erase the memory of the revolutionary martyr. Pure delusion is the thought that, with his death, the revolt against the exploitative regime has ended. Bolivia has more than doubled its military budget during the Barrientos tyranny. In view of the fact that Bolivia is at war with no one—that is, no outside enemy, large or small—it is clear that the 17% of the national budget spent on "defense" is spent on arms to fight its own masses. When the time is ripe, the cold-blooded murder of Che will be avenged by the Bolivian masses who will put an end to this oligarchal regime.

The Bolivian masses had once before succeeded in ridding themselves of a military junta soon after the end of the world war. But they also found that it is insufficient to succeed "at home" unless they also overthrew U.S.

imperialism's iron grip on the country's economy. It is this which Che's fight has highlighted.

To prepare themselves for the uphill struggle on two fronts it becomes necessary to also have a clear head, that is to say, a revolutionary theory, fully integrated with the self-activity of the masses. It is for this reason that we must not blind ourselves to the double tragedy of Guevara's death. Bravely he lived and bravely he died, but he did not do in Bolivia what he had done in Cuba: relate himself to the masses.

Social Revolution and Guerrilla War

Guevara's isolation from the mass movement arose from a certain concept of guerrilla warfare as a substitute for social revolution. *The impatience with the masses who do not rise at the call of the guerrilla leaders, the disdain for the city, which Castro had called "a cemetery for revolutionaries and resources," the scorn for theory—all adding up to isolating Guevara from the Bolivian masses at the moment he decided the time was ripe.* His tragic death makes it imperative that these facts become widespread because there is no other way to uproot oppression once and for all.

Che himself admitted, in tracing the development of the Cuban revolution, that

> the men who arrived in Havana after two years of arduous struggle in the mountains and plains...are not the same men, ideologically, that landed on the beaches of Las Coloradas....Their distrust of the *campesino* has been converted into affection and respect for his virtues; their total ignorance of life in the country has been converted into a knowledge of the need of our *guajiros*: their flirtations with statistics and with theory have been fixed by the cement which is practice.

However, the theory and practice of guerrilla warfare as if that were the only road to revolution led Guevara to disdain other forms of class struggles—from a minor strike to a general strike, from political struggles to theoretical development, including the separation of true Marxism from Communist perversions.

Because Guevara could not separate the one from the other, he became impatient and looked for shortcuts to revolution. Yet he himself did, at certain critical periods, understand that only *when* the working class and the peasants are united, "the first step toward definite liberation is taken."

Spontaneity and Theory

This is what the guerrilla fighter forgets when he becomes impatient and wishes to substitute himself for the masses. At those moments, Guevara argued against the statement of Lenin: "Without a revolutionary theory, there is no revolutionary movement." Instead he held that "even if theory is not known, the revolution can succeed if historic reality is interpreted correctly and if the forces involved in it are utilized correctly."

But it is not a question of "*utilizing*" the forces. A revolutionary who appreciated the elemental surge of the masses *learns from* them because he sees them as *reason, not* only as mass force and energy. The fatal flaw in the concept of guerrilla war, whether that be the concept of Guevara or Mao or Giap, is that it is taken to be the equivalent of social revolution.

It is impossible, however, to create revolutions from above. They arise from the spontaneous, creative self-activity of the masses. The theoretician who learns this prepares himself for the revolution.

To work out a new relationship of guerrilla fighting to social revolution, of theory to practice, of the class struggles of the factory workers and those of agricultural laborers remains the task. In this way alone can the death of Che Guevara become a movement toward so total a revolution that it will abolish decadent capitalism and create a totally new, humanist foundation for life and labor and thought—a new society.

∴

Shortcut to Revolution or Long Road to Tragedy? On Regis Debray's Revolution in the Revolution

News & Letters, ***March, April 1968***

Revolution in the Revolution? by Regis Debray, Grove Press, N.Y.

Jean-Paul Sartre was so impressed with Regis Debray's booklet that when the author was arrested in Bolivia, Sartre held that the reason behind the arrest was not any alleged guerrilla activity, but the authorship of a book which "removes all the brakes from guerrilla activities." Long before Debray's arrest, followed by the brutal murder of Che Guevara by the Bolivian military junta, the Cuban government had no less than 200,000 copies of *Revolution In The Revolution?* printed of the original Spanish edition. Since then it has undergone many translations and has become a must for all would-be Cuban type guerrilla fighters. The young French philosopher is, indeed, Fidel's alter ego, and, very obviously, Castro considers this booklet an accurate presentation of his views.

Insurrection or Revolution

Nevertheless, the very title of the book is quite deceptive. This is not a book about revolution either "as such" or "within." The Russian Revolution of 1917 is, for example, never once referred to as a revolution, but is called "the insurrection." Nor can the reader find a single word in the work that would inform him that *that* "insurrection" was the last, not the first, act of revolution, whose spontaneity as well as organization, dialectic of objective events as well as of theory, self-development of millions of people tearing the old society up by its roots in general strikes and battle of ideas, in anti-war struggles and in two revolutions, all led to the success of the insurrection.

Instead, spontaneity as well as organization—be it the mass type like Soviets or "the Party"—objectivity as well as theory seem to be dirty words. In their place we get the glorification of one, and only one, activity, guerrilla war.

But here, too, there is deception. Glorification of guerrilla warfare encompasses only Latin America (actually only Cuba). Upon it alone "the irony of history has willed... this vanguard role": it alone has evolved a "new style of leadership." The leaders of all other guerrilla wars, *including the Vietnamese*, are consigned to "the past." The booklet burns with missionary zeal "to free the present from the past."

The Poor Dialectic!

A greater deception than either that contained in the title of this pretentious little booklet, or in the alleged narrowing of the "terrain" of guerrilla war to Latin America, underlies the contention that, as against the abstractions of theory, this essay is based solely on "experience," facts, "the concrete."

As if a phrase like "the irony of history" was no more than the latest cigarette commercial—"Beats me. I don't know why. Taste just never quits."—Debray continues to sing the praises of details, especially military details. "Everything is a matter of detail," said Fidel. Under the guise of this untheory, the most pretentious theoretic declamations are asserted which indeed change the course, *not of details*, but of theory and fact, history and "a new dialectic of tasks." Dominating this "new dialectic" is the need to set up "military *focos*, not political *focos*'." Poor dialectics, what crimes have not been committed in thy name!

We're supposed, further, to extend the priority of the military over the political party to the point where it substitutes also for theory, indeed is its superior since it is contemporary and freed from such things of "the past" as Marx's theory of social revolution as an elemental outburst. It surely frees one of "theoretical orthodoxy," not to mention "historical orthodoxy" which might recall that the first act in the dialectics of liberation evokes a second negation or total reorganization of both reality and theory. According to Debray, even in the glorified field of guerrilla war, "theory does as much harm as good":

> One may well consider it a stroke of good luck that Fidel had not read the military writings of Mao Tse-tung before disembarking on the coast of

> Oriente, he could thus invent, on the spot and out of his own experience, principles of a military doctrine in conformity with the terrain.

Moreover, the "new dialectic of tasks" demands that physical fitness tower above "a perfect (sic!) Marxist education," clandestine work above open propaganda, now dubbed "armed propaganda," which is not only subordinated to the military, but put off, perhaps till even after power when it "facilitates the organization of production, the collection of taxes, the interpretation of revolutionary laws, the maintenance of discipline"....

The "Poor Peasant" and the Leader Maximum

Debray is as completely unconscious as to the *capitalistic* character of the concept he had just uttered as he was of the intellectualistic petty-bourgeois concept of the "backwardness" of the masses that he gave vent to when he stressed the need of being secretive around the peasantry:

> The poor peasant believes, first of all, in anyone who has a certain power... The army, the *guardia rural, the latifundista's* private police, or nowadays the 'Green Berets' and Rangers, enjoy a prestige all the greater for being subconscious.

It seems the poor peasant can be saved in only one way by guerrilla warfare carried out by small guerrilla bands irrespective of the ripeness either of the objective or the subjective situations. Instead of these dead-end streets, there is a "shortcut": it is the duty of revolutionaries "to make revolutions." As for the poor peasant, well, "Guerrilla warfare is to peasant uprisings what Marx is to Sorel." Nothing less!

As against the trusting peasant, the French philosopher shows his independence of authority by pontificating about the duality of politics and the military symbolized by Mao Tse-tung and Chu Teh, Ho Chi Minh and Giap. "Perhaps we could add Lenin and Trotsky"[2] but, glory be, "In Cuba, military

2 This linking of Lenin and Trotsky is, unfortunately, asserted, not in order to set the historic record straight in a country linked with Russia, but merely to give the proper show of "objectivity" as the author launches into a typical Stalinist diatribe: "Let us for the moment decide to take the Trotskyist conception seriously, and not as the pure and simple provocation that it is in practice...we have been told that Trotskyists are ultra-leftists. Nothing is further from the truth. Trotskyism and Reformism join in condemning guerrilla warfare, in hampering or sabotaging it." Although "the art of insurrection" had been Trotsky's strongest point both as practitioner and theoretician, the Trotskyist epigones not only did not rise to the defense of Trotsky, but in their high praise of Debray's book, never once mentioned that it contained these slanders. (See *The Militant*). The administrative mentality of those who thirst for power

(operational) and political leadership have been combined in one man: Fidel Castro." Then, with the help of a purported statement by Che, Debray reaches for the Leader Maximum:

> The guerrilla force, if it genuinely seeks total political warfare, cannot in the long run tolerate any fundamental duality of functions or power. Che Guevara carries the idea of unity so far that he proposes that the military and political leaders who lead insurrectional struggles in America can be 'united, if possible in one person'...

Marx should never have praised so highly the peasant wars in medieval Germany, much less dared criticize his closest collaborator, Engels, for "paying too much attention to military affairs" in the Civil War in the U.S. If only he had lived to learn the art of guerrilla warfare he would have seen how much easier it is to teach followers to concoct a Molotov cocktail than the theory of proletarian revolution, *especially if one does not himself have the foggiest notion of the Marxian philosophy of liberation.*

So dominated by the concept of the single leader maximum is Debray that he projects it on an international scale and into the future:

> When Comrade Che Guevara once again took up insurrectional work, he accepted on an international level the consequences of the action of which Fidel Castro, the leader of the Cuban Revolution, is the incarnation.
>
> When Che Guevara reappears, it is hardly risky to assert that it will be as head of a guerrilla movement, as *its unquestioned political and military leader.*

Part II

Throughout its 115 pages *Revolution in the Revolution?* has been one never-ending paean of praise to the guerrilla. So supreme is the military as means and end, as strategy and tactic, as leadership and manhood itself that it swallows up also theory and the political party. According to Debray, "the staggering novelty introduced by the Cuban Revolution" is this: *"The guerrilla force is the party in embryo."*

---

leads naturally to the preference of strange political bedfellows to an open clash of ideas. In both cases—Debray as a Castroite and *The Militant* reviewer as a Trotskyist—the style is truly the man.

"The Equivalent-Substitution"

No doubt, the peculiar style of untheory requires that a superficial noun, like "novelty," follows so extravagant an adjective like "staggering." Still, our stylist seems most anxious that the reader place *this* "novelty" on a pedestal of original contributions to Marxism. He, himself, credits the "staggering novelty" with no less a feat than having ended "a divorce of several decades' duration between Marxist theory and revolutionary practice."

Had it been achieved, the unity of theory and practice would surely have created a new universal of historic dimension. It turns out, however, that it is but one more re-statement of the supremacy of the military. "One cannot," Debray writes, "claim to train revolutionary cadres in theoretical schools detached from instructional work and common combat experience."

Debray, thereupon, pulls out from his fertile style a new expression—"the equivalent substitution" (military command). This is the end result of the Army replacing the Party, replacing the Proletariat, replacing the Peasantry only to be replaced by the know-it-all, see-it-all, be-it-all, "Equivalent-Substitution," the military command, which consists mainly of intellectuals of bourgeois extraction:

> One finds that a working class of restricted size or under the influence of a reformist trade union aristocracy, and an isolated and humiliated peasantry, are willing to accept this group, of bourgeois origin, as their political leadership.

No factionalism of any sort is permitted. This old chestnut of Stalinist totalitarianism is passed off as "The theoretical and historic novelty of this situation." The "proof" of "perfect understanding" lies in the acceptance (1) of insurrectional activity as *"the number one political activity,"* and (2) of the conclusion that "there is no longer a place for verbal ideological relation to the revolution, nor for a certain type of polemic." Along with monolithism comes the absorption of independent organizations: "The formation of a broad, anti-imperialist front is realized through the people's war."

Nothing is any longer itself; everything and everybody is from now on confirmed *through* another. Debray tells us:

> Furthermore, the best way of putting an end to vacillations is to pass over to the attack on imperialism...It will be up to the conciliators to determine their position *vis-a-vis* the revolutionaries, not vice versa. It is they who must define themselves in terms of the reality and with relation to a *fait accompli.*

That type of "transformation" of reality has, from time immemorial, been a principle of *capitalist* confrontation of the masses. The fact that *fait accompli* is now re-christened as a "staggering novelty" of the Cuban Revolution does not denude it of its class nature, much less transform monolithism into a "revolution in the revolution." But our petty-bourgeois French intellectual with a penchant for Maoist-type of mathematical equation concludes triumphantly, as follows:

> In a given historic situation there may be a thousand ways to speak of the revolution, but there must be one necessary concordance among all those who have resolved to make it.

The Style is the Man

Why did Debray take so involved a detour to reach so totalitarian a conclusion, and to say it in so poetic a style? After all, it was clear from the start that Fidel Castro, and Fidel Castro alone, was the true "original." Why, then, the cryptic illusions, which, even where they were supposed to be historic, were very hard to decipher? Why the elliptical style? Why the staccato sentences and yet the overly verbose first chapter?

The fact that Debray could not merely assert but had to attempt to prove Cuban originality on the question of guerrilla war ran into difficulties from the start.

The first Marxist theorist of guerrilla warfare was Mao Tse-tung, not Fidel Castro. Furthermore, the thesis of "freeing the present from the past" had to come face-to-face with the simple reality that it was Vietnam, not Cuba, which was presently engaged in guerrilla warfare on a massive scale against the biggest of all world's imperialisms, that of the United States.

Under the circumstances, Debray could not attack General Giap frontally. Our philosopher thereupon hit upon the idea of beginning with an attack on the Trotskyists, (always a safe bet for Communists), only after that could Debray attempt to move cautiously to a criticism of other concepts of "self-defense:"

> In Vietnam above all, and also in China[3] armed self-defense of the peasants, organized in militias, has played an important role...but...in no way did it bring autonomous zones into being. These territories of

---

3 Debray will not reveal his full hand on Mao until some 100 pages later; by then, however, his language becomes as unbridled and slanderous as Mao's. Debray speaks about the "pro-Chinese" faction "sabotaging the armed struggle," its "noisy opportunism," concluding: "Even if we assume, by violent exercise of the imagination, that a 'pro-Chinese' group were

> self-defense were viable only because total war was being carried out on other fronts...

Castro's total war includes a war on Marxist theory: first, Marx's own theory of revolution as the *objectively* produced elemental outburst of the masses; and, second, Lenin's dictum that there can be no revolution without a revolutionary theory. Che Guevara, when he spoke, not "through" Debray, but in his own words, was open enough about it:

> This is a unique Revolution which some people maintain contradicts one of the most orthodox premises of the revolutionary movement, expressed by Lenin: 'Without a revolutionary theory there is no revolutionary movement.' It would be suitable to say that revolutionary theory as the expression of a social truth, surpasses any declaration of it; that is to say, even if the theory is not known, the revolution can succeed if historical reality is interpreted correctly and if the forces involved in it are utilized correctly.[4]

Debray will have nothing to do with this open declaration of a deviation, much less an actual theoretical argument; instead, there are his devious diatribes, first against "Trotskyism," then Maoism, and only then "theoretically" against Giap.

The way he explains Castro's "heresy" leaves out the question of theory altogether. He writes, "Fidel Castro," "says simply that there is no revolution without a vanguard." That this is not the point in dispute among Communists, all of whom are passionate "vanguardists," does not seem to disturb our master of substitution, as he reduces theory to a literature of the absurd, by finding "a close tie between biology (yes, *biology!*) and ideology."

To save us from "the vice of excessive deliberation," and the fractionalism which is "a dead-end street," Debray points "a warning finger...to indicate a short-cut." It is a short-cut to nowhere. It is a long road to tragedy.

A Long Road, Not a Short Cut

Far from being a short-cut, much less the "guaranteed" way to achieve state power, guerrilla warfare is a long, protracted road which has more often failed than succeeded. Our post-war world is filled with guerrilla wars from the

---

to assemble fifty or so, scatter-brains, or degenerates..." etc., etc., etc. As Castro moves to the Maoist camp, will he now destroy this much touted booklet?

4 *Notes for the Study of the Ideology of Cuban Revolution* by Che Guevara.

Philippines to Burma, from Malaya to Indonesia, not to mention India and Japan, that have failed. That there is no "magic" to it, has been bitterly driven home by Che's tragic death. (See *News & Letters*, Editorial, November, 1967.)

Our post-war world, as against the post-war world fallowing the First World War, lacks "magic," the true magic, of the Russian Revolution which set the world aflame. Even today—a half century afterwards, when it has been transformed into its opposite—the original perspective remains the greatest force of world revolutionary development.

This, then, is our Marxist heritage, the past from which Castro's theoretician wishes "to free the present." He will not succeed. If it were merely the writing of a young French philosopher, it could be easily dismissed. Unfortunately, he speaks for a state power, one which pictures itself as revolutionary. Because short cuts to revolution look attractive, it was necessary to counter-pose reality to Debray's nimble-penned panacea.

The only "magic" is that of Social Revolution—a great mass in motion, in spontaneous, forward movement, propelled by a philosophy of liberation, a Marxist theory of proletarian world revolution in which the masses are not only mass and muscle, but also passion and Reason.

CHAPTER 16

State-Capitalism as a "New Stage of World Capitalism" vs. The Humanism of Marx

> *Stalin is but the Russian name for a world phenomenon.... [My study of the first Five Year Plans] was not embarked upon solely as a Russian study. It was done as a restatement of Marxism for our age....State intervention in the economy, whether totally or 'in part,' characterized both Hitler's Germany and Roosevelt's U.S. 'New Deal,' Japan's 'Co-Prosperity Sphere' as well as the 'Labor Government' in Great Britain....The State Plan had become part of the very organism of capitalism undermined by the Great Depression, fearful of proletarian revolution, determined to survive at all costs, be it state control or world war, or a nuclear holocaust—that is to say, destruction of civilization itself....Like the removal of an incubus from the brain, the death of Stalin, in March, 1953, released fantastic, elemental creativity on the part of the proletariat. Within three short months, the first uprising ever against Communist totalitarianism erupted in East Germany.*
>
> —DUNAYEVSKAYA, *"'Culture,' Science and State-Capitalism"*

The above summarizes the distinctiveness of Dunayevskaya's concept of state-capitalism. (1) It was not alone an economic analysis of Russia's transformation from a workers' state into a state-capitalist one. (2) She saw state-capitalism as a world phenomenon encompassing the capitalist economies' determination to survive the crisis of the Great Depression. (3) The analysis was part of her rethinking and restating Marxism in the post-World War II world, based in part on returning to the Marxism of Marx, particularly as found in the Economic-Philosophic Manuscripts of 1844 *and in* Capital. *(4) A crucial element for such a restatement of Marxism for her age was founded upon her focus on revolutionary subjects emerging from below, be it in the Russian satellites, within Russia itself, or in "the West," including workers, women, the Black dimension and youth within the United States.*

The Humanism of Marx is the Basic Foundation for Anti-Stalinism Today

News & Letters, *January 1966*

(As a contribution to the developing discussion on anti-Stalinism, the following article was submitted to Tokyo's Waseda University student newspaper by the author during her recent lecture tour of Japan.)

The death of Stalin, in March, 1953, marked the end of an era. DeStalinization began almost at once, not by Khrushchev from above, but by the East Berlin workers from below, who, on June 17, rose in spontaneous revolt for "Bread and Freedom" and against raising "work norms" (speed-ups). Within weeks the East German revolt was followed by one in the forced labor camps in Vorkuta inside Russia itself.[1] When the 20th Congress of the Russian Communist Party, in February, 1956, finally embarked on deStalinization, it brought to the surface the seething undercurrents of revolt throughout Eastern Europe, and, by October, 1956, Russian Communism was faced with a proletarian revolution in Hungary that demanded freedom from its overlordship. By the time the Sino-Soviet conflict reached the point of no return, in 1963, Mao Zedong was boasting of the fact that it was he who initiated the Russian armed intervention.

Thus did the Russian-Chinese *counter*-revolution begin and, hand in hand with it, came the campaign of slander against the Hungarian revolutionaries as "revisionists." However, because the revolutionary, creative restatement of Marxism for our age came from an elemental surge forward, and because the Humanist banner was soon seen also in Latin America, in Africa, in the whole new Third World fighting for freedom from Western imperialism as well, it was impossible any longer to consign the Humanist Essays of Marx to unreachable library shelves.

Philistines there are, in 1965, who declare that we should never have awakened the Economic-Philosophic Manuscripts, 1844 *from their century-old slumber. Serious thinkers, on the other hand, know that no other writing anywhere, at any time, has made history as have Marx's now-famous essays on "Private Property and Communism," "Critique of the Hegelian Dialectic," and "Alienated Labor." To look, even just cursorily, at the 121-year history of these essays is to embark on a journey of adventure which reveals the grandeur, the tragedy, and the challenge of our times.*

It is true that when the young Marx left his manuscripts "to the stinging criticism of the mice," it forbade no tragedy because the living Marx kept concretizing and developing his concept of alienation as it developed into the

1 See *Vorkuta* by Dr. Joseph Scholmer.

proletariat's "quest for universality."[2] This vision of "all-round" man was an integral part of the very organism of Marx, both as theoretician—be the theory that of revolution, the Paris Commune, or that of "the economic laws" of *Capital*—and as activist, as General Secretary of the first International Workingmen's Association.

Lenin's Independent Philosophic Breakthrough

Altogether different was the fate of those Humanist essays when the official heirs of Marx and Engels—the German Social Democrats—kept them sealed in vaults and thus deprived themselves of the concept of a new human dimension. With the outbreak of the first World War and the collapse of the German Social Democracy, Lenin had to recapture the unity of the ideal and the material through a painstaking return to the philosophic origins of Marx in Hegel, and only then moving it forward to the new historic plane, 1917, when the population "*to a man*" would not only abolish private capitalism, but would run production and the state, and thus initiate the break-down of the division between mental and manual labor that characterizes all class societies.

It took a Russian Revolution PLUS the tireless efforts of the great Marxist scholar, Ryazanov, PLUS money to pry the 1844 manuscripts out of the vaults of the Second International. But, once again, reaction intervened to rob the proletariat of its philosophic heritage. In Russia, the triumph of Stalin meant the beginning of the end of "the realization of philosophy," the Marxian concept of theory and of freedom. In Germany, the victory of Hitler marked the height of capitalist barbarism, the holocaust of World War II, the bankruptcy of bourgeois thought. Thrown into the savage inhumanity of a Buchenwald, who could think of philosophy?

And yet, World War II had no sooner drawn to a gory end with American imperialism's atom bombing of Hiroshima and Nagasaki, than, throughout Western Europe, everyone, from the Catholic theologians to the atheistic Existentialists, re-discovered those precious Humanist Essays. But the Communists were powerful enough to keep the debate confined in academic channels. The reality is this: yet another generation was born to face the challenge. No matter how young and new the present generation of anti-Stalinist revolutionary Marxists are, they must come face to face with these two overpowering facts: (1) World War II had come and gone without resulting in any successful proletarian revolution, and without starting a new stage in thought comparable to the one begun by Lenin at the time of World War I and his return to the Marxian origins in Hegel; and (2) nothing but a stillbirth had resulted from Leon Trotsky's gigantic labors to build an anti-Stalinist Marxist International.

---

2 Karl Marx, *Poverty of Philosophy*.

This, despite the fact that only Lenin had stood higher than Leon Trotsky in the leadership of the Russian October; despite the fact that Trotsky had tried to keep the Marxist banner unsullied by Stalin's betrayals and perversions of Marxism; despite the fact that he spent all the remainder of his life trying to build a revolutionary "vanguard party"; and despite, finally, the fact that he had succeeded in getting a few other outstanding revolutionary internationalists, such as the Dutch Marxist, Hendrik Sneevliet, to sign the Manifesto of the Fourth International.

Trotsky's Philosophic Failure

To this writer it has become all too obvious that Leon Trotsky failed because he had not been the theoretician that Lenin had been, had not prepared himself either for 1917, or for 1939, in the manner Lenin had or would have; that is to say, Trotsky had not met the twin political-philosophic challenges that each generation of Marxists must answer for itself: (1) what new stage of *production*, and with it, relations in production, had we reached? And (2) what *new* stage of workers' revolt and *new*, related underlying philosophy will now emerge? But, whether or not you, the readers, single out the Humanism of Marx as the theory of liberation for our state-capitalist age, you must find the link of *historic continuity*, if history has rejected Trotskyism—and the fact that the Fourth International has proved to be a still-birth seems to bear this out—then the new anti-Stalinist revolutionary forces must find the "why" of the failure of the first appearance of anti-Stalinist Marxism.

Not only is it impossible "to skip" historic stages, but one must face reality and note that, where the movement from theory to revolution proved a still-birth, the movement from practice did not. Quite the contrary. Whether you begin with the Hungarian Revolution openly unfolding the banner of Marx's Humanism[3] as a movement of freedom *from* Communism, or with Fidel Castro in Cuba, who, in fighting against *American* imperialism and its puppet Batista, claimed his revolution was both against capitalist exploitation and "communist political tyranny," was "humanist";[4] whether, instead, you begin with the year, 1960, "Africa's Year" when no less than 19 nations gained their independence from Western imperialism, again under the banner of Humanism,[5] or use that year as the new point of departure because of the mass demonstrations in Japan against the American Security Pact—and, indeed, those marvelous

3 See especially *Imre Nagy on Communism* and Tibor Dery's writings as well as *Po Prostu* for the whole year, 1956.

4 Fidel Castro, *History Will Absolve Me*.

5 See both Leopold Sedar Senghor, *African Socialism*, and Sekou Toure, *Africa's Path in History*.

"snake dancers" the TV screens brought us, the *second* America, the America of the proletariat, the youth, the Negro Revolution, the anti-Vietnam war fighters, promptly built an international bridge of solidarity between you and us—one truth stands out: everywhere the masses were in motion, and, from below, there was a dynamism of ideas unmatched in grandeur by the movement from theory that is bound to an elitist "vanguard" party.

Theoretic Void Denies Historic Action

No sadder commentary can be made about the 40 year theoretic void left by the death of Lenin than by quoting Chou Yang and realizing that his downgrading of the Humanism of Marxism reflects the views of some who call themselves anti-Stalinists: "The modern revisionists and some bourgeois scholars try to describe Marxism as humanism and call Marx a humanist…This, of course, is futile …"[6]

If a serious discussion on an international scale is to be started among anti-Stalinist Marxists, then we must begin here, just here. Chou Yang notwithstanding, it is not some "bourgeois scholars" who brought Marx's Humanism onto the historic stage, but masses in motion—masses in motion against established Communism, masses in motion against American imperialism, masses in motion against British, French, Belgian imperialism, masses in motion against all existing societies. The Marx of 1844 who could write of the Silesian weavers: "The Silesian uprisings began where the French and English uprisings ended, with the consciousness of the proletariat as a class," needs no lessons in class struggle from a representative of state power in China. Stalinism, be it in Russian or Chinese garb, should not be allowed to sully Marx's concept of revolution and vision of the "all-round" man.

It is the concept of individual as well as social freedom, the conditions of class society that had to be undermined, abolished, transcended. It is this we must now recapture, unfold, develop on the new historic plane of the 1960's.

Basis for a New Revolutionary International

There must be no more Hiroshimas and Nagasakis. And something a great deal less honorary than "a degenerated workers' state" should be reserved for retrogressionists, for any who expound the barbarous view that a "new civilization" can first be built on the ruins of what would be left of the world after a

6 Chou Yang, *The Fighting Task Confronting Workers in Philosophy and the Social Sciences*, Peking, 1963.

thermonuclear war.[7] In a nuclear age where the only war that can be won is the battle for the minds of men, it is high time for Marxists and other freedom fighters to clear their heads, and, in opposing both Western imperialism and private capital as well as state-capitalism that calls itself Communism, East and West, unfurl a banner of a classless society and *begin* laying the foundation for a new revolutionary Marxist International.

Tokyo, Dec. 28, 1965

The New Stage of World Capitalism: State-Capitalism

Nationalism, Communism, Marxist-Humanism and the Afro-Asian Revolutions, 1961

It is clear that World War II ended only because the two new world powers, Russia and the United States were exhausted. As if to prove to be only an uneasy interlude they put markers all along Germanys; two Koreas; two Vietnams.

While the Russians embarked on looting everything in sight from East Germany to Manchuria, the United States, the only rich victor, found it had to *give* rather than *take*. It promptly embarked on the Marshall Plan "to save" Western Europe from direct assault by proletarian revolution. The tide of colonial revolutions, which were putting an end to the empires of its "victorious allies," (Britain and France), it could not stem at all. The Far East, the Middle East, the Mediterranean, Africa—all were seething with revolt. It thereupon had also to embark on the "Point 4" program of aid to underdeveloped countries. Russia, too, found that if it wants to keep in the race for world domination, it better begin its own "help to underdeveloped countries."[8]

The problem for Russia, on the one hand, and the United States, on the other, is where to get the capital to give underdeveloped countries when capitalism, at this advanced stage of its development and decay, is suffering not from "overproduction" or "excess capital," but from a decline in the rate of profit in relation to the mass of capital invested. In a word, the total social capital needed for ever greater expansion is woefully inadequate.

---

7 For a more detailed analysis of Mao's position on thermonuclear war, see the chapter, "The Challenge of Mao Zedong" in *Marxism and Freedom.*

8 The first fairly comprehensive statement of this can be read in Joseph S. Berliner's *Soviet Economic Aid.*

Marx's Forecast

We live in an age when, even from a "purely economic" point of view, Marx's forecast of capitalist collapse has moved from theory to practice. Marx's theory of capitalist collapse was based on the fact that it would collapse out of its own inherent contradictions; that since surplus value comes only from *living labor*, and since an ever lesser amount of that is needed to set *in motion an ever greater amount of dead labor or capital*, that the system would fall if even "the full twenty-four hours a day...(were) wholly appropriated by capital."[9]

Lush as individual private profits are, and heavy as they feel on workers' backs on which they rest, the truth is that there isn't enough capital produced to keep the crazy capitalist system going with the self-same profit motive on an ever-expanding scale. At the heyday of imperialism, the superprofits extracted from the carving up of Africa and the colonization in the Orient *seemed* to contradict Marx's analysis and Marx's prediction. Not only bourgeois economists, but even Marxists, like Rosa Luxemburg, wrote that we might as well wait for "the extinction of the moon" as to wait for the decline in the rate of profit to undermine capitalism.[10]

Now, however, theory and fact have moved so close to each other that it would be hard to find anyone who would claim that there is an excess of capital anywhere in the world. This is obvious when you look at underdeveloped countries like India, China, Africa, and Latin America. It is just as obvious in Western Europe.

There are some discerning bourgeois economists who, seeing the hopeless impasse of capitalism, wish to sell the idea of a "Christian" internationalism to "the West." They feel that if they can invent some sort of installment plan on which to base this idea, it would not be "too heavy a burden" for the capitalist class to bear and, *at the same time*, be sufficiently palatable to the *leaders* in the underdeveloped areas that they would choose "democratic capitalism" against totalitarian Communism, i.e., state capitalism.

One such discerning economist is Barbara Ward, whom Nkrumah, Premier of Ghana, chose to deliver a series of "lectures on world affairs" at the University of Ghana. As the lady put it: *America's foreign ventures are barely one fifth of Britain's in the heyday of foreign lending...Shortage of capital is the world's trouble today, not the struggles of rival capitalists to go out and invest.*[11]

Nevertheless, Miss Ward wants to convince "the West" both to invest, and to give outright. She rightly cannot see the West "winning" in any other way. Hence, her knowledge of the shortage of capital does not stop her from

---

9 *Capital* Vol. III, p. 468, by Karl Marx.

10 Rosa Luxemburg, *Accumulation of Capital.*

11 Barbara Ward: *Five Ideas that Change the World,* p. 139.

propounding her thesis that the "have powers" can give the Afro-Asians what their economies *"at this stage"* can "absorb." Indeed, she insists that the total amount needed represents "not even one per cent of the United States' national income."[12]

The joker is in the words "at this stage". She emphasizes that it is really the backwardness of the workers ("the shortage of trained manpower is a severely limiting factor") that compels the economy to take only a little industrialization at a time. The doling out is to stretch over "4 or 5 decades," that is to say, no less than a half century. It is clear that the lady is in no hurry.

But mankind gaining its freedom is. It has no intention of stretching out its industrialization (not to mention land reform and caste reorganization) into centuries. It is precisely this snail's pace of modernizing the economy in India which has turned the colored world to look longingly at China.

The China Road

A seemingly new path to industrialization was being carried out by China. Usurpation of the Marxist banner of liberation in sweeping the corrupt Chiang Kai-shek regime out of power greatly enhanced the attractive power of Mao's China for the colored peoples of the world. Neither the Korean War, nor the first grabbing of Tibet, changed that impression of freedom, and newly-released creative energies for the reorganization of the semi-feudal regime on new beginnings. Compared to the snail's pace of industrialization in India, China, with its Russian-styled Plans, seemed to have leapt straightway into the technologically advanced world, challenging Britain's production of steel.[13]

It soon turned out, however, that whatever "great leap forward" was made was made on the bent backs of the masses, not for them. What was being established, as the result of toil from dawn to dusk, was not a new society, but state capitalist totalitarianism. The attempt of Mao's China to do Russia one better—through the establishment of barracks labor, barracks discipline, and barracks family life in what the Chinese Communist Party dared call "Communes"—made the new colored nations take a second look and drawback in revulsion at the crushing of Tibet.[14]

---

12 Barbara Ward: *Interplay of East and West,* n. 93.

13 Ygael Gluckstein: *Mao's China*; also the latest work *Economic Planning and Organization on Mainland China,* by Chao Kuo-Chin.

14 The most interesting as well as factual statements appear in the Yugoslav press. The "Communes" were of course covered in the daily, weekly, and monthly press; the *New Leader,* (July 15, 1959) has a special supplement on it.

It is not that this revolt matched the grandeur of the Hungarian Revolution with its Workers' Councils. Nor were the Tibetans the first to show revolt at the bureaucratic face of Communism—the Vietnamese peasants, who had not relented in their revolution against French imperialism and struggled to establish an independent nation, turned away from Ho-Chi-Minh years before. But then, the times were not ripe for other colored peoples to take a second look at present day Asian Communism. Now, the times are ripe, and the great African surge is ready to question that path to industrialization.

∵

"Culture," Science and State-Capitalism

News & Letters, *May, June–July 1971*

1971 is the eleventh year since the Sino-Soviet conflict first broke into the open. By the time, in August, 1966, that Mao launched the so-called Great Proletarian Cultural Revolution, not only had Mao succeeded in designating Russia as capitalist, state-capitalist, but all his opponents within China (all, that is, *except* the actual capitalists who continue to collect their five per cent interest on capital that they manage for the state) as "capitalist roaders."

There are young revolutionaries who are so enthusiastic about Mao's expose of "Khrushchev's phony Communism" (now called "Khrushchevism without Khrushchev") as capitalistic that they help cover up the greater truths, that (1) long before Khrushchev's "phony Communism" (deStalinized goulash), it was Stalin who lorded it over Russia and initiated the transformation of the first workers' state into its opposite, a state-capitalist society; (2) it was Mao himself who, in 1956, helped Khrushchev to crush the Hungarian Revolution with its Workers' Councils and struggles for a truly new social order; and (3), furthermore, Stalin is but the Russian name for a *world* phenomenon. Its [state capitalism's] appearance has nothing whatever to do with the Sino-Soviet conflict (which it antedated by three long decades), and everything to do with the Great Depression, and fear of proletarian revolution. Therein lies its crucial importance for our day.

The Stakes

The real question is: What, in this period of recessions that have come to take the place of the Great Depression nevertheless, makes the global crisis so total that even Mao's China is beginning to stretch out a hand toward a little "peaceful co-existence" with the U.S.? What is being outstretched is not the hand of a ping pong player (China's own brand of phony "people to people relations"), but that of Chou En-lai at the very top of the "new" Mao leadership.

Why is it that just as the recently concluded 24th Congress of the Russian Communist Party had all its pie-in-the-sky promises rest on "greater labor productivity," so Mao's Communism, purified of "capitalist roaders," continues to lash out against "the black[15] wind of economism"? It is this, *just this*, which makes both "socialist lands" bear such striking resemblance to that super-imperialist titan, the U.S.A.

State-capitalism, not as a mere swear word spewed out against dissidents, but as serious theory, does indeed reflect reality torn in twain by the decisive relations of men at the point of production, those exploitative relations of capital/labor which determine all else in society, especially its thought. *Which is why the proletariat, too, in its struggles, fights under totally new philosophic banners of liberation, as the 1968 Hunan Manifesto within China itself proved once again:*

> The form of political power is superficially changed...However, old bureaucrats continue to play the leading role in the 'new political power'... Chou En-lai (is) at present the general representative of China's Red Capitalist class...as the masses have said, 'everything remains the same after so much ado.'
>
> Victory of the Chinese proletariat and the broad masses of revolutionary people and the extinction of the new bureaucratic bourgeoisie are likewise inevitable...the 'People's Commune of China' will surely survive.[16]

In this, the 30th year of the elaboration of the theory of state-capitalism, and the 15th year of the rebirth of the Humanism of Marxism produced by the mass movements in East Europe in the 1950's, growing throughout the world in the 1960's, we must go back to theoretic origins not only to set the historical record

15 Evidently no one has told Mao that Black is beautiful. All the broadsheets that China directs to the Blacks in the U.S. notwithstanding, the word, black, has always (after the "Cultural Revolution" as before) been used in Mao's China as synonym for everything evil!

16 During the "Cultural Revolution" a new revolutionary youth organization sprung up in Hunan and called itself the "Hunan Provincial Proletarian Revolutionary Great Alliance Committee" (Sheng-wu-lien). Its Manifesto, quoted above, along with two other documents by it as well as all the official Maoist attacks on it have been reproduced in Klaus Mehnert's *Peking and the New Left: At Home and Abroad* (China Research Monograph #4, UC, Berkeley).

straight, but also to test the dialectic method of the state-capitalist theory against the dialectics of liberation today.

The Theory of State-Capitalism

Born under the impact of the shock of the Hitler-Stalin Pact, the outbreak of World War II, *and* Trotsky's calling for the defense of Russia, "a workers' state, though degenerate," the "state-capitalist tendency" decided to make its own study of the class nature of the Russian economy in strict relationship both to Marxism and the specific form of workers' resistance to the Five Year Plans. I happened to have been the first to make a study of the Plans from original Russian sources, but it was not embarked upon solely as a Russian study. It was done as a restatement of Marxism for our age. It was by no accident, therefore, that, in the process of analyzing the operation of the law of value, that mainspring of capitalism, that I rediscovered, in the early 1940's, Marx's now celebrated *1844 Economic-Philosophic Manuscript*. It was its concept of free labor as the shaper of history vs. alienated labor which is the mark of capitalism that governed the study, *The Nature of the Russian Economy*.[17]

Because the law of value dominates not only on the home front of class exploitation, but also in the world market where big capital of the most technologically advanced land rules, the theory of state-capitalism was not confined to the "Russian Question," as was the case when the nomenclature was used by others. Quite the contrary. The new in the theory of state-capitalism, its dialectics, its conclusions, demonstrated, first, that the State Plan, the State Party, the monolithic State, differed in no fundamental degree from the capitalism Marx analyzed, in *Capital*, where he showed that it was not the anarchy in the market, but the "despotic plan of capital" which labor confronted daily in the factory. Equally fundamental was the second point my study made, that the 1930's made it possible to prove, in the concrete, what Marx could only state in theory

17 A minority political tendency is always limited in the space accorded to it in the public press. Thus, the section of the study of the Russian economy that was based on the early essays of Marx and was entitled *Labor and Society* was not published either when Part I, *Analysis of the Russian Economy* appeared (*New International*, Dec., 1942, Jan., 1943, Feb., 1943), or when Part II, *Nature of the Russian Economy* (*New International*, Dec., 1947 and Jan., 1947), was finally published. *Labor and Society* finally appeared in mimeographed form in the Johnson-Forest interim period Bulletin No. 5 (1947). These documents form part of the *Raya Dunayevskaya Collection* (*Marxist-Humanism, Its Origin and Development in America, 1941–1969*) that is now available... from Labor History Archives, Wayne State University, Detroit. [*The Raya Dunayevskaya Collection, the Marxist-Humanist Archives* is now available in full on the Internet. www.rayadunayevskaya.org *"Labor and Society" can be found in Chapter 9 of this present study.*].

about the ultimate development of the concentration and centralization of capital "in the hands of a single capitalist or a single capitalist corporation."[18]

State intervention in the economy, whether totally or "in part," characterized both Hitler's Germany and Roosevelt's U.S. "New Deal," Japan's "Co-Prosperity Sphere" as well as the "Labor Government" in Great Britain. What the 1930's established is that under no conditions could The Plan be considered either "socialist" or only a "war measure" as it was during World War I. The State Plan had become part of the very organism of capitalism undermined by the Great Depression, fearful of proletarian revolution, determined to survive at all costs, be it state control or world war, or a nuclear holocaust—that is to say, destruction of civilization itself.

On the other hand, the proletariat has no intention whatever to let that happen. Its struggles against that are ceaseless, although the forms of resistance, of necessity, manifest themselves in new forms. Thus low labor productivity, far from being a sign of the "backwardness" of the Russian proletariat, *is the measure of his resistance to the State Plan, the State Party, the Leader.*

The masses have proven they cannot be brainwashed. All the means of communication may be in the hands of the state, but the heads belong to the same bodies that are being exploited, and *they think their own thoughts.*

By the time they openly revolt, their spontaneous outburst hews out new roads to freedom, to totally new human relations as well as to working out a new relationship between theory and practice. Such a new epoch opened in the 1950's when, at one and the same time, a second Industrial Revolution had begun with Automation, and the wildcats against it, in the U.S., and, in East Europe, revolts within totalitarian lands broke out.

Part II

Like the removal of an incubus from the brain, the death of Stalin, in March, 1953, released fantastic, elemental creativity on the part of the proletariat. Within three short months, the first uprising ever against Communist totalitarianism erupted in East Germany. This initiated a totally new epoch of

18 Karl Marx, *Capital*, Vol. I, p. 689. See also what I wrote in *Marxism and Freedom*: "The single capitalist, call him 'Collective Leadership under Khrushchev, Inc.,' if you will, will have at a certain stage a magnificent plant, completely automatized, or a jet bomber, but he cannot stop to raise the standard of living of the masses of the workers. He may be able to avoid the more extreme forms of ordinary commercial crises, but even within the community itself he cannot escape the internal crisis of production...That is why Marx, throughout *Capital*, insists that either you have the self-activity of the workers, the plan of freely associated labor, or you have the hierarchic structure of relations in the factory and the despotic Plan. *There is no in-between.*" (p. 136).

freedom struggles in East Europe. The "Polish October" had not actually developed into a full revolution, but the ideological struggles, especially among the youth, were open-ended, many-sided, passionate and brought Humanism of Marxism onto the historic stage.

The revolts culminated in a full-scale revolution in Hungary in 1956. With the establishment of a new form of workers' rule—Workers' Councils—the workers had created also the decentralized form of relationships for all other sectors of the population so that we had Councils of Revolutionary Youth, Councils of Intellectuals as well as a proliferation of parties, newspapers, free minds.

No matter what one's point of concentration was in those three-years between the East German uprising and the Hungarian Revolution—before the Russian tanks moved in to crush the revolution, when the Russians feared the possibility of revolution, they had launched a deliberately abstract discussion of the dialectic, "the negation of the negation"[19]—there was no doubt whatever that the masses in revolt were a new breed. Even so simple a slogan as "Bread and Freedom" pointed to new ways of uniting economics and philosophy.

The historic, the unique, the new initiated in East Germany in 1953, climaxed in Hungary in 1956, reborn in the 1960's throughout East Europe and culminating in Czechoslovakia in 1968,[20] and, as the Polish strikes at the end of 1970 showed, *the resistance has not yet ended.* All these epochal developments have yet to be grasped by intellectuals for what they were, are: *a movement from practice both to freedom and to theory,* a still developing new dialectics of liberation.

Paradoxically, the state-capitalist tendency which had looked towards just such spontaneous outbursts, had enthusiastically hailed the East German uprising, failed to meet the challenge to theory from practice. While I had begun to pose, the moment Stalin died, the question of the relationship between

---

19 See "Marx's Working Out of the Materialist Dialectics in the *Economic-Philosophic Manuscripts of the Year, 1844*" by V.A. Karpushin. This article (*Voprosy Filosofii* #3/1955) has never been translated into English. Although many other attacks appeared, none were as "strictly" philosophic. Nor is it possible, now that Khrushchev has become an unperson and the 21st Congress of the Party has been played down, to see, how from open attacks on the Humanism of Marxism, the bureaucracy suddenly tried to usurp it for its own use by having the reigning philosopher, Mitin, then declare Khrushchev's report to contain "the magnificent and noble conception of Marxist-Leninist socialist humanism" (!). I have traced through the changes of line on the subject of Humanism for the years, 1955–59 in *Nationalism, Communism, Marxist Humanism and the African-Asia Revolutions*, pp. 22–29 (Left Group, Cambridge University Labour Club, England, 1961.).

20 See *Czechoslovakia: Revolution and Counter Revolution* (News & Letters Pamphlet, 1968.).

philosophy and revolution, the working out of a new relationship between theory and practice that would be rooted both in actuality and in dialectics,[21] the co-founder of the Tendency was moving away from open Marxism. Whether that was due to the fact that McCarthyism was in full bloom in the U.S., or was due to his changed attitude to nationalism, the indisputable fact is that he glorified, first West Indian nationalism, then Cuba, and then raised Nkrumah to the level of Lenin, if not a notch above.

When I first read Johnson's statement, "In one of the remarkable episodes in revolutionary history, he (Nkrumah) single handedly outlined a programme based on the ideas of Marx, Lenin and Gandhi..." I wrote: "I admit that combining Marx, Lenin and Gandhi is quite a feat. But for a pamphleteer like J.R. Johnson who thundered so for the Soviet United States of Europe, Soviet United States of Asia, world revolution, the struggle against bureaucracy 'as such,' the self-mobilization of the masses and for new passions and new forces to reconstruct society on totally new beginnings—to end with Nkrumah as representative of the new, the new, is rather pathetic. There is nothing to add but to say with Hamlet, 'Alas, poor Yorick, I knew him.'" (*Afro-Asia Revolutions, supra*, p. 9 ftn.)[22]

---

21 "An Exchange of Letters on Hegel's Absolute Idea" (May 12, May 20, May 22, 1953) which appeared as Appendix in the mimeographed edition of Extracts of Lenin's *Philosophic Notebooks* (News & Letters, November, 1955). [The Letters can be found in Dunayevskaya's *Power of Negativity*]

22 Perhaps this is the place to comment not only on what J.R. Johnson had written on Nkrumah, but also on his sudden rewriting of the history of the state-capitalist tendency.

Johnson's pamphlet from which I quoted p. 77, was called *Facing Reality* and carried, as Appendix, a fantastic rewrite of the history of the state-capitalist tendency upon which I did not bother to comment. The deafness to reality calling itself *Facing Reality* has since then, however, not only rewritten the history of, but published the Tendency document itself, *State-Capitalism and World Revolution*, as if it were a product of C.L.R. James alone. If we are to believe Martin Glaberman, who writes the preface to this new publication, "the author was C.L.R. James. Perhaps this will help to place James, who wrote for a number of years under the pseudonym of J.R. Johnson, in a truer light as a major inheritor and continuator of the Marxist tradition."

One thing can be said for Martin Glaberman. As against the sudden long list of names appended as prefators to the republication of the document in England in 1956, all of whom had nothing to do with the writing of the document, and some of whom were adherents, not of the state-capitalist tendency, but of bureaucratic-collectivism, Martin Glaberman is an exponent of the state-capitalist theory. Too bad that since his grandiose *pronunciamento*, above, he too has separated himself from James, who had not only split the state-capitalist tendency, but also split from the co-author of *Facing Reality*. It was left to Paul Buhle and *Radical America* (Vol. IV, No. 4, May, 1970) to present "with the

Naturally this not only did not stop the Tendency's full development into Marxist-Humanism, but also, and, above all, the objectivity of the specific form of Marx's philosophy of liberation was embraced by great masses of people having nothing whatever to do with ideological battles that appear in factional form, and everything to do with their spontaneous struggles for freedom under a concrete banner of liberation. The socialism "with a human face" was embraced first by the East Europeans who were fighting for freedom *from Communism*, then by the African Revolutions gaining freedom *from Western imperialism*, and even, at first, by Castro defeating both internal reaction and U.S. imperialism.[23]

The whole new, Third World that was born sans any "leadership" from the Communist world led to the historic split in that orbit, *not* because either the Russian or Chinese Communist Parties were moving *together with* these new "storm centers of world revolution," but because both state powers were fighting for direction of and control over, (*especially the latter*), a world movement which emerged elementally, independent of all existing state powers—East and West, private capitalist, or state-capitalists calling themselves Communist.

It is true that, at first, Mao's Communism appeared as the greater force of attraction—in theory, with its dictum that "power comes out of the barrel of a gun"; in practice, with the "Great Leap Forward" which promised to skip both capitalism and socialism, and go "directly" to Communism. When, however, it had become clear that the "Great Leap Forward" had ended in great disaster, and when U.S. imperialism chose to throw the gauntlet (filled with devastating, barbaric bombs), not to mighty China, but to little North Vietnam,

---

encouragement of C.L.R. James" a new collection, without any compunction whatever to cite which are Tendency documents, and which are individual writings, on any subject whatever. It is a mishmash worthy of not-so-radical American eclecticism.

23 *The New Left Review*, Jan.-Feb., 1961, reproduced Fidel Castro's 1959 declaration: "Standing between the two political and economic ideologies or positions being debated in the world, we are holding our own positions... We have named it humanism, because its methods are humanistic, because we want to rid man of all fears, directives and dogmatisms. We are revolutionizing society without binding or terrorizing it. The tremendous problem faced by the world is that it has been placed in a position where it must choose between capitalism, which starves people, and communism, which resolves economic problems but suppresses the liberties so greatly cherished by man.... That is why we have said that we are one step ahead of the right and the left, and that this is a humanistic revolution, because it does not deprive man of his essence, but holds him as its basic aim...Such is the reason for my saying that this revolution is not red; but olive-green, for olive-green is precisely our color, the color of the revolution brought by the rebel army from the heart of the Sierra Maestra."

the Third World kept away from both ends of the Sino-Soviet conflict, solidarizing, instead, with North Vietnam.

1965 ended disastrously for all of China's "foreign policies," be they for Asia or Africa or Latin America, not to mention as contender for leadership of the whole Communist world. Yet the launching of a *preventive civil war, called the Cultural Revolution*, soon after the collapse of the hoped-for Peking-Djakarta axis to counteract both the U.S.-NATO Axis and the Moscow-Warsaw Pact Nations, was not so much the result of "foreign policies" as the product of a retrogressionist philosophy which originated in the failure of the Great Leap Forward, and now held that, in place of "one day equals 20 years," it would take no less than "a century"—"or more" (!) to establish socialism. What preceded the "Cultural Revolution" of 1966, and may, indeed, be called its first form—the Socialist Education Campaign (1962–3)—rested on an attack on Marx's Humanist Essays.[24] Though, in the 1960's, it was directed mainly against "Russian revisionism," the truth is that both Russia and China decided jointly to call the East European Freedom Fighters "revisionists." The Russian theoreticians maintained their leadership of the Communist world and grounded the struggle with alleged revisionism in a "critique" of Marx's *Economic-Philosophic Manuscripts* because that had become the banner of the revolutionary proletarian opposition to existing Communism.

The only contribution the Chinese Communists made to this struggle with revisionism was to constantly accuse their dissidents of wishing to establish "Petofi circles" in China.[25] Then, when the Sino-Soviet conflict erupted, the Chinese added the adjective, Russian, before the noun, "revisionism," *without, however, erasing either the adjective, Hungarian or Humanist. Clearly, a spectre is indeed haunting Communism, haunting it from below, from practice—the spectre of Marx's Humanism.*

Both giant Communist state powers were alike also in substituting science for the self-activity of the masses as the "proof" of the "superiority" of their

24 See Chou Yang, "The Fighting Task Confronts Workers in Philosophy and the Social Speeches," speech delivered at the 4th Enlarged Session of the Committee of the Department of Philosophy and Social Science of the Chinese Academy of Sciences, Oct. 26, 1963: "The modern revisionists and some bourgeois scholars try to describe Marxism as humanism...In particular, they make use of certain views on 'alienation' expressed by Marx in his early *Economic-Philosophic Manuscripts, 1844* ... in the early stage of development of their thought, Marx and Engels were indeed somewhat influenced by humanist ideas...But when they formulated the materialist conception of history and discovered the class struggle is the motive force of social development, they immediately got rid of this influence."

25 See especially Mao, *On the Correct Handling of Contradictions Among the People.*

social order, thereby proving, instead, the correctness of Marx's Humanist attack on science: "To have one basis for life and another for science is a priori a lie."

The Lie of Science

This is where state-capitalism calling itself Communism shows its affinity to private capitalism. Since, however, science's "equalizer" (the H-bomb) notwithstanding, Russia (much less China) has not yet "caught up" with U.S. industrial might, both Communist powers are looking for trade. And, since there is no way for U.S.'s industrial might to escape economic crises and strikes and opposition movements from youth to anti-war to Black revolutions, it too wants trade. The present mild flirtation with China has, of course, other "balancing" features in mind as it competes with Russia for world mastery. But nothing changes basics: the non-viability of state-capitalism, as of private capitalism, due to the exploitation of labor, reveals the more clearly science's impotence.

In a word, the lie of science shows itself nowhere more glaringly than in the attitude to labor. Thus, Khrushchev, at the height of his power, proclaimed: "It is only logical that the country of victorious socialism would have...blazed a trail into outer space." When, however, the paeans of praise to science came down to earth, they turned out to be pure capitalistic admonitions for workers to work hard and harder.[26] Thus, while Mao canonized the superiority of science into the Constitution itself, the dictum for labor remained what it had been through "Great Leaps Forward," all on the backs of that labor, most concretely spelled out: "Each person must work ten hours and engage in ideological studies for two hours a day. They are entitled to one day of rest every ten days."

By no accident whatever, glorification of science is the mark not only of the ruling classes in the age of "scientific and technological revolutions," but also of theoreticians busy revising Marxism. Not the deliberate statist misnaming of revolutionary proletarian opposition as "revisionist," but the genuine historic revisions have always used "science" in the fight against "the Hegelian dialectic" which turned out to be the fight against the proletarian revolution,

---

26 The just-concluded 24th Congress of the Russian Communist Party reiterated that it was mostly based on the 22nd Congress. Though none of the promises have been realized which were made at the Congress a full decade ago, the full concentration on labor productivity remains. And the 1961 Program was most explicit: "...it is necessary to raise the productivity of labor in industry by more than 100 per cent within ten years...To increase labor productivity and reduce production costs...implies a higher rate of increase in labor productivity as compared with remuneration...(and in) the second decade every family, including newlyweds, will have a comfortable flat conforming to the requirements of hygiene and cultured living."

for the "defense of the fatherland." Eduard Bernstein was the first, back at the end of the 19th century; Louis Althusser is the latest but he is sure not to be the last since, of necessity, these proponents of "science" and opponents of "philosophy" are sure to keep reappearing so long as capitalism is not torn up, root and branch, the world over.

What concerned us here was, on the one hand, the achievements of the state-capitalist theory which kept revolutionaries from tail-ending Stalinism into imperialist war, and, by relating the new stage of world capitalist development to the specific forms of workers revolt against it, aligning with the latter. On the other hand, the inadequacy of the state-capitalist theory which, without development into Marxist-Humanism, could not cope with the actual movement from practice that refused to be only the muscle of revolution and let the intellectuals do the theorizing.

The masses—all the new forces of revolution—have shown how different proletarian "subjectivity" is from petty-bourgeois subjectivity. They refuse any longer to be only the forces of revolution, for they are also its Reason, active participants in *working out* the philosophy of liberation for our age. Now that they have done so, isn't it time for intellectuals to begin, with them, to fill the theoretic void left in the Marxist movement since Lenin's death? At no time has this been more imperative than now when a new generation of revolutionaries has been born, but is so disgusted with "the old" as to turn away from both theory and history as if actions, without those unifying forces of historic and theoretic continuity, can devise shortcuts to revolution. Jean-Paul Sartre's advice to youth to reject history notwithstanding, a "newness" that treats history as if it weren't there dooms itself to impotence. A Hitler with his *Mein Kampf* could break with history; a revolutionary youth movement cannot. Nor can one continue to delude oneself that theory can be gotten "en route." To turn one's back on philosophy is as big a lie as is the lie of science separated from life.

Marx foresaw the impasse of modern science not because he was a prophet, but because he had made the human being the subject of all development and saw that there was no other answer to: can mankind be free in an age when the machine is master of man, not man of machine. There is still no other answer. It is from this ground that we today face what Hegel called "the birth-time of history" and Marx called the *unity* of theory and practice, of philosophy and revolution, of mental and manual labor, the new human dimension, "thoroughgoing Naturalism or Humanism."

May 1, 1971

State-Capitalism and the Dialectic

News & Letters, *May, 1975*

Two reasons prompted me, on this year's Spring lecture tour on the East Coast, to talk on the relevance of the relationship of philosophy to political economy today. One was that the New York Union of Radical Political Economists (URPE) invitation stressed the fact that Marxist historians should tackle the problems of the day in the U.S. The other was the re-emerging Maoist Stalinism, especially amongst those specializing in China studies. To the latter subject I will return in a future column. Here is an abbreviated abstract of my talk at the New School for Social Research.

I Concepts

"The law of motion" that Marx had set out to discern in his massive, rigorous study of the economic laws of capitalism "and its notions" led to two other discoveries. One was that the law of concentration of capital could lead to all capital concentrated in the hands of "a single capitalist...or single capitalist society" but changed nothing fundamental in the role of labor. Two was the creation of "new passions and new forces" from the absolute opposite of capital accumulation—workers' resistance at the point of production, the class struggles and passion for philosophy of liberation and reconstruction of society on totally new beginnings.

Until the first, classic Revisionism—Bernstein's *Evolutionary Socialism*—called for the removal of "the dialectic scaffolding" along with the indispensability of revolution, none questioned the integrality of economics and philosophy, philosophy and revolution, theory and practice.

Yet, though Rosa Luxemburg attacked Revisionism most profoundly in *Reform or Revolution?*, when she herself turned to analyze a still later stage of capitalist development, imperialism, and she found revolutionaries as well as reformists attacking her concept of "non-capitalist lands" being the reason for the State-capitalism and the extension of capitalism's life, she too, suddenly, spoke against "the roccoco" in Marx's style.

The truth is *none were practicing* dialectics, all Marxists merely "took it for granted." Only when the outbreak of World War I brought about the collapse of the Second International did Lenin finally feel the impulse to return to the origins of Marxism in the Hegelian dialectic. It is only then that Lenin turned to the study of Hegel's *Science of Logic*, not as abstruse, bourgeois philosophy, but as "algebra of revolution" that could help the rebirth of revolutionary Marxism.

Until 1917, or, more precisely, 1918–21, it would have appeared that Lenin held the same view of state capitalism as Bukharin, whose book on *Imperialism and the World Economy* he had favorably introduced. Only with the Revolution had "the dialectic" become the center of all his writings and deeds and perspectives for world revolution, so that even his Bolshevik coleader was characterized as "not fully a Marxist" because "he had never fully grasped the dialectic."

In a word, all the studies of the new stage of capitalism, from Hilferding's *Finance Capital* through Luxemburg's *Accumulation of Capital*, to Bukharin's studies both of world imperialism and the *Economics of the Transition Period*, were entrapped in the bifurcation of subject and object, economics and philosophy, history and revolution.

This was hardly helped by Trotsky—who, alone, was left to fight Stalinism—not facing the reality of the first workers' state in history having been transformed into its opposite, seeing the degeneracy as arising only from the fact that Stalin's Russia was "the policeman" arrogating to himself "distribution."

Since then, Marxist historians have either evaded the whole question by speaking of the imprecision of "advanced capitalism," or used "state capitalism" only against Russia as if it were not a world phenomenon, or as if Russia became that only when Mao so declared it to be—once the Sino-Soviet orbit became the Sino-Soviet conflict.

II Actualities

Today's "New Left" hardly helps illuminate today's problems when it forces a discontinuity from the past under the delusion that theory can be picked up "en route." To dig deep into the world reality, including that of the Third World, and, inseparable from that study of "object," to see what is truly new from below, from Subject, from the movement from practice, is the only way the theoretic challenge can be met for our age.

What are the continuities and discontinuities in actuality as well as in philosophic concepts, the totality demanding and expressing dialectics of liberation in the age of state-capitalism? The Great Depression, 1929–1939, had demolished completely private, competitive, "free enterprise" capitalism which went into a wild scramble to save the system through state intervention and thus hoped to keep the proletarian revolution at bay.

My study, from original Russian sources, was of the first three Five year plans and economic growth and degradation of labor. This was on a totally different basis than either that of the anarchists who were quick to throw "state capitalism" at the Russian workers' state from its very birth, or those like

Bruno R., who, in the shock at such a transformation into opposite, reverted to what totalitarianism was in feudalism, thus leaving room both for those who departed from Marxism as well as the early Shachtman who, though he saw "bureaucratic collectivism" as an "unforeseen, mongrelized reactionary part," nevertheless claimed it part "of the collectivist epoch of human history."

As distinct from that discontinuity of concepts, I retained the Marxian concepts of history and the basic relationship of labor/capital to study the actuality of Russia and there found the operation of the most basic law of capitalism: the law of value. *Stalinism was but the Russian name of the new stage of world capital: state-capitalism.*

A new world stage of development did begin in 1949 with the victory of Mao, but it was not of the scope of the Russian Revolution but of the national liberation struggles. In any case, Mao himself originally called his state "state capitalist," telling the Chinese masses not to worry because once they, through the Communist Party, held "the commanding heights," politically controlled the gun, then the state would be a "transitional one" only, leading to a classless society.

But in fact anything but that happened. State-capitalism mouthing Marxist phraseology doesn't change the conditions of labor for the masses, or their "superstructure," that is to say, their, freedom of thought. As is seen from the current debate in *The Black Scholar*, this is no more a question of China than the debate on Russian state-capitalism was a debate of Russia.

Rather, it is a question of world revolutionary perspectives, especially of the American Revolution. The governing point is that it is not "foreign," but involves us, American Marxists. The point is also that we will be entrapped in still another "faction" unless we begin with the new dialectic from practice which the masses established in the past two decades, whether it took the form of a liberation struggle from Communism, Russian Communism, as in East Europe, or *from* Western imperialism as it was in Africa, or from the Left *within* China, with the *Sheng Wu-lien* arising from within the "Cultural Revolution" that called for "a genuine Paris Commune" against "the red capitalist, Chou En-lai," or, finally the Black Revolution in the U.S. that stimulated the Free Speech Movement in academia as well as the totally involved youth in the anti-Vietnam war movement, thus giving rise to a whole new generation of revolutionaries, white as well as black, Women's Liberation as well as wildcats.

III Challenges to Marxist Historians: The Movements from Practice and from Theory

All history is contemporary history and all truth concrete. What were Hegelian concepts of dialectic were removed from ivory towers of thought and made into a new continent of thought and practice by Marx, who called his philosophy "a new Humanism" that united the ideal and the real, and saw history not as past but as present and as being shaped by living men and women.

There are no Marxes or Lenins today but we do have the maturity of the age and that movement from practice that is itself a form of theory. To think that, as American Marxists, we can only talk of class struggle without participating in it, or talk "Left" without mentioning the different tendencies, actually narrows Marxism from its world roots, and allows bourgeois ideology to prevail.

This doesn't mean that we will not concentrate on American studies. The very opposite is true both of concepts and of reality. When we attempt to restate Marxism for our age, when we study, in this age, be it the two-way road to revolution of Blacks in America and Blacks in Africa, or Nixon's "New Economic Policy," or the current deep recession, we cannot leave out the concepts of state-capitalism and the dialectic.

The dialectic is what makes us see the opposite in each unit and each unity and keeps us from the trap of one-dimensionality. Which is why Marx considered scientists as well as Utopians "abstract materialists," and warned against "a materialism which excludes history and its process." In this bicentennial year, as against the so-called objective historians, Marxist historians must dig deep both into the present and the past, not merely exposing the lie inherent in the Declaration of Independence which had made an abstraction of freedom, but in opening theoretical avenues for the second American revolution.

Only by listening to the masses from below—especially during these past two decades when on all fronts, from Black Revolution to anti-Vietnam war movement, from Third World and East European Revolts to Women's Liberation and Sheng Wu-lien, they far outdistanced theoreticians stuck in "fixed particulars" and one-dimensionality—can Marxist historians bring about a totally new relationship of theory to practice and thereby bring to life what Marx called "the realization of philosophy," that is to say, make freedom a reality.

CHAPTER 17

Battle of Ideas

"Battle of Ideas" was a crucial category throughout Dunayevskaya's life as a revolutionary. Whether in her pioneering analysis of Russia as state-capitalist which led to fighting not alone Stalinists but as well Trotskyists; in developing her view of Marx's humanism and Marxist-Humanism and in the process strongly critiquing those theoreticians and politicos who wished to imprison Marx and Marxism in their own narrow, often statist concepts; in analyzing ongoing events of revolution and counter-revolution from Africa, to Asia, to Latin America, to Europe, East and West, as well as the United States, she often presented her views in sharp contrast to other radical thinkers' views. See, for example, "The Battle of Ideas" (Section V of Volume XII of the Raya Dunayevskaya Collection). Below we present a brief selection of some of her critiques in relation to Russia and Communism.

Milovan Djilas' New Class

News & Letters, *October 1957*

Milovan Djilas, former Vice-President of Yugoslavia, has written a journalistic piece on the Communist system from which he has broken. This has been put between the covers of a book [*The New Class: an Analysis of the Communist System*. New York, Praeger, 1957] and given a million dollars' worth of free publicity by the "free" capitalist press. Thereupon followed rave notices in all the papers and magazines, including "the leftist" press. It was climaxed by *Life* magazine's claim that here is a book "that will rock Marxism." What astonishes us is not the presumptuousness of this claim but the naiveté of the journalists, book reviewers, editorial writers and State Department type thinking that believes this.

Here is a man who is a typical product of the Communist world—an alleged Marxist theoretician whose ignorance of Marxian theory is matched only by the enormity of the contradictions in his statements. Thus he claims that Marx "unintentionally" laid the basis for a new concept of the world. Otherwise, says Djilas, Marxian philosophy was so threadbare that it "would have been forgotten—dismissed as something not particularly profound or even original" IF—"if the political need of the working class movement in Europe had not demanded a new ideology complete in itself." That is how it happened that this philosophy which "was not important since it was based mainly on Hegelian and materialistic ideas" became "the ideology of the new, oppressed classes and especially of political movements" and as such "it marked an epoch, first in Europe, and later in Russia and Asia, providing the basis for a new political movement and a new social system."

Having thus cleverly slipped in present-day Communist totalitarianism under the Marxian theory of liberation, Djilas feels that he might be called to account for this sleight of hand, so he says magnanimously, "There is no other type of Marxism or Communism today, and the development of another type is hardly possible."

In this one-half of a sentence, that no other type of Marxism is possible, lies the whole secret for the naive belief that this poor excuse for a book will "rock Marxism." If ever whistling in the dark passed for a method of thought, this is it. Thereby "the West" itself has put the seal of bankruptcy on its own thought.

While hoping that the working people do not find Marxism in its original form of Humanism, what is it that Djilas is passing off as the needed philosophy in his book *The New Class*? According to Djilas, there is "an immutable law—that each human society and all individuals participating in it strive to increase and perfect production." This immutable law, to "perfect production," has us all sacrificing for "the cause." At least it has Djilas so much in its grip that he even forgives his present Communist enemies for their tyranny at least up until now since there was no other way to industrialize the backward countries.

Marx had a better name for this "perfect production." It was "production for production's sake" which drove the capitalists on, and they rode the workers so that it all ended in the two monstrosities, concentration and centralization of capital at the one hand, and the degradation of the worker to a cog in the machine at the other. Marx wrote:

> It is the fact that capital and its self-expansion, appears as the starting and closing point, as the motive and aim of production; that production is merely production for *capital* and not for vice versa, the means of production mere means for an ever expanding system of the life process for the benefit of the society of producers...*The real barrier of capitalist production is capital itself.*

The ultimate form of this is precisely its state-capitalist form now existing in Russia and Yugoslavia and calling itself Communist.

It is hard to believe that Djilas has chosen jail in order to expound the very philosophy which led to its form as state capitalism, and toward which the whole private capitalist world is moving. Djilas sheds very little light. The Communist tyranny has been analyzed long before he did it, and more seriously. He fails even to shed the light of experience on it. Indeed the one thing I did look for in this book—a live description of Tito's Yugoslavia—is entirely absent.

What then, prompted "the West" to give this threadbare book this spectacular send-off? We can see the answer not in what they say, but in the objective world situation. Little Rock, Ark. [The crisis over the racial integration of Central High School in Little Rock reached a climax in September of 1957 with President Eisenhower's deployment of U.S. army troops.] on the one hand, and the Sputnik, on the other hand, have combined to expose the hollowness of American democracy and the claims of superior technological know-how as well. Vice-President Nixon has been compelled thereby to call off his tour of Western Europe. The world sees U.S. aching for a war with Russia over who will dominate the world. It is true that Russia aims for precisely the same thing, but somehow Russia manages to march under the name of "Marxism" and thus is winning the colonial world. The desperation of "the West" can be seen precisely in this running after "the democratic socialist," the alleged Marxist, Milovan Djilas. They are running in vain. The American worker is not as dumb as they think, and not as helpless as the American intellectual without vision of a truly new society where the free and all-rounded development of the human being, not of "perfect production," is the sole motive force.

Intellectuals in the Age of State-Capitalism [On Herbert Marcuse's Soviet Marxism]

News & Letters, ***July and August–September 1961***

We live in an age of state capitalism which, at one end, Russia, persists in calling itself "Communist," and at the other end, America, still designates itself as "free enterprise." Not only are the conditions of production hardly distinguishable from each other, however, but so is the administrative mentality of the intellectuals at both poles of world capital. As befits one who chooses to defend the American side, a Daniel Bell will speak of "The End of Ideology" to mark the alleged end of a "proletarian cause." As befits one who chooses to whitewash the other power, an Isaac Deutscher will proclaim the near-identity of interests of the proletariat and the Russian state.

In each case the scholarship of the writer gets sucked into the veritable conspiracy between the two nuclear titans to force an identity between those two opposites, Marxism and Communism, although Marxism is a theory of liberation from capitalism while Communism is the practice of state capitalist enslavement. While, in origin, the administrative mentality dates back to the 1929 world crash that signaled the end of rationality of capitalist production relations, it is only with the nuclear age that the administrative mentality became the all-pervasive phenomenon it is now.

Take the Hegelian-Marxist philosopher, Herbert Marcuse. In the 1940's he produced the profound study, *Reason and Revolution*, which established a continuity of analysis by the young and mature Marx which went beyond the economics of production to the *human* relations. In the 1950's, however, he was impelled to the fantastic notion of establishing a "continuity" between Marxism and Stalinism.

Herbert Marcuse's "Soviet Marxism"[1]

Prof. Marcuse begins reaching for this feat with the very title of his book. While "Soviet" stands for councils of workers and peasants that achieved the Russian Revolution, and now exists in name only, the use of the word allows the author to cover Stalin with the same mantle as Lenin. At the same time the loose use of the word, Marxism, for the entire post-Marxist period makes it possible for Prof. Marcuse to straddle the historic fence.

We feel impelled to review the book now since it has just been published in a new paperback edition which, quite obviously, aims at a popular audience. Without explanation, this new addition leaves out the original introduction which explained his method of analysis as an "immanent critique." That stated "The critique thus employs the conceptual instrument of its object, namely, Marxism, in order to clarify the actual function of Marxism in Soviet society and its historical direction." (p. 1)

Furthermore, "the immanent critique," we were assured, can give us the "clue" not only to the causes of the "theoretical deficiencies," but also the "objective trends and tendencies which are operative in history and which make up the inherent rationality..." (p. 1) At least these are Prof. Marcuse's assumptions.

There is no end to the magical qualities of that instrument, "the immanent critique,": "For what is irrational if measured from without the system is rational within the system." (p. 86) This writer cannot guarantee that the irrational

---

1 1961 edition, Vintage Russian Library, Random House, New York $1.25; 1958 edition. Columbia University Press, N.Y. $6. Page references in this review are to the original edition.

can appear rational anywhere outside of a madhouse, but Prof. Marcuse has not only undertaken that feat, but also its opposite, that of endowing the rational with irrational features.

"The New Rationality"

Although Prof. Marcuse admits that "Neither the rise of the Soviet intelligentsia as a new ruling group, nor its composition and its privileges are any longer disputed facts..." (p. 107) he nevertheless dubs the totalitarian, state-capitalist society of Russia as "The New Rationality."

The reader must restrain his interest in motivation, and judge the author only by what he holds to be "the truth": (1) *Marx's* concept of the revolutionary nature of the proletariat is supposed to have "exploded" (p. 13) at the point of transition from capitalism to socialism, that is to say, the October Revolution. On the other hand, *Soviet* Marxism's hypostatization of that tenet into a ritual is judged to be nothing short of "an instrument for rescuing the truth." (p. 88)

The resulting play on words beggars rational description: "it (Soviet Marxism) is not 'false consciousness' but rather consciousness of falsehood, a falsehood which is 'corrected' in the context of the 'higher truth' represented by objective historical interest," (p. 91.) *And, of course, when all else fails, an intellectual can always blame "the backward population:" "The new form of Marxian theory corresponds to its new historical agent—a backward population which is to become what it 'really' is: a revolutionary force which changes the world."* (p. 89)

(2) *Lenin's* attempt to confront the post-Marxist phenomenon of imperialism by "redefining" capitalism and attempting "to draw the peasantry into the orbit of Marxian theory and strategy" is alleged to have suffered from "The refusal to draw theoretical consequences from the new situation." This, Prof. Marcuse concludes, "characterizes the entire development of Leninism and is one of the chief reasons for the gap between theory and practice in Soviet Marxism." (p. 30)

Not only is the unbridgeable gulf between Marxism and present-day Russian Communism blamed on the "theoretical deficiencies" of Lenin, the latter is made the author of the one original contribution of Stalin—the theory of "socialism in one country." Prof. Marcuse does not even bother to tell us that that is *what* he is doing; he merely quotes the one or two isolated statements as if these had never been called into question and that Stalin built on that. There is not a single reference to the voluminous writings of Leon Trotsky precisely on that one point over which so much blood flowed between Stalinism and Trotskyism over the meaning of Leninism.

Quotations out of context from Vol. IX of Lenin's "Selected Works" are used "to prove" that Lenin was for industrialization "without liberation." Nothing is said about Lenin actually inventing words to describe how "mortally sick" he was of "Communlies" (Communist lies.) Yet this is in that same profound Vol. IX (p. 346). As Lenin warned there: "History proceeds in devious ways...(Soviet state) has taken the road that will lead to the ordinary bourgeois state."

(3) While none of Lenin's castigation of the Communists' "passion for bossing" now that they had power comes through in Prof. Marcuse's *Soviet Marxism*, Stalin comes off with fairly clean hands. Even the reign of terror is very nearly justified: "The height of Stalinist terror coincided with the consolidation of the Hitler regime." (p. 75)

This, in this writer's view, is an inaccuracy. The height of Stalin's terror came during the First Five Year Plan which began with the expulsion of the Left Opposition and the exile of Leon Trotsky, and ended with forced collectivization, the institution of forced labor camps, the ruin of millions of human beings who, in turn, slaughtered thousands of heads of cattle and brought such havoc on the countryside and actual famine conditions that the whole regime nearly collapsed. At the same time Stalin's international policies did nothing to stop the *coming* of fascism. Insofar, however, as the Stalin period was one *continuous* reign of terror one could, in truth, designate very nearly any year as "the height of terror."

Obviously Prof. Marcuse prefers to substitute for the years, 1930–33, the period of 1936–39. But in that case the "immanent critique" must come face to face with the Stalin-Hitler Pact as something inherent in, not "outside of" Russia. But there is no time for a critique when the over-riding compulsion is "to prove" the thesis stated in the Introduction (missing from the 1961 edition): "There is theoretical continuity from the early Marxian notion of the Proletariat as objective truth of capitalist society to Soviet Marxist conception of *partinost* (partisanship.") (p. 9)

The Party, the Party

The loose translation of the word, *partinost*, party-ism, as "partisanship" is inexcusable in the crucial content of the Stalinist concept of the Party, the Party, which is alleged to be synonymous with Marx's concept of the proletariat as the gravedigger of capitalist society. To the extent that Marx developed any concept of a proletarian party it was, (and Prof. Marcuse admits this) of a party as the *self-organization* of the proletariat. The proletariat was *the* historic force which would establish "an association of free men." Under the circumstances how could Marcuse become party to the Stalinist sleight of hand substitution of their monolithic monstrosity for "the self-organization of the proletariat"?

Yet this is the inescapable consequence of this method of blaming everybody—Marx, Lenin, the proletariat, above all, the proletariat—in order to avoid facing the reality of the new stage of world capitalism—state capitalism—which manifested itself first on the historical stage in the Stalinist counter-revolution in Russia.

No wonder the promise of the "immanent critique" to reveal "the historic direction" just "perished" to use a Hegelian phrase, in the explosive contradictions of the "new rationality." The reader of the new as of the old edition must be content with the last paragraph:

> Ideological pressure there seems to tend in the same direction as technical-economic pressure, namely; toward the relaxation of repression...these forces, though unformed and unorganized, may well determine, to a considerable extent, the course of Soviet developments.

Truly the mountain has labored and given birth to...

The Flexible Dialectic

Although Prof. Marcuse admitted that "The difference between the first years of the Bolshevik Revolution and the fully developed Stalinist state are obvious," (p. 74), he has refused to admit that Stalinism, far from being a "continuation" of Marxism-Leninism is a break from it.[2] Indeed he puts the word, break, in quotation marks, and explains: "But if the dialectical law of turn from quantity

---

2 Professor Marcuse his much to say on Lenin's "Materialism and Empirio-Criticism," which gave the green light to vulgar materialism and which is now used as "the" philosophic text, without once mentioning Lenin's break with his own philosophic past emanating from his later, profound "Philosophic Notebooks." Yet this quintessential work is available in Russian, German, French and Italian, and, in an abbreviated version, appears in a first English translation as an appendix to my *Marxism and Freedom*. We saw above, that Prof. Marcuse also, failed to consider the Trotsky-Stalin controversy over "socialism in one country." One other word must be stated on Prof. Marcuse's selection of sources in the war and post-war periods. He makes a reference to the "spectacular public controversies" which are supposed to be less cogent than the more fundamental analysis he makes. But, while he manages not to make a single mention of either the 1943 reversal of all previous teachings of the Marxian law of value, or of the 1955 attack on the humanist essays of Marx, he does find space for the lesser linguistic controversy.

to quality was ever applicable, it was the transition from Leninism (after the October Revolution) to Stalinism." (p. 74)[3]

Obviously, Prof. Marcuse has been greatly influenced by the irrational becoming rational "within" a certain context. Here he is doing nothing less magical than equating *counter*revolution with revolution!

Nothing can stop him now. He concludes the one chapter ("Dialectic and Its Vicissitudes") which still shines with some fine Hegelian-Marxian perceptions with this astounding statement: "The Soviet Marxist 'revision' is 'orthodox.' Since Soviet Marxists maintain that Soviet society is a socialist society, they consistently invest it with the corresponding dialectical characteristics. What is involved is not so much a revision of dialectic as the claim of socialism for a non-socialist society." (p. 154)

In a word, all that is wrong are—the facts! Prof. Marcuse might at least have remembered what Hegel called the method of assuming what one should prove. The word was "barbarous." The method hasn't improved with age. Barbarous it is.

Jean Paul Sartre has recently (*Critique of Dialectical Reason*) shown anew that which has long characterized Existentialism—that all is fair not only in war and love, but also in the use to which the dialectic is put. But even a Sartre had to separate himself from Russia's brutal suppression of the Hungarian Revolution, and hail the Hungarian Freedom Fighters for breaking loose from all brainwashing. Not so Marcuse. So organic is his conception of the backwardness of the proletariat that, where he does admit that Russian rulers have "arrested" the dialectic in its classical Marxist sense of liberating "the subjective factor," he concludes that "the ruled tend not only to submit to the rulers but also to reproduce in themselves their subordination." (p. 191)

The Majesty of "The Ruled"

This vilification of the masses appears nearly a decade after the forced laborers struck in Vorkuta inside Russia itself, following the June 17, 1953 East German Revolt against Russian imperialistic rule there, and 5 years after the Hungarian Revolution of 1956 had demonstrated for all the world, even "the learned," to see that the courage, the fortitude, the humanism of "the ruled" can break through not only Russian brainwashing but Russian steel tanks!

---

3 Here too there is a looseness of expression. It is true that, after quality is transformed into quantity, the analysis continues "conversely." In strict Hegelian terminology, however, transcended quality is quantity, but transcended quantity is measure. Is Stalin now to be taken as "the measure" of the "new" society?

Though the ivory towers remain impervious to the self-activity of the masses, the majesty of "the ruled" beckons for all to join their life-and-death struggles for freedom.

∴

Western Intellectuals Help K[hrushchev], Inc. Rebury Lenin's Philosophic Legacy [On Gustav A. Wetter, David Joravsky, George Lichtheim, Eugene Kamenka]

News & Letters, ***Jan.–Feb. 1964***

1963 marked the tenth anniversary of Stalin's death. Many academic journals, in the West at any rate, celebrated the event by taking stock of every aspect of life—from the economic to the literary, and from the political to the philosophical—in Khrushchev's Russia, concentrating on the period since the de-Stalinization Congress in February, 1956.

Newsmen, too, summarized the year 1963 as a turning point in the Cold War. Very obviously the thaw in the Cold War, which resulted not merely in an abstract, limited Nuclear Test Ban Treaty, but also a real, cash, multi-million dollar sale of American wheat to Russia, whetted their appetite for prediction. One NBC newsman became so enamored of his prescience that he denied the very existence of the Cold War.

The "principle of coexistence," announced with such fanfare at that de-Stalinization Congress, seemed to have become the very way of life of Russian Communists, if not of their Chinese counterpart. Here we are interested neither in the self-proclaimed deStalinization, nor in the much-touted "peaceful coexistence," but in one of the lesser known aspects of that famous 20th Congress of the Russian Communist Party—the dictum on philosophy.

Death and Resurrection

It will be recalled that First Deputy Premier Anastas Mikoyan had, in his de-Stalinization speech, followed his attack on the historians for having failed to produce "an accepted history of the party for two decades"[4] by declaring: "One should say something, if even only two words, with regard to our philosophers—more insolvent even than historians and economists." The ossification of philosophy in the Soviet Union was ascribed to "the cult of personality,"

4 On that question see "Without A Past and Without A Future," *News & Letters*, March 30, 1956.

which had done its dastardly, terroristic acts not only in the lives and politics of the country, but in the "suppression of the creative development of Marxism-Leninism." The 20th Congress then decided that "the cult of personality" had suppressed "Lenin's philosophic legacy," and so decreed "The Creative Development of Marxism-Leninism Based on the Fullest Exploitation of Lenin's Philosophic Legacy."

Just as the Stalinist, Khrushchev, decreed deStalinization, so the Stalinist philosophers were put in charge of "saving" Lenin's philosophic legacy, specifically his Philosophic Notebooks, *from the deadening effect of Stalinism. And so began the rise in the Khrushchev hierarchy of the Stalinist philosophic clique of Mitin, Yudin, Rosental, Kanstatinov, Kedrov, Alexandrov and others.*

By 1958 they produced a "new" textbook on philosophy, and Western intellectuals wrote "learned treatises" on the "differences" between philosophic productions under Stalin and under Khrushchev. Whether this new attention paid to Communist philosophers was to make up for the previous neglect, or reflected the natural state of ossification of philosophy on this as well as the other side of the Iron Curtain, the Western output was threadbare indeed. Moreover, this characterized not only the output of articles, but of "authoritative" books.[5]

Where, however the Western intellectuals were "satisfied" with the "new" output Propaganda Chief Ilychev, in 1960, castigated the philosophers for not carrying out the dictum of either the 20th or 21st Congress. By October, 1961, when the 22nd Congress of the Russian Communist Party first "disclosed" that Stalin held Lenin's *Philosophic Notebooks* in "disfavor," the Sino-Soviet Rift, still then cloaked as a debate over Albania, overshadowed not only the philosophic "disclosure" but the announced purpose of that Congress for which the drums had been beaten for many months previous—the new Program, billed as a veritable new Communist Manifesto in the tradition of Karl Marx, which was to replace the one adopted in Lenin's time shortly after conquest of power.

5 In the West, too, so-called Marxology has become so institutionalized—and not only by theologians in Italy, West Germany, Switzerland, Holland, but now even "radicals" in France prefer working with their theologians than be exposed to more fundamental opposition to Marxists who believe in the philosophy rather than merely specialize in it for pay—that an independent work does not get the attention and circulation it should. Thus Gustav A. Wetter's *Dialectical Materialism*, built mainly on secondary sources, becomes the "standard," while David Joravsky's *Soviet Marxism and Natural Science, 1917–1932*, solidly based on primary sources and dispelling many of the myths in the former, is shunted aside as only for academicians. Unfortunately, we cannot use much of it in this review since it deals with a different period than that which is our concern, but we recommend it highly.

The West to the Rescue?

Surely it should have been easy to dispel the newly-created little myth that, with, *and only with,* the 1956 deStalinization Congress did Lenin's "philosophic legacy," specifically his *Philosophic Notebooks*, first come into its own. That this nevertheless was an impossible feat for bourgeois intellectuals tells as much of the ossification of Western philosophy as it does of regimentation of Communist philosophy.

The hardest thing for an intellectual to comprehend is his own fragmentation. Not only does he seem to feel that only workers are subject to fragmentation because they work in factories, but he is more likely than not "to value" his specialization since it is allegedly due only to the infinite scope of knowledge. *The one grain of truth in this is that the narrowness of vision of the intellectual is only in part due to specialization. Fundamentally it is rooted in the division between mental and manual labor. Or, more precisely put, to meet the specific point at issue, it is rooted in his isolation from reality.*

The "Theoretical" Practice of Stalin, Khrushchev, Mao

It is this which Stalin grasped at with all his might when he reduced theory to "practice," a word Stalin endowed with the all-ness *and nothingness* with which Humpty Dumpty endowed the word, glory: "it means just what I choose it to mean—neither more nor less." In the year 1929, when Stalin came face to face with the great agricultural crisis and declared himself to be the philosopher, "practice" meant the subordination of all abstract philosophy to the reality of the crisis and "therefore" the dictum "to liquidate the kulak as a class."

In his talk to the agronomists, Stalin took his first step in revising the Marxian theory of expanded reproduction, transforming the description of capitalist economy into the prescription for "socialist economy." What Stalin achieved in the 1930's with forced collectivization and the state-planned industry he crowned, in 1943, with another feat of revision, this time the Marxian theory of value, which included a break with the dialectic structure of Capital.

Even as the 1947 Stalin-Zhdanov order to philosophers "to replace" the Hegelian law of objective contradiction with "a new dialectical law"—"criticism and self-criticism"—is presently reaching its ultimate in Mao's perennial "thought reform" campaigns, so it has not been overthrown by Khrushchev who allegedly wanted "to return" to the true Lenin philosophic legacy. Because this is so, the Stalinist philosophers not only survived deStalinization but rose in the Khrushchev hierarchy. Because, on the other hand, the non-Marxist intellectuals persist in identifying Communism with its opposite, Marxism, they fail to see the true ideological continuity in Stalin-Khrushchev-Mao. A sort of built-in deafness to Lenin's break with his own philosophic past further assures Western intellectual incapacity to deal with philosophical writings in Russia.

Needed: Analysis of Class Nature of Communism

Take the standard: *Dialectical Materialism,* A Historical and Systemic Survey of Philosophy in the Soviet Union, by Gustav A. Wetter, S.J., which had first been issued in Italy in 1948, extensively revised in 1952 for its German edition, and, once again extensively revised for its fourth German, and first English and American translation in 1958, in order "to take account of the changes wrought by the deStalinization campaign."

Wetter follows the Communist break-up of dialectical philosophy into two separate divisions: dialectical materialism and historical materialism, and further he limits his field of inquiry to "dialectical materialism." Having achieved that amputation of the wholeness of Marxian dialectics, there inevitably follows the exclusion of controversies on Marxian economics. We do not get a whiff of the most startling Stalinist revision of the Marxian theory of value in 1943. Since, however, Marxian political economy is indivisible from Marxian dialectical philosophy, *which, in fact, imposed upon the Stalinist revisionists of the theory of value a break also with the dialectic structure of* [*Marx's*] Capital, Wetter has only succeeded in half-blinding himself in dealing seriously with the 1947 open break from Hegelian dialectics. The result is that when Wetter finally deals with Zhdanov's order to the philosophers to find a "new dialectical law"—"criticism and self-criticism"—to replace the objective law of contradiction as interpreted by Hegel and Marx, he can say nothing more illuminating than the fact that the 1947 and 1955 discussions of "criticism and self-criticism" first arose at the Fifteenth Congress of the Russian Communist Party (December 1927) which had proclaimed Stalin's victory over all opposition.

Precisely. This, however, needs to be understood, not as a mere listing of "firsts," but as a qualitative transformation into opposite. Because Stalin's victory over all opposition meant the abolition of all factions within the Party as well as without; because his one truly original contribution to Communism is the monolithic party; because this victory spelled out not only the transformation of philosophy into mere ideology, but the foundation for the centralized State Plan, the nationalized economy could, and did, create a state-capitalist ruling class.

Having been shown neither the class nature of Stalinism, nor the self-imposed blindness caused by specialization in the field of dialectics, Wetter finally brings us to the post-Stalin era and the "strictly" dialectic chapter—only to present the 1955 revision of the law of "the negation of negation" as a re-establishment of this nodal point of Hegelian and Marxian philosophy! The reason? The continuous use of quantitive measurements: (a) In his *Short History of the CPSU* (B), Stalin left out the law of the negation of the negation as one of the basic laws of the Hegelian dialectic. In *Questions of Philosophy* No. 3, 1955 Karpushin mentions it. (Never mind that he attacks it and perverts Marx's analysis of it; the point is he does mention it and Stalin didn't!) (b) Also Karpushin mentions the fact that the Early Essays of Marx have been dropped from the *Collected Works* of Marx. (Again, never mind that he regrets this omission only because he singles it out for attack and revision; obviously the point with our unregimented philosophers is to have everything in its proper chronological order.)

Forgotten altogether is that the Karpushin attack on the Humanism of Marx was not just revision of theory of past events, removed by 111 years, but preparation for next year's counter-revolutionary suppression of the Hungarian Revolution.[6]

Part II

In Part I of this article on the state of ossification of philosophy, East and West, I mentioned the built-in deafness to Lenin's break with his own philosophic past which has led to the Western intellectual's inability to cope with the deliberate emasculation of Lenin's philosophic legacy by the Communist theoreticians. I shall now develop this point.

Even so objective a study as David Joravsky's *Soviet Marxism and Natural Science, 1917–1932*, cannot escape the consequences of the failure to grapple with Lenin's *Philosophic Notebooks*, written at the time of the collapse of the Second International at the outbreak of the first World War, when Lenin felt compelled to return to the origins of Marxism in Hegelian philosophy.

Mr. Joravsky senses that Lenin's comments on Hegel's *Science of Logic* are "tantalizingly suggestive of a new turn in his thought" (p. 20). He profoundly exposes Stalin's transformation of Lenin's alleged "partyness" in the field of philosophy into pure Stalinist monolithism. He demonstrates that Lenin's aim, even in his *Materialism and Empirio-Criticism*, was "not to join the philosophical and political issues that Russian Marxists were arguing about; it was to *separate* them." (p. 34, emphasis added.) He proves conclusively that it is not

6 Here is what we wrote on this same Karpushin essay: "Nothing changed Marx's social vision: the vision of the future which Hegel called the Absolute and which Marx first called 'real Humanism' and later 'communism.' The road to both is by way of 'the negation of the negation' that is to say, the destruction of the existing system which had destroyed the previous system. That is what the Russian ruling class trembles at, as well it may, for it knows this movement not by the name 'negation of the negation' but by the reality of the revolution against it." (*Marxism and Freedom*, p. 66).

only the Communist theoreticians that pretend that Stalinist monolithism is the natural and only possible result of Lenin's concept, but that:

> Non-Communist authors have contributed to the confusion by an excess of boldness, by the proclivity that many have shown towards magisterial judgments on the basis of insufficient evidence. One author, for example, writing in a scholarly journal, based a history of the theory of relativity in Soviet physics and philosophy on three 'sources,' two of which were merely ambiguous passing references to Einstein's theory in Soviet articles on other subjects. (p. x)(The references is to Lewis S. Feuer's "Dialectical Materialism and Soviet Science," *Philosophy of Science*, April 1949.)

Nevertheless by excluding from his own work a serious analysis of Lenin's *Philosophic Notebooks*, Mr. Joravsky leaves the door wide open for lesser scholars to write as if there was a straight philosophic line from Lenin to Stalin, *instead of a transformation into opposite.*

Short of Philistinism

I am referring here not only to the sophomoric essays by American "experts" whose arrogance matches their Philistinism. George Lichtheim rightly calls the American contribution to Marxology by non-Marxists "a sort of intellectual counterpart to the late Mr. Dulles's weekly sermon on the evils of communism."[7] I am referring to Mr. Lichtheim himself and to such writers as Eugene Kamenka of Australia, whose *The Ethical Foundations of Marxism* places him In the sophisticated European tradition of non-Marxist analyses of Marxism.

Mr. Kamenka certainly appreciates the Humanism of Marxism and knows that Communist totalitarianism has nothing whatever to do with the Marxist theory of liberation. He has no organic anti-Leninist prejudices such as Mr. Lichtheim has. On the contrary, he sees in Lenin "a mind of the first order." Nevertheless, he feels that "philosophy was to him (Lenin) only of incidental

---

7 "Western Marxist Literature, 1953–63" in *Survey*, Jan. '64, Mr. Lichtheim's remarks follow his reference to Robert Tucker's *Philosophy and Myth in Karl Marx*. In casting the blame for such sophomoric performances on "the peculiarly American manner," Mr. Lichtheim conveniently disregards both Marxist Humanism in the United States and the fact that the "sort of intellectual counterpart to the late Mr. Dulles's weekly sermons on the evils of communism" to which Mr. Lichtheim refers covers also the Sidney Hooks, Daniel Bells, Lewis S. Feuers as well as their European counterparts. Furthermore, there is little difference between the professional anti-Leninist and professional fellow-traveler a la Sartre when it comes to a confrontation with the philosophic legacy of Lenin in his *Notebooks*.

interest" so that "the force of a first-class mind" needs to be discerned "through the frequent naiveté and dilettantism of his philosophical writings and notes." As if professionalization of philosophy were synonymous with original philosophic thought, Mr. Kamenka claims that contemporary "reformulations of the classical philosophical disputes" has robbed "Lenin's insights of most of their immediate impact and relevance."[8]

All this is said in passing supposedly because the subject matter under consideration is current Soviet philosophy. Allegedly for the same reason, no attempt whatever is made to deal with the text of Lenin's *Philosophical Notebooks*. And yet the allegations against him are made as if they were self-evident truths. We will see in a moment how the ravages of that eat into his expose of the superficialities of the Western treatment of Soviet philosophy.

First it should be stated that Mr. Kamenka magnificently exposes the ignorance of the learned. Needless to say, this is not his phrase. What other conclusion, however, can one draw from the following irrefutable facts? One, that for decades on end, the learned journal of the Royal Institute of Philosophy, edited by the illustrious Lord Acton carried not a single article on Soviet philosophy until January, 1963, when they published Mr. Kamenka's "Philosophy in the Soviet Union."

Two, even the *specialized* quarterly of the Institute of East European Studies at the University of Fribourg, Switzerland—*Studies in Soviet Thought*, edited by the eminent Professor Bochenski—has been so preoccupied with purely quantitative phenomena like the number of writers, the number of words written, the compilation of bibliographies, that it has hardly had time to present "actual translations" of Soviet articles, much less seriously answering the Soviet claims.

And yet, Mr. Kamenka suddenly concludes that what is needed to start a serious dialogue between "Western" philosophers and their Russian counterparts is for the latter to "acquire something of the integrity and sophistication of genuine philosophical argument…from the West…"

It is impossible to expose Khrushchevite pretensions about "a return to Lenin" without tracing Leninist philosophy to its source, *not excluding the quality in this heritage.* This is not an intra-factional dispute of interest only to Marxists, or their opposite, Communists. It is impossible to meet the challenge to thought, *to Western thought,* unless one fully appreciates the significance of Lenin's 1914–15 break with his own philosophic past.

8 "Soviet Philosophy Through Western Eyes," in *Survey*, Jan. 1964.

The Objective Compulsion to Thought

The point is this: the compulsion to break with this philosophic past, with vulgar materialism, came from *objective* conditions. The compulsion to thought was brought about by a world war, the first world war, a crisis in Western civilization, a crisis in all men's lives, Our post-World War II situation, with its little wars, The Cold War, threat of nuclear holocaust, is a daily reminder of the death throes of an older order, the birth pangs of a new one, the near-insoluble problems of this titanic conflict. In that respect Lenin's *Notebooks* can shed greater light than the "sophisticated" theses of today that keep philosophy hemmed in a tight little circle of the learned isolated from "politics."

Far from being "dated," Lenin's *Philosophic Notebooks*, as method, are as urgent as today's headlines. Far from being "Russian," they are as lacking in boundaries, in thought, as are the ICBM's in life. These are not only political problems. They are a challenge to thought as well as to life. As that encyclopedic mind of Hegel's said most profoundly when the philosophy of his day did not accept the challenge of changing times, did not grasp the French Revolution, as Idea, "it is the nature of truth to force its way to recognition." A philosophy that fails then to reorganize its very structure turns the learned into "'representatives,' who are like the dead burying the dead."[9]

Lacking such an attitude to objectivity, Western thought flounders and therefore falls into quantitative measurements instead of the measure of Man, the human aspiration, the thought that can lay the foundation for a reorganization of society. Khrushchev, and, yes, Mao,—have a State reason for burying Lenin's Notebooks—*the preservation of their respective state-capitalist tyrannies demands that the idea of freedom be buried along with freedom. But where, at least on the surface, the learned of the West need not be state philosophers, is it not time to end their ignorance of Marxist philosophy?*[10]

Naturally it is much easier to expose the superficiality of "the copy theory" of cognition expounded in Lenin's *Materialism and Empirio-Criticism*. But is that sufficient reason for serious thinkers to turn away from the compulsion to seek the significance of Lenin's *Notebooks* on Hegel's *Science of Logic* till they grasp the meaning of Lenin's statement, "Man's cognition not only reflects the objective world, but creates it"? Instead of helping Khrushchev, in the 35th year since the first Russian publication of Lenin's *Philosophic Notebooks*, once again, to perpetrate a live burial of these dialectic notes, isn't it high time finally to

9 Hegel, *The Phenomenology of Mind*, p. 130.

10 See Chapter X dealing with Lenin and the dialectic: a mind in action, in *Marxism and Freedom* as well as the new chapter "The Challenge of Mao Tse-tung;" in the paperback edition of *Marxism and Freedom*.

come to grips with their challenge to today's thought? Without such a meaningful encounter, the ossification of Western thought is sure "to outdistance" Communist putrefaction.

∴

Footnote on the Detractors of Lenin [On Cornelius Castoriadis (aka Pierre Chaulieu or Paul Cardan)]

News & Letters, *December 1969*

1970—the 100th anniversary of Lenin's birth—is sure to see a new facet of the Sino-Soviet conflict as the two state-capitalist giants calling themselves Communist vie with each other to grasp the revolutionary mantle of Lenin in order to cover up the reality of their respective exploitative systems. In this they will be aided not only by "Western" (private capitalist) ideologists who have always maintained that Stalinism flowed "logically" from Leninism, but also by some who, like Paul Mattick, consider themselves Marxists but have made a veritable profession of anti-Leninism.

The saddest aspect of the new outpouring of anti-Leninism is that some young revolutionaries show themselves to be not so new in their thought the moment they need to move from activity to philosophy. Thus, Daniel Cohn-Bendit, the freshest face and most spirited voice of the near-revolution in France, May, 1968, has found nothing newer to say in his *Obsolete Communism*, than the fact that he is a "plagiarist...of revolutionary theory and practice,"[11] which turns out, in the main to be that of *Socialisme ou Barbarie* (Pierre Chaulieu), Paul Cardan, etc. Since these departures from Marxism and restatements of *The Meaning of Socialism*[12] are being played up as "the left-wing alternative" to totalitarian Communism, it becomes important to take issue with these detractors of Lenin. In this footnote I will limit myself to Cardan, but it is only because what he says here is representative of all.

The Allegation

"For some strange reason," writes Cardan, "Marxists have always seen the achievement of working class power solely in terms of the conquest of political

11 *Obsolete Communism, The Left-Wing Alternative* by Cohn-Bendit, p. 18 (McGraw-Hill, N.Y.).

12 Solidarity Pamphlet No. 6 (London).

power. Real power, namely power over production in day-to-day life, was always ignored." This vitiation of Marx's philosophy of liberation is but prelude to the hammer and tongs approach to Lenin who, Cardan claims, was "relentlessly repeating *from 1917 until his death* that production should be organized from *above* along 'state-capitalist lines.'" (Emphasis added.)

I know of no greater lie, but, for the time being, we will let it stand in order to call attention to the foundation for the diatribe. As proof of the slanderous statement, Cardan quotes from *one* of Lenin's speeches, "The Immediate Tasks of the Soviet Government"[13] and then only those passages which relate to the possibility of utilizing the "Taylor system."

Never mind that the Taylor system was never introduced in Lenin's lifetime. Never mind that the "single" will was not a reference to foreman or managers of production. (The point of contention in that first year of revolution when the discussion revolved around "single" vs. "collective" referred to parallelism in organizations since the *first* national trade union organization arose only after the revolution, just when factory committees and Soviets likewise laid sole claim to running production.)

Never mind the objective situation, the backwardness of the economy, four years of imperialist war, civil war and countless counter-revolutionary attacks which were still going on as the new workers' state was struggling for its very existence. That speech was made when the state was but four months old. The references to "single will" and "iron discipline" are sufficient basis for Cardan to conclude: "We believe these conceptions, this *subjective* factor, played an enormous role in the degeneration of the Russian Revolution...we can see today the relationship between the views he held and the later reality of Stalinism."

Cardan is standing everything on its head. No "subjective" factor could ever have produced an objective situation—the new stage of capitalism. State-capitalism first arose during the world Depression, on the one hand, and, on the other hand, assumed its most mature form in Russia during the Five Year Plans and Stalin's most notorious Moscow Frame-up Trials.[14]

Were we to acquiesce to anything so idiotic that a single article could sum up a period covering the greatest proletarian revolution in history, would it not be incumbent upon the analyst at least to consider that article in its entirety?

---

13 *Selected Works*, Vol. VII, pp. 332, 342, 345.

14 For a full analysis of state-capitalism, see *Marxism and Freedom*, Chapter 13, "Russian State-Capitalism vs. Workers' Revolt." Lenin was warning of the possible return to capitalism throughout the last two years of his life. Especially important on state-capitalism is his speech to the 11th Congress of the Party, *Selected Works*, Vol. IX, 322–371.

That speech consisted of more, a great deal more than the passages singled out for quotation.

Lenin's Own Voice

The speech set forth the principal task of the proletariat to be "the positive or creative work of setting up an extremely intricate and subtle system of new organizational relationships extending to the planned production and distribution of the goods required for the existence of tens of millions of people. Such a revolution can be carried out only if the majority of the population, and primarily the majority of the toilers, display independent historical creative spirit…By creating a new Soviet type of state, which gives the opportunity to all the toilers and the masses of the oppressed to take an active part in the independent building of a new society, we solved only a small part of this difficult problem."[15]

Far from the Taylor system (which Lenin most certainly did *not* understand) being the ruling conception, proletarian democracy was the guiding line which permeated Lenin's speech. *This* is what the Soviets meant to Lenin. This is why he put the whole stress on the fact that the soviet form of organization is justified because "for the first time a start is thus made in teaching the *whole* of the population in the art of administration, and in their beginning to administer." And he warns against

> a petty-bourgeois tendency to transform the members of the Soviets into 'members of parliament,' or into bureaucrats. This must be combatted by drawing all the members of the Soviets into the practical work of administration…Our aim is to draw *the whole of the poor* into the practical work of administration…our aim is to insure that every toiler…shall perform state duties.[16]

Before and after Revolution

The four-months old workers' state was in "a period of waiting for new outbreaks of the revolution, which is maturing in the West at a painfully slow pace." And Lenin was holding fast to the new universal, that he had elaborated on the eve of revolution in *State and Revolution*, that unless the bourgeois state was so thoroughly smashed that production was run by the whole population *"TO A MAN";* and the state without bureaucracy, without a standing army, without

---

15 Vol. VII, pp. 315–316.

16 *Ibid*, pp. 345–347.

police, was administered by the whole population "TO A MAN," there would be no socialist society. Three months after gaining power, Lenin repeated:[17]

"We wanted the workers themselves to draw up, from below, the new principles of economic conditions." Indeed Lenin was willing to let a single distinction sum up the difference between the Second International that had betrayed the workers and the new Third International. That single distinction was that genuine Marxists "reduce everything to the conditions of labor."[18]

Lenin was concerned about how "shy" the workers still were. They had not "yet become accustomed to the idea that they are the ruling class now." He lashed out at "lackadasicalness, slovenliness, untidiness, nervous haste," of the "educated" which was due, he said, "of the abnormal separation of mental from manual labor." He urged upon these intellectuals to begin listening to these shy workers:

> every attempt to adhere to stereotyped forms and to impose uniformity from above gave a great example of how to combine initiative, independence, freedom of action, and vigor from below with voluntary centralism free from stereotyped forms...there is a great deal of talent among the people—it is merely suppressed. It must be given an opportunity to express itself. It, and it alone, with the support of the masses can save Russia and can save the cause of socialism.[19]

Nor was he talking only against "petty-bourgeois intellectuals." He was talking about Bolsheviks, his co-leaders now that they had state power; his appeal was to the initiative of the masses *from below*. The famous trade union debate of 1920–21 discloses how desperately he worked toward this one truth, how he differed even on the question of designating Russia as a workers' state. His contention was that a precise description would show instead that the designation of "workers' state" was an "abstraction" while the reality was that, it was a workers' and peasants' state "with bureaucratic distortions." In arguing against Trotsky's administrative mentality, Lenin insisted that the only assurance there is for the workers protecting that state is through giving them the freedom to protect themselves from the state: *"The entirely organized proletariat must protect itself and must utilize the workers' organizations for the purpose of protecting the workers from their own state."*[20]

---

17 *Ibid*, p. 227.

18 Vol. IX, p. 440.

19 *Ibid*, pp. 419, 420, 422.

20 *Ibid.* p. 9.

This was not just a visionary concept of a Marxist who has no state power. This was the demand of a Bolshevik who *had* state-power, a demand that his co-leaders, his Party, recognize that the workers' state can justify its existence only when the workers maintain their own *non-state* organizations to protect them from their own state. There is a veritable conspiracy between the Communists and the detractors of Lenin to portray Lenin's concept of the Party as if Lenin had never changed his position from 1903 to his death. Since space does not allow me here to deal with the question of "vanguardism," which I totally oppose, I must refer readers to *Marxism and Freedom*, Chapter XI, "Forms of Organization: the Relationship of the Spontaneous Self-Organization of the Proletariat to the 'Vanguard Party.'"

∵

Lukács' Philosophic Dimension

News & Letters, *February and March 1973*

Part I

1973 marks the 50th anniversary of the publication of *History and Class Consciousness*, and is sure to increase the deluge of articles, pamphlets and even whole books about its late famous author, George Lukács. These have been pouring forth the past few years from both the New Left[21] and the official Communist press.

1956 Stands between 1923 and 1973

In 1956, on the other hand, when Lukács briefly participated in the Hungarian Revolution despite a full quarter century of capitulation to Stalinism, the Hungarian Communists who helped the Russian counterrevolution destroy the revolution and execute its leader, Imre Nagy, expelled Lukács from the Party and unloosed still another vitriolic attack on his 1923 seminal study on Hegelian-Marxian dialectics.

---

21 As one example, see *Telos*, which not only devoted two special issues (Winter 1971 and Spring 1972) plus a "memorial statement" (Spring 1971), but this was preceded by a detailed study by Paul Piccone, " Lukács' *History and Class-Consciousness*, Half a Century Later" in the Fall 1969 issue. See also a book of essays, *The Unknown Dimension*, edited by Dick Howard and Karl E. Klare (Basic Books, N.Y.).

The tragedy lies not in any change in the stance of the Communist Party between 1973 and 1956; it hasn't changed its counter-revolutionary nature ever since the first workers' state, Russia, was transformed into its absolute opposite, a state-capitalist society. The tragedy lies in two altogether different spheres. One is Lukács' new, monumental work, *Social Ontology*, which he considered the greatest of his life, which he was completing when he died on June 4, 1971. Whether only because this philosophic work was abstract enough to be incomprehensible, or because in reality it was not all inimical to the ruling Communist Party, the fact is that we suddenly began seeing the belated publication of Lukács' 1923 work, *History and Class Consciousness*, with a most ambient new Preface included.[22]

The only reference the 1967 Preface makes to the 1956 Revolution is that there is no "inconsistency" between "the fact that in 1956 I had once again to take on a ministerial (!) post" (p. xxxi) and the fact that he had given up political activity in the mid-1920s. As if taking on political activities—"making revolutions"—hadn't related to revolutionary dialectics, and "giving up politics" hadn't "coincided" (in Stalin's day and now!) with renunciation of, and retreat from *History and Class-Consciousness*, Lukács concludes that he is glad to be out of politics since even when he was correct "there must be grave defects in my practical political abilities." (p. xxxi) Well, it isn't his "political abilities" we are concerned with. The reason for detouring to the Preface is not "politics" but the disjointedness of revolutionary philosophy from revolutionary activity.

The 1967 Preface

It isn't the *political* double-tonguedness that manifests Lukács' *philosophic* retreat from working out today's revolutionary dialectics in the forthcoming *Social Ontology* (to which we'll return later). In the Preface this manifests itself in places where he is full of praise of Lenin, but in fact doesn't stand on Lenin's philosophic ground. *And I don't mean Lenin's pre-1914 mechanistic* Materialism and Empirio-Criticism, *but his groundbreaking 1914–15* Philosophic Notebooks,[23] *which laid the philosophic foundation both for the Great Divide in Marxism, and for the Russian Revolution as well as for new world revolutionary perspectives.*

Lukács rightly shows how his work had caught the revolutionary spirit of the period, 1917–21: "A momentous world-historical change was struggling to

---

22 *History and Class Consciousness, Studies in Marxist Dialectics*, by Georg Lukacs, Merlin Press, London, 1971 (includes 1967 Preface).

23 See my article, "The Shock of Recognition and the Philosophic Ambivalence of Lenin" in *Telos*, Spring, 1970.

find a theoretical expression." (p. xxv) He also points to the truth that "undoubtedly one of the great achievements of *History and Class Consciousness* (was) to have reinstated the category of totality in the central position it had always occupied throughout Marx's work..." This, however, is followed up with a declaration about not knowing that Lenin was "moving in a similar direction." (p. xx) Suddenly there comes the arrogant and supercilious untitled reference to Lenin's *Philosophic Notebooks* as "philosophic fragments (that) were only published nine years after the appearance of *History and Class Consciousness*." (p. xx)[24]

Now, to have discovered, no matter when, that the revolutionary spirit of the age was not only caught as it objectively developed, *but prepared for* by Lenin back in 1914 via his "return" to Hegel after the collapse of the Second International, should have been so exciting an actual and philosophic adventure that the profound philosopher Lukács, couldn't have possibly slipped into factual dating of publications relative to one "knowing" or "not knowing" about these in 1919–22, if his 1967 ear had been attuned to the living revolutionary forces. Shouldn't his recollection of the "momentous world-historical change (that) was struggling to find a theoretical expression," 1919–1922, have led him to concretize his praise of "Lenin really brought about a renewal of the Marxist method," by grappling with Lenin's Notebooks instead of skipping over those "fragments"? *1967* is, after all, a good distance from 1932, by which time not only Lenin's Notebooks, but Marx's 1844 Humanist Essays had finally been published. It is true that Lukács' 1923 work had anticipated the essays on "Alienated Labor" and "Critique of the Hegelian Dialectic." But Marx's Essays also contained the sharp conclusion that "communism, as such, is not the goal of human development, the form of human society," which Lukács neither anticipated, nor knew how to relate to.

In any case, Lukács never reviewed either Lenin's or Marx's strictly philosophic works. This failure has nothing whatever to do with dates, but a great deal to do with the fact that Lukács is developing the dialectics, not of revolution, but of ontology. Whether his monumental work, *Social Ontology*, will

24 Actually, the dating is wrong. Even before Lenin's *Philosophic Notebooks* were published in Moscow, not in 1932, but in 1929–30, sections of them began to be published soon after Lenin's death, as various factional fights developed. In view of the fact that many among the "New Left," with malice aforethought, are deliberately mixing up the Comintern's June, 1924 attack on Lukács' work with Lenin's 1920 critique of the politics of the ultra-left in *"Left-Wing" Communism, an Infantile Disorder*, it should be made clear that Lenin lay on his deathbed, totally paralyzed, for 8 long mute tormenting months in 1923. Lenin's activity was finished when the second stroke hit him on March 10, 1923; he died Jam. 21, 1924.

prove to be not only his greatest work, but that dialectics of the concrete which the New Left expects all revolutionary forces to be grounded in, the indirect references to it in the new Preface to *History and Class Consciousness* does not help enhance that Preface. It isn't the Preface that will enter history, but the original work. The ambience of the Preface can no more detract from that epoch-making event than the author's renouncement of the book under Stalinism could keep it from having a most exciting underground life of its own. One final word must be said before we can finally turn to its contents, and that is that *History and Class Consciousness* isn't a book, i.e., a whole.[25] It is a collection of essays, and not all are of historic import. The two philosophic essays carried on a subterranean existence for a full half-century which has romanticized the whole, but the historic-philosophic breakthrough resides in those two central pieces—*What Is Orthodox Marxism?* and *Reification and the* Consciousness of the Proletariat. It is to these we now turn.

Part II

"What is orthodox Marxism?"

> Hegel's tremendous intellectual contribution consisted in the fact that he made theory and history dialectically relative to each other, grasped them in a dialectical reciprocal penetration ....
>
> LUKÁCS

It was the most unorthodox character of "What Is Orthodox Marxism?" that fired the imagination of German revolutionaries when it was first published in 1919 and again when it reappeared in revised form as part of the book, *History and Class Consciousness*, published in 1923.

When, by the end of the 1920's, the work was repudiated by its author as he made peace with Stalinism, the essay carried on many subterranean existences in many languages in different parts of the world: first, for those who had broken with Stalinism in the 1930's and 1940's; then for some of the "new philosophers"—French Existentialists, especially Merleau-Ponty—in the mid-1950s; and, finally, for those in the new generation of revolutionaries in the 1960's who, out of their own experiences, were turning away from sheer activism to reaching out for a "world view" of the dialectics of liberation.

---

25 Lukács himself, in the original (Christmas, 1922) Preface, made this clear with his very first sentence: "The collection and publication of these essays in book form is not intended to give them a greater importance as a whole than would be due to each individually." (p. xli.).

The enduring relevance of the essay is proof of the fact that its explosive effect was by no means limited to the fact that it had anticipated the rediscovery of Marx's now-famous 1844 Manuscripts which demonstrated how deeply rooted in Hegelian dialectics and theory of alienation were Marx's "Alienated Labor" and "Critique of the Hegelian Dialectic."

In re-establishing Marxism as a totality, never once separating the young Marx from the mature author of *Capital*, Lukács proved himself as uncompromising in his refusal to bow to scientism as to reformism.

The Revolutionary Dialectic

In naming names of those who had not worked out the full implications of the revolutionary nature of the Marxian dialectic, Lukács did not stop short of criticizing Marx's closest collaborator, Engels, who "does not even mention the most vital interaction, namely the dialectical relation between subject and object in historical process" (p. 3). The whole weight of this study in Marxian dialectics was its stress on "*the transformation of reality*": "It is at reality itself that Hegel and Marx part company. Hegel was unable to penetrate the real driving forces of history." (p. 17) It is true that Lukács himself so overstressed "consciousness" of the proletariat that it overshadowed its praxis which was both material force and reason so that it left room, at one and same time, for a slip back into the Hegelian idealism of "the identical subject-object," *and* into substituting the Party that "knows" for the proletariat.

But none noted this in the excitement generated by the essay's recapture of the revolutionary dialectical dimension of historical materialism which gave action its direction: "Marxist orthodoxy is no guardian of traditions; it is the eternally vigilant prophet proclaiming the relation between the tasks of the immediate present and the totality of the historical process." (p. 12) And that "historical process" was then concretized by the internationalism proclaimed in the *Communist Manifesto* and in the Paris Commune which Marx specified as having "no ideals to realize" but "to liberate the elements of the new society."

"Reification"

The essay, "Reification and Consciousness of the Proletariat" has neither the movement and verve of the first essay, nor its "orthodoxy" (and I'm using the word in the Lukaesian sense of *authentic* Marxism). There is no doubt, however, that it is the center of *History and Class Consciousness*.

This is not simply a matter of it being the longest, piece. (As against the 26 pages of the first essay, the essay on reification totaled no less than 139 pages.) Lukács could have called it a book, but, instead, took care to cast it in essay form. Where he shied away from claiming for it a totally new departure, a worked-out whole alternative, the intellectuals took it as such. It became the fashion to talk about "reification," "the reified world we live in." They may very well have anticipated, by three full decades, the intellectualistic rage around "One Dimensional Man," "One Dimensional Thought," "technological rationality," the move away from Reason to irrationality, or the retrogression from ontology to technology.

The "masses" (the rank and file) in the subterranean discussion of Lukács' book, on the other hand, kept their peace not merely because of lack of knowledge of "the history of philosophy," but because of a solid *proletarian* instinct that this was not merely a restatement of Marxism for a new epoch, *but rather that it contained elements deviatory from that which was authentic Marxism.*

First and most important of the distinctions between the two concepts of reification is that Marx had limited his analysis to the reification of *labor*, transforming it into *thing*, a mere appendage to a machine. Lukács on the other hand, had transformed reification into a universal, affecting the whole of society equally:

> Reification is, then, the necessary, immediate reality of every person living in capitalist society. It can be overcome *only by constant and constantly renewed efforts to disrupt the reified structure of existence by relating to the concretely manifested contradictions of the total development, by becoming conscious of the immanent meanings of these contradictions for the total development.* (p. 197)

Here, then, we see that reification is universalized, made a veritable "human condition"; "every person" is affected equally.

And "becoming conscious" is endowed with a "neutrality." Though Lukács is a revolutionary and quotes endlessly from Marx as to how the proletariat, and the proletariat alone, is the revolutionary force to create new human relations, it does not flow either logically or objectively, either historically or dialectically from his original theory.

Where Marx, the practitioner of the revolutionary dialectic, analyzes reification as resulting from the specifically capitalistic production process of the reification of labor, pounding labor into flung, and thereby creating in the laborer the absolute opposite—the "quest for universality" and the revolt—Lukács blurs totally the Marxian concept of "freely-associated labor" stripping the fetishism from commodities, overcoming alienation, shaping history.

Ironically enough, it was Lukács who—in recapturing the Hegelian dimension in Marx; in delivering mighty blows to the revisionists by showing how very inseparable was their reformism, their turn away from revolution with their abandonment of the dialectic—made his greatest contribution to authentic Marxism by interrelating and making central to his dialectic the interrelationships of the concepts of "totality" and "mediation."

In reviewing, in the 1967 Preface, what he had meant to do and what he had done, he thinks that, on the one hand, "alienation" sans objectivity was "in the air," and, on the other hand, "messianistic utopianism" led to a residue of idealism. And he adds that concerning the whole question of the relationship of "mediation to immediacy" of "economics and dialectics" that he had begun reworking in Moscow in the early thirties: "Only now, thirty years later, am I attempting to discover a real solution to this whole problem in the ontology of social existence." (p. xxxv)

Part III
The Hungarian Revolution vis-a-vis "Social Ontology"

The 1956 Revolution, with Lukács suddenly appearing as participant, revived hopes that, despite his quarter of a century of capitulation to Stalinism, Lukács would continue the revolution in thought he wrought in the early 1920's.

Every new stage of cognition is, after all, not born out of thin air. It can be born only out of *praxis*, the praxis of new revolutionary forces uprooting the existing social order; and the Hungarian masses were directing their revolt not against private capitalism which had already been abolished, but against the *existing* exploitative, ruling Communist state-power, or, more precisely put, state-capitalism calling itself Communism. With this new mass upsurge, its plunge to new freedom, there was every reason to expect the old philosopher would catch what, in the 1920's, he had called, "a momentous, world-historical change...struggling to find a theoretical expression."

The criticism levelled against Lukács by independent Marxists seemed to lose its validity, especially as much of it had the character of Monday morning quarterbacking raised to "wisdom" by the knowledge of some three to four decades of objective development. Considering the excitement of the new generation of Marxists over the philosophic dimension of Lukács and its impatient waiting for the comprehensive *Social Ontology* he had been writing for a decade and to which he had referred in his last years as having been the product of three decades of thought, it would indeed have been a joy to report so great a historic breakthrough—a new stage in cognition that met the challenge of the spontaneous upsurge from below, the Hungarian Revolution.

Unfortunately, nothing could be further from the truth. The truth is that, whatever deviatory—deviatory, not reinterpretative—elements were implicit in the "Reification" article, "reification of consciousness" affected Lukács, who reduced socialism to the perfection of industrial production achieving the Plan![26]

"Mediation"

Take a most crucial Hegelian category, and one central to Lukács' dialectics, Mediation. As concretized by Marx, and the one Lukács tried to extend, it was, first, inseparable from the most fundamental of all Hegelian categories, their summation, Subject. Secondly, and most important—since that revealed a totally new continent of thought, Historical Materialism—Marx historically, philosophically, dialectically spelled Subject out as Proletariat. In a word, Marx didn't simply stand Hegel "right side up," didn't only critically transform Hegel's concept of labor as process of man's becoming, much less leave it in the realm of thought. No, as laborer, the proletariat was both opposing the capitalistic exploitation and reduction of all his concrete labors to one abstract mass by that "pendulum of the clock," and seeking "universality." Thus, he *became reason as well as force, reshaped history, created new beginnings for totally new human relations.*

Whatever duality there was in Lukács, and whatever abstractions—because of the emphasis on "morality" and "ethics"—the point is that the concept of concrete totality escaped him, despite the fact that totality, itself, was one of his central categories. Having never grounded his concept in the concrete struggles at *the point of production,* in the factory he never entered; having never made the actual voices of the workers the new point of departure, *labor is seen not as the laborer in revolt; labor is no more than the exercise of labor power in the most specifically capitalistic form: socially necessary labor time.*

Where Marx used the category, socially-necessary labor time, to define that which is uniquely capitalistic, oppressive, chaotic, Lukács denudes it of its class character and makes it applicable to all societies. No wonder he begins this excursus with the statement: "Above all, we propose to examine what economic necessity consists of. At the outset, it would be emphasized this is not a

26 It no doubt is both incomplete and unfair to judge *Social Ontology,* since the work has not yet been published. But, no matter how the whole will reveal some partial brilliant flashes and dialectical insights, it is impossible to think that it could reverse the direction of what has been stated by Lukács in his many world interviews on the subject, in the references to it in the 1967 Preface to the 1923 work, and in the two chapters of his late writings. One was published in *Telos,* Fall, 1970. "The Dialectic of Labor: Beyond Causality and Teleology"; and the abbreviated publication of "The Ontological Foundations of Human Thought and Activity" in *Contemporary East European Philosophy,* Vol. Ill, 1971 (See especially pp. 223–224, pp. 228–230, the above quotations are from those pages.).

natural, necessary process, though Marx himself, in his polemic with idealism, occasionally used such an expression." As Lukács himself put it, he was ready "simply to skip over the most important mediating areas." By then mediation was no longer the class struggles, much less outright proletarian revolution. Mediation became subject-less; "totality" became cult.[27]

We hope we are wrong when we think that the attraction Lukács has for the New Left is due to the fact that they never were "weighted down" by any concept of the revolutionary role of the proletariat and, with Lukács at least philosophically, they are ready to scuttle Marx's theory of proletarian revolution.

∵

Tony Cliff Degrades Lenin as Theoretician

News & Letters, *May 1977*

The second volume of Tony Cliff's three-volume study of *Lenin,*[28] which has just been published, is a most curious compilation. Though subtitled, *All Power To The Soviets*, and although it follows the first volume which already had centered on *Building The Party* (and is so subtitled), it is that same vanguardist theme that permeates Volume II as well. Indeed, the Foreword explains that the reason for the book, when Trotsky's monumental *History of the Russian Revolution* had already covered that period so magnificently, is the latter's "serious defect": "The one thing noticeably missing is the Bolshevik Party: its rank and file, its cadres, its local committees, its Central Committee." (p. ix)

So weighted down is Tony Cliff with the concept of the vanguard party to lead and the "caliber of leadership," that he does not deign so much as to mention the philosophic break Lenin experienced at the shock of the simultaneity of the outbreak of World War I and the collapse of the Second International.

The Chronology does list: "23 August/5 September Lenin arrives in Berne (Switzerland)"—and then proceeds to mention that Lenin presented his thesis

27 Istvan Meszaros, who had once been a pupil of Lukács, and remains the most profound of his sympathetic critics, calls attention to the duality in Lukács' concepts. "Even the most recent Lukács"—the author of a massive *Social Ontology*—"insists on a duality, on a dual causality, and on an ultimate autonomy of "decisions between alternatives…on the basis of his Ontology, the positive outcome can only be envisaged as the impact of a 'sollen'… an *ought* to change their way of life." (pp. 53, 64, *George Lukács, The Man, his Work, and his Ideas*, ed. by G.H.R. Parkinson, Vintage, 1970.).

28 Tony Cliff, *Lenin*, Vol. II, Pluto Press, London.

on war to a Bolshevik conference. But neither there, nor in the whole 411 pages of text, Notes, and Index, is there a single word that Lenin repaired to the library to study Hegel's *Science of Logic* and that Lenin's "Abstract of Hegel's Logic" took from September to Dec. 17, 1914 to complete[29]—after which followed 1915 and more "On Dialectics" and everything from *Imperialism* to *Marxism and the State*, the first version of *State and Revolution*.

On Jan. 5, 1915, Lenin addressed a letter to *Encyclopaedia Granat*, for which he had written the essay, "Karl Marx." He was trying to recall it in order to make "certain corrections in the section on dialectics...I have been studying this question of dialectics for the last month and a half and I could add something to it if there was time..." Evidently there was no time—or at least the bourgeois *Granat* found no time—to allow Lenin to make his corrections, much less to try to figure out what had happened in those six weeks in Lenin's thought. No doubt it was hard to understand why Lenin, in the midst of a world holocaust, was so preoccupied with dialectics.

Sixty-one years later, a Marxist theoretician like Tony Cliff is still so little concerned with Hegelian dialectics that he fails to see its relevance either to Lenin or Marx—or *Imperialism*, to which he does devote Chapter 4. That chapter is the perfect proof that empiricists who are bereft of methodology cannot appreciate methodology in others *because* they so totally deviate from the revolutionary vision. Thus, Tony Cliff informs us that "in terms of the actual description of modern capitalism, Lenin is not original at all, and borrows practically everything from Bukharin." (p. 61) This follows a statement on what Lenin "owed to the people who had studied modern capitalism before—above all Hobson and Hilferding."[30]

---

29 When Moscow finally published Lenin's *Philosophic Notebooks* in English in 1961, they not only left out Adoratsky's Introduction to the first Russian edition of 1930, but also the Lenin Institute's listing of what books Lenin called for not just in Berne, 1914–16, but in Russia after taking power. It bears repeating Adoratsky: "Despite the fact...of the extreme situation and the necessity to give all attention and all energy to practical questions, Lenin continued to interest himself in questions of philosophy. This is evident from his readings...On June 24, 1921 he asked for a Russian translation of Hegel's *Logic* and *Phenomenology of Mind*...Lenin not only read but wrote on the question and philosophy. Nine-tenths of the remarks on Bukharin's *Economics of the Transition Period* concern the question of method."

30 Cliff picks out the quantitative fact of "148 books, 232 articles" that Lenin read and annotated, but says not a single word that while preparing the pamphlet he had read *Phenomenology of Mind*, much less any attempt to dig into the abbreviated "popular outline" to see there such dialectical principles as "transformation into opposite," or the relationship between Hegel's "attitudes to objectivity" and Lenin's analysis of those "other studies" that Lenin "owes" so much to.

That happens to be exactly what bourgeois economists—who have never *pretended to be concerned with dialectics as have Marxists (either as philosophy or as revolution.)— have always contended. Tony Cliff does them one better by drawing the further conclusion that "the difference between the two books (Bukharin's and Lenin's on Imperialism,) is radical—a difference between a theoretical treatise on imperialism and a political pamphlet on the same subject."* (*p. 61*)

The ground for this degradation of Lenin as theoretician is, in fact, laid in Vol. I (p. 256) where Cliff writes: "It was hardly an exaggeration for the Bolshevik historian M.N. Pokrovsky to write, 'You will not find in Lenin a single purely theoretical work; each has a propaganda aspect.'" In Vol. II, Cliff not only leads up to Chapter 4 by telling us (in the chapter on the National Question) that "many of the leading comrades in Russia did not understand why Lenin was so vehement in his opposition to Bukharin" (p. 56 ftn), but in the very chapter on Imperialism he skips to Lenin's *Will* (12/23–24/1922) to quote Lenin on Bukharin as the "biggest theoretician," *without so much as mentioning that a "but" follows: "but his (Bukharin's) theoretical views can only with the very greatest doubt be regarded as fully Marxian, for there is something scholastic in him. (He has never learned, and I think never fully understood, the dialectic)."*

What is this dialectic that made Lenin say—*and not just in a polemical way, but in his Will*—that his Bolshevik co-leader, Bukharin, who had never betrayed, who was always a revolutionary, who was, in fact, "the favorite of the whole party" and a "major theoretician," was "not fully a Marxist" because he had "never fully understood the dialectic"? The very work that Tony Cliff considers so theoretically superior to Lenin's popularization was the one that Lenin had first introduced favorably but after grappling with Hegel's dialectic, found so non-dialectical that he undertook his own study.

Secondly, and foremost, Lenin found Bukharin's opposition to self-determination not just bereft of the "dialectic of history," but so total an impediment to working with new national revolutionary forces, such as Irish revolutionaries, that he designated Bukharin's position as nothing short of "imperialist economism"!

Tony Cliff's singular empiricism—like all empiricism, bereft of all methodology—is beyond comprehension of Lenin's theory—*theory*, not just a "popular outline." By leaving out Lenin's *Philosophic Notebooks*,[31] Cliff not only skips

---

31 In Vol. I, Cliff does have one single reference (p. 291) to "dialectically terse and lively Philosophic Notebooks" at the point where he criticizes *Materialism and Empirio-Criticism*. One would have thought that, even if Cliff had no time for concretizing his terse single statement on the *Notebooks*, his preoccupation with the Party should have led him to see that, Stalinist detractors notwithstanding, Lenin himself had not a word on "partyness

over "philosophy," but the *dialectics of liberation as self-developing Subject, that is to say, the actual masses in revolt.* Thus by no accident whatever, the chapter on the "National Question," on which Cliff is supposed to agree with Lenin, not Bukharin, has not a word to say about the Irish Revolution, which was *the* concrete "topic" under discussion. What was decisive were live revolutionaries. Their appearances on the historic stage had sharpened to a fever pitch all the tendencies fighting Lenin's position.

This was not the Austrian Socialists in the 19th century (where Tony Cliff chooses to begin), nor even Poland, 1912, when the National Question was still debated just as "principle," as "theory," nor the Bund. Though he still keeps away from referring to the Easter Rebellion, Cliff is finally forced to quote Lenin: "The dialectics of history are such that small nations, powerless as an *independent* factor in the struggle against imperialism, play a part as one of the ferments, one of the bacilli, which help the *real* anti-imperialist force, the socialist proletariat, to make its appearance on the scene."

But meanwhile they hadn't. 1917 was still to be. And when it did come it was preceded by Lenin's *State and Revolution* that was first begun in those same critical years, 1914–16, when Lenin was grappling with Hegelian dialectics as philosophy, as politics, as economics, as self-developing Subject. "The dialectics proper"—Lenin's phrase—had to be shown as "the living tree of living, fertile, genuine, powerful, omnipotent, objective, absolute human knowledge" because "it is impossible fully to grasp Marx's *Capital*, and especially its first chapter, if you have not studied through and understood the *whole* of Hegel's *Logic*. Consequently, none of the Marxists for the past half century have understood Marx!"

By eliminating this from his study of Lenin, it is no wonder that Tony Cliff reaches the climax of his comprehension—I mean *non*-comprehension—of Lenin by singling out Lenin's "uncanny intuition. In a period of great changes, the number of unknown factors, not only in the enemy camp, but also in our own, is so great that sober analysis alone will not suffice. An unsurpassed ability to detect the mood of the masses was Lenin's most important gift." (p. 278)

What then of Cliff's indispensable party to lead? Ah. Cliff brings it all back in the penultimate paragraph: "The crucible of October furnished the supreme test of his (Lenin's) strategy, and of the caliber of his leadership of the party and the class."

---

of philosophy." Instead, Cliff's point is that it was supposedly only "in the period of reaction after the revolution" that "Marxist philosophy inevitably came to the fore" (Vol. 1, p. 289). No wonder he could not see the *Notebooks* as Lenin's philosophic preparation for revolution.

Bibliography

Aidit, D.N. May 23, 1965. "Intensify Revolutionary Offensive and First Oppose 'Five Devils,'" (Issue includes Peng Zhen's speech as well as excerpts from President Sukarno's address, "Indonesian C.P. Is a Thoroughly Progressive, Revolutionary Party.") *Beijing Review*, June 4,1965. http://www.massline.org/PekingReview/PR1965/PR1965-23-AiditSpeech.pdf.

Althusser, Louis. 1968. *Lenine et la Philosophie*. Paris: Colin.

American Quarterly for the Soviet Union. April, 1940.

Arnold, A.Z. 1937. *Banks, Credit and Money in Soviet Russia*. New York: Columbia University Press.

Ashai, Isoshi. 1939. *The Economic Strength of Japan*. Tokyo: Hokuseido Press.

Baran, Paul A. December, 1944. "New Trends in Russian Economic Thinking?" *The American Economic Review* Vol. 34, No. 4.

Baykov. December 1941. *The Economic Journal*. London.

Berle, Adolph and Means, Gardiner. 1932. *Modern Corporation and Private Property*. New York: MacMillan.

Berliner, Joseph S. 1958. *Soviet Economic Aid*. New York: Praeger.

Brokmeyer, Ron. 1984.The *Fetish of High Tech and Karl Marx's Mathematical Manuscripts*. Detroit: News & Letters.

Buhle, Paul. May 1970. Special Issue on C.L.R. James. *Radical America*. Vol. IV, No. 4.

Bukharin, Nikolai. *Ataka*, May, 1924. (Collection of Theoretical Articles) Moscow (in Russian).

Bukharin, Nikolai. 1926. *Historical Materialism* London: Allen and Unwin.

Bukharin, Nikolai. 1979. *Economics of the Transition Period*. Routledge. (English); 1920 (Russian).

Bukharin, Nikolai. 2003. *The World Economy and Imperialism*. London: Bookmarks.

Cardan, Paul (Cornelius Castoriadias). 1972. *The Meaning of Socialism*. London: Solidarity.

Carver, Terrell, ed. 1975. *Marx: Texts on Method*. New York: Barnes & Noble Books.

Castro, Fidel. 1953. *History Will Absolve Me* ("La historia me absolverá" spoken), Editorial de Ciencias Sociales, La Habana, Cuba. 1975. English translation: https://www.marxists.org/history/cuba/archive/castro/1953/10/16.htm.

Central Committee of the Communist Party of China. June 14, 1963. "A Proposal Concerning the General Line of the International Communist Movement," Beijing: Foreign Language Press.

Chao Kuo-Chin. 1963. *Economic Planning and Organization in Mainland China, 1949–1957*, a documentary study, Vol. 2. East Asian Study Center, Harvard University. Cambridge: Harvard University Press.

Chou Yang. Oct. 26, 1963. "The Fighting Task Confronts Workers in Philosophy and the Social Speeches," speech delivered at the 4th Enlarged Session of the Committee of the Department of Philosophy and Social Science of the Chinese Academy of Sciences.

Clark, Colin. 1940. *The Conditions of Economic Progress.* London: McMillan.

Cliff, Tony (Gluckstein, Ygael). 1957. *Mao's China.* Boston: Beacon Press.

Cliff, Tony (Gluckstein, Ygael). 1976. *Lenin 2, All Power to the Soviets.* London: Pluto Press.

Cohn-Bendit, Daniel. 1968. *Obsolete Communism, The Left-Wing Alternative.* New York: McGraw-Hill.

Correspondence. Mimeographed (Nov 1951 to June 1953); Printed (Oct. 1953 to March 1953) Detroit, Michigan. Selected issues available http://rayadunayevskaya.org/raya/ArchivePDFs/2180.pd (mimeographed) and http://rayadunayevskaya.org/raya/ArchivePDFs/2200.pdf (printed).

Crankshaw, Edward. February 12 and 26, 1961. *The London Observer.*

Debray, Regis. 1968. *Revolution In The Revolution? Armed struggle and political struggle in Latin America* New York: Grove Press, N.Y.

Denby, Charles. 1960, *Workers Battle Automation.* Detroit: *News and Letters.*

Denby, Charles. 1989. *Indignant Heart: A Black Worker's Journal.* Detroit: Wayne State University Press.

Deutscher, Isaac. 1954. *The Prophet Armed.* New York: Oxford University Press.

Deutscher, Isaac. 1959. *The Prophet Unarmed.* New York: Oxford University Press.

Deutscher, Isaac. 1963. *The Prophet Outcast.* New York: Oxford University Press.

Dewey, John. 1937. *The Case Of Leon Trotsky: Report Of Hearings On The Charges Made Against Him In The Moscow Trials.* New York: Harper (*Not Guilty: Report of the Commission of Inquiry into the Charges Made Against Leon Trotsky in the Moscow Trials*).

Doak, A. 1967. *China After Mao.* Princeton N.J.: Princeton University Press.

Draft Program of the 22nd Russian Communist Party Congress, released by *Tass* July 30, published in *The New York Times,* Aug. 1, 1961. *Foreign Language Press,* Beijing, 1963.

Dunayevskaya, Raya. *The Raya Dunayevskaya Collection—Marxist-Humanism: A Half-Century of Its World Development and Supplement to the Collection.* The most complete collection of Dunayevskaya's writings. The Collection, Supplement and Guides to the Collection are on the Internet at www.rayadunayevskaya.org.Originals are on deposit at Wayne State University Archives of Labor and Urban Affairs, Detroit, Michigan.

Dunayevskaya, Raya. *Raya Dunayevskaya Archive* in the Marxist Internet Archives. http://www.marxistsfr.org/archive/dunayevskaya/index.htm.

Dunayevskaya, Raya. (F. Forest) 1942, 1943. "Analysis of Russian Economy," *The New International.*

Dunayevskaya, Raya. (F. Forest). November, 1943. "A Restatement of Some Fundamentals of against Carter's Vulgarization," *Bulletin of the Workers Party*, March 1944. http://rayadunayevskaya.org/ArchivePDFs/167.pdf.

Dunayevskaya, Raya. 1943. "Labor and Society," http://rayadunayevskaya.org/ArchivePDFs/87.pdf.

Dunayevskaya, Raya. September, 1944. "Teaching of Economics in the Soviet Union," *The American Economic Review.*

Dunayevskaya, Raya. September, 1944 "A New Revision of Marxian Economics," *The American Economic Review.*

Dunayevskaya, Raya. September, 1945. "Revision or Reaffirmation of Marxism," *The American Economic Review.*

Dunayevskaya, Raya (Freddie Forest). December 1946; January, 1947. "The Nature of the Russian Economy," *The New International.*

Dunayevskaya, Raya. 1961. *Nationalism, Communism, Marxist-Humanism and the Afro-Asian Revolutions.* Left Group, Cambridge University Labour Club, England.

Dunayevskaya, Raya. 1967. *State-Capitalism and Marx's Humanism or Philosophy and Revolution.* Detroit: News & Letters.

Dunayevskaya, Raya. 1970. "The Shock of Recognition and the Philosophic Ambivalence of Lenin," *Telos.*

Dunayevskaya, Raya. May, June–July 1971. "'Culture,' Science and State-Capitalism," *News & Letters.*

Dunayevskaya, Raya. 1977. *Sexism, Politics and Revolution in Mao's China.* Detroit: Women's Liberation-News & Letters.

Dunayevskaya, Raya. 1980. *25 Years of Marxist-Humanism: A History of Worldwide Revolutionary Developments.* Chicago: News and Letters.

Dunayevskaya, Raya. 1991. *Rosa Luxemburg, Women's Liberation, and Marx's Philosophy of Revolution.* Champaign IL: University of Illinois Press.

Dunayevskaya, Raya. 1992. *The Marxist-Humanist Theory of State-Capitalism.* Chicago: News and Letters.

Dunayevskaya, Raya. 2000. *Marxism and Freedom: From 1776 until Today.* Amherst, New York: Humanity Books.

Dunayevskaya, Raya. 2002. *The Power of Negativity: Selected Writings on the Dialectic in Hegel and Marx.* Lanham, Maryland: Lexington Books.

Dunayevskaya, Raya. 2003. *Philosophy and Revolution, from Hegel to Sartre and from Marx to Mao.* Lanham, Maryland: Lexington Books.

Dunayevskaya, Raya. 2003. *American Civilization on Trial: Black Masses as Vanguard.* Chicago: News & Letters.

Dunayevskaya, R. and Andy Phillips. 1984. *A 1980s View: The Coal Miners' General Strike of 1949–50 and the Birth of Marxist-Humanism in the U.S.* Chicago: News & Letters.

Dunayevskaya, R. and Ivan Sviták. 1969. *Czechoslovakia: Revolution and Counter-Revolution*. Detroit: News & Letters.

Engels, Frederick. 1939. *Herr Eugen Duhring's Revolution in Science* (*Anti-Duhring*). New York: International Publishers, [Marx-Engels, *Collected Works*, Volume 25.].

Engels, Frederick. 1941. *Ludwig Feuerbach and the Outcome of Classical German Philosophy*. New York: International Publishers.

Fainsod, Merle. Nov.–Dec. 1961. "The 22nd Party Congress," special supplement of *Problems of Communism*, vol. 1. No. 6.

Fejto, Francios. 1957. *Behind the Rape of Hungary*. New York: David McKay Company, Inc.

Feuer, Lewis S. April 1949. "Dialectical Materialism and Soviet Science," *Philosophy of Science*, Volume 16, Number 2.

Fontaine, Andre. July 9, 1969. "Germany Remains Focal Point," *Le Monde*, Weekly Selection (English).

Gankin, O.H. and Fisher, H.H. 1940. *The Bolsheviks and the World War*. Stanford: Stanford University Press.

Gosplan (State Planning Commission for the Development of National Economy). 1933. Results of the First Five Year Plan, in Russian.

Gosplan (State Planning Commission for the Development of National Economy). 1939. Results of the Second Five Year Plan, in Russian.

Gosplan (State Planning Commission for the Development of National Economy). The Third Five Year Plan for the Development of National Economy of the USSR, 1939 in Russian.

Guevara, Che. October 8, 1960. *Notes for the Study of the Ideology of Cuban Revolution*. https://www.marxists.org/archive/guevara/1960/10/08.htm.

Hegel, G.W.F. 1894. *Philosophy of Mind*, Wallace translation. Oxford: Clarendon Press.

Hegel, G.W.F. 1929. *Science of Logic*, Johnston and Struthers translation. London: Allen & Unwin.

Hegel, G.W.F. 1931. *Phenomenology of Mind*, Baillie translation. New York: Harper & Row.

Herzen, Alexander. 1960. *Selected Philosophical Works*. Moscow: Foreign Languages Publishing House. https://archive.org/details/selectedphilosop032757mbp.

Howard, Dick, ed. 1971. *Selected Political Writings of Rosa Luxemburg*. New York: Monthly Review Press.

Howard, Dick and Karl E. Klare, eds. 1972. *The Unknown Dimension*. New York: Basic Books.

Hubbard, L.E. 1936. *Soviet Money and Finance*. London: Macmillan.

Hubbard, L.E. 1938. Soviet *Trade and Distribution*. London: Macmillan.

Hunan Provincial Proletarian Revolutionary Great Alliance Committee (Sheng-wu-lien). 1969. "Whither China?" translated in *Survey of China Mainland Press*,

Hong Kong, 4190, and appears in *International Socialism*, June/July 1969. Available also at https://libcom.org/library/whither-china-sheng-wu-lien.

Imre Nagy Institute. 1960. *The Review*, #4. Brussells.

Isaacs, Harold. 1938. *The Tragedy of the Chinese Revolution*. London: Secker & Warburg.

Iugov, Aron. [a.k.a. Yugow]. 1942. *Russia's Economic Front for War and Peace, An appraisal of the Three Five-Year Plans*. New York: Harper & Brothers.

Jacques-Francillon, J. 1963. "China's Borders," *New Republic*, 4/20/63.

James, C.L.R. (J: R: Johnson). April, 1943. "Production for Sake of Production – A Reply to Carter," *Workers Party Bulletin*. https://www.marxists.org/archive/james-clr/works/1943/04/production.htm.

Johnson-Forest Tendency. 1950. *State-Capitalism and World Revolution*, written by Johnson (C.L.R. James), Forest (Raya Dunayevskaya) and Ria Stone (Grace Lee). *Discussion Bulletin No. 4*, Sept. 1950, of *Socialist Workers Party*. http://rayadunayevskaya.org/raya/ArchivePDFs/1333.pdf.

Joravsky, David. 1961. *Soviet Marxism and Natural Science, 1917–1932*. New York: Columbia University Press.

Kahin, George McT. 1952. *Nationalism and Revolution in Indonesia*. Cornell: Cornell University Press.

Kamenka, Eugene. 1962. *The Ethical Foundations of Marxism*. London: Routledge & Kegan Paul.

Kamenka, Eugene. January, 1964. "Soviet Philosophy Through Western Eyes," *Survey*.

Kamm, Henry. June 10, 1969. "Rumanian, in Kremlin, Affirms Policy," *The New York Times*.

Karol, K.S. June 27, 1969. "Drawn Match at Moscow," *New Statesman*.

Karol, K.S. 1970. *Guerillas in Power: The Course of the Cuban Revolution*. New York: Hill and Wang.

Karpushin, V.A. 1955. "Marx's Working Out of the Materialist Dialectics in the *Economic-Philosophic Manuscripts of the Year, 1844*," *Voprosy Filosofii* #3.

Kedrov, B.M. 1970. "On the Distinctive Characteristics of Lenin's *Philosophic Notebooks*," *Soviet Studies in Philosophy*.

Konrad, George. December 2, 1982. "The Danger in Poland," *The New Your Review of Books*.

Lange, Oscar. March 1945. "Marxian Economics in the Soviet Union," *The American Economic Review* Vol. 35, No. 1.

Lenin, V.I. *Lenin Internet Archive* available on Marxist Internet Archives: http://www.marxistsfr.org/archive/lenin/index.htm.

Lenin, V.I. 1935. *Will*. First published by Trotsky as *The Suppressed Testament of Lenin*. Pioneer Publishers.

Lenin, V.I. 1937. *The Letters of Lenin*. New York: Harcourt, Brace and Co.

Lenin, V.I. 1943. *Selected Works*. Volume IV–XI, XIII. New York: International Publishers.

Lenin, V.I. *Collected Works*, 1963. Volume 19. Moscow: Foreign Language Publishing House.

Lenin, V.I. *Collected Works*, 1964. Volume 22. Moscow: Foreign Language Publishing House.

Lenin, V.I. *Collected Works*, 1964. Volume 26. Moscow: Foreign Language Publishing House.

Lenin, V.I. *Collected Works*, 1965. Volume 27. Moscow: Foreign Language Publishing House.

Lenin, V.I. *Collected Works*. 1965. Volume 30. Moscow: Foreign Language Publishing House.

Lenin, V.I. *Collected Works*. 1966. Volume 36. Moscow: Foreign Language Publishing House.

Lenin, V.I. *Collected Works* 1966. Volume 38. Moscow: Foreign Language Publishing House.

Lenin, V.I. *Collected Works*. 1970. Volume 45. Moscow: Foreign Language Publishing House.

Leont'ev, L.A. 1935. *Political Economy, A Beginner's Course.* New York: International Publishers.

Lewin, Moshe. 1968. *Lenin's Last Struggle.* New York: Random House.

Lichtheim, George. January, 1964. "Western Marxist Literature, 1953–63," *Survey.*

Lukacs, George. 1970. "The Dialectic of Labor: Beyond Causality and Teleology," *Telos.*

Lukacs, George. 1971. *History and Class Consciousness, Studies in Marxist Dialectics.* London: Merlin Press.

Lukacs, George. 1971. "The Ontological Foundations of Human Thought and Activity," *Contemporary East European Philosophy*, Vol. Ill.

Luxemburg, Rosa. 1937. *Reform or Revolution.* New York: Three Arrow Press.

Luxemburg, Rosa. 1951 (1913). *Accumulation of Capital.* London: Routledge and Kegan.

Luxemburg, Rosa. 1969 (1915). *The Crisis in German Social Democracy* (Junius pamphlet). New York: Howard Fertig.

Luxemburg, Rosa. 1974. *Gesammelte Werke,* Volume 4. Germany: Dietz.

MacFarquar, Roderick. 1966. *The Hundred Flowers Campaign and the Chinese Intellectuals.* New York: Praeger.

Malaka, Tan. https://www.marxists.org/archive/malaka/

Mao, Zhe-Dong. February 27, 1957. *On the Correct Handling of Contradictions Among the People.* https://www.marxists.org/reference/archive/mao/selected-works/volume-5/mswv5_58.htm.

Marcuse, Herbert. 1958. *Soviet Marxism.* New York: Columbia University Press.

Marcuse, Herbert. 1969. "Re-examination of the Concept of Revolution," *New Left Review,* Volume 56, July–August.

Marx, Karl. *Marx Engels Archive.* Marxist Internet Archives: https://www.marxists.org/archive/marx/index.htm.

Marx, Karl. *Critique of Political Economy*. 1904. Chicago: Charles Kerr; *Marx-Engels Collected Works 28*. 1976. New York: International Publishers.

Marx, Karl. 1906. *Capital, Vol. I.* Chicago: Charles H. Kerr; 1977. *Capital, Vol. I.* New York: Vintage.

Marx, Karl. 1975. "Private Property and Communism," in *Economic and Philosophic Manuscripts of 1844, Collected Works 3*. New York: International Publishers.

Marx, Karl. 1975. *The German Ideology. Collected Works, 5*. New York: International Publishers.

Marx, Karl. 1975 "Alienated Labor," in *Economic and Philosophic Manuscripts of 1844. Marx-Engels, Collected Works, 3*. New York: International Publishers.

Marx, Karl. 1976. *Poverty of Philosophy. Collected Works 6.* New York: International Publishers.

Marx, Karl. 1979. *The Eighteenth Brumaire of Louis Bonaparte, Collected Works, 11.* New York: International Publishers.

Marx, Karl. 1981, *Capital Vol. Ill.* London: Penguin.

Marx, Karl. 1980. *Collected Works, 16.* New York: International Publishers.

Marx, Karl. 1986. *Collected Works, 28.* New York: International Publishers.

Marx, Karl. 1988 *Civil War in France.* Chicago: Charles H Kerr.

Marx, Karl. 1990. *Collected Works, 26.* New York: International Publishers.

McVey, Ruth. January 1965. *Survey* devoted to "International Communism: The End of an Epoch."

Mehnert, Klaus. 1969. *Peking and the New Left: At Home and Abroad,* China Research Monograph #4. University of California Berkeley.

Mezaros, Istvan. 1970. "Lukacs Concept of Dialectic," in *George Lukács, The Man, his Work, and his Ideas.* (ed. by G.H.R. Parkinson). London: Weidenfeld and Nicolson.

Mikhailov, N.N. 1955. *The Great Constructions in the Land of the Soviets* London: Soviet News.

Mintz, Jeanne S. 1965. *Mohammed, Marx and Marhaen: The Roots of Indonesian Socialism.* New York: Praeger.

Mitchell, Kate L. 1942. *Industrialization of the Western Pacific.* New York: Institute of Pacific Relations.

Munis, Grandizo. 1946. *Los revolucionarios ante Rusia y el stalinismo mundial.* México: Editorial Revolución.

Nagy, Imre. 1957. *Communism: In Defense of "The New Course".* New York: Prager.

Neumann, Franz L. 2009 *Behemoth: The Structure and Practice of National Socialism.* with introduction by Peter Hayes, published in association with the National Holocaust Museum. Chicago: Ivan R. Dee.

News & Letters. 1955 to the present. Chicago. Published online at www.newsandletters .org.

Piccone, Paul. Fall 1969. "Lukács' *History and Class-Consciousness,* Half a Century Later." *Telos.*

Pipes, Richard. 1964. *The Formation of the Soviet Union: Communism and Nationalism, 1917–1923*. Cambridge, Mass.; Harvard University Press.

Prokopovicz (ed.). 1939. *Quarterly Bulletin of Soviet Russian Economics*, No. 1–2 (translated into English). Prague.

Rogin, Leo. March, 1945. "Marx and Engels on Distribution in a Socialist Society," *The American Economic Review* Vol. 35, No. 1.

Salisbury, Harrison E. 7/27/69. "Will There Be War Between Russia and China?" *New York Times Magazine*.

Scholmer, Joseph. 1955. *Vorkuta*. New York: Holt.

Schram, Stuart, 1963. *The Political Thought of Mao Tse-tung*. New York: Praeger.

Schumpeter, Allen, Gordon and Penrose. 1940. *Industrialization of Japan and Manchukuo, 1930–1940: population, raw materials and industry*. New York: Macmillan.

Sebestyen, Miklos. 1960(?). "My Experiences in the Central Workers' Council of Greater Budapest" *The Review*, Vol. III. Brussels: Imre Nagy Institute.

Sedov, Lev. 1936. *Le Livre Rouge du procès de Moscou.* Originally published in *Opposition Bulletin* (organ of the Russian Bolshevik-Leninists), edited by Sedoff in Paris. https://www.marxists.org/francais/sedov/works/1936/10/livrerouge.pdf.

Senghor, Leopold Sedar. 1964. *On African Socialism*. New York: Praeger.

Snow, Edgar. May 10, 1969. "Mao and the New Mandate." *The New Republic*.

Stanfield, Boris M. December 1941. "Private Property Rights in Russia," *International Conciliation* No. 375. New York: American Association for International Conciliation.

Toure, Sekou. *Africa's Path in History*. [(?) 1970 *África en marcha* La Habana: Editorial de Ciencias Sociales, Instituto del Libro].

Trotsky, Leon. The Trotsky Archives at Harvard College Library http://oasis.lib.harvard.edu/oasis/deliver/~hou00301.

Trotsky, Leon. *The Collected Writings of Leon Trotsky*: Trotsky Internet Archive https://www.marxists.org/archive/trotsky/works/

Trotsky, Leon. 1918. *Our Revolution-Essays 1904–1917*. New York: Henry Holt and Co.

Trotsky, Leon. 1931. *My Life*. New York: Charles Scribner's Sons.

Trotsky, Leon. 1931. *The Permanent Revolution* New York: Pioneer Publishers.

Trotsky, Leon. 1937. *The History of the Russian Revolution*. New York: Simon and Schuster.

Trotsky, Leon. 1937. *The Revolution Betrayed.* Garden City: Doubleday, Doran & Co.

Trotsky, Leon. 1937. *The Stalin School of Falsification*. New York: Pioneer Publishers.

Trotsky, Leon. March 1938. *Leon Sedoff, Son, Friend, Fighter.* New York: Young People's Socialist League (Fourth Internationalists), New York.

Trotsky, Leon. 1941. *Stalin*. New York: Harper & Bros.

Trotsky, Leon. 1958. *Trotsky's Diary in Exile, 1935*. Cambridge: Harvard University Press.

Van der Kroef, J.S. Nov.–Dec. 1958. "Communism in Indonesia" in *Problems of Communism*.

Varga, Evgenii. 1946. Changes in the Economy of Capitalism as a Result of the Second World War *Changes in the Capitalist Economy as a Result of World War II.* (in Russian only *Izmeneniia v ekonomike kapitalizma v itoge vtoroi mirovoi voiny.* Moscow: Gos. izd-vo polit. lit-ry).

Voznessensky, N. 1941. *The Growing Prosperity of the Soviet Union.* New York: Workers Library Publishers.

Voznessensky, N. 1947. *The Economy of the USSR During World War II.* In Russian, Moscow. (The American Council of Learned Societies produced a mimeographed English language translation.).

Ward, Barbara. 1959. *Five Ideas that Change the World.* New York: W.W. Norton.

Ward, Barbara. 1962. *Interplay of East and West.* New York: W.W. Norton.

Ward, Barbara. 1962 *The Rich Nations, the Poor Nations.* New York: W.W. Norton.

Waters, Mary-Alice, ed. 1970. *Rosa Luxemburg Speaks.* New York: Pathfinder Press.

Webb, Sidney and Beatrice. 1935. *Soviet Communism: A New Civilization* 2 vols. London: Longmans, Green and Co.

Wetter, S.J., Gustav A. 1959. *Dialectical Materialism,* A Historical and Systemic Survey of Philosophy in the Soviet Union. London: Routledge and Regan.

Wicker, Tom. 10/19/86. "Origins of the Collapse," *New York Times.*

Winter, Kamil. June 13, 1969. "Sell-out in Prague," *New Statesman.*

Yuan-Lu, Wu. 1956. *An Economic Survey of Communist China.* New York: Bookman Assoc.

Zagoria, Donald S. January 1965. "The State of the Parties: Asia," *Survey,* issue devoted to "International Communism: the End of an Epoch."

Zeman, Z.A.B. and Scharlau, W.B. 1965. *The Merchant of Revolution.* London: Oxford University Press.

Index